Classics in the Person-Centered Approach

Edited by David J. Cain

PCCS BOOKS
Ross-on-Wye

First published in 2002

PCCS BOOKS
Llangarron
Ross-on-Wye
Herefordshire
HR9 6PT
United Kingdom
Tel (01989) 77 07 07
website www.pccs-books.co.uk
email   contact@pccs-books.co.uk

This collection © David J. Cain 2002

Classics in the Person-Centered Approach

ISBN 1 898059 42 X (paperback)
ISBN 1 898059 48 9 (hardback)

Cover design by Denis Postle
Printed by Bookcraft, Midsomer Norton, Somerset, United Kingdom

Contents

PART C — CHILDREN AND THE FAMILY

PART D — EDUCATION

Foreword

Julius Seeman

This book is a selective compendium of articles that were published in the *Person-Centered Review* over a five-year span, from 1986 to 1990. The selection of the articles was made by David Cain, who was editor of the journal throughout that period of time. He was thus the person most conversant with the contents of the journal and therefore uniquely qualified to make the selection decisions for this book. All of the journal's articles had been reviewed by referees and by the editor and had therefore passed a prior test of quality in order to be chosen originally for publication. The articles chosen for this book have consequently passed a double test of their enduring significance and value.

A book authored by one person has its own kind of merit through the depth and extent with which it can examine a particular domain. A book of this kind, offering as it does the reflections of many authors, is also special yet in a different way. We are treated here to a panoply of viewpoints and breadth of scope unique to such a collection, a range and variety of viewpoints that a single-authored book cannot readily provide. Each paper in the book opens the door to a new idea uniquely representative of that author's thinking. Each of the six broad content areas represented by the papers introduces the reader to a different domain of the Person-Centered Approach. I found, for example, that I could satisfy some of my special interest in the thinking of Carl Rogers by reading the nine papers that constitute the section dealing explicitly with his ideas. Together the papers in that section constituted a biographical fabric that provided considerable insight into the ideas and the development of Carl Rogers. The same concentration of understanding is possible if one wished to focus on any other of the six areas covered by the articles.

The book has other possibilities, particularly in the domain of teaching. As a book of supplementary readings, it offers a broad sampling of interest areas that might not otherwise be encountered or even touched upon. In a similar vein, the articles could serve as a stimulus for discussion or for further exploration in depth with respect to any topics of special interest and appeal to group members.

Finally, the book has value as history. The authors of many of the book's papers are individuals who have made significant contributions to the history and literature of the Person-Centered Approach. Some of the authors are no longer living. It is a book worth having as part of one's personal library, a testament to the durability and value of the person-centered approach and to persons who helped shape that history .

Dedication

In celebration of Carl Rogers' 100th birthday and his profound and pervasive contributions to humankind

Introduction

During the 2000 meeting for the Association for the Development of the Person-Centered Approach (ADPCA), held in La Jolla, California, Pete Sanders and Maggie Taylor-Sanders approached me about the possibility of putting together an anthology of the best articles published in the *Person-Centered Review*. I felt heartened by their interest since I had considered such a project myself but never got around to it. For the next two years after the 2000 ADPCA meeting we began the process of selecting the articles for inclusion and attending to all the necessary details that go into the production of an anthology. A major criterion used in the selection of articles for inclusion was their timelessness. Like good art, good ideas endure. I believe the reader will find that the articles contained in this book will be relevant today and remain so in the future.

One of the reasons I was so pleased to embark upon this project was that I knew that some of the finest writings in the Person-Centered Approach had been published in the *Person-Centered Review*. Many of the articles published were contributed by persons who played a major role in developing Client-Centered Therapy and the Person-Centered Approach. Among these contributors were: Carl Rogers, Art Combs, Jules Seeman, Fred Zimring, John Shlien, Godfrey Barrett-Lennard, Charlotte Ellinwood, Tom Gordon and Leif Braaten—all of whom had worked at the University of Chicago Counseling Center during its pioneering years of the mid 1940s through 1957, when Rogers left for the University of Wisconsin. Almost every author contained in this book has made significant contributions to Client-Centered Therapy and the Person-Centered Approach over a substantial period of time. Therefore, we settled on the title *Classics in the Person-Centered Approach* in large part because the authors' writings seemed deserving of such an accolade. Fortunately many of the contributors continue to refine and advance person-centered theory, research and a wide variety of applications.

Classics in the Person-Centered Approach also contains articles by a number of prominent humanistic therapists including Clark Moustakas, Constance Fischer, Maurice Friedman, Salvatore Maddi, William Purkey, Flora Roebuck, Hobart Thomas, Ronald Arnett, Peter Reason, John Heron and Harold Greenwald. Further, this text is enriched by articles from some of the most prominent scholars of other persuasions such as Hans Strupp, Arnold Lazarus, Ernst Beier, Evon Guba and Yvonna Lincoln.

Sadly some of the authors of *Classics* are no longer with us. We have lost Carl Rogers,

Art Combs, John Shlien, Fred Zimring, Flora Roebuck and Maria Bowen in the last 15 years. Fortunately some of their seminal contributions will be preserved in this book. Many of those who have left us served as the teachers of the next generations of person-centered scholars and practitioners. Just as many of us stood on the shoulders of Carl Rogers, we now stand on the shoulders of those Rogers influenced. Many of these authors continue to contribute to our development through their research and writings and the students they taught.

One of the strengths of *Classics* is its breadth. Articles on and by Carl Rogers are prominent, but the book also contains provocative articles on psychotherapy by many of the most talented and creative therapists. Other sections include articles from the fields of 'Children and the Family', 'Education', 'Research' and 'Issues, Controversies, Discussions'. In short, there are articles for a wide range of reader interests.

The quality of the articles contained in *Classics* was assured, in part, by the careful editing and dialogue between the reviewers of the *Person-Centered Review* and the authors. A special tribute is owed to the associate editors of the *Person-Centered Review*. They carried an inordinate load of the work of reviewing and thus deserve my special thanks. These associate editors include: Jules Seeman, Art Combs, Brian Thorne and Jerold Bozarth. Great appreciation is also due to all of the persons who served as reviewers for the *Person-Centered Review*, most of whom also contributed articles to it. Thus, in a small way, *Classics in the Person-Centered Approach* celebrates and honors those who have contributed so much, in so many ways.

Finally, I wish to express my heartfelt appreciation to Pete Sanders and Maggie Taylor-Sanders for their vision, enthusiasm and great effort in bringing this book into being.

David J. Cain
Founder and Editor, *Person-Centered Review*
June, 2002

Part A

Carl Rogers and
the Person-Centered-Approach

30 Years with Rogers' Necessary and Sufficient Conditions of Therapeutic Personality Change: A personal evaluation

Leif J. Braaten   *University of Oslo*

The purpose of this article is to present a personal evaluation of Rogers' famous 1957 model of the necessary and sufficient conditions of therapeutic personality change after 30 years of clinical experience in a variety of person-centered activities. The author wishes to support and encourage his clinical colleagues to take the task of personalizing a therapy theory as seriously as it deserves. It must be emphasized that the conditions of accurate empathy, unconditional positive regard, and genuineness represent facets of a whole and that it is their totality that constitutes the therapist's contribution in treatment. After considerable intellectual and emotional battle with these conditions the author concludes with a strongly affirmative view of Rogers' exceedingly influential model.

The purpose of this article is to shed some light on the process and value of evolving a personal theory of psychotherapy. A personal theory is a function of at least three determinants: the personality of the theorist, the clientele, and the sociocultural context. The theories of Freud, Adler, Jung, Rank, Horney, Sullivan, Rogers, and others illustrate this point. In fact, all clinicians face the same basic challenge: how to reconcile personality, clinical experience, and current *zeitgeist.* Most psychotherapists typically begin their careers with an externally given therapy model and struggle along to determine whether they can truly come to own it or not. My hope for this article is to support and encourage my person-centered colleagues and other clinicians to take this task of personalizing a therapy theory as seriously as it deserves. More specifically, my task is to share with the interested reader my personal battle to come to terms with the client-centered therapy model (Rogers, 1957). I hope to convey that the model has challenged me both intellectually and emotionally. I also intend to convey that my whole personal background has both helped and blocked my endeavor to arrive at a personal theory of psychotherapy.

In order to appreciate my battle, the reader should know that I have about 30 years of clinical experience, mostly with young adults or adults with neurotic and personality disorders. During half of this period I worked extensively with college and university students in the United States and Norway. During recent years I have also specialized in various kinds of group work, such as sensitivity training, encounter groups, and group therapy. During most of this time I have held an academic position as a professor of clinical psychology, dividing my time between administrative work, teaching, research, and writing. My three books have dealt with the client-centered approach to therapy (Braaten, 1967), experiential learning through the group process (Braaten, 1974), and students' emotional problems (Braaten, 1980).

By a happy coincidence I was present on the historic occasion when Rogers first addressed the Counseling Center Staff at the University of Chicago on 'the necessary

First published in *Person-Centered Review,* Volume 1, Number 1, February 1986.

and sufficient conditions of therapeutic personality change' (Rogers, 1957). Little did we appreciate at that time what a seminal and far-reaching contribution his paper would turn out to be. My recollection is that both staff and graduate students were only moderately impressed. As critically trained academicians we responded with a few nice comments and tried to arrest Carl for his obvious oversimplification and omissions. As we all now know, this stubbornly simple but effective therapeutic model has been assimilated by thousands of clinicians all over the world. Probably hundreds of researchers have tried to assess its promise and validity.

Let me now attempt to summarize how Rogers' model has functioned for me. At the same time I invite the clinician reader to compare notes as to his or her own related struggle to come to grips with this challenge. Having recently watched myself for many hours on color videotape doing group therapy with adult educators, I was struck by how central *accurate empathy* has become in my work. I have learned to accept that my client also has a mind and wants to be correctly understood. I find myself actively listening with my 'third ear' (Reik, 1948) and my whole being, soaking up the combined cognitive and affective message from my client moment to moment, trying to communicate and verify my understanding. I believe we person-centered therapists are unique among our colleagues because we so carefully monitor whether we have gotten the message right. Uncommunicated empathy is no understanding at all in the experience of the client. The criterion for being right is the spontaneous recognition of the client. Such a respect for the phenomenological world of the client ensures a basic humility on the part of the professional helper. As my clinical experience has accumulated over the years, I have become increasingly daring by reaching to understand my client at deeper levels. My warning signal is not to go much beyond the client's awareness at any moment.

For a more scholarly discussion of emergent modes of empathy, the reader is referred to Bozarth (1984). Rogers (1980) himself has recently emphasized use of intuition. I have during recent years also been struck by what Tepper and Haase (1978) have pointed out as nonverbal aspects of accurate empathy, warm regard, and congruence.

At this point, I would like to share a personal note from my childhood because I am convinced that theory and one's personality must come to terms with each other. Only during my mature years have I discovered my lifelong yearning for accurate empathy because of its relative absence in my younger years. My well-meaning but ill-informed parents were in spirit missionaries, feeling obligated to tell me what I should think, believe, feel, and do. It was unheard of to attempt to take the position of the other person, to try to see the world from his or her perspective, to convey a basic respect for one's right to find one's own road to the good life and a possible salvation. However, it helps to realize that parents too are people, and that their lack of empathy is a deficiency of capacity and not simply ill will.

From a diagnostic perspective I have come to see an inability to empathize with others as a rather severe sign of psychopathology, not uncommon nowadays among many clients with personality disorders. If a person cannot be reasonably empathic, he or she is not properly individuated to have an appreciation for somebody else as a separate person. The I-Thou-boundaries Buber (1970) talks about are blurred. In effective treatment the client internalizes the therapist's empathy into accurate self-empathy. Kohut (1977) claims that especially clients with narcissistic disorders must have a considerable dosage of confirming empathy to restore the unstructured self. As far as training goes, I agree with Truax and Carkhuff (1967) that accurate empathy can, to some extent, be taught or learned. However, it is doubtful that graduate students can be trained to become truly accepting and/or genuine.

Among the errors I and many of my students have tried to correct in our attempts to show accurate empathy are the following: We have used too complicated language rather than plain, direct talk. We have tended to be a bit too compulsive by seeking to prove that we have understood clients correctly, rather than intervening only when it was truly facilitative. We have at times slipped into projecting a pet theoretical idea onto the client rather than being loyal to the client's unique perspective. We have had trouble meeting the challenge of the occasional client who demands perfect empathy. We have struggled to mobilize wholehearted empathy toward somebody we dislike or feel threatened by. Hence, for most of us, being accurately empathic implies hard work and considerable self-discipline.

Having now discussed my task in coming to terms with the concept of accurate empathy, I shall turn to the next basic person-centered therapy concept: *unconditional positive regard.* Let me readily admit that throughout my clinical experience I have had trouble with the unconditionality concept. Deep down in my gut I have felt an angry protest at the superhuman expectation that I should be unconditionally accepting of my client. It simply did not seem possible.

Here again, I shall insert a personal note to reveal the most important roots of my protest. During my formative years my Lutheran parents became eager adherents of the Western religious movement called the 'Oxford group' and later the 'Moral Rearmament.' According to their creed, with God's help one is supposed to be absolutely honest, unselfish, loving, and sexually clean. These absolutes fitted especially well with my mother's gruesome demands for perfection. In my late teens, in order to save my mental sanity I had to reject this heritage of absolutes. In a similar vein I suppose that I could not live with a professional demand that my positive regard for clients should be without conditions. One of my deepest personal discoveries in life was that I must have the courage to reject in order to fully accept. To me, the alleged unconditionally nice person is in fact a menace to significant others and him- or herself. Only a person who at times rejects me has credibility as an accepting helper or friend.

When I first wrote the last paragraph, I was struck by surprise. I probably could not have dared to admit such a view of a sacred person-centered concept until I had confronted Carl Rogers during the First International Forum for the Person-Centered Approach in Mexico in 1982, admitting to him and other colleagues publicly that I differed with him on certain theoretical and clinical matters. The deeper personal lesson at that time was that I was permitted to be loyal to my own best judgment without being rejected by the person-centered community. Put otherwise, if we agree on basics, we may differ on minor matters and refinements.

It will probably come as no surprise to the reader that I have had trouble even with the prefix *positive* regard. Persistently I have felt that my warm regard must be good enough, even if my therapeutic attitude reveals positive or negative feelings. With a great deal of resistance I have come to believe that my so-called positive regard must include a willingness to share my total self with significant others, including my anger and possible rejection. Only during recent years have I confronted my lifelong suppression of anger and antagonism. My two client-centered therapists were not especially helpful with this aspect of my personal problems. During a significant breakthrough of such feelings a few years ago I turned raving mad at everybody close to me. To my enormous relief and delight my relationships pretty much improved rather than deteriorated.

Since that time I have refrained my understanding of anger. I used to consider anger one of the biggest sins against the demand of absolute love. Now my experience is that I rarely turn angry at somebody I do not respect and love. Furthermore, I usually become angry when vital values are at stake. Thus my anger has changed into a signal to invest time and energy in improving a treasured relationship.

By now even the most sympathetic reader probably has started wondering whether there is anything left at all in the key concept of unconditional positive regard that remains intact for me. Let me therefore try to put into words the nature of my acceptance with the above reservations. I do accept my client unconditionally as a person, a fellow human being with a basic right to be in this world as I am. I try to help him or her with the two most basic therapy goals I can conceive of — namely, living in dialogue with significant others and individuation. At my best I feel a strong liking and a compassion for my client, both in regard to suffering and joy. In rare moments I marvel at the capacity of the human being not only to survive physically and mentally but at times even to transcend severely destructive influences. Occasionally I am in awe at a client's successful attempt to become a better, more fulfilled person than his or her parents. I tend to believe that there is such a thing as a unique, optimal human self to actualize.

One of the crucial tests of my capacity for persistent caring and regard comes with clients who are severely rejecting. Such an unfortunate person has been cheated of his or her right to be confirmed as a child, is unwanted, and literally senses the cold, stiff shoulder. For weeks and months I feel undercurrents of counterrejection and barely survive professionally as a helper with the aid of my accurate empathy. In fact, my salvation in confronting such a rejecting client is to exploit my skill of true understanding. I cannot love my client unless I know him or her. I agree with Rollo May (1969) that true love also presupposes a willingness and a disciplined effort to try to understand. If and when I manage to see this person accurately from the inside, my feeling of antagonism disappears at last, and I feel genuine acceptance.

During my personal therapy at the University of Chicago in 1956–1957 I was overwhelmed by the fact that I cried my eyes out. As a result of this classical catharsis I felt confident that 'I will not cry tomorrow.' Throughout the last three decades I have been hunting for the rock-bottom reason for all this crying. In my otherwise very helpful client-centered therapies I have (characteristically?) never gained such an insight. At long last, a few years ago in an international group therapy sequence with loving and committed colleagues I dared to regress (I think) and relived what I had experienced as my mother's rejection of me as a newborn infant.

Later I confronted my mother gently with this powerful experience. She was then a widow in her mid-eighties. She told me with considerable affect something she had never told anybody before. She had not really rejected me, but was exhausted after a long-drawn, complicated birth struggle. She felt physiologically and psychologically paralyzed and could not be the good mother she wished to be. At this point in her confession to me she exclaimed with tears in her eyes: 'You see, Leif, I have been so ashamed all my life ever since because I could not be a good mother to you when you were an infant.' At that point during our significant confrontation my heart melted. I felt a deep compassion for her nonperfection. I could finally accept her as belonging to the fallible human race and ended our meeting with a good hug, the first one in many years.

After reflecting on the last paragraphs about the concept of unconditional positive regard, it became obvious that becoming more fully accepting of others has been a lifelong battle. And the more I have become truly self-accepting, the more I can confirm and prize others. For a more scholarly discussion of this controversial basic attitude in client-centered therapy the reader is referred to Lietaer (1984).

I shall now proceed to examine the necessary condition of *genuineness*. I have come to prefer the concept of genuineness to the concept of congruence, although the latter emphasizes the theoretically important point of a harmony among inner experience, the symbolization of it in awareness, and the communication of it to the other individual.

First, I will summarize what I believe are the clinical advantages of genuineness in the therapist-client relationship. I have found it immensely freeing to be allowed to be my own person as a therapist and not merely perform a prescribed professional role. As is well known, the traditional psychodynamic model emphasized at most a well-meaning neutral attitude. Most of the time I experience myself as genuinely competent in my work, but at times I have used poor judgment. I admitted my errors to my clients and, fortunately, quite a few have told me that it felt good to know that their therapist also was a human being with shortcomings, struggling along with the rest of humankind. An important implication of this view of genuineness is that the therapist also must be considered good enough, even many years ago when he or she was less experienced and wise. Furthermore, even during personal crises and life stresses, sickness and accidents, a therapist can do a more or less adequate job as a helper and facilitator of mental growth.

Once 12 years ago, during the sad aftermath of my divorce, I ran one of my best weeklong therapy groups with graduate students in Gothenburgh, Sweden. The wooden bear mascot I received as a gift of deep appreciation still sits on my academic desk and perks me up when I am in some kind of passing despair. The best thing about the condition of genuineness is that it makes therapy a humanly possible career for a lifetime.

In addition, most clients are very sensitive people. They have an uncanny awareness of all kinds of faking, role-playing, hypocrisy, attempts at taking the easy route, double-talk, and incongruence between one's words and nonverbal cues. In fact, I stand little chance of helping unless I am my real self, mostly for the better, but sometimes for the worse. This observation also warns me that I better admit it when I occasionally fail with a client. The ethical decision is then to refer this 'difficult' client to a carefully selected colleague who presumably will be a more congenial helper.

Finally, I will consider some problems I have with the concept of genuineness or congruence. Not every kind of genuineness is facilitating for the client. Self-disclosure on the part of the therapist can be overdone in magnitude and kind. If, for example, I am very tired in a therapy session late in the afternoon, my constant yawning is disillusioning to the client. If I had a hostile encounter with a colleague just before another session, I must watch my step not to project some of that residual anger onto my client. On these and related occasions I have learned that it is best to tell the client about my state of mind to avoid confusion and even offer the client the option to cancel the hour.

In sum, I would like to argue that the art of psychotherapy demands the best of what I possess, but *not* perfection. My accurate empathy, warm regard, and genuineness must originate in my mind and my heart, and must be real.

In a recent personal communication, Carl Rogers reminded me that his therapy model puts no demand for perfection on any therapist. In true scientific spirit it says that, to the extent the therapist experiences accurate empathy, warm regard, and genuineness for his or her client, and to the extent that the client perceives it, the therapeutic personality change will follow as a consequence.

At this moment of writing, it strikes me how paradoxically therapist-oriented this person-centered model is, at least in terms of therapy theory. As everybody knows, the only alleged condition necessary and sufficient for the client is that he or she be anxious or vulnerable. No wonder this 'oversimplification' seemed a bit outrageous to clinicians committed to traditional diagnosis. For myself, especially in the first decade of my professional career, I found it helpful to make some judgment about the severity of psychopathology and, to a certain extent, about the kind of emotional disorder with which

I was faced.

Here, I would like to offer some thoughts about this key therapy concept concerning the state of the client. For me, perhaps the most important lesson is that I cannot perform effective therapy with a client who is not anxious or vulnerable. As the proverb says, you can lead a horse to water, but you cannot make him drink unless he is thirsty. A client can be manipulated to come to your office by an intimate partner or a boss, but you cannot make the client cooperate against his or her will. This important understanding lets me off the hook when I am in an omnipotent mood and believe I ought to be able to treat just about anyone who approaches me. Therapy is, in essence, a dialogical, cooperative endeavor. As necessary as the therapist is, he or she is never more than a catalyst or facilitator. The basic responsibility for constructive personality change lies with the client.

However, this argument does not imply that we as helpers may take the easy way out by getting rid of bothersome, threatening clients with the excuse that they are not properly motivated. Quite a few times I have begun therapy when the client appeared only vaguely to be vulnerable, and certainly not openly anxious. The client's behavior of keeping appointments often betrays a deeper commitment for constructive change that will surface in due time after considerable testing of the relationship with the therapist. During my first client-centered personal therapy in Chicago, I remember that it took me nine sessions before I finally admitted to my therapist that 'I really need your help.'

On the basis of my own group therapy research during recent years (Braaten, 1985), I have accumulated considerable empirical data supporting the theoretical claim that the typical client of today lacks the capacity for attachment/affiliation or interpersonal relatedness. I agree with Kohut (1977) that the therapeutic challenge is first to restore this capacity for interpersonal intimacy and afterward proceed with regular therapy. Incidentally, Kahn (1985) has just offered a timely comparison between Heinz Kohut and Carl Rogers. Kohut has succeeded in integrating many of Rogers' concepts of humanistic psychology into his version of psychoanalysis.

I have now completed my description of my struggle with Rogers' proposed necessary and sufficient conditions of therapeutic personality change. As I understand it, what we have here is a linear model. It argues: the more of these therapist conditions the better. Furthermore, the claim appears to be that the more anxious or vulnerable the client, the better. We allegedly obtain the best therapy results when these conditions are maximized. Generally speaking, I think there is a good deal of truth in this assertion. However, I agree with Dick Farson (1974) that there is an optimal range for these therapy conditions depending upon the circumstances.

A few examples will illustrate that these conditions do not operate independently but are parts of a whole having a range for autonomous expression. An overly obsessive-compulsive client will not tolerate a therapist who is perfectly empathic. A client who struggles to overcome unhealthy symbiosis may be threatened if the therapist is too warm and caring. A client who is attempting a more mature individuation may be overwhelmed if the therapist is uncritically genuine and self-disclosing. A client in an acute schizophrenic panic may have to be hospitalized for a while before the usual therapist conditions will take effect.

It must be emphasized that these three therapist conditions represent facets of a whole and it is their totality that constitutes the therapist contribution in therapy. This must be taken into consideration. All too often person-centered colleagues restrict themselves to discussing one condition, for example, accurate empathy or unconditional positive regard. The same criticism holds for research. I agree with Watson (1984, p. 40), who says, 'The studies that have focused on client perceptions of the relationship typically have not included all of the hypothesized conditions, thereby not testing the hypotheses as propositions of a *set* of necessary and sufficient conditions.'

My personal evaluation of Rogers' therapy model has come to an end, and I shall attempt to conclude. I hope I have been able to shed some light on the problems of evolving a personal theory of psychotherapy. The major problem with adopting somebody else's therapy model is that it is necessarily external to one's own personality. I feel convinced that such an external model is dysfunctional professionally. Our only chance of survival is to attempt to make it our own, with the necessary modifications. It helps initially that most clinicians intuitively seek out a congenial model. Nevertheless, for most of us it is a battle to develop a personalized therapy model. It takes a lot of integrity to examine an elegant and treasured model critically. But we have no choice except to advance on our own authority. I hope this anecdotal contribution has raised some doubts about the myth that building a theory of therapy is a purely academic and intellectual matter. I want to support and encourage all clinicians to undertake this task of personalizing a therapy model seriously. The reward is that we eventually are able to integrate our personality, clinical experience, the external model, and the zeitgeist for the benefit of our clients and ourselves.

In my estimation, Rogers' therapy model of 1957 is one of the most elegant and influential contributions ever made to therapeutic counseling and psychotherapy. For me, this model has turned out to be a very viable one, withstanding the ravages of clinical realities even with the mentioned reservations and clarifications.

AUTHOR'S NOTE

This article is a revised version of a presentation at the Second International Forum for the Person-Centered Approach in Norwich, England, July 14–21, 1984. I wish to acknowledge helpful comments from David J. Cain, C. H. Patterson, Jules Seeman, and John Keith Wood.

REFERENCES

Bozarth, J. D. (1984). Beyond reflection: Emergent modes of empathy. In R. F. Levant & J. M. Shlien (Eds.), *Client-centered therapy and the person-centered approach: New directions in theory, research, and practice* (pp. 59–75). New York: Praeger.

Braaten, L. J. (1967). *Client-centered counseling and therapy: A systematic introduction into the psychology of Carl R. Rogers.* Oslo: The University Press. (in Norwegian)

Braaten, L. J. (1974). *Psychotherapeutic learning in groups: An experiential approach.* Oslo: The University Press. (in Norwegian)

Braaten, L. J. (1980). *Students' emotional problems: A psychotherapeutic perspective.* Oslo: The University Press. (in Norwegian)

Braaten, L. J. (1985). Predicting symptom reduction and positive goal attainment from individually perceived cohesion early in group psychotherapy of one year's duration. Manuscript submitted for publication.

Buber, M. (1970). *I and thou.* New York: Charles Scribner.

Farson, R. (1974). Carl Rogers, quiet revolutionary. *Education, 95*(2), 197–203.

Kahn, E. (1985). Heinz Kohut and Carl Rogers: A timely comparison. *American Psychologist, 40*(8), 893–904.

Kohut, H. (1977). *The restoration of the self.* New York: International Universities Press.

Lietaer, G. (1984). Unconditional positive regard: A controversial basic attitude in client-centered therapy. In R. F. Levant & J. M. Shlien (Eds.), *Client-centered therapy and the person-centered approach: New directions in theory, research, and practice* (pp. 41–58). New York: Praeger.

May, R. (1969). *Love and will.* London: Souvenir Press.

Reik, T. (1948). *Listening with the third ear.* New York: Grove Press.

Rogers. C. R. (1957). The necessary and sufficient conditions of therapeutic personality change. *Journal of Consulting Psychology, 21,* 95–103.

Rogers, C. R. (1980). *A way of being.* Boston: Houghton Mifflin.

Tepper, D. T., & Haase, R. F. (1978). Verbal and nonverbal communication of facilitative conditions. *Journal of Counseling Psychology, 25*(1), 35–44.

Truax, C. B., & Carkhuff, R. R. (1967). *Toward effective counseling and psychotherapy: Training and practice.* Chicago: Aldine.

Watson, N. (1984). The empirical status of Rogers' hypotheses of the necessary and sufficient conditions for effective psychotherapy. In R. F. Levant & J. M. Shlien (Eds.), *Client-centered therapy and the person-centered approach: New directions in theory, research, and practice* (pp. 17–40). New York: Praeger.

Carl Rogers on the Development
of the Person-Centered Approach

Carl R. Rogers   *Center for Studies of the Person*

It is a new venture for me to have regular space available for the expression of my feelings and opinions on topics of current interest to me. I hope to use it in various ways. I will welcome feedback on what I write, and suggestions of topics for future columns. This time I am going to comment briefly on one important issue.

WHAT IS ESSENTIAL . . .?

The editor has asked all members of the Editorial Board to express their views as to what is most essential to the future development of the person-centered approach. Upon reading his question my immediate reaction was the following: 'What we need most is solid research!' Let me explain.

In the field of psychological practice the basic principles of client-centered therapy and the person-centered approach have gained respect and often acceptance, even though these principles frequently run counter to current ways of dealing with people. As therapists, as consultants, as educators, we have earned a place.

But in universities I feel we are underrepresented, badly misunderstood, mistakenly seen as superficial. We are underrepresented partly because we constitute a threat to the academically minded. We espouse the importance of experiential as well as cognitive learning. Such learning involves the risk of being changed by the experience, and this can be frightening to one whose world is intellectually structured. Perhaps partly due to this aspect, there are few faculty members who have been trained in, or even exposed to, a person-centered approach. Another reason for the paucity of person-centered faculty members is that the fascination of experiential learning tends to turn promising individuals away from the purely intellectual emphasis of academia. They go into private practice, or other activities within the helping professions.

But therapists in private practice do not significantly add to the development of a field of knowledge. They do not, with very rare exceptions, carry on research. Research is carried out, in large measure, by doctoral candidates in universities, often working on topics of interest to their faculty sponsors. Because those faculty sponsors are rarely interested in the person-centered approach, we have come full circle. There is relatively little new knowledge being developed in our field. This is a dilemma with serious implications for our future.

I have no neat solution to this dilemma. I can only point to two hopeful signs. Where humanistic psychology is well represented on the faculty — as in Union Graduate School, The University of Hamburg (West Germany), Saybrook Institute, the Center for Humanistic Studies, and others less well known — research on the hypotheses of the

First published in *Person-Centered Review,* Volume 1, Number 3, August 1986.

person-centered approach is possible, and is being done.

The prospects for research are also improved by new developments in the philosophy of science. Research has, in the past, often been a dirty word to therapists because it was seen as involving an impersonal, statistical approach to fragmented portions of the person and his experience. Now the logical positivist mode is no longer the only mode for behavioral science, and a variety of phenomenologically based methods are seen as sound ways of advancing our knowledge. I have tried to summarize some of these hopeful developments in a recent article (Rogers, 1985). Even the meticulous analysis of the single case is seen as a source of emerging knowledge and generative hypotheses.

There is only one way in which a person-centered approach can avoid becoming narrow, dogmatic, and restrictive. That is through studies — simultaneously hardheaded and tender minded — which open new vistas, bring new insights, challenge our hypotheses, enrich our theory, expand our knowledge, and involve us more deeply in an understanding of the phenomena of human change.

REFERENCE

Rogers, C. R. (1985). Toward a more human science of the person. *Journal of Humanistic Psychology, 25,* 4, 7-24.

Reflection of Feelings

Carl R. Rogers   *Center for Studies of the Person*

Although I am partially responsible for the use of this term to describe a certain type of therapist response, I have, over the years, become very unhappy with it. A major reason is that 'reflection of feelings' has been not infrequently taught as a technique, and sometimes a very wooden technique at that. On the basis of written client expressions, the learner is expected to concoct a 'correct' reflection of feeling — or even worse, to select the 'correct' response from a multiple-choice list. Such training has very little to do with an effective therapeutic relationship. So I have become more and more allergic to the use of the term.

At the same time I know that many of my responses in an interview — as is evident from published examples — would seem to be 'reflections of feeling.' Inwardly I object. I am definitely *not* trying to 'reflect feelings.'

Then I receive a letter from my friend and former colleague, Dr. John Shlien of Harvard, which still further complicates my dilemma. He writes:

'Reflection' is unfairly damned. It was rightly criticized when you described the wooden mockery it could become in the hands of insensitive people, and you wrote beautifully on that point. But you neglected the other side. It is an instrument of artistic virtuosity in the hands of a sincere, intelligent, empathic listener. It made possible the development of client-centered therapy, when the philosophy alone could not have. Undeserved denigration of the technique leads to fatuous alternatives in the name of 'congruence.'

Puzzling over this matter, I have come to a double insight. From my point of view as therapist, I am *not* trying to 'reflect feelings.' I am trying to determine whether my understanding of the client's inner world is correct — whether I am seeing it as he or she is experiencing it at this moment. Each response of mine contains the unspoken question, 'Is this the way it is in you? Am I catching just the color and texture and flavor of the personal meaning you are experiencing right now? If not, I wish to bring my perception in line with yours.'

On the other hand, I know that from the client's point of view we are holding up a mirror of his or her current experiencing. The feelings and personal meanings seem sharper when seen through the eyes of another, when they are reflected.

So I suggest that these therapist responses be labeled not 'Reflections of Feeling,' but 'Testing Understandings,' or 'Checking Perceptions.' Such terms would, I believe, be more accurate. They would be helpful in the training of therapists. They would supply a sound motivation in responding, a questioning desire rather than an intent to 'reflect.'

But in understanding the client's experience, we can realize that such responses do serve as a mirror. This is beautifully expressed by Sylvia Slack (1985, pp. 41–2) as she tells of her reactions in a therapy interview held in front of a large audience, and

First published in *Person-Centered Review,* Volume 1, Number 4, November 1986.

videotaped.

> Watching the tapes helped me to visualize the counseling process more clearly. It was like Dr. Rogers was a magical mirror. The process involved my sending rays toward that mirror. I looked into the mirror to get a glimpse of the reality that I am. If I had sensed the mirror was affected by the rays being received, the reflection would have seemed distorted and not to be trusted. Although I was aware of sending rays, their nature was not truly discernible until they were reflected and clarified by the mirror. There was a curiosity about the rays and what they revealed about me. This experience allowed me an opportunity to get a view of myself that was untainted by the perceptions of outside viewers. This inner knowedge of myself enabled me to make choices more suited to the person who lives within me.

As she hints here, and goes on to elaborate, it is important that the therapist's understanding be so sensitively correct that the mirror image is clear and undistorted. This means laying aside our own judgements and values in order to grasp, with delicate accuracy, the exact meaning the client is experiencing.

Thinking these thoughts and writing them out has been clarifying for me. I can continue, from the therapist's point of view, to test my understanding of my client by making tentative attempts to describe or portray his or her inner world. I can recognize that for my client these responses are, at their best, a clear mirror image of the meanings and perceptions that make up his or her world of the moment — an image that is clarifying and insight producing.

REFERENCES

Shlien, J. (1986, April 2). Personal correspondence.

Slack, S. (1985, Spring). Reflections on a workshop with Carl Rogers. *Journal of Humanistic Psychology, 25,* 35–42.

Reality, Illusion and Mental Health

David J. Cain   *Carlsbad, California*

Social psychologist Shelley E. Taylor of UCLA offers a challenge to the widely held notion that a clear sense of reality is a defining or essential characteristic of mental health. In the introduction to her book *Positive Illusions* (1989), she states,

> Rather than being firmly in touch with reality, the normal human mind distorts incoming information in a positive direction. In particular, people think of themselves, their future, and their ability to have an impact on what goes on around them in a more positive manner than reality can sustain . . . The normal human mind is oriented toward mental health and . . . at every turn it construes events in a manner that promotes benign fictions about the self, the world and the future. The mind is, with some significant exceptions, intrinsically adaptive, oriented toward overcoming rather than succumbing to the adverse events of life. In many ways, the healthy mind is a self-deceptive one. (p. xi)

ILLUSION AND TRADITIONAL VIEWS OF MENTAL HEALTH

This provocative thesis flies in the face of accepted and venerable conceptions of mental health and mental illness. Traditional conceptions (e.g., Jahoda, 1967; Jourard, 1974; Maslow, 1970) maintain that an accurate perception of reality is a cornerstone of the healthy, well-adjusted personality. Jahoda's views are representative of many personality theorists, especially those with a humanistic outlook: 'The perception of reality is called mentally healthy when what the individual sees corresponds to what is actually there' (in Taylor, 1989, p. 5). Rogers (1959) articulated a similar viewpoint in his description of the congruence of self and experience as a characteristic of optimal psychological adjustment and the fully functioning person. He states,

> When self experiences are accurately symbolized, and are included in the self-concept in . . . accurately symbolized form, then the state is one of congruence of self and experience. If this were completely true of all self-experiences, the individual would be a fully functioning person. (p. 206)

In contesting the view that accurate reality testing is a hallmark of mental health, Taylor addresses the development and maintenance of this viewpoint. She contends that mental health practitioners generally are trained in the established conventions of their professions, conventions that persist on both clinical and theoretical levels despite contradictory evidence. Summarizing this concern briefly, she states, 'Scientific bias is in favor of established beliefs' (1989, p. 5). Taylor then goes on to challenge this traditional view by presenting an enormous amount of evidence (over 500 references), including an impressive array of research studies, that provide a substantially different view of the

First published in *Person-Centered Review*, Volume 5, Number 3, August 1990.

nature of mental health. Her basic thesis is that 'Normal human thought and perception is marked not by accuracy but by positive self-enhancing illusions about the self, the world and the future' (p. 7). She further contends that these illusions are primarily adaptive and promote mental health rather than undermine it. Taylor defines illusions simply as biased perceptions and indicates that they fall into three categories: (1) self-enhancement, a perception of one's self, behavior, or enduring attributes as more positive than can be supported by reality; (2) personal control, an exaggerated belief in the degree of one's ability to bring about positive outcomes and prevent negative ones; (3) unrealistic optimism, a view of the future as unrealistically plentiful in opportunity and relatively devoid of negative events.

RESEARCH EVIDENCE

As Taylor points out, the view that illusion is characteristic of human perception is not new. However, most of the scientific evidence supporting this view is relatively recent, occurring mostly in the past 20 years. Some of the research findings cited by Taylor are the following:
1. Children tend to make grandiose assessments of themselves and their ability that are unresponsive to negative feedback until approximately age seven.
2. Most adults describe themselves as having many more positive than negative qualities and tend to downplay their weaknesses as unimportant or inconsequential.
3. People evaluate themselves more favorably than others do.
4. The enduring beliefs or self-schemas that people have about themselves guide the selection and interpretation of information in social situations.
5. Memory is organized egocentrically, and past events are likely to be recalled in a manner that reflects favorably on the self.
6. People take credit for good things that happen, deny responsibility for bad things that happen, and exaggerate the role they had in any task, particularly one with a good outcome.
7. People believe the world is controllable and that they have the ability to control it.
8. Most people are unrealistically optimistic about the future and expect it to turn out as they wish.

Taylor summarizes the literature as follows:
> What we see in the normal human mind does not correspond very well to the predominant view of mental health. Instead of an awareness and acceptance of both the positive and negative elements of their personalities, most people show a keen awareness of their positive qualities and attributes, an extreme estimation of their ability to master their environment, and a positive assessment of the future. Not only are these assessments positive, they appear to be unrealistically so. It is not just that people believe they are good, but that they think they are better than reality can sustain. Judgments of mastery greatly exceed the actual ability to control many events. Views of the future are so rosy that they would make Pollyanna blush. (p. 43)

BENEFITS OF ILLUSIONS

According to Taylor, not only are positive illusions characteristic of normal people, but they promote good mental health and effective living. They enable people to be happy; foster positive moods that help promote prosocial behavior; increase confidence in one's ability; enhance motivation, performance, and success; and promote recall, learning, creativity, and constructive thinking. By increasing their belief in personal control, positive illusions help people cope with stress more effectively. The optimism about the future and what they might become seems to enable people to use their illusions for constructive growth and change.

Taylor's ideas provoked a number of responses in me. One was that her views could dramatically alter the ways mental health professionals perceive and interact with normal people and those with varying degrees of cognitive, emotional, or behavioral impairment. Most of the people who become clients are impaired but have many qualities of normal and constructive behavior as well. As I reflected on the thousands of clients I've seen in a variety of inpatient, outpatient, school, and university settings over the last 20 years, it seemed to me that most were lacking in the positive illusions Taylor described and were instead characterized by poor or distorted self-concepts. It seemed, too, that many were having difficulty seeing the world as clearly as they might and that their 'distortions' about themselves, the world, their ability to control it, and their futures were more often negative than positive. I confess that one of my underlying assumptions about what promotes constructive growth is the capacity to see oneself and one's world more clearly. I find myself a bit reluctant to let go of that belief, but I do want to remain receptive to Taylor's impressive arsenal of research evidence and convincing arguments. I also want to keep in mind that my clients are not necessarily representative of persons who do not become clients. Taylor does make it clear that her conclusions are based on the normal person, although she never defines 'normal.' The research studies she cites are based predominantly on nonclinical populations. Therefore, her conclusions should be considered in this light.

ILLUSION AND DEFENSE

I wonder how it is that the normal thought of the typical person can be so self-deceptive. Perhaps Taylor doesn't distinguish between illusion and the variety of psychological defense mechanisms people employ to protect themselves from painful realities. Taylor, however, contends that positive illusions and defenses can be distinguished from each other. She argues that positive illusions are primarily adaptive and therefore unlike the defenses of denial and repression, which she views as maladaptive: 'Defenses distort the facts, leading people to hold misperceptions of external or internal reality. Through illusions, on the other hand, people make the most of bad situations by adopting a maximally positive perspective' (p. 126). As she sees it, the formation of positive illusions is a way in which people reframe events and experiences in a manner that promotes hope and positive self-appraisal. In contrast, defenses are viewed as maladaptive because they keep information from awareness as opposed to reconstruing it.

I find this to be a useful distinction but still find myself concerned about the potentially adverse impact of the self-deception involved in positive illusion. It seems to me that any distortion of reality, albeit positive, runs the risk of impairing learning. How can one learn from experience unless the experience reaches the organism in an undistorted manner? Taylor maintains that normal positive distortions are generally of a modest magnitude and have the effect of motivating and sustaining effective behavior. Simply stated, positive illusions are functional, constructive, and adaptive in that they enable people to do what they need to do to deal with a given situation. Further, Taylor argues, positive illusions don't prevent people from receiving and recognizing negative information about themselves or the world but rather may serve to soften the impact of the harsh realities with which all persons are confronted.

ILLUSION AND MENTAL ILLNESS

As mentioned earlier, Taylor's ideas are based primarily on research with normal populations. Therefore, you might legitimately question, as I do, whether or how her findings might apply to persons experiencing varying degrees of mental, emotional, and behavioral impairment. Here, Taylor is cautious about generalizing to a wide range of psychological disturbances because of the diversity of people variously categorized as mentally impaired. She does draw some interesting and relevant comparisons between mentally healthy persons and those experiencing depression and mania. These latter groups are especially relevant because there is a magnification of positive illusion in manic states and a deficit in depressed states. Taylor acknowledges that genetic and biochemical factors may well play a significant part in these disorders, especially in their extreme forms. At the same time, in their mild forms, mania and depression are experiences shared by most persons periodically. There is ample evidence too that depression is a frequent component of many varieties of emotional disturbance (e.g., Lehmann, 1985). In mania, positive illusions about one's abilities, talents, self-esteem, capacity to control things, and personal qualities are all greatly exaggerated. Creativity may be enhanced as well as one's leadership capacity. While in this state persons are sometimes extraordinarily productive and socially effective. One could argue that the exaggerated illusions that are part of the manic experience are not just disruptive but also functional and adaptive in their mild forms.

Depression, Taylor argues, represents an absence or loss of illusion: 'The depressed person regards the self, the world, and the future through mud-colored glasses' (1989, p. 211). Mental health theorists and clinicians have long believed that the person in a depressed state holds negative perceptions that are distortions of reality. Recent and accumulating evidence, however, supports the view that depressed persons may see the world more clearly than the normal person, at least in some aspects. Taylor summarizes this enormous body of research briefly as follows:

> Normal people exaggerate how competent and well-liked they are. Depressed people do not. Normal people remember their past behavior with a rosy glow. Depressed people are more evenhanded in recalling their successes and failures. Normal people describe themselves primarily positively. Depressed people describe both their positive and negative qualities. Normal people take credit for successful outcomes and tend to deny responsibility for failure. Depressed people accept responsibility for both success and failure. Normal people exaggerate the control they have over what goes on around them. Depressed people are less vulnerable to the illusion of control. Normal people believe to an unrealistic degree that the future holds a bounty of good things. Depressed people are more realistic in their perceptions of the future. (p. 214)

Taylor acknowledges that depressed persons are not always more accurate in their perceptions. Sometimes they are more negative and unrealistically pessimistic about the future than normal persons. People with mild levels of depression tend to see themselves and the world more clearly, whereas the more severely depressed are likely to be unrealistically gloomy in their outlook. The loss or absence of positive illusion in depressed persons, albeit temporary, does appear to have some adverse effects on their functioning. Taylor comments:

> Depressed people may actually be less capable of creative, insightful thought than nondepressed people . . . Depressed people show less complex thought processes . . . use fewer categories to make sense of information than nondepressed people, and the categories they do use tend to be quite simple ones. (p. 217)

Taylor speculates that the inability to hold or make use of positive illusions may make some persons more vulnerable to become or remain depressed. Interestingly, her conjectures are similar to those of Aaron Beck, a noted authority in the field of depression. He (Beck, Rush, Shaw, & Emery, 1979) believes that depression results, in part, from the person's tendency to form negative evaluations of the self, the world, and the future. Beck's cognitive approach to the treatment of depression places strong emphasis on enabling depressed persons to think more positively about themselves and the world. Taylor notes, 'When depressed people are no longer depressed, they show the same self-enhancing biases and illusions as nondepressed people' (1989, p. 223).

CONCLUDING THOUGHTS

An impressive body of evidence suggests that positive illusions about oneself, the world, and the future are characteristic of most persons most of the time. This evidence implies that positive illusions in our clients function more like assets than liabilities. In fact, it appears that the absence of these positive distortions of reality may signal depression and lowered functioning. One implication of this view for therapists of any persuasion is that acceptance and support of these apparently beneficial illusions may be more helpful than interventions that aim at disillusionment and 'better' reality testing. As students of psychotherapy, teachers, and supervisors, we may well benefit from reexamining our beliefs about what constitutes mental health and mental disturbance. On this issue, Taylor challenges all students of psychology and the helping professions to reconsider their beliefs.

> Increasingly, we must view the psychologically healthy person not as someone who sees things as they are but as someone who sees things as he or she would like them to be. Effective functioning in everyday life appears to depend on interrelated positive illusions, systematic small distortions of reality that make things appear better than they are. (1989, p. 228)

Taylor concludes her thinking by speculating that positive illusions may be evolutionary accommodations because of their adaptive function. Finally she suggests, 'The mind may be intrinsically structured so as to be healthy. It almost seems that good mental health is not something that a few fortunate people achieve on their own, but something intrinsic to human nature, at least for the majority' (p. 244).

Perhaps Taylor is right, or only partially so since she is subject to the same illusions that we all are. She seems to offer us a relevant and compelling challenge to reconsider our view of the person and the factors that contribute to adaptive functioning and well-being. Our own convictions and 'truths,' of course, are not immune from the effects of illusion. The predominantly positive view of the person that is held by person-centered theorists and practitioners is similar, in some ways, to the view that mentally healthy persons hold of themselves. Both views would seem to contain elements of truth and illusion. As scholars and practitioners attempting to advance our knowledge of persons and to facilitate their development, we must remain receptive to alternative views, regardless of whether they are compatible with our own. After all, even our sacred cows are just cows, though they may serve us well until we create better ones.

REFERENCES

Beck, A., Rush, A., Shaw, B., & Emery, G. (1979). *Cognitive therapy of depression*. New York: Guilford Press.

Jahoda, M. (1967). Toward a social psychology of mental health. In L. Rabkin & J. Carr (Eds.), *Sourcebook in abnormal psychology* (pp. 20–9). Boston: Houghton Mifflin.

Jourard, S. (1974). *Healthy personality*. New York: Macmillan.

Lehmann, L. (1985). The relation of depression to other DSM-III Axis I Disorders. In E. Beckham & W. Leber (Eds.), *Handbook of depression* (pp. 669–99). Homewood, IL: Dorsey Press.

Maslow, A. H. (1970). *Motivation and personality* (2nd ed.). New York: Harper & Row.

Rogers, C. R. (1959). A theory of therapy, personality, and interpersonal relations as developed in the client-centered framework. In S. Koch (Ed.), *Psychology: A study of science* (Vol. 3, pp. 184–256). New York: McGraw-Hill.

Taylor, S. E. (1989). *Positive illusions: Creative self-deception and the healthy mind*. New York: Basic Books.

Celebration, Reflection and Renewal:
50 years of Client-Centered Therapy and beyond

David J. Cain   *Carlsbad, California*

In this article, I will take a brief look at the roots and the major contributions of Carl Rogers and client-centered therapy, reflect on the current scene, and offer some thoughts about the future.

On December 11, 1940, Carl Rogers gave a speech to the campus chapter of Psi Chi at the University of Minnesota entitled 'Newer Concepts in Psychotherapy.' To a remarkable degree Rogers identified in this speech many of the elements that gave client-centered therapy its distinctive character for the next 50 years. Initially, Rogers was surprised at the intensity of the reaction to his talk:

> I was totally unprepared for the furor the talk aroused. I was criticized, I was praised, I was attacked, I was looked on with puzzlement . . . It struck me that perhaps I was saying something new that came from *me;* that I was not just summarizing the viewpoint of therapists in general. (Kirschenbaum, 1979, p. 113)

Such reactions would be familiar ones to Rogers throughout his professional career as it repeatedly became apparent to him that ideas that seemed so basic to him would seem so radical and controversial to others. Eventually, Rogers too realized that what he was saying and doing was indeed quite radical relative to other approaches to counseling and psychotherapy.

Rogers' impact (and that of his colleagues) on the fields of psychology, psychotherapy, education, and human relations in general can be variously described as momentous, pervasive, indirect, and elusive. At a time when the fields of counseling and psychotherapy were in their early stages of development in the United States, Rogers was a pioneer. He and his colleagues led the way in

1. Emphasizing the importance of the therapeutic relationship as a healing agent in therapy
2. Articulating a view of the person as inherently resourceful and self-actualizing
3. Developing the art of listening and understanding and demonstrating its therapeutic effect on the client
4. Introducing the term *client,* as opposed to *patient,* to convey greater respect, dignity, and equality for the person seeking help
5. Initiating the sound recordings of therapeutic interviews for learning purposes and informal research
6. Initiating scientific research on the process and outcome of psychotherapy
7. Paving the way for psychologists and other nonmedical professionals to engage in the practice of psychotherapy
8. Contributing significantly to the development of the encounter group movement
9. Offering a radical alternative to the field of education
10. Applying the person-centered approach to conflict resolution and world peace

First published in *Person-Centered Review*, Volume 5, Number 4, November 1990.

REFLECTIONS

Many of Rogers' concepts (e.g., self-concept) have been absorbed into mainstream psychology, often without recognition of their origin. To a large degree Rogers' impact has been indirect. Consequently, the magnitude of his impact is difficult to assess. If I were to venture a guess about how Rogers' contributions might be assessed on their 100th anniversary (2040), I would predict that the most enduring and meaningful contributions for which he will be remembered are the therapeutic impact of *listening* and the quality of the *therapist-client relationship.* Although many practitioners do not find Rogers' style of listening and responding congenial, most all recognize the importance of empathy and the desirability of a sound working relationship with the client.

One can only hope that the caricature of the client-centered therapist mindlessly repeating back the client's words will long be forgotten. Unfortunately, this notion of client-centered therapy is likely to persist in the foreseeable future because this constricted and mechanical way of responding is still practiced by many counselors who consider themselves client-centered. Although most students of client-centered therapy realize that the essence of the approach is to create a relationship that enables clients to identify and tap their resources, many rely heavily on an emphatic response mode to accomplish this end, often to the exclusion of other helpful response modes. Although careful listening and emphatic responding are basic and desirable components of client-centered therapy, they do not define its parameters. This limited view of how client-centered therapy is or should be practiced persists despite the fact that client-centered theory and values do not dictate reliance on any particular techniques or response styles. As Rogers himself commented on this issue:

> The approach is paradoxical. It is rooted in a profound regard for the wisdom and the constructive capacity inherent in the human organism—a regard that is shared by those who hold to this approach. At the same time, it encourages those who incorporate these values to develop their own special and unique ways of being, their own ways of implementing this shared philosophy. (1986, p. 4)

Rogers obviously recognized that there were individual differences in therapists' personalities and styles that would affect the way they could best create a growthful environment for the client. Part of Rogers' respect for the person of the therapist is this recognition that each therapist must develop a way of working that fits him or her, just as Rogers did. As client-centered therapists recognize that client-centered theory is not constrictive and can be implemented in diverse and creative ways, it is likely that its effectiveness will increase. In addition, the client-centered approach will likely become more appealing to graduate students and other professionals who will see that they can be client-centered and also be themselves.

For years there has been debate by client-centered practitioners and persons of other therapeutic persuasion over whether the six conditions specified by Rogers (1957) are 'necessary and sufficient' for therapeutic change. To my knowledge there is no definitive answer to this question. Although further research may throw more light on the issue, it may be an unanswerable question in general. This is because the personal qualities, skills, and adaptiveness of the therapist and the unique needs and personal style of the client must be factored into the equation of what contributes to the effectiveness of the therapy for a particular client. Rogers was a virtuoso in sensing the feelings and meanings of the client and communicating them in a clear and 'hearable' manner to the client. I doubt that there were few, if any, therapists who could do what he did as well as he did. Yet, I believe it is fair to say that other therapists might be as effective in assisting their clients by drawing on their individual strengths and skills, though they may well be different from those of Rogers.

One of my first graduate instructors, a person who found Rogers' therapeutic approach congenial, expressed a sentiment similar to Rogers' when he stated, 'You can best be yourself and nobody else.' My point is that Rogers' enormous skill and presence contributed greatly to his effectiveness. Others using similar response styles to Rogers', but without his personal characteristics, are not likely to be nearly as effective. However, other therapists may become increasingly effective by recognizing and drawing on their unique strengths and skills rather than by attempting to imitate Rogers' way of being. Thus, whether some therapist qualities are 'necessary and sufficient' for a particular client will vary enormously with the unique qualities of the therapist, the manner in which they are implemented, and the personal characteristics and needs of the client.

For some clients, the six conditions Rogers specified may be 'necessary and sufficient' when they are provided by an adequately skilled therapist. For other clients, conditions not yet specified by client-centered theory may be required for therapeutic change. Rather than ask whether six conditions are *sufficient*, I believe it would be more useful to identify a range of therapist and client factors that are *optimal* in promoting therapeutic growth for a wide variety of clients. Rainer Sachse has expressed a similar sentiment:

> The preservation of client-centered therapy in its present form is not reasonable because we are far from being able to offer the client an *optimal* or perfect therapy . . . What we need is the development of an *adaptive* therapeutic . . . strategy. The therapy must be adapted to the client and not the other way around. (1989, pp. 21–2)

Although the conditions that are optimal in fostering growth may include those specified by Rogers, they probably include others as well. Given the uniqueness of each course of therapy, one might expect that the client and therapist factors that would promote growth in one therapeutic endeavor would vary from those that would be optimally helpful in another. Only an open-ended and open-minded search for all the factors that critically affect the effectiveness of therapy will enable client-centered therapists to become maximally helpful to their clients.

However, we need more than speculation about such factors. In addition, various hypotheses about the critical elements in therapy must be tested with sound research. The facts can only be friendly because clients will be the ultimate beneficiaries of what is learned.

RENEWAL: THE NEXT 50 YEARS

As I anticipate what the next 50 years might hold for client-centered therapy and person-centered approaches, I see reason for optimism and cause for concern. In the United States and Canada there is relatively little interest in this approach. Client-centered therapy is not being taught in graduate programs in psychology, counseling, social work, psychiatric nursing, or psychiatry, except in rare instances. Part of the problem is that there are relatively few university faculty available who have the background or interest to teach client-centered therapy. To put this in perspective, however, one should note that other 'schools' (e.g., Gestalt, Jungian, Adlerian) of therapy appear to be in a similar position. Except for cognitive-behavioral therapy and to some degree psychoanalytic and systems approaches, most therapists become eclectic in their work. What this implies is that we need to be concerned about how we can reproduce ourselves.

Clearly, more graduate faculty will continue to be needed in U.S. universities. In addition, we must renew our research tradition and with it our legitimate place as one of the leaders in the field of psychotherapy. Another way to increase the visibility and impact of client-centered therapy is to address the pressing issues facing people throughout the world. Alcohol and drug abuse, physical and sexual abuse of children and women, the effect of divorce on families, conflict within and between countries, and violence against people are just some of the problems that might be addressed more systematically. Similarly, client-centered practitioners could contribute more significantly to the major issues facing psychology and other helping professions. Issues that come to mind include the training of helping professionals, the developing of new research paradigms, setting ethical standards for practitioners and researchers, and the developing more effective treatment for the severely disturbed.

By bringing their expertise and creativity to these problems and by *publishing* their findings in a variety of journals and books, client-centered therapists could increase their visibility and impact. As students and helping professionals *see* that client-centered practitioners have much to offer, they will want to know what we know and put it to use. To the degree that client-centered practitioners enter the mainstream, they will also reduce their insularity. Instead of talking primarily to each other, client-centered therapists could afford themselves the opportunity to enter into dialogue with, learn from, and influence helping professionals with other perspectives. By doing so, client-centered practitioners inevitably would increase their knowledge base and, ultimately, their effectiveness.

There is some evidence that such change is already occurring. During the 1988 International Conference on Client-Centered and Experiential Therapy, held in Leuven, Belgium, there was considerable diversity and dialogue among the participants. Papers were presented on a wide range of topics, including: process research and its implications for practice; treatment of clients with a wide range of problems (e.g., depression, mental retardation, schizophrenia); family, child, and marital therapy; dream work; comparison and/or integration of client-centered therapy with other approaches including experiential therapy; and various papers addressing theoretical issues. Most of these papers were written by persons from countries outside the United States where, in many cases, client-centered and experiential therapy has a wider and more enthusiastic following. A large number of these papers were published in a book entitled *Client-Centered and Experiential Therapy in the Nineties,* which was edited by Lietaer, Rombauts, and Van Balen (1990). This publication represents the first major book of articles published on client-centered therapy since Levant and Shlien's book in 1984. It clearly demonstrates that client-centered scholars and therapists are indeed evolving in their thinking and practice and are addressing issues of interest to therapists of other approaches.

In 1991, there will be a Second International Conference on Client-Centered and Experiential Therapy. It will take place at the University of Stirling, Scotland. In 1992, the Fifth International Forum for the Person-Centered Approach will be held in Holland. It is clear, then, that client-centered therapy continues to be of great interest to many professionals around the world. If this interest, energy, and commitment can be sustained, client-centered therapy may take its place once again as one of the leaders in the field of psychotherapy.

REFERENCES

Kirschenbaum, H. (1979). *On becoming Carl Rogers*. New York: Delacorte Press.

Levant, R. F., & Shlien, J. M. (1984). Client-centered therapy and the person-centered approach. New York: Praeger.

Lietaer, G., Rombauts, J., & Van Balen, R. (Eds.), (1990). *Client-centered and experiential therapy in the nineties*. Leuven, Belgium: Catholic University of Leuven Press.

Rogers, C. R. (1957). The necessary and sufficient conditions of therapeutic personality change. *Journal of Consulting Psychology, 21*, 95–103.

Rogers, C. R. (1986). Editor's introduction. *Person-Centered Review, 1*, 3–4.

Sachse, R. (1989). Proposals for the future of client-centered and experiential therapy. *Person-Centered Review, 4*, 21–2.

An Interview with

Carl Rogers

David Ryback

Editor's Note: This interview was conducted at Carl Rogers' home in La Jolla in April 1985. It presents Rogers' views, toward the end of his life, on a number of issues that continue to be relevant as we approach the coming decades.

Carl Rogers first became known to me while I was a graduate student at San Diego State University. Following a guest lecture at one of my classes, I remember walking him back to his car and asking about romantic love — something about Romeo and Juliet and the nature of intense longing as contrasted to his concept of unconditional, nonpossessive love. I forget his exact answer but what remains with me is my complete respect for his ability to unflinchingly tackle any question with utmost candor and open-hearted sincerity. It was this quality that pulled me to him. I first came to his attention by name when I invited him to keynote the second conference on Humanistic Education which I had founded in 1974. I picked him up at the airport in Atlanta and during the next few days of the Conference we became friends. I visited his home in La Jolla a number of times, staying in the guest room behind his garden of succulents. It was during one of these visits that I invited Carl to the following discussion.

David Ryback: All education is a moral enterprise fundamentally. That is to say, whether it is person-centered or traditional, it deals with the development of youngsters by providing an environment for their optimal growth. We have some visions of a positive life experience when we propose any curriculum. I'm struggling with the assumption of morality intrinsic in education, particularly of the young. What are the moral principles on which you base your person-centered curriculum and, second, on what personal experience do you base this?

Carl Rogers: That's certainly a very serious and profound question. I sympathize with your asking of it. I think it's a difficult question. I think that, for me — and this may be much more than you would want to agree with — I don't believe there is a goal out there toward which I should be trying to develop students — a moral goal or any other kind of goal. I believe that, whatever morality there is in the point of view that I hold, it is in the belief in the worth of the person as an individual, and the fact that, given a free opportunity to choose, he will move in directions that are socially constructive. So I think this is a truly moral point of view but not in the sense of knowing the goal to which he will arrive. And to me that makes a great deal of sense in the modern world. I don't know which of us is wise enough to say that a student today should be, 15 years from now, such and such a kind of person. The world is changing so rapidly that I don't know anyone who's wise enough to set that kind of goal. But, if I trust the student to make responsible choices right now, he's going to move in directions that are constructive, and, the more practice

First published in *Person-Centered Review,* Volume 4, Number 1, February 1989.

he gets in moving in such directions, the more likely he is to move in what I regard as socially moral or socially constructive directions as his life goes on. And I mean that very seriously. For example, to pick up one very debatable point these days, I know, and I'm sure you do, too, of many, many young people who are living together without marriage. Is that moral or not? It takes a wiser man than I am to know whether that's moral but as I've talked to some of these people and find the very high ideals they have for their relationship — not all of them necessarily, but certainly a number that I know — the more I would say that they are making significant moral choices with which I would not be inclined to disagree, despite the fact that my own youth started at such an age when such a thing would have really been quite unthinkable. So that's my response to your question. It's certainly not a complete answer to it, but that's some of my thinking.

David: So your morality, if we can call it that, stems from your continuing affirmation and belief in the worth and the power of the individual, the client, and the student, as he or she continues to experience and learn. Do you still maintain that belief as the years go by? And, if so, more strongly?

Carl: I think the answer to that is really quite simple. Yes, I do maintain it — if anything, more strongly. I think the more experience I've had, the more reason I see to believe in the person who is open to his experience. Let me try to put that a little bit more fully. When I trust a person and try to facilitate his learning, whether in therapy or in education or in encounter group or whatever, I am trying to make it easier for that person to be open to what's going on within — the feelings and reaction and so on that he's having — and also to be more aware of the various stimuli that are impinging on him from the external world. In my mind the person most to be trusted (this is kind of a theoretical principle as well as a practical one) is the person who is most open to his experiences, both inner and outer. A person who comes anywhere near fulfilling that criterion, and none of us approach it very closely, though I think we try to move in that direction, is trustworthy in the extreme. I would be willing to trust him as a scientist, educator, philosopher, you name it. I feel that that person is perhaps one of the few basic things that I trust. If the person is really aware of all of the options, open to as much as possible of his experience, I'll bet on him as being the person who is going to move in sensible directions and ones that, in the long run, will prove to be worthwhile.

David: So if I were more open to my feelings, I'd make more sensible decisions. I guess I'm still moving in that direction. As a teacher and professor years ago, I was one of those who exercised a great deal of control when I first began. Over the years, I gradually relaxed more and more. I'm not sure where I am on the continuum now, but I discovered that it was a very slow and somewhat painful process for me. I'm still moving in that direction to trust others and to trust myself. And I'm thinking that there may be others out there (though I'm only speaking for myself now) who would like to move more in the direction of giving up some of that control. What steps could we take? What steps can I take? What are some of the things that I may do or feel within myself to become this sort of facilitator?

Carl: Well, that's a heavy question. First, let me deal with one part of it. It isn't the central point but I'd like to comment on it. You said that it's been painful moving toward a more person-centered point of view and I certainly found that, too, in every respect where I've tried it. For example, it's much more painful to move in the direction of being person-centered than it is to continue being a good, conventional, authoritarian teacher. And I'm sort of puzzled over that. It seems to me that one reason is that we never know what happens when we maintain the conventional point of view. We never know the real outcomes and so we can be quite happy with it, for example— 'I gave a series of good lectures so they must have learned a lot.' On the other hand, when you try to facilitate a group and let them express themselves, you find that some of the things you hoped were happening don't seem to be happening, and you feel you were trying to trust them and they don't feel very trusted. And the whole thing is a painful growth process where you know what's happening, so it's much more raw somehow than when you give a nice, packaged bit of education in the older sense.

As for your main question: I don't know of any one simple way that I can tell you that one can increase his facilitative attitude. I just think that it is a continual process of growth. I held a workshop some years ago and had the pleasure of working with my daughter on the staff. In fact, she was the one who initially proposed the idea. I personally thought of myself as being quite open as to what was going on and as being quite facilitative and someone made the remark that some of the things that were going on in that large morning discussion could easily be topics for special subgroups. I said, 'Yeah, that's so. Some of the things that *he* said, and that *he* said, and that *he* said, would all make very good topics.' And my daughter just flew up in a rage. She said: 'Where are the women? Why don't you mention any of the women who spoke up?' And that really hit me where I live. I thought for a while and then I said, 'Well, I guess my awareness hasn't extended to that point yet.' As I thought it over, a number of the women had said things that were just as valuable as the things that the men had said. And yet the old habits persist. We find that in any situation. So, I'm quite convinced that it's a lifelong process of trying to learn from each experience to be a little more open than we were before. And then, too, I find it very valuable to try continually to get feedback because then I find that trusting people has been worthwhile. I'm lucky in being older in that I get letters from people I dealt with a long time ago. Sometimes, where I felt the contact was superficial or not very good, I then found later that because I did trust them it had a lot of meaning for them. We gradually learn from feedback that it's worthwhile to place more trust in people and to be more open to them.

David: This is a practical question, something that comes to my mind when you allude to the competitive attitude that some men may have toward women. Many school systems have done away with the system of honor graduates and the honor roll. This has concerned a lot of parents as well as teachers. They say that doing away with competition or the competitive spirit will make for mediocre students and for mediocre performance. What can we tell these parents when they raise this issue?

Carl: I think that competitiveness is so deeply built into our culture that any attempt even to modify it is bound to bring a lot of adverse reaction. I suppose that (I'm thinking out loud and perhaps these are not very practical answers to a practical question) it would be interesting to see if those students who wanted to be honor students and to have that kind of system could go ahead and have that and those who didn't like it could go ahead and do away with it. We often forget that you can give people alternatives. I don't like to 'impose' freedom or impose a new set of values, and that might be one way of gradually sorting it out. My guess would be that if there were a division along those lines, no matter how it went, that gradually the students who were all gung-ho for honors would feel, 'But, gee, these people seem to be having a much more interesting time—they're all doing what they want to do. They're not quite so worried and anxious.' I feel the same kind of choice exists between the conventional and the person-centered kinds of classes. I've quite admired some school systems which have been able to say, 'All right, if some children and their parents want their learning to be primarily reading, writing, and arithmetic, here are some classes where that's possible. And for those who would prefer a more open system, that's possible, too.' I realize you can't do that in every situation. But I admire that attempt because I think it begins to educate people in making choices. It begins to educate parents and students themselves so that they don't feel that you're abolishing something, but that you're giving them a chance to choose between two systems.

David: You're known as one of the earliest innovators of encounter groups, as they were then known. I would like to know what you feel about encounter groups or group process now that they seem to have peaked. I can remember, in the past three decades, excitement about all kinds of group process, ranging from Paul Bindrim's nude marathons to Bell & Howell tapes and leaderless groups. Currently there seems to be a decline in groups. Even Werner Erhard's Forum seems anticlimactic compared to the wild days of EST. And many people suggest that the original advent of groups reflected the fact that we were very much out of touch with ourselves and our bodies and that groups were an attempt to get back in touch with them. Perhaps we could now attribute the decline in the popularity of groups to the fact that we are now more in touch with ourselves than we were previously.

Carl: No, that wouldn't be my answer. I think that the decline in interest in encounter groups is probably directly connected with the faddish nature that they came to assume. I feel it's been quite a while since I'd heard of a nude marathon — no, but I remember one now, just a few weeks ago. At any rate, the situation gets worse as more and more people get into it to gain notoriety or to exercise their control over people, because an encounter group can become a terribly gimmicky experience that is really just another way of pushing people around. And I think that has tended to give groups a bad name. I have sometimes said that it is quite possible that a phrase like *encounter group* may become as socially unpopular as the phrase *progressive education,* for instance. Progressive education was a good idea and most of the changes that have gone on in education can be traced back to some of the ideas that have grown from the whole progressive education movement. But because for a time it became so faddish and so overdone, giving way to such captions of cartoons as 'Mother, do I have to do what I want to do?' and so on, that it gradually became a very unpopular term and yet, underneath that, is a steady movement in the direction of what, if it wasn't an unpopular term, we could still call *progressive education.* And my feeling is that people have a desire for closeness, for acceptance, for finding relationships where they can really be themselves and be accepted. I don't think that's diminished at all. I think that's a very dominant need in today's life, and that whether the term *encounter group* dies out or not, I just feel quite certain that the kind of impulse, and the kind of experience that that represents at its best, is going to continue under one guise or another.

David: Certainly teachers, so susceptible to burnout because of deteriorating conditions in school systems, need as much support and acceptance as anyone else. Assuming a system in which most learners are committed to a continued process of growth, do you see an ongoing group experience for teachers who are in training?

Carl: Yes, I indeed most assuredly do. I don't know of anything that might revolutionize teacher training institutions quite as quickly as the introduction of an intensive group experience for teachers in training, where they would learn to be more aware of themselves, and more aware of how different people are from their facades and surfaces, where they would get acquainted with other people who at first may seem unlikable or whatever. And then they find that when they get underneath — here's a real person worthy of respect. One of the things that I suggest is that a way to change attitudes within educational institutions, which often are very rigid and very conventional, would be to institute a series of intensive groups. I wouldn't care if only a small minority joined such groups. They would begin to create a ferment which would reach far beyond the number of student teachers involved. I guess what I'm talking about is the possibility of extending democracy clear down to the grass roots. If we can appreciate that education belongs to the learners, and that parents are also learners, then they have to learn to exercise responsibility, too. And this, to my mind, is very exciting.

David: So one of your values appears to be related to grass-roots democracy. Earlier, you made an allusion to socially constructive directions — that which would benefit society, I imagine. I wonder if that was as close as you'd come to a value-laden statement on your part. Would you feel that when you make a statement like that you probably reflect not quite the ultimate in openness or the philosophy you seem to project otherwise in your own person? Do you always feel an emotional integrity and ideological synthesis of everything you believe in, as expressed in your books and your public statements?

Carl: I'm not entirely sure that I get the whole drift of your question. If you mean, am I trying to say that I am that person — no! But if you're asking, was I really proposing one value above others — yes! I most assuredly was. I think I'm willing to stand by valuing the person above anything else, and a lot of things flow from that if you really believe that. I'm not really sure that answers your question.

David: It does. I'm trying to lead into something. It has to do with us as helpers sometimes needing help or perspective ourselves. One of my own clients is a counselor in a secondary school. She deals mostly with student clients. Then she turns around and sees administrators and teachers who also express tremendous inner need. So one of the issues we're dealing with relates to the personal/emotional needs of the helper. For example, the teachers and administrators might ask: 'When do I suddenly become an emotional person, and stop talking about my students? When do my students quit "becoming" and when do I start "becoming"?' What are your feelings on that particular aspect?

Carl: I have very strong feelings on that but I'm not sure how practical they are. I think the most exciting thing a school counselor could do would be to gradually shift her clientele from students to teachers. I've only known one or two counselors who have been able to do that. Often the job is defined in such a way that you can't do that. But school counselors — college counselors, too, for that matter — are so often working with the faulty end product of a system. It would be far more economical and efficient and make a lot more sense if they were dealing with the people who were helping to create some of these difficulties and who need understanding. I'm not trying to deride the teachers — they need understanding. They need to become and they are eager for that, and it's just very unfortunate that in our culture, to be a young person and say, 'Hey, I'm in trouble — I need your help,' that's okay. But for an adult to say, 'I don't know where I'm going, I'm all mixed up, I don't know just what I want to do,' and to turn to a counselor in a school system for that kind of help is unheard of. I'm sure that that person would be looked down upon. So it's a subtle thing but one which I feel very, very deeply. We probably would be making much more efficient use of money spent for school counselors if they dealt with teachers mainly rather than with students only.

David: So a lot of processing is appropriate at the higher levels of power, not only at the grass roots. In the past few years, you've spent a good deal of your energy on promoting world peace through person-centered negotiations. Having entered the arena of world politics, have you ever felt you were used politically by one group or another? And, conversely, have you gained some degree of political power to influence others?

Carl: Now, if I understand your question, has any pressure ever been put on me to try to work toward a particular type of manipulative goal? Not that I can recall. I think they would get a quick answer, so maybe such attempts have been made and I don't remember them. I think you touched on something that I'd like to say a word about. Two things that make me unhappy. One is when people sort of mindlessly try to follow me or anybody else. One of my favorite Zen sayings is: 'When you meet the Buddha—kill the Buddha.' I think that's extremely good advice. When you find the guy who has all the answers, the person you really ought to follow, the person that shows you the way to go, well . . . I'd try and get rid of him psychologically. I hope you don't really kill him, but, at any rate, get rid of him psychologically. Then the other thing that I wanted to comment on is that one of the things that makes me most unhappy is when people adopt some of these notions in a pseudo fashion and that can be done. That is, you can talk an awfully good game of humanistic education, or having regard for the worth of the person or something, and really turn that into a game, into a pseudo-something that isn't the real thing. That makes me terribly unhappy. I'd much rather have someone really stoutly opposed say, 'I don't like your ideas— I'm 100% against them,' than to have someone say, 'Oh, I'm for your ideas.' Then, when I watch him at work, I find that he's really making a pseudo-something out of it that's very false and phony.

David: A number of social critics have proposed this to me so I'll pass it along to you for your reaction. They've argued that we live in a very hierarchical society where poverty is solidly stratified in the social structures, and the elite power groups maintain this. The schools are the major vehicle for it. But then, when you propose that humanistic education or person-centered education would be one way to improve schools, they return with the criticism that that's a cop-out and all that does is salve things over well enough so that the system can continue without facing the basic problems. Do you have a reaction?

Carl: Yes, I do. One of the themes that is continually brought up is that a person-centered point of view is all right if you are talking about the affluent middle class, where you're dealing with people who have plenty and so on, but if you're dealing with people who are really repressed it's no good at all. I think that a person-centered approach to minorities has a great deal to offer to such groups. In other words I don't think it is a cop-out because I think if it's applied across the board in administration, in our dealing with minorities in education, and so on, it makes a total web of a new kind of society. I've written of some examples in my books of the way in which powerless groups, when they recognize their own strength as persons, become decidedly powerful. That, I think, is true of minority groups **and oppressed** groups in general. Incidentally, I think students are one of the oppressed groups. That's why it's dangerous to teach only one class in a school in a student-centered fashion. Because then those students acquire a sense of their own worth, of their own independence, their own chance to make choices, and they begin to make trouble all through the school system. That's what people object to, why they get all upset, because it is rocking the boat, and they get disturbed.

David: Since we're talking about oppressed groups, what about the emerging equality of women? In all of American history, women have been an oppressed group. Until recently, they have felt a sense of powerlessness. Has that affected the personal growth of women? Has their lack of freedom inhibited individual or personal growth?

Carl: Oh, I think that feeling a sense of powerlessness inhibits individual growth a great deal. It's been true of women, it's been true of Blacks, and I think it's true of all minority groups. I think it's true of students when they feel that they have no power. On the other hand, the women's liberation movement, in spite of certain excesses perhaps, by and large is a very person-centered thing. They believe in women as persons, as individuals. When that begins to happen then women begin to grow as individuals. I think of a number of women whom I know who really have undergone quite a transformation as they realized, 'My gosh, I can be an independent person. I don't have to be just a second-rate citizen.' So I think the answer is, yes. If the person feels powerless, that really does inhibit his personal growth or her personal growth. But as he or she begins to get a sense of his or her own worth and the possibility of independence—Wow! that's a real stimulant to individual growth.

David: Getting back to group process for a moment, some individuals have urged against using group process with people who might have daily interaction with one another. This has implications for those in industry as well as in education. Would you care to comment on that?

Carl: Yes, I would. I've come to hold just the opposite point of view. I think that the most *dramatic* groups I've had are encounter groups where you see tremendous transformations in people that often last over the years. On the other hand, a lot of people who come to stranger groups get all fired up and get new insights and so on and go back home and that rapidly diminishes. Now you take a group of people who are working together, they are going to be much more cautious in exposing themselves. You're not likely to have such a dramatic group. They know that they're going to be seeing you tomorrow. And they're not sure just what you're going to make of the things they say. They're not sure they trust you enough. It's easier to trust strangers than it is to trust the person you work with in your office. But, I think, in the long run, that the smaller and less dramatic changes that occur in a group that's been working together have a more lasting impact on the organization and on the individual than the perhaps more dramatic stranger group. So, I've tried increasingly to work with groups that are going to be working together. For example, years ago one of our staff members started a group on 'Human Dimensions in Medical Education' and they were successful in getting a lot of medical educators into the conferences which were essentially encounter group experiences and we found that they really took to that. They really enjoyed that. One great drawback was that in order to recruit a group we drew from various parts of the country, rarely more than one person from a medical school. We tried slowly to change that. Pretty soon there were three or four coming from one medical school. That was better. They went back home and had their own support groups. Finally, we got to the point where it was sufficiently accepted that there were two or three medical schools which were asking the staff to come and put on such a conference at their medical schools, and I think that turned out to be much better and to have a much more lasting impact.

David: Sort of a social facilitation effect, as social behaviorists might call it. In that regard, what about the age-old debate between free will and determinism? Do humanists need any further new arguments against those who feel choice is an illusion and that we have no choice?

Carl: Yes, I expect we need more arguments, but I don't think they'll do any good. I think that that's a question of one's deepest philosophy, really, and it's not too likely to be changed by arguments. On the other hand, people who have experienced choice in their own lives and who have found that it really makes a difference in the direction that they take—they don't particularly need intellectual arguments to decide which philosophy is for them. I don't get awfully excited about arguing that philosophical point. But I do find a great deal of satisfaction in helping people discover experiences which give them the opportunity of significant choice and living with those significant choices and feeling, 'I do have a part in shaping my life.' To me, that then becomes a living philosophy, not a question of which intellectual philosophy they believe.

David: So you enjoy helping other people gain a sense of significance and personal power, more than debating a worn philosophical issue. Are you still doing individual therapy and, if so, how much has your point of view been changed by some of the more recent developments in the therapeutic field? And, if I'm not being too personal, what are you learning about yourself?

Carl: Since I moved to California, about 20 years ago, I haven't done any individual therapy. I came to realize that I couldn't hold to the kind of schedule that is necessary for individual therapy. I get the same kind of kick and the same kind of psychological nourishment out of dealing with occasional encounter groups where the experience is not really all that different. I'm a tough old bird and I'm not too much influenced by all the new developments in therapy. I feel that in my own experience I have grown to be much more expressive of myself than I used to be, but expressive of my own feelings, trying to express them in a way that I own them as my own feelings and not as something I'm trying to say that is true about the other person. I don't know whether that distinction gets across, but it's really a very important distinction in experience because you can cast all kinds of judgments in feeling terms. I feel you're no good and say that's a feeling—well, no, it isn't. It's a judgment. On the other hand, if I express a real feeling that I don't like you very well, then that's a feeling in *me*, one that you and I then both have to deal with. It's that kind of thing that I have certainly learned to express more of—both negative and positive feelings, more than I used to do.

David: Thank you, Carl.

Theory as Autobiography:
The development of Carl Rogers

Julius Seeman   *George Peabody College of Vanderbilt University*

This paper examines the thesis that Rogers' theoretical formulations evolved in close relationship to his development as a person—in short, that his conceptual formulations may be seen as an approximation of his professional autobiography. The paper examines samples of Rogers' writings in the three domains of personality theory, therapy theory, and research philosophy and shows how these writings mirrored his more general development. The paper concludes that clinical theory by its nature contains elements of professional and personal autobiography.

It should come as no surprise that clinical theories, far from being intellective abstractions, are living theories shaped by the observations and experiences of the theorist. It can be no other way. The very subject matter of clinical theory concerns the core of human experience. The theorist who chooses to observe these experiences and to frame them in a conceptual structure cannot stand aside and escape personal involvement, for it is through his or her person that these observations must filter. Thus, the question is not whether the theorist as a person is involved in the theory. The question rather has to do with the nature of that involvement.

It is this question that I will address here, and concretely, through an examination of the life and writings of Carl Rogers. The two parts of the title above convey the directions that this examination will take. First, I will explore the continuities between the writings of Rogers the theorist and Rogers the person. Second, I will examine Rogers' work from a longitudinal perspective, on the ground that his work reveals strong developmental trends in the growth and richness of his theory and his person. Thus, to understand Rogers the person and Rogers the theorist, we must look at the course of his development.

But the conception of theory development that I have propounded here brings new questions in its train. Theories were never intended to be private reflections. They are on the contrary intended as public statements, general in application and subject to the discipline of public verification. The validity issue thus needs to be addressed, and will be in its appropriate context.

THE PARAMETERS OF THEORY

A discussion of Rogers the theorist requires the selection of writings that most centrally represent his work. At first glance such a selection may appear to be a formidable task, for Rogers was a prolific writer, and his bibliography contains nearly 300 entries. But Rogers has himself indicated the papers that held special value for him. These indications, blended with judgments of my own, produce the list that follows. I have chosen papers

First published in *Person-Centered Review,* Volume 5, Number 4, November 1990.

in three major areas of Rogers' interest: personality theory, therapy theory, and research, as well as one comprehensive theory paper.

A Comprehensive Theory Statement
  1. 'A Theory of Therapy, Personality and interpersonal Relationships as Developed in the Client-Centered Framework' (Rogers, 1959a)

Personality Theory
  2. 'A Theory of Personality and Behavior' (1951)
  3. 'The Concept of the Fully Functioning Person' (1963)

Psychotherapy Theory
  4. 'A Process Conception of Psychotherapy' (1958)
  5. 'The Necessary and Sufficient Conditions of Therapeutic Personality Change' (1957)

Research
  6. 'Persons or Science? A Philosophical Question' (1955)

The first and fourth of the foregoing entries were invited by the American Psychological Association (APA). The first, in Koch's multivolume work, was part of an ambitious project that undertook to report the contemporary status of the entire science of psychology. This paper is arguably Rogers' most comprehensive theory statement. He more than once expressed pride and satisfaction with it. The fourth was invited in connection with a Distinguished Scientific Contribution Award made to Rogers by the APA. The respect accorded to Rogers' work is symbolized by the fact that this award was granted in the first year that the award system was instituted. Rogers commented, 'Never have I been so emotionally affected as I was by the scientific contribution award and its accompanying citation' (Kirschenbaum, 1979, p. 221).

As for the other papers, the second represents the earliest comprehensive formulation of personality theory produced by Rogers. The third, on the fully functioning person, is my own choice of a paper that combines an unusual depth of analysis and an almost poetic style of writing. The fifth turned out to be a highly provocative paper, so much so that it has produced well over 500 published reports of research and evaluation (Patterson, 1984). Finally, the paper on research depicts with special clarity the developmental aspects of Rogers' thinking about research.

PERSONALITY THEORY

For Rogers, the process of theory formulation was in itself a developmental process. Although Rogers had displayed a fascination for science since his youth, his early professional work was thoroughly clinical in nature. His first book on psychotherapy (1942) was virtually devoid of theory, and indeed the term *theory* does not appear in the book's index. Moreover, Rogers' early work showed a distinct preference for clinical practice and a disinclination to theorize.

It was not long, however, before his impulse for organization and understanding manifested itself in efforts at theory development. His early efforts centered on issues of personality change associated with therapy. The first two clear-cut theory papers appeared in 1947 and 1950. Both highlighted what was to be a major dimension of his theoretical work, namely, a formulation of the key role of the self in personality structure, development, and change.[1]

The basic ground of Rogers' self theory appeared in its most systematic form a year later as a final chapter in his book *Client-Centered Therapy* (1951). The first two propositions of the theory provide the key to its structure; all other propositions flow from the premises of the first two: (1) 'Every individual exists in a continually changing world of experience of which he is the center,' and (2) 'The organism reacts to the field as it is experienced and perceived. This perceptual field is, for the individual, reality' (pp. 483–4). What is so significant about these propositions is that they embody an approach that, as we shall see, goes to the core of Rogers' whole way of functioning — namely, a thoroughgoing phenomenological approach.

For Rogers, the early 1950s turned out to be a highly fertile period of theory building, for it was just two years later, in 1953, that Rogers produced in prepublication form the paper on the fully functioning person. This paper has a strategic place in Rogers' theoretical writings for two reasons: it is his most complete and articulate description of optimal personality organization, and it is a useful bridge between personality theory and psychotherapy theory.

The paper delineates the personal characteristics of an individual who has experienced and completed a theoretically ideal process of psychotherapy. Three related characteristics are paramount: such persons would be open to their experience, they would live in an existential fashion, and they would find their organisms a trustworthy source of experiential data for arriving at satisfying decisions and action.

THERAPY THEORY

Papers 4 and 5 in the foregoing list represent systematic theory statements with respect to psychotherapy. Paper 4, on a process theory of psychotherapy, is particularly significant from two standpoints. First, its content charts a framework that helps us to highlight the developmental aspects of Rogers' professional self. Second, the mode of inquiry that Rogers used to create the paper marks a special stage in Rogers' own development.

Rogers described in some detail his mode of approach to the process theory paper. He felt a special responsibility to make the paper a significant representation of his work, because he had to present it as part of the Distinguished Scientific Contribution Award. After having entertained a number of possible themes, he abandoned all effort to summarize or conceptualize any part of his work and chose instead to make a fresh start toward a new understanding of the therapy process. To this end he immersed himself for a year in recorded therapeutic interviews, 'trying to listen as naively as possible' (Rogers, 1961, p. 128). In this process he continued to avoid broad abstractions, allowing the data to speak for themselves and himself to sense 'the simplest abstractions that would describe them' (p. 128).

From this inquiry Rogers discerned and reported a continuum that included seven sequential stages of the therapy process. Few if any individual clients would span the entire continuum, but it marked the possible range that could characterize clients as a whole. The continuum dealt centrally with modes of experiencing and communication

---

1. Rogers (1959) later let us know that these papers were written at some emotional cost. He said that "the self" was at that time a somewhat despised construct. For this reason, it was with some fear and trembling that I advanced the facts and theories contained in this paper' (p. 435).

exhibited by clients at different stages of personal development. These modes reflected more than anything else the extent to which a client was in touch with his or her own immediate experiential process.

In the first stage, there is a rigidity and remoteness from immediate awareness of any experiential process, a blockage of internal communication. By the third stage, there is much freer reporting of past feelings and somewhat more conceptualization than expression of current feelings. In the seventh stage, experiencing of present feelings occurs with immediacy and richness, and there is comfort and trust in the experiencing process. Situations are experienced in their newness; internal communication is clear.

What is evident in this formulation is the congruence between this empirically derived framework for describing psychotherapy and the earlier conceptual paper on the fully functioning person. Both formulations emphasize in-touchness, richness of experiencing and expression, and trust in self.

THERAPY THEORY AND PERSONAL EXPERIENCE

It is in these descriptions of the therapy process and outcomes that Rogers' theory and experience come together most clearly. His early descriptions of the counselor's function were couched in distant impersonal terms, but with each successive description he became less distant, more open, more expressive. For example, in *Counseling and Psychotherapy* (1942), his description was tentative and cautious:

> From the counselor's point of view, however, this is a definitely controlled relationship, an affectional bond within limits . . . The counselor frankly recognizes that he becomes to some extent emotionally involved in this relationship . . . but that this involvement must be strictly limited for the good of the patient. (p. 87)

Eight years later, in *Client-Centered Therapy* (1951), Rogers was exploring the possibilities of a deeper and more intimate relationship: 'The client moves . . . to the realization that he is accepted, respected, and loved, in this limited relationship with the therapist . . . Here she finds complete acceptance — or love if you will' (p. 159). In this description we see an emerging commitment to a closer relationship, accompanied still by a note of tentativeness in the use of the term *love.*

By 1955, the tentativeness is gone and the commitment to a personal relationship is unconditional: 'I launch myself into a relationship . . . I risk myself . . . I let myself go into the immediacy of the relationship where it is my total organism which takes over' (p. 269).

Fourteen years later, again on the place of love in psychotherapy, Rogers wrote:

> I have found it to be a very enriching thing when I can truly prize or care for or love another person and when I can let that feeling flow out to him. Like many others, I used to fear that I would be trapped by this . . . I think that I have moved a long way in the direction of being less fearful in this respect. (1969, p. 233)

The contrast between the cautious, constrained, distant style of the 1942 statement and the progressively more open and expressive statements is plain to see. These contrasts were not limited to statements concerning therapy, but were more broadly characteristic of Rogers' development toward openness, self-awareness, and expressiveness.

One index of this development comes through in Rogers' use of personal pronouns — specifically in the use of the first person singular. Table 1 shows the average frequency of use per page for the pronoun *I* in four of Rogers' books spaced over a period of 38 years.

I derived the frequencies by selecting seven pages, spaced over the length of the book, and averaging the number of times per page that *I* was used on these pages. The same page numbers were used for all four books listed in the table.

Table 1: First-person singular usage in four books by Rogers

Name of Book	*Date of Publication*	*Average Per-Page Use*
Counseling and Psychotherapy	1942	0
Client-Centered Therapy	1951	0
On Becoming a Person	1961	6.9
A Way of Being	1980	9.7

There was a parallel development in still another way with respect to Rogers' immediacy and use of self in speaking and writing. He began to decrease the use of general concepts and turned more and more toward experientially based expressions of self as the basis of his talks. There were two reasons for this development. One reason was that over time Rogers was less and less inclined to make statements that might be experienced as a way of guiding or instructing others. The second reason, the more central one, was that Rogers was coming more and more to rely on his own experiences as a way of communicating to others.

DEVELOPING VIEWS ABOUT RESEARCH

The course of Rogers' development in his thinking about research paralleled in many respects the changes that I have just reported in his thinking about psychotherapy. When Rogers embarked on an academic career at Ohio State University in 1940, the positivist model of research was the prevailing model in American behavioral science. There was emphasis upon operational definitions, attention to instrumentation, and reliance on detachment of self from data.

Rogers readily accepted this model of detachment, rigor, and objectivity. Indeed, he played a key role in demystifying the process of therapy and bringing it within the orbit of scientific scrutiny. His 1942 volume contained the first published example of a verbatim recording of an entire therapy case. In 1946 he wrote the first published review of psychotherapy research, a review that reflected his pride in the conduct of positivist-oriented research by his students. Concerning these studies, he wrote, 'The end of cultism is predicted by these studies, which would substitute patient scientific investigation for argument, and controlled measurement of results for elaborate but unsubstantiated claims' (p. 588).

In spite of the landmark character of the research that Rogers stimulated, he came to feel growing discordance between his values as a therapist and his work in research. The objectivity and detachment required by the positivist model came to be more and more discrepant from the growing personal and subjective involvement he experienced as a therapist. He voiced these doubts in several papers (e.g., 1955, 1959). In the 1959 paper, he wrote:

The logical positivism in which we were professionally reared is not necessarily the final philosophical word in an area in which the phenomenon of subjectivity plays such a vital and central part . . . Is there some view, possibly developing out of an existentialist orientation, which might preserve the values of logical positivism and the scientific advances which it has helped to foster and yet find more room for the existing subjective person who is at the heart and base even of our system of science? (p. 251)

Several years later, Rogers put forth a statement of growing decisiveness with respect to his view of science and inquiry. He had found for himself the view of science that worked for him. In a passage that he labeled 'How do we know?' he answered:

The more one pursues this question, the more one is forced to realize that in the last analysis, knowledge rests on the subjective: I *experience*; in this experiencing, I *exist*; in thus existing, I in some sense *know*, I have 'felt assurance.' All knowledge, including all scientific knowledge, is a vast inverted pyramid resting on this tiny, personal, subjective base. (1968, p. 60)

From this basic premise Rogers went on to discuss in greater detail the process of inquiry with which it was compatible. He emphasized the use of all personal avenues of knowing, leaning here on his view that 'knowing' involved pervasive organismic processes not limited to intellective knowledge. He spoke also of laying aside prior preconceptions and allowing new patterns to emerge. These developing views brought a greater sense of personal harmony between Rogers the therapist and Rogers the scientist/theorist.

THEORY AS AUTOBIOGRAPHY: A SYNTHESIS

This paper began with the thesis that a theory in the human sciences is autobiography. The theory will come from the deeper ground of the theorist's experiences and from the intellective structure by which the theorist organizes those experiences. So far the case has been made for this thesis by pointing out for each element of Rogers' theory the resemblance between his formal theory statements and the more general ground of his views and actions. For example, I pointed to Rogers' process theory of psychotherapy and indicated the ways in which his own development as a therapist was congruent with the theory.

Such resemblances between theory and person are pertinent, but they may be only at the periphery of the issue. It turned out that, for Rogers, there was a single central dynamic that integrated all of the disparate threads of his work. That dynamic was his steady development toward a thoroughgoing phenomenological construction of his own life and work. In such a pervasive context, theory and autobiography dissolve as separate entities and serve only as external labels for a deeper unity.

Rogers came to see this dynamic clearly and took it as his personal credo, stating it explicitly toward the midpoint of his career:

Experience is, for me, the highest authority. The touchstone of validity is my own experience. No other person's ideas, and none of my own ideas, are as authoritative as my experience. It is to experience that I must return again and again, to discover a closer approximation to truth as it is in the process of becoming in me. (1961, pp. 23–4)

Here Rogers unknowingly made a link with history; he created anew, with remarkable fidelity, the historic touchstones of phenomenology as developed by Husserl (1965) and others (e.g., Carr, 1987). Husserl's quest was ambitious. He envisioned a philosophy that reached toward a protoscience, a basic structure for discerning the realities upon which a science must be built. As part of the quest, Husserl delineated approaches to both content and method that yielded the most basic available data—the direct phenomena of consciousness, undiluted by preconceptions and conceptualizations that necessarily departed from the data of direct experience. As to the means for arriving at these experiential data, he devised the method of epoché and reduction to maximize access to the data. This procedure involved bracketing and setting aside the natural attitude with which one ordinarily views events, an intentional relinquishing of any pre-existing way of looking at the world, precisely in order to focus one's gaze more clearly at events of immediate experience, including events within the natural attitude (Zaner, 1975). In a general sense, the procedure has been characterized as one of disciplined naïveté.

We see in Rogers' development an inexorable movement in this direction toward phenomenology, suffusing all elements of his approach to theory building as well as to his way of working. It is evident from the very start of his work in non-directive therapy. As Shlien (1970) pointed out some years ago, Rogers' first therapy invention, 'reflection of feeling,' was designed to highlight the basic data of the client's experiential world, and this invention was just the starting point of a long developmental sequence. It will be recalled, for example, that in Rogers' major theory paper on a process conception of psychotherapy (1958), he devised his own version of the epoché and reduction, setting aside all preconceptions and going back to the basic data of the therapy experience. In his research philosophy, his success with traditional research methods was not enough to win him to that tradition. He was restive until he found a philosophy congruent with his attachment to direct experience. And, finally, we have seen in his own credo about the primacy of experiencing an explicit acceptance of his phenomenological center.

On validity

Theorists do not write for themselves alone but choose to propose general truths. Thus the question of validity arises. We expect theory propositions to withstand scrutiny and to confront questions about veracity. But the issue of validity is not a simple matter. We may have to begin by giving up the fiction that there are fixed approaches to the tests of validity. What at first glance may appear to be standard criteria—construct validity, content validity, and the like—are in fact ideologically linked to particular theoretical presuppositions about the nature of knowledge. It turns out that the question, 'How do we know?' does not have a single answer but is subsumed under particular theories of knowledge and has multiple answers.

For our purposes, then, we may inquire about phenomenologically based touchstones of validity. As I have indicated, Husserl engaged the issue of validity directly, and indeed his interest in phenomenology was based on the premise that the method itself spoke to the question of validity. He argued that by setting aside all presuppositions about a phenomenon and by approaching the phenomenon anew, purely on its own terms, the inquirer would be most open to the experiential data. The phenomenological method itself was proposed as a method leading to validity.

But a further step is required. Since theories are designed to encompass general truths, they require shared understandings. Validity in this sense comes through persons' seeing eye to eye about phenomena, through shared realities. Carr (1987), speaking from a phenomenological perspective, characterized this process as aspects of intersubjectivity:

> Intersubjectivity is in fact one of the most important new features to be noticed when Husserl begins to speak . . . If our experience is always already meshed in a world, it is a world we share with others. The objectivity of its objects is really their public character;

our conviction that they are not ours alone is a function of our interaction with others and our sense that we all experience and are part of the same world. (p. 11)

Sullivan (1953) offered a similar framework for reality testing. In his discussion of development with respect to modes of perception, he characterized the most advanced and mature mode of perception as the syntactic mode, a mode that maximized consensual validation. It is through this avenue of consensual validation, of shared realities, that the phenomenologist discovers and asserts validity.

FURTHER PERSPECTIVES, OTHER CONTRIBUTIONS

The idea that personality theory engages the personal involvement of the theorist is a widely recognized idea. Writers who have dealt with this issue have pursued it at two levels of discourse, levels that may be labeled respectively as *descriptive* and *structural.*

At the descriptive level, critics have identified particular aspects of a theory and described influences or characteristics in the life of the theorist that could have shaped the theory statement. Atwood and Tomkins (1976), for example, begin with the assertion that 'every psychological theory arises from a background of personal factors and predisposing subjective influences' (p. 170). They illustrate this premise by citing examples from the theories and personal histories of Freud, Adler, Jung, and Rogers. With respect to Rogers, they cite the concept of 'conditions of worth' and trace it to Rogers' strict religious upbringing by orthodox parents. Similar comparisons between theory and life experiences are made concerning the other theorists. Atwood and Tomkins explore in considerable detail the life and work of Jung, dwelling in particular on Jung's emphasis upon opposite tendencies (e.g., introversion-extraversion) and calling attention to Jung's personal problems with conflicting personality dispositions that fit the introversion-extraversion thesis.

Another example of descriptive comparisons is provided by Homans (1979), who offered comparative analyses of Freud and Rogers. With regard to Rogers, Homans also selected the concept of conditions of worth as a basic construct in Rogers' theory and cited life experiences that fit the concept. This illustration, and others discussed by Homans, all fit the descriptive method whereby theory statements are ascribed to the theorist's life pattern.

The second kind of explanatory principle advanced to account for autobiographical influences on theory is what I have called structural explanations. These center on the inherent characteristics of knowledge itself. The structural argument proposes that knowledge itself cannot be unconditional, standing in veridical isolation. Knowledge is regarded as relative and contextual, conditioned by both individual and cultural influences that shape the experiences and perceptions of the theorist.

Atwood and Tomkins (1976) argue that unless we take into account the role of personal factors in the structure of knowledge we are misunderstanding what knowledge is about. In this regard they concentrate on the role of personal subjectivity in theory building. Thus, they emphasize the psychology of knowledge and offer the avenue of psychobiographical study as a way of assessing the role of subjective factors in theory building. Homans (1979), on the other hand, is concerned not only with individual influences but also with the role of cultural influences, and in particular the role of mass society, in setting inherent boundaries on the experiences and perceptions of the theorist. In this sense Homans is concerned with the sociology of knowledge and the ways in which it conditions theory building.

And so we take note of the manifold influences that shape theory building and the broader spectrum of ideas that we call knowledge. These influences are often described in ways that imply defects in the theorizing process. But that is not necessarily the case. These influences may also provide relevant contexts for theories that apply to particular times and places. There is, after all, no final authority to declare what knowledge is about. Perhaps Rogers was as near to the mark as anyone when he said, 'Man lives essentially in his own subjective world . . . Thus there is no such thing as Scientific Knowledge; there are only individual perceptions of what appears to each person to be such knowledge' (1959b, p. 192).

REFERENCES

Atwood, G. E., & Tomkins, S. S. (1976). On the subjectivity of personality theory. *Journal of the History of the Behavioral Sciences, 12,* 166–77.
Carr, D. (1987). *Interpreting Husserl.* Boston: Martines Nijhoff.
Homans, P. (1979). The case of Freud and Carl Rogers. In A. R. Buss (Ed.), *Psychology in the social context* (pp. 368–92). New York: Halsted Press.
Husserl, E. (1965). *Phenomenology and the crisis of philosophy.* New York: Harper & Row.
Kirschenbaum, H. (1979). *On becoming Carl Rogers.* New York: Dell.
Patterson, C. H. (1984). Empathy, warmth, and genuineness in psychotherapy: A review of reviews. *Psychotherapy, 21,* 431–8.
Rogers, C. R. (1942). *Counseling and psychotherapy.* Boston: Houghton Mifflin.
Rogers, C. R. (1946). Recent research in nondirective therapy and its implications. *American Journal of Orthopsychiatry, 16,* 581–8.
Rogers, C. R. (1947). Some observations on the organization of personality. *Am. Psychologist, 2,* 258–68.
Rogers, C. R. (1950). Significance of the self regarding attitudes and perceptions. In M. L. Reymert (Ed.), *Feelings and emotions* (pp. 374–82). New York: McGraw-Hill.
Rogers, C. R. (1951). *Client-centered therapy: Its current practice, implications, and theory.* Boston: Houghton Mifflin.
Rogers, C. R. (1953). The concept of the fully functioning person. Unpublished mimeograph.
Rogers, C. R. (1955). Persons or science? A philosophical question. *American Psychologist, 10,* 267–78.
Rogers, C. R. (1957). The necessary and sufficient conditions of therapeutic personality change. *Journal of Consulting Psychology, 21,* 95–103.
Rogers, C. R. (1958). A process conception of psychotherapy. *American Psychologist, 13,* 142–9.
Rogers, C. R. (1959a). A theory of therapy, personality and interpersonal relationships as developed in the client-centered framework. In S. Koch (Ed.), *Psychology: A study of a science. Vol. 3. Formulations of the person and the social context* (pp. 184–256). New York: McGraw-Hill.
Rogers, C. R. (1959b). Significance of the self regarding attitudes and perceptions. In L. Gorlow & W. Katkovsky (Eds.), *Readings in the psychology of adjustment.* New York: McGraw-Hill.
Rogers, C. R. (1961). *On becoming a person.* Boston: Houghton Mifflin.
Rogers, C. R. (1963). The concept of the fully functioning person. *Psychotherapy: Theory, Research, and Practice, 1*(1), 17–26.
Rogers, C. R. (1968). Some thoughts regarding the current presuppositions of the behavioral sciences. In W. Coulson & C. R. Rogers (eds.) *Man and the Science of Man* (pp. 55–72). Columbus Ohio: Charles E. Merrill.
Rogers, C. R. (1969). *Freedom to learn.* Columbus, OH: Charles E. Merrill.
Shlien, J. M. (1970). Phenomenology and personality. In J. T. Hart & T. M. Tomlinson (Eds.), *New directions in client-centered therapy* (pp. 95–128). New York: Houghton Mifflin.
Sullivan, H. S. (1953). *The interpersonal theory of psychiatry.* New York: Norton.
Zaner, R. M. (1975). On the sense of method in phenomenology. In E. Pivcevic (Ed.), *Phenomenology and philosophical understanding.* London: Cambridge University Press.

The Evolution of
Carl Rogers as a Therapist

Jerold D. Bozarth   *University of Georgia*

This article examines two questions: Did Carl Rogers alter his fundamental views of client-centered therapy? and Did Carl Rogers change his operational functioning as a therapist? In relation to the first question, there is a review of Rogers' comments in his writings and on three demonstration tapes with 'Miss Mun,' 'Gloria,' and 'Kathy' in the years 1955, 1965, and 1975. In relation to the second question, the responses of Rogers during the three demonstration tapes are examined using a simple classification system. The results of another analysis of a demonstration by Rogers in 1985 are also reported. The conclusions are that Carl Rogers neither altered his fundamental views of client-centered therapy nor changed his operational stance as a therapist. He remained dedicated to discovering the perceptual world of the client.

This article considers questions about the evolution of Carl Rogers as a therapist during his lifetime. These questions are: Did Carl Rogers alter his fundamental views of client-centered therapy? If so, what were these alterations? and Did Carl Rogers change his operational functioning as a psychotherapist? If so, what changes occurred?

The importance of this inquiry is to affirm or refute the increasing references, both formal and informal, asserting that Rogers' thinking and functioning significantly changed during his work with schizophrenics and during his involvement with the 'Basic Encounter Group' beginning in the 1960s. Boy (1985), for example, believes that Rogers' Basic Encounter Group is no longer client-centered because such groups include behaviors that are akin to eclectic behaviors by group leaders of other encounter group models. The implication is that Rogers altered his fundamental theoretical stance. Coulson (1987) and Frankel (1988) contend that, in essence, Rogers significantly changed his thinking after having moved to California in the 1960s. They suggest that there was a 'Carl Rogers 1' prior to his move to California and a 'Carl Rogers 2' after the move. Periodically, I have heard educators and graduate students espouse this belief also. The assumptions that Rogers altered his fundamental stance and method of operation as a therapist may promote the belief that client-centered (or person-centered) therapy has joined the mainstream of psychotherapeutic approaches that lead to the therapist's directing, diagnosing, and intervening in the life of the client.

METHOD OF INQUIRY

Information concerning the first question was acquired from Rogers' comments in the literature and from his remarks prior to and after several of his more notable demonstration tapes.

Information concerning the second question was acquired from examining the

First published in *Person-Centered Review,* Volume 5, Number 4, November 1990.

dialogue of three demonstration tapes. These are the classic films of Rogers with 'Miss Mun' (Rogers & Segal, 1955), 'Gloria' (Rogers, 1965), and 'Kathy' (Shostrom, 1975).

DID CARL ROGERS ALTER HIS FUNDAMENTAL VIEW OF CLIENT-CENTERED THERAPY?

The conclusion here is that Rogers did not alter his fundamental view of client-centered therapy. He did become more explicit in stating that the underlying assumptions of client-centered/person-centered therapy are the attitudinal qualities and the presence of the therapist, which relate to a 'way of being' rather than to techniques (Baldwin, 1987; Heppner, Rogers, & Lee, 1984; Hobbs, 1985; Rogers, 1986, 1987). However, early in his career he concluded that it was the attitude of the therapist that was important in successful therapy (Rogers, 1939). In his most formal statements (1957, 1959), he emphasized the importance of the attitudes of the therapist — for example, that the therapist *be* genuine or integrated and *experience* empathy and unconditional positive regard toward the client during the therapy session. Rogers' earlier writings (1942, 1951) include examples that emphasize the intent to be empathic through oral dialogue. Later writings (1967, 1970) are more explicit about the importance of the relationship and the conditions of therapist genuineness and unconditional positive regard. Rogers' comments after 1967 referred more to therapists' using their own experiences and unsystematic modes of inquiry to attempt to understand (be empathic with) their clients. The facilitative conditions were manifested in more diverse ways (Bozarth, 1984, 1990). Nevertheless, Rogers' comments in the literature did not fundamentally change over the course of his career. He simply became more explicit about and prolific with his basic philosophy.

Rogers' comments about his therapy sessions with Miss Mun, Gloria, and Kathy also reveal his continuing dedication to a basic philosophy. In the session with Miss Mun, he states that what he thought went on in psychotherapy 'is that you [referring to the therapist] feel enough caring for this person to really let him or her process his own feelings and live his own life.' He adds, 'What the individual experiences in therapy is the experience of being loved.'

His comments in 1965 preceding the session with Gloria reaffirm his emphasis upon the attitudinal qualities of the therapist as being crucial for establishing the proper climate for therapeutic personality change. He also expressed at this time the importance to him of the question, 'Can I be real in the relationship?' He continued:

> I am real when my experiencing inside is present in my awareness and comes out through my communication . . . when I am all in one piece in the relationship . . . when I want to be willing for my client to see all the way through me so that there would be nothing, nothing hidden, and when I'm real in that fashion that I'm trying to describe, then, I know that my own feelings will often bubble up into awareness and be expressed in ways that won't impose themselves on my client. (Shostrum, 1965, p. 3)

Rogers states after his session with Gloria that he found himself 'bringing out of my own inner experiences statements that seem to have no connection with what is going on but usually prove to have a significant relationship to what the client is experiencing.'

Again, with Kathy in 1975, he emphasized the importance of the attitudinal qualities of the therapist. He also indicated that he wanted to meet the 'client as a person, for the encounter to be that of two persons.' He viewed himself, the therapist, as being 'responsible for doing my best to create a facilitative climate in which she can explore her feelings in the way that she desires and move toward the goals that she wishes to achieve.'

It is clear from statements by Rogers in the literature and his comments on the demonstration tapes that his fundamental views of client-centered theory remained consistent. However, he became more explicit about his view of the importance of therapist genuineness and the importance of the use of the self of the therapist in a person-to-person therapeutic encounter. It is more accurate to describe any change in Rogers' fundamental belief as evolutionary clarification rather than as a shift of fundamental philosophy.

DID CARL ROGERS CHANGE HIS OPERATIONAL FUNCTIONING AS A PSYCHOTHERAPIST?

The conclusion here is that *Rogers did not change his operational functioning as a psychotherapist.* This question was examined by categorizing Rogers' responses in the three demonstration tapes into a schema that would identify the types of responses and by considering Temaner's (1988) analysis of a demonstration session by Rogers at the Phoenix Evolution of Psychotherapy Conference in 1985. The following schema was used in the analysis of the three sessions (Miller, 1972):

Continue Frame: *This frame included responses that were considered to foster the idea: 'I'm giving you my full attention, please continue.' Such responses included 'Uh huh,' 'Tell me more,' and 'I don't understand.'*

Check Frame: *This frame included responses that were considered to foster the idea: 'This is what I understand you to be saying.' Such responses included summaries, reflections, and therapist restatements of the clients' comments.*

Focus Frame: *This frame included responses that were considered to foster the idea: 'Tell me your feelings and/or thoughts on the subject to give me an idea of how you are feeling and thinking about it.' Such responses included 'Tell me more about that' and 'Tell me about that part of what you are saying.'*

Switch Frame: *This frame included responses that were considered to foster the idea: 'Perhaps we should talk about something else' (or 'consider this separately'). Such responses included 'Tell me about your family' and 'Tell me about your work.'*

Declarative Frame: *This frame included responses that were considered to foster the idea: 'Here is new and additional information from me that we might consider as we go along.' Such responses included 'Here are the requirements of the school' and 'Here are your test scores.'*

Three different raters examined each of the three demonstration tapes. Ebel reliability ratings among the raters were Miss Mun: 0.98; Gloria: 0.92; and Kathy: 0.89. Figure 1 depicts the results of these analyses. 'Continue' and 'check' responses were the types of responses most indicative of attempts to understand the perceptual world of the client. These categories predominated in Rogers' responses in the three sessions. With Miss Mun, 100% of his responses were categorized as continue and check responses. With Gloria, 90% were categorized in a similar way. The session with Kathy had 80% check responses. The frequency of Rogers' responses increased slightly from 1955 with Miss Mun to 1975 with Kathy. He made 37 responses to Miss Mun and 57 responses to Gloria during the 31-minute sessions. He made 97 responses to Kathy during the 35-minute session.

Temaner's (1988) analysis of Rogers' demonstration in 1985 applied a different but comparable system. Temaner discovered that 100% of his responses were 'empathic understanding responses' (or responses similar to check and continue responses in the analysis of the three sessions). It seems clear that Rogers remained dedicated to the client's

	Demonstration Tape Length			
Categories	Miss Mun (31 min.)	Gloria (31 min.)	Kathy (35 min.)	Percentage of Responses*
Continue	2	8	18	15
Check	35	45	64	76
Focus	0	0	3	1.5
Switch	0	0	0	0
Declarative	0	3	0	1.5
Miscellaneous	0	4	8	6
TOTAL*	37	60	93	100

Figure 1: Therapist Responses
*Six percent of the 191 responses in the three sessions were too difficult to classify in these categories. Most of these were in the Kathy demonstration.

pace, direction, and way of being. He had no intentions to direct the client in any predetermined way. His responses over these years as illustrated by these demonstration tapes were predominantly dedicated to the unspoken question, 'Is this the way it is in you?' (Rogers, 1986, p. 376).

SUMMARY

This article has examined two questions: Did Carl Rogers alter his fundamental views of client-centered therapy? and Did Carl Rogers change his operational functioning as a therapist? In relation to the first question, the article reviewed Rogers' comments in his writings and on three demonstration tapes with Miss Mun, Gloria, and Kathy in the years 1955, 1965, and 1975.

In relation to the second question, Rogers' responses during the three demonstration tapes were examined using a simple classification system. The results of another analysis of a demonstration by Rogers in 1985 were also reported. The conclusions are that Rogers neither altered his fundamental views of client-centered therapy nor changed his operational stance as a therapist. He remained dedicated to discovering the perceptual world of the client.

REFERENCES

Baldwin, M. (1987). [Interview with Carl Rogers on the use of self in therapy.] In V. Satir & M. Baldwin (Eds.), *The use of self in therapy* (pp. 45–52). New York: Haworth Press.
Boy, A. V. (1985). Mainstreaming the basic encounter group. *Journal for Specialists in Group Work,*

10(4), 205–10.

Bozarth, J. D. (1984). Beyond reflection: Emergent modes of empathy. In J. Shlien & R. Levant (Eds.), *Client-centered therapy and the person-centered approach: New directions in theory, research and practice* (pp. 59–75). Boston: Praeger.

Bozarth, J. D. (1990). The essence of client-centered/person-centered therapy. In G. Lietaer, J. Rombauts, & R. Van Balen (Eds.), *Client-centered and experiential psychotherapy in the nineties* (pp. 44–51). Leuven, Belgium: Catholic University of Leuven Press.

Coulson, W. R. (1987, November). The Californication of Carl Rogers. *Fidelity,* pp. 20–31.

Frankel, M. (1988, May). The category error and the confounding of the therapeutic relationship. Paper presented at the Second Annual Meeting of the Association for the Development of the Person-Centered Approach, New York.

Heppner, P. P., Rogers, M. E., & Lee, L. A. (1984). Carl Rogers: Reflections on his life. *Journal of Counseling and Development, 63,* 14–63.

Hobbs, T. (1985). The Rogers interview, *Changes, 2,* 3–14.

Miller, L. A. (1972). Resource-centered counselor-client interaction in rehabilitation settings. In J. D. Bozarth (Ed.), *Models and functions of counseling for applied settings and rehabilitation workers* (2nd ed.) (pp. 75–98). Hot Springs: University of Arkansas Press.

Rogers, C. R. (1939). *The clinical treatment of the problem child.* Boston: Houghton Mifflin.

Rogers, C. R. (1942). *Counseling and psychotherapy: New concepts in practice.* Boston: Houghton Mifflin.

Rogers, C. R. (1951). *Client-centered therapy.* Boston: Houghton Mifflin.

Rogers, C. R. (1957). The necessary and sufficient conditions of therapeutic personality change. *Journal of Consulting Psychology, 21,* 95–103.

Rogers, C. R. (1959). A theory of therapy, personality, and interpersonal relationships as developed in the client-centered framework. In S. Koch (Ed.), *A study of a science. Vol 3. Formulations of the person and the social context* (pp. 184–256). New York: McGraw-Hill.

Rogers, C. R. (1965). *Three approaches to psychotherapy 1* [Film]. Psychological Films.

Rogers, C. R. (1967). Client-centered therapy. In A. M. Freedman & H. I. Kaplan (Eds.), *Comprehensive Textbook of Psychiatry* (pp. 1225–8). Baltimore: Williams & Wilkins.

Rogers, C. R. (1970). *On encounter groups.* New York: Harper & Row.

Rogers, C. R. (1986). Reflection of feelings. *Person-Centered Review, 1*(4), 375–7.

Rogers, C. R. (1987). Client-centered? Person-centered? *Person-Centered Review, 2*(1), 11–13.

Rogers, C. R., & Segal, R. H. (Producers). (1955). *Psychotherapy in process: The case of Miss Mun* [Film]. Pittsburgh: Pennsylvania State University Psychological Cinema Register.

Shostrom, E. (1975). *Three approaches to psychotherapy* [Film]. Santa Ana, CA: Psychological Films.

Temaner, B. T. (1988, August). Carl Rogers' therapy. Paper presented at the national convention of the American Psychological Association, Atlanta, GA.

A Characteristic of
Rogers' Response to Clients

Fred Zimring   *Case Western Reserve University*

Rogers had a unique and cohesive set of beliefs about the person. An important characteristic of his response to clients, based on this unique set of beliefs, and not on responding to any particular content, is described and contrasted to a pattern of responding to a particular content. The effect of Rogers' pattern in achieving his goal of freeing the self-actualizing tendency is described.

Carl Rogers, like all great psychotherapy innovators, proposed a startlingly different approach to people and to psychotherapeutic change. His assertion that people would change if they were understood in a particular manner was unique. The characteristics of this understanding and how it was manifested in his responses to people are the subject of this article.

I start with a brief description of some of Rogers' beliefs about people. Then an aspect of Rogers' way of responding to clients in therapy interviews is described and examined. Rogers' way of responding will then be compared to another way of responding, and the effect of his method will be discussed.

Rogers had a unique vision of what a person is and what motivates the person. For him, the person was a single, indivisible unit. Whatever the person did was seen as being done by the total person, not by a part or subsystem. The person was not a group of parts or systems like the ego, id, and superego. Action or behavior did not come from a part or subsystem of personality. It was not a part of the person that was seen as dealing with the world, nor were feelings seen as coming from a part. Instead, it is the person as a whole that decides or feels. This emphasis on the unitary person can be seen in the fundamental propositions stated in Rogers' book *Client-Centered Therapy* (1951). Proposition II was that 'the organism reacts to the field as it is experienced and perceived. This perceptual field is, for the individual, reality' (p. 484). Proposition III was that 'the organism reacts as an organized whole to this phenomenal field' (p. 486).

Rogers saw in human beings, as in all of nature, an actualizing tendency: 'The most impressive fact about the human being seems to be his directional tendency towards wholeness, towards actualization of his potentialities' (1963, p. 4). Significantly, he did not see himself as directly changing the person:

> I have not found psychotherapy effective when I have tried to create in another individual something that is not there, but I have found that if I can provide the conditions which make for growth, then this positive directional tendency brings about constructive results. (1963, p. 4)

If the person is seen as a series of subsystems or parts and you want to change some behavior or perception, *and you think that your method can change that subsystem,* you will

---

First published in *Person-Centered Review,* Volume 5, Number 4, November 1990.

try to change that subsystem. You will try to bring change by working with content from that area or subsystem. Later in this paper, trying to bring change in this way is referred to as 'responding to content.' How you will try to help the person change will be very different if the unitary person is seen as the source of perception and action and *if change can happen only by freeing and helping the actualizing tendency,* a property of the total person. Rogers facilitated the actualizing tendency by responding to the experiencing self. He responded to the experiencing self by understanding and responding to the internal frame of reference. In Proposition VII, he says that 'the best vantage point for understanding behavior is from the internal frame of reference of the individual himself' (1951, p. 494). Rogers defined the internal frame of reference as all of the realm of experience which is available to the awareness of the individual at a given moment. It includes the full range of sensations, perceptions, meanings and memories which are available to conciousness' (1959, p. 210).

It cannot be assumed that the individual, in his or her daily life, will respond in terms of these sensations, perceptions, and so forth, which comprise the internal frame of reference; that is, even though these sensations, perceptions, and meanings are available, they may not be, for the individual, the object of attention. For Rogers, the degree to which we attend to our internal frame of reference was important. For him there was a continuum of types of knowledge. At one end of this continuum is the subjective knowledge we have when we attend to our frame of reference. Thus, to use Rogers' example: 'If I decide whether I love him by focusing on my experience, by looking at my perceptions and reactions, I am using subjective knowledge' (Rogers, 1961). At the other end of this continuum is objective knowledge. Again, to use Rogers' example: 'If I try to find if I love him by checking with others, then I am observing myself as an object, am viewing myself from an external frame of reference' (1961, p. 67). Thus, even though I may have an internal frame of reference, I may not use it.

Rogers found 'an accurate and sensitive empathy communicated by the therapist crucial' to helping the actualizing tendency (1963, p. 10). Empathy involved responding to the client's internal frame of reference (1959). To understand how he actually responded—a main goal of this paper—a distinction between two parts of the client's present internal frame of reference should be noted. Assume that a woman client chooses to talk about a particular topic, say an argument with her husband. One aspect of her frame of reference is manifest in what she says about the interaction. She may say that her spouse does not understand her, does not try to see what is important to her. Not being understood in this way may be part of the habitual way in which she sees her world, an important part of her frame of reference.

There is also a different, and important, aspect of the frame of reference in existence when the client is discussing the husband's lack of understanding. It is this aspect with which this paper is concerned. This is the client's intention in communicating, her present perception of why she chose the topic, and how she feels about talking about the topic. Thus, she may have chosen the topic because she feels helpless about the husband's lack of understanding. Perhaps she is puzzled about why what happened bothers her. Also, she may be a little ashamed, at the moment, to be bothered about the topic. If the therapist only responded to the frame of reference in what she says about the incident, that is, that she did not feel understood by the husband, the therapist would be neglecting her present puzzlement or helplessness.

Rogers responded to both parts of the person's present frame of reference. He responded to the part that has to do with the present communicative act—that is, to the person's intentions at the moment and with how the person felt about talking about the topic, the puzzlement or helplessness in the above example. Rogers also responded to the part of the frame of reference that was manifest in the topic itself.

It has been thought that Rogers responded to something other than the two aspects of the frame of reference mentioned above, that he responded to the 'hot' emotion or feeling. This perception has led to the view that the main client-centered response is the 'reflection of feeling.' This was not Rogers' view of his goal in responding (Rogers, 1986).

CASE EXAMPLES

The lack of emphasis on responding to strong feelings, and the differences in responding to the two parts of the present frame of reference mentioned above, can best be seen by examining Rogers' actual responses to clients. In 'Mrs. Ett,' which was recorded and transcribed at the Counseling Center of the University of Chicago many years ago, we find the following interaction (in which C stands for client and T for therapist):

C1: *Yes, they are very strong, they're there. I'm getting so emotional I can't talk. What I meant to say is that they are there and I feel them very strongly and, ah, oh, I don't know, it's like little demons inside of me at work all the time, it doesn't give me a chance to sit and rest quietly to read, there's always conflict. It's either that or this. Such a great indecision; I can't tell you the – if I were to tell anybody the amount of indecision, it's almost pathological. I have a maid, a new maid now, and I'm very much upset about this. She's the epitome of efficiency and yet I hate her. I can't stand her, I think I'll have to let her go just because she's too efficient. She is, ah, taking away Bonnie from me. If I hold Bonnie in my arms, whoops, she's right out of my arms and she is re-diapering the baby, feeding her, and many times I would tell her that these are her duties and those are mine, but she has entered as the matriarch of the house – a colored woman – very nice, the type of a person, we hired her because of her appearance, very efficient and intelligent, but I find – oh my God! It didn't occur to me until just now that she's beginning to represent a mother figure to me. Isn't that – I never thought of it until right now, that I resent her because she's domineering, she's oh, she's very much like my mother.*

T1: *So that you resent her not only for her efficiency and her struggle to take over Bonnie but perhaps even more deeply because she is a mother.*

C2: *Oh, yes. Well, not so much a mother person as perhaps the type of a person my mother is, because I notice that if I tell her something she won't listen to me, but she will continue to do it her way, which is what I have as the problem with mother all the time. And yesterday, Mr. L., towards the end of the evening I was in such a fog, I was so undecided and so unhappy without knowing why, and now, darn it, I see why it is, it's that. I think I'll have to get rid of her for that reason, or what do you think I should do? Should I hang onto her and fight it out myself and use this as a good opportunity to vent out a lot of my feelings? It might be the ideal opportunity to struggle within myself against mother and then ultimately win, or should I dismiss her because she is rubbing me the wrong way at a time when I shouldn't be rubbed the wrong way. I mean what would your opinion be, I'm sure you won't give me an opinion, because you always turn everything back to a question, but from a clinical –*

T2: *It's not a question, you mean, but it's to know how to go at it – because you see yourself all that I would see there – ah, you might get rid of her because she represents your mother and you dislike her, or conceivably you might be able to adjust to her, which would certainly be a step toward adjusting to your mother, but, ah –*

C3: *I might have an awful lot of struggle, a lot of tension. I think there would be. Because for the past two or three days there's been an awful lot of tension in – I didn't know it until just now that she represents the mother figure to me, which is sometimes acceptable, very acceptable, and desirable, but at the other time, which is so upsetting for me.*

T3: *You feel pulled two ways by it, as you do with your own mother.*

C4: *I know that eventually she, if she stays long enough – you know how it is with help – but she has managed to take everything over. I've never in my life seen anything like it. At one time she appeals to my, the feeling of efficiency, even if I personally don't have it – but, ah – on the other hand I resent it terribly when she takes Bonnie from me. So much so that I worry about it now. I worry that Bonnie won't realize that I am the mother, she'll think that, ah, Daisy is the mother.*

T4: *You're afraid that she might transfer her affection and loyalty.*

C5: *It's possible, isn't it? Or don't you think, I mean certainly it's been Ribble's opinion that ah, a child responds to the person who is mothering it. Of course, Bonnie is almost nine months old and the basic mothering I have done, so perhaps it won't be as decisive and I'm always there for the, ah – she won't even let me bathe the baby [laugh] it's the most peculiar thing. And to me, the bath is the most personal time of the baby and ah, I was very upset yesterday, I was in a mess, really I couldn't, I couldn't get down to make supper, I couldn't get organized as to what I'd make, I couldn't get organized to take care of Evelyn. It was constant fighting, I couldn't drive this Daisy out of my mind – should I fire her, should I keep her, should I fire her, yes, I'll keep her because look at all the freedom she's going to give me, complete lack of responsibility to the house, and on the other hand I have to fire her because she's too assertive, she's too domineering. Aunt Sadie can't see it. She thinks I'm crazy, she thinks I'm out of my head completely, and what I'm trying to explain to Aunt Sadie, not very successfully is the fact that I'm very emotional about it, and I didn't realize it until now that that's what it is, definitely [pause].*

T5: *You really were pretty deeply confused by that whole issue and consequently not able to organize yourself very effectively.*

C6: *Yesterday, it was awful. I'm very efficient in the kitchen. I mean, when I cook anything I have everything planned out in a little column and it's very good because I can prepare a meal in three seconds flat and if Arnold calls up at the last minute, which he very often does, and brings somebody over, I'll have a spread out in perhaps an hour, which is good – things ready – and salad made and everything like that. Yesterday I couldn't peel the onions, I'd drop it and then I'd run out, watch Daisy with the baby, and then I'd drop it and start again and bawl Daisy out, Daisy because she was trying to get into the kitchen, and oh, I was very much upset yesterday. And, ah, you say one point is good and the other point isn't, but I don't know what – to do [laugh]. I do know that I'm not as calm as I should be in the house because of that and for the benefit of the children, maybe by talking about it, it might alleviate the situation, the tension.*

T6: *It might help to get it out of your system.*

C7: *Oh, how I* hate *my mother! I mean it just overwhelms me at times. Not so much hate but the strong emotion the drive, mother, mother, it hasn't — it wasn't that way a year ago. There was always this undercurrent of emotion toward mother, but it's just coming to a peak, it's like, it's overwhelming me, it's over me, it's like I'm being sunk in a wave, and I don't know what to do.*

T7: *It's a very overpowering feeling of all the emotions about her.*

C8: *I always had it, I never was without it, it was always a subconscious undercurrent, only when I would see her would that tremendous feeling come out, but now it's even without seeing her. Maybe it's because I'm here, maybe it's like a boil coming to a head would be. I haven't really talked about it so much so deeply as I'm doing now. It feels like sickness.*

There were several aspects of C1 to which Rogers could have responded. One was the 'hot' emotions Mrs. Ett had at the moment she was talking, the feelings of being overwhelmed and of the 'little demons inside of me.' The second aspect to which Rogers could have responded, and the aspect to which he chose to respond, is what she discovered in the moment, her resentment of the maid being like her mother. Also, Rogers could have responded to the feeling or experience of this resentment.

Whatever aspect he chose to respond to would have had consequences, might have led her to follow a particular path in her exploration. If Rogers had chosen to respond to the first part of the first aspect, her experience of getting very emotional and being overwhelmed, she might have explored this feeling more deeply. Perhaps this exploration would have led to realization of what this loss of control, of being overwhelmed, felt like. In the second part of the first aspect to which Rogers might have responded, Mrs. Ett described her experience of indecision, the 'little demons' inside. If Rogers had chosen to follow this feeling, she might have gone deeper into the feeling of being conflicted, might have experienced these reasons as feeling alien, as coming from others. If Rogers had chosen to respond to these present aspects of feelings, Mrs. Ett might well have become involved in following the experience of the 'little demons' and might not have come to the realization of her resentment of the maid as a mother figure.

Although in T1 Rogers responded to her resentment, it is not the 'feel' or sensation of the resentment to which he responded. Instead, he chose to couple her present reaction, her resentment of her maid, with her present perception of her maid as mother. Rogers could have emphasized the feelings, the anger and loathing that Mrs. Ett seemed to feel for the maid. Instead, Rogers responded to the connection between the relationship that Mrs. Ett saw between her present reaction and elements of her world (maid's efficiency and being a mother).

In C2, Mrs. Ett was trying to decide what to do about the maid and was weighing the various alternative courses of action and the feelings to which each is connected. Rogers simply reflected these alternatives without trying to heighten their feeling aspects.

In C3 Mrs. Ett repeated the connection between the tension of the past few days and the realization of the maid as a mother figure. In addition, she described her ambivalence about the mother figure. It is this ambivalence that Rogers responded to in T3, not her feeling of tension. Again, it is her present reaction ('You feel pulled two ways') to the content of her perception ('as you do with your mother') that was of primary importance, not the qualitative, emotional aspects of her tension and struggle.

This happens again in C4 and T4. It was Mrs. Ett's present response ('You're afraid that') to her concerns ('that she might transfer her affection and loyalty') in which Rogers was interested and to which he responded. It was her present reactions to her concerns and not the content of these concerns to which Rogers chose to respond.

At the beginning of the first interview of a case recorded at the Counseling Center of the University of Chicago in the late 1940s, Mrs. Oak says:

C1: *Well . . . apparently things with Peggy seem to be going well, and of course we might as well get to the point where it isn't Peggy. It's me. And what'll we do? Are we . . . where we find the source I don't know, I mean, I'm confused, I'm shocked . . . I know it's this, that apparently I have made this girl my only link with life. I have a . . . I've sublimated everything. And I have, I don't know. But it isn't fair, I mean, it's a shocking situation. [Pause] There's a kind of transference, something, I've come to the point which of course I don't know, where I simply identify myself with her. Of course there are these terrible tensions and the anxiety feelings. But the shocking part of it is that the, the awful part to face, I mean I'm not saying it all now, I naturally won't . . . is that it's really me . . . I mean it's, I'm afraid for myself, you see.*

T1: *Then you think that, you really feel it's almost as though your life is her life, or her life is your life, whichever you want to put it, and that this recent, this recent upset on her part has made it shockingly evident to you. Is that . . . ?*

C2: *Yes. Yes. My own . . . what should I say . . . my own sort of, well, unpleasantness of the thing, the unwholesomeness.*

T2: *M-hm. I see.*

C3: *I mean, I . . .*

T3: *It sort of hits you that this isn't the right kind of relationship.*

C4: *That's right, that's right. It's not good. It's not good for her and it's certainly not good for me. I mean I'm too young for that sort of thing. Too, it shocks me. It shocks me to the point where, as I say, as yet, I can't go into the thing and I can't verbalize the whole thing. The . . . how it happens, I don't know.*

T4: *Sort of feel all of a sudden that there is something that is unwholesome, wrong somehow, it's wrong for me. And yet . . . just what all that is, you can't say or can't even be sure probably in your own mind.*

As in the case of Mrs. Ett, though Rogers responded to both the problem with which the person is concerned and to her present relation to that problem, he emphasized the latter. In C1, Mrs. Oak spent most of her time explaining her present concern. In T1, after indicating his understanding of her concern, Rogers stated her present reaction to that concern that 'has made it [transference and sublimation] shockingly evident to you.'

Again, in T3, Rogers was concerned with her present reaction to the problem when he said that it 'hits you that this isn't the right kind of relationship.' And in T4, when Rogers said that she 'sort of feel[s] all of a sudden that there is something that is unwholesome, wrong somehow . . . just what all that is, you can't say or can't even be sure probably in your own mind,' he responded to her present reaction to the problem rather than to the problem itself. In other words, Rogers could have responded to the problem, the sublimation and transference, or he could have responded to her experience of this, of how it felt when she was not living her own life but was living life through her daughter. Instead, he responded to her present reaction to her perception that she was living her life through her daughter.

Even though the responses discussed above were made to different clients in different circumstances, there was consistency. These responses, like all consistent patterns of responses, direct the attention of the client to particular material and stimulate the synthesis of this material by the client.

CHARACTERISTICS OF ROGERS' RESPONSES

A consistent pattern of responses operates much as a series of instructions might. If we were to translate Rogers' responses into a series of instructions, they might be:

> What I am interested in is what is important to you at the moment and what your present reaction is to it. What I would like you to do is to find an area of your life that feels important to you right now. Tell me how you see that area, what is true about it for you, and what your present reaction is to it.

These instructions ask the person to search both for an area of life that is important and for his or her present reaction to that area. This importance is not defined in terms of deep experience, emotional intensity, or meaningfulness. Clients are not, for example, asked to search for important feelings or meanings. Mrs. Ett explored her relationship to her maid. The thrust of Rogers' pattern of responding is to direct the client's attention to the client's present response to his or her world. If a client were to talk about earning money, Rogers would probably not have responded to the details of what was done to earn money. Instead, he would have been more interested in the problem that the client saw at the moment of speaking about earning money, or in what the client's present response was to the problem of earning money.

Rogers' focus was on the person's present reaction to and interest in his or her problem or concern, as well as on the problem or concern itself. 'Client-centered' has been taken to refer to the person being worked with as a client rather than as a patient. Instead, for Rogers, his responding was client-centered rather than problem- or feeling-centered.

CONTRASTING ROGERS' PATTERN OF RESPONDING

To understand Rogers' pattern of responding more fully, it will be useful to contrast it to another pattern of responding. In this pattern of responses the therapist emphasizes one type of content: the client's feelings in the situations about which the client speaks. The therapist did not choose to respond to either the client's present intentions in choosing the topic or to the client's response to the topic at hand.

The following interaction was presented at the 1988 Annual Meeting of the Association for the Development of the Person-Centered Approach. How the therapist responded and how Rogers might have responded will be contrasted.

C1: *A familiar topic. Well, um, a week ago today I had an interview about my placement, my diagnostic placement. And at that point the fact that I'm in the master's as opposed to the Psy. D. program was brought up, and I was, I was really shaken by it, in that it was emphasized over and over that it is not automatic for one to go from the master's to the Psy. D. Um, she was saying that not everyone does get accepted, a n d that, it really the message was coming across [sic] that there are no certainties, no guarantees and that has been bothering me much more than I thought it would. I seem to have the attitude of well, of course I'll be accepted. I mean, why wouldn't I? I have all these wonderful qualifications. And yet, ever since that meeting I'm having a hard time because it seems like I want to do extremely well in school now. The more pressure I put on myself to do things par excellence, the harder it is to do them. It's almost as if what I've done before is put it aside and go about my business and I thought I was doing well, I was happy with what I was doing.*

T1: *So, in that meeting, it helped to kind of introduce a problem about your feelings about how you're working in school. It reminded you with its repeated references that not all master's students get in, that you can't take that for granted and you've been more concerned about it since. If I'm understanding it, the concern is actually sort of counterproductive. It makes you more uptight.*
[Aside: The therapist responded to what happened at the meeting and emphasized both the client's concern about being admitted to the Psy. D. program and the consequence of this concern: that it makes her more 'uptight.' In addition to mentioning the concern (but probably not mentioning the concern about being counterproductive), Rogers might have mentioned her observation about herself. This was that she was more bothered than she thought she would be and, perhaps, was surprised at this. She was surprised about being concerned since she believes that she should be accepted given her 'wonderful qualifications.']

C2: *Very.*

T2: *It's not helpful.*
[Aside: Note that the concern about her admission's causing problems for her remained the focus of the therapist's response. This has a mechanistic flavor: this cause-and-effect sequence is almost separate from her self.]

C3: *Exactly. And it seems before that there was a possibility of that but it seems that I was able to not dwell on it and I was able to enjoy the work much more. And it seems from that meeting there wasn't enough encouragement to balance that this may be a real possibility, that this may be a terminating point. A master's. That, I don't know, I'm just.*
[Aside: The fact that the client agrees with what the therapist has said indicates that the the therapist is correct about what took place in the incident, or is correct about how the client had felt in the past. The client's agreement does not, of course, indicate that the therapist is responding to the client's present feelings or responses about the topic.]

T3: *Most of the emphasis at the meeting was on that side and that wasn't so good for*

*you to have that emphasized and no encouragement. In spite of the fact that it
sounds like you've done pretty well in your prior performance and you've felt good
about how you've worked and have enjoyed the material.*
[Aside: The therapist emphasized the lack of encouragement. Rogers' response
might have included, 'And so you have difficulty not dwelling on the negative
possibility.']

C4: *Exactly. I'm having a great time in school. And I'm just wondering whether what I
consider good is not what the school might consider good enough to go on to the
Psy. D. program.*

T4: *Uh huh. It shook your confidence in your own judgment, whether what you feel is a
good performance, if they'll agree with that.*
[Aside: The therapist mentions the loss of confidence. Although this is true, it is
not what the client is attending to. Instead the client's present concern may be
about whether she was right about what was required to enter the program.]

C5: *Right. And all of a sudden it is as if the rules were changed and I'm wondering
maybe I should find out what they really are. What are the criteria. I thought I knew
what the criteria were and it seems as though . . .*

T5: *I see, it left you with that impression that maybe you had a misunderstanding about
what the criteria are for getting ahead in the Psy. D. [Yeah] And you think maybe
you should seek clarification of that.*
[Aside: Although the therapist emphasized the client's desire for correct
information, the client was, in fact, talking about both the lack of information and
the fact that she thought she knew what the rules were but they were changed. It is
this sort of self-relevant material to which Rogers might have responded. He might
have said something like, 'You thought you knew the rules and all of a sudden you
find you don't,' leaving it to her to decide in the next remark whether she was to
follow the subjective side of the change in rules: 'Yes, it felt like the rug was pulled
out from under me,' or the more objective focus: 'Yes, they changed the rules
arbitrarily.']

C6: *Yeah. And perhaps [Laughs nervously] there's some information that I am just not
taking in because I'm living in a fool's paradise. I want to know what the truth is.
I'm not clear on that.*

T6: *You're not sure now. You're saying that it is possible that you've been living in a
fool's paradise and kidding yourself about what the standards really are.*
[Aside: Again, the therapist responded in terms of the immediate past: 'you've
been living in a fool's paradise.' In his response Rogers would also have noted the
present desire to 'know what the truth is.']

There is a consistency in the responses of this therapist. The therapist responds in terms
of the client's circumstances and the reactions that had taken place in these circumstances.
He did not talk about her present reactions to these circumstances even when these
reactions were the focus of her attention. It was as if the therapist was talking to a parent
(the client) about the behavior and reactions of a child (what the client had experienced

previously). The therapist, perhaps reasoning that the child and not the parent was his client, was not interested in the reactions of the parent (the client's present self) to these behaviors and reactions.

THE RESULTS OF THESE DIFFERENT PATTERNS OF RESPONDING

A consistent pattern of responses helps create a particular world. The responses in the last example will create a world in which these reactions and feelings of the client have an important, independent existence. Rogers, by responding to the reactions of the client to what is being said, created a world in which the client's self had an independent existence and served as a basis for the client's choices.

Methods of responding give rise to knowledge. Rogers' method of responding to the person's relation to the problem will give rise to knowledge about the self's relationship to decisions, feelings, and events. Methods that focus on feelings and experience will give rise to knowledge about the person's feelings.

In addition to giving rise to knowledge, these patterns of therapist responding will give rise to structures. Knowledge frequently results in structures that are used to interpret the world. As an example, if you learn the differences between younger and older trees, see pictures of each kind, and so on, then, when you subsequently see a tree you will automatically see it as a younger or older tree. Similarly, after a number of therapist responses, structures in which we interpret the world will be created and will change the way in which we see the world.

If the structures of your world have to do with your feelings, your feelings, especially those that are not clear, will be of primary importance. When you sense a feeling or meaning that is not clear you will attend to it. If you are successful, you will have increased knowledge about your feelings. In addition, you will be more likely to remain vigilant for other unclear feelings to which you will attend. For example, as I write this, there is a vague feeling about my automobile insurance bill. It seems too high and yet I do not know what I can do. As I begin to attend to this feeling-tinged situation, it starts to change, and feelings that are part protest and part helplessness begin to emerge. If I were to continue to focus on my feelings about this over a number of occasions, first I might feel more comfortable as my helplessness in this type of situation became familiar and then, perhaps, I might eventually change the situation.

Contrast this to what would happen if I were talking to a client-centered therapist who responded as Rogers did above. Here, a different structure would be created. If I were to say that thoughts and feelings of helplessness about the insurance company intruded when I was trying to write, the therapist might respond in terms of my reaction to the intrusion by the concern about the insurance. Attending to the fact of intrusion might lead me to explore the importance for me of completing things, perhaps finding that I respect myself less when I don't complete things. This response leads to my knowing more about what I prize, leads to knowledge of what I, as a person, value and like or dislike. This knowledge might lead to a structure in which I automatically evaluate choices in terms of their utility and value for the self.

After psychotherapy oriented to feelings and past reactions, like that in the last example of typescript, the next time I write and a feeling begins to intrude, I focus on the feeling and hope to resolve it before it becomes a serious problem. After client-centered therapy, because of what I have learned about my self-respect, I might choose not to focus on the feeling. Thus, the experiential method as exemplified in the last typescript example, like other methods that are concerned with a particular content, can free me from some control by that content. However, as a result of this method, I may be controlled in another way. I may find myself constantly vigilant about, and dealing with, my feelings. Rogers' method may remove some of our negative feelings but will not, to the same extent, leave me as a servant who has to take care of my feelings. Instead, Rogers' method of responding to the internal frame of reference will lead to its being more central for the person regardless of the type of problem with which the person is concerned. If my frame of reference is of critical importance for my therapist, and is constantly referred to by him or her as a valid source of information, I am more likely to find it important and use it as a basis for decisions. My actions will become more based on internal considerations. More importantly, being responded to in this way might lead me to make choices and act on the basis of what is good for the self, not just on the basis of negative or positive feelings.

There may be another outcome of the freeing of the self-actualizing tendency that results from Rogers' method of responding. There are times in our lives when we have an abundance of energy. Rogers talks about the self-actualizing tendency as leading the individual to be an 'active initiator' (1963). The self-actualizing tendency is seen as a force. It may be that we have more energy when our actions are the outgrowth of this tendency.

REFERENCES

Rogers, C. R. (1951). *Client-centered therapy.* Boston: Houghton Mifflin.
Rogers, C. R. (1959). A theory of therapy, personality, and interpersonal relations. In S. Koch (Ed.), *Psychology: A study of a science: Vol. 3. Formulations of the person and the social context* (pp. 184–256). New York: McGraw-Hill.
Rogers, C. R. (1961). *On becoming a person.* Boston: Houghton Mifflin.
Rogers, C. R. (1963). The actualizing tendency in relation to 'motives' and to consciousness. In *Current Theory and Research in Motivation. Vol. II: Nebraska Symposium on Motivation.* Lincoln, NE.
Rogers. C. R. (1986). Reflection of feelings. *Person-Centered Review, 1,* 375–7.

Part B

Psychotherapy

Rogers, Kohut and Erickson: A personal perspective on some similarities and differences

Carl R. Rogers   *Center for Studies of the Person*

The article has two purposes. The first is to present some misunderstood major aspects of client-centered therapy: the view of human nature, the actualizing tendency, the nature of empathy, the place of intuition, the therapeutic relationship, the reorganization of self, and the place given to theory. The second purpose is to relate each of these to the comparable aspects of the thinking of Kohut and Erickson, pointing to agreements and disagreements. One point of sharp differences is in the application of therapeutic principles in other fields. Neither Erickson nor Kohut was involved in this area, so only my work is described.

I have several purposes in these remarks. I wish to present some of the major elements in my work, especially elements that I feel have often been misunderstood. I wish to acknowledge the fact that the work that I and my colleagues have done is being increasingly compared with the work of Heinz Kohut, a major innovator in psychoanalysis, and Milton Erickson, an innovator who went far beyond hypnotherapy (Graf, 1984; Gunnison, 1985; Kahn, 1985; Stolorow, 1976). Finally, from my limited knowledge of the work of these two men, I should like to give my view (undoubtedly biased) of some of the similarities and differences that I see. I hope I can do this in a way that will provoke fresh thought around some of the basic issues of psychotherapy.

FUNDAMENTAL HUMAN NATURE

This is an element whose importance has, I believe, been underestimated. Thirty years ago I wrote,

> My views of man's most basic characteristics have been formed by my experience in psychotherapy . . . I have discovered man to have characteristics inherent in his species, and the terms which have at different times seemed to me descriptive, are such terms as positive, forward moving, constructive, realistic, trustworthy. (Rogers, 1957)

My belief in that statement has been confirmed by continued experiences in individual therapy, in small groups, in large groups, and in groups consisting of antagonistic factions. It is borne out by experience with very troubled and psychotic individuals and individuals with powerful defenses. If one is able to get to the core of the person, one finds a trustworthy, positive center.

I am pleased to find that on this point Kohut and Erickson agree with what I have stated. Kohut specifically rejects the idea that the most basic element of human nature is 'a wild beast.' He maintains, 'We are born as an assertive whole, as an affectionate whole,

First published in *Person-Centered Review*, Volume 1, Number 2, May 1986.

not as a bundle of isolated biological drives — pure aggression or pure sexual lust — that have to be gradually tamed' (Kohut, quoted by Graf, 1984, p. 74).

Erickson used the term 'unconscious' to represent the core of the person. He saw the therapeutic task as being that of arranging the conditions that would encourage and facilitate the emergence of the unconscious as a positive force. He says, 'Unconscious processes can operate in an intelligent, autonomous and creative fashion. . . . People have stored in their unconscious all the resources necessary to transform their experience' (Gilligan, 1982).

This similarity of views — seeing the human organism as essentially positive in nature — is profoundly radical. It flies in the face of traditional psychoanalysis, runs counter to the Christian tradition, and is opposed to the philosophy of most institutions, including our educational institutions. In psychoanalytic theory our core is seen as untamed, wild, destructive. In Christian theology we are 'conceived in sin,' and evil by nature. In our institutions the individual is seen as untrustworthy. Persons must be guided, corrected, disciplined, punished, so that they will not follow the pathway set by their nature.

THE ACTUALIZING TENDENCY

It is my experience that in the nurturing climate I endeavor to create, the actualizing tendency becomes evident.[1] In client-centered therapy, the person is free to choose any direction, but actually selects positive and constructive pathways. I can only explain this in terms of a directional tendency inherent in the human organism — a tendency to grow, to develop, to realize its full potential.

> It is confirming to find that this is not simply a tendency in living systems but is part of a strong formative tendency in our universe, which is evident at all levels.
>
> Thus when we provide a psychological climate that permits persons to be — whether they are clients, students, workers, or persons in a group — we are not involved in a chance event. We are tapping into a tendency which permeates all of organic life — a tendency to become all the complexity of which the organism is capable. And, on an even larger scale, I believe we are tuning in to a potent creative tendency which has formed our universe, from the smallest snowflake to the largest galaxy, from the lowly amoeba to the most sensitive and gifted of persons. And perhaps we are touching the cutting edge of our ability to transcend ourselves, to create new and more spiritual directions in human evolution . . . This kind of formulation is, for me, a philosophical base for a person-centered approach. It justifies me in engaging in a life-affirming way of being. (Rogers, 1980, p. 134)

One aspect of this basic tendency is the capacity of the individual, in a growth-promoting environment, to move toward self-understanding and self-direction.

When I look at Erickson's work, I find that he also seems to trust this directional aspect in the person. This is indicated in the quotation I have already given. Both of us find that we can rely, in a very primary way, on the wisdom of the organism.

I believe Kohut's trust is of a more limited nature. He makes it clear that it is the analyst who is responsible for movement in therapy, not the patient. Even in a talk given a short time before his death (Kohut, 1981), he states that the analyst cures, by giving explanations. He is wedded to the medical model of therapy. His trust in the actualizing tendency is sharply limited.

---

1. Note that the self-actualizing tendency may be opposed to the more basic actualizing tendency. See Rogers (1959, pp. 196–7).

THE SIGNIFICANCE OF EMPATHY

I wish now to turn to what is for me one of the most important elements in therapy. I have endeavored to define my perception of this element as follows:

> The way of being with another person which is termed empathic has several facets. It means entering the private perceptual world of the other and becoming thoroughly at home in it. It involves being sensitive, moment to moment, to the changing felt meanings which flow in this other person, to the fear or rage or tenderness or confusion or whatever, that he/she is experiencing. It means temporarily living in his/her life, moving about in it delicately without making judgments, sensing meanings of which he/she is scarcely aware, but not trying to uncover feelings of which the person is totally unaware, since this would be too threatening. (Rogers, 1980, p. 142)

To my mind, empathy is in itself a healing agent. It is one of the most potent aspects of therapy, because it releases, it confirms, it brings even the most frightened client into the human race. If a person can be understood, he or she belongs.

Kohut, too, was greatly interested in empathy. Let me present a beautiful statement.

> Empathy, the accepting, confirming, and understanding human echo evoked by the self, is a psychological nutrient without which human life as we know and cherish it, could not be sustained. (Kohut, 1978, p. 705)

I read this carefully, and felt myself very much in tune with him. Then I came across a most contradictory statement, published later.

> Empathy is employed only for data gathering; there is no way in which it could serve us in our theory building. In the clinical situation, the analyst employs empathy to collect information about specific current events in the patient's inner life. After he has collected these data with the aid of empathy, he orders them and gives the patient a dynamic or genetic interpretation. (Kohut, in Goldberg, 1980, pp. 483–4)

Here is where we part company. This cold, impersonal use of the capacity for understanding is abhorrent to me.

We differ in another way. It is my practice to test my empathic understanding by checking with the client. Sometimes I tie together or integrate some of these understandings into a more general picture. These I am especially careful to check, to see if this is actually the way the client sees it.

Kohut, too, makes tentative tests of the interpretation he wishes to give. He says,

> The analyst may use empathic testing maneuvers [once he has] tentatively formulated his dynamic and, especially, his genetic interpretations, before he decides to communicate them to the analysand. (Kohut, in Goldberg, 1980, p. 484)

I believe that a transcript of one of my integrative responses would look very similar in form to one of Kohut's preliminary tests of his interpretations. But the intent would be very different. I would be testing to see if I was deeply in tune with my client, because this 'in-tune-ness' is in itself healing, confirming, growth-promoting. Kohut's intent would be to see if his patient was ready to accept his explanation, the explanation that cures.

Erickson, though he worked in ways very different from my own, gave great importance to sensitive understanding.

> [Erickson believed that] An attitude of empathy and respect on the part of the therapist is *crucial* to insure successful change. (Erickson & Zeig, 1980, p. 335)

Gunnison describes the manner in which Erickson was empathic:

> Erickson expressed his understanding of the inner world of his patients in a way different from Rogers'. It was 'through the use of the client's own vocabulary and frames of reference, pacing, and matching, a powerful kind of empathy developed that forms the interpersonal connection.' He recognized that this was similar to the approach Rogers took to therapy. (Gunnison, 1985, p. 562)

INTUITION

In recent years, I have given more importance to another aspect of my functioning.

> As a therapist, I find that when I am closest to my inner, intuitive self, when I am somehow in touch with the unknown in me, when perhaps I am in a slightly altered state of consciousness in the relationship, then whatever I do seems to be full of healing. Then simply *my presence* is releasing and helpful. There is nothing I can do to force this experience, but when I can relax and be close to the transcendental core of me, then I may behave in strange and impulsive ways in the relationship, ways which I cannot justify rationally, which have nothing to do with my thought processes.
>
> But these strange behaviors turn out to be *right* in some odd way. At those moments it seems that my inner spirit has reached out and touched the inner spirit of the other. Our relationship transcends itself and has become a part of something larger. Profound growth and healing and energy are present. (Rogers, in press)

One has only to read some of Erickson's cases to realize the masterful quality of his intuitive reactions and responses to his patients. He seems to be unmatched in his ability to sense their deepest feelings, and to react to these in ingenious, spontaneous, creative ways.[2]

Due to his own early suffering and pain, Milton Erickson discovered for himself much about altered states of consciousness. This undoubtedly helped him in being intuitively sensitive to his patients. 'He was so "in touch" with his own inner experience and so trusted the "wisdom of *his* unconscious", that he was capable of incredible understandings of his patients' worlds' (Gunnison, 1985).

THE PERSONAL QUALITIES OF THE THERAPEUTIC RELATIONSHIP

For me therapy is a person-to-person experience. Of the various conditions I have described as essential to effective psychotherapy, the outstanding element is congruence — a genuineness or realness, in which the therapist is being him- or herself. This not only means striving to understand the client, when that is the therapist's purpose, but also means a willingness to communicate other feelings — even negative ones — when they are persistently experienced. Thus boredom, anger, compassion, or other feelings may be expressed, when these are a significant and continuing part of the therapist's experience.

So, for me, therapy proceeds most effectively when the relationship contains the therapist's experiencing of sensitive, even intuitive, empathy; of prizing or caring for the client; and, above all, of congruence, in which the therapist is willing and able to express his or her true feelings.

---

2. In analyzing Erickson's every move, in studying 'pacing,' 'matching,' 'seeding,' and other detailed aspects of his work, his followers may run a risk of losing the spontaneity of his intuition.

It seems strikingly clear that for Erickson, too, therapy was a highly personal affair, a deeply involving experience different for each person. He thought about his patients, he reacted to them in very personal ways—challenging, abrupt, patient, soft, hard—always being himself in the interest of his client. He sometimes took individuals into his home, or used pets, or told of his own life—doing whatever would keep him in close personal touch.

It appears equally clear that for Kohut the therapeutic relationship was cooler, less personal. The analyst was observing, gathering data through his empathy, preparing for the all-important explanations. His attitudes are perhaps most transparently shown in an incident where he departs from his usual style, and is more personal. He describes this in one of his last talks.

He was working with a woman who was strongly suicidal.

> In one session she was so badly off that I thought, 'How would you feel if I let you hold my fingers for a little while?' I am not recommending it, but I was desperate, so I gave her two fingers to hold. I immediately made a genetic interpretation to myself. It was of the toothless gums of a very young child, clamping down on an empty nipple . . . I reacted to it even then as an analyst to myself . . . I wouldn't say that it turned the tide, but it overcame a very difficult impasse at a dangerous moment (the analysis went on for years and was reasonably successful). (Kohut, 1981)

It seems clear that in this interaction Dr. Kohut is experiencing desperation, caring, and compassion. He found a beautifully symbolic gesture that enabled him to express something of what he was feeling. Yet he is apologetic about this, about giving her his fingers to hold. Even more astonishing—and sad—is his interpretation to himself that he is giving her a dry nipple. He appears unaware that by giving something of himself—of his own deep and persistent feelings—he is giving her the nourishing human caring and compassion that she so desperately needs. Being thus openly feeling with her is most therapeutic. Yet he seems dubious and apologetic about his action. He appears to be unaware that being openly himself in the relationship was the most healing thing he could have done.

It is obvious that I differ deeply from Dr. Kohut in the value I give to being one's own whole person in the relationship.

THE REORGANIZATION OF THE SELF IN THERAPY

One of the satisfactions of my professional career has been to advance a theory that is later confirmed by research. Such a pattern is evident in my thinking about the reorganizing of the concept of self as a central aspect of therapeutic change.

In 1946 I was elected president of the American Psychological Association. During the ensuing year I prepared my presidential address, which centered upon the changes in perception of self and reality that took place in therapy. It was with real trepidation that I wrote this paper, for it seemed totally unlike the presidential presentations that preceded it. With some inner uncertainty, I led up to the statement that in the therapeutic relationship it is the absence of threat, and 'the assistance in focusing upon the perception of self, which seem to permit a more differentiated view of self, and finally the reorganization of self' (Rogers, 1947, p. 368). The paper was received with polite acceptance.[3]

I had no hard evidence for this statement. I could only give illustrations from recorded interviews to support my theory. It was therefore very satisfying to be able to publish research findings on the subject in 1954. Using Stephenson's new 'Q-technique,' in an original adaptation, we were able to objectify this very subjective entity, the concept of self, and to measure in great detail the changes that took place during therapy.

We found, much as I had hypothesized earlier, that clients showed certain characteristic change in self-perception during therapy. They became less anxious, guilty, driven, hostile, dependent. They became more secure, self-confident, more aware of experiences and conflicts previously denied to awareness, and more able to give and receive love. This reorganization of the self was clearly in a direction perceived as healthy (Rogers & Dymond, 1954, esp. Chap. 4, 15).

Erickson uses different words, but it is clear that these changes in perception are also important to him. He speaks of the process of therapy as a loosening of the cognitive maps of the patient's experience, 'helping them break through the limitations of their conscious attitudes to free their unconscious potential for problem-solving' (Erickson, Rossi, & Rossi, 1976, p. 18). This is very similar to my view that in a sound therapeutic relationship, 'all the ways in which the self has been experienced can be viewed openly, and organized into a complex unity' (Rogers, 1947, p. 366).

Kohut is in general agreement. The restructuring of the self is central to his whole concept of therapy, and we share many common ideas.

THE PLACE AND NATURE OF THEORY

There is another element of my work that I feel is not completely understood. It is the kind of importance I give to theoretical hypotheses, and the place I see for theory. I spelled out some of my views quite explicitly in the major presentation of my theoretical views (Rogers, 1959).

I see the formulation of a theory as 'the persistent, disciplined effort to make sense and order out of the phenomena of subjective experience' (Rogers, in Koch, 1959, p. 188). To be of value, such formulations should be tentative. This makes them more stimulating to further creative thought. They should also be testable because a theory has minimal truth value until it is subjected to some sort of rigorous test, through empirical or phenomenological research (see Rogers, 1985b).

It was and is important to me that in my exposition of the theory of client-centered therapy, all of the major statements are testable through empirical means. It is gratifying that a considerable number have been so tested, with generally confirmatory results. (For a review of the studies of the therapeutic conditions, see Patterson, 1984.) To me there seems little value in a theory that cannot be tested. It means that it must remain static. There is no possibility for growth or correction. As I emphasized in this theoretical paper, 'There is only one statement which can accurately apply to all theories — and that is that at the time of its formulation, every theory contains an unknown (and perhaps at that point unknowable) amount of error and mistaken inference' (Rogers, in Koch, 1959, p. 190).

I see science itself as a directional flow into which our theories and research find

---

3. The acceptance was very minimal. When the chairman of the meeting, John Anderson, and I went to the men's room after the address, we could hear the loud buzz of comment and conversation as we opened the door. As I entered, the sound dropped to absolute silence. There was not a word of greeting or comment. As we left, I could hear the loud buzzing recommence. Never have I experienced so vividly being a 'loner' in my profession.

their place. 'If the movement is toward more exact measurement, toward more clear-cut and rigorous theory and hypotheses, toward findings which have greater validity and generality, then this is a healthy and growing science. If not, it is a sterile pseudo-science . . . Science is a *developing* mode of inquiry, or it is of no particular importance' (Rogers, 1959, p. 189).

One aspect of my purpose in formulating theory is often overlooked. Throughout my professional life I have been interested in the process of change in personality and behavior, and this is the major focus of both my theory and practice. I have been much less interested in the way in which personality develops or in its structure. These two are, however, the major foci of Freudian theory, so comparison is often difficult.

Neither Erickson nor Kohut have such a commitment to science as I feel. Erickson did place great value on flexibility of thought and action, and warns against too much loyalty to a method, a school of thought, a mentor, or a technique. He says, 'Remember that whatever way you choose to work must be your own way, because you cannot really imitate someone else' (Erickson, in Haley, 1967, p. 535). This is very similar to the statement I have often made to students and those in training: 'There is one *best* school of therapy. It is the school of therapy you develop for yourself based on a continuing critical examination of the effects of your way of being in the relationship.'

Kohut was much interested in the formulation of a theory of the development of personality. His concepts are intriguing and complex. What troubles me is his lack of interest in testing his theories.

Let me give an example. Kohut sees the self as developing along two lines, beginning in infancy: the 'grandiose self' and the 'idealized parent image.' He postulates 'that in early self-development the infant's narcissistic exhibitionism and idealization become established as independent constituents of a "nuclear" self: the grandiose and the re-internalized ideal parent image' (Graf, 1984, p. 82).

Without quibbling about definitions, this is an interesting basic theory. It can never be disproved. By the same token, however, it can never be proved or validated. There is no present way by which we can enter the infant's conceptual world to know if in fact there are these two lines of development. So this theoretical formulation, like most psychoanalytic theories, exists only in a speculative realm. It thus becomes a matter of belief or disbelief rather than a matter of confirmation or disconfirmation.

I have been puzzled by the lack of interest in the testability of theories exhibited by Kohut—and others. I see it as perhaps due to two factors.

First is a European tradition that sees theory as an entity in itself rather than as a step toward more solid knowledge. (Einstein's theory of relativity was only that—a theory—until it was confirmed by observational findings.)

The second factor is Kohut's belief that a 'genetic' explanation of his patient's behavior is essential to cure. This means that the analyst must know and understand the patient's past. Hence there must be theories concerned with the way in which behavior develops. The analyst must know the past history—the inner and outer history—of the patient's infancy and childhood, in order to make a useful and valid genetic interpretation.

But this overlooks a most important fact. We can never know the past. All that exists is someone's present perception of the past. Even the most elaborate case history, or the most extensive knowledge of a person's free associations about the past, reveal only memories present now, 'facts' as perceived now. We can never know the individual's past. I have pointed out earlier that 'the effective reality which influences behavior is at all times the perceived reality. We can operate theoretically from this base without having to resolve the difficult question of what "really" constitutes reality' (Rogers, 1959, p. 223).

I believe Kohut is mistaken in thinking that data gathering—through empathy or otherwise—is a key to an accurate and helpful causal explanation of present behavior.

I do not minimize the importance of dealing with the past as it is remembered in the present. But my client is the one best able to see the significant patterns in this remembered past. I cannot, no matter how much I desire it, give my client an account of his or her 'real' past.

Because of this assumed importance of 'genetic' interpretations, Kohut must know the patient's past, and the course of his or her development. This leads to theories about personality development that are of necessity speculative and untestable.

Thus Kohut and I differ sharply over the nature of theory, and particularly over our ability to know and interpret a 'real' past history of our clients/patients.

THE APPLICATIONS OF THERAPEUTIC PRINCIPLES

In one respect the work that I and my colleagues have done is completely different from that of Erickson, Kohut, and most other psychotherapists; namely, my interest in using the principles I feel I have learned in therapy in fields quite divergent from that in which they have originated.

Why have I been involved in the application of therapeutic learnings? In part I believe it is due to the fact that a very important part of me is a scientist. I can fully understand the enthusiastic exaggeration of Archimedes when he discovered that the forces operative in the lever could be described in a mathematical formula. 'Then,' he said, 'If I have a lever long enough, I can move the world!' I, too, have dreamed of that long lever!

I expressed something of this sort a decade ago, when I was in a large workshop in which I felt we were discovering important things.

> If we can find even one partial truth about the process by which 136 people can live together without destroying one another, can live together with a caring concern for the full development of each person, can live together in the richness of diversity instead of the sterility of conformity, then we may have found a truth with many, many implications. (Rogers, 1977, p. 175)

Since writing this I have had increasing opportunities to test some facilitative principles in practice. There have been many cross-cultural workshops, a number of interracial groups, and more and more a focus on groups containing antagonistic factions (Rogers, 1977, Chap. 6, 7; 1984).

It has been a privilege and a challenge to deal with a group from Belfast, containing militant Protestant and Catholic members (Rogers, 1977, pp. 129–34); a group in Dublin containing persons from Northern and Southern Ireland as well as participants from many other countries; a black/white group in South Africa (Sanford, 1984); a group of international leaders from Central and South America as well as from other interested countries that focused on 'The Central American Challenge' (Rogers, 1986). In my wildest dreams I could not have imagined participating in such an exciting series of events.

In each of these I have learned a great deal. In each one there have been disappointments. In no case have there been miracles. But in each of these situations there has been a decrease in bitterness, an improvement in communication, and constructive actions taken by members after the workshop.

I find a deep satisfaction in discovering that some of my basic learnings in psychotherapy apply to other areas of life. This is not a one-way street. I have learned about therapy from these experiences in very different fields. But to find that the sort of climate that is so important in the therapeutic relationship is also important in education, in administration, in dealing with interracial, intercultural, and even international tensions and conflicts, is a richly rewarding experience. To have the opportunity to test such principles in three of the world's 'hot spots' — Northern Ireland, Central America, and South Africa — has been incredibly meaningful. I am well aware that these opportunities have been small in scale — test-tube experiments, really — but I hope they have helped to set precedents for a more human interaction that may move us in the direction of peace.

REFERENCES

Erickson, M. H., Rossi, E. L., & Rossi, S. I. (1976). *Hypnosis realities: The induction of hypnosis and forms of indirect suggestion.* New York: John Wiley.

Erickson, M. H., & Zeig, J. K. (1980). Symptom prescription for expanding the psychotic's world view. In E. L. Rossi (Ed.), *The collected papers of Milton H. Erickson on hypnosis.* vol. 4 (pp. 335–7). New York: Irvington.

Gilligan, S. G. (1982). Ericksonian approaches to clinical hypnosis. In J. K. Zeig (Ed.), *Ericksonian approaches to hypnosis and psychotherapy* (pp. 87–103). New York: Brunner/Mazel.

Goldberg, A. (Ed.). (1980). *Advances in self-psychology. With summarizing reflections by Heinz Kohut.* New York: International Universities Press.

Graf, C. L. (1984). Healthy narcissism and new-age individualism: A synthesis of the theories of Carl Rogers and Heinz Kohut. Unpublished Ph.D. dissertation, State University of New York (Stonybrook).

Gunnison, H. (1985, May). The uniqueness of similarities: Parallels of Milton H. Erickson and Carl Rogers. *Journal of Counseling and Development, 63,* 561–4.

Haley, J. (Ed.). (1967). *Advanced techniques of hypnosis and therapy: Selected papers of Milton H. Erickson, M.D.* New York: W. W. Norton.

Kahn, E. (1985, August). Heinz Kohut and Carl Rogers: A timely comparison. *American Psychologist, 40,* 893–904.

Kohut, H. (1978). The psychoanalyst in the community of scholars. In P. H. Ornstein (Ed.), *The search for self: Selected Writings of H. Kohut,* three vols. New York: International Universities Press.

Kohut, H. (1981, October 4). *Remarks on empathy* (film). Filmed at Conference on Self-Psychology, Los Angeles.

Patterson, C. H. (1984). Empathy, warmth, and genuineness in psychotherapy: A review of reviews. *Psychotherapy: Theory, Research and Practice, 21,* 431–8.

Rogers, C. R. (1947, September). Some observations on the organization of personality. *American Psychologist, 2,* 358–68.

Rogers, C. R. (1957). A note on the nature of man. *Journal of Counseling Psychology, 4,* 199–203.

Rogers, C. R. (1959). A theory of therapy, personality and interpersonal relationships as developed in the client-centered framework. In S. Koch (Ed.), *Psychology: A study of a science, Vol. III. Formulations of the person and the social context* (pp. 184–256). New York: McGraw-Hill.

Rogers, C. R. (1977). *Carl Rogers on personal power.* New York: Delacorte.

Rogers, C. R. (1980). *A way of being.* Boston: Houghton Mifflin.

Rogers, C. R. (1984). One alternative to nuclear planetary suicide. In R. Levant & J. Shlien (Eds.), *Client-centered therapy and the person-centered approach: New directions in theory, research and practice* (pp. 400–22). New York: Praeger.

Rogers, C. R. (1985a, May). Reactions to Gunnison's article on the similarities between Erickson and Rogers. *Journal of Counseling and Development, 63,* 565–6.

Rogers, C. R. (1985b, Fall). Toward a more human science of the person. *Journal of Humanistic Psychology, 25*(4), 7–24.

Rogers, C. R. (1986, Summer). The Rust Workshop: A personal overview. *Journal of Humanistic Psychology, 26.*

Rogers, C. R. (in press). A client-centered/person-centered approach to therapy. Chapter in I. L. Kutash & A. Wolf (Eds.), *Psychotherapist's casebook: Theory and technique in practice.* San Francisco: Jossey-Bass.

Rogers, C. R., & Dymond, R. F. (Eds.). (1954). *Psychotherapy and personality change.* Chicago: University of Chicago Press.

Sanford, R. (1984). The beginning of a dialogue in South Africa. *Counseling Psychologist, 12* (3), 3–14.

Stolorow, R. D. (1976). Psychoanalytic reflections on client-centered therapy in the light of modern conceptions of narcissism. *Psychotherapy: Theory, Research and Practice, 13,* 26–9.

Experiencing Level as a
Therapeutic Variable

Marion N. Hendricks   *Illinois School of Professional Psychology*

Specific transcript material is presented to help therapists recognize clients' immediately sensed, but implicit experience. The observational markers of High Experiencing (EXP) process defined in the research instrument, the EXP Scale, are shown to specify clinical interventions and training procedures for therapists. One kind of therapist response that points toward the implicit is explained and the difference such a response makes to the client's subsequent responses is illustrated. The therapist's capacity to respond toward the implicit is a kind of empathy, different from either an accurate grasp of content or emotion.

In this article, I will present brief therapy excerpts and show exactly what part of a client's statement, if responded to, is likely to lead to therapeutic movement. Client-centered therapists respond to 'feelings,' but what this means when one looks at a client's statement is not always clear. The theory and research on Experiencing are useful for specifying what can be responded to that is not yet obvious.

The concept of Experiencing (EXP; Gendlin, 1962, 1981, 1984) refers to a client's immediately sensed, but implicit, experience. One feels 'something' but one does not yet know what. In a High EXP process, a client attends directly to this implicit sense and thereby allows its verbal expression. This is a step of therapeutic change. In a Lower EXP level process, a client may fail to discriminate this initially vague sense and get stuck in an intellectual or repetitively emotive process.

RESEARCH ON EXPERIENCING

An EXP Scale (Klein, Mathieu, Gendlin, & Kiesler, 1970) that operationalizes this variable has been found to be correlated with successful therapy outcome in a number of studies. These early studies are summarized in *The Experiencing Scale Manual* (Klein et al., 1970) and in Mathieu-Coughlan and Klein (1984). As summarized in Klein et al. (in press), some recent studies have also found significant correlations between EXP level and therapy outcome. Klein et al.'s summary of studies includes the following: Nixon and Fishman found significant correlations with outcome. Fishman also found that EXP change correlated with both patient and therapist success ratings. Jennen found EXP level correlated with outcome scores on the inner support subscale of the Personal Orientation Inventory. Custers found EXP change correlated with MMPI and Q sort success measures.

Bommert and Dahlhoff (1978) found a clear relationship of EXP to outcome in their middle session segments. They also found a significant rank order correlation between EXP level and measures of client well-being.

First published in *Person-Centered Review,* Volume 1, Number 2, May 1986.

Although not an outcome study, Wexler (as cited in Mathieu-Coughlan & Klein, 1984) found a correlation between EXP level and indices of client richness and depth.

Klein and Mathieu-Coughlan (in press) also cite some studies that did not find a correlation between EXP level and outcome.

THE EXPERIENCING PROCESS

Until recently (Mathieu-Coughlan & Klein, 1984), what successful therapist and client behavior look like in a transcript has been known only by the research raters. The observational cues of the scale constitute not only research specificity but enable an equally specific training and practice. The EXP Scale defines clients' implicit beginning and leads. These are points when the client is momentarily sensing something that, as yet, has no words or images. There is the sense of a whole thing present, which is not explicit. The therapist wishes to pick up and respond to such openings. Therapists and clients frequently understand content and emotions correctly, but miss or close off these implicit leads. In the transcripts I will make these leads visible, and distinguish implicit experiencing from explicit content and emotions.

It is often assumed that what is not explicitly expressed by the client can only be inferred. If that were so, interpretation would be necessary. But the client's implicit meaning is directly sensed — not inferred. It is expressed, but through the particular uses of language and silence that will be detailed in this article.

Low experiencing level

The EXP concept refers not to the content but to the manner in which a person relates to his or her experience. The client may speak of memories, fantasies, or the relationship with the therapist, but any of these contents may be processed in a High or Low manner of experiencing. On a Low EXP level, the client narrates events (inner or outer) with no explicit references to their currently felt meaning. We are all familiar with clients who only report *what* happened since the last session. They don't attempt to sense or explore the events' implicit personal significances. The process feels flat and static. Similarly, people in a psychotic process function at a Low EXP level, but narrate the inner events, images and contents of delusions or hallucinations. Similarly, 'acting out' is a Low EXP process — the person acts the meaning behaviorally rather than experiencing its felt significance.

Middle experiencing level

At Middle EXP levels, the client can at least identify some emotions and may also think about events in terms of personal connections, but there is no 'focusing' on a felt sense.

High experiencing level

At High EXP levels, the client refers to the implicit meaning of an event. This is not a speculative attempt to 'figure out' or deductively reconstruct probable significance. Nor is it a matter of recognizable emotions, however intense. The implicit significance is spoken of as a concrete, bodily 'sense' of a whole situation. Gendlin calls this a *felt sense*. It is preverbal, a bodily felt whole that is not at first clear. When a client says, struggling, 'It is so hard to put in words,' a felt sense is experienced. The client has an 'it' that is sensed bodily. But 'it' does not yet have words or images. The meanings of it are not yet explicit.

At the High EXP client 'focuses' on this felt sense, exact words 'move it,' 'shift it' so that the client says, 'Oh yes, *that's* what it is!' This 'felt' shift is accompanied by bodily relief — a deep breath, tears, a sigh.

Such an experienced opening of what was *sensed but not known* is a bit of therapeutic change. High EXP clients have these small steps of change during the hours. We think of them as 'good' clients. The EXP Level specifications allow us to pinpoint exactly why they are.

These three levels will be illustrated below. Their characteristics will be exactly defined so that therapists can recognize this variable minute by minute, and respond to maximize it.

CLINICAL EXAMPLES OF LOW, MIDDLE AND HIGH EXPERIENCING LEVELS

The following three excerpts illustrate Low, Middle, and High EXP level.[1]

Low EXP level

> One day he [the doctor] called me and said, 'I'm afraid she won't last long. She's spreading like wildfire.' They couldn't get all of it. It was too late. And so that's about the extent of it, you know. She went into a coma, she lasted for about three or four months. All together from the time she became ill, the entire time was about two years. After he performed the operation he said, 'I'm surprised she lasted that long.' We didn't know it had gone all the way back. There was no sign of it, nothing. But it was there all the time. Can you imagine that.

Middle EXP level

> A_____ and I . . . spent about two hours talking over the luncheon about his problem. And I've never known him, until that time, to be so low and despondent about his future in science. He said, 'You won't believe this Dad, until I tell you, that it has been over six months since I had a test-tube in my hand' . . . and after listening I was very much disturbed *by what he said because this was a very serious conversation, and it dealt with what I felt had to do with a decision he had to make regarding his work and his marriage, and they were both at stake . . .* I said, 'But A_____, don't you think if J_____ were made *to realize how desperate the situation is that she would elect to allow you to do more of your science . . .'* And there was silence for a moment or two and he shook his head, and said, *'She will never change.'* Now when he said that I felt he had already made a decision . . . to divorce rather than to continue . . . I felt absolutely consternated *by that because I knew they really loved each other, I knew they could have a harmonious relationship for many years to come if only she could understand.*

High EXP level

> It almost like . . . it kind of feels like . . . *sitting here looking through a photo album. And, like each picture of me in there is one of my achievements. And, I think [inaud] because I wasn't achieving for me. I was always achieving for . . . someone else so they'd think I was good enough.* It's like it feels right to me to say . . . *that* . . . I don't know quite how to say it . . . It's like the feeling is there, but I can't quite put words on it. It feels right somehow to say it's like *I've chosen this man as my challenge . . . knowing*

---

1. Thanks to Melanie Bryan, Paula Kirshner and Cindy Keene and their practice 'clients' for permission to use these excerpts.

> *that I'd be defeated. That this person wouldn't respond to me in the same way. So that I could kind of buy right back into the photo album being flipped through. I didn't have what it took [T: Uhhum] to get what I wanted. Which is kind of . . .*

Reading these excerpts side by side one can see the differences.

Low experiencing level

Let's characterize the first segment exactly, in terms of our variable. The therapist is being told about a series of events: the course of his wife's illness, her death, what the doctor said. Many details about the events are told. A characteristic of Low EXP process is that it is *externalized.* The therapist learns a lot about behaviorally observable situations. Anyone familiar with the situation could give the same information. One does not hear about any inner process. There are few, if any, self-referent statements. In spite of the highly painful content, the client does not name his feelings about the events or the inner meanings of the events for him. One can guess that he feels angry at the doctors and bereaved, sad, and lonely about the loss of his wife. But he does not tell any of this. The closest he comes is his statement, 'Imagine that.' One can hear a suppressed shock, outrage, anguish in this comment. Again one can guess what he would be feeling if he could 'open up' this statement. 'How could something so awful happen with no warning, no signs'; 'It's terrible to feel so helpless to save someone you love'; 'I'm furious that they didn't diagnose her properly.' But he is not exploring any of this kind of inner detail.

The therapist cannot know what his wife's death actually means to him. One gets a sense of the client's discomfort with his feelings when he tells about the doctor informing him of the terminal nature of the illness. In the midst of telling this surely grief-laden material, he says, 'So that's about the extent of it, you know.' It's as though at the point where feeling might break through, he flattens or distances from the feelings, as though he were saying, 'There is nothing *more* here; I've told you the whole thing and that's it.' He's closing down, moving away from any larger, implicit, textured sense of that whole situation. He doesn't seem to want to cry or feel angry or let himself begin to have an actual bodily sense of the whole situation.

Events are described as flat and self-evident. If emotions are acknowledged, they too are seen as obvious, self-evident, just what they are. There is not a sense that, by attending to one's whole bodily sense of some situation, new and specific meanings will emerge and thereby change one's sense of the situation. One has a sense that this man's experience will remain blocked, silent, and pained for many years until time blurs its sharpness.

In a Low EXP manner, the client primarily uses past tense. What happened is reported without immediate processing of his current direct experience of those events.

To summarize, Low EXP Level has the following characteristics:

1. Use of past tense.
2. Reporting of external events.
3. Events or emotions are described as flat and self-evident.

Middle experiencing level

In segment two, an event is being reported to the therapist—this man's conversation with his son. Some of what he tells could be gotten from a tape recording of their interaction. He describes the setting, their behavior, and their exchange: 'He said . . . and then I said . . .' However, there is a difference from segment one. This man refers to his feeling about the conversation and his son's situation: 'I was very much disturbed by what he said . . .' 'I felt absolutely consternated by that . . .' At this Middle EXP Level the narration of events is interspersed, parenthetically, with the client's impressions, feelings, and inner personal sense of the situation. We get some account of how he is affected by the events he describes.

However, references to personal meanings remain parenthetical to the event-story. Peculiarly, each of these statements has the structure, 'I felt X because . . .' and what follows is more about the son than the father. 'I felt disturbed because they (son's marriage and career) were both at stake.' 'I felt consternated because they loved each other, they could have a harmonious relationship.' One doesn't hear what it is that is disturbed in him in response to his son's situation. What is it about the potential divorce that so disturbs him? The therapist does not and cannot know unless she can get him to differentiate inwardly his whole sense of that situation, the sense that he is calling 'disturbed.' What is it exactly that feels so disturbing? Again we can guess: it hurts him to see his child in pain. He's scared his son's career will be jeopardized because he needs his son to succeed so he can feel like he is someone through his son. If his son claims what he needs, and divorces, perhaps it raises issues about the father's own marriage and how he stayed at too great a price to his self-hood. These are, of course, pure speculations. We cannot know what's actually in the 'disturbedness' this father felt as he listened to his son's struggle. Quite possibly, the client himself couldn't tell us what his 'disturbed' feeling was even if we asked him, or at least not at first. He would probably give us some obvious answer at first. 'Well, any parent would feel upset about his child's marriage breaking up. We want the best for our children.' Or some such 'commonsense,' 'self-evident' conventional answer. (And, of course, that would be true in a way.) A person at this Middle EXP Level is not used to turning and attending to the body sense of a situation and letting it articulate itself.

As in segment one, the past tense is used. Even when feeling is referred to, it is a present report about what was felt then. There is not now an ongoing sensing of the problematic situation.

Middle Level EXP has the following characteristics:

1. Mainly a descriptive narrative of events.
2. Personally felt meanings are referred to, but briefly, without internal elaboration.

HIGH EXPERIENCING LEVEL

Segment three illustrates a High EXP level process. There is almost no narration of events. It isn't even clear what the client is talking about in terms of time, place, event. There is only a brief, vague reference to 'a person' who 'won't respond' to her. This is the exact reverse of segment two. The events are parenthetical to the inner exploration, which is the main focus. If one had to summarize what each segment is about one could say: Segment one, 'wife's death'; Segment two, 'upset about son's divorce.' But what shall we say of the third? The first two are about someone else. This is about the client herself, her own sensing of inner meanings. The entire process is self-referent.

In the other two segments one could make guesses about what the implied meanings might be, but here one can't even guess. She is working at a level where the process is unique, specific to the individual. What comes next can only arise out of her wholistic sensing of whatever she's working on.

Second, much of the segment is in the momentary present tense, for example, 'if I could . . .' 'it sort of feels like . . .' 'The feeling is there.' When the past tense is used it is to articulate a felt sense she experiences currently.

Third, she isn't afraid to let something come—an image, a phrase for a whole sense of something. 'What comes . . . what comes to me . . .' She is able to let new content emerge freshly from her immediate sensing. We see this again when she says, 'I don't know quite how to say it . . . it's like the feeling is there but I can't quite put words on it . . . it feels right somehow to say . . .' She has an immediately present tangible sense, but she does not yet 'know' cognitively what it is. She lets words (or images) come from it directly. (Some capacity to 'let' something come is common to basic therapeutic change processes across models, for example, free associations, active imagination, gestalt.) When they come, she learns something about herself that she didn't articulate previously. Her process is also characterized by pauses as she attends to the bodily felt but preconceptual sense and waits for symbols to come from it (instead of trying to fill in or deduce what it must be). She has to grope for words that will 'fit' the sense just right. This body sensing is individually specific. Clichés and ordinary uses of language have little power. She creates metaphors to get at the exact specific quality of the experience. Metaphors are a use of language marked by 'it's like . . .' (Your eyes are like stars). She is using language this way when she says, 'it kind of feels like . . . (pause as she gropes for words and lets them come) sitting here looking through a picture album.'

To summarize, in a High EXP process, the client has specific, observable characteristics:

1. An inner exploration of personally felt meanings is the main focus. Events are referred to only as a base from which to sense inwardly into one's whole body sense of a situation.
2. Present tense is being used.
3. There are pauses as one waits to let words or images come from the felt sense.
4. One uses language metaphorically: 'The feeling is like . . .'
5. One uses language to point to the implicit: 'it,' 'that,' 'something,' what is sensed but not yet known.

IMPLICATIONS FOR **EXP** VARIABLE FOR CLINICAL PRACTICE

The therapist who is familiar with this variable can move toward the implicit at each moment. This includes several modes of therapist response.

First, the client can be helped to stay with the felt sense if the therapist recognizes when the client is indeed speaking from such an implicit sense of the situation. The client will be groping, pausing, struggling to find words to describe something that can be sensed but that does not yet have words. The therapist waits while the client tries to explicate (find symbols for) the preverbal, preconceptual sense of the situation, or speaks of it as that sense that cannot yet be defined. The unaware therapist may consider this hesitant manner, the silences, the initial vagueness as resistance, confusion, or unproductive process. Instead of helping the client to stay with the felt sense, the therapist may try to clarify the process and end up with only an intellectual understanding.

The therapist can also help the Low EXP client find this level of processing by direct instruction or by integrating focusing instructions into the ongoing therapy process (see Gendlin, 1984).

The following excerpts illustrate differences between therapists who do not know this variable and those who do.

Therapist failure to recognize client's High EXP level process

In the following excerpt the student-therapist is not aware of the EXP variable.

CLIENT: *Yuh . . . it's really gone . . . And yet,* like I feel . . . there's . . . there's something underneath it all but I don't know what . . . *and if I kind of knew what it was . . . I might feel differently, I don't know. But* it's vague *right now.*

THERAPIST: *Okay . . . if things could be a little more definite. If you were really able to identify the cause . . . you really think that you'd be able to cope with it then. But right now you can't seem to put your finger on what the real problem is.*

CLIENT: *Yuh . . . and . . . that . . . like when you say that . . . that makes me mad because I feel . . . you know like I'm . . . intelligent. I can figure things out. And yet . . . right now I don't know what the hell's going on with me.*

The client here is in a High EXP level process. In her first statement she literally describes focusing on a felt sense, 'Something (there) . . . but I don't know what.' She is concretely sensing the presence of some whole thing, but it is implicit. She does not yet know what is in this sense. Such an implicit sense is often felt as 'vague' initially. It doesn't yet have a sharp, definite, explicit form. The possibility of something new, some change, arises only when working in direct contact with what is not yet known. The client can sense that if this sensed 'something' would become explicit, it might shift her whole context or bring some release. Notice the High EXP characteristics: pauses, not being able to find words immediately, the use of 'something' to point to what is there without prematurely labeling or imposing definition on it.

The therapist reflects the feeling level of the manifest communications. His response is not inaccurate. We can see what he responds to, with each of his phrases. 'More definite' and 'identify the cause' refer to client's 'if I kind of knew what it was.' His 'be able to cope' refers to 'vague.' However, every major word the therapist has chosen ('definite,' 'identify causes,' 'cope,' 'the real problem') is closed, explicit, 'definite.' His message seems to be, 'Stop being so tentative and vague . . . let's uncover and label the cause and solve the problem.' The therapist seems to need a tighter, more explicit problem-solving process. He moves away from the implicit in this response.

The therapist is often defined by the client as having power and expertise. When there is trouble in the interaction, as there is here, clients may define it as something wrong with them. Most clients would feel vaguely put down without knowing why, give up the attempt to articulate the felt sense of the issue, and shift to a more cognitive, problem-solving, speculative manner of process, or feel badly about their ineptitude. Fortunately, this client is somewhat able to hold onto her experiential response, after her initial verbal agreement with the therapist. But he doesn't recognize the problem as a therapist error. She defends herself against the implied message that she is cognitively inadequate. 'I'm intelligent,' 'I can figure things out.' Notice she has shifted to the therapist's cognitive framework, 'figure out,' and away from her original felt sense, 'I feel . . . I might feel differently.'

Another typical pitfall is to try to 'help' a client by filling in, guessing at what the sensed 'something' might be. At other times one might appropriately offer an interpretation or a hypothesis, but not when the client is directly sensing and differentiating his or her own experience. That is a time for the therapist to contain his or her own anxieties about silence, control, and performance. No other person can supply a word (or image or action) that exactly 'gets' or carries forward the client's complex, preverbal sense of the situation. So much that is idiosyncratic functions in a felt sense. It is all the unique meanings the situation has for this individual at this point.

How would the therapist respond in our excerpt if he had recognized the client's High EXP process? He might have said, 'You can feel something right there . . .' Or, 'You can feel it right there underneath . . .' Therapists can use open pronouns that function as pointers *toward the implicit* without labeling or defining it. The therapist would acknowledge and reflect that the client has a direct referent, a 'something' concretely felt. He might say that neither the client nor he as yet knows what it is. In this way they both turn their attention toward it, to let words come from it.

A few minutes later in the same session there is a repetition of the above interaction. But the therapist's response is better and thus we can make some further distinctions about therapeutic responses.

> CLIENT: Like the, uh . . . like I feel almost like I'm *trapped in my own self* or something
> that . . . It's hard to describe the feeling . . . Like that . . . that it's *not going to*
> *get better* . . . And I guess like . . . like you said . . . that there doesn't seem to be a
> light at the end for me and I can't see right now . . . or at least I can't see the light.
> [8 sec.]
>
> THERAPIST: *There's an element of . . . of . . . hopelessness. Perhaps that's too strong a word,*
> *but an element at least that you don't immediately see any hope of resolving your*
> *. . . present feelings and frustrations.*
> [20 sec.]
>
> CLIENT: *Well . . . It looks pretty hopeless to me right now. But then, when you said that*
> *what came to me was . . . I sort of had an angry place that . . . Hopeless maybe, but*
> *I'm not helpless . . . like that bugs me if someone thinks I'm helpless because . . . even*
> *though it does look hopeless right now . . . Like I've always been able to fight and*
> *work things out before . . . for myself . . . But if . . . I don't know — somewhere inside*
> *me there's . . . there's something that's real . . . hurtful . . . [12 sec. silence] . . . And*
> *like my reaction to that is that I just don't care . . . [sobbing].*

Again, her first statement shows High EXP characteristics: she pauses, she uses words metaphorically, 'almost like I'm trapped.' She has to grope for words that will articulate what she senses: 'It's hard to describe.'

The therapist does respond to the felt level with his word, 'hopeless,' but still seems to have a cognitive bias ('element,' 'resolving,' 'frustrations'). Why exactly does the client react so negatively to the word 'hopeless?'

First, the therapist has offered his own word instead of staying closer to the client's words. At a High EXP level clients choose words very carefully. One tries to let each word or phrase come from the felt sense. One then carefully checks it against the felt sense to see whether it exactly gets it (moves it, opens it). The client is struggling to get just the right words to capture the quality, 'trapped in my own self,' 'not get better,' 'can't see.' A better response would be to repeat these key words, pointing with her toward that 'hard to describe' felt quality.

Second, the therapist's word simplifies too much. He tries to sum up in one commonly used emotion word what the client experiences in a much more finely differentiated way.

Third, if one does want to offer a word or phrase, it must be as a question, or be offered tentatively: 'Sort of *like* this?' The therapist's words must also be used metaphorically to point toward the implicit. He might have said something like, 'Closed in by yourself?' Client and therapist need to use words as pointers. If given words don't evoke some response from the felt sense (such a response is experienced as a change in the body), they are dismissed by both therapist and client.

Fourth, any time one is trying to articulate a sensed experience, one is in process. High EXP process has an inherent positive change directionality. It is a kind of change. Even though the client expresses hopelessness, her very willingness to turn toward that sense, to try to get at what it is, to let it open up is living in a hopeful manner. The therapist responds to the hopelessness in the content and misses the process events going on in the moment.

'That bugs me if someone thinks I'm helpless' is most likely a reference to the therapist, as well as to others in her life. Her comment, 'Somewhere inside me there's something that's real hurtful,' is probably both an attempt to return to her interrupted process and the hurt from this interaction. One might speculate that this client has conflicts around dependence, boundaries, asking for help, self-sufficiency. But to pursue these hypotheses now would stop the client's process in favor of a therapist-created problem. It is the therapist's poor responding that has produced this issue now. He is, of course, unaware of his contribution to the difficulty.

These examples demonstrate some of the problems arising from a therapist's insensitivity to the EXP level variable. Even very intuitive therapists are helped by discriminating and labeling the process consciously.

Therapist facilitation of client High EXP process

In my next excerpt, both client and therapist are functioning at a High EXP level. This continues from the High EXP sample presented earlier. (See High EXP Level sections.) It illustrates the change process made possible when a therapist is familiar with the EXP variable.

> CLIENT: *Yeah. I think so. I think so because . . . this person feels inaccessible. Yet, not so inaccessible that it's a total impossibility. So it's like I keep trying out my worth . . . on him . . . and keep coming up against, 'Yeah, I like you, but . . .'*
>
> THERAPIST: *O.K. So, how about, 'Yeah, I like you, but . . .' Does that fit? Is that exactly right to that whole feeling?*
>
> CLIENT: *Yeah, it really is. Really is.*
>
> THERAPIST: *'I like you, but . . .'*
>
> CLIENT: *That's how I feel when my mother 'liked me.' That we related. I like you but . . . But, there was always something missing. Some big flaw that was so awful, she just couldn't quite love me because of it.*
>
> THERAPIST: *Couldn't quite love. It's always qualified somehow.*
>
> CLIENT: *Yeah . . . It feels like such a hurt spot [Client begins to cry] And, I always had to . . . I always had to . . . be a star or she wouldn't love me.*

Through several steps at a High EXP level, an inner shift and release occurs. She gets to the core of what she sensed and, this 'felt shift' is bodily. It is experienced as a release of tears, but it might have begun as a sigh or a burst of laughter — some involuntary, whole-body release.

The therapist takes the client's key phrase, 'I like you but' and asks her to check and see if that really gets at her whole implicit sense of this relationship. I call this a 'focusing reflection' in the initial response. The therapist is directing the response toward the implicit. 'Do these words get at that whole thing?' The client checks back with her felt sense and affirms, 'Yes,' that phrase really does get the felt quality of the relationship with this man. She feels a differential response in her body as she says the phrase silently to herself. The therapist helps her to stay in direct contact with the felt sense. This phrase connects her to it, is a 'handle' for it. The felt sense 'stirs' when she says it. This leads to new material, a memory. The therapist again points by repeating client's key words. Then 'hurt' emerges.

The present tense tells us she is experiencing directly an aspect of her past. It is characteristic of High EXP process that past material emerges freshly. The connections are directly sensed now, not deductively 'reconstructed.' That she repeats an old pattern from her relationship with her mother with the current man in her life is felt. She now senses the underlying similarity. Sensing it in this manner begins to let it change.

The client does not merely 'discharge' or 'relive' a hurtful memory. She goes on to let that whole sense of 'hurt' begin to articulate itself: 'I always had to be a star.' The discharge, crying, is always within a context. The point is not the emotion itself. The client doesn't 'get into,' 'act out,' or feel contained within the emotion. She lets the sense of the whole thing she's tracking unfold further. What emerges in this kind of process is usually new to both client and therapist.

The client's feeling of 'always having to be a star' for her mother may be a derivative reference to the current therapist-client interaction. The client is performing, on tape, to meet the therapist's needs to do this assignment well. This structure is hurtful and repeats her early interaction with her mother. Even in this difficult context, the therapist's ability to respond to the client's implicit, direct experience allows this hurt to emerge into awareness. As it is articulated it would be probable that the client could then become aware that this is also how she feels now in this interaction, if that is the case.

The following excerpt from a therapy session again illustrates a therapist facilitating High EXP Level process in her client.[2] The client has become aware of a feeling of fear about an upcoming meeting with her ex-husband.

C1:   *. . . But, why in the hell do I get so scared? I mean, I'm just sick to think I have to meet him. I get this feeling like some pressure's gonna come on me. Like . . . like when I was talking to him on the phone today, he goes, 'I've really missed you. I've really been lonesome for you.' Wouldn't you think that would make me feel good?*

T1:   *It feels like pressure, you say. Can you sense what is the quality of that pressure?*

C2:   *I don't know. I mean . . . I . . . I just feel like . . . like he could make me do something that I didn't want to, or something. Now what could he make me do that I don't wanta do? I don't know.*

T2:   *Why don't we just slow down and see if you can sense that. It feels like pressure, like you could do something you don't wanta do. What is that all about?*

C3:   *Gee, I'm not sure . . . [deep breath] . . . [long pause] . . . This is kinda dumb; you know, I was thinking that . . . [tears] . . . I mean, what if I even liked him more or something? Or something. I don't know what it is [tears].*

T3:   *That you might like him more than you wanta like him.*

In C1, the client is posing a potential focusing question to herself. She has noticed an 'afraid' feeling and is puzzled by it. She does not yet know what is in this feeling. She has a whole, specific, felt experience about the upcoming visit without it yet being differentiated into explicit (symbolized) aspects. The phrase, 'like some pressure's gonna come on me,' is descriptive of the quality of this still vague, but present feeling texture. But the client immediately notices that this mass of feeling doesn't make logical or conventional sense. Clients who are unfamiliar with focusing often stop here and disavow the felt sense: 'That's not important,' 'That's stupid,' 'That's silly.' It is dismissed because it 'doesn't make sense.' Then they continue to talk about the situation.

---

2. My thanks to the therapist, Barbara Harro, and her client for permission to use this material.

In T1, the therapist does not get caught by this. She refers to the unclear feeling by going back to the phrase, 'pressure's gonna come on me.' She asks the client to stay in relation to that whole sense of pressure. This is a facilitative response. First, the therapist has recognized which of the client's words actually resonate with the client's felt texture ('resonate' means that, when the word is said, the client feels something stir in her). The therapist does not get sidetracked. By repeating her words, the client is helped to regain her access to the whole sense. The therapist then directly points the client to the opening, asking her to invite more to come from it. This is not an invitation to a cognitive speculation but a movement of attention toward a concrete, implicit, bodily sense of something.

In C2, the client does allow further words to emerge. Notice the pauses, the groping quality, the exploration of something unclear that is currently felt. The words, 'or something,' indicate the client's awareness that the phrase, 'He could make me do something,' does get the feeling, but not altogether. The client than moves too quickly and seems to shift to a cognitive mode. Again, she implies that this doesn't make sense. Or she may just feel blank or stuck for the moment.

In T2, the therapist slows her down and, by repeating the words that were closest to the feeling, invites the client to focus again on the whole feeling. Again, the therapist is pointing toward the implicit.

In C3, the client focuses deeply. Notice the body release as she lets herself down into her body sense (deep breath) and waits. She tolerates waiting. She is willing to stay with what she does not yet know, but senses. This is focusing. Something new does emerge. The client again struggles past the critical, blocking tendency 'kinda dumb' and in saying what has come ('what if I liked him more'), experiences a beginning release and knowing of her feeling about the meeting. This is a small felt shift, marked by the body release of tears, as she becomes able to 'know' what she feels. The phrase 'Or something. I don't know . . .' again implies that more is to come. The explication is not complete.

As the client continued to focus in this session, she found what was involved in 'what if I like him more.' She felt fear that their old pattern would repeat. Her husband would seem emotionally available and invite her to trust him. When she would rely on that and feel close to him, liking him, he would pull away and feel she was too demanding. She would feel hurt again just when she had become open. As this is articulated, she is able to sort out what she needs in the meeting. She does not need the more global closeness she desired in the past, but does need to tell him how hard it feels to deal with the children alone. She would like him just to hear that with some concern for her. She can now approach the meeting with more inner clarity and less fear. She will probably behave differently.

Vague is nevertheless there

In C1 the client has noticed this sense of fear, of 'pressure's gonna come on me.' She does not know what this pressure might be, or what is involved in her anxiety. Looking back, it is clear that her inability to know what she felt did not mean she had nothing present. Her whole implicit sense was vividly present. Many clients believe that only what can already be spoken or known exists. Then, their unclear but present texture is skipped as not being anything important (too vague, 'meaningless,' 'too hard to express') or is not discriminated at all. To focus, one must allow a felt sense to form without immediately knowing what it is.

The content that emerges is not determined by our conscious, directed thought. What emerges may surprise us. The process is not our familiar way of thinking; it is bodily anchored. Many clients (and therapists) are not used to trusting the orderedness of this level. There is a very exact sequencing in the experiencing process. The person is living forward what is organismically implied. In the last segment, there is an exact four-step sequence:

1. scared
2. pressure
3. make me do something
4. like him more

If the client had not stayed with 'scared,' she would not have gotten 'pressure.' The therapist brought her back to 'pressure.' She had already gone on, not trusting that anything could come from something that did not fit her expectations. When she returned to pay attention to the 'pressure,' 'make me do something' came. She then questioned 'what can he make me do?' The therapist did not reflect this question. She invited the client slowly to go back into her sense of apprehension. And so, a step came with crying and a deeper movement.

RECOGNIZING INTERNAL ATTACKS ON THE PROCESS

As pointed out, in just this short excerpt the client verges on attacking what she finds in her own emergent process. ('Why in the hell,' 'wouldn't you think,' 'this is kinda dumb.') These imply that what is forming does not make sense. This occurs almost universally. What is being noted is her unfamiliarity with a process that is experientially rather than logically ordered. Clients can be helped to recognize this rather than dropping their process. Or, as in this segment, the therapist can help the client move past that problem by responding directly to the felt sense rather than to the attack.

FRIENDLY ATTITUDE

When clients have not yet found this level of process in themselves, they may not know to value the actions involved in it. An inwardly gentle, receptive, welcoming attitude is necessary to focus. One must want to hear from oneself and be able to welcome what comes, no matter what the content is.

Focusing cannot be inwardly coerced and whatever comes needs to be received and treated with respect. That is the reality of what is there now. By letting it be, further steps become possible. The client needs to be helped to respond to internal processes in a nurturing, respectful manner, very much as the therapist is responding to the client in their interaction.

CONCLUSION

In our concern to protect the client's autonomy, we can get caught in a superficial interaction. There may seem to be no movement. If the client does not find or connect internally to a process of his or her own, therapy does not deepen. An acceptance of this state in the client is very valuable, but not enough. Only acceptance may leave the client floundering. Many clients do not have any experience with what an internally connected process is or feels like. They may be 'locked out' of their experience or enmeshed in bad feelings that are experienced repetitively. To 'refeel' them endlessly, even in a caring interaction, is not enough. Most clients do not know how to focus on their experiences. They do not know that they can attend to their more vague, implicit sense of something and that such attending leads to steps of change. Once a client discriminates this level, there is an internal directionality and momentum. It is important to understand that many clients really have no idea of this. The therapist who is aware of this fact can help the client learn this process.

REFERENCES

Bommert, H., & Dahlhoff, H. D. (1978). *Das Selbsterlehen (Experiencing) in der Psychotherapy.* Urban and Schwarzenbnery, Munchen.

Gendlin, E. T. (1962). *Experiencing and the creation of meaning.* New York: Macmillan.

Gendlin, E. T. (1981). *Focusing.* New York: Bantam.

Gendlin, E. T. (1984). The client's client. In R. Levant & J. M. Shlien (Eds.), *Client-centered therapy and the person-centered approach.* New York: Praeger.

Klein, M. H., Mathieu, P. L., Gendlin, E. T., & Kiesler, D. J. (1970). *The Experiencing Scale: A research and training manual.* Madison: University of Wisconsin Extension Bureau of Audiovisual Instruction.

Klein, M. H., & Mathieu-Coughlan, P. (in press). The Experiencing Scales. In L. S. Greenberg & W. M. Pinsof (Eds.), *The psychotherapeutic process: A research handbook.* New York: Guilford.

Mathieu-Coughlan, P., & Klein, M. H. (1984). Experiential psychotherapy: Key events in client-therapist interaction. In L. N. Rice & L. S. Greenberg (Eds.), *Patterns of change.* New York: Guilford.

Heuristic Inquiry as Psychotherapy:
The client-centered approach

Maureen O'Hara   *Center for Studies of the Person*

The dialogical process of client-centered therapy is viewed as a joint study of the nature and meaning of human experience as seen from the client's point of view. It is proposed that one way to understand the 'healing process' in dialogical therapy is to view growth and expansion of consciousness as natural consequences of successful moments in this inquiry, when the client achieves deeper contact with, and makes a commitment to, some larger truth. Also described is the syntactical nature of such discoveries and, by use of examples from therapy transcripts, how this is experienced by the client. The role of the therapist is seen as one of service to the client's inquiry. Issues of power and authority as they impinge upon the collaborative enterprise are discussed.

Carl Rogers has devoted his professional life to the scientific study of human experience. His studies have included applied research (Rogers, 1951), which led to the development of one of the most widely practiced approaches to psychotherapy and counseling—the person-centered approach. Like all master-craftsmen throughout history, he developed and refined his therapeutic system in the crucible of practice. Beginning with the naked phenomenon of the therapeutic encounter between therapist and client, and subjecting his observations to rigorous testing and evaluation, the art and science of client-centered therapy evolved.

Not content to rely solely upon his own subjective judgment, and mindful of the natural human propensity for selective perception, distortion, and self-deception, Rogers and his colleagues developed strategies by which to evaluate objectively the effectiveness of their therapeutic approach. They were the first psychotherapists to open up the process of therapy to sound-recording technologies (Covner, 1942a, 1942b). Rogers accumulated thousands of hours of recorded therapeutic interviews that he and his colleagues pored over for months afterward.

For the first time, a system of psychotherapy could be developed using recordings of actual therapeutic encounters as a guide to the most effective kinds of therapist behavior. Rogers dreamed of taking the arcane mystification out of the therapeutic endeavor and of laying it open to all those who wished to help others in the process of growth.

Rogers and his team of brilliant, enthusiastic graduate students had access not only to material pertaining to the effectiveness of client-centered therapy but also to verbatim accounts of hundreds of persons in the process of becoming. Also, for the first time, the exquisitely delicate web of associations, feelings, thoughts, experiences, fantasies, silences, and meanings that are the client's story could be appreciated and studied, not only by the therapist in the private world of the therapeutic session but also by Rogers and his team of researchers. From this treasure house of material, along with tens of thousands

First published in *Person-Centered Review*, Volume 1, Number 2, May 1986.

of hours of face-to-face encounters with individuals, families, small groups, and community groups, Rogers has developed a view of persons—of the whole human predicament—that has been embraced by a generation. His concept of the 'emerging person,' a person motivated by an inherent directionality toward growth and transcendence, acknowledges an organismic 'actualizing tendency' in the whole of nature, including human nature. This optimistic view of people is based in concrete, dialogical experience with individuals and groups and clearly identifies Rogers with the Third Force in psychology (Rogers, 1961, 1980).

HEURISTIC INVESTIGATION AS THERAPY

There is one feature of human science that distinguishes it from all other forms of science—the focus of the inquiry is other conscious beings like ourselves. And in Rogers and his colleagues' work, the therapist/scientists were not the only ones engaged in research. In the dialogical process of client-centered therapy, both therapist and client become engaged in a joint study of the rich and mysterious world of the client. Client-centered therapy is, itself, a heuristic investigation into the nature and meaning of human experience. In his work with clients, Rogers discovered that when a person is engaged passionately and skillfully in the search for his or her own truth *the process itself is therapeutic.*

Rogers found himself in the happy situation (for a humanistic scientist) in which both scientific and therapeutic gains could be made at the same time. For the client, knowledge gains lead to psychological growth; and for the therapist, to advances in knowledge of psychology. In looking for a more effective therapy Rogers discovered an approach to human science that was expansive rather than reductive.

THE SYNTAX OF DISCOVERY

The process of discovery in a session of client-centered therapy follows a syntax that is identical to the steps characteristic of a scientific breakthrough, an intellectual insight, and the process of Gestalt formation. In the numerous verbatim accounts of therapy sessions published by Rogers and his coworkers, these stages are clearly visible (Rogers, 1951).

The process of discovery begins with the client's experience of disquiet about something amiss. The problem draws attention. Through delicate and painstaking exploration of present experience of reality, the investigation deepens, revealing piece after piece of the puzzle. Sometimes the piece discovered is an emotion, sometimes an idea, sometimes a new body sensation, a dream, or a memory. As each piece surfaces it adds to the complexity and, at first, plunges the searcher further and further into confusion. The old paradigms, the old concept of how things are, cannot accommodate all these new pieces. In Rogers' discussion of the sixteenth interview with Alfred this process is described most vividly:

> I certainly think in a way the problem is a lot clearer than a while ago, yet—maybe—It's like the ice breaking up on a pond in the spring, it's—while things are a lot nearer to—While the pond is a lot nearer to being nothing but clear water, yet things are much more unstable now, possibly, than when the pond was covered over with the ice. What I'm trying to bring out is that I seem to be so much in a terrible fog all of the time lately, but I do feel a lot better off than I was before, because then I didn't realize what was the matter. But maybe all this fog and so-called trouble is due to the fact of two opposing forces in me now. You know it's not really a case of letting one be superior, but it's kinda breaking up

and reorganizing that's going on now that makes things seem doubly bad. So maybe I'm better off than I think. (Rogers, 1951, p. 80)

This new world is different, alien, incomprehensible, and apparently without much order. As Gestalt psychologists have demonstrated, people find this situation intolerable. All the psychological resources of the individual will be mobilized to find some order in the complexity. If this cannot be done, one may experience a reality of unconnected pieces and great psychological distress that in extreme cases can precipitate psychotic-like states or severe disorganization. A Gestalt must be formed either by finding an order that accounts for all the new pieces—in which case there will be a shift toward greater integration and expanded consciousness—or by ignoring some of the strangely shaped pieces, or by creating new ones. The course taken will depend on the state of consciousness of the searcher.

Rogers and others often have found that, in moments of true revelation, there is an irreversible shift toward congruence. This has been variously described, depending on the situation in which the discovery occurs, as a healing moment, a growth step, a moment of insight, a cosmic connection, a 'Eureka' experience, satori, a paradigm shift, and so on. This shift of consciousness is cherished in most traditions as a moment of wisdom (Wood, 1977).

Fundamental to the nature of mind is our fascination with puzzles and mysteries. We struggle, often mightily, to unravel all kinds of knots. If the mystery that calls us is our own existence, we may be caught irresistibly. As a piece of the puzzle yields and we catch a new glimpse of our own story, it is therapeutic in the most profound sense. There is an expansion of consciousness, a widening of vision, an increase in wisdom.

Moments like these are sometimes experienced with joy and excitement—even ecstasy. Miss Har describes this experience:

> I shall never forget the happiness, excitement, elation and peak of self-satisfaction that I felt during the first part of the seventh interview when I had just come from proving to myself that I could face in the presence of someone other than the counselor the feeling that had been with me for years. (Rogers, 1951, p. 84)

Sometimes the process is much more terrifying and confusing, as can be seen from this session with a young woman client of mine, Felicia.

> *There is nothing beneath me. I feel like I am leaning out into hell. All my beliefs, all my fucking Marxist-feminist-humanist ideas have deserted me. I can't stand the confusion [agonized cry]. Ten years and a Ph.D.-full of certainty have failed me. I know nothing useful. I don't know how to love my own son. I saw him, I mean saw — today. He said he loves me — he's proud of me [sobs]. He said he loved me. Maybe he can teach me — actually I think he already has, you know? [smile]*

As the person moves closer to the felt meaning, consciousness shifts. The closer to a felt truth the person feels, the more complete the change (Gendlin, 1962), the greater the growth, and the more profound the healing. Moments like these may mark the end of a small paragraph or chapter in an ongoing, unfolding therapeutic process or may signal the end of the volume and the termination of therapy.

THERAPIST AS CORESEARCHER

This view of psychotherapy, which can be called 'search-as-therapy,' places a different set of burdens on the shoulders of the therapist than does the presently predominating therapy-as-search view. This view acknowledges healing as a *natural consequence* of a successful moment in a progressive search for truth.

In this situation the therapist need not, and indeed cannot, assume the role of healer, nor can the process be aided by the offering of ready-made truths because it is the moment of shift in consciousness that is experienced as a healing moment. The specific content of any new formulation must have relevance to the individual, but need not reflect any generalized concepts or be in accordance with a 'theory of personality.' An 'Ah Ha' may be about anything from domestic to cosmic. It may even be soon abandoned for yet another formulation as the process continues.

In this heuristic process, the function of the therapist becomes more like that of the research assistant[1] in a scientific laboratory. The therapist's contribution is to help bring pieces of the puzzle to awareness. Using faculties of perception and discernment to enlarge the client's awareness of existent realities, the therapist helps the client to put into words vague, unclear ideas, feelings, and sensations. In this way, the therapist helps draw attention to overlooked elements of the puzzle. Using expressive capacities to communicate as clearly as possible, offering faith that there is an order in the unfolding picture even if it is currently hidden, the therapist makes a wholehearted commitment to the other's search. This last challenge is demanding, delicate, and not without risk for the therapist.

INDWELLING AND PSYCHOTHERAPEUTIC BREAKTHROUGH

In a psychotherapeutic investigation, it frequently occurs that the client arrives at a point where there are so many new pieces of the puzzle that previously held beliefs about the nature and meaning of reality must be surrendered. This moment is often marked by intense fear and extreme psychological vulnerability. As is obvious to anyone who has tried to perform a task requiring even the minimum levels of concentration, this is not the state most desirable for puzzle solving! The presence of a supportive coinvestigator at these moments can be very important, as in the following example with Felicia.

FEL: *I don't know what's happening. Why is this happening? I am out of control. The pain is . . . [groan] the pain – like a knife . . . This is senseless. I know I could stop this. I could stop this right now. But there's part of me doesn't want to stop it. I want it somehow.*

THER: *Even though it's painful you want to let it continue?*

FEL: *Yes – Oh! It's coming faster now. Worse. [She stops breathing – looks very frightened]*

THER: *Your breathing just stopped and you began to stiffen up. As you did that you looked very scared.*

FEL: *[Breathing deeply, panting] Oh! My god! I know what's happening. It's Andrew, it's Andrew. He's coming [loud cry at first in pain changing to joy followed by a long silence, easy breathing and a gentle body position]. You know I never felt him born. I had a general anaesthetic. It was Caesarian. When they gave him to me I really didn't know where he had come from.*

THER: *You never had bodily experience of becoming a mother. You didn't feel it . . .*

FEL: *Until now. I never let my body have any say in anything. Now I feel like I had to do* body *work* here, *to cry. I had to let it take me over, not fight.*

THER: *You had to surrender . . .*

---

1. I thank William Coulson for this view of therapist as research assistant.

FEL: *To myself — to me — to being a woman. Holy shit!*

At this point the therapist must voluntarily suspend his or her own particular view, to indwell in the complexity of the experience by the other. Briefly they are both there at the focus of the client's sphere, experiencing reality from a similar perspective. No matter how fearful this position is for the client, for whom this represents an existential predicament, the therapist is free from this burdening emotional experience. It is not, after all, the therapist's life. The therapist can therefore use this detachment from this particular existential predicament to fully enter the unknown with the client.

It is important to stress here that I am referring to detachment from the client's *fear* of the experienced predicament and not detachment from the *person* of the client or the situation we are in together. Indeed, it seems unlikely that anything short of love would induce anyone, even a psychotherapist, to leave his or her own comfortable place in the universe to risk taking a look at it from someone else's.

In this state of surrender (Wood, 1977), indwelling (Polanyi, 1958), or empathy (Rogers, 1951), as it has variously been called, the therapist can bring to bear tacit faculties, such as intuition, knowledge and experience, reason, and subtle body sensations, to arrive at an understanding currently out of sight of the confused client. Any order discovered, any gestalten formed, represent the therapist's best attempt to discover hidden order. The therapist's discovery can then be offered to the client for acceptance, rejection, or further exploration. As Gendlin (1962) has pointed out, even incorrect interpretation by the therapist can point the way toward deeper awareness and understanding if the therapist and client have entered into a shared search together.

COLLABORATION, POWER AND CONVICTION IN PSYCHOTHERAPY

This kind of collaboration raises the question of power and authority in the relationship between client and therapist. Rogers has pointed out that if the therapist's understanding is a faithful reflection of the client's puzzle, it can be a powerful catalyst for a similar organization within the client's own consciousness. In this way consciousness expands, and the client is now aware of a greater truth and makes a commitment to this new view, experiencing a breakthrough.

This process is clearly demonstrated in the vignette 'Nancy Mourns,' written about an incident in a person-centered approach workshop:

> At least two other possible bases for her strong feelings were caringly and tentatively suggested to her. To the first she said, 'I'm trying on that hat, but it doesn't seem to fit.' To the second she said, 'That doesn't fit either.' ... Then Ann said, 'This may be inappropriate, but I am going to say it anyway ... I wonder if there is any connection between you and your father and Carl?' 'That's it.' Nancy sobbed as though she had been struck by a bolt of lightning. She collapsed into herself, weeping her heart out. (Rogers, 1980, pp. 221–2)

But it is well known that, at these moments, there are many factors at play that will predispose the client to accept what the therapist suggests. For example, a person will frequently see what he or she has been told is there. There is no avoiding this. When we speak we influence each other. Psychological distress will also propel the client to accept any solution that lessens the discomfort. This, together with the client's trust in the authority and honesty of the therapist, makes the pressure very great for the client to grasp for the therapist's conclusions.

The delicate issues of authority and power cannot be altogether avoided, nor do I believe they should be. The potential of these therapist-client investigations lies in the collaboration itself. The 'research team' of a principal investigator, the client, with the research assistant, the therapist, are as susceptible to error as any researchers in any field. Each is capable of leading the other down any number of false trails.

What is remarkable, however, is how the process of mutual exploration, with all its inherent pitfalls, so often results in the client's greater awareness and understanding of his or her truth. Clients commit to this view new truth, not because the therapist says so but because they know truth when they experience it. This is what Coulson has recently called the *recovery of conviction*, which occurs when the client can once again believe in his or her capacity to perceive and make meaning of the universe from a unique vantage point. It is a supremely personal act. The nature of this conviction or commitment is influenced by everything that the person has ever experienced. But even so, when a person comes to this commitment, he or she does it independently and does it as Polanyi (1958) has said, with *universal intent*. This means that we have enough confidence in our perception, and enough grasp of things, to believe that if someone else were to see the world from our unique point of view, they would conclude what we have concluded. As Coulson has said, a significant consequence of this universal intent is that it urges those with convictions to speak up, to make contact, and to engage passionately with their fellows. The poet through poems, the scientist through writings, and clients to those close by all make public their personal knowledge, to influence and be influenced in return. Our willingness to declare our knowledge becomes part of an unfolding collective dialogical search for truth. In this way the private 'research project' by the client of his or her own experience may become part of everyone's knowledge as it provides the client with self-knowledge and expanded consciousness.

LIMITATIONS OF HEURISTIC APPROACHES

Because the focus of the encounter between the therapist and client is the discovery of truth as the client sees it, there is no way of knowing whether the client is right or wrong. The person could be a pathfinder, the first person ever to have seen or to have understood the world in this way. If so, the discovery will become the property of all of us. But only after future confirmation by others. On the other hand, the person's view may be idiosyncratic and in error, describing only a private world of meaning.

There is also no guarantee that the investigation will yield any new configuration for the client. It requires considerable skill whether in art, science, or psychotherapy to find a frontier of investigation that, though demanding enough to stretch the searcher beyond previous certainties, is not beyond the searcher's present capacity to reach.

In looking for direction in this shared investigation, Rogers insisted that the client's choices are the most reliable guide regarding where to begin. We may trust the push from the client's own sense of urgency to point to the promising leads. It must be acknowledged, however, that not all puzzles can be solved quickly, and some of the grandest puzzles may only yield their final secrets at death, or even beyond.

The therapist, as coinvestigator, can suggest more promising areas or more fine-tuned research techniques, but must accept (and so must the client) that the client may leave therapy with more puzzle pieces and more confusion than when he or she began.

Most decidedly of all, heuristic approaches cannot promise positive outcomes the way more technologically oriented therapeutic approaches do. Because, by definition, what is to be discovered is unknown, there must always be risk in such a process. Discovery is irreversible; we cannot bury it again without burying those committed to it. We can only go beyond it to future discoveries. Not all societies, whether domestic, institutional, or political, welcome new discoveries that destroy past convictions. They may even exert considerable pressure to suppress or destroy those who bring a new vision.

The heuristic psychotherapist is primarily concerned with truth, expansion of knowledge, and consciousness. In a sense, such a therapist is indifferent to the practical consequences of the discovery. Of course, such a therapist must believe that wisdom is preferred over ignorance or illusion, but makes no claims that wisdom will necessarily bring happiness or even tranquility.

Conclusion

Any promise claimed by therapists engaged in a heuristic process with clients must proceed from the faith that the universe of which we are part is not random and arbitrary but has a preestablished harmonic order. Perhaps more important for the therapeutic process, it also must be based in a belief that human life is not random but is essentially meaningful. We proceed with the faith that a progressive, open-ended search will bring the searchers into deeper contact with this harmony and meaningfulness.

The therapist and client are not engaged in idly turning over stones, simply to satisfy a desire for novelty, but are engaged in an active exercise of their faith in a rational universe and a comprehensible human experience.

There is substantial evidence that at moments of revelation people move toward psychological health, whether in a religious, scientific, artistic, or therapeutic context. This is the only basis for claims that this mutual exploration is, in fact, a valid form of psychotherapy.

But perhaps this is not a modest intention. We are living at a time when 'truth' is a word uttered almost with embarrassment. We live in a world of 'separate realities' and 'bottom lines,' where 'truth' is increasingly taken as being synonymous with 'ideological consensus,' where technological achievements have massively outstripped our moral development, where knowledge and wisdom are increasingly confused with expertise.

I believe that a strong case can be made for an enterprise that has as its only goal the progressive uncovering of the mysteries of human existence, and that perhaps, alongside problem solvers, technicians, and behavioral and strategic therapists, there is still a place for explorers, even in the field of psychotherapy.

References

Coulson, W. R. personal communication.

Covner, B. F. (1942a). Studies in the phonographic recording of verbal material: I. The use of phonographic recordings in counseling practice and research. *Journal of Consulting Psychology, 6,* 105–13.

Covner, B. F. (1942b). Studies in the phonographic recording of verbal material: II. A transcribing device. *Journal of Consulting Psychology, 6,* 149–53.

Gendlin, E. T. (1962). *Experiencing and the creation of meaning.* New York: Free Press.

Polanyi, M. (1958). *Personal knowledge.* Chicago: University of Chicago Press.

Rogers, C. R. (1951). *Client-centered therapy.* Boston: Houghton Mifflin.

Rogers, C. R. (1961). *On becoming a person.* Boston: Houghton Mifflin.

Rogers, C. R. (Ed.). (1967). *The therapeutic relationship and its impact: A study of psychotherapy with schizophrenics.* Madison: University of Wisconsin Press.

Rogers, C. R. (1980). *A way of being.* Boston: Houghton Mifflin.

Shlien, J. M., & Zimring, F. M. (1971). Research directions and methods in client-centered therapy. In J. T. Hart & T. M. Tomlinson (Eds.), *New directions in client-centered therapy* (pp. 33–57). Boston: Houghton Mifflin.

Wexler, D. A., & Rice, L. N. (Eds.). (1974). *Innovations in client-centered therapy.* Boston: Houghton Mifflin.

Wood, J. K. (1977). Shadows of surrender: Notes on person-centered approaches. Talk given in Sao Paulo, Brazil.

Personality Differences
and Person-Centered Supervision

Maria C. Villas-Boas Bowen   *Center for the Studies of the Person*

Two types of person-centered supervision are considered; one emphasizes the preservation of 'pure forms,' the other a basic philosophy of life. The philosophy-of-life-oriented supervision is characterized by taking individual differences into account, and by emphasizing the development of the supervisee's internal locus of evaluation through self-awareness and trust in the supervisee's own intuition. Some approaches to developing self-awareness are discussed. Two kinds of empathic responses are hypothesized: supportive responses and integrative impressions. It is postulated that intuition is manifested through integrative impressions of which four kinds are described. It is recommended that the supervisee's preferred mode of expressing integrative impressions be honored, even when different from the supervisor's. Thus the same principles that guide therapy are also present in supervision: the trust of the supervisee's inner resources, and capacity for self-determination and self-direction.

One of Carl Rogers' greatest contributions to the field of psychology has been his trust in the person's capacity for self-regulation, self-direction, and self-determination. The belief that people have within themselves the necessary resources to enhance their own lives and the lives of those around them has had a profound political implication: power and expertise came to be shared between client and therapist instead of being concentrated only on the therapist. Therapists learned to trust the client's capacity to find his or her[1] own direction and to respect the client's unique way of being.

As early as 1956, Rogers had begun to apply these same principles of therapist-client interaction to the supervisor-supervisee relationship. Rogers (1956) stated that by providing the supervisee with an accepting, empathic, and genuine atmosphere, the supervisor would not only model how to create those conditions, but would also offer an atmosphere in which the supervisee might freely explore the feelings, blocks, and difficulties that emerge while learning to become a therapist. The implication was that supervisors need to create an atmosphere where supervisees could experience their own expertise and power. There is evidence that this approach to supervision is also in agreement with the expectations of supervisees who indicated that they desired the freedom to explore and develop their own style (Gysbers & Johnston, 1965). Also, research showed that supervisees who received empathy, acceptance, and genuineness became significantly more open to their own experiences (Hansen & Barker, 1964) and were more successful in developing these helpful behaviors in themselves (Blane, 1968; Pierce, Carkhuff, & Berenson, 1967).

---

1. Although the author has conformed to the APA guidelines for nonsexist language she wishes to state her preference for the alternation of the gender of pronouns to achieve this end. This was the form she used in the original draft of this article.

First published in *Person-Centered Review,* Volume 1, Number 3, August 1986.

Undoubtedly, person-centered supervisors will agree with Rogers' ideas about supervision; yet how their understanding of these ideas is implemented in practice may differ considerably according to two major orientations: form-oriented and philosophy-of-life-oriented supervision.

FORM-ORIENTED SUPERVISION

In this approach, the primary commitment is to the preservation of a single mode of doing psychotherapy that seems to take the forms inspired by Rogers' style of therapy during the 1940s and 1950s: it is nondirective, uses reflection of feelings as the primary way of expressing empathy, and avoids the introduction of anything that the client had not already brought up during the session. Shlien and Levant (1984) mention that they feel nostalgia for these 'pure forms,' which they seem to consider as 'classical types.' These authors are concerned that by being pragmatic, in introducing 'whatever works' in therapy, it becomes difficult for the researcher to identify which element is working in a specific situation.

The commitment to the preservation of 'pure forms' continues to influence the practice of supervision. Coulson (1984), for example, seems to emphasize telling supervisees what *not* to do, so that they won't diverge from the 'pure forms,' but will learn to listen better, and learn specific therapeutic responses through 'apprenticeship' with the supervisor. Temaner (Bozarth & Temaner, 1984, p. 11) writes about the supervisor 'providing the student with an initial way to relate to and interact with practice clients that almost completely eliminates the need for the student to make decisions about how and when to respond.' Because of the possibility of misunderstanding the client, she discourages beginning therapists from 'idiosyncratic responses' that emphasize transparence, the role of intuition, and immersion in the process. Temaner (1982) indicates when, under what circumstances, and the criteria the therapist uses to make explicit empathic responses.

In form-oriented supervision, the supervisor seems to have a preconceived idea of how supervisees should behave in order to preserve the forms the supervisor is committed to. The supervisee is discouraged from styles of expression that do not fit the supervisor's model. Although the atmosphere of warmth, empathy, and congruence may be present, a basic philosophical principle of the person-centered approach seems to be missing: the trust in the supervisee's capacity for self-direction and self-determination—that is, the belief that the supervisee has the inner resources to develop his or her own style of being an effective therapist. It seems that the basic philosophy is sacrificed to the preservation of 'pure forms.'

PHILOSOPHY-OF-LIFE-ORIENTED SUPERVISION

The primary commitment of this type of orientation is to a basic philosophy of being, which is reflected in the way one does psychotherapy. This approach may be considered 'pragmatic' in the sense that it may take any form that will be helpful to the client as long as this form is guided by respect for the client's capacity for self-direction and self-determination, and trust that the client has the inner resources necessary for self-understanding, changes in self-concept, attitudes, and behavior. Like form-oriented supervisors, supervisors with this frame of reference believe that, in order to tap the client's resources, a climate of acceptance, empathy, and congruence is needed. But they also believe that the form that those necessary conditions take depends on the personality of the therapist, the personality of the client, and the type of interaction that develops between the two.

The philosophy-of-life orientation seems to be inspired by Rogers' ways of interacting after he became deeply involved with group work in the 1960s and afterwards. Group process, with its variety of human experiences, including angry confrontation by group members, seemed to have deeply affected the way Rogers responded to others. He increased his repertoire of responses in dealing with people and, consequently, his way of doing individual psychotherapy changed. Rogers (1986) has given a fine description of the person-centered approach as a philosophy that guides his psychotherapy:

> The person-centered approach, then, is primarily a way of being which finds its expression in attitudes and behaviors that create a growth-promoting climate. It is a basic philosophy rather than simply a technique or a method. When this philosophy is lived, it helps the person to expand the development of his or her own capacities. When it is lived, it also stimulates constructive change in others. It empowers the individual, and when this personal power is sensed, experience shows that it tends to be used for personal and social transformation.

I believe that philosophy-of-life-oriented supervision has two main characteristics: (1) personality differences are taken into consideration, and (2) there is an emphasis on the development of the internal locus of evaluation of the supervisee.

PERSONALITY DIFFERENCES

It is important to take into consideration that different persons respond in their own unique ways to the same stimulus according to their personality and past experiences. Consequently, it is important that the supervisor enter the frame of reference of the supervisee, even when different from the supervisor's. Research by Reising and Daniels (1983) points out the importance of taking individual differences into account in supervision. They state that any style of supervision that does not vary from trainee to trainee assumes incorrectly that all trainees are in need of the same thing.

During a recent supervision group with Carl Rogers the importance of valuing and using personality differences in supervision was impressed upon me. The group was reviewing the audiotape of a demonstration interview that Rogers had conducted recently. I allowed myself to imagine how I would respond if I were the therapist. I saw myself responding in ways similar to Rogers' in many instances. Rogers often describes himself as responding to the feeling that is most important to the client at any one moment. Because my responses were similar to his, I felt I was right on target. But, quite frequently I also saw myself responding differently from him — or reacting to different aspects of what the client had said. I felt puzzled at those moments and wondered if I was failing to respond to the feelings that were most important to the client at that moment. But, even though I admired the high quality of Rogers' responses, I also felt that, although different from his, my responses were also appropriate and on target. I then realized that both of us were responding according to our own personalities and to our own ways of perceiving things. I shared this experience with Rogers, and in response he (1985) wrote:

> I was very much struck by the truth of your notion that when I try to respond to the feeling that is most important to the client, my choice of what is most important is certainly influenced by my own personality, past history, and so forth. I agree that that is most

assuredly true and I don't think I ever had said that. I have approached it in a back-handed way by saying, 'I try to respond to what is most important to the client.' . . . I deplore the notion that if a therapist responds in much the same way I do she or he is 'on target,' and if he or she responds differently they are making a mistake. I think, however, that your thoughts about this give all of us a new way of avoiding that. If it is openly recognized that such responses are partly shaped by the therapist's perception, and that this perception is shaped both by the client's expression and by the therapist's personality, we may be able to avoid imitative 'modeling.'

Just as therapists' perceptions and responses are inevitably shaped by 'their personality, past history and so forth,' it follows that the supervisee is going to perceive and act differently from the supervisor. It is important that the supervisor respect these differences and trust that supervisees have the resources necessary to develop their own effective ways of doing therapy. The function of the supervisor, then, is to create the atmosphere that will enable the supervisee to find her or his own style of being a therapist. By doing so the supervisor also models the growth-promoting environment of congruence, acceptance, and empathy.

Having stated the above one might ask: If the supervisee has the freedom to develop his or her own style, does it mean that supervision is a laissez-faire situation, and that anything the supervisee does is acceptable? If so, what purpose would be there for supervision?

My belief is that supervision is *not* a laissez-faire situation. On the contrary, I see supervision as a very rigorous and active process of careful examination of the interaction between supervisee and client. By placing portions of the session's interaction under careful scrutiny through the review of audio or videotapes, process notes, role playing, or demonstration interviews (Kagan & Werner, 1977), supervisees become increasingly aware of how their behavior affects others, and how, in turn, they are affected by others. Through the development of this kind of self-awareness supervisees learn to be the judge of their own performance, developing in that way an internal locus of evaluation that will guide their actions.

DEVELOPMENT OF INTERNAL LOCUS OF EVALUATION

Rogers (1959, p. 210) uses the term *locus of evaluation* to indicate the source of evidence for one's values: 'Thus an internal locus of evaluation, within the individual himself, means that he is the center of the valuing process, the evidence being supplied by his own senses.' In order to facilitate supervisees' capacity to trust their own inner processes, I believe that the supervision should be focused on the development of two main personality qualities: (a) self-awareness and (b) trust in one's intuition.

Development of self-awareness

One of the functions of the supervisor is to create an environment that will facilitate the supervisee's openness to continued growth and learning, a willingness for deeper self-knowledge and assessment of the ethics and effectiveness of his or her work. In order to achieve the courage for inner exploration, the supervisee needs to listen empathically to himself or herself, to develop a discerning self-acceptance, and to be aware of the disharmonies within. By learning to be that way with oneself, the supervisee can then genuinely be empathic, acceptant, and congruent with clients.

Here one might ask if the supervisor has the same function as the therapist, and whether or not the supervisor acts as the supervisee's therapist. Much has been written over the years about the role of the supervisor. Arbuckle (1963), for example, maintained that the only appropriate way for counseling students to learn to do psychotherapy was for them to engage in the same interpersonal process with their supervisors. In contrast, Patterson (1964) took exception to Arbuckle's conceptualization of the supervisor as counselor, arguing that supervision is not therapy, although it is therapeutic. To do therapy with the supervisee, according to Patterson (1964, p. 49), is 'to impose counseling on a captive client.' Studies of Rogers' style of doing supervision (Goodyear & Bradley, 1983; Goodyear, Abadie, & Efros, 1984; Hackney & Goodyear, 1984) show that he focused primarily on helping the supervisee to clarify and explore the attitudes, beliefs,and feelings that emerge in the context of the relationship with the client.

Although Rogers perceives psychotherapy and supervision as having parallel goals and processes, it seems to me that there is a major distinction: in psychotherapy the client has absolute freedom to talk about any realm of experience, but in supervision there is a primary focus – the interaction between the supervisee and the client. On one hand, in spite of the fact that many factors in the life of the supervisee have relevance to his or her way of doing therapy, the concentration on outside problems would divert from the rigorous exploration of how the behavior of the supervisee is affecting the client. On the other hand, when the behavior of the clients brings out in the supervisees feelings or attitudes that interfere with their ability to listen and to understand, it becomes important to explore in supervision the factors in the supervisees' life that might be contributing to their difficulty in being empathic. Although at such moments the focus of supervision becomes the relationship of the supervisee with someone other than the client, it is only relevant because it is interfering with the supervisee's interaction with the client.

As I examined the interaction between supervisee and client over many years, it became clear to me that most beginning therapists have the tendency to be too active. The ability to listen well and to appreciate the moments of fecund silence is often lost in a barrage of interventions. Instead of discouraging these spontaneous reactions, the philosophy-of-life-oriented supervisor draws attention to them in an attempt to facilitate the supervisee's self-awareness. The hope is that supervisees will learn to recognize on their own the inappropriateness of some of their interventions and in that way develop an internal locus of evaluation.

In my experience three elements contribute to the beginning therapist's tendency to be too active: (1) the need to be helpful, (2) the need to be relevant, and (3) the lack of contact with one's own unconscious.

The need to be helpful

Most beginning therapists, moved by the client's suffering, feel eager to find solutions to ameliorate the client's pain. Impatient with the slowness of the process, they try to accelerate it by giving advice, by challenging the client's interpretations and explanations, by confronting the client's 'irrationality,' and sometimes even by preaching to the client. Consequently, their behavior becomes too cognitive and too much oriented toward problem solving while not giving enough consideration to the client's feelings. In turn, the client feels pressured and judged. Feeling overly responsible is common among beginning therapists. The function of the supervisor is to help them understand that the power to change lies with the client, and to help them develop patience, respect, and trust in the client's own rhythm and capacity to find her or his own solutions. In doing so, the supervisor facilitates the supervisees' capacity for acceptance.

The need to be relevant

Usually, beginning therapists want to know that they are having an effect on the process of therapy. They want to make sure that the client knows that they are listening and understanding well. In order to try to ensure good rapport, they are likely to work hard to be likeable and to provide the 'necessary and sufficient conditions' for change. There is a tendency to rephrase what the client is saying, to give reassurance, and to make warm and 'empathic' comments. Usually such comments, when stemming from the need to be relevant, come across as platitudes. They introduce incongruence into the interaction and put pressure on the client to respond to the therapists' comments while interrupting the client's flow. This need to be relevant also interferes with the process of listening well; therapists become so concerned with providing the 'right' kind of response that their attention becomes focused on the search for this 'right' response instead of on the client. The function of the supervisor, then, is to help supervisees to identify when and how their needs for recognition and approval are interfering with the process of the client. They then learn to distinguish between responses that are coming from their own needs, and those that stem from an authentic inner feeling. The ability to make such distinctions, along with the understanding that the client's needs come first, enable supervisees to stop their own inappropriate responses and to be more authentic with the client. In that way congruence is developed.

The lack of contact with the unconscious

In affirming his difference from Freud, Rogers circumvented the concept of the unconscious. He stated that material that is significantly inconsistent with the self-concept, although experienced at a subliminal level, cannot be directly and freely admitted to awareness. When this incongruity between self-concept and experience emerges without the person's awareness, then the person is potentially vulnerable to threat, anxiety, and disorganization. In order to deal with the incongruence, the person becomes defensive by distorting in awareness, or by denying into awareness, that material that is inconsistent with the concept of self (Rogers, 1959). For the purpose of this article, *unconscious* is defined as experiences that are not integrated with the self or available to awareness, yet are powerful in affecting one's feelings, perceptions, and behavior.

There is an increasing belief that the unconscious is more than the denial and distortion of material that is inconsistent with self-concept. Milton Erickson (Lankton & Lankton, 1983) conceptualizes a creative unconscious, which is the organizing aspect of the personality. Brown (1980, p. 6), a pioneer in biofeedback research, considers the unconscious a manifestation of 'the existence of a superior intelligence within every person, a mind born of the brain, but existing apart from the brain, a mind with extraordinary, unacknowledged potency and range of powers.' In my opinion, this superior intelligence is manifested through intuition. *Intuition* is defined in this article as the process of instantaneously coming to direct knowledge without inference or reasoning.

When therapists are not in contact with their own fears, needs, attachments, and aversions, and other unconscious forces, these forces can interfere insidiously with the client's process. Interventions that divert the client from the course that is subliminally uncomfortable to the therapist become frequent. Highly charged emotional issues such as sexuality, illness, and death become particularly absent from therapy, even though they might be central in the client's life at the moment. I believe that the therapist's unconscious forces per se do not interfere with the client's process — everyone has fears, attachments, aversions, needs, and so on. What hinders therapy is the lack of awareness of their presence, and the lack of recognition of their effect on the therapist's interaction with the client. When the existence of those forces is recognized, and their effect acknowledged, they might even become catalytic for the client to work with her or his own fears, needs, aversions, attachments and so on.

There are at least three powerful ways of sharpening this kind of awareness in the supervisee: (1) review of the supervisee's session, (2) co-therapy, and (3) demonstration interviews.

Review of the supervisee's session

The supervisor and supervisee go over an audio or videotape of a supervisee's session together. When the supervisor notices any incongruence, awkwardness, or intervention that divert from the client's feelings, the supervisor interrupts the tape and invites the supervisee to go inward in search of what he or she was feeling at that particular moment. Initially, the supervisee is often only in touch with a sense of disharmony or incongruence, sometimes almost imperceptible. Soon she or he learns to identify such impressions as warning signs that something is amiss and to use them as invitations to check inside. With practice, looking within and facing whatever is there, self-awareness increases. The unconscious becomes conscious and is therefore less likely to interfere with the process. Another way of reviewing the session is through process notes. The supervisee writes his or her perceptions of what went on during the session and shares them with the supervisor. Although it is easier to miss the supervisee's blind spots with this method, the process of reconstructing the session step-by-step, helps the supervisee become more aware of the process that goes on during therapy.

Co-therapy

Two therapists working together will often respond differently to the client. When they process the session afterwards, they give each other feedback and discuss their similarities and differences, thereby increasing their self-awareness. The co-therapist might be the supervisor, or another student with both co-therapists having the same supervisor. The important precondition is that a high level of trust exists between them in order to increase their willingness to search within.

Demonstration interviews

During these interviews either the supervisor observes the supervisee, or the supervisee observes the supervisor doing therapy, either by being in the same room, or by viewing the session through a one-way mirror. By being present the supervisor and supervisee can react to the client at the same time, and the comparison of their reactions become an important source of input for the supervision session.

As supervisees become more aware of their own inner processes, intuition becomes increasingly accessible. Supervisees will discern when the urge to say something during the session is coming from self-indulgence, unresolved conflicts, or unrecognized needs and fears. They will increasingly trust that other forces that transcend the conscious mind might be at work. With the ability to listen within, and to discriminate which of the unconscious forces are at work at any given moment, comes the development of empathy.

Development of intuition

It is my belief that person-centered psychotherapy is more than listening empathically and creating a climate where the client can feel safe to express whatever comes to mind. Recently Rogers (1986) described one more characteristic of the best moments in therapy, and that has yet to be investigated by research: *the ability of the therapist to be close to his or her intuitive self.* This quality guides the therapist in enabling the client to move into a new integration: 'What I wish is to be at her side, occasionally falling a step behind, occasionally a step ahead when I see more clearly the path we are on, and only taking a leap when guided by my intuition' (1986, p. 27) wrote Rogers referring to the client whose session he described.

The fact that Rogers acknowledges that there are times when he might be one step ahead of the client, might see the path they are on more clearly, and might allow himself to take a leap when guided by his intuition, shows how much his ideas have evolved since the 1940s and 1950s.

The existence of two different types of empathic responses is hypothesized: (a) supportive responses and (b) integrative impressions. My hypothesis is that intuition is manifested in therapy through the specific kind of empathic response that I call integrative impressions.

Supportive responses

Supportive responses are therapist responses whose purpose is to communicate understanding to the client. They help the client feel affirmed, appreciated, encouraged, and cared for. Although their presence is important in therapy, they do not necessarily lead to a new integration at that moment.

Integrative impressions

Integrative impressions are responses that enable clients to integrate fragmented and confusing parts of their experience into a higher order of coherence and understanding. In order for this type of response to be possible an I-Thou relationship (Buber, 1958) has to be present, one in which the boundaries between client and therapist disappear. The therapist becomes at one with the client, and in this way enters the disorganized, confused, irrational experiences the client experiences at that moment. The therapist then has an impression that, in magnet-like fashion, draws together the client's fragmented and disconnected bits of experience into a single meaningful configuration. The therapist reflects back to the client that integrative impression, which enables the client to order her or his chaotic experience, and to see it in a new light. That moment of reorganization is the essence of the therapeutic process. According to the physical chemist Prigogine (1981), with each new organization that is achieved, the organism becomes able to change into a pattern of a higher order of coherence and complexity. He won the Nobel Prize in 1977 for his explanation of how some energy events dissipate themselves into a state of increasing order, paradoxically reversing entropy while attaining a nonreversible gain in complexity. He uses the term *dissipative structure* as a collective term for entities that exchange materials and energy with their environment. Because dissipative structures cannot accommodate entropic disorder beyond a critical point, they suddenly reconfigure themselves into more highly ordered arrangements that can accommodate the increased entropy. As this reconfiguration is achieved, change occurs. My hypothesis is that integrative impressions are the catalysts for personal reorganization.

I believe that there are several kinds of integrative impressions. Four of them, with respective examples, are as follows:

(a) *Reflection of feelings.* The therapist has an impression that summarizes the feelings of the client and reflects it back to the client. For example:

CL: *I feel that I am in a panic situation. I am 35 years of age, and I've only got another five years 'til 40. It's very difficult to explain. I keep turning around and I want to run away from it.*

TH: *It's enough of a fear that you — it really sets off a panic in you.*

CL: *Yes, and it's affecting my confidence as a person.*

(b) *Identification of underlying issues.* The therapist has an impression that depicts the underlying issues that are contributing to the client's feelings and reflects it back to the client. For example:

TH: *And you didn't have those feelings very much until perhaps a year and a half ago. [pause] Was there anything special at that time that seemed to set you off?*

CL: *Not that I can recall, really. Well, my mother died at 53, and she was a very young and very bright woman in many ways. But I think maybe that has something to do with it. I don't know.*

TH: *You sort of felt that if your mother died at that early age, that was a possibility for you, too. [pause] And time began to seem a lot shorter.*

CL: *Right! . . .*

(c) *Creation of metaphors.* The therapist has an impression that suggests a likeness or analogy to the client's experience, and by reflecting it back to the client, it makes explicit an implied comparison. For example:

CL: *That's another thing, of course, that's going on in my mind: it's a part of my development, as it were. But I feel that it's not enough; I must have physical contact. . . . Somebody I can relate to . . .*

TH: *Somebody you can relate to. And I guess that . . . this may seem a silly idea, but — I wish that one of those friends could be that naughty little girl. I don't know whether that makes any sense to you or not, but if that kind of sprightly, naughty little girl that lives inside could accompany you from the light into the dark — as I say, that may not make sense to you at all.*

CL: *[in a puzzled voice] Can you elaborate on that a little more?*

TH: *Simply that maybe one of your best friends is the you that you hide inside, the fearful little girl, the naughty little girl, the real you that doesn't come out very much in the open.*

CL: *[pause] And I must admit — what you had just said, and looking at it in retrospect I've lost a lot of that naughty little girl. In fact, over the last 18 months, that naughty little girl has disappeared.*

All the examples quoted are excerpts from a single interview with Carl Rogers (1986) as the therapist. In the last one he uses 'the naughty little girl' as a metaphor to enable the client to get in touch with a part of her that she is missing.

(d) *Use of experiments.* The therapist has an idea for an experiment that might facilitate the organization of the client's experience at that moment, and shares it with the client. It is the client's choice whether or not to pursue the experiment. Although such experiments might be structured, they are integrative impressions because they are tailored to a specific client, and emerge in the context of a specific situation. They differ from a 'technique' because, with techniques, the structure is chosen beforehand, and an assumption is made that it will fit all clients. Individual differences are not taken into account. For example:

CL: *Life is too much trouble . . . What's the use of going on with it? Where does it get me?*

TH: *What feels so bad? Give yourself a peaceful minute and see what feels so bad.*

CL: *I didn't get my period. I'm scared I'm pregnant . . . I miss Ted so much! And now my period is late. What if I'm pregnant? Oh God, what's going to happen to me?*

TH: *Just stand back, now, and take each thing that's bad, and stash it in front of you. One by one. See what each thing is that feels bad.*

The above example is the excerpt from a focusing session with Gendlin (1978) as the therapist. Another example of the use of experiments as integrative impressions is the work of Natalie Rogers and Frances Fuchs (1986) with groups. They use movement, art, sound, journal writing, guided fantasy, and dream work to expand self-awareness and consciousness.

The preference for the use of one kind of integrative impression over another will vary from therapist to therapist. Rogers, for example, seems to have a preference for reflecting feelings. For many years he was identified as using only this kind of integrative impression. But, as evidenced by the examples given in his therapy, he also uses the identification of underlying issues and metaphors. I have even witnessed occasions when, in group situations, Rogers has suggested experiments (although always very gingerly).

I believe that it is important for supervisors to honor supervisees' preferred modes of integrative impressions and to help them trust the way in which their intuition is manifested. Sometimes when the integrative impression of the supervisee is of a different type than the one preferred by the supervisor, it is difficult for the supervisor to recognize its value and to accept it as legitimate. A good criterion for its acceptability is the effect it has on the client. If it facilitates insight, integration, or helps the client move closer to feelings, then that particular integrative impression is an effective intervention. In that way the criterion of acceptability is a pragmatic one.

CONCLUSION

A distinction was made between two approaches to supervision: the form-oriented and the philosophy-of-life-oriented. If individual differences are taken into account, that distinction may reveal itself to be spurious. To some therapists, the form-oriented way, which preserves the 'classical' forms, is syntonic with their own way of being, hence, they should maintain their commitment to that mode of doing therapy. For others, different forms may emerge, and attempts to force themselves into a preestablished mold would only give rise to artificiality. Whether individual differences really affect the preference for form-oriented or philosophy-of-life-oriented supervision is a question for future research.

There seems to be concern among some person-centered therapists that the variety of forms that are replacing a single mode will make research difficult. I hope that the opposite will be true. The expansion of the conceptual framework and the identification of new variables may provide new challenges for researchers. An example is the construct of intuition. Because it has not yet been operationalized does not mean that it is not in operation. Instead, I would like to see researchers try to define it operationally and to assess its role in therapy. A recent article by Wicker (1985) challenges researchers and theorists to get out of their conceptual ruts and to develop new and exciting ways of studying phenomena, Carl Rogers himself is a good model for the importance of expanding conceptual frameworks. His ideas have evolved over the years, and he himself is a person in process. It is no wonder that his theory is also constantly in process. He has always seemed to shy away from orthodoxy, preferring instead to encourage creativity and change.

Another expressed concern is that the person-centered approach to therapy will be lost, diluted into a morass of eclecticism, if the original forms are not preserved. I do not share this fear. I believe that the person-centered approach will always have its distinctive features as long as the work of the therapist and supervisor is guided by the three basic philosophical beliefs about the nature of the person: the person's capacity for self-determination, the person's capacity for self-regulation and self-direction, and the existence within the person of all resources necessary for enhancing her or his life and the lives of others.

REFERENCES

Altucher, (1967). Constructive use of supervisory relationship. *Journal of Counseling Psychology, 14,* 165–70.

Arbuckle, S. D. (1963). The learning of counseling: Process, not product. *Journal of Counseling Psychology, 10,* 163–8.

Blane, S. M. (1968). Immediate effect of supervisory experience on counselor candidates. *Counselor Education and Supervision, 8,* 39–44.

Bozarth, J. D. (1984). Functional dimensions of the person-centered approach in therapy. *Renaissance, 1,* 1.

Bozarth, I. D., & Temaner, B. S. (1984). Client-centered/person-centered psychotherapy—a statement of understanding. Paper prepared for the Second International Forum on the person-centered approach. Norwich, England.

Brammer, L. M., & Wassner, A. R. (1977). Supervision in counseling and psychotherapy. In D. J. Kurpius, R. D. Baker, & I. D. Thomas (Eds.), *Supervision in applied training.* Westport, CT: Greenwood.

Brown, B. B. (1980). *Supermind.* New York: Harper & Row.

Buber, M. (1958). *I and Thou.* New York: Scribner.

Coulson, W. R. (1984). The form of relationship in client-centered therapy. *Renaissance, 12,* 1–2.

Gendlin, E. T. (1978). *Focusing.* New York: Everest.

Goodyear, R. K., & Bradley, H. (1983). Theories of counselor supervision: Points of convergence and divergence. *Counseling Psychologist, 11,* 59–67.

Goodyear, R. K., Abadie, P. D., & Efros, F. (1984). Supervisory theory into practice: Differential perception of supervision by Eckstein, Ellis, Polster and Rogers. *Journal of Counseling Psychology, 31,* 228–37.

Gysbers, N. C., & Johnston, J. A. (1965). Expectations of a practicum supervisor's role. *Counselor Education and Supervision, 4,* 68–74.

Hackney, H., & Goodyear, R. K. (1984). Carl Rogers' client-centered approach to supervision. In R. F. Levant & J. M. Shlien (Eds.), *Client-centered therapy and the person-centered approach.* New York: Praeger.

Hansen, J. C., & Barker, E. N. (1964). Experiencing and the supervisory relationship. *Journal of Counseling Psychology, 11,* 107–11.

Kagan, N., & Werner, A. (1977). Supervision in psychiatric education. In D. J. Kurpius, R. D. Baker, & J. D. Thomas (Eds.), *Supervision of applied training: A comparative review.* Westport, CT: Greenwood.

Lankton, R. L., & Lankton, C. H. (1983). *The answer within: A clinical framework of Ericksonian hynotherapy.* New York: Brunner/Mazel.

Patterson, C. H. (1964). Supervising students in the counseling practicum. *Journal of Counseling Psychology, 11,* 47–53.

Pierce, R., Carkhuff, R. R., & Berenson, B. G. (1967). The differential effects of high and low functioning counselors upon counselors in training. *Journal of Clinical Psychology, 23,* 212–15.

Prigogine, I. (1981). *From being to becoming.* San Francisco: W. H. Freeman.

Reising, G. N., & Daniels, M. H. (1983). A study of Hogan's model of counselor development and supervision. *Journal of Counseling Psychology, 30,* 235–44.

Rogers, C. R. (1956). Training individuals to engage in the therapeutic process. In C. R. Strother(Ed.), *Psychology and mental health.* Washington, DC: American Psychological Association.

Rogers, C. R. (1959). A theory of therapy, personality, and interpersonal relationships, as developed in the client-centered framework. In S. Koch (Ed.), *Psychology: Study of a science.* New York: McGraw-Hill.

Rogers, C. R. (1985). Personal communication. January 16.

Rogers, C. R. (1986). A client-centered, person-centered approach to therapy. In I. L. Kutash, & A. Wolf (Eds.), *A psychotherapist's casebook: Theory and technique in practice.* San Francisco: Jossey-Bass.

Rogers, N., & Fuchs, F. (1986). *A person-centered approach to expressive therapy.* Brochure announcing an international training program. Santa Rosa, CA.

Shlien, J. M., & Levant, R. F. (1984). Introduction. In Levant, R. F. & Shlien, J. M. (Eds.), *Client-centered therapy and the person-centered approach.* New York: Praeger.

Temaner, B. S. (1982). Criteria for making empathic understanding responses in client-centered therapy. Paper prepared for the First International Forum on the Person-Centered Approach. Oaxtepec, Mexico.

Wicker, A. W. (1985). Getting out of our conceptual ruts. *American Psychologist, 40,* 1094–103.

Carl Rogers and Martin Buber:
Self-actualisation and dialogue

Maurice Friedman   *San Diego State University*

In their 1957 dialogue Rogers stressed total mutuality between therapist and client in opposition to Buber, who stressed the 'normative limitations of mutuality' in therapy: the therapist can practice 'inclusion,' imagine the real, whereas the client cannot be expected to experience the therapist's side of the relationship. Rogers saw what is deepest in the individual as something that can be trusted so that when it is released the forward moving processes of life would take over. Buber saw man as polar — to be trusted and not to be trusted — and in need of that 'confirmation' that will strengthen the force of direction in him, something that can be discovered by the therapist's accepting love. Rogers sometimes uses empathy as Buber uses inclusion by stressing that he remains himself in the dialogue, but sometimes uses it in the narrower sense of losing one's own ground. Unconditional positive regard and congruence too can be understood dialogically. If dialogue were seen as goal and self-actualization as by-product, it would strengthen the consistency of Rogerian therapy.

MARTIN BUBER: PARTNER IN DIALOGUE

When Carl Rogers and Paul Tillich carried on a dialogue in the early 1960s, it was easy enough to identify Tillich as a theologian, though as one who had profound interests in philosophy and psychotherapy. When Martin Buber and Carl Rogers had their dialogue in 1957, it was not so easy to categorize Buber. Buber was, to be sure, a philosopher and a philosopher of religion. Beyond that, he was a philosophical anthropologist, one concerned with the wholeness and uniqueness of the human. He was not a theologian, if one means by that term someone who proceeds on the basis of certain assumptions taken on faith or, to use Tillich's terminology, one who finds in the tradition the essentialist answers to the existentialist questions with which we are confronted. Tillich, as he described himself, lived on 'the border,' but he was, above all, the intellectual. Buber was a person who not only wrote about the philosophy of dialogue but lived it — in ever renewed immediacy with each person who came to see him. At the end of the chapter on 'The Discovery of Hasidism' in *Martin Buber's Life and Work: The Early Years,* I wrote of Buber: 'He did not become a leader of a genuine community, but he withstood the thousandfold questioning glance of countless sorely troubled persons and constantly measured the depths of responsibility with the "sounding lead" of his presence and his words' (Friedman, 1982, p. 123).

When Carl Rogers asked Buber at the beginning of their dialogue, 'How have you lived so deeply in interpersonal relationships and gained such an understanding of the human individual, without being a psychotherapist?' Buber replied by telling Rogers,

First published in *Person-Centered Review,* Volume 1, Number 4, November 1986.

first of all, of his early interest in psychiatry, and his study with Wundt, Mendel, Bleuler, and Flechsig. But, Buber (1965, pp. 167–8) added,

> About what mainly constituted what you ask, it was something other. It was just a certain inclination to meet people. And as far as possible to change something in the *other,* but also to let *me* be changed by *him* . . . I began as a young man. I felt I have not the right to want to change another if I am not open to be changed by him as far as it is legitimate . . . I *cannot* so to speak be above him and say, 'No, I'm out of the play. *You* are mad.' There were two phases of it. The first phase went until the year 1918, meaning until I was about 40. And then I, in 1918 . . . felt that I had been strongly influenced by . . . the First World War . . . I was compelled to . . . live it . . . You may call this *imagining the real.* Imagining what was going on. This imagining, for four years, influenced me terribly. Just when it was finished, it finished by a certain episode in May 1919, when a friend of mine, a great friend, a great man, was killed by the antirevolutionary soldiers in a very barbaric way, and now again once more—and this was the last time—I was compelled to imagine just this killing, but not in an optical way alone, but may I say so, just with my *body* . . . From now on, I had to give something more than just my inclination to exchange thoughts and feelings . . . I had to give the fruit of an experience.

Later on in this same dialogue Buber said of himself that he met with problematic persons for whom life has become baseless, persons who need to know that the world is not condemned to deprivation, degeneration, destruction. A year later Buber said that he had founded his entire philosophical thinking on a study of actual human beings from the time of his youth (Friedman, 1984, p. 344).

HEALING THROUGH MEETING

In a discussion of Ludwig Binswanger's 'The Case of Ellen West,' which he entitles 'The Loneliness of Contemporary Man,' Carl Rogers (1980, pp. 164–80) points to Martin Buber's 'healing through meeting' as the center of therapy. Ellen West was a woman who was written up at great length by Ludwig Binswanger; only Binswanger never treated her; he just gave a phenomenological description of her case. The greatest weakness of Ellen West's treatment, in Rogers' opinion, is that no one involved in it seems to have related to her as *a person* whose inner experiencing is a precious resource to be drawn upon and trusted. She was dealt with as an object, and helped to *see* her feelings, but not to *experience* them. She herself recognized that the doctor can give her discernment, but not healing. She utters a desperate cry for a relationship between two persons, but no one hears her.

'She never experienced what Buber has called healing through meeting,' writes Rogers. 'There was no one who could meet her, accept her as she was.' Rogers draws from the case of Ellen West the lesson that whenever or however the therapist makes an object of the person—'whether by diagnosing him, analyzing him, or perceiving him impersonally in a case history, he stands in the way of his therapeutic goal.' The therapist is deeply helpful only when he relates as a person, risks himself as a person in the relationship, experiences the other as a person in his or her own right. 'Only then is there a meeting of a depth which dissolves the pain of aloneness in both client and therapist' (Rogers in Friedman, 1973, pp. 484–5).

In *Client-Centered Therapy* (1951), Rogers states that the role of the counselor in 'nondirective' therapy is not, as is often thought, a merely passive laissez-faire policy, but rather an active acceptance of the client as a person of worth for whom the counselor has real respect. Client-centered therapy stresses above all the counselor's assuming the internal frame of reference of the client and perceiving both the world and the client through the client's own eyes. It is important in the process of the person's becoming that the person experience understanding and acceptance by the therapist. This means an active experiencing with the client of the feelings to which expression is given, a trying to get *within* and to live the attitudes expressed instead of observing them. This implies, at the same time, a certain distance and absence of emotional involvement — an experiencing of the feelings from the side of the client without an emotional identification that would cause the counselor to experience these feelings as his or her own. Finally it implies a laying aside of the preoccupation with professional analysis, diagnosis, and evaluation in favor of an acceptance and understanding of the client based on true attitudes of respect that are deeply and genuinely felt by the therapist (Rogers, 1951, pp. 20–45, 55). Rogers is willing to extend this respect and trust even to a patient in danger of committing suicide or one who has been institutionalized.

> To enter deeply with this man into his confused struggle for selfhood is perhaps the best implementation we now know for indicating the meaning of our basic hypothesis that the individual represents a process which is deeply worthy of respect, both as he is and with regard to his potentialities. (Rogers, 1951, p. 45)

A corollary of client-centered therapy is the recognition that good interpersonal relationships depend upon the understanding and acceptance of the other as a separate person who is 'operating in terms of his own meanings, based on his own perceptual field' (Rogers, 1951, p. 521). Rogers sees the recognition of the separateness of others as made possible through a relationship in which the person is confirmed in their own being. A person comes to accept others through self-acceptance, and this, in turn, takes place through the acceptance of the child by the parent or of the client by the therapist. The real essence of therapy, correspondingly, is not so much the client's memory of the past, explorations of problems, or admissions of experiences into awareness as it is the client's direct experiencing in the therapy relationship.

> The process of therapy is, by these hypotheses, seen as being synonymous with the experiential relationship between client and therapist. Therapy consists in experiencing the self in a wide range of ways in an emotionally meaningful relationship with the therapist. (Rogers, 1951, p. 172)

As early as 1952 Rogers defined the person as a fluid process and potential in rather sharp contrast to the relatively fixed, measurable, diagnosable, predictable concept of the person that is accepted by psychologists and other social scientists to judge by their writing and working operations. The person as process is most deeply revealed, Rogers wrote, in a relationship of the most ultimate and complete acceptance, a relationship Rogers described in Martin Buber's terms, as a real I-Thou relationship, not an I-It relationship. The person moves in a positive direction toward unique goals, that the person can but dimly define (Rogers, 1961).

In his book *On Becoming a Person*, Rogers (1961) tells how he changed his approach to therapy from the intellectual question of how he could treat the patient to the recognition that changes come about through *experience* in a *relationship*. He found that the more genuine he was in relationship, the more aware he was of his own feelings, the more willing he was to express his own feelings and attitudes, the more he gave the relationship a *reality* the person could use for his own personal growth. He also found that the more he could respect and like the client, showing a warm regard for the client as a person of unconditional self-worth while accepting each fluctuating aspect of the other, the more he was creating a relationship the client could use. This acceptance necessarily includes a continuing desire to understand the other's feelings and thoughts, which leaves the other really free to explore all the hidden nooks and frightening crannies of his or her inner and often buried experience. This includes, as well, complete freedom from any type of moral or diagnostic evaluation.

As a therapist, Rogers (1961, pp. 201–2) writes,

> I enter the relationship not as a scientist, not as a physician who can accurately diagnose and cure, but as a person entering into a personal relationship. Insofar as I see him only as an object, the client will tend to become only an object. I risk myself, because if, as the relationship deepens, what develops is a failure, a regression, a repudiation of me and the relationship by the client, then I will lose . . . a part of myself.

The therapist conducts the therapy without conscious plan and responds to the other person with his or her whole being, that is, total 'organismic sensitivity.'

> When there is this complete unity, singleness, fullness of experiencing in the relationship, then it acquires the 'out-of-this-world' quality which therapists have remarked upon, a sort of trance-like feeling in the relationship from which both the client and I emerge at the end of the hour, as if from a deep well or tunnel. In these moments there is, to borrow Buber's phrase, a real 'I-Thou' relationship, a timeless living in the experience which is *between* the client and me. It is at the opposite pole from seeing the client, or myself, as an object. It is the height of personal subjectivity. (Rogers, 1961, p. 202)

Through the therapist's willingness to risk, and his or her confidence in the client, the therapist makes it easier for the client to take the plunge into the stream of experiencing. This process of becoming opens up a new way of living in which the client feels 'more unique and hence more alone,' but at the same time is able to enter into relations with others that are deeper and more satisfying and that 'draw more of the realness of the other person into the relationship' (Rogers, 1961, p. 203).

In 1967, Rogers placed an even stronger emphasis on the centrality of healing through meeting than in any of his earlier writings, claiming that it is the 'existential encounter which is important, and that in the immediate moment of the therapeutic relationship consciousness of theory has no helpful place' (Rogers, 1967b, p. 189). Healing through meeting occurs when the meeting between therapist and client is the central as opposed to the ancillary aspect of the therapy. Practically every therapist sees the relationship as having some importance as structure, or support, but only when the relationship is the *central factor* in the healing is it properly called 'healing through meeting.' From this we can see how strong a place Rogers occupies in healing through meeting.

Thinking about theory during the relationship itself, as opposed to afterward, is detrimental to the therapy because it leads the therapist to be more of a spectator than a player, writes Rogers, who believes that theory 'should be held tentatively, lightly, flexibly, in a way which is freely open to change, and should be laid aside in the moment of encounter itself' (Rogers, 1967b, p. 190).

In 1967, Rogers published a brief statement that can well serve as a summation of his own view on healing through meeting.

> I find that when I am able to let myself be congruent and genuine, it often helps the other person. When the other person is transparently real and congruent, it often helps me. In those rare moments when a deep realness in one meets a deep realness in the other, it is a memorable I-Thou relationship, as Buber would call it. Such a deep and mutual personal

encounter is experienced by me as very growth enhancing. A person who is loved appreciatively, not possessively, blooms and develops his own unique self. The person who loves non-possessively is himself enriched. (Rogers, 1967c, pp. 18–19)

SELF-ACTUALIZATION AND DIALOGUE

For Rogers, healing through meeting works both ways. Meeting is sometimes seen as an end in itself and sometimes only as the means to the end of personal becoming and self-actualization. This ambiguity comes through particularly clearly in Rogers' most recent book, *A Way of Being* (1980), in which he puts forward two different and in some ways incompatible touchstones of reality. The two touchstones of reality he puts forward are self-actualization and the I-Thou relationship. In one place Rogers writes of the actualizing tendency as the fundamental answer to the question of what makes an organism tick. In another he writes:

> In those rare moments when a deep realness in one meets a deep realness in the other, a memorable I-Thou relationship, as Martin Buber would call it, occurs. Such a deep and mutual encounter does not happen often, but I am convinced that unless it happens occasionally we are not living as human beings. (Rogers, 1980, p. 9)

Although they reside comfortably together in Rogers' thought, these two touchstones of reality are not really compatible. *Either* the I-Thou relationship is seen as a function of self-actualization, and the real otherness of the Thou is lost sight of in the emphasis on the development of the organism, *or* the I-Thou relationship is seen as a reality and value in itself, in which case self-realization becomes a by-product and not a goal and, what is more, a by-product that is produced not through a pseudobiological development, but rather through the meeting with what is really other than the self.

THE BUBER-ROGERS DIALOGUE

The issues that arose in the dialogue between Martin Buber and Carl Rogers that I moderated at the University of Michigan in 1957 are subtle ones. Rogers began with a description of his own approach to therapy and ventured that it was, as he himself had often written, an I-Thou relationship:

> I feel that when I am being effective as a therapist I enter the relationship as a subjective person, not as a scrutinizer and not as a scientist. I feel too that when I am most effective that somehow I am relatively whole in that relationship. To be sure, there may be many aspects of my life that are not brought into the relationship, but what is brought into the relationship is transparent. There is nothing hidden. When I think too that in such a relationship I feel a real willingness for the other person to be what he is, I call that acceptance. I don't know that that's a very good word for it, but my meaning there is that I am willing for him to possess the feelings he possesses, to hold the attitudes he holds, to be the person he is. But then another aspect of it that is important to me when I think of those moments when I am able to sense with a good deal of clarity the way his experience seems to him. Really viewing it from within him, yet without losing my own personhood or sacrificing in that. And then, if in addition to those things, on my part, my client or the person with whom I am working is able to sense something of those attitudes in me, then it seems there is a real experiential meeting of persons in which each of us is changed. I

think sometimes the client is changed more than I am, but I think both of us changed in that kind of experience. (Rogers in Buber, 1965, pp. 169–70)[1]

It is not surprising that Buber characterized what Rogers had said as a very good example for a certain moment of dialogic existence. For there are present here all the elements that Buber himself emphasizes: meeting the other as a partner and not an object, experiencing the client's side of the relationship without losing one's own, bringing oneself as a whole person, accepting the other as the person they are in their otherness. It is important to note that in this description Rogers does not claim total mutuality. Rogers as therapist sees the client from within whereas the client's inclusion is limited to something of the therapist's attitude toward the client. It does not touch on the therapist as a person with problems of his or her own.

At first glance it appears as if Rogers is talking about total mutuality. He never is. He never suggested that the client is concerned with Carl Rogers' problem, however much the client may help Rogers. Buber stressed that in this situation, which therapist and client have in common, the person comes to the therapist for help and insisted that this makes an essential difference in the role of therapist and client.

> He comes for help to you, you don't come for help to him. And not only this, you are *able,* more or less, to help him. He can do different things to you, but not help you. You see him, just as you said, as he is. He cannot, by far, cannot *see you.* Not only in the degree but even in the kind of seeing. You are, of course, a very important person for him. But not a person whom he wants to see, and to know, and is able to. He is floundering around, and comes to you. He is, if I may say, entangled in your life, in your thoughts, in your being, your communication and so on. But he is not interested in you as you. It cannot be. You are interested in him as this person, this kind of detached presence he cannot have and give. (Buber, 1965, p. 171)

In Buber's philosophical anthropology there are two movements—distancing and relating. Buber is saying that this person, because of his or her problems, has lost that capacity for distancing that enables one to appreciate the other from where he or she is. This does not mean that it is difficult for a therapist and client to have an I-Thou relationship. I-Thou is mistakenly thought of as total mutuality. It is mutual in friendship and love, but there are certain relationships that still are I-Thou yet have what Buber calls the 'normative limitation of mutuality.' The therapy relationship is one of them. Putting it another way, you have mutuality of contact, mutuality of trust, and from my own experience I would add a third, mutuality of the sense that you have a common problem. Every problem brought in is part of the whole communal reality. It may be focused in you, but you and I are both concerned with this at the moment. That's another sort of mutuality. But mutuality in the sense of inclusion, of experiencing the other side, cannot be demanded.

Years ago I gave Erich Fromm a copy of an article on Buber and psychotherapy entitled 'Healing Through Meeting.' When I saw him some time later, Fromm said, 'I like that title very much; in fact, my patients heal *me.*' I'm sure that there is no therapist who is not in some way healed by his or her clients, and there is no good teacher who is not to some extent taught by his or her students. But you don't set it as a goal, you don't make that a demand and say, 'This has been a bad session because you haven't healed Dr. Fromm, or taught Dr. Friedman.' That is what I see as the difference. It's still an I-Thou

---

1. The dialogue between Buber and Rogers is printed as the Appendix to Martin Buber, *The Knowledge of Man* (Buber, 1966).

relationship, not an I-It. It is an I-It only when the other becomes just an object that you know and use and manipulate. The relation between parent and child is I-Thou even though parent and child are not fully mutual and fully equal. When the child grows up to really experience the other side of the relationship, he or she is no longer a child at that point.

Buber went on to say that in the therapy situation Rogers was able to observe and know and help the client from both his own side and that of the client. The therapist can experience bodily the client's side of the situation, feel touched by the client, whereas the situation itself makes it impossible for the client to experience the therapist's side of the relationship. 'You are not equals and cannot be. You have the great self-imposed task to supplement this need of his and do rather more than in the normal situation. I see you mean being on the same plane, but you cannot. These are the sometimes tragic limitations of simple humanity' (Buber, 1965, p. 172). Rogers agreed that if the client could really experience the therapist's side of the situation fully, the therapy would be about over, but he also insisted that the client's 'way of looking at his experience, distorted though it might be, is something I can look upon as having equal authority, equal validity with the way I feel life and experience it. It seems to me that really is the basis of helping' (Buber, 1965, p. 172).

What Rogers said here is the essence of what I call the 'dialogue of touchstones' (Friedman, 1985, chap. 18). But that does not change the fact that the situation is not equal however much Rogers feels the equality. 'Neither you nor he look on *your* experience,' Buber said to Rogers. 'The subject is exclusively him and his experience.' In response, Rogers suggested that what Buber said applies to the situation looked at from the outside; this has nothing to do with the actual therapy relationship that is 'something immediate, equal, a meeting of two persons on an equal basis even though in the world of I-It it could be seen as a very unequal relationship.' Buber replied that effective human dialogue must be concerned with limits and that these limits transcend Rogers' method, especially in the case of the schizophrenic and the paranoid.

> I can talk to the schizophrenic, as far as he is willing to let me into his particular world that is his own. But in the moment when he shuts himself, I cannot go on. And the same, only in a terrible, terrifyingly strong manner, is the case with the paranoiac. He does not open himself, he does not shut himself, he *is* shut. And I feel this terrible fate very strongly. Because in the world of normal men there are just analogous cases. When a sane man behaves not to everyone but behaves to some people just so, being shut. And the problem is if he could be open, if he could open himself, this is a problem for the human in general. (Buber, 1965, pp. 172–6)

In my own role as moderator of this dialogue between Buber and Rogers I suggested that the real difference was that Buber stressed the client's inability to experience Rogers' side of the relationship, whereas Rogers stressed the meeting, the change that takes place in the meeting, and his own feeling that the client is an equal person whom he respects. Rogers replied that in the most real moments of therapy the desire to help is only a substratum. Although he would not say that the relationship is reciprocal in the sense that the client wants to understand and to help him, he did assert that when real change takes place it is reciprocal in the sense that the therapist sees this individual as he or she is in that moment, and the client really senses this understanding and acceptance. To this Buber replied that Rogers gives the client something in order to make him equal for that moment. This is a situation of minutes, not of an hour, and these minutes are made possible by Rogers, who out of a certain fullness gives the client what the client wants in order to be able to be, just for this moment, on the same plane with the client.

ACCEPTANCE AND CONFIRMATION

Rogers uses Buber's phrase 'confirming the other,' accepting the person not as something fixed and finished, but as a process of becoming. Through this acceptance, Rogers says, 'I am doing what I can to confirm or make real his potentialities.' If, on the contrary, writes Rogers, one sees the relationship as only an opportunity to reinforce certain types of words or opinions in the other, as Verplanck, Lindsley, and B. F. Skinner do in their therapy of operant conditioning, then one confirms him or her as a basically mechanical, manipulatable object and then tends to act in ways that support this hypothesis. Only a relationship that 'reinforces' *all* that one is, 'the person that he is with all his existent potentialities' Rogers concludes, is one that, to use Buber's terms, confirms him 'as a living person, capable of creative inner development' (Rogers, 1961, pp. 55–6).

Rogers, however, tended to equate acceptance and confirmation, while Buber said no, I have to distinguish between the two. I begin with acceptance, but then sometimes to confirm this person I have to wrestle with, against, and for him or her. Although one part of you has direction, the other part of you is an aimless whirl. I have to help you in taking a direction rather than just remaining with the aimless whirl.

In the course of his 1957 seminars at the Washington School of Psychiatry, Martin Buber threw out some hints concerning confirmation in therapy and its relation to healing through meeting. The therapist's openness and willingness to receive whatever comes is necessary in order that the patient may trust existentially, Buber said. A certain very important kind of healing — existential healing — takes place through meeting rather than through insight and analysis. This means the healing not just of a certain part of the patient, but also of the very roots of the patient's being. The existential trust of one whole person in another has a particular representation in the domain of healing. So long as it is not there, the patient will not be able to disclose what is repressed to the therapist. Without such trust, even masters of method cannot effect existential healing.

The existential trust between therapist and patient that makes the relationship a healing one in the fullest sense of that term implies confirmation, but of a very special sort. Everything is changed in real meeting. Confirmation can be misunderstood as *static*. I meet another — I accept and confirm the other as he or she now is. But confirming a person *as he or she is,* is only the first step. Confirmation does not mean that I take the person's appearance at this moment as representative of the person I want to confirm. I must take the other person in his or her dynamic existence and specific potentiality. In the present lies hidden what can *become.*

This potentiality, this sense of the person's unique direction, can make itself felt to me within our relationship, and it is that I most want to confirm, said Buber. In therapy, this personal direction becomes perceptible to the therapist in a very special way. In a person's worst illness, the highest potentiality of this person may be manifesting itself in negative form. The therapist can directly influence the development of those potentialities. Healing does not mean bringing up the old, but rather shaping the new: it is not confirming the negative, but rather counterbalancing with the positive (Buber, 1969, pp. 169–73; Friedman, 1966, pp. 38–9).

Buber's insistence that confirmation is not static, but rather is a confirmation of the potentialities hidden in the worst illness of the patient, touches on the issue that arose in the dialogue between Buber and Rogers concerning the difference between *accepting* and *confirming.* True acceptance, Rogers holds, means acceptance of this person's potentialities as well as what the person is at the moment. If we were not able to recognize the person's potentiality, Rogers says, it is a real question whether we could accept him or her. If I am accepted exactly as I am, he adds, I cannot help but change. When there is no longer any need for defensive barriers, the forward-moving processes of life take over. Rogers holds that we tend to be split between our 'should' part in the mind and a feeling part in the stomach. We don't accept ourselves, so if the therapist accepts us we can somehow overcome that split. If we overcome it we will become the person we are meant to be. In his stress on an unqualified acceptance of the person being helped, Rogers says that if the therapist is willing for the other person to *be what he is* – to possess the feelings he possesses, to hold the attitudes he holds – it will help him to realize what is deepest in the individual, that is the very aspect that can most be trusted to be constructive or to tend toward socialization or toward the development of better interpersonal relationships. Human nature, for Rogers, is something that can be trusted because the motivation toward the positive or constructive already exists in the individual and will come forward if we can release what is most basic in the individual. What is deepest in the individual can be released and trusted to unfold in socially constructive ways (Rogers in Buber, 1965, pp. 179–80).

Buber replied that he was not so sure about that; for what Rogers saw as most to be trusted, Buber saw as least to be trusted. This does not mean that Buber saw man as evil while Rogers saw man as good, but that Buber saw man as polar. It is precisely Rogers' assumption that the processes of life will always be forward-moving that Buber (1965, pp. 180–1) questions:

> What you say may be trusted, I would say this stands in polar relation to what can be least trusted in this man . . . When I grasp him more broadly and more deeply than before, I see his whole polarity and then I see how the worst in him and the best in him are dependent on one another, attached to one another.

This doctrine of polarity leads inevitably to Buber's distinction between acceptance and confirmation; for confirmation means wrestling with the other against his or her self in order to strengthen the one pole and diminish the power of the other:

> I may be able to help him just by helping him to change the relation between the poles. Not just by choice, but by a certain strength that he gives to the one pole in relation to the other. The poles being qualitatively very alike to one another. There is not as we generally think in the soul of a man good and evil opposed. There is again and again in different manners a polarity, and the poles are not good and evil, but rather yes and no, rather acceptance and refusal. And we can strengthen, or we can help him strengthen, the one positive pole. And perhaps we can even strengthen the force of direction in him because this polarity is very often directionless. It is a chaotic state. We could bring a cosmic note into it. We can help put order, put a shape into this. Because I think the good, what we may call the good, is always only direction. Not a substance. (Buber, 1965, pp. 180–1)

Rogers speaks of acceptance as a warm regard for the other and a respect for the other as a person of unconditional worth, and that means an acceptance of and regard for a person's attitudes of the moment, no matter how much they may contradict other attitudes he or she has held in the past. In response to my question as moderator as to whether he would not distinguish confirmation from acceptance of this sort, Buber said:

> Every true existential relationship between two persons begins with acceptance . . . I take you just as you . . . But it is not yet what I mean by confirming the other. Because accepting, this is just accepting how he is in this moment, in this actuality of his. Confirming means first of all, accepting the whole potentiality of the other and even making a decisive difference in his potentiality, and of course we can be mistaken again and again in this, but it's just a chance between human beings . . . And now I not only accept the other as he is,

but I confirm him, in myself, and then in him in relation to this potentiality that is meant by him and it can now be developed, it can evolve, it can answer the reality of life ... Let's take, for example, man and a woman, man and wife. He says, not expressly, but just by his whole relation to her, 'I accept you as you are.' But this does *not* mean, 'I don't want you to change.' Rather it says, 'Just by my accepting love, I discover in you what you are meant to become.' ... it may be that it grows and grows with the years of common life. (Buber, 1965, pp. 181–2)

Rogers, in his reply, recognizes that we could not accept the individual as is because often he or she is in pretty sad shape, if it were not for the fact that we also in some sense realize and recognize the individual's potentiality. But he went on to stress the acceptance as that which makes for the realization of potentiality: 'Acceptance of the most complete sort, acceptance of this person as he is, is the strongest factor making for change that I know' (Rogers in Buber, 1965, pp. 182–3). To this Buber (1965, pp. 182–3) replied:

There are cases when I must help him against himself. He wants my help against himself ... The first thing of all is that he trusts me ... What he wants is a being not only whom he can trust as a man trusts another, but a being that gives him now the certitude that 'there *is* a soul, there *is* an existence ... The world *can* be redeemed. *I* can be redeemed because there is this trust.' And if this is reached, now I can help this man even in his struggle against himself. And this I can do only if I distinguish between accepting and confirming.

Rogers says, in effect, 'I will come to you and I will be concerned about you, I'll have unconditional positive regard for you, I'll have empathic understanding of you, but I can only do so if I do it authentically as the person I am.' That is what Rogers calls congruence. But confirmation, as distinct from congruence, has to do with the other person. People do not just naturally develop so that all I have to do is accept them — in this I agree with Buber. They are in a struggle themselves about their own direction. While I cannot impose on them what their direction should be, I can help them in their struggle.

I don't confirm you by being a blank slate or blank check. I can confirm you only by being the person I am. You'll never be confirmed by me by simply putting myself aside and being nothing but a mirror reflecting you. Confirming the other may mean that I *don't* confirm him in some things, precisely because he's not taking a direction. It's not just that he is wrestling with himself; I am wrestling with him. There's an added factor here that is not what one calls being empathic. It's not just that I'm watching him wrestle with himself, but I am also entering into the wrestling. It means I wrestle with you, not just that I provide a ground for your wrestling, even though I may not impose myself on you, and say 'I know better than you.' It's only insofar as you share with me and we struggle together that I glimpse the person you are called to become (Friedman, 1983, Chaps. 6 and 7).

EMPATHY AND INCLUSION

Rogers' 'deep empathic understanding,' which enables him to see his clients' private world through their eyes, is close to Buber's 'experiencing the other side,' or 'inclusion.' Rogers states that 'when I hold in myself the kind of attitudes I have described, and when the other person can to some degree experience these attitudes, then I believe that change and constructive personal development will *invariably* occur' (1961, p. 35). This faith in the latent potentialities that will become actual 'in a suitable psychological climate,' seems to expect of 'healing through meeting' an effectiveness that goes beyond the concrete situation with its often tragic limitations. If the parent creates such a psychological climate, 'the child will become more self-directing, socialized, and mature,' says Rogers (1961, p. 37). Through relationship, the other individual will experience and understand the repressed aspects of himself, will become better integrated and more effective in functioning, closer to the person he would like to be, 'more of a person, more unique and more self-expressive,' and 'will be able to cope with the problems of life more adequately and more comfortably' (Rogers, 1961, p. 38).

Empathy, in the strict sense of the term, means to feel oneself in the client by giving up the ground of one's own concreteness. One experiences the other side of the relationship through an imaginative aesthetic leap. In making this leap one ceases for the time being to experience one's own side. One brackets or suspends one's awareness of oneself, as it were, in order to understand the other better. Carl Rogers' earlier uses of empathic understanding often suggest this with its emphases upon client or person-centered therapy, on the becoming of the client, on acceptance of the client by the therapist, and on unconditional positive regard. Empathy was never, to be sure, an aesthetic category for Rogers, but it seemed to be one in which one tended to lose sight of oneself and one's own side of the relationship.

In contrast to empathy, inclusion means a bold imaginative swinging 'with the intensest stirring of one's being' (Buber, 1965, p. 81) into the life of the other so that one can to some extent concretely imagine what the other person is thinking, willing, and feeling, so that one adds something of one's own will to what is thus apprehended. It means grasping the other in his or her uniqueness and concreteness. A person finds himself or herself as person through going out to meet the other, by responding to the address of the other. One does not lose one's center, one 's personal core, in an amorphous meeting with the other. If one sees through the eyes of the other, experiences the other side, one does not cease to experience the relationship from one's own side. We do not experience the other through empathy or analogy. We do not know another's anger because of our anger; the other might be angry in an entirely different way from us. But we can glimpse something of the other's side of the relationship. That is because real persons do not remain shut in themselves or use their relations with others merely as a means to their own self-realization. Inclusion or 'imagining the real' does not mean at any point that one gives up the ground of one's own concreteness, ceases to see through one's own eyes, or loses one's own touchstone of reality. In this respect it is the complete opposite of empathy in the narrower and stricter sense of the term.

It is striking that in his later formulations of empathic understanding Rogers stressed this very point. Rogers said to Buber, in describing his own therapy, 'I am able to sense with a good deal of clarity the way his experience seems to him, really viewing it from within him, yet without losing my own person-hood or separateness in that' (Rogers in Buber, 1965, p. 170). In his later essays Rogers stresses accurately seeing into the client's world *as if* it was his own without ever losing that 'as if' quality. This too is very close to Buber's definition of inclusion as the bipolar experiencing of the other side of the relationship without leaving one's own ground. The therapist runs the risk of being changed by the client but never loses his or her own separateness or identity in the process. Rogers' placing of congruence before both empathic understanding and unconditional positive regard in these later essays also represents a swing in this direction.

Carl Rogers' more recent statements on empathy belie our attempts to point to a clear chronological progression. In his 1980 essay 'Empathic: An Unappreciated Way of Being,' Rogers quotes his own 1959 definition of empathy as sensing the other's inner feelings as if they were one's own without losing sight of the 'as if' and falling into identification. In this same essay, however, he updates his view on empathy in a way that sometimes resembles inclusion and sometimes empathy in a narrower sense.

> An empathic way of being with another person means entering the private perceptual world of the other and becoming thoroughly at home in it, as well as being sensitive moment by moment to the changing felt meanings that flow in this other person — his fear or rage or tenderness or confusion or whatever he or she is experiencing. It means temporarily living the other's life, moving about in it delicately without making judgments. (Rogers, 1980. pp. 142–3)

Entering the private perceptual world of the other and temporarily living in the other's life suggest empathy in the narrower sense of losing one's own ground, whereas communicating one's sensings of the person's world with fresh and unfrightened eyes and checking as to the accuracy of one's sensing suggest inclusion.

Those who are used to using 'empathy' in the customary way may well ask what practical difference is made by the fine distinctions between empathy in the stricter sense and inclusion. A first answer would be that empathy (in the narrower sense) is a very limited means of understanding, within therapy and outside of it; it relies on only one side of the relationship. A second, deeper answer is that empathy, in the strict sense, cannot really confirm another person, since true confirmation means precisely that *I* confirm *you* in your uniqueness and that I do it from the ground of my uniqueness as a real other person. Only inclusion, or imagining the real, can confirm another; for only it really grasps the other in his or her otherness and brings that other into relationship with oneself.

CONGRUENCE AND UNCONDITIONAL POSITIVE REGARD

The three chapters that Rogers contributed to *Person to Person* (Rogers & Stevens, 1967a), chapters he wrote in 1962 and 1963, have in common the assertion that the traits in the therapist that most facilitate effective therapy are congruence, unconditional positive regard, and empathic understanding. Of these three the most indispensable, says Rogers, with an emphasis that was relatively late in his thinking, is *congruence*:

> Personal growth is facilitated when the counselor is what he *is*, when in the relationship with his client he is genuine and without 'front' or facade, openly being the feelings and attitudes which at that moment are flowing in him . . . It means that he comes into a direct personal encounter with his client, meeting him on a person-to-person basis. It means that he is *being* himself, not denying himself. (Rogers, 1967a, p. 90)

For Rogers, even when the therapist is annoyed with, bored by, or dislikes his or her client, it is preferable for the therapist to be real than to assume a facade of interest and concern and liking that is not felt. What the therapist can do is recognize that it is his or her feelings of being bored that are being expressed and not the supposed fact that the client is a boring person. When the therapist expresses this feeling, which has been a barrier between the therapist and the client, the client will express himself or herself more genuinely in turn because the therapist has dared to be a real, imperfect person in the relationship. Although the qualities of unconditional positive regard and empathic understanding may be easier to achieve, it is better for the therapist to be what he is than to pretend to possess these qualities (Rogers, 1967a, pp. 90–2).

The client will pick up what the therapist actually feels and will experience dissonance between how the therapist appears and the way the therapist wants to appear. One of the questions that is often raised concerning Rogers' approach to psychotherapy is how his emphasis on congruence in the therapist is to be reconciled with the importance he places on unconditional positive regard. This latter emphasis is an older one in Rogers' thought, and means a warm, positive and accepting attitude toward the client. The therapist meets the client in a totally nonpossessive way rather than placing conditions upon his or her acceptance, thereby making constructive change more likely to occur. One answer that might be given to this question is that the therapist cares what the client is as a person and not just what the client does. Another is that, if the two principles conflict, then the therapist must be genuine, that is, congruent, but need not turn his or her feelings toward the client into a judgment on the client.

In his essay 'Learning to be Free' Rogers (1967a) makes unconditional positive regard the second essential condition of good therapy. In 'The Interpersonal Relationship' (Rogers 1967a) he places it third after empathic understanding, as he calls it in the earlier essay. Rogers' stress on accurately seeing the client's private world *as if* it were the therapist's own, without ever losing that *as if* quality, is very close, as we have seen, to Buber's definition of 'inclusion' as the bipolar experiencing of the other side of the relationship without leaving one's own ground. In marked contrast to his earlier statement about 'complete unity' Rogers (1967a, p. 93) writes: 'When the counselor can grasp the moment-to-moment experiencing occurring in the inner world of the client as the client sees and feels it, *without losing the separateness of his own identity* in this empathic process, then change is likely to occur.' At the same time, Rogers warns that when therapists are truly open to the way that life is experienced by their clients—making the clients' world their own and seeing life as they do—then therapists run the risk of being changed themselves. But therapists must also succeed in communicating the fact that they have or are trying to have empathic understanding of their clients if meaningful change is to occur (Rogers, 1967a, pp. 92–3).

In his discussion of empathy Rogers adds a caution that was largely absent from his earlier work and that serves as a corrective to his assertions that change is *bound* to occur:

> I have learned, especially in working with more disturbed persons, that empathy can be perceived as lack of involvement; that an unconditional regard on my part can be perceived as indifference; that warmth can be perceived as a threatening closeness, that real feelings of mine can be perceived as false. (Rogers, 1967a, p. 96)

Rogers would *like* to behave in such a way that what he is experiencing in relation to the client would be perceived unambiguously by the client. But Rogers recognizes that this is complex, and hard to achieve. In the case of a severely disturbed person, even this would seem to be an understatement! Yet at the end of 'The Interpersonal Relationship' Rogers (1967a) asserts that congruence, empathy, and unconditional positive regard 'will have a high probability of being an effective, growth-promoting relationship' not only for maladjusted individuals who come on their own initiative seeking help, but also for 'chronically schizophrenic persons with no conscious desire for help' (p. 101).

This extension to schizophrenia of his approach to therapy represents an important change in Rogers' thinking since his dialogue with Martin Buber in 1957. Commenting on a study of psychotherapy with schizophrenics in his third and final contribution to *Person to Person* (1967b), Rogers begins by recognizing that the clinic client's inevitable focus on exploring and experiencing self once having tasted its 'bitter-sweet satisfactions' does not hold for the hospitalized schizophrenic. Nonetheless, Rogers reported that 'the more successful schizophrenic shows the greatest increase in depth of self-exploration from early to late, greater even than the successful neurotic cases' (p. 184). The schizophrenic who improves does so because he has really entered into therapy, spontaneously and feelingly expressing personally relevant material in an active, struggling, fearful exploration of self (pp. 184–5).

If the therapeutic relationship has little to do with theory or ideology, says Rogers, it also has little to do with techniques. 'In this respect I believe my views,' says Rogers,

> have become more, rather than less, extreme. I believe it is the *realness* of the therapist in the relationship which is the most important element . . . Probably this is a 'trained humanness' . . . but in the moment it is the natural reaction of *this* person. For one, an impatient, no-nonsense, let's put-the-cards-on-the-table approach is most effective, because in such an approach one is most openly being himself. For another it may be a much more gentle, and more obviously warm approach, because this is the way *this* therapist is. Our experience has deeply reinforced and extended my own view that the person who is able *openly* to be himself at that moment, as he is at the deepest levels he is able to be, is the effective therapist. Perhaps nothing else is of any importance. (Rogers, 1967b, pp. 186–7)

If Rogers does not arrive at an explicit recognition of the *difference* between acceptance and confirmation that Martin Buber stressed in the 1957 dialogue between Rogers and him, he *seems* to imply it in his comment on one of the therapists in this study:

> One in particular is moving more and more toward allying himself with the hidden and unrevealed person in the schizophrenic, and openly 'clobbering' the defensive shell. In his work there is a real similarity to John Rosen and Carl Whitaker. He is sensitively and obviously committed to the person who is hiding, but he is quite violently and sometimes sarcastically critical of the psychotic symptoms, the fear of relating, the defenses and avoidances. Perhaps partly because this approach is congenial to him as a person, he is finding it effective. (Rogers, 1967b, pp. 187–8)

The last sentence, of course, is meant to illustrate 'congruence' and shies away from any general recognition that the therapist may have to struggle with the client against himself, as Buber says in his distinction between confirming and accepting the patient.

Rogers concludes by expressing his great personal satisfaction 'that we have been able to help withdrawn, bizarre, hopeless individuals become human beings' (1967b, p. 191) and to Rogers this means persons, whether they are labeled schizophrenics or not:

> Behind the curtains of silence, and hallucination, and strange talk and hostility and indifference, there is in each case a person . . . if we are skillful and fortunate we can *reach* that person, and can live, often for brief moments only, in a direct person-to-person relationship with him. To me that fact seems to say something about the nature of schizophrenia. It says something too about the nature of man and his craving for and fear of a deep human relationship. (Rogers, 1967b, pp. 191–2)

There is no suggestion here of full mutuality between therapist and client. Also there is a realism about the fact that the person-to-person meeting is often a matter of moments only. This realism is very close to Buber's position in his dialogue with Rogers five years earlier.

CONCLUSION

Rogers' emphases upon the I-Thou relationship in therapy, healing through meeting, acceptance, empathy, unconditional positive regard, and congruence are not only compatible with Buber's philosophy of dialogue but could be strengthened, clarified, and made more consistent by being seen within that framework. I would like to see person-centered therapy move in the direction of recognizing the origin of the person in person-to-person relationship. I would like to see the recognition that persons become themselves and reach self-actualization not by directly aiming at these goals but as a by-product of dialogue. At the very least, holding Carl Rogers' views in tension with those of Martin Buber could make the dialogue between the two more fruitful in the thought and practice of person-centered therapists.

REFERENCES

Buber, M. (1965). *The knowledge of man: A philosophy of the interhuman* (M. S. Freidman, Ed.; M. S. Friedman & R. G. Smith, Trans.). New York: Harper & Row.

Buber, M. (1969). *A believing humanism: Gleanings* (M. S. Friedman, Ed. and Trans.). New York: Simon & Schuster.

Friedman, M. S. (1966) Introductory essay. In M. Buber, *The knowledge of man: A philosopy of the interhuman.* New York: Harper & Row.

Friedman, M. S. (1973). *The worlds of existentialism: A critical reader.* Chicago: University of Chicago Press.

Friedman, M. S. (1982). *Martin Buber's life and work: The early years – 1878–1923.* New York: E. P. Dutton.

Friedman, M. S. (1983). *The confirmation of otherness: In family, community, and society.* New York: Pilgrim.

Friedman, M. S. (1984). *Martin Buber's life and work: The later years – 1945–1965.* New York: E. P. Dutton.

Friedman, M. S. (1985). *The healing dialogue in psychotherapy.* New York: Jason Aronson.

Rogers, C. R. (1951). *Client-centered therapy.* Boston: Houghton Mifflin.

Rogers, C. R. (1961). *On becoming a person: A therapist's view of psychotherapy.* Boston: Houghton Mifflin.

Rogers, C. R. (1967a). The interpersonal relationship: The core of guidance. In C. R. Rogers & B. Stevens (Eds.), *Person to person: The problem of being human. A new trend in psychology* (pp. 89–103). Lafayette, CA: Real People Press.

Rogers, C. R. (1967b). Some learnings from a study of psychotherapy with schizophrenics. In C. R. Rogers & B. Stevens (Eds.), *Person to person* (pp. 181–92). Lafayette, CA: Real People Press.

Rogers, C. R. (1967c, summer). Article in *Voices.*

Rogers, C. R. (1980). *A way of being.* Boston: Houghton Mifflin.

Rogers, C. R. & Stevens, B. (Eds.), *Person to person: The problem of being human. A new trend in psychology.* Lafayette, CA: Real People Press.

Attaining Mastery:
The shift from the 'Me' to the 'I'

Fred M. Zimring   *Case Western Reserve University*

Increases in feelings of mastery as a result of client-centered therapy are discussed from a self-theory perspective. Two modes of relating to the world, the 'I' and the 'me' are described. Client-centered therapy starts the process of shifting the person to the 'I,' the self-mode with more mastery, by responding to particular contents. This responding stimulates attention to the self and changes clients' beliefs about their selves.

To help people increase the mastery of their lives is the goal of client-centered psychotherapy, as articulated by Carl Rogers at the 1977 American Psychological Association convention. The achievement of mastery will be examined using concepts drawn from self-theory, a framework central to Rogers' explanation of therapeutic change. These self-theory concepts have to do with the perceived relationship of the self to the world. Different relationships to the world result in the person experiencing various amounts of mastery. Two relationships thought to be important have been characterized as the 'I' and the 'me' modes of the self.

DEVELOPMENT OF THE SOCIALIZED SELF—THE 'ME'

The most important theorist in this area was George Herbert Mead (1934) who preceded Rogers at the University of Chicago. According to Mead, the self is not innate. Rather, the self comes from social experience. The very substance of the self is social. The self begins with the infant's interactions with parents and other significant individuals. In these interactions the child perceives, and eventually incorporates, the attitudes of these 'significant others.' The self consists of these attitudes. During this early stage the responses of the child to the world are very specific and reflect the particular attitudes incorporated as a result of contact with significant others. The next stage of the development of the self occurs upon entering school, when the child interacts with groups. Through play and participation in games the child incorporates both the rules and the structure of group interaction. This process leads to the formation of the 'generalized other.' Here, the attitudes of the others involved in the same activity are generalized and viewed as the attitudes of the whole community. These attitudes become part of the self and are responded to as the child formerly responded to the attitudes of the significant others.

Conversations and interactions with others are also incorporated into the self by the child. Thinking is the mental occurrence of these conversations and interactions. This constellation of attitudes, conversations, and interactions with the significant and generalized others is termed the 'me' by Mead.

First published in *Person-Centered Review,* Volume 3, Number 2, May 1988.

The 'me' is the social self. The social world has become the person's internal world. In the 'me' mode the self consists of the social aspects of the person.

The 'me' serves many functions. One is to guide behavior. By the very nature of the 'me,' the person knows what should be done from the perspective of the significant other or group. These 'shoulds' are one kind of morality. The 'me' also enables one to solve social problems. In deciding how to go about obtaining something from another person, incorporated interactions guide the choice of the correct method. This incorporated social knowledge also explains the ease with which one can understand a gesture or posture.

One of the appealing aspects of Mead's formulation is that it corresponds to much of our day-to-day experience. We spend a significant amount of time and energy having internal interactions with others. The voices of significant others are experienced as telling us what we should do. In this sense, the world is experienced as that of the others, seems external and not under our control. We are observers.

The 'me' is a recipient self, which, although busily interactive, is passive in its lack of initiating. The passivity of the 'me' is reflected in our language. When one is an object one talks about 'What happened to me.' The 'me' incorporates only past learnings and does not allow for innovative action.

THE PERSONAL SELF — THE 'I'

Mead postulated another aspect of the self as the source for creative action. These aspects, which he did not describe as fully as he did the 'me,' he termed the 'I.' Recently, there have been a number of theorists (Coulter, 1979; Harré, 1983; Shotter, 1984) who have discussed the nature and genesis of the 'I.' They contrast the social definition of the 'me' to the personal definition of the 'I.' The 'I' is that which results from the concept that one has about what type of person 'oneself' is.

The aspect of the 'I' most relevant to mastery is that of agency, the ability of the self to behave independently. In respect to this Harré (1983, p. 29) says:

> To be an agent is to conceive of oneself as (hold a theory that one is) a being in possession of an ultimate power of decision and action. A pure agent is capable of deciding between alternatives, even if they are equally attractive or forceful. A pure agent is capable of overcoming temptation and distraction to realize its own plans. It can adopt new principles and it can curb its own desires.

For Mead, the 'I' reacts to the attitudes and interactions with others that make up the 'me.' To say to oneself 'I know I should do X but somehow it's not right for me now' is an 'I' judgment about a 'me' attitude. The 'I' changes the response of the self as the attitudes of others to something more idiosyncratic. The 'I' responds in terms of plans and goals. This involves values that are that of a different nature than the 'shoulds' generated by the 'me.'

An important aspect of mastery is the setting of goals. Taylor (1979), an English philosopher, talks about two types of relationships to goals corresponding to the relationships to goals that occur in the 'me' and in the 'I.' At the superficial level the goals are set by others or by the logic of the situation. One merely chooses between alternative means to an end (e.g., choosing the best way of getting to the airport). This more superficial valuing process also involves making preferences, in deciding, for example, which of two restaurants one prefers.

The other level of evaluation, according to Taylor, occurs at a deeper level and involves decisions regarding the value or worth to the self. Using the first level of evaluation, one may prefer Chinese to Italian food. On the deeper level one may decide that because of a resolution to lose weight, neither Chinese nor Italian food would be advisable.

The most common complaint of a beginning client, at least of those in academic settings, is that they are oppressed by 'shoulds.' Growth in therapy, for these clients, can frequently be measured by freedom from these 'shoulds.' These 'shoulds' are oppressive because 'should' is the application of a moral value to the 'me,' where only the superficial level of evaluation is appropriate. Thus if I am trying to make a choice between Chinese and Italian food for lunch and my spouse remarks that I am gaining weight and should not eat either, this interferes with making a choice and will be resisted. In contrast to the 'me' mode, when operating in the 'I' mode, the opinion can be evaluated on the basis of self-respect. Perhaps one's self-respect would be greater if neither type was eaten. Morality and values become useful only when in the 'I' mode.

SHIFTING BETWEEN THE 'ME' AND THE 'I'

The very different worlds of the 'I' and the 'me' are relatively independent and cohesive. When one is in either the 'me' or 'I,' many aspects of living are present. When one changes from one to the other, these aspects change together. For example, upon going from the 'me' to the 'I,' one stops interacting internally with other people, playing roles, attending to 'shoulds,' and begins to attend to the self, to values, and responds fluidly.

This shift between the 'me' and the 'I' may not occur easily. The cohesion of each world means that when one is firmly in either the 'I' or 'me' world, it is difficult to move into the other. This is especially true when in the 'me' mode. Once one begins to justify oneself to others internally and to respond to the objections of the 'significant others,' additional objections to the desired course of action emerge. At that moment standards independent of the opinions of others do not occur and problems cannot be resolved in new ways.

Client-centered therapy often results in a shift from the 'me' to the 'I' because the response of the client-centered therapist is typically directed toward particular contents. Directing attention to these contents directs the client's attention to his or her self.

Three 'contents' are important for the shift from the 'me' to the 'I.' These contents are values, feelings, and intentions. Some illustrations of their use in facilitating a shift from the 'me' to the 'I' can be drawn from daily life. For example, one might experience difficulty in beginning a task such as writing a paper or paying bills. Despite having logical reasons, one doesn't begin. Thinking of more reasons doesn't help. At this point one is in a fervid 'me' interaction with oneself. To consider feelings about the matter is sometimes helpful but frequently not decisive. In addition, intentions, plans, and purposes should be considered. In considering these (as is also true of feelings) one is considering information stemming from the 'I.' Assume that in the given example what is valued about the day is considered and assume also that paying the bills frees one to do something of value. Then it may suddenly be possible to pay them. The futile, repetitive 'me' interaction will have stopped when consideration of what was important to the 'I' (what you valued in the day) occurred.

ILLUSTRATIONS

The shift from the 'me' to the 'I' frequently involves values and valuing. It will be recalled that the 'me' is concerned with values determined by others, the 'I' is more involved with

TABLE 1: Comparison of the 'Me' and 'I' Modes of Functioning

Me	*I*
(1) Socially defined self.	(1) Personally defined self.
(2) Behavior guided by incorporated social standards.	(2) Goals set by own plans and values.
(3) Morality defined by society's values.	(3) Personal values and morality.
(4) Agenda for what has to be done is set by others.	(4) Agenda set by self.
(5) Enables problem solution according to social standards.	(5) New, creative solutions.
(6) Repository of social knowledge and expectations.	(6) Contains self-knowledge.
(7) Provides social viewpoint in line with assimilated social values.	(7) Reacts creatively to 'me' attitudes and interactions.
(8) Passive recipient of reactive self.	(8) Proactive.
(9) Concerned with past and future.	(9) Experiencing the present.
(10) Focus on others.	(10) Focus on self.
(11) Lives in roles.	(11) Acts from present personal values.

personal values. An interesting example of a client's shift to a consideration of values occurs in a demonstration tape, the 'Case of Mike' (AAP, 1960). Here a misstatement by Rogers moves Mike to consider his values. Mike has been talking about his hatred for his father and Rogers responds:

ROGERS: So, for about eight years you've lived with someone for whom you have no respect and really hate.

MIKE: Oh, I respect him.

ROGERS: Excuse me. I got that wrong.

MIKE: I have to respect him. I don't have to, but I do. But I don't love him. I hate him. I can't stand him.

ROGERS: There are certain things you respect him for, but that doesn't alter the fact that you definitely hate him and don't love him.

MIKE: That's the truth. I respect anybody who has bravery and courage, and he does.

ROGERS: I see.

MIKE: And I still, uh, though I respect him, I don't like him.

ROGERS: But, you do give him credit for the fact that he is brave, he has guts or something.

MIKE: Yeah. He shows that he can do a lot of things that, well, a lot of men can't.

ROGERS: M-hm. M-hm.

MIKE: And, also, he has asthma, and the doctor hasn't given him very long to live. And he, even though he knows he is going to die, he keeps working and he works at a killing pace, so I respect him for that, too.

Here Rogers' attempt to have Mike attend to his anger had the paradoxical effect of directing Mike's attention to his values. In most cases the therapist directs attention to the client's values by selecting and summarizing the client's valuing activity. Thus after a long story from the client about visiting his mother, the therapist may reply, 'You really didn't like being forced to pretend to be happy.'

Directing the client's attention to these values, feelings, or intentions and attending to the client's exploration of experience does more than enable clients to have knowledge of their experience. This exploration of experience is also exploration of the self. When the therapist directs attention to experience, the client shifts from attending to others to attending to the self. To cite an example from a typescript made at the University of Chicago (1947), Mrs. Ett was concerned about her daughter Bonnie's relationship with her caretaker Daisy.

MRS. ETT: I worry that Bonnie won't realize that I am her mother. She'll think that, ah, Daisy is the mother.

ROGERS: You're afraid that she might transfer her affection and loyalty.

This is a reasonably accurate paraphrase. Like many client-centered responses, it emphasizes two aspects of the client's statement. The 'afraid' part of the 'you're afraid' emphasizes the client's feeling. The other emphasis is also important. The 'you' in the 'you're afraid' directs the client's attention to the self having the fear. If the client was then to say, for example, 'Yes, but I'm ashamed also,' the client may have been considering both the self and the emotion. This direct consideration of the self is an 'I' activity. In addition, Rogers' response may have shifted Mrs. Ett's attention from concern about her role as a mother to self or/and to her emotions. This is a shift away from a typical 'me' activity, concern with one's role.

In another example, a friend of mine went from repetitive 'me' interactions to 'I' valuing by considering his self. The friend was bothered about a possible sexual relationship. On one hand, he felt that he should not get involved, that there might be some seriously negative social consequences. On the other, he had a strong physical desire for the woman. He had been vacillating between alternatives and couldn't decide what to do. As we talked, he first expressed his desire for the woman and how he felt about being denied her company. As I indicated my understanding not only of both alternatives but also of his experience of the dilemma, he examined his perspective about the dilemma. The focus of his attention changed from his feelings about her being denied to him to his appraisal of the rightness or wrongness of the situation for himself. He decided that he would not respect himself if he began a relationship with her. Once the decision was made on that basis, the anger at being denied disappeared.

He had started in the 'me' mode. As is true of that phase, the opinions of significant others immediately occurred to him. Since these opinions felt external to him, he began resisting and resenting them and became locked into a vacillating battle. It was only when he approached the problem from within the 'I' mode using standards of his own that he was able to resolve the problem. His shift into the 'I' state was facilitated by my focusing on his experience of the dilemma that served to redirect his attention from the woman to himself. Focusing attention on other aspects of his experience were also important. For the sake of this discussion, assume that he had said 'I really want a relationship with her but know that I shouldn't,' and I had paraphrased this, saying 'You feel you shouldn't, even though you want to.' If he had attended to the 'you feel' part of my response and had focused on the inner conflict between the shouldn't and the wanting, his attention would have been on himself rather than on his wanting the relationship with her. Considering the self as one is examining a course of action may evoke different standards than arise when considering a course of action without considering the self. Asking oneself, 'What about doing X?' may evoke logical, reality-based standards. Asking oneself, 'Should I do X?' may evoke questions about 'X's' relevance for oneself. Asking someone else 'Should I do X?' may involve yet a third set of standards (the opinions of others).

One aspect of what Harré meant in the quotation given earlier — by 'agency' — the ability to choose, is easy to understand. The quotation also stated that agency depends upon the theories that one holds, something more difficult to understand. A recent experience illustrates how these personal theories are formed. While visiting at a zoo with a two-year-old boy and his parents, I found that his parents continually asked the boy about his wants and intentions. For example, as we approached the monkey house, although the boy was quiet, the parents repeatedly asked whether he wanted to see the monkeys. While eating, his hand was near a drink and they asked whether he wanted the drink. This type of verbalization occurred continually. As a result the boy will learn that certain actions and inner experiences are 'wants' or 'intentions.' Other parents might give their child a different concept of wants and intentions. The nature of wants or intentions depends upon what the child has learned from significant others.

These considerations give rise to another way in which client-centered therapy enables the client to become more 'I' oriented and attain more mastery. It will be recalled from the above quotation by Harré that agency is partially based on the theory that one has of 'oneself.' Client-centered therapy changes the client's theory about 'oneself,' giving the client a theory with more agency. The client usually begins therapy in a 'me' phase with corresponding theories of 'oneself.' At this point 'oneself' is seen as 'father,' 'mother,' 'son,' and so on, and is defined in terms of roles, relationships, accomplishments, and the like. The important actions of 'oneself' are felt to be those that occur in relation to others and the criterion for decisions is what others think.

Client-centered therapy helps the client reform these theories of 'oneself.' Clients frequently enter therapy assuming the therapist to be an expert and that 'oneself' will be changed only as a result of expert advice: that the power to change oneself resides in the other. Client-centered therapy counters this assumption by refusing to give advice. Also, the therapist does not ask about or discuss the history of, or the objective reasons for, the client's problems. Thus the therapist's behavior deemphasizes the assumption with which the client begins. When the therapist focuses on the client's experience, the client learns that experiential knowledge residing in oneself is an important basis for decisions and action. This is a shift from a theory of 'oneself' based on a world of others to a theory of 'oneself' as defined more by one's experience.

CONCLUSION

In this article the argument has been made that the 'I' and the 'me' are important self-configurations with different degrees of mastery. The attainment of mastery is the change from the self-configuration with less mastery to the configuration with more. Several ways in which client-centered therapy facilitates this shift from the 'me' to the 'I' configuration have been described. Increased attention to the self results from working with feelings, intentions, and values. Exploring the values and experiencing of the client enables the client to develop a theory of 'oneself.'

It should be emphasized that change in mastery results from changes in the self rather than from knowledge of contents such as feelings, experience, or meanings. This emphasis has been a constant in Rogers' theorizing. He was not interested in responding to particular contents but rather in responding to the totality of the person. Rogers sometimes termed this totality the 'person' or the 'client' and sometimes the 'self.' What changes as a result of the therapist responses is the whole person, not the content. The client's knowledge of content is important only when it leads to changes in his or her framework.

This analysis has many implications for the practice of client-centered therapy. One is that the client is learning about the efficacy of the self, the validity of one's experience. This means that responding to particular contents, such as feelings, may not be important per se. Rather, it is important to respond to the self at the moment, to any self-relevant aspects of the client's communication.

REFERENCES

American Academy of Psychotherapists. (1960). *The case of Mike.* AAP Tape Library, Vol. 7.
Coulter, J. (1979). *The social construction of the mind.* Totawa, NJ: Rowman & Littlefield.
The Counseling Center, University of Chicago. (1947). *The Case of Mrs. Ett.*
Harré, R. (1983). *Personal being.* Oxford: Basil Blackwell.
Mead, G. H. (1934). *Mind, self and society.* Chicago: University of Chicago Press.
Shotter, J. (1984). *Social accountability and selfhood.* Oxford: Basil Blackwell.
Taylor, C. (1979). What is human agency? In T. Mischel (Ed.), *The self: Psychological and philosophical issues.* Oxford: Basil Blackwell.

Some Current Issues for Person-Centered Therapy

Arthur W. Combs   *Greeley, Colorado*

The author proposes compilation of a list of issues in therapy in need of attention, clarification, dialogue, and research. To begin such a project, he suggests and briefly discusses six areas currently in need of such exploration: the need for a comprehensive theory of personal meaning for psychology, a consistent humanist view of the therapy process, the goals of therapy and its importance for the teaching role of the counselor, the efficiency of therapy, person-centered research and the societal implications of person-centered thinking. The article closes with the hope that other counselors will be moved to contribute further problem areas to the discussion.

To celebrate Carl Rogers' seventy-fifth birthday, the American Psychological Association Convention offered a series of programs dealing with his contributions to various aspects of psychology and the social scene. Commenting on these sessions in the course of a quiet chat between programs, Carl told me, 'You know, Art, I really can't get excited about looking back. I'd much rather push forward to new horizons.' In that spirit, now that the immediate sadness of Carl's death is fading, I find myself thinking less about what he brought us and more about where therapy needs to go next.

To that end I propose that the *Person-Centered Review* open its pages to a problems census in which members of the profession might:
1. Propose current problems for exploration.
2. Define and explore their ramifications through dialogue.
3. Invite solutions from the profession.
4. Provide a pool of important problems for research.

To get the ball rolling, this article suggests six major problems currently in need of attention.

THE NEED FOR MORE ADEQUATE THEORY

A person-centered therapy requires a person-centered psychology on which to base its thinking and practice. Persons in the helping professions, especially, need clearly stated, trustworthy principles to provide guidelines for action and point the way toward possible innovations for exploration and improvement.

To serve these purposes adequately a supporting theory should meet at least these criteria—it ought to be comprehensive, accurate, internally consistent, systematic, appropriate to its problems, and adaptable to changing demands and conditions. At this point, most person-centered therapists do not have a theory that can meet such criteria. We have pieces of general theory such as the growth principle, the self-concept, the

First published in *Person-Centered Review,* Volume 3, Number 3, August 1988.

exploration of meaning, or we have concepts related to practice such as empathy, congruence, and unconditional positive regard. A comprehensive fundamental psychology, however, still eludes us.

We are currently in transition from one frame of reference to another, from behaviorism to humanism. Despite the inadequacies of behavioral approaches to psychology, it gave its adherents comprehensive, systematic, easily understandable and demonstrable principles. In the humanist revolt against that view, we relinquished the security of the behavioral tradition and have not yet found a comparable humanistic psychology to replace it.

Some practitioners have never gotten beyond the revolt and operate 'by the seat of the pants.' Some have become 'eclectic,' picking up pieces of concepts from many sources only to produce a framework full of inconsistencies. Others eschew any hint of theoretical interest whatsoever. Some, such as Victor Raimy (1971), have made important contributions to humanistic theory as they searched for theoretical explanations of the phenomena they observed in the course of practice. Carl Rogers carried this process further in the theory of therapy he proposed in 1959. Such contributions have provided valuable units for inclusion in a humanistic psychology. We need now to formulate a more comprehensive, systematic position capable of providing the support and direction person-centered theory and the humanistic practice of counseling require for healthy growth.

The humanist movement came about with the recognition, primarily among practitioners in the helping professions, that behavior is only a symptom, that the 'causes' of behavior lie inside people — in personal meanings, such as attitudes, beliefs, understandings, hopes, fears, and aspirations. Counselors in the 1940s and 1950s who practiced 'nondirective' therapy, for example, learned to focus the client's attention upon personal meaning by use of the 'recognition and acceptance of feeling' technique. Today, person-centered therapy is primarily understood as a process for helping clients discover new and more satisfying personal meanings about themselves and the worlds they inhabit. To help us organize our thinking and guide our practice in that endeavor, *we need a comprehensive theory of meaning.* But meaning lies inside people and is not readily open to direct observation. Is it possible, then, to construct a viable systematic psychology of meaning?

I believe it is.

In 1949 Donald Snygg and I, in a book entitled *Individual Behavior: A New Frame of Reference For Psychology,* proposed a framework for a systematic, comprehensive theory of psychology from a phenomenological orientation. The frame of reference was updated in 1959. It was revised again with Anne Richards and Fred Richards in 1975 as *Perceptual Psychology: A Humanistic Approach To The Study of Persons* and reissued in 1988. This perceptual-experiential view of persons is capable of incorporating most of the concepts and research in person-centered therapy. It has provided support and direction for much of my own thinking and practice. In the foreword to the first edition, the authors expressed their hope that their presentation was 'if not the truth, then very like the truth' (1949, p. ix). I believe this point of view could be developed into the theory we need. Perhaps others may find it a useful place to begin the search for a truly comprehensive, systematic psychology of meaning.

THE PROCESS OF THERAPY

Humanistic-perceptual-experiential psychologies ascribe the origins of behavior to people's perceptions or meanings. If that is true, then the process of therapy can be fully understood only in terms of the belief systems of the client and therapist. The process of person-centered therapy is designed to facilitate client exploration and discovery of meaning. We have recognized the need for therapists to be keenly in touch with client perceptions (empathy). We have also sought techniques to facilitate changes in client meanings and tried to map ways in which client beliefs about self and the world change in the course of treatment. Our studies of the counselor and the therapeutic process, however, have been, for the most part, from an objective point of view, focusing on behavior and techniques. This concentration on behavior is likely to be no more productive than going to a physician who dealt only with our symptoms.

Despite hundreds of studies designed to demonstrate the superiority of one or another method in the helping professions, we are still unable to designate any method as necessary for effective practice. There are good reasons for this: (a) methods are extremely complex; even the simplest methods must fit an enormous number of factors, and (b) the effect of any technique is not inherent in the method but in the perceptions of those who experience them.

In another paper (1986a), I summarized the findings of a whole series of studies demonstrating that good helpers could be clearly distinguished from poor ones on the basis of the belief systems of the helper. If it is counselor beliefs, rather than methods, that make the difference, we need to shift attention from counselor behavior and methods to counselor perceptions and belief systems.

Preoccupation with methods and behavior extends into educational programs. The assumption of most programs is that persons become counselors by learning about counseling and practicing its methods. Emphasis is generally upon content and learning *how to counsel,* with heavy dependence upon observation, 'practice counseling,' the dissection of therapy transcripts, and analysis of live or taped therapy sessions. If counselors, like their clients, behave in terms of their belief systems, the acquisition of trustworthy belief systems must become a prime objective of educational programs. The task of training must be seen as a problem in personal becoming rather than the traditional 'how to' concept. Implementing such a concept means rethinking every aspect of the educational process (Combs, 1986b).

A belief system approach seems to me to have widespread implications for person-centered therapy. For example, it suggests the following:

a) The need to shift from methods and techniques to the counselor belief systems that determine them.

b) A pressing need for research focused on client and counselor perceptions or meanings.

c) The need for reexamination of the fundamental assumptions of therapy and their implications for both preservice and in-service training programs.

GOALS AND TEACHING

Two matters generally given scant attention in person-centered thinking have to do with the goals of therapy and the teaching role of the counselor. Person-centered therapy began with 'nondirective' counseling. The tradition of noninvolvement in client choices has continued through 'client-centered' and 'person-centered' phases of development. Most counselors in this school of thought typically eschew authority and the idea of 'teaching' clients is generally anathema. Indeed, the concept of teaching, for many therapists, is practically an epithet, synonymous with autocrat or dictator. I think these attitudes are unnecessarily inhibiting.

Counseling is essentially a learning process designed to help clients learn new and more satisfying ways of being in the world. People learn from all their experiences, especially those with significant others. Being a significant other in the life of the client is just what counselors try to be. Counselors cannot avoid the teaching role for clients learn from counselor behavior, verbal or nonverbal, whether therapists are aware that this is happening or not. If this is true, we ought to acknowledge the teaching role and use it, purposefully, for positive ends. To do that effectively requires that therapists

a) be aware of what clients are learning from their experiences in therapy;

b) have accurate and usable concepts of the learning process as guidelines for the interventions they make;

c) possess clear conceptions of the desirable goals of counseling since such goals are necessary to provide objectives for teaching and guidelines for counselor choices in practice.

Most discussions of the goals of person-centered therapy are focused on the enabling process — facilitating client exploration and discovery of new meaning. Some counselors carry this thinking so far as to deny that they possess any goals for clients whatsoever. Such a denial is self-delusion. The therapeutic process is designed to help and the goal of helping is better psychological health, however that is defined by a given therapist. What is more, the counselor's conception of the nature of mental health will inevitably be conveyed to the client. Therapists behave in terms of their beliefs and clients are deeply sensitive to their counselors' attitudes and behavior. To assure the communication of facilitative messages, then, requires a clear grasp of the goals of therapy. Accordingly, the possession of a truly accurate and defensible conception of the nature of healthy personality must be a crucial concept in an effective counselor's belief system.

For this counselor, the most appropriate and useful concept stems from modern conceptions of self-actualization. Definitions of the supremely healthy human being have been approached from two frames of reference; objectively, in terms of characteristic traits and behaviors (Goble, 1970; Maslow, 1954) and internally, in terms of personal meanings and perceptions (Combs et al., 1988). The latter seems to me most congruent with humanistic thinking. Observed phenomenologically, self-actualizing persons seem characterized by three typical perceptual organizations: (a) they see themselves in essentially positive ways, (b) they are open to experiences (willing to confront themselves) and accepting of self and the world, and (c) they are deeply identified with and experience feelings of oneness with others. These concepts provide me with a set of ultimate goals for my clients, outcomes both of us hope to achieve. They also provide me with guidelines for the choices I make in practice. For example, to implement a more positive self, I may ask myself, 'How can a person feel liked unless someone likes him or her?' or 'How can one feel she or he is a person of dignity and integrity unless someone treats him or her so?' The answers I find to such questions provide direction for the choices I make from moment to moment in the counseling hour. Besides using these goals as determiners of my own behavior, on occasion, I have discussed one or more of them openly with clients to good effects.

I do not believe perceptual concepts of self-actualization are the last word in defining the healthy self. They are, however, the best I have found to date and I will continue to use them until something better comes along. Meantime, I believe the teaching role of the therapist and the definition of the supremely healthy human being are vital topics for all the helping professions, but especially for counseling and psychotherapy. It is time such crucial questions are given the attention they deserve.

The efficiency of therapy

The fourth area that I believe needs attention has to do with the efficiency of the therapy process. It seems immoral to let people suffer pain or deprivation any longer than absolutely necessary. If there are faster ways to help clients, it seems to me, therapists are obligated to use them. Person-centered therapy's stricture against authority, teaching, and telling, however, make counselors hesitant to experiment with means to accelerate the process. Most therapists have had unhappy experiences in which efforts to move clients along more rapidly, produced, instead, resistance and delay. As a consequence, some counselors tend to give up the search for more expeditious ways of working. Others experiment with techniques from other schools of thought and some give up person-centered therapy altogether.

As a perceptualist, I am keenly aware that choice both opens and closes opportunities. The choice of a particular approach to counseling opens that field to the counselor, but preoccupation with it can make it unlikely that he or she will appreciate alternatives when change becomes necessary or desirable. I have watched well-meaning teachers try to be so person-centered and tuned in to children's adjustment, that the children failed to learn to read or write effectively. Similarly, though the application of person-centered techniques to administration often creates better atmospheres, it can also reduce the efficiency with which tasks are accomplished. And, anyone who has watched a group of person-centered counselors decide where to go on a picnic must surely have asked themselves whether there are not speedier ways of reaching good decisions. Problems such as these ought not be swept under the rug. They merit attention, not just defensively in order to avoid criticism, but positively, because finding solutions may improve the efficiency of the therapy process.

Person-centered research

One of Carl Rogers' greatest contributions to therapy was his fearless insistence upon opening the transcripts of therapy sessions to critical examination and the application of research technology to counselor-client dialogue. Psychotherapy was thus exposed to public scrutiny and subjected to the rigors of research analysis. Those first efforts in the 1940s were followed over several decades by a whole series of studies exploring the counseling process. More recently, this early momentum has slowed almost to a standstill and comparatively few of today's practitioners engage in any form of research. I believe there are four reasons for that:
1. The humanistic revolt against behaviorism has been so complete for many psychologists that participation in anything that smacks of the old days seems like a form of surrender. Accordingly, objectivity, systematic research, and discipline are terms that have few advocates among today's practitioners.
2. Most psychologists interested in therapy are engaged in private practice or in agencies providing therapeutic services. This effectively separates them from settings where research is valued and carried on.
3. Lack of adequate theory in the profession leaves us without essential foundation for effective research.
4. We lack effective research techniques for the exploration of phenomenological problems.

Whatever the reasons, I believe the profession badly needs a recommitment to the importance of research and the devotion of substantial efforts to the encouragement and support of promising research efforts. Without a firm research base, the practice of counseling becomes difficult to defend and the profession is cut off from a valuable source of growth.

I have already pointed out, early in this article, the need for a comprehensive, systematic psychology as a basis for practice. It is equally important as a foundation for research and a source of hypotheses for exploration. Fortunately, there are promising beginnings afoot and before long this handicap may begin to disappear (Aspy, 1972; Howard, 1987; Lambert, 1986; Reason & Heron, 1986). To this point a majority of studies have concentrated upon the techniques or conditions of practice, leaving many further questions in need of research virtually untouched. In addition to areas already suggested earlier in this article, I would add such further problems as

- the dynamics of the therapy process
- the nature and functions of learning and their application in the therapy process
- the dynamics of changing perception or personal meaning
- the nature and function of need
- the dynamics of challenge and threat

In addition to such substantive areas in need of exploration, there is the technical problem of research methodology. How does one conduct research from a phenomenological orientation? Some humanistic or person-centered problems can be studied by using time-honored techniques from our behaviorist past, such as counting client and counselor responses. But personal meanings and perceptions lie inside people and cannot be explored by direct observation. New frames of reference in any science generally require the invention or application of new modes of study. The shift from behaviorism to humanism in the profession, however, has seen little thought given to appropriate research techniques for the exploration of perception and meaning.

Most attempts to explore personal meaning and belief have approached the problem through self-reports or introspection. Each of these, however, has fatal flaws. Self-reports are not perceptions but behaviors, symptoms of personal meanings with indeterminate relationships to the perceptions producing them (Parker, 1966; Soper, 1957). They are, nevertheless, widely reported in the literature as synonymous with perception or self-concept. Introspection is also error prone because the act of examining one's perceptions changes the perceptual field.

A more promising strategy, it seems to me, is to explore personal meaning by reading behavior backwards; that is, by making inferences from a sample of observed behavior. If behavior is, indeed, the product of perceptions or personal meanings, then it should be possible to observe behavior and infer the nature of the perceptions that produced it. This is, in fact, what everyone does almost automatically in our daily interactions with others as we attempt to infer what they are thinking, feeling, or intending. It is also the primary basis for much of psychotherapy since empathy requires putting one's self in the other person's shoes. Unfortunately, the use of inference in psychological research has a bad name with psychologists in the behavioral tradition and that prejudice has carried over to the humanist persuasion where it does not apply. The use of inference in science has a long and respectable history in biological and physical science and there is no reason why it should not be acceptable for person-centered studies.

Inferences made by carefully trained observers can provide valuable data about the inner life of persons. In a series of investigations into the perceptual organization of good and poor helpers in five helping professions, for example, trained observers made inferences about the ways subjects perceived themselves (self-concept), other people, the significant data of personal interactions, the purposes they were seeking to accomplish, and so on. These inferences showed high levels of reliability when compared to those of other observers and with the observer's own perceptions at a later time (Combs, 1986, 1969). What is more, these results were obtained by observers after unexpectedly short periods of training and from surprisingly small samples of behavior. Such results are promising, indeed, and call for further exploration of inference as a research tool for humanistic problems.

The search for effective research techniques ought not stop with the exploration of inference. There must be appropriate ways of studying our subject matter waiting to be discovered. A major effort devoted to such a search might yield exciting new possibilities to advance the kinds of research person-centered thinking requires.

Societal applications

Just before his death, Rogers and his colleagues were engaged in a series of workshops or encounter groups involving people caught up in religious, racial, political, and ideological conflicts. The reports we have about these efforts are astounding and deeply moving. People from groups with supposedly irreconcilable differences, ancient prejudices, anger, suspicion, hostility, and despair apparently learned to communicate with each other, appreciate one another as persons of dignity and integrity, and find ways to peaceful resolution of interpersonal and intergroup relationships. Such applications of person-centered therapy to the larger social scene seem to me to have implications as momentous and far reaching for group therapy as Rogers' introduction of nondirective counseling was for individual treatment almost 50 years ago.

To this point, most of the reports from these seminars have been in the form of testimonials from participants, reports about notable events or behaviors in the course of sessions and deeply moving narrative evaluations from the leaders. Anyone reading or hearing of these sessions must surely be impressed with the enormous potential they hold for contributing to the solution of some of the world's and society's most pressing problems.

These tantalizing glimpses into new areas of human interaction need continuance and expansion on a practical level, for the world sorely needs them. It is good to know, also, that groups have formed to continue these investigations.[1] For the sake of science and the profession, I hope we shall also see a major effort to explore the dynamics of these processes so that we may understand and research them successfully.

Conclusion

We are a very young profession with an enormous potential for contributing to human growth and fulfillment. For most of us the helping role is deeply satisfying and fulfilling, so much so, that it is easier to commit our energies to the growth of clients than the growth of the profession. But professions, like clients, grow by confronting problems,

1. See Carl Rogers Institute for Peace, 1125 Torrey Pines Rd., La Jolla, CA 12037.

defining them clearly, searching for solutions, and incorporating new concepts into a dynamic matrix of meaning. In the forward-looking spirit of Rogers I have, therefore, presumed to suggest areas of our discipline that seem to me to need exploration and development. I am sure that others perceive equally pressing problems in need of consideration, debate, and investigation. I have requested that the editors of the *Person-Centered Review* open its pages to a general stock taking for the profession. I hope that sharing our concerns may provide a problems census for stimulating discussion, research, and the advancement of the profession.

REFERENCES

Aspy, D. N. (1972). *Toward a technology for humanizing education.* Champaign, IL: Research Press.

Aspy, D. N., & Roebuck, F. N. (1974). From humane ideas to humane technology. *Education, 9S,* 163-171.

Combs, A. W. (Ed.). (1969). *Florida studies in the helping professions.* Gainesville: University of Florida Press.

Combs, A. W. (1986a). What makes a good helper? *Person-Centered Review, 1,* 51-61.

Combs, A. W. (1986b). Person-centered assumptions for counselor education. *Person-Centered Review, 1,* 72-82.

Combs, A. W., Richards, A. C., & Richards, F. (1988). *Perceptual psychology; A humanistic approach to the study of persons.* New York: University Press of America.

Combs, A. W., & Snygg, D. (1949). *Individual behavior: A new frame of reference for psychology.* New York: Harper & Row.

Combs, A. W., & Soper, D. W. (1963). Perceptual organization of effective counselors. *Journal of Counseling Psychology, 10,* 222-6.

Goble, F. G. (1970). *The third force: The psychology of Abraham Maslow.* New York: Grossman.

Howard, G. S. (1987). The person in research. *Person-Centered Review, 2,* 50-64.

Lambert, M. J. (1986). Future directions for research in client-centered therapy. *Person-Centered Review, 1,* 185-201.

Maslow, A. H. (1954). *Motivation and personality.* New York: Harper & Row.

Parker, J. (1966). The relationship of self report to inferred self concept. *Educational and Psychological Measurement, 26,* 691-700.

Raimy, V. C. (1971). *The self concept as a factor in counseling and personality organization.* Columbus: Ohio State University Libraries.

Reason, P., & Heron, J. (1986). The paradigm of cooperative experiential inquiry. *Person-Centered Review, 1,* 457-77.

Rogers, C. R. (1959). A theory of therapy, personality and interpersonal relationships as developed in the client-centered framework. In S. Koch (Ed.), *Psychology: A study of a science.* New York: McGraw-Hill.

Snygg, D., & Combs, A. W. (1949). *Individual behavior: A new frame of reference for psychology.* New York: Harper & Row.

Soper, D. W. (1957). The self, its derivate terms and research. *Journal of Individual Psychology, 13,* 134-45.

Wasicsko, M. M. (1981). *Becoming a teacher: A personal journey.* Fort Worth: Texas Wesleyan College.

The Relationship between Emotions and Cognitions: Implications for therapist empathy

Reinhard Tausch   *University of Hamburg, Psychological Institute III*

In recent years there has been extensive clarification of the relation between emotions and cognitions. According to Richard Lazarus' theory, emotions are closely linked with cognitions. This view supports and differentiates Carl Rogers' 1951 theory. In a pilot study it was shown that (1) there are differences in the extent to which psychotherapists of different schools attend to their clients' emotions and/or cognitions; and (2) that therapists have a distinct influence on their clients' attention to emotions and/or cognitions. The positive and negative effects of therapists' different approaches are discussed. In a pilot study, an analysis of Carl Rogers' interaction with a client showed that two-thirds of his responses refer to the client's cognitions, about one-fourth to the client's emotions. This seems appropriate on both the theoretical and practical level. Theoretical clarification of the relationship between emotions and cognitions facilitates a better differentiation and understanding of many therapeutic processes.

Many clients come to psychotherapy with disturbing emotions such as fear, dejection, despair, guilt, and anger. One might ask: 'With which other psychological processes are these emotions connected?' Understanding this theoretically is important for a scientific foundation of the practical work of the psychotherapist. Person-centered psychotherapists are empathic to their clients' emotions, probably to a much greater extent than psychotherapists with a behavioral, cognitive, or psychoanalytic orientation. One might ask if this empathic understanding of the client's emotions is helpful? If so, why? What are the effects? In this article I will first discuss Richard S. Lazarus' theory of emotions and their relation to cognitions which, in my view, complements and differentiates Rogers' theory.

LAZARUS' THEORY OF EMOTIONS AND COGNITIONS

I will present, briefly, Lazarus' theory and its relevance to the person-centered psychotherapist (Lazarus, 1982; Lazarus & Folkman, 1984; Lazarus, Kanner, & Folkman, 1980). His main points are as follows:

1. Emotions (e.g., fear, anger, jealousy) are the consequences and 'products' of cognitive processes. Thus emotions are closely related to cognitions. Cognitions are essential for what we feel.
2. The term *cognition* is easily misunderstood. Cognitions, as defined here, are perceptions of meanings and/or appraisals of events with respect to their significance to one's own well-being and/or thoughts-assumptions-ideas persons have about themselves and their environment. They are person-related processes (e.g., perceptions, thoughts) that refer to oneself and one's relation to the

First published in *Person-Centered Review,* Volume 3, Number 3, August 1988.

environment. They are shaped by each person individually and have meaning in the individual's everyday life. As defined by Lazarus (1982, p. 1022), 'the cognitive activity in appraisal does not imply anything about deliberate reflection, rationality, or awareness.'

3. Feelings vary with persons' perceived meanings, appraisal of events, specific thoughts, views, and imaginations they have about their environment and themselves. Emotions are the result of one's perceived meanings, appraisals, and thoughts. Every emotional reaction is caused by a complex cognitive perception and appraisal of the meaning of events for one's own well-being. Cognitive processes determine the emotional processes of people in their everyday lives.

4. The cognitive processes and the perception of meanings are influenced by past experiences, opinions, personal theories, commitment, and so on. If we have experienced an animal (e.g., a bear) to be threatening to our well-being, then, in the future, we will regard this animal to be threatening. We appraise it as something threatening to our well-being.

5. The intensity of one's emotions is dependent on the importance the event may have with respect to one's well-being.

6. According to Lazarus, appraisals may be classified in two categories: primary appraisal refers to what is valued as relevant for one's own well-being in the encounter with the environment. Secondary appraisal refers to the appraisal of oneself in a situation, that is, one's sources of help, control in the situation, and possibilities of coping with it.

7. Frequently, one makes reappraisals of one's circumstances and of oneself, on the basis of new experiences or new information. This leads to a differentiation of perceived meanings and appraisals. Inadequate appraisals of one's own resources are also changed by experience.

8. Cognitions and emotions are closely related to one another. With few exceptions, one does not appear without the other. Essentially, emotion and cognition can be regarded as inseparable. Emotions generally are not free of cognitions, nor are cognitions free of emotions. Thus it follows that when a perceived meaning disappears, the emotion disappears too. However, though closely connected, it should not be concluded that cognitions and emotions are the same. They have a distinctly different quality, independent of their joint appearance.

9. 'Every emotion has its own cognitive theme' (Lazarus et al., 1980, p. 200). In other words, every emotional quality and intensity is related to a specific cognitive activity.

10. The reverse can also be true: emotions can affect cognitive processes (Lazarus et al., 1980, p. 190). This seems to happen less often and it is less clear how it happens. The way in which emotions are perceived and appraised may be a significant factor.

11. The clinical implication of this phenomenologic-cognitive theory can be stated as follows: 'if one changes what the person thinks and believes one can also change the pattern of emotional reactions to ordinary social transactions' (Lazarus et al., 1980, p. 191).

ROGERS' THEORY

Lazarus' theoretical conceptions are not accepted by some person-centered psychotherapists even though they are similar to those of Carl Rogers. Rogers' (1951, pp.

481–524) theory is as follows:

1. A person reacts and behaves toward his perceptual field in the way in which she or he experiences and perceives it. In Lazarus' terminology this means one behaves and reacts in response to one's cognitions.

2. An important part of the perceptual field is the self, the way in which a person perceives her- or himself. If a client says: 'I'm a failure,' this is an expression of her or his concept of self, the way she or he perceives the self. These cognitions about one's self clearly determine one's behavior. According to Rogers, one's self-concept is a perception of great significance. According to Lazarus, this cognition of the self has a significant effect on emotions and behavior.

3. In Rogers' view, the intensity of one's emotions is closely related to the perceived meaning of an event. Lazarus believes the type and intensity of emotions depends on the person's appraisals-cognitions of an event.

ROGERS' VIEW OF EMOTIONS AND COGNITIONS IN PSYCHOTHERAPY

In person-centered psychotherapy, the psychotherapist has an empathic understanding for the inner world of the client and tries to communicate this to the client without evaluating it. One might ask: 'Which part of the client's world does the therapist try to understand and to what does the therapist respond?' Rogers (1983, p. 23) states, 'The activity of the psychotherapist becomes apparent in his ability to perceive his client's experiences and emotions and their personal meaning for him in a precise and sensitive way. This is an immediate sensitivity for the here and now of the inner world of the client with all the private and personal meanings.'

Rogers therefore focuses on emotions as well as perceived meanings. His definition of the frequently employed expression *feeling* helps to understand Rogers' (1959, p. 198) concept:

> This is a term which has been heavily used in writings on client-centered therapy and theory. It denotes an emotionally tinged experience, together with its personal meaning. Thus it includes the emotion but also the cognitive content of the meaning of that emotion in its experiential context. It thus refers to the unity of emotion and cognition as they are experienced inseparably in the moment.

Therefore, there are similarities between Rogers and Lazarus: both take the view that emotions appear jointly with cognitions. Apparently, for Rogers, every specific emotion is linked with a specific cognitive meaning. Empathic understanding therefore means that the psychotherapist is empathic toward the client's emotions *and* those personal meanings that are closely related to them. Possibly, for some person-centered psychotherapists, this aspect of Carl Rogers' thinking is not well known.

IMPLICATIONS FOR THERAPEUTIC ACTIVITY

What are the implications that follow from the theoretical relationship between cognitions and emotions? How can we help clients change the perceived meanings and appraisals of themselves and their environment, and, as a consequence, their emotions? Should psychotherapists exclusively attend to their clients' cognitions, or to their emotions, or to both?

The necessity for theoretical clarification becomes apparent from the results of a pilot study (Schlegel, 1986) where significant differences were found between therapists of varying orientations with respect to the extent to which they attended to cognitions or emotions. The consequence of this differing empathic understanding is reflected in the varying extent to which clients would express themselves in emotional or cognitive terms.

Using Schlegel's *pilot study* we looked at extracts from counseling sessions of psychotherapists that were available in the German language. The therapists were (1) David Burns (1983), a representative of cognitive therapy (Beck, 1976), (2) Carl Rogers, and (3) a German psychotherapist, Wilhelm Gerl, who combines person-centered psychotherapy with the focusing method of Eugene Gendlin (1978). For each therapist three extracts were chosen, each with at least five consecutive client-therapist sequences. These were given individually to three 'blind' raters. On the basis of a five-point scale they ordered the therapists' utterances and, separately from these, the clients' utterances according to cognitive or emotional content, respectively. Interrater reliability was .85 and .82, respectively.

There were strong and statistically significant differences in the extent to which therapists were attending to cognitions and emotions. For Rogers M = 3.3 for cognitions; M = 2.3 for emotions. For Burns M = 4.3 for cognitions; M = 1.5 for emotions. For Gerl, M = 1.7 for cognitions; M = 2.8 for emotions.[1] The same was found for their clients. Some of the results are mentioned in the following pages. At present, we are in the process of conducting a more extensive empirical study with a much larger sample.

THERAPIST EMPATHY FOR CLIENT COGNITION

Beck (1976), a cognitive therapist, assumes that emotions, particularly depressive emotional states, have their origin mainly in thoughts, appraisals, perceptions and convictions with respect to oneself, the environment, and the future. Another cognitive therapist, Burns (1980, p. 23) states:

> The first principle of cognitive therapy implies that all your emotions are elicited by your cognitions or thoughts. A cognition is the way in which you perceive things, [including] your consciousness, your opinions and convictions. It also includes the way in which you interpret your environment, or the way in which you picture a person or situation to yourself. The emotions you feel right at this very minute are closely related to the thoughts that you have at this moment.

In Schlegel's (1986) study the therapists' behavior supported this theory (as well as the behavior of a German rational-emotive therapist who applies Ellis' method). When assessed on a five-point scale, the cognitive therapist's comments with respect to his empathic understanding for his clients' cognitions were rated at 4.3, for emotions the rating was 1.5. This difference was significant, t(19) = 11.38, p < .01. Further, in all his utterances the therapist showed more empathic understanding for the cognitions than the emotions of the client.

In 85% of his or her utterances, the *client* attended more to his cognitions than emotions, in 7% equally to both, and in 8% more to his emotions than cognitions. Clients

---

1. Comparisons of means for cognitions: (1) Burns versus Rogers, t(34) = 3.11, p < .01; (2) Burns versus Geri, t(39) = 9.13, p < .01; (3) Rogers versus Geri, t(35) = 4.72, p < .01. Comparisons of means for emotions: (1) Burns versus Rogers, t(34) = 2.71, p < .05; (2) Burns versus Gerl, t(39) = 4.98, p < .01; (3) Rogers versus Gerl, t(35) = 1.5l, p < .10.

also attended more to their cognitions (M = 3.9 on a five-point scale) than to their emotions (M = 1.7). This difference was statistically significant: $t(19) = 6.97$, $p < .01$.

The approach of the cognitive therapist appears to have the following *advantages:* (1) The negative emotions of depressive patients are not reinforced nor do they have to pay special attention to them; (2) when clients realize that their emotions are determined by their thoughts and appraisals, and when there is a good relationship with the therapist, they may question and partially change their appraisals. Since the conversation centers on cognitions related to the person, and on cognitions and appraisals that clients have with respect to themselves, their environment, and their future, I do not see any danger that clients will develop rationalizations for their reactions. However, the following *disadvantages* may arise: (1) Clients may not feel that they are deeply understood and accepted, since their emotions are also part of their reality. This possibility could be reduced if therapists explained to their clients why they are not attending to their emotions. (2) Therapists show their clients their mistaken cognitions and offer them alternative cognitions. This rather directive approach seems justifiable with patients who have very distorted perceptions and cognitions, but seems questionable with clients who have minor complaints.

THERAPIST EMPATHY FOR CLIENT EMOTIONS

Some psychotherapists encourage clients to be more sensitive to their emotions. In the second phase of our pilot study, we reviewed the published counseling session of a German psychotherapist (Gerl, 1982), who combines person-centered psychotherapy with Gendlin's method of focusing. Gerl's mean values on a five-point scale for empathic understanding of cognitions was 1.7; for empathic understanding of emotions it was 2.8, $t(20) = 3.77$, $p < .01$. In 65% of his utterances the therapist attended more to his client's emotions than his cognitions, and in 16%, he attended more to the cognitions than emotions. Gerl's client attended more to his emotions (M = 2.5) than his cognitions (M = 2.0), but this difference was not significant, $t(20) = 1.36$, p, n.s.

Some *advantages* for the empathic understanding of clients' emotions are as follows: clients feel they are understood, that their emotions are taken seriously and that they are accepted. This leads to increased relaxation and facilitates a good relationship with the psychotherapist. Further, the expression of emotions frequently leads to a reduction of stress, immediately during the session and for some time afterwards.

The possible *disadvantages* of this method are that
1. Cognitions that trigger these emotions may remain hidden for both psychotherapist and client. As a consequence, the client pays only little attention to them.
2. Clients with strong psychological disturbances attend predominantly to their negative emotions. This may reinforce their negative emotions. Some depressive clients quite understandably resist this attention to their emotions.
3. Some psychotherapists encourage clients to 'let *out* aggressions.' This frequently leads to a reduction of tensions. However, the emotions are not really admitted *into* consciousness. Therefore, the clients do not develop an understanding of the relationship between their emotions and their origin, the cognitions. As a result, there is rarely a lasting change.
4. Clients' intensive and predominant attention to their emotions makes them more open and sensitive to their emotions. If, however, their emotions are experienced as something frightening and disturbing and/or other persons reinforce this,

psychological disturbances in the client may be stronger after psychotherapy than before since the client is more open and vulnerable. Even though such clients may have greater sensitivity to their feelings, when faced with difficult conditions in their environment, their psychological disturbances are likely to increase. Burns (1983, p. 60) makes a similar observation: 'If you feel better after the treatment by an empathic and caring therapist your relief will only be short-lasting, if you have not definitely changed your self-assessment and your attitude to life . . . If the therapist does not show his objective viewpoint of the reliability of your self-assessment, you conclude that he agrees with you. This may indeed be the case. In the end you will feel only more incapable.'

Hammond, Hepworth, and Smith (1980, p. 155) offer a similar view: 'With emotionally overexpressive individuals . . . empathic responsiveness, especially that which focuses on the feelings presented, may indeed foster cathartic and temporary symptomatic relief, but it may also defeat the aims of therapy by permitting, reinforcing and perpetuating the client's dysfunctional mode of coping. Such clients need more to encourage their rational processes than to express their emotions freely. They might be better directed to evaluate and analyze than to experience feelings.'

I believe that intensive empathic response to the client's emotions tends to lead to a prolongation of the therapy and to less changes, particularly since most of the emotions that clients express are mainly burdening emotions.

THERAPIST EMPATHY FOR CLIENTS' COGNITIONS AND EMOTIONS

This approach is closest to the conception of Carl Rogers (1951): the psychotherapist has empathic understanding for clients' emotions and their personal meaning (cognitions). In our study the verbal behavior of Carl Rogers (1965) in his 'Gloria' interview showed that his theoretical conceptions correspond to his actual behavior. On a five-point scale, the mean values of Carl Rogers' behavior were the following: attention to cognitions 3.3, attention to emotions 2.3. These differences were statistically significant, $t(15) = 2.52$, $p < .05$. In 67% of his responses Rogers attended more to the client's cognitions than emotions, in 13% he attended equally to both, and in 21% more to emotions than cognitions. This seems to have had a parallel effect on the client's behavior. In 56% of the cases the client expressed more cognitions (M = 3.4) than emotions (M = 2.7), in 25% this was equal, and in 19% more emotions than cognitions. These differences between means were statistically significant, $t(15) = 2.11$, $p < .05$. A high level of empathic understanding for the client's cognitions *and* emotions was present in 23% of Rogers' responses. For the cognitive therapist it was 8%. For the person-centered experiential therapist it was 5%.

Carl Rogers' empathic understanding of the client's cognitions in approximately two-thirds of his comments seems to be an appropriate and helpful therapeutic approach, since it avoids the disadvantages that arise with the exclusive attention to cognitions or emotions only.

Positive consequences of the empathic understanding of clients' cognitions: (1) Since cognitions have a crucial influence over the client's emotions, changes in clients' cognitions should result in changes in their emotions. (2) Even if the problem is about internal or external conditions that cannot be changed, a change in clients' appraisal of these internal or external conditions may result in a crucial change in their emotions. (3) Continuous empathic understanding in the therapist for the client's cognitions *and* emotions seems appropriate because all emotions are addressed and connected with specific cognitions and vice versa.

Advantages of empathic understanding of clients' emotions that are connected with their cognitions: (1) When clients' feelings are deeply understood, positive relationships are facilitated with their therapists. Further, when the client feels that the therapist has really understood his or her emotions, a state of relaxation often occurs. If clients can relax while they explore their cognitions, they are less likely to become rigid, which in turn increases the possibilities for change. (2) Changes in cognitions may lead to changes in emotions, which the client may then perceive more consciously. In turn, changes in emotions may facilitate a change in cognitions. (3) As a result of the therapist's attention to both cognitions and emotions, clients are more likely to attend to both. Consequently, clients may become more conscious of instances where they wrongly attributed specific emotions to particular cognitions. (4) If the therapist addresses both cognitions *and* the appropriate emotions, there is less danger that the client will overemphasize the importance of thoughts or feeling states. (5) Because of the continuous attention to both cognitions and their appropriate emotions, there is no need for the therapist to guide the client in any way. Clients are then free to explore and examine their cognitions largely on their own. (6) The therapist's empathic understanding and acceptance of the client's emotions increases the accessibility of the corresponding cognitions. If emotions that have been denied or ignored are now admitted into consciousness, the possibility for altering the corresponding cognitions is increased. (7) Since emotions are usually more conscious and easily accessible to the client than cognitions and appraisals, the client has an identifiable framework from which to identify the related cognitions.

SUMMARY AND CONCLUSIONS

According to Lazarus' theory, emotions are closely connected with cognitions. The type of cognition has a distinct influence on the type and intensity of the emotion. The main implication of this theory is that psychotherapists should respond empathically to clients' cognitions.

Our pilot study reinforces the presumption that there are distinct differences between therapists in their attention to clients' cognitions and emotions. These differences have a significant effect on clients' attention to their own emotions and cognitions and, in my opinion, on clients' outcome as well.

As we found in our pilot study with Carl Rogers, empathy for both cognitions and emotions appears to be more beneficial than exclusive attention to cognitions or predominant attention to emotions. We don't yet know what the optimal balance is. Maybe it is 50% to each. Research may answer this question.

Some further considerations that extend beyond the scope of this article: the close connection between cognitions and emotions is not unidirectional. I have emphasized the influence of cognitions on emotions in order to understand better this connection. However, emotions also exert their effect on cognitions, a phenomenon that has, so far, been little understood. The feeling of relaxation, for example, facilitates the emergence of pleasant cognitions, and possibly changes in cognitions. On the other hand, tension produces unpleasant cognitions.

Depending on the intensity, tension may restrict a person's perception, openness to new information, and flexibility to change her or his cognitions. An important factor, here, is the person's cognitive appraisal and perception of her or his emotions. In addition, since emotions can be influenced considerably by physiological processes (e.g., brain metabolism or hormones), cognitions may also be affected. This realization led me to modify my therapeutic work: I now pay greater attention to clients' states of tension and stress, as well as possible disorders of their metabolism, and if necessary, I cooperate with other specialists who treat these disorders. Therefore, I would like to propose the following:

- Self-exploration can be regarded as a discovery of the connection between cognitions and emotions, and of any contradictions between them.
- If the therapist accepts the client's emotions and cognitions, then the client may also appraise them less negatively. This increases the possibility for change in distorted perceptions or in emotions that are attributed to faulty cognitions.
- Congruence in the psychotherapist can be helpful to the client, if the client is also able to express and explore her or his own perceptions fully while being accepted by the therapist.
- In a group, clients may learn how they appraise themselves and others. Someone who feels like a failure, when accepted by the other group members, may change his or her self-appraisal (self-cognition) and perceive him- or herself as someone worthy of acceptance. Accordingly, the person's feelings are likely to change.
- The therapist's empathic understanding and nonjudgmental acceptance of the client's emotions and cognitions may have the effect of a paradoxical intervention that facilitates changes in client's cognitions.
- Information about personal cognitions, when expressed by a group member or the therapist, may affect the client's intensive self-exploration and facilitate a change in the client's cognitions and emotions.
- We can evaluate therapeutic procedures in terms of the extent to which they help change cognitions. For example, physical activity may have a positive effect on relaxation and mood states and, consequently, may change self-cognitions.
- Meditation and Hatha Yoga, since they are nonevaluative exercises, may increase relaxation and positive physical sensations, and thereby facilitate a change of appraisals of oneself and others.
- When Gendlin's experiential focusing is considered in the light of Lazarus' theory of cognitions and emotions, it is possible that the client may sense a complex emotion (felt sense) then find the appropriate cognitions on his own or with the therapist's help. However, in person-centered therapy, where the therapist has empathic understanding for both cognitions *and* emotions this is nearly always the case.
- Changes in cognitions and appraisals with respect to oneself and the environment appear to be the key to a reduction of psychological disturbances and to positive psychological functioning.
- Since these theoretical conceptions can be tested scientifically, we can develop a more differentiated view of the psychotherapeutic process. Therefore, person-centered psychotherapy could, once again, become an integral part of scientific psychology in the universities.

AUTHOR'S NOTE

I am very grateful to Frau Silke Püngel, Hamburg, for her translation of the article into English, Jules Seeman, Ph.D., C. H. Patterson, Ph.D., and Fred Zimring, Ph.D., for their valuable comments that helped the scientific clarification of this article, and David Cain, Ph.D., for his intensive work that helped to improve the article throughout.

REFERENCES

Beck, A. T. (1976). *Cognitive therapy and the emotional disorders.* New York: International Universities Press.

Burns, D. (1983). *Angstfrei mit depressionen umgehen.* [Feeling good, the new mood therapy.] Pfungstadt: Minotaurus.

Gendlin, E. T. (1978). *Focusing.* New York: Everest House.

Gerl, W. (1982). Kombination von gesprächspsychotherapie mit focusing nach E. T. Gendlin. In J. Ho)we (Ed.), *Integratives handeln in der gesprächspsychotherapie* (pp. 221–48). Weinheim: Beltz.

Hammond, D. C., Hepworth, D. H., & Smith, V. G. (1980). *Improving therapeutic communication.* San Francisco: Jossey-Bass.

Lazarus, R. S. (1982). Thoughts on the relations between emotion and cognition. *American Psychologist, 37,* 1019–24.

Lazarus, R. S., & Folkman, S. (1984). *Stress, appraisal and coping.* New York: Springer.

Lazarus, R. S., Kanner, A. D., & Folkman, S. (1980). Emotions: A cognitive-phenomenological analysis. In R. Plutchik & H. Kellerman (Eds.), *Theories of emotion. Vol. I. Emotion: Theory, research and experience.* New York: Academic Press.

Rogers, C. R. (1951). *Client-centered therapy.* Boston: Houghton Mifflin.

Rogers, C. R. (1959). A theory of therapy, personality and interpersonal relationships, as developed in the client-centered framework. In S. Koch (Ed.), *Psychology: A study of a science, Vol. III. Formulations of the person and the social context* (pp. 184–256). New York: McGraw-Hill.

Rogers, C. R. (1965). Client-centered therapy. Film No. 1, in E. Schostrom (Ed.), *Three approaches to psychotherapy. A therapeutic interview with Gloria.* Psychological Films, 189 N. Wheeler St., Orange, California.

Rogers, C. R. (1983). *Therapeut and klient.* Frankfurt: Fischer.

Schlegel, J. (1986). *Eingehen auf konzepte oder emotionen: Eine empirische untersuchung von psychotherapeuten verschiedener orientierungen.* Diplomarbeit, Fachbereich Psychologie, Univ. Hamburg.

Self-actualization:

A reformulation

Julius Seeman   *George Peabody College of Vanderbilt University*

This article reexamines the concept of self-actualization. It starts with the premise that the current formulation is too general and too encompassing to provide a basis for empirical analysis. The article explores a formulation that is more closely and more clearly anchored in observable organismic processes. The formulation offered is a human-system model that is characterized by self-regulative open system processes. The presumed advantages of the model are that (a) it permits a comprehensive analysis of human functioning, and (b) it permits us to study with some specificity the attributes that characterize the fully functioning person. Implications for psychotherapy are considered.

The concept of self-actualization is one of the most basic and durable concepts in person-centered theory, yet in its present form it remains for me a vague and unsatisfying concept. My purpose here is to explore a formulation that amends some of the current weaknesses that I see. In pursuing this task I will deal with three topics: a critique of the current formulation, a presentation of an alternative formulation, and an exploration of the way in which a revised formulation explains variety in therapist styles.

THE CURRENT FORMULATION

First, let us look at the concept as it is generally stated. Kurt Goldstein (1939) gave the concept its early expression. In his extensive study of brain-injured persons he came to be impressed with the ways in which even deeply injured persons developed alternative pathways of cognitive and affective capacity. Goldstein concluded that 'experiences with patients teach us that we have *to assume only one drive, the drive of self-actualization . . .* ' (p. 197, italics in the original).

Twelve years later, Carl Rogers (1951) formulated a theory of personality consonant with his observations in client-centered therapy. In Proposition IV (1951, p. 487) he said: 'The organism has one basic tendency and striving — to actualize, maintain, and enhance the experiencing organism.'

This concept was central to Rogers' thinking, and he continued at subsequent times to pursue and explore its ramifications. Some of his later statements are much more tentative than the 1951 proposition quoted above. For example, as recently as 1980 (Rogers, 1980, p. 133) he said, 'I hypothesize that there is a formative directional tendency in the universe . . . This is an evolutionary tendency toward greater order, greater complexity, greater interrelatedness.' There is no indication here that Rogers saw this formative tendency as the sole developmental tendency.

First published in *Person-Centered Review,* Volume 3, Number 3, August 1988.

Maslow (1970) is also well known for his interest in self-actualization, and for his enumeration of attributes that characterize self-actualizing persons. Maslow specified a hierarchy of needs and drives, making it clear in this way that he did not regard self-actualization as the sole drive.

Patterson (1985) has reviewed aspects of the self-actualization literature and argues from his review that 'the single basic motivation of all human beings is the actualization of one's potentials' (p. 34).

A CRITIQUE OF THE FORMULATION

There are two limitations to the current formulation of self-actualization as it is generally proposed. The major limitation is that, in its present form, it is much too general and abstract to be tested empirically. Consequently, we cannot pursue inquiries into the validity or truth value of the concept. From a scientific standpoint, therefore, the concept has limited utility. It is important to determine whether there are ways to reformulate the proposition in such a manner that it is amenable to empirical testing.

David Wexler (1974) has advanced a similar critique of the concept, arguing that it is so molar and ambiguous as to make it unamenable to empirical investigation. Wexler has gone further in his critique, arguing that the theoretical grounding of client-centered therapy did not require the concept since client-centered theory rested on concepts of experiencing and information processing — that is, on current observable processes.

The second limitation of the predominant formulation of self-actualization concerns the assertion that it is the sole human drive. There are formidable problems with this assertion from the standpoint of the logic of scientific method. One would have to demonstrate, for example, that all human behavior could be explained by some variant of a self-actualization drive. I do not see this as a logical way to explain murder, suicide, rape, child abuse, war, or the extermination of total populations.

At this writing, the country of Mozambique is torn by strife, and a majority of its people are starving. There is a band of Mozambique 'rebels' reputed to be supported by the neighboring South Africa apartheid government; these rebels destroy crops and engage in wholesale murder of Mozambique people. It strikes me as utterly tortuous to explain these behaviors by any variant of a self-actualization drive. To do so would be to forfeit all meaningful use for the term. There is little logic and no need to follow such a course in order to assess the role and significance of a self-actualization drive in its own terms, as a powerful constructive force in human development.

A REVISED FORMULATION OF SELF-ACTUALIZATION

The chief function of a revised formulation is to bring it more fully within the orbit of a testable proposition, not only to facilitate an assessment of its validity but also to connect it more closely with the therapeutic process.

As I approach this task, I will start with a statement that I made some years ago (Seeman, 1956). In that statement I said:

> We may accept as a premise that the body is governed not by anarchy but by a series of biologically given developmental laws of regularities. When we refer to the drive for self-actualization, we are referring to the tendency of the organism to stay within the orbit of these developmental laws. In our complex culture the chances for intra-psychic disturbance

of these laws are manifold, and thus the need for therapy arises. In these terms we may think of therapy as the removal or assimilation of these intra-psychic disturbances and the return to organic order or integration, and the motivating force for therapy as inherent in the integrative potential itself. (p. 99)

The foregoing statement makes two points: first, it treats the concept of self-actualization not as a concept but as a metaphor for something more tangible and testable. Second, that more tangible something is 'a series of developmental laws or regularities.' Here we have a foothold for empirical analysis, for if we can ascertain the character and function of these developmental laws, we will be on the way to understanding how we develop and thrive as humans.

The first step in this task is to search for a model that will fit the data. The best fit here appears to be a human-system model because it is comprehensive enough to encompass all relevant organismic processes. What do we mean by a 'system'? Angyal (1941) has defined the term with simplicity and elegance. He refers to a system as '*unitas multiplex*,' which is to say that a system consists of a series of components or subsystems bound together by unifying processes that link every part. No part exists by itself but, rather, is so basically connected that its very definition depends on this conceptual linkage process. In this context, the human-system model permits us to address all aspects of human functioning and thus to discern with some specificity the characteristics of optimal human functioning: that is, the operational expression of self-actualization.

Two processes are at work here: communication and regulation. These are the processes that make the system work. Our human system, with its billions of cells, is a marvel of intricacy and complexity, yet each of us is a single entity. And that unitary aspect is possible because our subsystem components connect through a communication hierarchy that suffuses our entire system, going from the micro communication between individual cells, through more molar communication at the perceptual-motor level, the cognitive level, and finally on to the interpersonal level. All of these organismic levels participate in self-actualization and all may be studied empirically.

I would like first to discuss the regulative aspect of organismic functioning, an aspect that is perhaps the most central expression of personal integration. It is in the aspect of self-regulation that we find the clearest operational expression of Carl Rogers' (1963) concept of the fully functioning person. Differences in the efficacy of self-regulation also mark the points at which a person's functioning level leads to distress and the need for therapy.

Organismic regulations have engaged the attention of several theorists who have put forth detailed analyses of these regulative processes. One of the early expositions is the one developed by Cannon (1932) in his analysis of homeostatic processes.

A later contribution to regulation theory is to be found in Wiener's (1948, 1954) extensive description of cybernetics. Wiener characterized cybernetics as the science of communication and control. He pictured a system (human or physical) as one that was governed by an internal communication process that was regulative in nature — that is, the communication served the purpose of guiding and maintaining the system's proper level of functioning. Communication as regulation can be seen most clearly in the process of feedback, a process in which information loops that are an integral part of the system make it possible for an organism to remain informed about its own functioning and to take action when aberrations are detected.

The heart of this self-regulative process is the phenomenon of negative feedback. In order to understand the concept of negative feedback, the first requisite is to discard entirely the usual evaluative connotation of the term *negative,* because this evaluative connotation only gets in the way of comprehending the concept as it is used here. A useful way to illustrate the function of negative feedback is to take the mundane example of a thermostat. A thermostat regulates temperature because it has two capabilities: it has the capacity to receive feedback about the current temperature and it has the capacity to act upon that information in order to maintain the temperature within a preset norm or reference point. When the thermostat receives information that the room has gotten too cold, it goes into action to *reduce the discrepancy* between the existing temperature and the norm or reference value. This is what negative feedback is about: it is feedback that reduces deviance and keeps the functioning within normative boundaries.

Here, then, is the heart of our organismic regulative process: for all of the major subsystems in our bodies there are preset norms or reference values. They are built-in regulators of our human functioning (e.g., basal heart rate, blood pressure, respiration, and hormonal activity). When these functions deviate from the norm, signals are given and corrective action takes place through negative feedback. This model of organismic regulation leads to a working definition of self-actualization: *persons are maximally actualizing when as total human systems they are functioning at peak efficacy.*

While we do not know all of the elements that go into maximally effective functioning (e.g., genetic and constitutional factors), the model itself suggests a key element, namely, maximally complete and open communication within and between subsystems. Such communication maximizes the information that is available to the system. Wiener (1954, p. 27) supported this view in his discussion of cybernetic processes when he said 'To live effectively is to live with adequate information.' Person-centered theory has developed more extensively this concept of open communication. Rogers (1963) in particular has characterized 'openness to experience' as one of the three key hallmarks of a fully functioning person. In the context of the human-system model, such open communication likewise fulfills the key function of providing reality data to the system. The more open the communication, the more available are reality data as a basis for judgment, decision, and action. In this sense reality data serve almost literally as psychological nutrition to make possible optimal self-regulation.

There is one more step required in this description of organismic self-actualization, and that is to provide more detailed empirically based illustrations of self-actualization in action. The research literature of the past two decades is replete with such illustrations. Three such examples may suffice to indicate the point.

EMPIRICAL EVIDENCE

In a study of biofeedback, Rebecca Cooley and I (Cooley & Seeman, 1979) hypothesized that highly integrated persons would make maximal use of biofeedback information to regulate their peripheral skin temperature. The task given to each person was to increase his or her skin temperature. After obtaining baseline skin temperature, we provided first a no-feedback condition and then a feedback condition in which each person received continuous auditory information as to changes in skin temperature. According to the human-system model that I have described earlier in this article, two behavioral subsystems, the cognitive and the physiological, are engaged in information exchange. The model proposes that efficacy in information utilization would result in the capacity to alter skin temperature, and that effective human systems would be able to respond in that way. We defined 'effective human systems' through the use of a self-concept scale

(Fitts, 1965), which has repeatedly shown itself to be a valid indicator of high-functioning persons. We divided the group at the median on the self-concept measure to create a high group and nonhigh group.

What we found was that the high group was able to use the feedback information to increase their skin temperature while the nonhigh group showed no temperature change. This result is congruent with the human-system model, which asserts that efficacy in information utilization is a key variable in personal effectiveness.

A second study similarly shows differences in information utilization related to personal effectiveness (Seeman, 1966). The study was a concept formation study, conducted with college women. Each participant was given the following instructions: 'Think of three persons that you know well. Now state all of the ways in which two of these persons are similar to each other and different from the third person.' Here the task is a cognitive challenge, requiring the person to generate concepts that will differentiate persons whom she knows. The results of the study were in accord with the model: when the group was divided at the median in personal integration on the basis of their self-descriptions, the high group was shown to have generated more than twice as many constructs to describe their friends. What this result suggests is that persons relatively high in personal integration have a richer and more complex way of understanding and describing their interpersonal world. The result is also congruent with an openness-to-experience explanation.

The third study, by Swan (1970), illustrates the proposition that high-functioning persons have the capacity for effective interpersonal behavior. More specifically, Swan hypothesized that in an intensive encounter group the behavior of high-functioning persons would be recognizable in terms of Rogers' (1957) 'three necessary and sufficient conditions of therapeutic personality change': empathy, unconditional positive regard, and congruence. Swan's premise here was that these qualities were not limited to psychotherapy but were more general qualities of effective interpersonal functioning.

Swan took advantage of the fact that many prior studies had shown that an affirmative concept of self was a central process related to personal integration in general. He therefore used high self-concept scores as an index of high functioning. His sample consisted of 17 persons who had enrolled for a two-week basic encounter group experience. On the last day of the group, Swan secured peer ratings of the three conditions for all of the group. He divided the group at the median on the basis of the self-concept scores. The group functioning higher according to this measure received significantly higher ratings on empathy, unconditional positive regard, and congruence than was the case for the lower group. We thus note that from two separate perspectives of observation — phenomenological and interpersonal — we can identify high-functioning, self-actualizing persons.

The foregoing three examples serve to illustrate the possibilities of the human-system model in discerning empirically the characteristics of self-actualizing persons. Following this model, we may observe at any organismic level the kinds of subsystem functioning that are maximally effective.

APPLICATIONS TO THEORY

The final section of this article explores the application of the human-system model to psychotherapy. One of the goals in writing this article was to define self-actualization in ways that bring the model closer to observable variables in person-centered theory. One way to implement this goal is to see how well the model helps to explain the therapeutic process. In effect, the model identifies the characteristics of an open system, and postulates that self-actualization involves the development of maximal information exchange within the system (including interpersonal exchange). Does this postulate fit the facts of the therapy process? In my view this is the common thread that unifies the various emphases in the person-centered approach.

If, for example, we examine the emphasis that Carl Rogers has brought to the therapy process, we note that he too was enhancing information flow. First of all, he was freeing the person to experience more fully the internal organismic awareness that was dimly felt and hardly understood. Rogers' intent listening, and his clarifying responses, helped the client to make sense of these phenomena. In other words, Rogers' procedures were linking multilevel sources of information and making them available in an integrated and usable way, a process that I have referred to as 'experiencing with meaning.'

If we analyze Gendlin's emphasis on focusing (e.g., Gendlin, 1978) we note that his theory centers on enhancing the person's awareness of bodily processes and on linking them with cognitions about these precognitive signals. Gendlin's whole theory argues that we as humans have information not only in our heads but throughout our bodies, and his method is designed to make that information available as a basis for self-understanding and action.

A third illustration of a person-centered emphasis can be noted in Godfrey Barrett-Lennard's writings on the interpersonal relationship in therapy (e.g., Barrett-Lennard, 1984). He has long been interested in the connection between what he has termed 'interactive systems and inner experience' (1984, p. 222). With respect to the 'interactive systems' he has elaborated in considerable detail the differential phenomenological meanings of different interpersonal combinations (e.g., dyads, triads, and quartets). Barrett-Lennard has argued that each of these combinations represents distinctive interpersonal processes and therefore represents differential dimensions of inner experience. It follows that therapist sensitivity to these differences can contribute to deeper self-understanding by the client. Here, too, we note that explanations of personal experience are sought through a study of the multilevel subsystems that constitute the human system.

A final illustration of the diverse formulations that have evolved in the person-centered approach is one put forth by Laura Rice (e.g., Rice, 1984). One of her central premises is that 'a successful client-centered therapy involves the resolution of a series of cognitive-affective reprocessing tasks' (p. 183). The governing phrase here is 'cognitive-affective reprocessing,' a phrase that tells us that multiple subsystems are activated in the service of therapeutic change. In this process, new information is brought to bear and channels of communication are opened between behavioral subsystems.

In closing this article, I want to say a personal word about the differences in therapeutic approach that I have just described. It has been my observation that the varied approaches to therapy that have evolved within the person-centered framework have sometimes engendered tension and conflict, a sense that the proper boundaries of the person-centered philosophy have been breached. It is my belief that the human-system theory that I have propounded here leads to an understanding of these differences and provides alternative ways to view their contribution. For it is the case that the human system consists of multiple subsystems, all connected and unified. Given this situation, we may be able to enter the human system in any of a number of ways and at any of a number of points, and rest assured that the underlying unity of the systems will lead to central processes within the person. The multiplicity of our own experiences leads quite naturally to variation in our own frames of reference and what we perceive to be core processes within the person. Thus it is equally natural for us to place emphasis in different places.

My observation here is in no way intended to suggest that any approach will work, nor that just any approach fits within the framework of person-centered theory. Rather, the point is to recognize the underlying unity of the human system, and to recognize the varied ways in which we may make contact with that system. Experience suggests that so long as we remain in meaningful contact, our clients' lawful organismic processes are quite likely to take them to their own center.

REFERENCES

Angyal, A. (1941). *Foundations for a science of personality.* New York: Commonwealth Fund.

Bandura, A. (1982). Self-efficacy mechanism in human agency. *American Psychologist, 37,* 112–47.

Barrett-Lennard, G. T. (1984). The world of family relationships: A person-centered systems view. In R. F. Levant & J. M. Shlien (Eds.), *Client-centered therapy and the person-centered approach.* New York: Praeger.

Cannon, W. B. (1932). *The wisdom of the body.* New York: Norton.

Cooley, R. S., & Seeman, J. (1979). Personality integration and social schemata. *Journal of Personality, 47,* 228–304.

Dismukes, R. F. (1979). New concepts of molecular communication among neurons. *Behavioral and Brain Sciences, 2,* 409–48.

Fitts, W. H. (1965). *The Tennessee self-concept scale manual.* Los Angeles: Western Psychological Services.

Gendlin, E. T. (1978). *Focusing.* New York: Everest House.

Goldstein, K. (1939). *The organism.* New York: American Book Co.

Maslow, A. H. (1970). *Motivation and personality.* New York: Harper.

Patterson, C. H. (1985). *The therapeutic relationship: Foundations for an eclectic psychotherapy.* Monterey, CA: Brooks/Cole.

Rice, L. N. (1984). Client tasks in client-centered therapy. In R. F. Levant & J. M. Shlien (Eds.), *Client-centered therapy and the person-centered approach.* New York: Praeger.

Richard, W. C. (1971). An approach to the study of personality integration and autonomic responsivity. *Journal of Consulting and Clinical Psychology, 36,* 298.

Rogers, C. R. (1951). *Client-centered therapy.* New York: Houghton Mifflin.

Rogers, C. R. (1957). The necessary and sufficient conditions of therapeutic personality change. *Journal of Consulting Psychology, 21,* 95–103.

Rogers, C. R. (1963). The concept of the fully functioning person. *Psychotherapy: Theory, Research, and Practice, 1,* 17–26.

Rogers, C. R. (1980). *A way of being.* Boston: Houghton Mifflin.

Seeman, J. (1956). Client-centered therapy. In D. Brower & L. Abt (Eds.), *Progress in clinical psychology.* New York: Grune & Stratton.

Seeman, J. (1966). Personality integration in college women. *Journal of Personality and Social Psychology, 4,* 91–3.

Sherrington, C. S. (1906). *The integrative action of the nervous system.* New Haven, CT: Yale University Press.

Swan, A. C. (1970). Personality integration and perceived behavior in a sensitivity training group. Unpublished doctoral dissertation, George Peabody College.

Wexler, D. A. (1974). A cognitive theory of experiencing, self-actualization, and therapeutic process. In D. A. Wexler & L. N. Rice (Eds.), *Innovations in client-centered therapy.* New York: Wiley Interscience.

Wiener, N. (1948). *Cybernetics: Control and communication in man and the machine.* Cambridge: MIT Press.

Wiener, N. (1954). *The human use of human beings.* New York: Avon.

Listening

Godfrey T. Barrett-Lennard   *Center for Studies in Human Relations*

This article begins by discriminating seven general properties of listening as it occurs in a wide range of life situations. Each of these is presented as a briefly stated proposition, which is then elaborated and discussed illustratively. The fruits of this first step establish a distinctive context for the ensuing focus on sensitive, emphatic listening, considered as a special case within the broader framework. Effects of sensitive listening, in particular, are then examined, under four headings: personal healing and growth, relationship enrichment, tension reduction and problem solving, and knowledge advancement. The article seeks to make careful distinctions and weave a whole cloth of meaning that is primarily descriptive but implicitly conceptual as well.

Listening to others is a universal human activity. The extent of our practice might suggest that little could be said on the topic that is not already a part of common human experience, or of well-established knowledge. Even accepting that human problems typically involve disturbed relationships and faulty communication, a focus on listening might seem too simple or elementary to be useful as we work to understand and resolve these problems. I think otherwise. It is my own view that we get into and out of difficulties with each other to a large extent by the way we listen and by what we hear, mishear, and fail to hear. Further, the topic is far from simple. It is many-sided and a continuing challenge to our understanding.

It may help to clarify my terms a little at this point. In ordinary language, listening to another person refers essentially to the process of attending to his or her communication. While at times a passive response, listening clearly can also be very active, as we tune into and actually engage with the other's felt experience and meaning. In active listening, we may have all our 'antennae' out, with the concern and aim of receiving the whole range of signals the other is using, reading the other's central meaning, sensing other's feeling, and being in touch with the *other's* listening and response to us. Hearing is the product of our listening. It may include not only what the other is pointing to—the overt, content message—but where the other is pointing from—their feelings, attitude, outlook.

Let me now point to the overall scope of the ideas I wish to share. My article has three main parts. The first part is a fresh exploration of properties of listening generally, in its everyday diversity. This provides a foundation from which to approach the second focus—a description of sensitive or empathic listening as a special kind within the broader framework. In the last part, I will draw various threads together and share my perspective on the wide-ranging effects of sensitive listening.

First published in *Person-Centered Review,* Volume 3, Number 4, November 1988.

GENERAL PROPERTIES OF LISTENING

To speak exhaustively about the general nature of listening is quite beyond my present goal. However, it does seem instructive to ask the question, 'What can be said about listening that is true generally? What properties apply over a very wide range of contexts, purposes, and sensitivity in listening?' In careful outline, the seven such properties that have occurred to me are as follows:

1. *Listening is always selective and incomplete in relation to the potential meanings in the speaker's expression.* Yes, for practical purposes, I do mean 'always.' Either we do not pick up all of the verbal and nonverbal communication signals or we do not read and resonate to these signals in a manner that allows their whole spectrum of meaning to come alive in us. Rarely, if ever, does this meaning have only one element. Typically, it includes messages on more than one level that unfold as we tune in to them. Even where it is produced spontaneously and quickly the meaning expressed results from a complex process in a unique individual communicating in a particular situation. It is almost a truism that different listeners hear different specific messages and overtones of meaning when confronted with the same total expression. Thus the message sent is not the same as the message received. The two may be close, different but overlapping, far apart or even opposite.

2. *Qualities of the listener and the relationship or context, as well as the signals sent, govern what is heard.* More specifically, what we hear is conditioned by our own interests, by what we want at the time, our expectations in the situation, our own fears or conflicts, and by other conditions that stem from our general view of the speaker and the association between us. Our response is an outcome of experience in many communication situations moderated or shaped by the ambience and personal meaning of this relationship situation, even by the particular occasion or interplay of contexts. Let me give a partial illustration.

In a classroom teaching situation, different intentions, expectations, attitudes, and personal needs may operate, for any one of us, than those that would apply in our family situation. If our own children show, in a family context, that they are feeling overlooked, unhappy, or humiliated, we are quite likely to catch the gist of their felt message. In a classroom, we may very easily overlook such messages from children, or choose to ignore them. Sometimes we confuse another person because we pick up what they are telling us at one time but completely fail to register the same message on another occasion. Underlying this discrepancy is the influence of context on what we are open to, and on the differing ways we read the 'same' signals.

3. *We seldom if ever distinguish or express all that registers in us while exposed to another's communication.* I think that we do register at some level more than comes to mind consciously, and certainly more than we express. In the moment of encounter with another person we seldom notice, integrate, and have at the tip of our tongue all the impressions we are getting from that person. Sometimes, a strong sense of what the other person was really conveying comes to us later, after the interchange. For example, we might say, as we reflect afterwards, '*That* was what he was trying to tell me.' Or we might recognize a person's mood that we hadn't formulated to ourselves at the time. Without realizing it, we had registered information or cues that took shape afterwards to give us a powerful impression of the meaning of the other person's communication or experience.

In practice, often we are unable to lift the full meaning from what we do notice or recall. We might sense that there is something unmanageable or threatening there, while protecting ourselves from having to deal with it. Or we might just be preoccupied with some other ongoing activity and concern that doesn't leave room at the time for full

151

attention to what the other person is expressing. Or we may have a rather fixed view of that person, which permits some meanings to surface but not others. In these and countless other ways, information can be passed over or not processed. Our response typically reflects only part of what we have in some sense heard. Thus a fuller awareness of another's experience and meaning than we realize and articulate is within our reach.

4. *What we hear affects and can profoundly influence the other person's further communication.* Usually, we give some clues to the other person about what it is we are hearing and the extent to which we have taken in and heard what was meant. Our response may also add to the other's impression of what we generally listen to, listen for, and hear. Frequently, when a person is trying to communicate something, one tunes in to the intellectual content only (what the person is pointing to) and misses the person's feelings, or one may fail to sense the other's personal involvement with his or her ideas. If one disagrees with the other, without this awareness (perhaps only meaning to dispute the expressed idea or reasoning), the other person feels rejected and not fully heard. If, on the other hand, one first acknowledges one's understanding of the other's meaning and the other's attachment to this meaning one may then place one's differing view beside the other's with helpful effect.

5. *To a point, we cannot help but listen. It is not possible to hear nothing while exposed to another person's communication.* It is often difficult to tune in accurately but is awfully hard, as well, to tune out totally, *completely* ignoring the other person's signals and message. We may try to do this, perhaps to avoid a (perceived) demand with which we feel we cannot cope at the time, or because we want to focus our attention elsewhere. However, I think that such attempts to avoid receiving another individual's messages only partially shield us from them. The other person tries harder to get through or makes stronger or more persistent demands on our attention. He or she may, for example, resort to nonverbal actions that sharply express feelings of hurt, rejection, or resentment. When we *try* hard to tune out or evade the other's communications, we are really still responding to them, and conveying a message. Someone has said, wisely, that we cannot *not* communicate. If we are in any kind of encounter with another person, what we don't do as well as what we do *will have meanings to that person.* Thus it is also true that one 'cannot not listen' in any first-hand encounter, even if one's impressions are fragmentary, or grossly inaccurate.

6. *Listening in everyday interchange is, as a rule, accompanied by an evaluative reaction to what is heard.* Often, we attend to the other with the conscious purpose to assess, compare, or judge. Even if this is not a conscious aim, rarely is our response in a listening situation without elements of approval-disapproval, agreement-disagreement, distaste or appreciation. Typically, we are not simply registering what the other conveys, but sifting, judging, translating, labeling, or refashioning the other's communication in a way that says as much about ourselves as about the other's meaning. To the extent that we openly receive and allow the other's melody to play in us before forming an opinion of it, there is the possibility of enrichment—on the other's part, one's own, and in the relationship.

7. *People* need *to hear others and to be heard by them.* We need the effects of hearing other people as well as the fruits of their hearing us. Although some of us can survive in relative isolation, most of us hunger for connection with our own kind, and depend on being in close or intimate contact with at least one other person (Barrett-Lennard, 1986a). Basic to such connection and close contact is a sense of being known and experiencing companionship in one's own right; and of reaching out and being there for the other, with awareness of the other. Such mutual, informed relationships cannot develop without listening, hearing, and being heard.

This completes my outline of listening in general. As another bridge to the thought that follows, I wish to share excerpts from a talk by Carl Rogers (1965b), given in Australia. These passages are as transcribed from the live recording.[1]

> The first simple feeling that I want to share with you is my enjoyment when I can really hear someone. I guess perhaps this is telling a long-standing characteristic of mine. I can remember, even in my very early school days, a child would ask the teacher a question and the teacher would give a perfectly good answer to a question that hadn't been asked — a kind of miscommunication that is so extremely frequent. A feeling of pain and distress would always strike me in that situation. My reaction was: 'But you didn't *hear* him.' I felt a kind of childish despair at the failure of communication that is so very common.
>
> I think I know why I'm satisfied to hear someone. When I can really hear someone it puts me closely in touch with him. It enriches my life. It's also true that it's through hearing people that I have learned all that I know about individuals, about personalities, about inter-personal relationships. Then, there is another peculiar satisfaction — I'm not sure I can communicate it — but when I really hear someone there is something in it of listening to the music of the spheres, if that doesn't seem too romantic to you. Beyond the immediate message of the person, no matter what that might be, there is the universal and the general. It is hidden in all the personal communications that I really hear. There seem to be orderly psychological laws, aspects of the awesome order that we find in the universe as a whole. So there is both the satisfaction of hearing *this* person, and also the satisfaction of feeling ourselves in some sort of touch with what is universally true. (Rogers, 1965b)

Rogers' eloquent communication continued and, while speaking of the kind of listening he most valued, he recounted the following episode:

> Not long ago, a friend called me long distance on the telephone about a certain matter. We concluded the conversation and I hung up the phone. Then, and only then, did the tone of voice really hit me. I said to myself that behind the subject matter we were discussing there seemed to be a note of distress or discouragement or even despair, which had nothing to do with the matter at hand. I felt this so sharply that I wrote him a letter saying to this effect: 'I may be all wrong in what I am going to say and if so you can toss this letter in the waste basket, but to me after I'd hung up the phone it sounded as though you had been in real distress and pain.' And then I attempted to share with him some of my own feelings about him and about this situation in ways that I hoped might be helpful. I sent off the letter with some real qualms, thinking that I might have been ridiculously mistaken. I very quickly received a reply. He was extremely grateful that someone had heard him. I'd been quite correct in hearing his tone of voice and I felt pleased within myself that I had been able to do so and hence make possible a real communication and a deeper relationship. So very often, as in this instance, the words convey one message and the tone of voice conveys a sharply different one; and this time I had been able to hear both. (Rogers, 1965b; see also Rogers, 1980)

While the quality of listening exemplified in this cited episode is unusual, it is not outside the framework I have described so far. Within this broad framework, it is a special kind that I will simply call sensitive listening. I could alternatively have used the term empathic listening — as implied in my next heading.

---

1. I was present at Rogers' talk, and had played a part in organizing it. The actual presentation, to a large and responsive audience, was audio tape recorded — a recording that I still have. The passages quoted here are taken from excerpts used in my own talk from which this article grew.

SENSITIVE OR EMPATHETIC LISTENING

Sensitive listening refers broadly to listening in which individuals feel that their communication — and thus potentially their inner self — is heard and understood. Such listening is not only directed to the other's intended verbal messages but also, as Rogers illustrates, to messages that come in other ways, perhaps without clear awareness on the sender's part. In sensitive listening, one is receptive to the full spectrum of the other's experience. The other person feels that you have tuned in, that you have indeed heard him or her, perhaps that you may almost know at this moment how the other's world is. Generally this is also accompanied by a feeling of being prized or accepted and trusted. This is so because this particular kind of listening, in its full expression, is rare and implies that the listener is not standing apart but is close to the point of touching the other's understanding.

In a related vein, sensitive listening implies giving others an opportunity to be heard on their own terms. It reflects an openness to receiving and responding to the internal frame of reference of the other person. Mostly, I believe we want to be heard in the full depth of our experience and meaning, not only in some narrow aspect of our awareness. At best, the listener can pick up and reverberate to any level of communication, and to any content in the other's experience and meaning.

If one can be this way with another individual, in a sustained manner, then it isn't long before the other is likely to begin to disclose aspects of his or her experience that are seldom expressed. And, if the helping relationship is a continuous one, many aspects of the person's inner world, which were previously not in clear consciousness, can now be seen and shared. This, of course, also happens outside a formal helping situation, and is one of the factors that enable people to form deep relationships with each other.

In sensitive listening, judgment of the other person is absent or largely suspended. One is not listening to gain advantage for oneself, or with any ulterior aim. One is listening from genuine interest, from desire to be in contact with the other, and to know the *other's* reality. The listener does not presume that this reality is fixed and immutable but rather is aware that experience and meaning are living processes that move and change in the flow of open sharing. Thus the deepest listening does not come from conscious and deliberate intention to bring about change in the other. Such change, when it occurs, is a natural by-product of a large process of self and interpersonal engagement in which deeply perceptive listening is a crucial element.

Listening beyond the other's words means hearing the literal content of those words but, *in addition,* responding to the other's manner of expression, gestures, and to the other nuances interwoven in the total communication. With such broad and deep listening, we may pick up diverse or conflicting messages, as though from different voices in the other person. If, when we hear the more submerged voice, we neglect the other's spoken words, our listening will have become selective in another way and, to that extent, insensitive. Sometimes, what we hear or sense may go beyond what we feel the other person could bear to have acknowledged. It is as though our sensitivity has made us an intruder in the other's private world. However, if we truly have heard the other, and are not ill at ease from the impact, then usually it is safe and helpful to let the other know what we are aware of — especially if we then continue to listen sensitively.

I would like to quote from another article of mine, written many years ago. In the extract that follows, I am speaking of helping relationships and discussing the crucial part that empathic understanding plays. Such understanding flows from sensitive listening.

The helping person . . . recognizes or senses what is real and meaningful to the other at any given time. He cares to know how the other person sees things, how he feels about himself, what his own subjective experience is in regard to any aspect of his life process. He is able to sense or infer the . . . feelings and meanings underlying the other's outward communication. In a certain real sense the other person's experience becomes alive in him also, although he does not confuse feelings and perceptions originating in the other with those that originate in himself. (Barrett-Lennard, 1965, pp. 1–2)

It is challenging and difficult to maintain a clear distinction between meanings originating in oneself and in the other person. Our concern to avoid such confusion requires the attitude that our 'understanding' is always open to correction and change. Expression of this attitude by checking our sense of the other's meaning with the other is a basic, frequent element in sensitive listening.

EFFECTS OF SENSITIVE LISTENING

This final section of my paper offers a distillation of four kinds of outcomes of sensitive listening. All of these effects are manifestations of one larger consequence. Sensitive listening fosters knowing. It helps to uncover what is partially hidden and to free experiencing and extend consciousness. It brings about fuller contact and deeper relationships between the listener and the person heard. It can open and enhance communication between groups, and facilitate new understanding of human nature. Let me elaborate.

1. Personal healing and growth. Sensitive, nonjudgmental, empathic listening, which leads to the experience of being deeply understood, helps to open inner channels and serves as a powerful bridge to others. By being clearly and distinctly heard around some acute but unclear concern, we hear or see ourselves more clearly, and often with less fear. Inner divisions or boundaries tend to dissolve, doors we may have shut on some of our experience begin to open. We may feel freer, more whole, released from some bondage or drain that had been sapping us. We realize we are not alone at the moment of understanding and are freshly aware of what this is like. If this understanding recurs, our sharing can develop a self-propelling quality.

Just the fact that our experience has made sense to someone else can help it to make sense to us. The experience of acceptance and understanding, especially during relatively unguarded communication, lessens our need to be on guard. Being listened to and heard, particularly in the context of struggle and felt limitation, helps to validate and empower us. We see ourselves in the other's mirror and know our humanity and that we are not alone. We see that our image is many-sided and changing and feel a movement toward new possibilities. Implicit is an element of healing or growth.

Growth on the part of the *listener* can also flow from sensitive listening. In a valuable earlier paper, Rogers and Farson (1957, p. 4) speak to this point in the following vein:

Not the least important result of [active, sensitive] listening is that change takes place within the listener himself. Besides the fact that listening provides more information than any other activity, it builds deep, positive relationships and tends to alter constructively the attitudes of the listener. Listening is a growth experience.

The listener need not be seeking any intrinsic gain. It is a by-product, a 'bonus' in the case of a professional helper. Sensitive listening and contact with the inner life of others is potentially deeply affirming and deeply challenging to any of us, as fellow humans on our own personal journeys. To give nourishment that is freeing to the other can nourish and free us, too. We see ourselves in the other's depth while also discovering a consciousness distinct from our own—which moves as we respond. Our relationship acquires a life and quality that act on us both. To listen and understand deeply is often to walk where we have never been.

2. Relationship enrichment. Sensitive listening has a major role in the quality and prospects of an established relationship. Where it falls within the repertoire of both members of a twosome—or each person in a family or other small unit—there is potential for a relationship that is enhancing to the selfhood of each member. Such qualities as respect and caring are enriched, perhaps even made possible, by two-way listening. Where this reciprocal listening is occurring, the *dyad* is effectively listening to itself. Besides being directly healthful or integrative, such capacity for inner listening gives promise of openness and sensitivity to others.

Sensitive listening can be difficult or impossible to sustain in a relationship where participants have felt deeply hurt or where trust is low. Sometimes, however, a third person who listens very well in interaction with both people can reverse the downhill spiral and open the way for each participant to take in what the other is experiencing, and thereby show that this awareness matters to each. I do not mean to suggest that listening is a panacea in distressed relationships, for it is part of a larger matrix in which the component elements are interdependent. However, if changes in quality of listening do come about, this can work like a motor in propelling communication forward.

3. Tension reduction and problem solving. Personal relationships may deteriorate to the point where any improvement hinges on the contribution of a third party: an informally skilled person or a professional helper. The helper's capacity to hear deeply each person and appreciate his or her reality is likely to be crucial in producing change in the quality of listening in distressed relationships. So, too, with groups in conflict. As Carl Rogers (1965a, p. 7) has pointed out, such opposing groups typically each hold two beliefs: 'I am right and you are wrong,' and 'I am good and you are bad.' These attitudes can be stated in many ways. Rogers (1965a, p. 8) offers the following extended expression:

> I am correct and accurate and sound in my view of the situation, my perception of its elements, my interpretation of its meaning. My view is the right and true one. You are unfortunately mistaken and inaccurate in your view of the situation and in your analysis of what it means. Your view is false and wrong, yet you stubbornly hold to it.
>
> I am honest and straightforward and fundamentally good in my approach to our relationship and its problems. Unfortunately, you are none of these things. You are essentially bad and evil and untrustworthy in your approach to the whole situation. My motives are good. Yours are not.

I will presume that the opponents can agree to accept help in trying to get through such an impasse and will sketch the ensuing process in briefest terms. First, the consultant-helper listens very closely to individuals on each side, genuinely taking their concerns and views most seriously. The helper demonstrates that this can happen, that no damage results, and that this step begins to diminish threat. Then, step by step, with the helper's determined and perceptive listening the antagonists each come to see the other's concerns and 'character' in a different light. Finally, with assistance and with renewed capacity to hear each other, the parties can converse first-hand. Assuming this is effective, tensions will have been sharply reduced, and the improving communication will have a self-perpetuating quality. Such change could not take place without effective listening playing a vital role.

4. Knowledge advancement. A different effect of sensitive listening is that it can be a fertile route to knowledge of human nature, especially the nature of experiencing. Gaining knowledge of how humans, as a species, experience themselves and others, and make sense of their world, has long been of interest in varied fields of study. As is the case of basic knowledge in other fields, many particular applications can flow from such enlightenment about our essential nature. Broad areas of application include the fields of personal helping, interpersonal and group relations, *and* communications fields. Most of what we know stems from observing and listening. The latter *can* be a kind of closed circuit listening, attuned only to predetermined signals over a limited range, and similarly limited to a band of meanings the listener determines in advance. Such listening can test hypotheses but scarcely generate them. We can't learn anything new and unexpected from it. Open, sensitive listening, on the other hand, releases in-depth communication and contact, minimizes 'filtering' and promotes new vision, new hypotheses, and expanded knowledge.

The passage from Rogers' talk, already cited, includes his eloquent testimony on the issue of knowledge-via-listening: 'It's also true that it is through hearing people that I have learned all that I know . . . about interpersonal relationships,' and 'there is both the satisfaction of hearing *this* person and also the satisfaction of finding ourselves in some sort of touch with what is universally true.' Note the phrase 'some sort of touch.' Our best generalizations are not cast in stone but held, perhaps, as first approximations of some larger truth, new dimensions of which we perceive as we work to uncover it and push out the boundaries of what is known. It is in this spirit that I mean to offer the observations and thoughts presented here.

CONCLUSIONS

These concluding remarks are not a literal summary but a summing up, with added brush-strokes of meaning. I began by advancing a number of general propositions in regard to listening. Some of these propositions would justify more extended discussion and teasing out of component meanings. No doubt, additional generalizations could be advanced, also. Those presented may warrant further refinement, especially in light of research yet to come. My immediate aim, however, relates less to research and more to the hope that what I have advanced may speak to readers in directly useful ways. It will be a bonus if ideas have been added here that help to spark fresh inquiry into the nature of listening, either in everyday communication or helping relationships.[2]

My intention, in the second part of the article, was to introduce sensitive listening as a special case within the broader framework of listening in general. Looking back now, however, I wonder whether this special listening has been made to seem so unlike the usual variety, so exceptional and powerful, that it stands apart as altogether different in kind. My perspective may become clearer in light of one or two further points. With less

---

2. I am pleased to have been able to discuss sensitive listening without drawing much on the language of empathy in its more specialized aspects. This feature reminds me of the remark of a therapy client, dating back to my own internship days. The client told me *how* he could tell that I had understood him. The most compelling evidence to him was that of hearing his exact meaning *expressed in completely different words than he had used.* My words, here, also seem to me to rely substantially on fresh arrangement and language for the illumination I have attempted. The research-interested reader will find my previous work on empathy partly contained and fully referenced in Barrett-Lennard, 1986b.

than total understanding and knowing of each other, a certain aloneness by nature, is a price we pay for individuality and complexity of being. Sensitive listening brings us in contact despite our uniqueness. Far from leading us to become copies of one another, it works to protect our own individuality. Each of us has his or her continual flow of experience, including that which comes from memory and reflection. We are always in motion in some way, changing even as we learn and conserve. There is little wonder that listening, at its best, results in two, or more, pathways crossing in an encounter of understanding; but that it cannot connect these pathways in a flawless zippered seam of continuous mutual knowing.

In relation to my third and last focus, knowledge of effects can contribute to the importance we place on sensitive listening and, in this indirect sense, help give rise to it. It is part of my thesis, however, that *in action* listening cannot simply be a means to a calculated end and at the same time be sensitive. The effects I have spoken of are outcomes of such listening; they can advance it but not produce it. Listening takes place in a many-sided context, of interest and aim, of relationship, of opportunity and capacity. Such factors vitally influence what is heard and the ensuing communication. Communication runs deaf without the ears of listening, and has hearing to the degree that the listening is sensitive. An authentic process of sensitive listening is deeply absorbing for its own sake. This is so, in the final analysis, because it is satisfying to hear, to know, and to be in human contact.

AUTHOR'S NOTE

This article had its origins in an invited talk to the Kitchener-Waterloo System Guidance Workshop, given not long after I joined the faculty of the University of Waterloo in 1966. A transcription of the talk lay in my files for many years and was the point of departure for the rewritten and much developed version presented here. Carl Rogers and I had been in frequent and close contact at the time of my original talk. The references to his work from that period continue to fit and also grace this article, which I now dedicate to his memory. (My address, for reprints or feedback, is P.O. Box 144, West Perth, W.A., Australia 6005.)

REFERENCES

Barrett-Lennard, G. T. (1965). Significant aspects of a helping relationship. *Mental Hygiene, 47,* 223–7; and *Canada's Mental Health,* Supplement No. 47, July/August, 1965.

Barrett-Lennard, G. T. (1986a). On loneliness. *Ceshur Connection, 1*(2&3), 3–8.

Barrett-Lennard, G. T. (1986b). The Relationship Inventory now: Issues and advances in theory, method and use. In L. S. Greenberg & W. M. Pinsof (Eds.), *The psychotherapeutic process: A research handbook* (pp. 439–76). New York: Guilford.

Rogers, C. R. (1965a). Dealing with psychological tensions. *Journal of Applied Behavioral Science, 1*(1), 6–24.

Rogers, C. R. (1965b). Audio-recorded address given at the University of New South Wales, Sydney, January 18th.

Rogers, C. R. (1980). Experiences in communication. In C. R. Rogers, *A way of being* (pp. 5–26). Boston: Houghton Mifflin. (See also 'Empathic: An unappreciated way of being,' pp. 137–63 in this volume.)

Rogers, C. R. & Farson, R. E. (1957). *Active listening.* University of Chicago: Industrial Relations Center (and, University Library).

What is Dialogic Communication?
Friedman's contribution and clarification

Ronald C. Arnett *Manchester College*

This article examines two major approaches to dialogic communication: (1) the work of Carl Rogers, and (2) the contribution of Martin Buber. It critiques and clarifies the similarities and differences in the respective approaches. The work of Maurice Friedman is used as the foundation for the examination of the scope of the term *dialogue* and the conceptual contributions made by Rogers and Buber toward an understanding of dialogic communication.

Do you mean what you say? Do you say what you mean? Such guidelines are necessary for accurate and ethical communication in everyday discourse, including discussion of theory about human behavior. In a dialogue with Carl Rogers, Martin Buber (1965) stated that not all relational communication could be referred to as 'dialogue' (pp. 180–4). The question this articles explores is, if Buber and Rogers can disagree about what constitutes dialogue, how can we fully understand what the notion means?

The purpose of this article is to reveal (1) how some practitioners of Buber's and Rogers' theories conceptualize their respective understandings of dialogue very differently, (2) how this confusion of what constitutes dialogue has limited scholarship in the area, and (3) how Maurice Friedman's recent work moves beyond this unnecessary deadlock.

INTERPRETATIONS AT VARIANCE

In order to describe the significance of differing interpretations of dialogue attributed to Buber and Rogers, I provide below a brief summary of a debate over this issue between Anderson (1982) and myself (Arnett, 1981, 1982). The work of Anderson and myself illustrates the need for Friedman's clarification of 'What is dialogue?' In essence, this articles critiques my own position and that of Anderson as limited; Friedman's recent work clarifies and lends sophistication to the issue.

The Anderson-Arnett article exchange in 1981 and 1982 concerning what constitutes dialogic communication made visible a more widely conceptual confusion, evident in Ayres' (1984) review of interpersonal communication literature in the *Western Journal of Speech Communication,* a 1983 symposium on empathy (Anderson, 1984), and Ayres' comments on the controversy at the 1986 Speech Communication Association convention in Chicago. In addition, Ayres' (1984) review of interpersonal communication literature claimed that dialogic communication has begun to wane in significance (pp. 421–2). This claim is verified by the fact that no major article on dialogic communication has been published in a national or regional communication journal since 1982 and no major

---

First published in *Person-Centered Review,* Volume 4, Number 1, February 1989.

textbook currently assumes this approach, with the exception of Stewart's *Bridges Not Walls: A Book About Interpersonal Communication,* now in its fourth edition (1986), and my own *Communication and Community: Implications of Martin Buber's Dialogue* (Arnett, 1986).

The confusion over what actually constitutes dialogue is illustrated by two general areas of disagreement between Anderson and myself. First, how many approaches to dialogue exist? Anderson (1982) spoke of one large generic category called *dialogue:*

> The works of Buber, Friedman, Maslow, and Rogers, each with its unique emphases, are conceptually supportive in many more ways than they are divergent. Certainly it is not 'inappropriate' to consider them 'under the same generic term' of dialogue. (p. 357)

On the other hand, I spoke of two distinct approaches — one grounded in phenomenology (Buber) and the other rooted in psychology (Rogers):

> Buber and Rogers are both significant contributors to interpersonal communication theory and each world-view is strong enough to stand alone. Rogers need not be lumped with Buber to be worthy of study and vice versa.
> ... An extension of Buber will not come from a study of Rogers; the world- views are too different. (Arnett, 1982, p. 372)

The essence of the 'How many approaches to dialogues?' controversy is that I differentiated the dialogic contribution of Buber from that of Rogers, while Anderson did not see value in such a distinction.

The second major point of disagreement between my interpretation and Anderson's is the location of the focus of meaning in a communicative situation — a major point of separation between particular communication theories (Fisher, 1978, pp. 83–4, pp. 95–6). I contended that Rogers has more of an internal focus than does Buber, with Buber being more interested in the ontological reality of the 'between.' Anderson stated that there is little need to make such a distinction between the work of the two men on the locus of meaning issue, because of their agreement on the relational nature of communication. Anderson (1982) stated, 'If Arnett's problem with "internalization of meaning" is that it is anti-Buber in its essence, it is also anti-Rogers' (p. 357). I, on the other hand, suggested a significant difference in the two approaches:

> Martin Buber's and Carl Rogers' works are cited together, despite the fact that Rogers' emphasis on the psyche, 'internal locus of control,' 'congruence between self and organism,' and 'the innate goodness of the organism,' is incompatible with the fundamental dialogical notion of the 'between.' Each of these concepts is based in an internal understanding of communication. The meaning of communication remains *inside* the person, not 'between' persons. (Arnett, 1981, p. 204)

The above variance in interpretation between two people who appreciate the work of Rogers *and* Buber — even as they interpret the work of the two men quite differently — requires us to ask: (1) Are such divergent interpretations of what is dialogue valid? and (2) Do Buber and Rogers conceptualize meaning as emerging from different places in their communication paradigms, and, if so, what is the significance of that difference?

FRAMEWORK FOR CRITIQUE

As we examine the variance in 'dialogic' interpretations offered above, it appears that I sought too much differentiation in the dialogical approaches of Rogers and Buber (Arnett, 1981,

1982), while Anderson (1982) did not recognize enough important differences. In examining this contrast in interpretations, three keys to this analysis need explication. First, this particular examination of different interpretive frameworks is grounded in a constructivist hermeneutic (an interpretive framework that builds on givens), in contrast to a deconstructivist hermeneutic (an interpretive framework that looks for underlying and hidden meanings beyond apparent givens); the former reflects interpretation that stretches and pulls, while the latter tears apart and analyzes motivations, as in the case of the psychological work of Freud or the social-economic critiques of Marx and more recently Habermas (Bleicher, 1980, pp. 3–5). The struggle between constructivist and deconstructivist hermeneutics is an issue of contention between Gadamer and Habermas (Habermas, 1981, 1983).

Following Gadamer's (1980) lead, this interpretive study does not ask how psychological, economic, or social conditions prompted such different interpretations; rather, it asks what *fundamental question* guided each inquirer. The interpretive research of Anderson and myself was framed by different questions. I asked, 'What is the difference between the dialogic approaches of Buber and Rogers?' Anderson's question was, 'What are the similarities in the respective approaches to dialogue?' These different interpretive keys naturally resulted in contrasting interpretive pictures of what constitutes a dialogic approach to interpersonal communication.

Since a major key to Gadamer's understanding of interpretive research is the clarification of the questions before commencing the inquiry, it is important to explicate the interpretive 'question,' or what Bernstein (1983) called the 'enabling prejudice' (pp. 126–31), that guides this article: how can we restore conceptual clarity to dialogic research with the diverse interpretations of Anderson and myself? This article does not consider our works inaccurate, but limited by the questions that initiated their inquiries. The remainder of this article brings the contributions made by Anderson and me into creative synthesis, with the aid of recent scholarship by Maurice Friedman.

FRIEDMAN ON DIALOGUE

How many approaches to dialogue?

In a letter responding to one of my articles, Friedman indirectly affirmed the positions of both Anderson and myself on the question of 'How many approaches to dialogue?' He described three distinct examples of dialogic communication approaches: Buber's narrow ridge, Rogers' individualistic dialogue, and Jung's psychologized dialogue. At first glance, Friedman seems to indicate that multiple approaches to dialogic communication do exist. He concurs with my earlier work on that score, but his description of three dialogues (Buber's narrow ridge, Rogers' individualistic dialogue, and Jung's psychologized dialogue) simultaneously affirms Anderson's thesis as well.

A generic notion of dialogue

Friedman recognizes a generic category called *dialogue,* while concurrently understanding the theoretical benefit of separating the different types of dialogues with qualifiers describing the specific kind or type of dialogic communication being discussed. Friedman described this dual position of multiple dialogues within one generic title in his 1985 work, *The Healing Dialogue in Psychotherapy.* Friedman used the generic name *dialogue* in a way similar to Hans Trüb's *Healing Through Meeting* (p. 1).

161

The generic term *dialogue* means 'meeting' the other as a person, not as an object, being sensitive to the relational nature of communication, responding to the unique, concrete other, and recognizing that one must start with oneself, but 'real' living begins in the partnership of dialogue (Friedman, 1976c, pp. 57–61). In reference to this generic dialogue, Friedman uses the metaphor 'healing through meeting' and emphasizes the importance of 'mutuality.' Those who to some degree affirm such an orientation in therapeutic relationships are indeed numerous, including individuals such as Rogers, Jourard, Fromm-Reichman, and Searles (Friedman, 1985b, 1976b). Friedman (1972) has also recognized the connection between the general term *dialogue* and humanistic psychology.

Other researchers have similarly described dialogue in this humanistic fashion, emphasizing personness, noninterchangeability of persons, and the transactional or partnership nature of a communication exchange (Johannesen, 1971; Stewart, 1986). In essence, it is appropriate and defensible to use the generic term *dialogue* simply defined as humanistic communication that is person-centered and grounded in the concrete moment of authentic human meeting.

Dialogic distinctions

As Friedman provides us with the generic notion of dialogue, he also breaks down the notion into smaller, more precise theoretical units. The following provides a brief description of three distinct dialogic communication orientations. The goal of this section is not to provide fine details, but to identify general differences in these dialogic orientations.

Jung's psychologized dialogue. Friedman discussed Jung's 'psychologized approach to dialogue' as involving a commitment to dialogue through a recognition of the importance of the relation between doctor and patient, and mutual 'unconscious' exchange. In Jung's (1958) classic work, *The Undiscovered Self,* he outlined the necessity of treating the person, not just a symptom, recognizing the importance of 'healing through meeting.' Jung's approach requires a mutual dialogical relationship in which the patient is responded to as unique and significant and is encouraged toward ever-increasing *individuation*.

However, as Jung emphasized the importance of meeting the other, he placed the psyche at the center of his psychotherapeutic system:

> Jung emphasizes the mutual, *unconscious* influence of therapist and patient. The therapist is in danger of 'psychic infection,' of getting entangled in the neurosis of his patient; yet if he tries too hard to guard against this influence, he robs himself of his therapeutic efficacy. (Friedman, 1985a, p. 23)

As suggested above, Jung's orientation is psychologized, according to Friedman, due to the emphasis on the psyche. 'Psyche' is the inner mental world of the unconscious that motivates the actions of a person. This view, of course, is somewhat similar to that of Jung's former teacher and mentor, Sigmund Freud. Friedman (1985a) contrasts placing the unconscious within the realm of the psyche, which locates the dynamic force of life *within* the person, not *between* persons as in Buber's dialogue, which rejected the dualisms of inner and outer and the separation of the physical and the psyche (pp. 48–55). The following form of psychologism is what Buber rejected:

> Holding that the unconscious must be simply psychical, places the unconscious *within* the person . . . As a result, *the basis of human reality itself comes to be seen as psychical rather than the interhuman, and the relations between person and person are psychologized.* (Friedman, 1985a, p. 145)

Jung is a representative of a dialogic effort of 'meeting the other,' but he places the psyche, not the 'interhuman' or the 'between,' at the center of his theory (Friedman, 1975, p. 256). Jung's version of psychological health is discovered in therapy as the psyche of one person meets the psyche of another in mutual conversation. The notion of psychologized dialogue will be examined later in this article in discussion of my inappropriate labeling of Rogers' dialogue as a psychologized dialogic approach to interpersonal communication.

Rogers' individualized dialogue. The second form of dialogue that Friedman described was Rogers' 'individualized dialogue.' Rogers' dialogue is referred to throughout this interpretive analysis, but in brief Friedman views Carl Rogers' approach as emphasizing the person and the importance of human relationship, fitting within the 'healing through meeting' metaphor, which is the broadest definition of dialogue used by Friedman. Rogers' work is also considered much closer to that of Buber's than the approach of Jung, which makes the task of identifying their similarities and differences more demanding, but nevertheless necessary, if we are to respect the unique contributions of both Rogers and Buber.

Rogers followed in the footsteps of Otto Rank in emphasizing the therapeutic relationship, and he has often referred to Buber's emphasis on 'healing through meeting' (Friedman, 1985a, p. 48). But Friedman does not consider the I and Thou of Buber to be equivalent to the self-actualization of Rogers; he conceptualizes their approaches as two different understandings of dialogic communication.

Rogers uses metaphors such as 'organismic impulses' (Friedman, 1983b, pp. 150–1), 'self-actualization' (Friedman, 1976c, pp. 5–34; Geller, 1982), 'human as basically constructive'(Friedman, 1982b, p. 99), and 'self-directing' or 'becoming' (Friedman, 1984, p. 107) in order to describe the nature of individual growth, according to Friedman. Rogers' desire is to unleash the innately constructive individual self and permit it to grow to maturity. The dialogic relationship pointed to by Rogers, whether invited by therapist, friend, or parent, is a vehicle for propelling the other toward more autonomy and self-reliance.

> If the parent creates such a psychological climate, 'the child will become more self-directing, socialized, and mature' says Rogers. Through relationship, the other individual will experience and understand the repressed aspects of himself, will become better integrated and more effective in functioning, closer to the person he would like to be, 'more of a person, more unique and more self-expressive,' and he 'will be able to cope with the problems of life more adequately and more comfortably.' (Friedman, 1985a, p. 50)

The striving toward self-reliance and autonomy that marks the goal of self-actualization is most appropriate for our culture. Individuality has been a trademark of American life since the early frontier. It is no wonder that Rogers' biographer has called his approach 'as American as apple pie' (Kirschenbaum, 1979, p. 138). As helpful and as common as this approach may be for our culture, it is still different from that of Buber's dialogue, according to Friedman. Friedman contends that Rogers' mixing of the I-Thou vocabulary of Buber and his commitment to self-actualization makes the I-Thou relationship a function of or a way to promote or achieve self-actualization.

> Although they [self-actualization and the I-Thou relationship] reside comfortably together in Rogers' thought, these two touchstones of reality are not really compatible. *Either* the I-Thou relationship is seen as a function of self-actualization, and the real otherness of the Thou is lost sight of in the emphasis on the development of the organism, *or* the I-Thou relationship is seen as a reality and value in itself, in which case self-realization becomes a by-product and not a goal and, what is more, a by-product that is produced not through a

pseudo-biological development, but rather through the meeting with what is really other than the self. (Friedman, 1985a, p. 55)

Friedman conceptualizes Rogers as a major contributor to the general notion of dialogic communication, but he does not see Rogers duplicating the work of Buber. Where Rogers is most concerned about the development of individuality and self-reliance that will be naturally socially constructive, Buber is more intent on examining the tensions that must be played out between the unique person and the group and each person's 'polar tendencies of good and evil' (Buber, 1965, pp. 180–4; 1953). Rogers places his trust in the biological impulses of the individual (Friedman, 1982a). Rogers' trust is in the person. Buber, on the other hand, visualizes the oxymoronic tension, the unity of opposites, of the interplay between the unique person and tradition (Friedman, 1976c, p. 3). Buber's trust was an understanding of dialogic life as the unity of contraries, gathering together what others would place in separate and irreconcilable camps. Buber accepted life as played out not in either/ors, but in the intermix of yes and no, good and evil, individual and group, spontaneity and tradition, permanence and change.

Is it any wonder that Friedman, who has worked with Buber's material for so many years, would agree with both Anderson and me on the question, How many approaches to dialogue? His position of affirming both orientations is at the heart of Buber's effort to seek third alternatives to either/or propositions and to walking the 'narrow ridge' between the abyss of one extreme or another (Friedman, 1976c, p. 3).

Buber's narrow ridge dialogue. Friedman provides his most thorough account of Buber's dialogue in his classic piece, *Martin Buber: The Life of Dialogue* (1976c) and in his three-volume 'dialography' of Buber's life and work (Friedman, 1981, 1983a, 1983b). In his first major publication stemming from his dissertation, *Martin Buber: The Life of Dialogue*, Friedman (1976c) distinguished between Buber's dialogue and a psychologized version:

> The unfolding of this sphere Buber calls 'the dialogical.' The psychological, that which happens within the souls of each, is only the secret accompaniment to the dialogue. The meaning of his dialogue is found in neither one nor the other of the partners, nor in both taken together, but in their interchange. (p. 85)

Psychologism. I referred to Rogers' dialogue as psychologized, and Anderson countered by stating that there is little difference between the orientations of Buber and Rogers. I am now convinced that the difference between the dialogic orientations of Buber and Rogers does not revolve around psychologism. Rogers' approach does not place the focus of communication within the psyche, as does Jung's. Rogers' focus of communicative meaning is in the organismic impulses of the individual, not the psyche.

Buber's (1969) brief but classic essay 'On the Psychologizing of the World' described the nature and significance of this problem (pp. 144–56). Friedman (1974), in *Hidden Human Image*, vividly outlines the nature of psychologism, in which the center of life becomes the individual psyche.

> Psychologism is a habit of mind. It is the tendency to divide the reality that is given to us into two parts—one of which is an outer world into which we fit ourselves and the other of which is an inner psyche into which we fit the world. (p. 280)

When I claimed that Rogers was psychologistic, the case was overstated (Arnett, 1981). I misinterpreted the significance of the following quotation from Friedman (1974):

> To seek to 'have' an experience is already to risk not having it; for the more we focus on it as a goal, the more we are in danger of removing it into ourselves, of psychologizing it.

> The word *psychologism* is in no sense an attack either on psychology or psychotherapy when these observe their proper limits. It is an attack on the tendency to make the reality of our relationship to what is not ourselves . . . into what is essentially *within* ourselves.
>
> The very notion of *having* experience, whether it be psychedelic, mystical, sexual, travel, or adventure, robs us of what experience once meant — something which can catch us up, take us outside ourselves, and bring us into relationship with the surprising, the unique, the other. (p. 280)

I used the above quote to establish Rogers' significant reliance on the inner person. Friedman (1983c) makes this same point in *The Confirmation of Otherness in Family, Community, and Society* (pp. 149–51), but he does not consider Rogers to be advocating a psychologistic model. Rogers' metaphors of 'organismic impulses,' 'an ever developing and changing self,' and the importance of 'self-actualization' do not locate meaning in the psyche; he conceptualizes communicative meaning emerging from the individual organism, not from the deep recesses of the human mind. In essence, Buber's (1969) work can be called a radical critique of psychologism' (pp. 149–51). But such a stance should not be considered a critique of Rogers. Rogers is interested in getting persons in touch with their inner tendency toward self-actualization. His work has an individual focus, not a psychologized emphasis.

Self-actualization and I-Thou. To suggest that Rogers relies primarily on the psyche fails to comprehend the difference between Rogers' commitment to self-actualization and Buber's notion of the I-Thou relationship. It is in Friedman's most recent work that he differentiates Buber's (I-Thou) dialogue from an individualized, not psychologized (self-actualization) dialogue. In personal conversation Friedman has called this issue of self-actualization versus the I-Thou relationship the fundamental distinction between Rogers and Buber. In addition, this is the central point in Friedman's (1986) most recent examination of Buber and Rogers, which he recently published in the *Person-Centered Review,* appropriately titled, 'Carl Rogers and Martin Buber: Self-Actualization and Dialogue.'

Rogers uses the relationship (which he sometimes calls the I-Thou relationship) to increase individuality and self-actualization. Buber, on the other hand, welcomes the relationship on its own merit, regardless of its eventual contribution to individual growth. At this point Rogers' self-actualization and Buber's understanding of the I-Thou 'meeting' are at odds. Rogers' ties the I-Thou to enhancing the individual. Buber permits the I-Thou to be a means in itself, with individual growth occurring as a by-product, not the goal of the relationship.

I must, however, add a cautionary note at this juncture. It would be another misreading to suggest that Rogers *always* subordinates the I-Thou to self-actualization. Rogers provides us with mixed messages — sometimes suggesting that the I-Thou is an end in itself and at other times that it is used to promote self-actualization. It is the latter emphasis that Friedman (1986), in his reading of Buber, rejects (p. 416).

Basic I-Thou notions. In order to understand more fully Buber's unique view of I-Thou dialogue and how it differs from an individualized dialogue, four major terms are of significance: 'narrow ridge,' 'between,' 'common center,' and 'community.' The metaphor of the 'narrow ridge' signifies walking between extremes in an effort to locate a third alternative. The 'narrow ridge' is a 'concrete' home between extremes — such as individual and group, good and evil, and potentiality and reality. Life is to be lived in the tensions of the demands emerging from contrasting places of expectation. In contrast, Rogers' dialogue is one in which demands of the individual take precedence.

165

The narrow ridge is the foundation of 'community' for Buber, because it recognizes the strain between individual and group demands. Due to Friedman's appreciation of Buber's 'narrow ridge' commitment to community, he cannot affirm what he considers Rogers' trust of the individual versus a mistrust of society as a whole. Friedman wants to maintain a tension of a 'unity of contraries' — the place where opposites come together in support of one another, in the tension of a third alternative that rejects extremes.

> Equally serious is the tendency on Rogers' part to see what is happening . . . in terms of an Either/Or — the individual versus the society or the organic whole, the inner versus outer. Either [Friedman quotes Rogers] 'the welfare of the total organism, the state or nation, is paramount . . . and each person is helped to become conscious of being but one cell in a great organic structure' or there is 'a stress on the importance of the individual.' Rogers fails to see the third alternative that lies at the 'community of otherness' [where the individual is affirmed, but not at the expense of the common good]. (Friedman, 1983c, p. 150)

If Buber had forgotten this tension and sided with the individual, he would have followed the path of Rogers' dialogue. If he had ignored the struggle between contrasting demands and followed the group, he would have tended toward the collectivism of Lenin. Buber's understanding of community can happen only when the tension of individual and group concerns is focused on a 'common core' or mission. In the psychological language of Sherif (1961), a superordinate goal must bring the contrasting expectations together. 'Buber's community . . . was a community of choice around a common center, the voluntary coming together of men in direct relationship' (Friedman, 1981, p. 238). In Buber's dialogic communication it is the 'common center' of concern that brings individual and group hopes and aspirations together long enough for dialogue between persons.

It is not just in community but in the dyad that one can recognize the importance of the notion of a 'common center.' The 'common center' is the rhetorical vision or collectively accepted mission or task that brings people together in conversation. Interestingly, what keeps the conversation going is not total agreement, but the tension between the persons attempting to contribute to a 'common center.' In communication theory, the work of Fisher (1984, 1985) provides another way of understanding this notion of 'common center'; perhaps we can call it a narrative that binds people together — a story that is larger than any one of the participants and that cannot be viewed as the sum of their interaction. I would go so far as to call Buber's 'between,' or what he often referred to as the 'interhuman' (Buber, 1965), a story in which partners in conversation participate as they simultaneously engage in the writing of the narrative. More than anything else, the notion of the 'between' means that one is not the center, but rather a vital participant in a 'common center' or narrative.

Interestingly, Friedman (1981) refers to Buber as a 'philosopher of speech' (pp. 291, 310). Buber had concern for speakers in conversation joining and adding to an ongoing narrative. Willingness to participate in this 'common core' or narrative may hold people together, even when the relationship or affective reaction to another cannot. One may dislike another, but still find it necessary to continue conversation. Buber's (1972) classic description of a 'Conversation with an Opponent' (pp. 34–40) is actually an invitation into a 'common core' or narrative, which in this case is the importance of being in dialogue even in the midst of disagreement.

Buber's narrow ridge understanding of dialogue does not ensure commonality of thought; rather, it is a narrative of 'keeping the conversation going and responding with one's whole person to another.' Buber called that narrative or story (narrow ridge dialogue) the 'last revolution,' one in which proletariat and capitalist can both participate. It is a story of listening with one's whole being, confirming the other in the midst of disagreement, and agreeing that keeping the lines of conversation open may ultimately be the most important ingredient in our 'hope for this hour' (Buber, 1967). For dialogic communication to be invited and 'successful,' the partners in conversation must take up the 'common core' or narrative of the importance of 'keeping the conversation going' — the attitude of dialogue.

Buber's I-Thou can be summarized in three respects. First, Buber does not consider self-actualization the goal of life. At best, it is a by-product of human interaction. Second, Buber places more trust in tensions played out between persons than in any one individual. Third, Buber affirms the importance of a 'common center' to be as significant as the participants themselves. It is the 'common center,' not self-actualization, that is at the heart of Buber's dialogue.

IMPLICATIONS FOR FURTHER RESEARCH IN DIALOGIC THEORY AND PRACTICE

The objective of this article has been to place dialogic research back on track and to reveal its contemporary value. To reenergize research on human dialogue we must recognize that the term *dialogue* has both general and specific meanings. Future research in the area of dialogic theory and practice should specify whether general or specific use of the term *dialogue* is in operation. Using Friedman's language, there is a general dialogic term implying 'meeting' and 'relationship' *and* specific orientations rooted in psychologism (e.g., Jung), the individual organism (e.g., Rogers), and the narrow ridge of Buber's notion of the 'between.' With Friedman's research so helpfully answering 'What is dialogue?' we should now move on to research questions such as the following: What is the significance of the generic term *dialogue* in a more pragmatic and less 'relationship conscious' era? How do the three varied approaches to dialogue reflect a different rhetorical or persuasive perspective? For instance, do not the metaphors of psyche, individual, and narrow ridge lead to significantly different interpretations of what takes place in a relationship?

The second major point of clarification is that Buber did struggle against psychologism, but this was not his complaint against Rogers and should not be presented as such. The contrast of Buber's work with that of psychologism can best be seen by examining his work in opposition to others assuming a deconstructive hermeneutic. Individuals such as Freud, Marx, Habermas, Jung, and other 'ideological slayers' can be contrasted with Buber's critique of psychologism. Similarities between Buber's and Frankl's writings on the danger of psychologism would be of interest, as well. Both recognize the occasional use of psychologism and the need to unmask hidden motives sociologically and psychologically, at times, but not as a common stance (Frankl, 1978).

Third, Buber and Rogers do skew their views of dialogue differently, with Rogers propelled by the psychological and affective and Buber by the common center or narrative. As Marcel (1967) stated about Buber, affective issues were not as important to him as the 'common center' or 'narrative' that emerged 'between' persons. It was this 'common center,' not feelings, that could provide the long-term ground for community. Buber (1958) clearly believed that human feelings are important, but not fundamental (p. 44). Buber saw the 'common center' or narrative around which a community could be gathered as more fundamental than the psychological realm.

Buber's emphasis on 'common center' or 'narrative' led him away from the assertion that the 'meaning is in the person.' This general semantic orientation is at the heart of Rogers' individual dialogue. For Buber, the meaning is in the narrative, 'the common center' between persons. The narrative is co-constituted, created by the partners in dialogue.

> The true community does not arise through people having feelings for one another (though indeed not without it), but through, first, taking their stand in living mutual relation with a living Centre, and, second, their being in living mutual relation with one another. The second has its source in the first, but is not given when the first alone is given. Living mutual relation includes feelings, but does not originate with them. The community is built up out of living mutual relation, but the builder is the living effective Centre. (Buber, 1958, p. 45)

The notion of the 'common center' is central to Buber's dialogue. Buber's 'common center' is akin to the concept of 'narrative.' Exploration of 'narrative' may lend further insight into dialogic interaction (Gadamer, 1980, pp. 146–50).

In summary, the recommendations for future research are as follows. First, differentiate a constructivist and deconstructivist hermeneutic using dialogic theory. The constructivist hermeneutic offers an image of the human being that is closer to Friedman's dialogic vision of persons stretching rather than limiting one another in interaction. Second, examine how emphasis on the individual and self-actualization are different from focus on the I-Thou. And third, it would be interesting to resurrect the old 'message versus receiver' debate in light of Buber's notion of the 'common center' and Fisher's recent work on narrative. The theoretical and practical task of exploring dialogic ways of associating with others is not completed, only temporarily taken off track. While the Anderson-Arnett exchange led to a pause in research in dialogic interaction, it has not resulted in a victor or vanquished, but in the dialogic reality that much of life rests in our creative search for the unity of opposites of seemingly separate camps.

References

Anderson, R. (1982). Phenomenological dialogue, humanistic psychology, and pseudo-walls: A response and extension. *Western Journal of Speech Communication, 46*, 344–57.

Anderson, R. (1984). Responses to the symposium of articles dealing with empathic listening. *Communication Education, 33*, 195–6.

Arnett, R. C. (1981). Toward a phenomenological dialogue. *Western Journal of Speech Communication, 45*, 201–12.

Arnett, R. C. (1982). Rogers and Buber: Similarities, yet fundamental differences. *Western Journal of Speech Communication, 46*, 358–72.

Arnett, R. C. (1986). *Communication and community: Implications of Martin Buber's dialogue.* Carbondale: Southern Illinois University Press.

Ayres, J. (1984). Four approaches to interpersonal communication: Review, observation, prognosis. *Western Journal of Speech Communication, 48*, 408–40.

Ayres, J. (1986, November). Religious values implicit in contemporary interpersonal communication theory and research: A response. Paper presented at the annual meetings of the Speech Communication Association, Chicago.

Barnlund, D. (1962). Toward a message-centered philosophy of communication. *Journal of Communication, 12*, 197–211.

Bernstein, R. J. (1983). *Beyond objectivism and relativism.* Philadelphia: University of Pennsylvania Press.

Bleicher, J. (1980). *Contemporary hermeneutics: Hermeneutics as method, philosophy, and critique.* London: Routledge & Kegan Paul.

Buber, M. (1953). *Good and evil.* New York: Scribner.

Buber, M. (1958). *I and thou.* New York: Scribner.

Buber, M. (1965). *The knowledge of man: A philosophy of the interhuman* (M. Friedman, Ed & Intro.; M. Friedman & R. G. Smith, Trans.). New York: Harper & Row.

Buber, M. (1967). Hope for this hour. In F. W. Matson & A. Montagu (Eds.), *The human dialogue: Perspectives on communication* (pp. 306–12). New York: Free Press.

Buber, M. (1969). *A believing humanism: Gleanings.* New York: Simon & Schuster.

Buber, M. (1972). *Between man and man.* New York: Macmillan.

Fisher, B. A. (1978). *Perspectives on human communication.* New York: Macmillan.

Fisher, W. R. (1984). Narrative as a human communication paradigm: The case of public moral argument. *Communication Monographs, 51,* 1–22.

Fisher, W. R. (1985). The narrative paradigm: An elaboration. *Communication Monographs, 52,* 347–67.

Frankl, V. (1978). *The unheard cry for meaning.* New York: Simon & Schuster.

Friedman, M. (1972). Dialogue and the unique in humanistic psychology. *Journal of Humanistic Psychology, 12,* 7–22.

Friedman, M. (1974). *Hidden human image.* New York: Dell.

Friedman, M. (1975). Healing through meeting: A dialogical approach to psychotherapy. *American Journal of Psychoanalysis, 35,* 256.

Friedman, M. (1976a). Aiming at the self: The paradox of encounter and the human potential movement. *Journal of Humanistic Psychology, 16,* 5–34.

Friedman, M. (1976b). Healing through meeting: A dialogical approach to psychotherapy and family therapy. *Psychiatry and the Humanities, 1,* 191–233.

Friedman, M. (1976c). *Martin Buber: The life of dialogue.* Chicago: University of Chicago Press.

Friedman, M. (1981). *Martin Buber's life and work: Vol. 1. The early years, 1878–1923.* New York: Dutton.

Friedman, M. (1982a). Comment on the Rogers-May discussion of evil. *Journal of Humanistic Psychology, 12,* 93–6.

Friedman, M. (1982b). Psychotherapy and the human image. In P. Sharkey (Ed.), *Philosophy, religion, and psychotherapy: Essays in the philosophical foundations of psychotherapy.* Washington, DC: University Press of America.

Friedman, M. (1983a). *Martin Buber's life and work: Vol.2. The middle years, 1923–1945.* New York: Dutton.

Friedman, M. (1983b). *Martin Buber's life and work: Vol. 3. The late years, 1945–1965.* New York: Dutton.

Friedman, M. (1983c). *The confirmation of otherness in family, community, and society.* New York: Pilgrim.

Friedman, M. (1984). *Contemporary psychology: Revealing and obscuring the human.* Pittsburgh: Duquesne University Press.

Friedman, M. (1985a). *The healing dialogue in psychotherapy.* New York: Aronson.

Friedman, M. (1985b). Healing through meeting and the problematic of mutuality. *Journal of Humanistic Psychology, 5,* 7–40.

Friedman, M. (1986). Carl Rogers and Martin Buber: Self-actualization and dialogue. *Person-Centered Review, 1,* 409–35.

Gadamer, H. G. (1975). *Truth and method.* New York: Seabury.

Gadamer, H. G. (1980). *Dialogue and dialectic: Eight hermeneutical studies on Plato.* New Haven, CT: Yale University Press.

Geller, L. (1982). The failure of self-actualization theory: A critique of Carl Rogers and Abraham Maslow. *Journal of Humanistic Psychology, 22,* 56–73.

Habermas, J. (1981). *The theory of communicative action: Reason and the rationalization of society.* Boston: Beacon.

Habermas, J. (1983). *Philosophical-political profiles.* Cambridge: MIT Press.

Johannesen, R. L. (1971). The emerging concept of communication as dialogue. *Quarterly Journal of Speech, 57,* 373–81.

Johannesen, R. L. (1983). *Ethics in human communication* (2nd ed.). Prospect Heights, IL: Waveland.

Jung, C. (1958). *The undiscovered self.* Boston: Little, Brown.

Kirschenbaum, H. (1979). *On becoming Carl Rogers.* New York: Dell.

Marcel, G. (1967). I and thou. In P. A. Schilpp & M. Friedman (Eds.), *Philosophy of Martin Buber.* La Salle, IL: Open Court.

Sherif, M. (1961). *Intergroup conflict and cooperation: The robber's cave experiment.* Norman: University of Oklahoma.

Stewart, J. R. (1978). Foundations of dialogic communication. *Quarterly Journal of Speech, 64,* 183–201.

Stewart, J. R. (1986). *Bridges not walls: A book about interpersonal communication* (4th ed.). New York: Random House.

Trüb, Hans (1971). *Heilung aus der Begegnung.* Stuttgart: Klett

Client-Centered Therapy:
The art of knowing

Janet M. Sims   *University of San Diego*

Knowing oneself is a skill that has technical and artistic components. Technical knowing, because it is formalizable, can be learned from various articulate means, such as self-help books and personal journals. Artistic knowing, because it is partially inarticulate, can be learned only through indwelling as guided by the authority of a master. Artistic knowing of oneself is achieved in client-centered therapy when the therapist makes the client (rather than a theory) the master and indwells him or her. In turn, the client submits to the authority of the therapist, who embodies tacit dimensions of the client. Through this process the client learns about both him- or herself and the art of indwelling. Client-centered therapy is distinct from other therapies because its framework is primarily a process rather than a theory of personality. As such, it can uncover those aspects of the client that are inarticulate and unanticipated, even by the therapist.

> The client is the master. When the client knows what the master knows, the client is healed.
> (Bill Coulson)

The various schools of psychotherapy differ greatly with respect to the nature and goals of treatment, but there is at least one tenet to which most all concede, that is, the process of psychotherapy allows the client to 'know' aspects of him- or herself that are currently unknown or forgotten. For example, a psychoanalytic therapist would help the client know and experience unconscious conflicts from the past. A behavioral therapist would help the client know the particular reinforcements that shape behavior. A client-centered therapist attempts to create an atmosphere in which the client can know whatever seems to need knowing, as determined by the client.

Broadly speaking, then, the goals of any school of psychotherapy are (1) to expose something of the person to him- or herself, and (2) to make this knowledge useful by integrating the newly exposed information meaningfully. In this article we will look at both the contents and processes of knowing oneself as well as the unique contribution of client-centered therapy to these areas.

The works of Michael Polanyi contributed significantly to my understanding of the process of knowing. All of the theory, many of the explanations, and some of the examples used here to describe the contents and process of self-knowing are derived from his writings, especially his book, *Personal Knowledge* (1958). In it, Polanyi articulates a cogent and thorough explanation of how it is that we can 'know' anything at all.

It is Polanyi's thesis that any act of knowing requires a passionate and personal contribution from the knower, in the form of an intellectual commitment, and that this component is 'no mere imperfection but a vital component of his knowledge' (p. viii). Such personal involvement is strictly antithetical to the traditional scientific prescription

First published in *Person-Centered Review,* Volume 4, Number 1, February 1989.

of knowing via detached observation. While most of Polanyi's arguments focus on knowing in science, this article expands the concept to knowing oneself.

As used here, the terms *technical* and *technique* refer to the categories of knowledge or skill that can be reduced to such detail as to be completely describable to others. *Artistic* and *art* refer to a higher logical type of knowledge within the same discipline, such as the skill of applying technical skills appropriately, gracefully, aesthetically. There is a logical gap between technique and art, a gap that is crossed in a leap as opposed to by discrete, prescribable steps. For this reason, artistic knowledge can be demonstrated in its wholeness, but a description of it — including this description — is discrete and distorted. One can be technically skillful and lack artistic expertise, but the reverse is not possible. For example, Olympic ice skaters must pass technical tests to qualify to proceed on in competition; it is understood that there must be a certain level of technical skill before artistic expression can occur. As the skaters advance, their complete routines are judged with two sets of marks — one for technical merit and one for artistic expression. Artistic expression is of a higher logical type and relies on but is not equivalent to technical skill. *Knowing oneself is a skill that is only partly formalizable.*

Knowing oneself is a skillful performance. As such, it can be learned and perfected just as any other skill is learned and perfected. But any skillful performance — be it riding a bicycle, playing the piano, performing surgery, or knowing oneself — is accomplished by following rules, some of which are not totally specifiable. That is, some of the rules used in the performance are tacit; they cannot be isolated and described; they may not even be known consciously but are used in the performance nevertheless. We know, for example, that creating meaningful visual images from perceptions picked up by the retina is a skill that infants must acquire, yet it is not possible at any age to perceive the processes whereby these images are created (Bateson & Bateson, 1987, p. 96). Similarly, there are many books written on the technique of learning to play the piano, but not everyone who reads and practices these books becomes a great pianist. This is because the master pianist does something more than the books can describe, more than even the master can describe. To use Polanyi's (1958) words, 'By acquiring a skill, whether muscular or intellectual, we achieve an understanding which we cannot put into words' (p. 91). Knowing oneself is also a skill that has specifiable and unspecifiable, technical and artistic components. When we know ourselves we achieve an understanding that we cannot totally put into words but that is nevertheless crucial to being ourselves.

This unspecifiable knowledge, this understanding, is artistic skill as opposed to technical skill. Since no prescription for it exists, it can be learned only by submitting to the authority and demonstration of a master who has already acquired the particular artistic skill. This fact has been recognized and accepted by artisans, scientists, and tradespeople of every civilization with a developed culture. In all developed cultures we see some tradition allowing for the master-apprentice transfer of information (Polanyi, 1958, p. 53). We also see instances where a particular art died with the master because there was no apprentice to carry it on. Even with all our elaborate modern technology, we are unable to replicate the musical quality of the Stradivarius violin. Masters cannot say or write down all that they know, but they can show it to someone through example.

Our parents are most often the first masters we have relative to the skills of being a person and knowing ourselves as persons. We imitate and relate to them and in doing so acquire both technical information about our culture and the art of being in our culture. Later on, friends, teachers, television personalities, and others all exert their mastery over us. Much of what we learn from them is tacit — rules, beliefs, attitudes of which we are not aware focally even as we use them to make sense of the world. Some tacit information may be unknown but knowable, such as beliefs and attitudes. Other tacit information may be forever unknown to our consciousness but used successfully nevertheless, for example, the process whereby we make meaning from retinal images. To know oneself more thoroughly, one's tacit information (artistic, unspecifiable, subsidiary) must be exposed and consciously integrated as much as possible.

TECHNICAL VERSUS ARTISTIC KNOWING OF ONESELF

It is important to understand the difference between technical and artistic skills as they apply to self-knowledge. As was stated before, technical skills are formalizable. They can be observed, analyzed, and written down in the form of instructions, prescriptions, maxims, algorithms, and so on. They can be learned by reading books. In fact, the enormous self-help book industry consists of precisely this kind of information. Self-help books are technical manuals for improving the quality of our lives, whether through enhancing self-esteem, changing bad habits, altering destructive thought processes, understanding the mechanics of relationships, or making other changes. These books are very good at presenting information that can be observed about human behavior.

All of these techniques for gaining information about ourselves are valid and useful, but *using the information correctly* is a skill that falls in the artistic category. Contrary to what advertising suggests and what people would like to believe, it is doubtful that people receive lasting gain from self-help psychology books unless their application is supplemented with psychotherapy (Rosen, 1987, p. 47). Often people come into therapy saying, 'I *know* what I should do but still can't do it.' Why is it so difficult to use information about ourselves in a meaningful way? I believe it is because there is subsidiary or background information (beliefs, attitudes) that prevents a meaningful integration of what is known focally (that is, what is in the foreground). Or sometimes the subsidiary clues needed to use the knowledge are absent—the person has no framework for organizing what is perceived focally. He or she doesn't know how to *be* any different. Client-centered therapy is an art that facilitates assimilation of the contents and processes of self-knowing, which in turn lead to a more integrated way of being.

INDWELLING

Any knowledge, be it a theory or a personal insight, is made useful by *dwelling in it.* To indwell means that one makes the knowledge part of one's personal framework by living in it and using it as an extension of oneself. The master *demonstrates indwelling of the knowledge* for the apprentice, though exactly how the demonstration is accomplished cannot be described completely with words. In order to learn to dwell in the new knowledge the apprentice must submit to the authority of the master, whom he or she trusts to be skilled in the artistic use of the knowledge. The musician dwells jointly in the instrument and in the notes to create music. The carpenter may dwell so completely in the tools that they seem to be extensions of his or her body. Scientists live in theories and use them to create visions of the universe beyond the frameworks in which they dwell. By watching, listening, and practicing with a master we learn likewise to indwell the new framework and incorporate it into our being so that it becomes part of us. We may then use it as our own. The act of indwelling is an artistic skill.

The term *indwell* was taken from Michael Polanyi (1958), but Carl Rogers (1951) describes the same process with different words in his explication of client-centered therapy. Indwelling is immersion of oneself in the subject at hand in order to 'know' it in a way that is impossible with detached observation. The subject may be a theory, a musical instrument, a work of art, or a person. Through intense contemplation one pours oneself into the subject. One participates completely in that which one contemplates. This does not imply observation or control of the subject, but rather living in it, surrendering oneself to it. As clients in psychotherapy, the framework we are trying to dwell in and make useful is ourselves. As psychotherapists in psychotherapy, the framework we are trying to dwell in is the client.

While we are indwelling a subject the particulars that compose the subject are not part of our focal awareness; we are aware of them only subsidiarily. A hammer is most efficiently used when it feels like an extension of one's arm rather than a foreign object; it is not watched as it strikes the nail any more than the hand is watched when one pours a glass of milk. When contemplating a piece of music, we do not listen to individual notes and pauses; in fact, to do so would ruin the musical effect. Instead, we experience the piece as an evolving whole. Similarly, when contemplating a painting we do not focus on so many blobs of paint interspersed with white space; such an approach would render the painting meaningless. When indwelling, we see the subject as a whole. The particulars are held in our awareness only as background, subsidiary to that which is the focus of our attention.

The process is the same when the subject of our contemplation and indwelling is a person. In this context both the therapist and the client are endeavoring to know the framework that *is* the client as well as the cognitions the client uses to comprehend and manipulate the world. If one focuses on the person's clothing, haircut, particular behaviors one wants to reinforce, then one is detached, merely observing them. When indwelling a client, all of the particulars are released to subsidiary awareness. They become background as one becomes immersed in or filled by *who* the person is. This process is described by Raskin in this way:

> At this level counselor participation becomes an active experiencing with the client . . . the counselor makes maximum effort to get under the skin of the person . . . tries to get *within* and to live the attitudes expressed instead of observing them . . . then there is simply no room for any other type of counselor activity or attitude; if he is attempting to live in the attitudes of the other, he cannot be diagnosing them . . . [He is engaged in] the most intense continuous and active attention to the feelings of the other, to the exclusion of any other type of attention. (quoted in Rogers, 1951, p. 29)

It is here that the various theories of psychotherapy differ. Traditional psychoanalytic therapies suggest we adopt a detached but interested view toward the client. Then, inferences from a theory of personality and development are compared and applied to the client as a means for understanding and explaining the client to him- or herself. The focus is upon having the client compare him- or herself to a preexisting conceptual framework and then embrace this as his or her own; that is, to see him- or herself with the therapist's prescribed framework. Similarly, behavioral strategies emphasize the observation of behaviors and reinforcements. Clients are asked to watch (not dwell in) themselves and explain what is seen from a reinforcement model. Both the psychoanalytic and behavioral models are useful for particular explanations or naming discrete phenomena, but this same usefulness becomes a hazard when trying to comprehend the whole, immediate, continuous process that a person is. In these models the client cannot discover more than the therapist's framework can explain. Such a result is very different from that obtained with participatory indwelling, a process for which the outcome cannot be precisely predicted in advance or ever completely explained once it has occurred.

INDWELLING AND CLIENT-CENTERED THERAPY

As was pointed out earlier, there is a technical and artistic component to any act of knowing. Technical skills can be learned through various analytic processes, but artistic skills are learned through indwelling the example of the master as he or she indwells the subject. Knowing oneself requires indwelling of oneself.

It is in the area of artistic self-knowing that client-centered therapy makes a unique contribution. Unlike other schools of psychotherapy that make a theory of personality or human development the subject in which they dwell and in which they teach the client to dwell, *client-centered therapy makes the client the subject.* Rather than asking the client to live in a predetermined framework based on the therapist's beliefs about personality, the client-centered therapist endeavors to indwell the client, to experience life from the client's framework, to discover the client's beliefs and embody them. The therapist must be prepared to dwell in and find meaning in a new framework with each new client. The client-centered therapist sees the client as the master and dwells in the client's world to discover who the client is and what the client means.

Indwelling is an important process offered by client-centered therapy, but it would be useless if the therapist didn't also break out of the client's framework from time to time and show the client what the therapist has seen or experienced. Because one cannot see the framework in which one lives, it is a precious and revealing experience to have someone live in one's skin who can also get out of it and report back what he or she has seen of the framework and beliefs from which one operates. This is knowledge that cannot be obtained from books or exercises or even from a therapist who does not practice the art of indwelling with clients.

The indwelling demonstrated by a therapist in client-centered therapy is different from the use of a tool or instrument. The master can literally demonstrate indwelling of the tool or instrument by picking it up, using it, and showing the apprentice how to operate it artistically. The therapist cannot actually be in the client's life and operate from the client's framework—cannot, for example, drive the client's car or think the client's thoughts as the day goes by. Rather, the therapist indwells the client's verbal report of some event and the immediate feelings or images the client is having about the report in the therapy session. More important, *the therapist indwells the subsidiary dimensions of the client* – those beliefs, attitudes, feelings, and so on that form the background while attention is focused elsewhere. This is important because subsidiary beliefs may be determining observable feelings and behavior. Sometimes, the client may be well aware of what he or she believes focally, but his or her tacitly held beliefs are invisible. The client uses them but cannot see them, just as one uses one's eyes for sight but cannot see them without a mirror. In other instances, indwelling allows the therapist to become aware of feelings the client has pushed into subsidiary awareness. In either case the client-centered therapist offers a mirror to the client's tacitly held beliefs, attitudes, and feelings. By embodying thoughts and feelings that were previously unknown, or only partially acknowledged and understood, the therapist gives legitimacy and form to these events. When they are treated as valuable and meaningful in themselves it gives the client confidence to accept them as valuable and meaningful. If they were disowned they can now be reowned; if they were not understood they can now have meaning; the client is more able to dwell in them and use them in life outside the therapist's office.

But it is not enough that the therapist indwell the client and then break out to offer a picture of what was seen. *The client must also submit to the authority of the therapist* to learn the indwelling of him- or herself. When the therapist offers the client a vision of him- or herself and the client trusts the therapist enough to surrender to this vision and indwell it, the client is in fact submitting to a part of him- or herself that was momentarily embodied by the therapist. In this process, the therapist, intent upon making the client the subject and indwelling him or her, is actually *making the client the master* and submitting to the authority of the client's framework, whatever it might be. Subsequently, when the client makes the therapist the master and submits to the authority of the therapist's framework, the client is really surrendering to the mastery of his or her own framework. The client can see him- or herself in the therapist because the therapist is willing to forgo momentarily his or her own personal framework (or diagnosis or psychological theory) and embody the client's framework.

Tacit dimensions of the client's framework become available as he or she experiences them focally as embodied by the therapist. As these pieces of information are integrated, the client begins to know what he or she *means* rather than just what he or she thinks or feels. Artistic knowing yields meaning as well as information. As clients experience tacit meanings via the therapist, they have the opportunity to reassert belief in what they mean or modify the meaning until it is believable to them. At this point one often hears the client ask, 'Did I really say that?' or 'Is that what I really mean?' Through therapy, the client (1) calls into question tacit assent to prior beliefs and meanings, (2) makes the assent explicit, and (3) renews the assent to believe or changes the meaning to one that is believable. The accreditation of our own meanings, and acceptance of our own beliefs, even though they are unprovable, is the basis for the conviction we need to act confidently and masterfully in our lives.

This back-and-forth dialectic of the therapist indwelling the client and the client indwelling the therapist to discover, reintegrate, and indwell him- or herself has a rhythm and flow that one must experience to understand. When it is done correctly and artfully, both people are moved and changed by the experience yet cannot say at the moment exactly what has happened. Even later, when the moment of exploration or discovery has passed, words can only point at what has taken place. They are as a map is to the territory. As therapists (and clients) we have all had the frustrating experience of attempting to share a particular therapy session with an outsider, but finding the words lifeless and incomplete compared to the phenomenon. We know that we 'know' something more than before the therapy session, but we cannot say completely what it is. When done skillfully, the exposure of a person to him- or herself is very much a work of art—it can speak for itself, but it cannot be explained.

The only limits to this process are the skill of the therapist to indwell the client and articulate his or her framework, the ability of the client to trust the authority of the therapist, and the receptivity of the client. It is the nature of any psychotherapy that clients begin to see aspects of themselves that were previously forbidden or too painful to know. Not all clients are willing to trust the therapist to this degree or to accept the view of themselves exposed by the treatment. In many instances, however, the willingness of the client-centered therapist to embody forbidden thoughts or feelings without judgment gives the client implicit permission to acknowledge these qualities too. Clients learn to dwell in themselves more completely. They not only know more about themselves, but they are more able to *be* themselves. Enabling clients to *be* what they know (rather than just know what they know but not be able to act on it) is the art of client-centered psychotherapy. The art of being involves knowing what one means, believing what one knows, and dwelling in this framework with one's actions.

CLIENT-CENTERED PHILOSOPHY

It is important to look at the nature of the client-centered framework that allows the therapist to dwell in the client without interference. As was suggested earlier, it is the very framework of other theories that *inhibits the framework of the client from emerging* without bias. A psychoanalytic therapist is looking for old conflicts in the content the client presents because psychoanalytic theory teaches that these are the most important aspects to assess. A behavioral therapist is taught to listen for reinforcers that maintain behavior.

In contrast, the task of the client-centered therapist is to adopt attitudes that foster indwelling and report to the client what he or she sees as a result of the indwelling. The theory teaches us to make the client the framework. The therapist is a master of indwelling and surrenders to the mastery of the client's tacit knowledge and learns the client's framework from the client. Congruence, empathy, and unconditional positive regard all assist both the indwelling of the client by the therapist and the indwelling of the client in him- or herself. By adopting these attitudes the therapist can more completely indwell and experience *who* the client is and share this knowledge. By experiencing these attitudes, clients can more completely be whoever they are.

The inferences of client-centered theory are very general, low-level statements about human behavior, for example, 'The individual has the capacity to deal constructively with all those aspects of his life which can potentially come to conscious awareness' (Rogers, 1951, p. 24). Rogers' assumptions can be criticized for their lack of specificity and predictive ability, but it is precisely these features that make possible a focus on the client's own framework rather than the therapist's prescriptions about what should or should not be found in the content of client material. It might be more accurate to characterize the client-centered framework as a meta-framework; it is a framework for understanding frameworks. It functions as a process that allows individual frameworks to emerge rather than prescribing itself as a framework to be adopted by the client. Client-centered therapy doesn't predict what growth should or will happen or particular course that therapy must take. This fact makes learning client-centered therapy very frustrating for students who want to know techniques that are clear and specifiable, and for clients who want to know in advance the direction their growth will take. In fact, client-centered therapy is trivialized by those who want to make concrete what is essentially an artistic endeavor. It's like a painting being reduced to blobs of paint and white space. Yes, at one level this is what it is, but to be meaningful it can't be reduced to this level. In client-centered therapy the client may learn and become more than the therapist knows or can articulate. Because client-centered therapy teaches a discipline of indwelling rather than a theory of personality, it grants each person the authority to develop his or her own theory and to be more than the therapist's conception of the person. This theory based on attitudes allows for conceptions beyond itself. Because it predicts no particular outcome (only that something of the person will be revealed), it can never know in advance exactly what its practices will yield. Just as lasting scientific theories continue to embrace discoveries centuries later that were unanticipated by their originators (e.g., Copernicus' theory of heliocentrism), client-centered therapy allows for personal revelations unanticipated by Rogers or subsequent practitioners.

CONTRADICTIONS AND LIMITS

The obvious contradiction in this article is that it attempts to formalize something that is claimed at the outset to be unformalizable, that is, the *art* of knowing oneself. It is important to the pursuit of self-knowledge to persist in the effort to identify and formalize knowledge that is tacit, despite knowing from the outset that it is impossible to eliminate the tacit dimension totally.

As we focus on a part of ourselves that was previously known subsidiarily, we still hold and use other information subsidiarily. We may shift our focus and expose new tacit items as often as we are able, but we can never see the whole framework focally because we must use tacitly some portion of it to be able to see at all. The paradox comes from the fact that we can *use* the complete framework by dwelling in it but can *never see* the complete framework because we can never be totally detached from it and still be able to see it.

Another aspect of this article that may be perceived as a contradiction is the notion of client-centered therapists asking clients to submit to their authority in some fashion. Client-centered therapists may make such a request because they are submitting to the authority of a tradition that demands that their own framework be put aside so as to indwell and express the client's framework. The client is then merely being asked to submit to him- or herself. If there is a danger, it lies in the client placing faith in a therapist who is not genuinely committed to the client-centered tradition or in one whose skill at practicing it is inadequate.

It is also important to mention briefly the phenomenon of the self-taught master. When writing this article, I was asked by nearly everyone who critiqued it about the case of persons who have not been taught by a master but have somehow developed mastery on their own. Basically, such persons have the capacity for indwelling primary phenomena, holding in subsidiary awareness preexisting thoughts or ideas and allowing themselves to become a part of whatever is 'out there,' so to speak. There is still an act of surrender, but it is to the phenomenon itself (e.g., a fish, a sonata, a rainbow) and is subject to the conditions of the particular place and time the person inhabits. In other words, a person who lives in a society with no piano or who has no way of hearing piano music is not likely to become a master pianist. However, there are many skilled musicians who never had professional training or learned to read music, but learned by listening to the music of others and tinkering with instruments until the instruments taught the musicians about themselves. These people surrender to the experience. They seem naturally skillful in indwelling.

It must be remembered that indwelling takes place at many different levels of sophistication. Infants, having no elaborate cognitive systems for mediating the world, are in an almost constant state of indwelling. As adults, we may have to relearn indwelling. It may require some effort for us to suspend our cognitive boundaries, participate in experiences, and allow them to fill us rather than be filled with our ideas about them. The more complex the subject, the more artful our indwelling must become. In such cases we come to rely more on the teacher or master. The master helps us, either by providing experiences that will empty us of preconceived ideas (e.g., the Zen koan) or by instilling practices that are more likely to lead to a proper indwelling of the subject matter (e.g., the basic scales of a musical instrument). The self-taught master is able to accomplish these tasks alone, dwelling in the phenomenon with the anticipation that there is something there (some process, some organized framework) and the faith that he or she will recognize it when it appears.

Finally, a few words must be said about the limits of the master. As was mentioned above, masters are limited to the conditions and circumstances of the particular place and time in history to which they belong. The boundaries and accomplishments of a master scientist who lived before the advent of electricity are very different from those living today, yet this does not take away from the accomplishments of the earlier scientist. It is one of the hallmarks of masters that they may see beyond the current thinking of the time (e.g., Leonardo da Vinci's vision of flying machines), but the absence of relevant contributions from masters of collateral fields makes the gap too great for the visionary's dream to become reality at the time. More important, however, nothing in this article is intended to suggest that the master is more than a human being. It is Polanyi's contention that everyone is capable of intentions and actions that can be subjective, personal, or universal. In the areas of their expertise, masters are able to communicate universal intention via ongoing personal participation in and commitment to their crafts. But no matter what the level of the master's skill, the master is still simply a person and does not always perform masterfully. Art attempts to bring form to that which is formless. Under such constraints even the most skilled master is destined from the outset to fall short of the goal.

REFERENCES

Bateson, G., & Bateson, M. C. (1987). *Angels fear.* New York: Macmillan.
Polanyi, M. (1958). *Personal knowledge.* Chicago: University of Chicago Press.
Rogers, C. R. (1951). *Client-centered therapy.* Boston: Houghton Mifflin.
Rosen, G. (1987). Self-help treatment books and the commercialization of psychotherapy. *American Psychologist, 42,* 46–51.

Janet M. Sims

Part C

Children and the Family

Family Therapy in the Client-Centered Tradition:
A legacy in the narrative mode

Wayne J. Anderson   *Psychological Resources, Olympia Fields, Illinois*

Psychotherapy is a social, dialogical, and storied enterprise. It is something people do together. It is a refined or special version of what Bruner (1986) calls the narrative mode, the telling and hearing of stories in social contexts. A legacy of the client-centered tradition lies in its careful attention to narrative. The implications of this legacy are explored for their relevance to couple and family therapy, an area little reported or written about in the client-centered tradition.

> Each of us is moving, changing with respect to others. As we discover, we remember; remembering, we discover; and most intensely do we experience this when our separate journeys converge. (Welty, 1983, p. 112)

Psychotherapy is something people do together. It is a social, dialogical, and storied enterprise. Psychotherapy is a special, or refined, version of what Bruner (1986) calls the narrative mode — the lending of coherence and meaning to our lives by the telling and hearing of stories in social contexts.[1]

A legacy of the client-centered tradition lies in the careful attention to narrative in the psychotherapist's empathic responding to personal and subjective experience. Thus a story told is a story heard when its *meaning* for the teller is not imposed, extracted, or reflected, but created in the social dialogue of psychotherapy. It is a legacy in the narrative mode.

My objective in this article is to expand upon this legacy in the narrative mode and to stress its relevance to psychotherapy with couples and families. My view, also proposed by Levant (1978), is that empathic responding is possible not only to personal and subjective experience, but also to shared social and collective experience. If, as Rogers and Sanford (1988) propose in their concept of empathic responding, the therapist's 'sensitive and accurately empathic understanding of the client's feelings and meanings' (p. 15) leads to a 'powerful growth experience' (p. 17), the same is possible for empathic responding to social and collective experience.

Rogers did not extend his concepts of empathy, prizing, and therapist congruence to couple and family therapy, though he did write (1961) on the implications of client-centered therapy for family life. He also wrote a book on couple relationships but it was not related directly to couple therapy (Rogers, 1972). He never addressed, to my knowledge, the direct application of his ideas to couple and family therapy. That task fell to others.

---

1. Bruner (1986) takes his text from William James and contrasts the narrative mode with the paradigmatic mode. 'How to know truth' is the paradigmatic mode (e.g., logic, mathematics, science). 'How to endow experience with meaning' is the narrative mode (e.g., stories, poems, music, dance). Bruner sees the narrative mode as by far the most pervasive in daily life, and he seeks to explicate its most refined forms in drama, fiction, and poetry.

First published in *Person-Centered Review*, Volume 4, Number 3, August 1989.

There were promising beginnings. Ellinwood (1959), in a pioneering paper, wrote of work with parents in a child therapy program. Van der Veen (1969) and Raskin and van der Veen (1970) conceptualized and researched the family concept. More recently, Levant (1978, 1982) drew on the implications of client-centered theory for studies of and applications in couple and family therapy. Yet the fact remains that little has been reported or written in the client-centered tradition about psychotherapy with troubled, conflicted, or incongruent couples and families.

One factor in this neglect, no doubt, is the tradition's deep conceptual and empirical roots in self-theory, a framework strikingly set forth by Rogers (1959) 30 years ago. A less recognized factor is that the tradition is largely viewed as experiential in its epistemology although it is also social. Psychotherapy is, after all, something people do together.

THE NARRATIVE MODE: STORY TELLING AND HEARING

So pervasive in our lives is the telling of stories that the power of narrative is scarcely noticed.[2] Perhaps even less noticed is the dialogue that narrative implies. As Gergen (1985) puts it in a broader context, 'Knowledge is not something people possess in their heads but rather, something people do together' (p. 270).[3] And if knowledge is so fashioned, so too must be the coherence and meaning of our lives.

Stories are not arbitrary and capricious. They bear intent.[4] They are told, enacted, framed, and constructed around affective themes and meanings.[5] Each of us is a dramatist, or fictionist, busy in dialogue with ourselves and others in daily life and in psychotherapy.

One need only notice certain characteristic expressions in social dialogue and psychotherapy to see their narrative potential. 'End of story,' a client might say, or, 'Let me tell you what happened,' or, 'Oh, my God, I've had a horrible week' or, 'To make a long story short,' and so on.

The telling and hearing of stories in daily life and psychotherapy is largely verbal and spoken. Yet such exchanges rely as heavily on the narrative mode as does the reading and 'decontextualization' of written texts now seen by some as a significant conceptual enterprise in philosophy and psychology.[6] At stake is not only what is written or said, but also what the reader or the listener brings to what is read or heard—a joint endeavor to establish

---

2. One researcher, Peggy Miller (1989), who has videotaped families in their homes reports that about eight stories an hour were told in these settings. She acknowledges being 'amazed' by the frequency of story telling in families.

3. Gergen (1982, 1985) makes a strong case for the socially constructed origins, development, and validation of all knowledge and meaning, even in areas of scientific endeavor. For an overview of the constructionist movement see Fiske and Shweder (1986).

4. That stories may be used to deceive, baffle, instruct, amuse, confuse, and so on is a topic apart from this article. My concern is with stories enacted or told in psychotherapy and how stories told in therapy are heard by psychotherapists. For a view of deceptive intent, see Watzlawick (1976).

5. The storied aspects of memory were recognized more than 50 years ago by Bartlett (1932) in his classic studies on remembering. He found that, over a period of time, specific details of experiences were eroded or lost. What he called schemas remained, schemas fraught with affective overtones, by which those experiences could be recreated with the meaning still intact, but with details altered to fit that meaning. This is fiction, at its best, no doubt, but is it true recall? Hardly.

6. The role of hermeneutics, the decontextualization of texts, and of narrative in psychotherapy and psychology, in general, is being increasingly noted and analyzed (e.g., Frank, 1987; Sampson, 1985; Sarbin, 1986).

coherence and meaning.

Bruner (1986) suggests in his analysis of the narrative mode that there are both constraints and possibilities in story telling and story hearing. As he puts it, 'What is at the core of a literary narrative as a speech act . . . [is] an utterance whose intention is to guide a search for meanings among a spectrum of possible meanings' (p. 25). The search is not random. A story carries intent which 'guides reactions and prevents it from being arbitrary' (p. 25). Yet the same intent leaves open to a degree the significance or meaning of the story to the teller and to the listener.

Briefly, what is at the heart of the narrative mode is the joint search of the teller and the listener for coherence and meaning in a story's intent. Once that coherence and meaning is found, narration turns into narrative: a story told, a story *heard*. 'That's it,' a client might respond. 'That's exactly the way it is,' or, 'No, that's not it. It's more like this,' or, 'I really hadn't been aware of how angry and lonely I am.' The heard coherence and meaning of the intent of a story is what gives it its narrative form, its distinctive voice.

A strong sense of the narrative mode is given by Rogers (1970) in a chapter on facilitating groups:

> There is no doubt that I am selective in my listening, hence 'directive' if people wish to accuse me of this. I am centered in the group member who is speaking, and am unquestionably much less interested in the details of his quarrel with his wife, or of his difficulties on the job, or his disagreement with what has just been said, than in the *meaning* these experiences have for him now and the *feelings* they arouse in him. It is to these meanings and feelings that I try to respond. (p. 47)

Note how Rogers speaks of attending to the feelings and meanings, the unifying and thematic aspects which form and integrate the story being told. He also recognizes the social and dialogical implications of what he is doing when he speaks of being selective, perhaps even directive, in his listening, and states that he will try to respond to what gives narrative its true impact, not just facts and details, but the meaning that ties facts and details together.

It seems clear in the quote here that Rogers implicitly recognized the social, dialogical, and storied aspects of psychotherapy; but these aspects of psychotherapy are addressed more explicitly by the concept of the narrative mode. The nature and origin of knowledge and meaning, an epistemological issue, appear to reside not only in personal, but also in collective, experience. As Keen and Fox (1974) suggest, 'Every person is plural. There is no I without we' (p. 42).

Nowhere is this interplay of personal and collective experience more evident than in the dialogue of couple and family therapy; an 'I hate living in this family. It's a disorganized mess,' from one family member, no matter how clearly empathically responded to by the therapist, may be met by a different claim from another family member, 'I don't know how you can say that. We're the most organized family I know. It's just your personal problems that make our family seem disorganized.'

IMPLICATIONS FOR FAMILY THERAPY

Unlike the therapist doing individual therapy, the couple or family therapist is faced with many versions of personal and social experience, not just one. In couple and family therapy, personal, couple, and family stories are told. Just how and at what point to respond emphatically to such stories is complex, since there are so many perspectives from which to draw meaning as a listener.

Take a bit of dialogue from a family I recently saw — a husband and wife in the mid-fifties and their son in his early twenties.

> WIFE: *I feel worthless. I'm not contributing anything.*
>
> HUSBAND *(quietly, almost under his breath): Oh, my God.*
>
> WIFE: *I've never been that depressed. [She is referring to a recent episode at home when she felt very detached and isolated.] I'm so sick of this with myself. I'm so tired of this.*
>
> HUSBAND *(to therapist): This was really bad.*
>
> WIFE: *I was just sliding down into darkness.*
>
> SON *(to father): Well, you do that too.*
>
> WIFE: *I know. I feel guilty. He's having problems.*
>
> SON *(to mother): Don't you think part of it is Dad?*
>
> HUSBAND *(to wife): It doesn't do anything to me. You don't feel you are doing anything for us, and you are.*
>
> WIFE: *I keep everybody clean.*

At this point, three perspectives developed: the wife's concern over a miserable childhood and a sister diagnosed as manic-depressive; the husband's view that she feels worthless because she is not doing enough for him and their son; their son's version that she is feeling sad and depressed because she is not doing enough for herself.

> WIFE *(after the foregoing perspectives were explored): I'm just a bore, a big bore.*
>
> THERAPIST: *Just a big, crashing bore.*
>
> WIFE: *We never eat together.*
>
> HUSBAND: *I like to eat off a plate and watch TV, and you say, 'Can't we ever eat at the table?'*
>
> THERAPIST *(to wife): It sounds to me like 'I'm a bore' translates into 'We're a bore.'*
>
> WIFE: *How'd we fall into this pattern of living?*
>
> SON: *Probably when I went to school.*
>
> WIFE *(to husband): We don't have anything to talk about.*
>
> HUSBAND: *I didn't know you thought that.*
>
> THERAPIST: *I hear [wife] saying she's bored, bored, bored, and 'Come on, let's do something.'*
>
> WIFE: *I'd love to go to the zoo. I could just watch the gorillas all day. Or a day at the Art Institute. [She pauses, studies her husband for a moment.] What do you want?*
>
> HUSBAND *(after a long pause): Money.*

I would like to draw attention to two points. The first point is to emphasize the wide spectrum of possible meanings in the intent of stories told in couple and family therapy. The second point is to illustrate what I call a frame shift, a shift from empathic responding to an individual, subjective frame of reference to a social, collective frame of reference.

The wife in the session said, 'I'm just a bore, a big bore,' to which I responded, 'Just a big crashing bore.' She then shifted to the plural, saying, 'We never eat together.' The husband then replied in his own frame of reference, but I stayed with the wife's plural frame of reference and said, 'It sounds to me like "I'm a bore" translates into "we're a bore."' I emphasized this again in saying, 'I hear [wife] saying she's bored, bored, bored' and 'Come on, let's do something.'

A frame shift moves personal and subjective experience into the realm of social and collective experience in the telling and hearing of stories in the context of couple and family therapy. It is a shift from the 'I' to the 'we.' It is not a shift called for in individual therapy where all social relationships are dealt with in a personal, subjective frame of reference.

Couple and family therapy evoke what Bruner (1986) sees as hallmarks of the narrative mode: the triggering of presuppositions and multiple perspectives and, more than anything, the *subjectification* of reality — or the depiction of reality through the consciousness of protagonists. To be in the subjective mode, he writes, is 'to be trafficking in human possibilities rather than settled certainties' (p. 26). Whose depiction, whose subjectification of reality, is the family therapist to choose? There are no settled certainties here, only trafficking in human possibilities. But, is there a 'shared' as well as an 'individual' consciousness? Perhaps.[7]

The notion of 'shared consciousness' in families has been raised by van der Veen in his work on the *family concept* (van der Veen, 1969; Raskin and van der Veen, 1970). His concepts and research are directly related to the client-centered tradition. He and Raskin write, 'The family concept consists essentially of the feelings, attitudes, and expectations each of us has regarding his or her family life' (p. 389).

The family concept, in brief, is analogous to the self-concept, as Levant (1978) notes in an elaboration of the construct, 'in that it is an organized cognitive-perceptual schema with associated affects, which is based on experience' (p. 38). The family concept is a 'shared consciousness by the parents and their children of their experience together' (van der Veen, quoted in Levant, 1978, p. 35).

A family concept can be explicated, even operationalized in the Q-sort as van der Veen (1976) and van der Veen and Olson (1983) demonstrate. It is a valuable research construct, but, more important for clinical practice, it offers the idea of a family schema that coexists and coevolves with the self-schema.

In my clinical work, I try to keep in mind that I am dealing with self, family, and other social, storied, and dialogical schemas that are all in concert. I also remind myself over and over again that the persons with whom I am in dialogue, individually and collectively, are using the narrative mode to lend coherence and meaning to their lives; that self, couple, and family stories are often subtly interwoven; that I am trying to help persons hear as clearly as possible the meaning of the intent of their stories; and that the empathic understanding of self, couple, and family stories is a powerful growth experience.

In the family session quoted previously, self stories predominated at times and relationship or family studies predominated at other times. The constant interplay of personal and collective experience is typical of couple and family psychotherapy. There are many stories in couple and family therapy. Some are agreed upon by family members; some not. The meanings of stories, empathically framed by the therapist and often by family members, are found, followed, elaborated, or discarded. Some are finally judged as effective and meaningful by mutual accord.

FURTHER IMPLICATIONS: THE FRAME SHIFT

What I think of myself doing as a family therapist is empathically responding, as in individual psychotherapy, to self stories. I also remain alert to fitting those stories into social frames of reference, or relationship stories, that might expand the meaning of the

---

7. Sampson (1988) presents a sophisticated analysis of self/nonself-boundaries in our culture and proposes an alternative.

self stories. I referred earlier to this as a frame shift.

A frame shift is a tilt or movement out of a self frame of reference toward a relationship frame of reference. In making a frame shift, I seek to stay in tune with what is being told and expressed but to move what is being told and expressed into a context of the self *and* social relationships. Frame shifts are not interpretations or observations of couple or family process. They are empathically responsive to the sensed individuality and mutuality of my clients' lives. However, since smooth frame shift is not always possible in couple and family therapy, I will give an illustration of a more radical frame shift.

An irate father, divorced and remarried, tells me loudly and clearly that his daughter Betty, age 16, is a slut, and he has slapped her when she mocks him. I paraphrase and articulate his anger to which I get a confirming response. 'Yes. I'm angry as hell. She wanted to come and live with us and now this.' Everyone in the family is silent in the face of the father's anger. So I do a frame shift. I leave the father's frame of reference, his anger, and I ask other members of the family (a blended family with three children of the father and two of the mother in their remarriage) how they see this 16-year-old. I might even say, 'I've heard Dad's story, and it seems clear. How do others of you feel about Betty?'

The youngest child, age nine, not living in the family, but still at the sessions, says, 'Betty's not a bad kid. I kind of like her. I tease her a lot, but I think she's okay.' An older brother, age 17, adds, 'She's okay. Just crazy about boys.' A younger sister says, 'I hate her. She steals my blouses and makeup.' The wife (Betty's stepmother) sides with the father.

Through story telling and hearing, multiple perspectives are offered and a sharpening, keener awareness of what it is like to live in this family is coming into focus. Selves are emerging in a special context, the family, in the presence of a therapist. Children and parents are learning how to dialogue, how to keep talking in the face of problems, how to exchange views, how to listen to, expand upon, and respond to each others' stories, and how to hone in on individual and collective experience.

When I watch video tapes of the 'masters' in the family therapy field, I often imagine what a great family therapist Rogers would have been. Not only did he have a genius for empathic responding to stories, but also an abiding respect for persons as they are and of creating a safe, tolerant climate for persons individually or together. As he wrote:

> If there is one thing I have learned and relearned in recent years, it is that it is ultimately very rewarding to accept the group [read family] exactly where it *is*. If a group [read family] wishes to intellectualize, or discuss quite superficial problems, or is emotionally very closed, or very frightened of personal communication, these tendencies rarely 'bug' me as much as they do some other leaders [read family therapists]. (Rogers, 1970, p. 48)

Though written by Rogers in the context of facilitating groups, I think it speaks directly to the creation of an accepting and tolerant climate in doing couples and family psychotherapy. It also speaks to the ideals and values inherent in any kind of therapy in the client-centered tradition.

Not too long ago, I saw a family in which the youngest son, age 20, had attempted suicide while away at his first year in college. At the first session after his return to home, all family members were present — two older brothers, not living at home, an 18-year-old sister still living at home, and the mother and the father. Not long into the session the talk turned to the family's dog, Dusty, and 20 minutes or so were devoted to stories about the dog and his cherished place in the family. The father finally exploded in anger, saying,

'What in the hell are we doing talking about our dog when what is at hand is my son's trying to kill himself?' A productive dialogue then ensued about the giving and receiving of affection in the family and the recognition of how isolated family members felt from each other, if not from Dusty.

The simplest of stories may provide safety in couple and family therapy, yet also touch on issues of deep significance to couple and family relationships. There are no lifeless stories in psychotherapy, only stories brought to life by an empathic responding to their intent.

CONCLUSION

Psychotherapy with couples and families in the client-centered tradition is the process of empathically responding to the intent of self, couple, and family stories. The process is one which lends coherence and meaning to individual *and* collective experience — a legacy in the narrative mode. As Kundera (1986) writes:

> To take, with Descartes, the *thinking* self as the basis of everything, and thus to face the universe alone, is to adopt an attitude that Hegel was right to call heroic.
>
> To take, with Cervantes, the world as ambiguity, to be obliged to face not a single absolute truth but a welter of contradictory truths . . . to have as one's only certainty the *wisdom of uncertainty* requires no less courage. (pp. 6–7)

AUTHOR'S NOTE

This article is based on an earlier presentation to the Third PCA Forum, in La Jolla, California, in 1987, entitled 'The Family Therapist in Carl Rogers: A Legacy in the Narrative Mode.' Charlotte G. Ellinwood and Fred M. Zimring have been dear and devoted friends throughout my efforts to write about my ideas. David J. Cain and Christian B. Anderson, my son, also contributed with their editorial comments and suggestions. Ferdinand van der Veen also deserves special note. His ideas about and empirical research on psychotherapy with families are truly unique contributions to the client-centered tradition.

REFERENCES

Bartlett, F. C. (1932). *Remembering.* Cambridge: Cambridge University Press.
Bruner, J. (1986). *Actual minds, possible worlds.* Cambridge, MA: Harvard University Press.
Ellinwood, C. (1959). Some observations from work with parents in a child therapy program. *University of Chicago Counseling Center Discussion Papers, 5*(18).
Fiske, D., & Shweder, R. A. (Eds.) (1986). *Metatheory in social science: Pluralism and subjectivities.* Chicago: University of Chicago Press.
Frank, J. D. (1987). Psychotherapy, rhetoric, and hermeneutics: Implications for practice and research. *Psychotherapy, 24*(3), 293–302.
Gergen, K. (1982). *Toward transformation in social knowledge.* New York: Springer-Verlag.
Gergen, K. (1985). The social constructionist movement in modern psychology. *American Psychologist, 40*(3), 266–75.
Keen, S., & Fox, A. (1974). *Telling your story: A guide to who you are and what you can be.* New York: Signet.
Kundera, M. (1986). *The art of the novel.* New York: Grove.
Levant, R. F. (1978). Family therapy: A client-centered perspective. *Journal of Marriage and Family Counseling, 4*(b), 35–42.

Levant, R. F. (1982). Client-centered family therapy. *American Journal of Family Therapy, 10*(2), 72–5.

Miller, P. (1989, February 2). Miller looks at effects of 'everyday stories' on children. *University of Chicago Chronicle,* p. 6.

Raskin, N. J., & van der Veen, F. (1970). Client-centered family therapy: Some clinical and research perspectives. In J. T. Hart & T. M. Tomlinson (Eds.), *New directions in client-centered therapy* (pp. 387–406). Boston: Houghton Mifflin.

Rogers, C. R. (1959). A theory of therapy, personality, and interpersonal relationships as developed in the client-centered framework. In S. Koch (Ed.), *Psychology: The study of a science* (Vol. 3, pp. 184–256). New York: McGraw-Hill.

Rogers, C. R. (1961). *On becoming a person.* Boston: Houghton Mifflin.

Rogers, C. R. (1970). *On encounter groups.* New York: Harper & Row.

Rogers, C. R. (1972). *Becoming partners: Marriage and its alternatives.* New York: Delacorte.

Rogers, C. R., & Sanford, R. C. (1988). Client-centered psychotherapy. In H. I. Kaplan & B. J. Sadock (Eds.), *Comprehensive textbook of psychiatry* (Vol. 5). Baltimore: Williams & Wilkins.

Sampson, E. E. (1985). The decentralization of identity: Toward a revised concept of personal and social order. *American Psychologist. 46*(11), 1203–11.

Sampson, E. E. (1988). The debate on individualism: Indigenous psychologies of the individual and their role in social functioning. *American Psychologist, 46*(11), 1203–11.

Sarbin, T. R. (Ed.) (1986). *Narrative psychology: The storied nature of human conduct.* New York: Praeger.

van der Veen, F. (1969). Family psychotherapy and a person's concept of the family: Some clinical and research formulations. *Institute for Juvenile Research Reports, 6*(16).

van der Veen, F. (1976). *Perception and interaction in the family: Establishing an empirical base.* (Available from F. van der Veen, P. 0. Box 73, Encinitas, CA.)

van der Veen, F., & Olson, R. E. (1983). *Manual and handbook for the family assessment method.* (Available from F. van der Veen, P. 0. Box 73, Encinitas, CA.)

Watzlawick, P. (1976). *How real is real?: Confusion, disinformation, communication.* New York: Vintage.

Welty, E. (1983). *One writer's beginnings.* New York: Warner.

190

The Person-Centered Approach and Family Therapy:
A dialogue between two traditions

Charles J. O'Leary   *Center for Studies of the Person*

This article places the person-centered approach, as described by Rogers, in dialogue with perspectives common among family therapists. The person-centered approach is strongest in articulation of the subjective, individual, and nondetermined side of reality, while family therapists deal with the objective, systemic, and deterministic perspectives that are also valid in understanding people. Gabriel Marcel's distinction between problem and mystery are a way of discussing the incompleteness of both points of view. Needed contributions of the person-centered approach to family therapy are highlighted. The unique challenges of work with families are explored in relation to the concepts of therapists' unconditional positive regard, empathy, and congruence.

Family therapy offers a way of welcoming people back into the human community as does the person-centered approach to therapy as developed by Carl Rogers. However, family therapists and Rogers refer only rarely to each other and differ at least superficially in all of their most important values. While Rogers emphasizes the person's subjective reality, most family therapists emphasize that the person shares family group reality. Rogers writes about freedom, while family therapists describe families in terms of what determines them. Rogers writes about autonomy; many family therapists describe the never completely winnable struggle for differentiation. Rogers creates an atmosphere for recovery from the harmful effects of past and often well-intentioned behaviors; many family therapists plan strategies for interventions. This article will attempt to place the differing approaches in dialogue.

THE UNIQUE GENIUS OF ROGERS

Carl Rogers, over a career of more than 55 years, worked clearly, consistently, and scientifically on the task of never treating anybody like an object — including the therapist. He reported again and again the discovery that treating persons in a way that does *not* distract from their unique experiences has a healing and life-enhancing effect. The following (in Kirschenbaum, 1979, p. 123) is a clear expression of his approach:

> The primary technique which leads to insight on the part of the clients is one that demands the utmost *in self-restraint* on the counselor's part . . . To recognize that insight is an experience achieved, not an experience which can be imposed is an important step in progress for the counselor.

His approach in the 1940s and early 1950s focused as much on training therapists what not to do as what to do. As Rogers states (quoted in Kirschenbaum, 1979, p. 89),

First published in *Person-Centered Review,* Volume 4, Number 3, August 1989.

[It] is the client who knows what hurts, what directions to go . . . It began to occur to me that unless I had a need to demonstrate my own cleverness and learning, I would do better to rely on the client for the direction of movement in the process.

Rogers developed a powerful method for creating second-order change, although the terminology would be foreign to him. Second-order change is that change that involves a significant shift in the cognitive framework and habitual behavior of an entire system. First-order change, on the other hand, refers to a shift in one particular behavior, which, having no effect on the system in which it is enclosed, will be canceled by it eventually. Rogers would make an enormous impact — the equivalent of a bolt of lightning — on an individual human system: he would refrain from intervening! He would refrain from claiming superior knowledge to his client. Faced with such restraint, *clients* would be enabled to see their own capability and would change or not change, respond or not respond as would be appropriate for their lives. Rogers was not unaware of the paradox here — the influence of his 'not doing' on human self-concept and behavior. He was fond of quoting the following from Lao Tse (Rogers, 1980, p. 42) in many of his talks and dialogues:

A leader is best when people barely know he exists,
Not so good when people obey and acclaim him,
Worst when they despise him . . .
But of a good leader, who talks little,
When his work is done, his aim fulfilled,
They will all say 'We did this all ourselves.'

The discovery of the power and necessity of restraint is, along with Rogers' development and research of the necessary and sufficient conditions of therapy, a discovery not often discussed in the literature on family therapy. Restraint for Rogers was never a tactical move, but was a choice made in service of the client's own capacity to behave constructively and responsibly. Rogers did not pretend that the client knew better than he which direction to choose, he considered this a fact established again and again by his experience and research. 'If the insight is real insight and not insight imposed by the therapist, then positive actions based on the insight are almost inevitable' (Rogers, quoted in Kirschenbaum, 1979, p. 127).

Feldman (1979) addressed Rogers' impact on family therapy in his summary of types of family therapy strategies. Referring to Rogers (1957), he described the necessity for all family therapists to have and demonstrate the qualities of empathy, genuineness, respect, and caring. He found these the conditions upon which *all* strategies (in his formulation — modeling, insight, paradox, reinforcement/education) must build. He presented his description of these qualities using quotations only from family therapists; for example, Minuchin (1974) on empathy: [the therapist] 'should feel a family member's pain at being excluded or scapegoated, and his pleasure at being loved, depended upon or otherwise confirmed within the family' (p. 123); Whitaker (1973) on respect/concern: 'A family that is worth treating is worth loving' (p. 27); and Whitaker (1973) on congruence in his emphasis on the significance of the therapist's 'presence and the quality of his person' (p. 5).

Family therapy, as Feldman presents it, is dependent on the same virtues and human validation upon which individual therapy is built. It might be said that Feldman is echoing a finding of Rogers' colleague Fiedler (1950) that most experienced therapists, of whatever school, are more like each other than they are like less experienced therapists of their own schools. Feldman's article links Rogers' precise formulation with the work of family therapists but does not describe *how* these dimensions work in the active pursuit of systems strategies.

On the other hand, the practice of empathy, congruence, and unconditional positive regard may not be sufficient in work with whole families unless further developed. Effective attention to individuals' subjective development relates to, but does not fully address, the question of their objective presence in the world of their significant others. People can get in each other's way even while attempting to set each other free. The question, 'Who are we?' may be best responded to by a restrained invitation to keep exploring. The question, 'How are we?' may invite the more challenging responses described in the approaches to family therapy described next (S. Covington: personal communication, September 26, 1988).

THE UNIQUENESS OF THE FAMILY THERAPY MOVEMENT

The family therapy literature has focused consistently on describing the social processes in which people get trapped, even while intending to maintain their own freedom and that of others. It has described from many perspectives the same phenomenon: individual intentionality is at least in part *determined* by the cognitive and behavioral patterns of a person's social group. This finding is of course not new to anthropological literature.

In a concise formulation, Barrett, Falicov, and Margolis (1984) detailed the essential observable dimensions of a family. Each family can be described according to stage and tasks in the life cycle; structure (i.e., subsystems, boundaries, hierarchies, and triangles); and ecological forces (e.g., job, school, and other specifics of relations to the external world). Other dimensions they did not address include the influence of preceding generations, living and dead, and the effects of ethnic customs and historical experience. The questions of the family therapist are an attempt to understand a family by a careful examination of their internal patterns and external contingencies.

Family therapy is based on general systems theory and is necessarily deterministic. Without denying the possibility of subjective experiencing, a family therapist works to discover the repeating sociopsychological pattern that keeps the family from functioning well and *acts* to change it. For an intergenerationally oriented therapist, the problem might be unintegrated introjected childhood images carried into adult life by the parents in a family (Framo, 1970). The family treatment, therefore, is a carefully prepared-for meeting in the present as an adult with one's family of origin. For a family systems therapist, difficulties result from failure to emerge from one's undifferentiated family ego mass. The therapist must coach an individual step by step in establishing person-to-person relationships with family members without surrendering his or her capacity to think autonomously (Bowen, 1966). For a strategic family therapist, the problem is the repeating sequences of behavior that take place between three or more people. The therapy then interrupts that sequence often by means of paradoxical directives (Madanes, 1981). For a structural family therapist the problem might be a coalition between one parent and a child, developed because of lack of intimacy between parents. The therapist's intervention might be directed toward clarifying boundaries appropriate to each person's age and family role (Minuchin, 1974). Family therapy deals with the problem that family members act as if other family members are objects to each other, whether they acknowledge it or not. Actively facing that dimension is an important assignment of the therapist.

Intervention alone seems both risky and incomplete for one who has seen Rogers demonstrate the surprising change that occurs when a person is accepted without judgment. Can a family receive help from someone who ignores its particular reality? Effective therapy may require active debate between the subjective and objective experiences of family members. This issue will be addressed in the following case.

A CASE EXAMPLE

A family came in to see me—father, 44, mother, 40, and teenage daughter. The daughter, 14, had begun experimentation with drugs and boyfriends and had stopped being (to her parents) the friendly, reliable, moderately achieving person they had known. They had become restrictive, angry, accusing, suspicious custodians and had stopped being the supportive, agreeable, understanding, interesting individuals that she had known. The father and daughter had been particularly close and mutually supportive in the past, but are now engaging in combat and mutual blaming.

Some of the following interventions might be helpful from a systems point of view: (1) the mother might be encouraged to be more involved in the day-to-day discipline in the house, while the father takes a sabbatical; (2) the parents might be encouraged to examine possible subtle and not-so-subtle disagreements about what to expect from their daughter and to strive to reach greater clarity; (3) the expectations of all might be examined in terms of normal age-related roles as well as the unique needs of all family members; (4) the parents might be encouraged to become more socially active together and thus take subtle pressure off their daughter for their unfulfilled relationship needs; or (5) a ritual might be planned that expresses both the reality of the daughter's coming of age and an affirmation of the deeper values of the social system in which she is growing up.

These ideas, based on a variety of family approaches, and each with a rationale based on enabling a family to adapt to developmental change, might be useful in freeing this family from a painful logjam blocking their individual and family movement through life.

In my experience, however, each family member described here by his or her role is also undergoing a personal transformation and personal sufferings, only partly contained in their mutually experienced family dilemma. Although a family therapist might intervene effectively in one or more of the ways described here, the family may also need to be met and understood at a level beyond the solution of its problems. Family members have perceptions, feelings, and sufferings that can be understood only in their particular language and metaphor. A therapist who knows the foregoing perspective and its rationale will be effective only if additionally he or she can show awareness and be present in a manner responsive to the personally experienced meanings of the individuals and group living with these problems.

PROBLEM AND MYSTERY

Existential philosopher Gabriel Marcel's distinction between problem and mystery may be helpful in this dialogue. A problem, according to Marcel, is something that can be seen clearly from the outside, admits of solution, involves elements that are interchangeable, and can be viewed with emotional detachment. The term *mystery*, on the other hand, describes data of which the observer is inextricably a part (and therefore is never able to claim the position of outside observer), that is insoluble because its ongoing reality is constantly interactive with the reality of the observer, and has the quality of being unique and, therefore, is not interchangeable with any other experience (Gallager, 1962). A family in difficulty may be usefully conceptualized as *both* a problem and a mystery. Seeing people *only* as mystery avoids making use of skills and perspectives which could remove a particular roadblock to a family's capacity to move through their developmental tasks. Seeing people as only problems may not only miss the essential in their life experience, but also lead to an interference in their long range development. A good family therapist makes use of skillful problem description as a helpful tool without confusing it with a summary of the family's character, needs, or possibilities.

A COMMON PERSPECTIVE

At the heart of Rogers' approach is his assumption that people in distress suffer from a discrepancy between their self-concepts and their experiences. Because of real or perceived conditions of worth, individuals reject their experience in favor of perceptions shaped by others. Perceiving this discrepancy as necessary for acceptance by significant others, the individual develops less and less ability to perceive things as they really are and becomes less able to function effectively.

In family distress the process is very similar to that experienced by the individual. Family members usually come in for therapy concerned with presenting an image of themselves as being in control. They believe that if other family members would try harder their problems would diminish. They try harder to identify a clear villain (identified patient) who, if changed, would restore their family to a much hoped for normalcy. Their experience, however, includes frequent confusion, anxiety, fear, and depression. They maintain that they are very close to 'having it all together,' while showing feelings of hopelessness and paralysis. The family described in the case example might see themselves as needing a competent father, but, because of other needs, they remain unwilling to let their father function as such. The family's statement might be: 'We have a father who can handle everything and whom we like to please; and we have a father who can do nothing right and whom we need to defy; and we are also a family with no contradictions.'

Unconditional positive regard, empathy, and congruence may be most effective in resolving this alienated condition in families as well as in individuals. The following discussion attempts to describe the application of these therapeutic qualities in work with families.

UNCONDITIONAL POSITIVE REGARD

In Rogers' theory unconditional positive regard is essential for the healing process to take place. This same attitude may be necessary if a family is to move away from the distorted thinking and incongruent actions that are the result of their struggle with the discrepancy between how things should be and how things are. Family members need to be validated as they are and assured that their distress and perceived shortcomings are also acceptable. If the therapist acts in such a way as to create an experience in which the individual feels valued and unique, personal development and problem solving will be facilitated.

The family therapist's unconditional positive regard must adapt to the opportunities and challenges of the family. The therapist shows awareness of both the family's unity and its dividedness. The therapist responds to the family in terms of each person's roles as well as to each person's unique individuality. The therapist also must pay attention to the family reality: that someone is mother, someone is father, someone is stepparent, someone is older than someone else, and so on. The therapist makes use of both the presenting problem and the family history and demographics to show awareness that the family is *both* presently troubled *and* possesses a history of and future potential for successful functioning. The therapist must demonstrate awareness that any family, no matter how confused or angry, has within itself sources of strength, healing, and cohesion (many of which will never be expressed during therapy sessions).

The concept of unconditional positive regard takes on new dimensions when there is an entire family involved. The therapist must show acceptance for individual family members without acting as someone whose acceptance is superior to that of other family members (parents, for example). The unconditional positive regard shown to a family must be compatible with a therapist's realization that a family may indeed demonstrate resistance to the very change its members seek. Levant (1984) has contrasted Rogers' accepting attitude with many family therapists' expectation of resistance to change. It is often helpful if the therapist can demonstrate understanding that the family is both willing to change and also resistant to it.

What family therapists call 'reframing' is an attempt to be responsive to the need for unconditional positive regard. Reframing deliberately bypasses a conventional explanation for a behavior and is an attempt to define it in a way that is more encouraging or challenging. The 'motivation for the behavior is defined positively not the behavior itself' (Papp, 1984, p. 45). Influenced by Rogers, a therapist would be congruent and truthful in such reframing because of the constructive intention contained in any words or actions.

EMPATHY

Empathy, or the ability to show understanding of the unique point of view of another, is a demanding task in individual therapy. A family therapist must manage person-to-person empathy without losing a sense of empathy for the family as a whole. Boszormenyi-Nagy and Ulrich (1981) have called this 'multidirected partiality' and describe it in a manner congenial to many person-centered therapists. 'Towards the participants, the therapist does not adopt a stance of impartial contemplation of all competing interests. The therapist is multidirectionally partial, i.e., directing empathy, endorsement, listening to one person, then in turn to that person's adversary' (p. 178).

The therapist must show sensitivity for the family situation as well as empathy for individual personal expressions. For example, a father who becomes angry and punitive while his daughter responds to a question of the therapist must be understood in terms of the feelings he is showing, the timing of his response, and its meaning about the session. To treat the communication with an attempt to clarify what he might be saying to his daughter would distract from what he is saying about the whole context. He may be calling the therapist's attention to a type of interaction that takes place at home and has not yet surfaced in the session; he may be expressing annoyance at some perceived slight in the progress of the session. The therapist's desire to show empathy may be frustrated and confusing if he is too quick on the active listening trigger.

Since in family therapy a therapist is most often called upon to take a more active role than in individual therapy, empathy might take the form of behavioral responsiveness. Sitting next to someone in trouble, sitting between two people who seem stuck, or getting up and opening a window when someone says he or she feels trapped can be sometimes more communicative than words.

Some strongly interventive family therapists have described empathy in terms of fine-tuned responsiveness to a family's response to a suggested ritual or homework assignment. Cloe Madanes remarked in a 1984 workshop on strategic family therapy that the family will tell you by their responses whether an intervention will be relevant to them. She described a therapist's sensitivity to client responses in a manner that recalls Rogers' descriptions of the tentative quality of his reflections to clients. Nonempathic therapist responses are often ignored by clients, or provoke agitation that shows that the therapist is failing to understand (see also Madanes, 1981).

Empathy requires an ear to hear and the articulateness to express the positive intentions implicit even in the angry words and deeds of family members. For example, a mother's complaint about the current state of her relationship with her teenage daughter may include the implication that she once was like that child and felt comfortable relating to her. Her criticism of her daughter implies a longing to be closer to her and affirms past success in that relation. The therapist's awareness of that dimension may open the mother to a storehouse of positive past experiences.

Implicit in many of these observations is my belief that a family therapist is called on to be more active than an individual therapist. The client's self-direction is facilitated less by the therapist's restrained communication than by his or her deference to the client's sense of what is on track and what is not.

CONGRUENCE

Therapists must use themselves—their unique combination of inclinations, thoughts, feelings, and talents—to make a difference in the family. The word *congruence* is used to describe the consistency of outward expression and inner experience that enables the therapist's unique personality to emerge. Clients need someone to understand how they feel *and* to react authentically to them. The effective therapist's reactions bring about change when balanced with respect and actively demonstrated empathy. For example, in a family in which two members hotly and unfairly accuse each other, therapists can speak of their own discomfort, concern, or frustration without needing to join one of the contendents against the other. This disclosure is founded not on therapists' position of superior knowledge of the way one should act, but on the natural rights they claim as humans. Family members can make use of therapists' authentic responses to let go of rigid positions without losing self-respect.

Therapists' personal reactions provide guidance to unfinished business, overlooked strengths, fears, and unfair bases for solutions to family problems. A congruent therapist may be trusted by the family because of his or her ability to face conflict without assigning blame.

Congruence relates to the concept of 'taking the "I" position' (Bowen, 1966). 'My "I" stands, all based on experience, are in terms of what I will do and will not do, and are never in terms of "what is best"' (Bowen, 1966, p. 371). The therapist models taking action as an autonomous person whose fallibility does not interfere with the therapist acting on his or her own beliefs.

A CASE EXAPMLE

Intermittently, over a period of several years, I have counseled the family of a single mother, Mary, aged 35, and her two daughters Linda and Kathleen, now aged 13 and 14 (not their real names). Recently, this family had to deal with the difficulties stimulated by the death of the girls' father who had left them during the girls' early childhood. He had paid no support and had very rarely contacted the girls, and his unpaid debts after he left had resulted in additional damage to the family. This man's death brought about tremendous struggles between Mary and her daughters. Mary's anger over her former husband's treatment of her was increased at the time of his death by her discovery that he had been living relatively comfortably while she and the girls had suffered tremendous poverty. The girls, on the other hand, had recent contact with their father's family. They had discovered that their pictures were prominently displayed in his apartment, and they were experiencing a surge of grief, affection, and loyalty to their father.

Highly involved with one another, this small family fought to express its discordant reactions to this event. Each was insistent on having her feelings understood, but also on having those feelings acknowledged as the only correct and appropriate ones possible. In the midst of all this anger and grief, each felt abandoned by the others at a most crucial moment in their lives.

As a therapist I had to draw on already established foundations of realness, acceptance, and interest in each family member's point of view. While listening to all sides, all at once, I had to show understanding of their grief, anger, and strong desire to have support from each other. I had to acknowledge that the girls wanted help from a mother who had a precisely opposite point of view. I also made use of the possibilities of my office. I had Mary sit in one chair as a person who experienced a particular loss and ill treatment, and who had a rightful anger. Next I asked her to sit in another chair as the mother of two girls who had lost and rediscovered their father. Using the trust we had already established, I also was able to speak forcefully about my strong objection to their handling their strong feelings by mutual accusations and unanswerable demands. At other times I discussed the nature of crisis and the inevitability of ambivalent feelings at such a time. I also made use of my information that this family had handled crises and radical differences before with great success. At one point I defined the family's disputes as a successful beginning of the work of adolescence, with its task of learning to develop differing world views as parents and children while staying in relation to each other.

My empathy in this case took the form of reflective listening under fire, so to speak. It also included sharing the perception that each person felt strongly justified for not hearing the others' point of view at that time. It included empathy for the whole family, which, as a whole, was experiencing rage and abandonment and the effects of unfairness. My congruence meant an active role in the whole discussion as well as genuine expression of sympathy, not only about their years of losses now being acutely relived, but also at their distress at being unable to suffer on the same side. My unconditional positive regard took the form of the ability to acknowledge that both the crisis and the divided response to it were in the natural order of things and could be worked with. Seeing the crisis as a time in which normal struggles of adolescence could be faced was also important. Additionally, unconditional positive regard was present because this family and I had achieved that state with each other. We managed to like each other; and they knew that I thought their lives made sense and that they were capable of facing what life dealt them.

Conclusion

The family therapy literature tends to overemphasize the objective tasks of the therapist and to take for granted the art of human relations developed so painstakingly by Rogers and his associates. On the other hand, the person-centered therapist must go beyond the therapeutic attitudes and address the integration of those attitudes into the active role most family therapists feel called upon to take. The field of family therapy developed after most of the concepts of the person-centered approach had been articulated. Person-centered family therapy has not yet been defined clearly. Person-centered therapists should consider the possibility that the manner in which the therapeutic conditions are conveyed may require, at times, a different operational form when working with families.

Family therapy helps to welcome a family back into the human community by concretely addressing their dimensions as a living system. Family members need to be received as subjects while being encouraged to face their reality as part of a system with patterns not entirely in their consciousness or control. They need to be acknowledged as mysteries as well as confronted with the limits and unacknowledged potential in their interpersonal living.

References

Barrett, B., Falicov, C., & Margolis, E. (1984). Major theoretical tools. Unpublished manuscript.

Boszormenyi-Nagy, I., & Ulrich, D. (1981). Contextual family therapy. In A. S. Gurman & D. P. Kniskern (Eds.), *Handbook of family therapy* (pp. 159–86). New York: Brunner/Mazel.

Bowen, M. (1966). The use of family theory in clinical practice. *Comprehensive Psychiatry, 7,* 345–74.

Feldman, L. (1979). Strategies and techniques of family therapy. In J. Howells (Ed.), *Advances in family psychiatry* (pp. 411–27). New York: International University Press.

Fiedler, F. E. (1950). A comparison of therapeutic relationships in psychoanalytic nondirective and Adlerian therapy. *Journal of Consulting Psychology, 14,* 436–45.

Framo, J. L. (1970). Family of origin as a therapeutic resource for adults in marital and family therapy: You can and should go home again. *Family Process, 15,* 193–210.

Gallager, K. (1962). *The philosophy of Gabriel Marcel.* New York: Fordham University Press.

Haley, J. (1982). *Reflections on therapy and other essays.* Chevy Chase, MD: Family Therapy Institute of Washington, DC.

Kirschenbaum, H. (1979). *On becoming Carl Rogers.* New York: Delacorte.

Levant, R. F. (1984). From person to system: Two perspectives. In R. F. Levant & J. M. Shlien (Eds.), *Client-centered therapy and the person-centered approach* (pp. 243–61). New York: Praeger.

Madanes, C. (1981). *Strategic family therapy.* San Francisco: Jossey-Bass.

Minuchin, S. (1974). *Families and family therapy.* Cambridge, MA: Harvard University Press.

Papp, P. (1984, January/February). Setting the terms for therapy. *Family Therapy Networker,* pp. 42–7.

Rogers, C. (1957). The necessary and sufficient conditions of therapeutic personality change. *Journal of Consulting Psychology, 21,* 95–103.

Rogers, C. (1980). *A way of being.* Boston: Houghton Mifflin.

Weakland, J. H., Fisch, R., Watzlawick, P., & Bodin, A. M. (1974). Brief therapy: Focused problem resolution. *Family Process, 13,* 141–68.

Whitaker, C. (1973). Process techniques of family therapy. Unpublished manuscript.

The Necessary and Sufficient Conditions for Change:
Individual versus family therapy

Ned L. Gaylin   *University of Maryland*

Over 30 years ago, Carl Rogers delineated six 'necessary and sufficient' conditions for psychotherapeutic personality change in individual psychotherapy. This article presents and expands these conditions in an effort to demonstrate their relevance to the practice of family psychotherapy. The similarities and differences of the conditions within these two contexts is explored. The intent of this endeavor is to identify and define those elements common to psychotherapy regardless of context, in order to maximize the understanding and efficacy of the therapeutic process in family therapy.

It has been over 30 years since Carl Rogers delineated the six conditions he deemed 'necessary and sufficient' for therapeutic personality change (Rogers, 1957). Rogers' intent was to discern the inherent unity within the process of psychotherapy, regardless of the psychotherapeutic persuasion practiced. His conceptualization was seminal in that it led to a brief golden era of rigorous empirical examination of the process of psychotherapy. It facilitated research primarily for two reasons: (1) the model had an elegant parsimony, and (2) the conditions could be operationalized. The conditions Rogers delineated helped distinguish those elements common to all therapeutic practices from those variables primarily stylistic in nature.

The increasing professional acceptance and growing popularity of marriage and family therapy has spawned a plethora of schools of practice, but there has been little coherent, theoretically based empirical research actually focusing on the process by which change occurs. For students and practitioners, as well as for theorists and researchers, the situation is at best confusing. The intent of this article is to identify the similarities and differences between client-centered therapy with individuals and that with couples and families, in order to establish definable criteria within the process of family therapy[1] which will facilitate an understanding of the process of change.

By and large, despite some minor modifications (e.g., Rogers, Gendlin, Kiesler, & Truax, 1967), the six conditions as put forth originally have withstood the test of time and clinical practice with individuals. Furthermore, although the literature is scant, some theorists (e.g., Levant, 1978, 1984; Thayer, 1982; van der Veen & Novak, 1969) have attempted to apply the basic principles of client-centered theory to the practice of family therapy. Interestingly, however, little attention has been given to the six conditions that Rogers deemed a shibboleth for therapeutic change. Thus the conditions as originally stated by Rogers are presented, reexamined, and elaborated upon to elucidate their validity, relevance, and modification for applicability to the practice of family therapy.

---

1. For simplicity's sake, the term *family therapy* as used throughout this article should be understood to refer to work with couples and families.

First published in *Person-Centered Review,* Volume 4, Number 3, August 1989.

Rogers' (1957, p. 96) six conditions are:

1. Two persons are in psychological contact.
2. The first, whom we shall term the client, is in a state of incongruence, being vulnerable or anxious.
3. The second person, whom we shall term the therapist, is congruent or integrated in the relationship.
4. The therapist experiences unconditional positive regard for the client.
5. The therapist experiences an empathic understanding of the client's frame of reference and endeavors to communicate this experience to the client.
6. The communication to the client of the therapist's empathic understanding and unconditional positive regard is to a minimal degree achieved.

No other conditions are necessary. If these six conditions exist, and continue over a period of time, this is sufficient. The process of constructive personality change will follow.

PSYCHOLOGICAL CONTACT: THE THERAPEUTIC RELATIONSHIP

The first condition of therapeutic change, that of psychological contact between the client and the therapist, is assumed in the practice of individual psychotherapy by Rogers. Little explication was offered. This lack of explanation is somewhat deceptive, however, as the quality of the relationship is really elaborated upon under the last three conditions, unconditional positive regard, empathic understanding, and the client's perception of the therapist. Thus Rogers really suggests that the client at least minimally 'subceive' the therapist as engaged in the relationship, and that this engagement will enable the client to perceive the therapist as both caring and understanding.

Therefore, even without elaboration, in individual therapy the assumption of psychological contact seems straightforward and obvious; in family therapy, however, the therapeutic relationship is neither obvious nor simple, and requires explanation. The establishment of a relationship between the therapist and client is complex in family therapy because the psychological contact most often includes more than one client. The issue, however, is one about which many practitioners of family therapy are divided.

For therapeutic change to take place in family therapy, many maintain that the therapist must sustain a relationship with the system as a whole (i.e., the couple or family). Some (e.g., Minuchin, 1974) believe that the entire therapeutic process is likely to be far more effective if the therapist not only relates to the system but also, to some extent, becomes part of that system as well. Still others (e.g., Bowen, 1975) maintain that it is sufficient if a relationship exists between at least one member of the system and the therapist.

How the family system is defined becomes an issue for the family therapist. Barrett-Lennard (1984), for example, delineates a range of the complex interrelationships within various nuclear family constellations with which the family therapist must deal, whereas Speck and Rueveni (1969) propose that the system include extended kin and even quasi-kin (e.g., neighbors).

Despite the debate, it becomes clear that therapists who work with families conceive of and relate to clients in a somewhat different fashion from therapists who work with individuals. To begin with, the family therapist is given entirely to the multiple perspectives of the various family members present. This affords the family therapist a rich multidimensional view of the individual members and their intimate environment, one to another or to the family as an interactive whole—a view rarely available to the individual therapist. Thus, in contrast to the individual therapist who has only the perspective of a single client, the family therapist becomes aware of and attentive to the subtle ecology of the family context through the complex interactions played out directly in the therapy hour. It is common for individual therapists who begin doing family therapy to report that once they have become immersed in family therapy process, the experience subtly but significantly alters the manner in which they think about and do therapy, even with individuals.

Thus psychological contact between therapist and client, a relatively simple variable in individual therapy, becomes in family therapy a multifaceted investigable variable by which the effectiveness of intervention strategies might be evaluated. Ironically, this very basic condition is perhaps one of the least explored in both individual and family therapy.

INCONGRUENCE: THE STATE OF THE CLIENT

The state of the client, perhaps more than any of the other five conditions, differentiates individual from family therapy. The concept of incongruence as used by Rogers in the context of individual psychotherapy defines psychological distress as resulting from a disparity between the actual experience of the individual and the individual's image of self.[2]

Incongruence is relative (as are all of the conditions) in the sense that few if any of us fully meet our expectations of ourselves. When this discrepancy is within tolerable bounds, we may experience mild dissatisfaction, vulnerability, anxiety, or guilt. Such states may indeed be functional in that they may motivate us in various directions, endeavors, and so on. On the other hand, when more severe, the discrepancy may cause us anguish to the point of incapacity. The latter state we term 'psychological distress'. The reasons for, or even the extent of, the distress may or may not be conceptualized fully by the individual. More simply put, this condition states that the client must be experiencing some psychological distress for therapy to be effective. While Rogers never articulated it, what he certainly implied is that personal incongruity motivates the client to seek change.

Transposing the concept of incongruence to the milieu of the family extends its richness: the incongruence of each family member, as well as the incongruence of the system as a whole, requires attention. The concept of familial incongruence to some degree parallels personal incongruence. Van der Veen and Novak (1969) demonstrated that, like a concept of self, each of us has a personal concept of family (a similar concept has been discussed more recently by Reiss and Klein (1987) called a 'family paradigm').

To some degree each individual family member's perception of their family is a shared experience. However, each individual's perception is also colored by their unique experiences as individual family members: e.g., the extended family histories of the spouses, the difference created by order of birth of each of the children, etc. These experiences are augmented by the individual's separate observation of other families, both real (our extended families, friends, and neighbors) and unreal (those we read about

---

2. The concept of incongruence (as well as its obverse, congruence) is an ipsative (as opposed to normative) means of defining psychological health or distress. It is empirically grounded (see Butler & Haigh, 1954) in Q technique (Stephenson, 1980), and has been, in large measure, responsible for facilitating evaluation of the effectiveness of individual client-centered psychotherapy.

in books and see in movies and television).

Thus one form of familial incongruence exists when there is a discrepancy between how an individual perceives the family and the individual's actual experience of his or her family. A common example of this often occurs when the spousal relationship begins deteriorating. Children, believing (or needing to believe) that their parents care about each other, often attribute the parental difficulty to their own behavior: that is, if they had been better behaved, or achieved better academically, or related better to their siblings, and so on, the marriage would not be troubled.

In turn, the child may withdraw, refuse to go to school, fight with his or her siblings, or exhibit other behaviors — any or all of which might create an incongruence (i.e., anguish, pain, distress) for virtually all family members, and consequently impel the family to seek help. The latter condition, where there is consensual distress, may be termed a 'system incongruence'. Thus a family may seek aid because of the distress (i.e., severe incongruence) of one or more of its individual members, an incongruence within one of the familial subsystems (i.e., spousal, parent-child, or sibling) and/or a generalized incongruence within the system as a whole.

Systemic incongruence may result from a temporary acute stress placed on an individual or on the system (e.g., severe illness, financial difficulty, death, etc.). Alternately, the incongruence may be chronic, having developed over a long period of time (e.g., a husband's and wife's disaffection, a child's failure to meet parental expectations, etc.). It is not unusual for an individual's incongruence to create a familial incongruence. When the family comes to a family therapist with the incongruence of an individual as the presenting problem, the therapist's question is often whether or not the incongruence of that individual is primary or, rather, an expression of the incongruence of the family system.

This last situation is commonly observed in family therapy: an individual is presented as 'the family's problem' when, in fact, the individual may actually be one of the more congruent family members, but is being used by the family to deflect or express the incongruence of the system (as might well be the case in the foregoing example of children who blame themselves for their parents' marital problems). In this situation, the individual who impels the family to seek therapy is commonly referred to as a 'lightning rod' or 'scapegoat.' However, the mechanism that may have begun as a temporary measure to maintain family congruence may become fixed because of its initial success. So reinforced, the lightning rod or scapegoat becomes entrenched in the role, thus creating a new set of problems with which the family must come to grips.

Similarly, the individual who expresses the incongruence of the family may be analogous to an individual psychosomatic disorder. The 'identified patient' may indeed be incongruent, but his or her incongruence may be the result of, and/or in conjunction with, the familial incongruence. In this case, the individual bearing the symptom may be the most vulnerable member of the family, and thus the expresser of both the individual's and the family's incongruence.

Another example is that of the family with a handicapped member. In this complex situation, the issues may include: (1) the individual's incongruence related to the handicap itself, (2) the corresponding incongruences of other members surrounding their relationship to the handicapped individual, and (3) the incongruence of the family system. It should be noted that these last two examples are in sharp contrast to the family with a relatively strong individual serving as the family scapegoat or lightning rod.

The discovery and unraveling of these complexities by the family are often a vital part of family therapy. With respect to the concept of incongruence, the difference between working with individuals and with families is subtle but pivotal. In individual therapy, when the client begins feeling more congruent, the assuaging of psychological distress is experienced and the individual feels freer, more integrated, and so on. This is often accomplished through a coming to terms (i.e., becoming more realistic) with expectations of oneself. An internal rather than an external locus of evaluation is experienced. In the family session, that kind of simple congruence seldom suffices. Rather, the family often seeks a kind of consensual congruence consistent with each individual member's internal locus of evaluation. This is neither so simply nor so easily accomplished as the mitigation of incongruence in individual therapy. The interplay of these states of congruence and their continually changing patterns (both in response to internal and external forces) is the essence of the family therapy process.Thus despite the manifestations of progress through the course of family therapy regarding the resolution of conflicts and/or the diminution or elimination of those presenting problems that brought the family to seek help, certain (and in some cases, all) family members, ironically, may experience greater discomfort and distress than they did at the outset of therapy. Much of this has to do with individual family members' differing levels of frustration tolerance, the timing of change, and the lowering of individual protective defenses (see Gaylin, 1966). Indeed, apparent therapeutic 'failure' or abortion of the course of therapy may actually be engineered (usually unconsciously) by one or more family member(s) for whom the process may be going too rapidly or taking a frightening direction, creating intolerable distress. When the lightning rod is removed, other difficulties—including those for which the lightning rod may have been created—may become more easily discernible. This point in the therapeutic process is often the critical juncture, where the family must decide to tolerate the potential anxiety of the unknown and to create new and perhaps unfamiliar behavior patterns for dealing with each other and the world, or to return to former familiar (albeit dysfunctional) behavior patterns.

Awareness of these system dynamics, and the differing responses of individual family members to them and to the therapeutic process, requires assiduous concentration as well as 'openness to experience' (see the following) on the part of the family therapist.[3] However, as a counterbalance to this effort, the richness of these interplays affords great opportunities for the facilitation of change in the therapeutic hour. Finally, dealing with the complexity of multiple levels of potential incongruence within the family may help clarify previously equivocal family therapy outcome results by delineating and separating variables which may appear to have counteracting influences.

CONGRUENCE: THE GENUINENESS OF THE THERAPIST IN THE RELATIONSHIP

One of Rogers' major contributions to the understanding of the practice of psychotherapy was his emphasis on the therapist as a person (i.e., one with a history, values, feelings, etc.) in the therapeutic relationship. Rogers defines the congruence of the therapist in very personal terms—that is, the therapist is 'freely and deeply himself.' What is implicit in the notion of therapist congruence is the concept of 'openness to experience'—the obverse of defensiveness—a key concept introduced and elaborated upon in a later paper

---

3. The compounded complexity of the incongruence in family therapy (over that in individual therapy) tends to support the case for the use of cotherapist teams (as suggested by Rubenstein & Weiner, 1967; Napier and Whitaker, 1972), or 'multiple impact family therapy' (McGregor, 1971). This complexity may also account for the extensive use of 'live supervision' (through a one-way mirror with telephone contact) in the training and practice of family therapy.

by Rogers (1959). The therapist must be able to perceive both himself and the client as accurately as possible. As in the other conditions, that of the therapist's congruence is relative. However, the contrast between the degree of incongruence of the client (condition two) and the degree of congruence of the therapist is focal. This relative absence of defensiveness and facade on the part of the therapist is considered to be a powerful force for therapeutic change. Although Rogers never really elucidates the reason for its power, it is my belief that part of the therapeutic process may be an emulation by the client(s) of the therapist's genuineness.

Congruence of the therapist is often more difficult to achieve in family therapy than in individual therapy. Family therapists must communicate openly with more than one individual — often simultaneously. Ideally, the family therapist needs to feel and express a genuine prizing and empathy (see next two conditions) for each family member — even though these individuals may be in open conflict with one another. Family therapists must be able to draw upon many aspects of their being and experience in order to empathize with individuals of different gender, age, and life experience. Moreover, family therapists must do this even when faced with reflections of their own feelings about situations which may evoke old and perhaps unresolved family conflicts. Indeed, I have found this relatively unexplored therapeutic variable the linchpin of the supervisory process. When I am in doubt about a problem presented by a consultee, I seek out the potential incongruence of the therapist.[4]

UNCONDITIONAL POSITIVE REGARD: PRIZING THE CLIENT

Perhaps none of the six conditions has been so poorly understood as the need for the therapist to maintain unconditional positive regard for the client. Part of this misunderstanding may originate in the apparent absolute nature of the terminology. It should be made clear that, like all of the other conditions, unconditional positive regard is relative. It is therefore perhaps not quite so 'unconditional.' Rather, Rogers means that the client experiences in therapy an acceptance that is much less conditional than that which he would likely experience outside therapy. It requires that therapists suspend their personal values (to the extent possible) in order to maintain a nonjudgmental stance toward clients. Unconditional positive regard should be read as a caring or prizing attitude toward the client, regardless of the feelings the client presents. In other words, therapists at least should feel positively about their client.

In family therapy, there are complications regarding the unconditional positive regard of the therapist for the client(s). The therapist must maintain a prizing attitude toward more than one individual. It is not unusual for the therapist to maintain this attitude in

---

4. A cautionary note is in order here. I have grown somewhat uncomfortable having observed the therapist's expressed need for congruence to provide an excuse for everything from psychological to sexual abuse of the client. The concept of genuineness (later used and extended by Jourard, 1971, and Gendlin, 1978, as 'transparency' and 'self-disclosure') should not be taken to mean that therapists must act upon or even express perceived incongruences within themselves. What is crucial is that therapists be aware of their reactions and feelings and continually be in touch with their own internal frame of reference. Then the therapist may be sensitized as to whether or not the client is evoking certain reactions within the therapist, or, conversely, whether or not the therapist, by dint of his or her own experiences, is bringing his or her own feelings to the relationship. This process is crucial to the use of the person of the therapist as an instrument of change.

the face of expressions of acrimony by family members toward each other. Thus there is a contrast presented to family members when the therapist expresses feelings of unconditional positive regard to individuals who claim to have lost any positive regard for each other, and where feelings of caring and prizing have been replaced by those of judgment and condemnation. As in the preceding condition, therapists may serve, in part, as role models for their clients. In so doing, they may also remind individuals of their positive attributes and worth.

A further complication arises (often in the case of marital discord, or parent-child conflict) when one or more family members attempt(s) to place the family therapist in the role of arbiter. In these cases the family members may be locked into a struggle in which validation of their position requires the invalidation of another's. It is not at all unusual for family members to resist the nonjudgmental stance of the therapist initially. It is natural to seek validation for one's position in a conflict. Family therapy is no exception. If the family therapist can maintain a nonjudgmental stance toward all parties, the family may be able to 'reframe' (see Watzlawick, Weakland, & Fisch, 1974) the situation from a winner-take-all conquest to a new and, ideally, mutually acceptable view of the situation. Especially in these circumstances, unconditional positive regard is closely related to empathy (see the following).

EMPATHIC UNDERSTANDING

The therapist's ability to maintain an empathic stance toward the client is undoubtedly the most widely accepted and commonly discussed of Rogers' six conditions. Rogers elegantly describes empathy as follows:

> To sense the client's private world as if it were your own, but without ever losing the 'as if' quality ... When the client's world is this clear to the therapist, and he moves about in it freely, then he can both communicate his understanding of what is clearly known to the client and can also voice meanings in the client's experience of which the client is barely aware. (1957, p. 99)

Ironically, empathy has become so accepted a concept in psychotherapy that few appreciate the intricacies of its nuances and power. It is neither so simple nor so easily accomplished as many a beginning therapist supposes. It requires rigorous attention and concentration to foster and maintain. While some come by it more naturally than others, empathic ability is nonetheless a skill that cannot be taken for granted. It, like musical virtuosity, requires both talent and continuous practice.

One of the difficulties in dealing with empathy as an identifiable (and therefore researchable) variable is its easy confusion with its isomorphs: sympathy and identification. The sympathetic observer maintains distance, not allowing himself to enter the internal frame of reference of the other person. On the other hand, a person who is identified with another does not maintain any distance. While sympathy does not engender therapeutic change, identification is more dangerous to the therapeutic process because it permits the therapist to project motivations onto the client which may be outside the client's frame of reference. It is the delicate balance of significant, but separate, understanding that defines the empathic stance and gives it its power. Empathy empowers metaphor as a therapeutic tool (Watzlawick, 1978), just as the empathic communication of metaphor enables poetry to express the universality of the human condition.

While it is difficult enough for a therapist working with individuals to maintain an empathic stance in the therapeutic hour, it is far more difficult for a therapist to achieve and maintain this condition effectively in family therapy. However, if the therapist is able to convey empathy for each individual, family members may be led to the inevitable conclusion that there may indeed be separate realities: that each person sees through lenses that have been uniquely colored by his or her experience. If these separate realities can be accepted by the family, then rich complementarity can supplant clashing polarity. Thus a reconceptualization of the situation is made possible, one that may engender greater empathy among family members.

It is the family therapist's ability to experience empathically the internal frame of reference of each family member that not only facilitates intrafamilial empathy, but also sheds new light on 'unresolvable' conflicts. When a family member concurs with the therapist's reflection of his or her internal frame of reference, it is not uncommon for another member — who is listening to the therapist — to exclaim in wonder, 'I never realized you felt that way!' or, 'I never understood what you meant when you said that before!' Johnson & Greenberg (1988) have identified this 'increased accessibility and responsiveness' and labeled it 'softening.'

Furthermore, in the family therapy session, the therapist may often have an empathic understanding of the entire system, an understanding not easily available to family members since they are emotionally involved and invested in their family. In such cases the therapist's reflection of a systemic vantage point may have the impact of holding up a mirror to the family, ideally enabling the family members to see their interactions in a new light. Often such reperceiving can help cut through (or at least loosen) the family's Gordian knot.

THE CLIENT'S PERCEPTION OF THE THERAPIST

The final condition is that the therapist's acceptance and empathy be perceived to some degree by the client. This last condition harkens back to the first in that it delineates the special boundaries of the therapeutic relationship. Here, finally, the family therapist may have it easier than the therapist working with individuals. Insofar as the condition indicates at least a minimal perception by the client(s), it may be sufficient if at certain times only some members perceive the therapist as caring and understanding. However, as noted throughout the preceding discussion, the more the therapist can communicate these attitudes to each family member, and thus to the system at large, the more likely the therapist will be able to facilitate change. Conversely, when some family members see the therapist as the obverse (i.e., insensitive and condemning) the likelihood of an abortion of the therapeutic process is increased because of withdrawal and/or sabotage by the alienated family member(s). However, even when only parts of the system have been 'reached,' additional change may be facilitated from within after the direct relationship with the therapist has been ended. That is, once the family experiences its actualizing potential, a process of growth has been set in motion and is likely to continue.

CONCLUDING COMMENTS

These are the only conditions postulated by Rogers. In the years I have applied them to the practice, consultation, teaching, and supervision of family therapy, I have found these conditions to be a good foundation for the refining and clarifying of processes occurring within the family therapy hour. Furthermore, I have found them useful for identifying dimensions for research into the process of family therapy. Thus this article is not intended to suggest yet another form of family therapy; rather, it is an attempt to identify and harness the warp threads common to the fabric of all therapeutic endeavor on which we as therapists with different styles, personalities, and theoretical persuasions apply our weft, whether the context is individuals, groups, or families.

Neither did I intend to elaborate the total panoply of differences between the practice of family therapy and other therapeutic endeavors. There are distinct differences in the tools necessary to do family therapy — particularly family therapy in which young children are involved. One of these very crucial differences that is certainly worthy of note is that family therapists need to have some knowledge of child development, and on occasion shift from 'therapeutic' to 'guidance' mode. For example, it is one thing to listen empathically to distraught parents lament over their sense of inadequacy, concern for their offspring, and so on. It is another story to hear the complaint that their child, at a year and a half, is 'willful' because she does not succumb to the parents' efforts at toilet training. There are relatively immutable normative developmental parameters regarding biological functions such as sphincter control (or talking, walking, reading, etc.). To ignore these parameters may maintain unrealistic parental expectations, which could indeed have deleterious effects on all family members in this situation. Thus I make a clear distinction in my work with families as to when I am doing child guidance and when I am doing family therapy. For my family therapy endeavors, the conditions as discussed here serve admirably.

Some readers may be disappointed that I did not delve more deeply into the underpinning theoretical concepts that parallel those of individual client-centered therapy. One of the most important of these is the concept of family actualization. In many respects, following the organismic base of Rogers, it is easier to make a case for family actualization than it is for self-actualization. The 'self' is a construct not unlike that of ego, id, or superego. Family is an observable, and to some degree a biological, entity: it is indigenous to who we are, and defines us as a species (see Gaylin, 1985). An elaboration of these issues here would have distorted the intent of the foregoing exposition.

Finally, some readers may feel the need for more case examples to flesh out the conditions. However, this article was not intended as a recipe book on how to do family therapy. Rather, I had hoped to demonstrate that the practice of client-centered family therapy has natural (and familiar) parallels to that of individual therapy. The practice of both and the ideas underpinning that practice are inductively derived and based on therapeutic process. By design, the structural elements have been minimized. The summary goal of this discussion was the specifying of the elements and important philosophical parallels between the practice of client-centered therapy in both individual and family contexts, these being a deep and inherent respect for the client (individual or family) and the facilitative stance of the therapist.

REFERENCES

Barrett-Lennard, G. T. (1984). The world of family relationships: A person-centered systems view. In R. F. Levant & J. M. Shlien (Eds.), *Client-centered therapy and the person-centered approach* (pp. 222–42). New York: Praeger.

Bowen, M. (1975). Family therapy after twenty years. In S. Arieti, D. X. Freeman, & I. E. Dyrud (Eds.), *American handbook of psychiatry. V: Treatment (2nd ed.)* (pp. 367–92). New York: Basic Books.

Butler, J. M., & Haigh, G. V. (1954). Changes in the relationship between self-concepts and ideal-concepts. In C. R. Rogers & R. F. Dymond (Eds.), *Psychotherapy and personality change* (pp. 55–75). Chicago: University of Chicago Press.

Gaylin, N. L. (1966). Psychotherapy and psychological health: A Rorschach structure and function analysis. *Journal of Consulting Psychology, 30,* 494–500.

Gaylin, N. L. (1985). Marriage: The civilizing of sexuality. In M. Farber (Ed.), *Human sexuality: Psychosexual effects of disease* (pp. 40–54). New York: Macmillan.

Gendlin, E. (1978). *Focusing.* New York: Everest House.

Johnson, S. M., & Greenberg, L. S. (1988). Relating process to outcome in marital therapy. *Journal of Marital and Family Therapy, 14,* 175–83.

Jourard, S. (1971). *The transparent self* (rev. ed.). New York: Van Nostrand Reinhold.

Levant, R. F. (1978). Family therapy: A client-centered perspective. *Journal of Marital and Family Therapy, 2,* 35–42.

Levant, R. F. (1984). From person to system: Two perspectives, in R. F. Levant & J. M. Shlien (Eds.), *Client-centered therapy and the person-centered approach* (pp. 243–60). New York: Praeger.

McGregor, R. (1971). Multiple impact psychotherapy with families. In J. G. Howells (Ed.), *Theory and practice of family psychiatry* (pp. 890–902). New York: Brunner/Mazel.

Minuchin, S. (1974). *Families and family therapy.* Cambridge, MA: Harvard University Press.

Napier, A. Y., & Whitaker, C. A. (1972). A conversation about co-therapy. In A. Ferber, M. Mendelsohn, & A. Napier (Eds.), *The book of family therapy* (pp. 480–506). New York: Science House.

Reiss, D., & Klein, D. (1987). Paradigm and pathogenesis. In T. Jacob (Ed.), *Family interaction and psychopathology* (pp. 202–55). New York: Plenum.

Rogers, C. R. (1957). The necessary and sufficient conditions of therapeutic personality change. *Journal of Consulting Psychology, 21,* 95–103.

Rogers, C. R. (1959). A theory of therapy, personality, and interpersonal relationships, as developed in the client-centered framework. In S. Koch (Ed.), *Psychology: A study of a science: Vol 3. Formulations of the person in the social context* (pp. 184–256). New York: McGraw-Hill.

Rogers, C. R., Gendlin, E. T., Kiesler, D. J., & Truax, C. B. (1967). *The therapeutic relationship and its impact: A study of psychiatry with schizophrenics.* Madison: University of Wisconsin Press.

Rubenstein, D., & Weiner, O. R. (1967). Co-therapy teamwork relationships in family psychotherapy. In G. H. Zuk & I. Boszormenyi-Nagy (Eds.), *Family therapy and disturbed families* (pp. 206–20). Palo Alto, CA: Science and Behavior Books.

Speck, R. V., & Rueveni, U. (1969). Network therapy: A developing concept. *Family Process, 8,* 182–91.

Stephenson, W. (1980). Newton's fifth rule and Q methodology. *American Psychologist, 10,* 882–9.

Thayer, L. (1982). A person-centered approach to family therapy. In A. M. Horne & M. M. Ohlsen (Eds.), *Family counseling and therapy* (pp. 175–213). Itasca, IL: F. E. Peacock.

van der Veen, F., & Novak, A. L. (1969). Perceived parental attitudes and family concepts of disturbed adolescents, normal siblings and normal controls. *Family Process, 8,* 327–41.

Watzlawick, P. (1978). *The language of change.* New York: Basic Books.

Watzlawick, P., Weakland, J., & Fisch, R. (1974). *Change: Principles of problem formation and problem resolution.* New York: Norton.

Empathy and Strategy in the Family System

Margaret S. Warner

Chicago Counseling and Psychotherapy Center and
Illinois School of Professional Psychology, Chicago

Some families get caught in a web of indirect communication and interaction in such a way that traditional client-centered approaches, such as empathic listening, problem solving, or communication skills training, are ineffective. Client-centered therapists can increase their effectiveness in working with these families if they have an understanding of strategic communication and the sorts of experience that often underlie indirect styles of interaction. A model of communication is presented that incorporates elements of strategic family systems thinking and critiques core elements of the theory.

Some families get caught in a web of strategic communication that blocks much of the empathic understanding and open communication that is crucial for effective client-centered therapy. 'Strategic' communication, as I am defining it here, is communication in which there is a discrepancy between what people are saying and doing and what they intend to accomplish. This communication is not simply manipulative. Often family members are trying to get their own needs met while protecting other family members. Strategic communication can make therapist empathy difficult, since people's intentions are not what they seem to be on the surface. An even more crucial problem arises because members of families that communicate strategically often have become so anxious about the possibility of being dominated or criticized that they react to attempts to clarify what family members mean with an escalation of indirect communication. The purpose of this article is to describe strategic communication in families, help therapists to understand its functions, and assist family members in communicating more effectively.

Since direct communication is blocked, such families often have a backlog of serious, unresolved problems. Yet the indirectness of family maneuvers can make it difficult for outsiders to help in ordinary ways. High levels of frustration are often generated in both family members and mental health professionals. In attempting to gain control over the situation, family members may become sick or violent or behave in crazy ways. Mental health professionals often find themselves becoming punitive and rigidly bureaucratic or overinvolved and depleted.

Metaphorically, a person in a strategic family is like a spy at a cocktail party at enemy headquarters who is afraid he may be found out and killed, but is still trying to maintain polite chatter to cover the situation. Suppose you were at this party and wanted to offer understanding or help to this man. If you simply take his surface behavior seriously — he is perhaps chatting about the weather and local events — you will miss the point of his situation entirely. Yet if you are sensitive to undercurrents in his presentation, and comment on them — noting perhaps that he seems a little nervous and on edge or that he seems to be looking out the window a lot — he is likely to do everything in his power to disqualify

First published in *Person-Centered Review*, Volume 4, Number 3, August 1989.

your communication and change the subject. If you openly challenge his behavior he is likely to be even more upset, and may take some drastic action to stop you from continuing in a way that threatens to expose him.

Strategic family interaction raises important issues about the nature and impact of empathy under complex communicational circumstances. Ordinarily, client-centered therapists take people's self-presentations at face value and assume that, if relevant, other versions of the situation will emerge in time. However, if family members feel that open communication is dangerous, empathy that is directed at their surface communication may seem to be beside the point. They are likely to feel that the therapist just does not understand what people are really doing and saying in the family. Under these circumstances, family members are likely to decide not to risk more direct communication in that setting. Usually if a client-centered therapist is feeling confused about what people mean, he or she will simply raise the issue and discuss it with the clients, but if raising issues directly results in an escalation of indirect communication and maneuvers aimed at changing the subject, this means of clarification is blocked.

Under these circumstances, it is extremely difficult for a therapist to maintain a stance that is empathic, congruent, and prizing of all family members and, at the same time, work effectively on family issues. Strategic family communication raises issues that are not easily resolved within a client-centered framework. Yet I believe that the client-centered tradition, with its sensitivity to interpersonal power issues and its concern for the dignity of the individual, brings an invaluable perspective to such families.

STRATEGIC FAMILY SYSTEMS THEORY

Although they conceptualize it somewhat differently, strategic family systems theorists have focused intensively on the sort of family process described here. The understanding of strategic communication presented in this article is grounded in recent work by philosophers and linguists on the negotiation of meaning (Austin, 1961; Harre & Secord, 1972; Pearce, 1976). It is a view that incorporates and reinterprets many of the phenomena explained by strategic family systems theorists without losing any of their core insights. To understand this reinterpretation let us first look at the history of strategic family systems theory.

When it was first presented in the 1960s and 1970s, strategic family systems theory offered an exciting new way of understanding serious psychopathology. A group headed by Gregory Bateson had developed a systems theory of communication in families in the 1950s, suggesting that families of schizophrenic patients communicate in 'double-binding' ways (Bateson & Jackson, 1964). Jay Haley extended this thinking to suggest that all communication is strategic and popularized the use of 'paradoxical' communication by family systems therapists (Haley, 1963, 1973). In the 1970s, strategic thinking was often combined with structural family therapy, an approach that focuses on creating a clear hierarchy of power between grandparents, parents, and children in families (Minuchin, 1974). The two models are often referred to together as 'structural-strategic' family therapy.

Systems theorists[1] observed that individual problems are often part of ongoing patterns of family interaction. Deep change in the system will occur if the therapist can interrupt the ongoing patterns in the systems that contain problematic behaviors.

---

1. Many theoretical positions originally developed by strategic theorists have been adopted broadly within family systems theory. 'Family systems theory' as used in this article includes 'strategic family systems theory.'

Sometimes this can be done directly, but strategic therapists will often intervene with 'paradoxical' directives that are chosen for their ability to make it difficult for the family to continue in existing patterns. Such directives are chosen without consideration for whether they are 'true' in the usual sense of the word.

Strategic approaches to family therapy reached the height of their popularity in the late 1970s and early 1980s when some therapists saw paradoxical maneuvers as the treatment of choice for virtually all problems (Andolfi, Angelo, Menghi, & Nicolo-Corigliano, 1983; Bergman, 1985; Papp, 1983; Selvini-Palazzoli, Cecchin, Prata, & Boscolo, 1978; Weeks & L'Abate, 1982). However, many practitioners found therapeutic paradoxes difficult to implement and got varied results with clients. Humanistically oriented therapists were troubled by the ethical implications of practicing therapy without regard to issues of authenticity in client or therapist communication. In spite of these difficulties, strategic family therapy offers the only well-developed theory of indirect communication in family systems.

Strategic systems theorists propose that all families maintain existing patterns of behavior in homeostatic ways, and that the only way to understand such patterns is to ignore individual experience and to concentrate on sequences of family behavior.[2] My view is that this situation occurs only when families are communicating strategically, and that it is actually a sign of family dysfunction. All communication is not equally strategic. When it is necessary for the therapist to ignore expressed feelings and intentions in order to get a good understanding of what is actually going on in a family, one can usually assume that family members do not trust each other enough to interact openly on core family issues. The fact that family members cannot communicate openly contributes to unresolved problems and eventually leads to rigid sequences of interaction. The approach to understanding strategic communication presented in this article offers two advantages over traditional family systems thinking that are particularly relevant to client-centered therapists. The therapist can understand and respond to strategic interaction and rigidly patterned family behavior without dismissing the experience of the individual. In addition, neither therapists nor family members need to behave inauthentically in order to develop a realistic view of the complexity of the family's strategic interaction.

THE NATURE OF STRATEGIC COMMUNICATION[3]

To reinterpret strategic family systems, one first needs to explore the nature of strategic communication. When people communicate strategically, their purposes are not indicated by the overt content of their verbal and nonverbal communication. For example:

- A mother may say 'I don't think you are well enough to go away to school' to get a son to stay home when she is afraid of facing her husband by herself.
- A daughter may throw a temper tantrum so that her parents will be so focused on her problems that they are distracted from their difficulties with each other.
- A man may try to look sick on the bus in the hope that someone will offer a seat.

2. See, for example, Watzlawick, Beavin, and Jackson (1967, p. 42); Haley (1980, pp. 86–7); and Selvini-Palazzoli et al. (1978, p. 26).

3. The analysis of the negotiation of meaning used in this article is most strongly influenced by Austin (1961), Harre and Secord (1972), Pearce (1976), and Searle (1969). The definition of strategic communication and the separation of truth and impact considerations are my own. For a fuller consideration of these issues, see Warner (1983).

There is almost always more than one plausible way to construe social behavior. In ordinary communication, people use both truth considerations and impact considerations in assessing situations. A version that has high truth value will offer a good account of all the information available and will have some predictive value as to what people are likely to do next and why. For example, if a woman is 'really sick' as opposed to 'lazy' when not completing a work assignment, it can be assumed that she is likely to perform responsibly once she is better. If she is 'lazy' it is likely that she will think of another excuse when there is more work to do.

In everyday communication, people are also expected to consider the impact of construing situations in one way as opposed to another. For example, a spouse may think, 'If I worry about every little thing, I'll just make myself feel insecure. I should probably give my wife the benefit of the doubt and assume that she didn't mean to be late.' The use of impact considerations allows the individual to choose among alternative versions of reality, selecting ones that are personally appealing or that seem likely to create desired outcomes in social interactions.

Although people are expected to use both truth considerations and impact considerations in framing their interpretations of events, general social norms dictate that impact considerations should not overshadow or eclipse truth considerations unless there are exceptional circumstances. For example, if a man was being held hostage, playing a poker game, or talking to someone who is senile, he might be seen as justified in shaping his communication to achieve desired outcomes. Under ordinary circumstances, however, if an individual's communication persistently offers an unreliable account of what is going on, the individual risks being seen as insincere, manipulative, self-deluded, or crazy.[4]

When people communicate strategically, impact considerations are dominant in shaping their verbal and nonverbal behavior. As a result, their outward expressions give a poor account of their intentions, and offer little guidance about their likely future behavior. Individuals may or may not be aware that they are communicating strategically. For example, whenever her mother gets depressed a daughter may misbehave in such a way that her mother's energy is mobilized without the girl's knowing that this is the reason for her behavior. People may be aware of their motivations, but feel that the risks of open communication are too great. For example, a husband who feels worthless may feel that his wife would stay only if he is sick and in need of her care, and, as a result, he consciously plays up the seriousness of his disability. Many times there is some mix of self-deception and covert intention in strategic situations. People are afraid to look too closely at their intentions for fear that to do so will make things worse in a situation in which they feel out of control.

COMMON FORMS OF STRATEGIC COMMUNICATION

Several kinds of situations offer potential strategic advantage within families. The following are some of the most common:

The appearance of emotional and physical disability. The appearance of need can allow a family member to call on others for care and attention, thereby relieving him- or herself of ordinary obligations. This is even more true if the disability is out of the person's control, since the person cannot be expected to take care of his or her needs independently under those circumstances.

---

4. For a more extended discussion of this point, see Warner (1983).

Perceiving others as needing caretaking. Conversely, if a family member is seen as being in need of care, a rationale is provided for other family members to take control of certain aspects of that person's life.

Offering the appearance of love. The appearance of love or care for another person's well-being can offer strategic advantage to the caretaker by motivating that person to continue investing in the relationship. The person will then be tempted to forget past difficulties without clarifying or resolving underlying issues.

Undermining alternative relationships or activities. Communication that undermines or devalues a person's ability to function successfully in other situations can offer strategic advantage by cementing the individual's dependence on the family.

STRATEGIC COMMUNICATION AND THE FAMILY SYSTEM

Some amount of strategic communication occurs in all relationships since most individuals are never fully aware of their own motivations or able to express them in a straightforward manner. Strategic communication is not likely to cause great difficulty if it is limited to a few sensitive subjects or if family members can openly discuss issues that really concern them. However, if strategic communication dominates core family issues over an extended period of time, the family system itself becomes altered in ways that exacerbate the seriousness of its problems and block commonsense problem-solving efforts. This occurs because strategic communication has the indirect effect of making open communication less and less effective, and because strategic maneuvers need to become stronger over time to maintain their effectiveness. Let us look at how this develops.

Strategic communication is often quite rewarding in the short run since it can offer immediate relief from difficult situations without the pain and uncertainty involved in open communication. Initially, quite mild strategic moves can have a positive effect. If a person seems mildly sick or upset, family members are likely to be solicitous and not expect much in return; but if a person is always sick or upset when something uncomfortable is to be faced, family members are likely to be less and less responsive. Initially, a husband might stay home if his wife has the flu, but later will do so only if she has severe asthma attacks. If an individual is always upset, he or she will soon have to be seriously impaired or suicidal to get a response from family members. Therefore, if a family begins to rely heavily on strategic maneuvers in order to maintain a sense of control, individual members may escalate the intensity of disability and kinds of dysfunctional behavior over time.

If the appearance of love or self-disclosure is often used to gain strategic advantage, family members will learn to become more suspicious when others seem most sincere and open. Over time, family members will become anxious and self-protective in response to any appearance of love, openness, or concern, because they have so often been tricked by these appearances before. If strategic communication becomes the norm, family members will learn to disregard open communication and look for other clues in the environment, such as nonverbal signs or patterns in a person's behavior, in an attempt to determine another person's motives. They are likely to learn to avoid revealing their deepest desires and hopes because these can be used against them in strategic moves by other family members.

Since strategic advantage is often gained by undermining the other's self-confidence, family members are likely to become extremely criticism-sensitive—shifting communication away from any topic that might result in their being blamed, or away from any suggestion that some other behavior might work better for them; and because family maneuvers involve attempts to control each other's behavior, family members can become very reactive. Consequently, they will often do the opposite of any suggestion made by the therapist or any family member.

Over time, then, a family system that is dominated by strategic communication can become impermeable to open communication. Attempts at open communication are likely to be seen as a ruse or as a weakness of which others can take advantage. Attempts to problem-solve are likely to set off criticism, sensitivity, and reactivity in the family. As a result, the original issue is lost and plans made in therapy are undermined. If some family members do communicate more openly because of the therapist's urging, they may well put themselves at a disadvantage in the family, risking further hurt and disillusionment.

Under these circumstances, family members are likely to develop an intense hunger for intimacy. Since they cannot afford to understand their own motives or to express them openly if they do understand them, they can never feel fully understood. Because their overt behavior cannot be understood, they never have the experience of knowing that they are cared for in their own right. Their hunger for intimacy makes family members even more vulnerable to family maneuvers since their need to have contact is so great.

A different sort of intimacy does develop in a strategic family — the intimacy of knowing intuitively and being able to operate within the framework of each other's strategic moves. There is a certain drama that develops as family members make moves and countermoves to control each other, and excitement in the possibility of winning the next round in the family drama. Because strategic communication often involves the desire for intense attachment and future love, family members often have the feeling that a quality of family life beyond that of ordinary people is unattainable, or they have the sense that they live in a family with special needs, that they are indispensable to each other in a life and death way. Since the dramas of strategic families involve increasingly severe disability, out-of-control behavior, and sabotage of family members' attempts to function outside of the family, the longer members have been involved in a strategic family, the less confident they are about whether they could function elsewhere. Given their feeling that family members cannot function without each other, they find it harder and harder to leave the family without feeling guilty.

Young children are likely to pick up and respond to the unacknowledged feelings and purposes of their parents in strategic families, especially if they sense a high level of anxiety around such issues. For example, if a parent is overwhelmed with fear whenever a child expresses excitement, the child may become very subdued to avoid eliciting that reaction; or if parents strongly need to believe that they have a perfect family, children may learn to pretend that all family situations are perfect and help their parents to avoid situations in which any lack of perfection would have to be acknowledged to the parents. On the other hand, if parents are fighting destructively, even quite young children will learn that creating a scene can calm things down. In each of these situation, children are learning to become incongruent internally and/or in their communication as a way of preserving the stability and sense of well-being of the family. By doing this, they learn to mislabel their own experiences and purposes.

Although children may have little conscious awareness of the dynamics of their family, they may come to have a more functional awareness of these dynamics than their parents have because they need to manage their self-presentations in response to their parents' unspoken needs. For example, children of parents who are overwhelmed by the needs of others may learn to pretend that they do not want anything even if their parents offer to give them wonderful presents. Children in such families may become aware of the reason for their behavior at quite a young age. 'Mom says that she wants to buy me something, but she'll get angry if I say I want it and won't buy it anyway.' Often children develop a complex double consciousness in which they are at least partially aware of family maneuvers and of their own countermaneuvers. However, they tend to see such behaviors as part of their badness or craziness.

THERAPIST EMPATHY AND STRATEGIC FAMILY INTERACTION

Empathic understanding of strategic family interaction requires that the therapist be aware of two levels of communication: (1) the surface meaning and (2) the strategic meaning. Strategic communication is likely when patterns of behavior that are not related to family members' expressed intentions recur. Underlying purposes can often be understood if the therapist tries the following formula:

a) Observe sequences of behavior while disregarding family members' expressed reasons for behaving the way that they do.

b) Assume that each behavior is intended to elicit the results that occur, even if the outcome seems quite undesirable on the surface.

c) Assume that the reason for desiring the outcome is positive, that is, that some attempt to self-actualize oneself and/or be helpful to the other person is involved.

d) Assume that all members of the family may be served by a particular outcome, not just the person who seems to be initiating the behavior.

For example, the daughter whose mother had complained for years about her being overweight began a serious diet. The next time she went to visit, her mother said she was making 110 cupcakes for the church bazaar the next day. The daughter did not eat any cupcakes while making them. Her mother packed some in a food package that the daughter was taking home, with a note that they were for the rest of the family. After the daughter complained of this to her mother, her sister called to say that she was treating her mother badly. The daughter resisted family pressure for a while and then regained all the weight she had lost.

The intensity and persistence of this pattern suggested that the whole family was in some way invested in keeping this woman overweight. One might ask how this pattern might be serving the self-actualizing tendencies of the people involved. The mother may feel that her daughter will want to relate to her only if she feels so unattractive that she is unable to succeed with other people. The daughter and mother may both feel that real closeness occurs only when there are serious problems to worry about. The daughter may sense that her mother's fears of worthlessness are relieved when the daughter has problems. Thus she 'helps' her mother by continuing to have problems.

Therapists' formulations that interpret family interactions in terms of their positive strivings may sound very strange to most of us. Yet they often turn out to offer much better explanations of family behavior than commonsense, negatively framed versions. Why, for example, would a mother need her daughter to feel unattractive to believe that she would want to relate to her? Is she not just being perverse and selfish? In my experience, families that interact strategically are trying to avoid the emotional disintegration of family members while keeping their relationships intact. They often feel that these strategic relationships offer the only alternative to complete aloneness for some family members, and provide the only way that family contact can be maintained.

Once it becomes clear that family members are maintaining certain patterns, the therapist needs to consider what emotional outcomes could be so bad that this behavior makes sense. The therapist needs to appreciate how terrifying emotional disintegration can be to such family members. Violent relationships may be preferred to suicidal despair. Psychosis may feel preferable to losing family relationships altogether. Never being close to anyone may feel better than having relationships that stir up incest memories. If the therapist perceives family members as perverse or self-centered in their interactions with each other, it is likely that some element of the emotional experience of the family members has not been fully understood.

When family interaction is looked at in this way, the therapist can often begin to understand the family's 'code.' Full understanding is not essential. Often it is enough to understand that the family members seem to be cooperating in order to maintain a certain sequence, and that this sequence is probably helping them avoid something worse. For example, in the case of the woman who wanted to lose weight, it is enough to understand that her relationship with her mother is probably felt to be necessary in order to avoid an emotional disintegration in one or both of them. Empathy for the emotional reality underlying strategic interaction in a family is likely to assuage the therapist's experience of impatience and frustration with family members. Strategic families are often frantic about doing something about serious problems, yet family members often undermine sensible change efforts. Empathy for the surface level of communication allows the therapist to understand that family problems are genuinely frightening and burdensome. Understanding the strategic meaning of the interaction can allow the therapist to understand that existing problems may help avoid outcomes that are seen by family members as worse than their problems are.

COMMUNICATION WITH STRATEGIC FAMILIES

Because strategic families are often sensitive to criticism, any negatively framed communication is likely to elicit defensiveness in family members. For example, if a mother is afraid that she is worthless, a simple therapist question (e.g., regarding why she did not follow through on a homework assignment) may trigger her worst fears about herself. She may hear it as an indictment of her as a mother, and to avoid this implication she may launch into a subtle attack on other family members or on the therapist. Sensing her distress, other family members may cooperate in changing the subject or creating distractions.

The therapist can increase his or her understanding of family interaction a great deal by simply noticing what subjects trigger sensitivity to criticism in the family. If the therapist conceptualizes the family in terms of self-actualizing motives, it is easier to avoid critical, negatively framed communication. When family members increase their indirect maneuvers, it often signifies that an underlying sensitivity in some family member has been touched. If the therapist will review communications mentally, he or she can often infer what sensitive areas have been triggered.

Strategic families are often reactive. That is, some or all family members will do the opposite of anything they are asked to do. They may ask for suggestions and then find fault with any that are offered, or they may agree to suggestions and then find reasons to avoid following through. Again, the therapist can understand a great deal about the purpose of family interaction by noticing whether people avoid doing anything that is asked of them. The therapist can avoid escalating strategic interaction by making very few demands or suggestions. Family agreements should be very clear and result from thorough family discussion that takes everyone's point of view into account.

Raising the possibility that positive strivings may be involved in apparent disabilities is often quite helpful in strategic families. Family members tend to get caught up in blaming themselves and other family members for their problems while finding themselves unable to change. An interpretation that identifies a positive striving in each family member's behavior often gives family members their first chance to see each person as valuable and sensible. For example, in the family described here, the therapist could ask if they have considered the possibility that the daughter's weight problem gives them a way to be close to each other.

If the therapist can understand strategic maneuvers within the family and still maintain a sense of empathy and prizing for family members, an overall atmosphere of trust can develop in the family. By communicating in ways that are positively framed and undemanding, the therapist can avoid triggering family anxieties. Situations in which family members have upset each other can often be defused by clarifying what caused the reaction and looking for underlying positive strivings that were involved in each person's interaction (Warner, 1980).

As family members begin to feel safe in the therapy situation, they can begin to discuss the issues that have been expressed indirectly in the past. Then the therapy can focus on making room for the full expression of each family member's point of view and for problem-solving around family issues.

CONCEPTUALIZING FAMILY SYSTEMS THEORY AS APPLIED TO STRATEGIC FAMILIES

Family theorists often assert that all families tend to maintain states of homeostasis much the way that a thermostat will make adjustments to keep house temperature constant. These homeostatic responses are described as relatively automatic. As one family systems theorist commented, 'It is as much the nature of systems to maintain dynamic equilibria as it is the nature of the tiger to eat the goat, or, for that matter, of the goat to be eaten' (Papp, 1983, p. x).

Family members' feelings, beliefs, or rationales for acting are seen as irrelevant to homeostatic systems corrections because (1) they occur at a different system level, that of the individual, and (2) they follow a linear cause-effect logic rather than a circular systemic logic.[5] As a result, strategic theorists suggest that *all* families are best understood by attending to sequences of behavior while disregarding the feelings and intentions displayed overtly by family members. Some families may be seen as more 'rigid' than others, allowing too little room for individuality or change in the system (Anderson & Stewart, 1983; Andolfi et al., 1983; Weeks and L'Abate, 1982). However, systems theorists offer little explanation as to why some families would adopt rigid homeostatic patterns while others maintain higher levels of openness to individuality and change.

Saying that families tend to maintain patterns of behavior *because they are systems* begs the question of how, when, and why families do change. Clearly groups of people sometimes behave in predictable, patterned ways and at other times behave in ways that are novel and unexpected. Many family patterns exist because of the conscious and easily acknowledged purposes and values of family members. When this is true, family members might have difficulty solving a particular problem, but their expressed feelings and beliefs

---

5. See Watzlawick et al. (1967, p. 42); Haley (1980, pp. 86–7); and Selvini-Palazzoli et al. (1978, p. 26).

would be highly relevant to understanding what is going on and finding alternatives. Some patterns may not be maintained homeostatically at all if they are incidental to other events or goals in the family.

Many homeostatic qualities attributed by strategic systems theorists to families in general are actually side effects of strategic communication and are atypical of families that communicate in other ways. When family patterns result from strategic maneuvers by family members, their expressed feelings and beliefs *are* likely to be irrelevant to understanding what family members are doing and why. Since open communication is blocked, they are likely to settle into rigid, homeostatic patterns that are resistant to commonsense attempts at change.

The family systems strategy of ignoring overt communication while looking at repeating patterns can be quite effective in understanding strategic families. However, this is not because the family is a 'system.' In healthy systems, people's overt expressions have a great deal to say about what is happening and why. If it is necessary to ignore overt communication in order to understand a family, it is usually a sign of family dysfunction.

Strategic systems theorists often recommend 'paradoxical intention,' that is, by suggesting ways that family problems could be seen as representing a benefit to the family. Systems theorists often justify paradoxical suggestions with premises said to apply to all families. They are:

1. that people tend to do the opposite of what they are told to do, and
2. if the therapist positively reframes the symptom, the family will be forced to let go of its existing homeostatic pattern because it will be put into a paradoxical position. If they keep the symptom it will be seen as something beneficial to the family and encouraged by the therapist. If they rebel against the therapist they will have to give up the symptom and develop a new homeostasis. Therefore, the family cannot avoid doing something that the therapist wants.[6]

The understanding of strategic families presented in this article offers quite a different way of understanding the impact of 'positive refraining' and 'prescribing the symptom.' Since out-of-control, symptomatic behavior often has strategic value, consideration of possible benefits of the symptom can have considerable truth value in understanding the family's situation. Such formulations often offer more coherent versions of what people have done in the past and what they are likely to do in the future than more commonsense, negatively framed interpretations of events. Understood in this way, positive refraining is similar to the client-centered strategy of trying to understand 'positive strivings' or 'self-actualizing tendencies' embedded in seemingly negative behavior.

COMPARISON OF CLIENT-CENTERED AND STRATEGIC SYSTEMS APPROACHES

In traditional forms, both family systems approaches and client-centered approaches can have serious weaknesses in therapy with strategic families. While family systems thinking can uncover underlying dynamics in strategic families and offer ways to get past some forms of family resistance to change, the underlying theory can easily create distance between the therapist and family members. If therapeutic maneuvers are seen as ploys to

---

6. For presentations of this position, see Weeks and L'Abate (1982, pp. 3–37) and Papp (1983, pp. 6–26).

gain leverage within the family, the therapist can easily lose awareness of the experiential reality behind family behavior. When the therapist's communication becomes strategic it is likely to diminish the therapist's sense of authenticity in relation to the family.

Family systems theory itself tends to undermine any valuing of authenticity in intimate relationships by implying that any way of framing experience is as good as any other as long as it creates a favorable outcome. The present analysis of strategic families suggests the opposite—that when communication becomes dominated by impact considerations, the functioning of the system is undermined and serious dysfunction is likely to result. Family systems theorists often do not distinguish between families that communicate relatively openly and those that are involved in strategic patterns of interaction. Techniques such as positive reframing and prescribing the symptom may identify an underlying reality in strategic families, but they are likely to demoralize and confuse a family that is communicating openly about a problem.

On the other hand, a client-centered therapist can easily remain at a superficial level of understanding of strategic families by taking family members' statements completely at face value. Under these circumstances, the therapist is likely to feel increasingly frustrated and confused as it becomes apparent that many family behaviors do not seem to make sense.

Attempts by the therapist to address the incongruence are likely to be perceived as criticism by the family and to set off the same reaction as any other negatively framed communication (blaming, discrediting, distorting, making the communication disappear), without having any noticeable positive effect. Various family members are likely to try to get the therapist to participate in their strategies or to undermine attempts to go against their perceived needs. If the therapist is easily taken in by indirect family strategies, family members are not likely to trust the therapist with vulnerable issues, and they are not likely to feel deeply understood either.

The approach suggested in this article combines elements of traditional family systems therapy and client-centered approaches. Patterns of family interaction are used to infer unstated purposes involved in family interaction and the personal experiences likely to lie behind such strategies. By understanding family members in this way, the therapist is more likely to be able to communicate with family members without escalating strategic maneuvers in the family. As family trust is increased, more traditional communication and problem-solving approaches are likely to be helpful.

Although it can be more intrusive than other forms of client-centered therapy, this way of working with strategic families retains an intense respect for the ultimate autonomy and self-actualizing potential of family members. The therapist will always try to respond with the lowest level of interpretation and intrusiveness possible to allow empathic contact to be maintained. Individuals in a strategic family have often given up on the idea that they could be fully understood and still be prized. The most powerfully healing experiences seem to occur when therapists are able to comprehend covert levels of communication while maintaining a sense of care and respect for the existential dilemmas that result in family members expressing some of their deepest needs indirectly. The therapist's core aim remains the same as that of any person-centered relationship: maintaining an attitude of empathy, congruence, and prizing toward each family member and toward the family as a whole.

REFERENCES

Anderson, C. M., & Stewart, S. (1983). *Mastering resistance.* New York: Guilford.

Andolfi, M., Angelo, C., Menghi, P., & Nicolo-Corigliano, A. M. (1983). *Behind the family mask.* New York: Brunner/Mazel.

Austin, J. L. (1961). *Philosophical papers.* New York: Oxford University Press.

Bateson, G., and Jackson, D. D. (1964). Some varieties of pathogenic organization. In Association for Research in Nervous and Mental Disease (Ed.), *Disorders of communication.* Baltimore: Williams and Wilkins.

Bergman, S. (1985). *Fishing for barracuda.* New York: Norton.

Haley, J. (1963). *Strategies of psychotherapy.* New York: Grune & Stratton.

Haley, J. (1973). *Uncommon therapy.* New York: Norton

Haley, J. (1980). *Leaving home.* New York: McGraw-Hill.

Harre, R., & Secord, P. F. (1972). *The explanation of social behavior.* Oxford: Basil Blackwell.

Minuchin, S. (1974). *Families and family therapy.* Cambridge, MA: Harvard University Press.

Papp, P. (1983). *The process of change.* New York: Guilford.

Pearce, W. B. (1976). The coordinated management of meaning: A rules-based theory of interpersonal communication. In G. R. Miller (Ed.), *Explorations in interpersonal communication* (pp. 17–35). Beverly Hills, CA: Sage.

Searle, J. R. (1969). *Speech acts.* London: Cambridge University Press.

Selvini-Palazzoli, M., Cecchin, G., Prata, G., & Boscolo, L. (1978). *Paradox and counter-paradox.* New York: Jason Aronson.

Warner, M. S. (1980). Trust in the family system. Unpublished manuscript.

Warner, M. S. (1983). Soft meaning and sincerity in the family system. *Family Process, 22,* 523–35.

Watzlawick, P., Beavin, J. H., & Jackson, D. D. (1967). *Pragmatics of communication.* New York: Norton.

Weeks, G. R., & L'Abate, L. (1982). *Paradoxical psychotherapy.* New York: Brunner/Mazel.

The Young Child
in Person-Centered Family Therapy

Charlotte Ellinwood   *Psychological Resources, Olympia Fields, Illinois*

Early review of the literature on family therapy (e.g., Zuk & Rubenstein, 1965; Haley, 1971) tend to emphasize the importance of communications theory and systems theory in the development of family theory and its application to family therapy in the early studies of schizophrenia. These reviews also mention that in the 1940s and 1950s, persons in the field of child therapy and child guidance were beginning to think of the family as a unit and began to explore the possibility of working with whole families, for both diagnostic and treatment purposes. The pioneers in this shift in point of view from child to family therapy were at the Judge Baker Child Guidance Clinic in Boston (Ackerman, 1958).

Actually, family therapy (broadly defined) has always been an integral part of child therapy, regardless of the theoretical orientation of the therapist, although it was not always so designated. Some adult, usually a parent, has always initiated therapy for a child. How that adult has been viewed and how involved he or she was in the therapy process has depended on the orientation of the therapist. Often parents have been seen simply as sources of historical and clinical data about the child and as contributing factors to the child's disturbance. Until recently, their relationship with the child was not the focus of therapy (except by Guerney, 1964). If the parents so desired, they could enter individual therapy for themselves, or child guidance could be provided, individually or in parent groups; however, they were not included in therapy sessions with the child. The focus of the child's therapy was on the inner experience of the child. This was true in client-centered child therapy as well as in other approaches to child therapy.

In the late 1940s, the 'bible' of client-centered (then nondirective) child therapists was Virginia Axline's (1947) book, *Play Therapy*. Her focus was on the individual child, just as Rogers' focus was on the individual adult. She stated emphatically that 'while therapy might move ahead faster if the adults [parent or parent-substitute] were also receiving therapy or counseling, *it is not necessary for the adults to be helped in order to insure successful play-therapy results*' (p. 68, italics in original). In contrast to the emerging views of the relationship of family dynamics to emotional and behavioral problems of children, she focused on the child and that child's ability to change, to develop his or her potential with his or her own inner resources, based on a belief in the self-actualizing tendency and the inherent capacity of the individual — child or adult. A similar emphasis was evident in Dorfman's (1951) chapter on play therapy, although she did mention that parents might be involved. Actually Axline also met, on occasion, with the parents of children who were in therapy; she just emphasized that such involvement was not necessary. Neither she nor Dorfman mentioned the possibility of seeing the parents and children together. However, it is interesting to note that there were hints in their writings (and the writings of Rogers) of a recognition of 'systemic' effects within a family. It was their view

First published in *Person-Centered Review,* Volume 4, Number 3, August 1989.

that a therapeutic change in the attitudes or feelings of one member of a family would result in changes in that person's relationships with others in the family and in the attitudes and feelings of other family members (see Rogers, 1953/1961, pp. 314–28). Bolstered by Axline's firm stand, and the stated implications of Rogers' theory, client-centered child therapists felt justified, and some still do, in providing individual therapy for a child. There was discomfort, however, with the exclusion of the parents. Thus it may be that the early seed of client-centered family therapy can be found in the efforts made to include them. An examination of University of Chicago Counseling Center staff memos written by Nathaniel Raskin in 1950 and Edyth Barry in 1951 demonstrate this early discomfort and concern. Later this concern was evident in an attempt to relate the details of Rogers' (1959) theoretical formulations to work with parents in a child therapy program (Ellinwood, 1959). In no instance was *family* therapy considered.

However, in the 1960s, influenced by the current thinking about families and family therapy, client-centered child therapists took tentative steps toward family therapy. At the University of Chicago Counseling Center, in addition to individual or couple therapy for parents, a sibling or a parent might be invited to a session by the child. The child's request was accepted as his or her way of moving toward self-actualization, or of resolving an interpersonal problem within the family. Then we began to offer conjoint therapy — child and sibling or child and parent, as a unit rather than with one person being a 'visitor' in the child's session. Finally, by the time the Counseling Center closed in 1971, we were experimenting with total family sessions, as an adjunct to individual therapy, or in some instances as the only form of therapy. In addition, other client-centered therapists were relating client-centered theory to client-centered family therapy (e.g., Raskin & van der Veen, 1970). Some were experimenting with family therapy in different settings and exploring different theoretical orientations of family therapy in an attempt to clarify the similarities and differences between the client/person-centered approach and other approaches, for example, strategic, structural, systems (Levant & Shlien, 1984).

The articles in this special issue of the *Person- Centered Review* continue this exploratory process and demonstrate how client-centered theory has expanded to meet the new demands of family therapy while retaining its basic principles. Perhaps the shift to the use of the term *person-centered approach* exemplifies this expansion.

It is clear, then, that some person-centered therapists are doing family therapy of some sort, that is, therapy with whole families or with family subgroups (couples, parent-child), applying client-centered theory to this aspect of their work. Many others are undoubtedly doing the same.[1] It is our hope that these articles will stimulate further sharing of thinking and experience in this area. One hope I have is that there will be more sharing of experience with young children (under 8–9 years old) in family therapy. I am concerned about what happens to the young child when family therapy is a method rather than an orientation.

In their article in this issue, the Guerneys have described a clearly formulated structured program in which the emphasis is upon teaching the parents while concurrently,

---

1. At the present time 'family therapy' is used to refer to therapy with any group or subgroup of a family. Whether or not a group is considered a family depends on the chosen definition of a family. One that seems useful to me is that given by Zilbach (1986): 'A family is a special kind of small, natural group in which members are related by birth, marriage or other form which creates a home or a functional household unit' (p. 6). Thus, using this definition of a family, family therapy can include therapy with couples with or without children, with single parents and children, with separated or divorced parents and children, with total family units — everyone in the household, or with any subgroups within the unit.

as an important aspect, providing a therapeutic experience for the child, and for the parent-child relationship. Gaylin (thisvolume pp. 200–9) implies that in working with families with young children, he sometimes finds it necessary to shift into the 'guidance' role with the parents of these children. I suspect all children in a family are included in Gaylin's family sessions, but it is not clearly so stated. Anderson (this volume pp. 183–90) refers to a nine-year-old in one of his case examples in his article and includes his 'story' among the views being expressed. In my view, it would be useful to know more about how he and other therapists respond to younger children and involve them in a session. O'Leary (this volume pp. 191–9) mentions that he had been working with one family for several years. The girls were 13 and 14. I wondered how he responded to them when they were younger and whether, in these examples, the focus was on the parent(s) and older children. My concern is whether young children in client-centered family therapy are responded to with unconditional positive regard, genuineness, and *empathy,* and if they are truly heard. Is their contribution to the family interaction and family concept noted and appreciated? Is it possible to respond empathically to a young child in a family session without some understanding of basic principles of child development and some familiarity with the young child's mode of expression?

In a recent book, *Young Children in Family Therapy* (1986), Joan Zilbach has expressed concern about the tendency to exclude young children in family therapy sessions. She also notes that Montalvo and Haley (1973) expressed a similar concern in their article 'In Defense of Child Therapy': 'A child therapy orientation may prevent one of the most recent and common errors of family therapy — that of overfocusing on the couple and losing the child in the process' (quoted in Zilbach, 1986, p. 43). My concern is that therapists may be focusing primarily on the adults and older children. Zilbach (1986) points out that when Ackerman introduced a family therapy training program at the Judge Baker Child Guidance Clinic, training in play therapy was included. She also points out that little has been written in the field about the inclusion of play (or child) therapy in family therapy sessions.

As the field of family therapy has developed, the training of students usually has emphasized an understanding of family dynamics, development (family life cycle), and communication patterns. However, it has not included an understanding of the children in a family, especially young children, based on an understanding of their level of physical, cognitive, and emotional development, and on the therapist's experience interacting with them in a therapeutic relationship. Whether or not young children are included in family sessions in the clinical setting apparently depends on the therapist's comfort with them. This comfort might come from previous training and experience in child therapy or child guidance settings, or sometimes simply from a natural ability to relate to children. Zilbach indicates that the program at the Judge Baker Clinic was an effort to formalize child therapy training as a part of training in family therapy.

I believe the failure to include, or at least to discuss, the young child in family therapy is an issue or problem in person-centered family therapy. It is a problem or issue that has not been addressed directly, at least in the literature. One possible solution has been that of the Guerneys: teach parents how to do play therapy and in the process facilitate their learning of the attitudes and skills considered important in the healthy social and emotional development of their child. This approach assumes that the training therapists are familiar with issues of child development and have had experience in child therapy. Another approach, which is similar to the one described by Zilbach within the psychodynamic framework, is to include individual experience with children as well as with adults in the training of family therapists. Within the client-centered framework such training would involve an understanding of child development, of family systems or dynamics, and of client-centered theory. Given this kind of background I believe most therapists would be comfortable with young children (including infants) in family sessions. They would be able to understand children's communications and their view of the family. Therefore, the therapist and the family would reap the benefits of their inclusion.

REFERENCES

Ackerman, N. W. (1958). *The psychodynamics of family life: Diagnosis and treatment of family relationships.* New York: Basic Books.

Axline, V. (1947). *Play therapy.* Boston: Houghton Mifflin.

Dorfman, E. (1951). Play therapy. In C. R. Rogers (Ed.), *Client-centered therapy* (pp. 235–77). Boston: Houghton Mifflin.

Ellinwood, C. (1959). Some observations from work with parents in a child therapy program. *University of Chicago Counseling Center Discussion Papers* (Vol.5, No. 18). Chicago: University of Chicago Counseling Center.

Guerney, B., Jr. (1964). Filial therapy: Description and rationale. *Journal of Consulting Psychology, 28,* 303–10.

Haley, J. (1971). A review of the family therapy field. In J. Haley (Ed.), *Changing families: A family therapy reader* (pp. 1–13). New York: Grune & Stratton.

Levant, R. F., & Shlien, J. M. (Eds.) (1984). *Client-centered therapy and the person-centered approach: New directions in theory, research and practice.* New York: Praeger.

Montalvo, B., & Haley, J. (1973). In defense of child therapy. *Family Process, 12,* 227–44.

Raskin, N., & van der Veen, F. (1970). Client-centered family therapy: Some clinical and research perspectives. In J. T. Hart & T. M. Tomlinson (Eds.), *New directions in client-centered therapy* (pp. 387–406). Boston: Houghton Mifflin.

Rogers, C. R. (1959). A theory of therapy, personality, and interpersonal relationships as developed in the client-centered framework. In S. Koch (Ed.), *Psychology: The study of a science* (Vol. 3, pp. 184–256). New York: McGraw-Hill.

Rogers, C. R. (1961). The implications of client-centered therapy for family life. In C. R. Rogers, *On becoming a person* (pp. 314–28). Boston: Houghton Mifflin. (Original work published 1953.)

Zilbach, J. J. (1986). *Young children in family therapy.* New York: Brunner/Mazel.

Zuk, G. H., & Rubenstein, D. (1965). A review of concepts in the study and treatment of families of schizophrenics. In I. Boszormenyi-Nagy & J. L. Framo (Eds.), *Intensive family therapy: Theoretical and practical aspects* (pp. 1–31). New York: Harper & Row.

The Case Against Disciplining Children
at Home or in School

Thomas Gordon   *Effectiveness Training, Solana Beach, California*

The article examines and evaluates the commonly held belief that children must be disciplined (controlled) by parents and teachers. Semantic imprecisions in books authored by discipline advocates are illustrated, and more precise definitions are provided for such terms as *discipline, authority, power, control,* and *influence*. Why both rewards and punishments are ineffective and hazardous to the mental and physical health of children is extensively documented. Finally, alternatives to disciplining children are proposed, illustrated, and supported by research findings. These include methods that encourage the involvement of children in family and classroom rule-setting, methods that foster participation in all phases of the learning process, skills that influence children to solve their problems themselves and control their behavior out of consideration for the needs of others, and a nonpower method of resolving adult-child conflicts so that neither loses (or both win).

I am grateful for the opportunity to put my thoughts about discipline in print in a journal devoted primarily to the dissemination of theory, research, and applications of what has come to be widely known as the person-centered approach. It seems fitting for me to share this first summary of my analysis of discipline with colleagues and students of Carl Rogers, since he had such a profound influence on my choice of occupation, my early professional development, and my philosophy of human relationships.

I deeply regret that Carl will read neither this article nor the book on discipline that follows it, for I believe he would clearly see evidence of his personal influence on some of my thinking.

For example, my emphasis in this article on increasing student participation in the learning process as a way of decreasing disciplinary problems can be traced as far back as 1946, when the Counseling Center teaching staff at the University of Chicago made our first stab at 'student-centered teaching' with the V.A. trainees. Each of us — Carl, E. H. Porter, Doug Blocksma, and I — experienced his share of anxiety when we discarded the traditional and comfortable role of 'instructors' and 'lecturers' in favor of that of 'facilitators.'

I can also trace my advocacy of the classroom teacher as a kind of democratic leader back to the democratic model of leadership Carl practiced as administrator of the Counseling Center. His style of leading our staff greatly influenced me to attend the third National Training Laboratory for Group Development in Bethel, Maine, in the summer of 1949, from which I returned to write my chapter on 'Group-Centered Leadership and Administration' for Carl's book, *Client-Centered Therapy* (Rogers, 1951).

Finally, my emphasis on classroom teachers' needing to learn the listening skills of the client-centered counselor can easily be traced to a quarter of a century of using client-

First published in *Person-Centered Review,* Volume 3, Number 1, February 1988.

centered skills, first as a practicing psychologist and then as an instructor of many classes of Parent Effectiveness Training and Teacher Effectiveness Training.

Returning now from the past to the present, it is my strong belief that an in-depth analysis of the practice of disciplining children at home and in the schools is long overdue. Any idea so universally accepted and so rarely questioned deserves to be evaluated. As an avowed person-centered therapist, student-centered teacher, and group-centered leader, I bring strong biases to this analysis. These are tempered, however, by the findings from the many pertinent research studies I have discovered and by a quarter of a century of teaching parents and teachers viable alternatives to discipline — effective nonpower methods. Some of these methods are rooted in the person-centered philosophy so ably championed by Carl Rogers — methods that grant children a lot of freedom but freedom within limits, methods that promote self-discipline and self-responsibility, methods that foster motivation, creativity, and emotional health.

THE DISCIPLINE ISSUE

Discipline has surfaced as an important issue in our country — a political, legal, educational, religious, and family issue. President Reagan himself declared in 1984:

> American schools don't need vast new sums of money as much as they need a few fundamental reforms. First, we need to restore good old-fashioned discipline . . . We need to write stricter discipline codes; then support our teachers when they enforce those codes.

U.S. Supreme Court Justice Powell, writing for the majority in the case of *Ingraham v. Wright,* defended the right of schools to discipline students by corporal punishment:

> The school child has little need for the protection of the eighth amendment . . . Paddling of recalcitrant children has long been an acceptable method of promoting good behavior and instilling notions of responsibility and decorum into the mischievous heads of school children. (1976)

A Gallup poll revealed that less than 20% of parents disapprove of the use of corporal punishment in schools. Strict discipline of children both in our schools and in the family is currently preached vigorously by conservative religious spokespeople. James Dobson, author of *The Strong-Willed Child* (1978), urges parents to use their 'authority' to discipline (including 'spankings that really hurt'). His view is that children must learn *early* to 'yield and submit' to *all* adult authority, including teachers, school principals, police, neighbors, employers:

> By learning to yield to the loving authority (leadership) of his parents, a child learns to submit to other forms of authority which will confront him later in life . . . while yielding to the loving leadership of their parents, children are also learning to yield to the benevolent leadership of God Himself. (1978, p. 171)

In a sample of more than two thousand American parents surveyed by Strauss, Gelles, and Steinmetz and later reported in their book, *Behind Closed Doors: Violence in the American Family* (1980), it was found that in the year prior to the survey

> 86% of three-year-olds had been victims of some form of parental violence, 82% of five-year-olds, 54% of those between 10 and 14 years, and 33% of those between 15 and 17 years.

In recent years, thousands of schools throughout the United States have adopted a system of rigorous discipline called 'Assertive Discipline,' a creation of behaviorist Lee Canter (1976), who prescribes how teachers can make use of their authority in graduated disciplinary steps from mild to severe with the ultimate goal being obedience in the classroom.

And, as many parents have discovered, the shelves in bookstores during the last decade or so have been loaded with books urging parents to use their power to discipline children. They can be identified easily by such titles as: *Dare to Discipline, Assertive Discipline for Parents, Parent Power, Parents on the Run: The Need for Discipline, Power to the Parent, Your Acting Up Teenagers, Survival Kit for Parents, Toughlove,* and (believe it or not) *Spank Me If You Love Me.*

However, it took one particular book to jar me into making a decision several years ago to investigate this pervasive discipline issue. I remember the day I was reading *Parent Power* (1980), authored by a prominent American psychologist, Logan Wright, who subsequently was elected to the presidency of the American Psychological Association. I recall dropping this book into my lap utterly amazed after reading his first two sentences:

> The order of the day for any parent who wants to retain some semblance of sanity, is to get and maintain control. But, the most important reason for seizing control is that *you must be able to control a child before you can really support and love him.* (p. 17, italics added)

I thought, 'What's going on here? Why is a prominent, licensed and apparently respected colleague giving advice that I consider actually harmful?' In my first book for parents, *Parent Effectiveness Training – P.E.T.* (Gordon, 1970), I had never mentioned the word 'discipline,' convinced as I was that power-based control had no place in effective parenting (or teaching).

Dr. Wright's book so disturbed me that, then and there, I made the decision to embark on an in-depth study of discipline to learn for myself what was known about discipline and to look for answers to the many questions that were nagging me. The project eventually led me to review all the research studies I could find, as well as to read all the 'parent power' and 'dare-to-discipline' books available. In the end, the project produced a book, soon to be published.

One objective of this article is to describe some of the principal learnings I acquired and to share my own thoughts about disciplining children. A second objective is to point out some alternatives to discipline, which, in my judgment, not only would help parents and teachers acquire *more* influence with youngsters but also make for warm relationships and social environments that foster psychological health.

Throughout the article I will refer to both parents and teachers and cite research conducted both in families and in schools. Needless to say, much of the content of the article is also applicable to other caretakers of children and youth.

SEMANTIC PROBLEMS

One of my first discoveries was that people writing about discipline were not using the same definitions of certain words they were commonly employing. This made for muddy waters and widespread misunderstandings, to say the least.

Take the word *discipline* itself. As a noun, the definition of which is 'behavior and order in accord with rules or regulations,' discipline provokes no controversy. Everybody appears to be in favor of discipline in the classroom or good discipline of a basketball team. The noun conjures up order, organization, cooperation, following rules and policies, and consideration for the rights of others.

The verb, 'to discipline,' has two quite different meanings. The first is 'to train by instruction and exercise; to drill, edify, enlighten.' This variety of discipline, too, seldom causes arguments. However, the second meaning of the verb, 'to discipline,' is what makes hot and heavy controversy. Here are some synonyms for the second kind of discipline, which is a controlling-restricting-chastising-punishing type of action:

> correct, direct, keep in line, regulate, restrain, check, curb, contain, arrest, govern, oversee, manage, harness, bridle, rein in, leash, muzzle, restrict, constrain, confine, inhibit, chastise, reprimand, reprove, rebuke, criticize, make an example of, punish, castigate, penalize.

Clearly, the teach-train-inform kind of disciplining is an effort *to influence* children, while the second kind of disciplining is an attempt *to control them.* Most teachers and parents want nothing more strongly than the ability to *influence* youngsters, but in their zeal to do so, fall into the trap of using control methods— imposing limits, making rules, sending commands, coercing, punishing, or threatening punishment. Control methods don't really influence children to choose particular ways of behaving, they merely coerce or compel them to do so.

We must also recognize two radically different kinds of the control type of discipline: externally imposed or internally imposed, other-imposed or self-imposed, discipline by others or self-discipline. I didn't find anyone *against* self-discipline, although most of the dare-to-discipline advocates fail to mention it. There is controversy, however, and it's quite widespread, over what is the best way to foster self-discipline in children and youth—a conflict over the 'means' to achieve the agreed upon and valued 'ends'—namely, self-disciplined children. Most teachers and parents, I suspect, take the position that children 'internalize' adult-imposed discipline, hoping it will be eventually transformed into self-discipline, a theory championed by Freud and by most psychologists who advocate disciplining to control children. Seldom did I find anyone challenging this traditional belief, as I shall do later.

Another source of semantic confusion comes from the term *authority.* Everybody who writes about discipline uses this word, but few authors recognize the existence of the various meanings the term has.

First, there is the authority derived from a person's special expertise: 'He is an authority on corporate law,' 'He speaks with authority.' This is often referred to as earned authority. I've adopted the convention of labeling it Auth E—for expertise.

Second, there is the authority derived from the job (or role) a person occupies in life. Airline pilots ask passengers to fasten seat belts, and they usually comply; a committee chairperson is given the authority to open and close its meetings and to guide and direct what goes on in between. I've termed this kind of authority Auth J—for job.

A third kind of authority is derived from understandings, agreements, rules and contracts people make in their relationships with others. I agree to drive my daughter to the auto repair shop; in our family we have an understanding (policy) that we knock before entering another's bedroom; we have agreements as to who does each and every one of the many jobs in our house. Call this Auth C—for contract.

Finally, there is the authority derived from possessing power over another—power to control, dominate, coerce, bend one's will, and so on. Call this Auth P—for power. This type of authority is what people mean when they talk about 'obedience to authority,' 'exercising your authority,' 'a breakdown of authority,' 'rebelling against authority.' Understandably, it is the authority many teachers believe they need to discipline (control) children at school.

I found countless examples of cloudy thinking due to failure to recognize the difference among these four kinds of authority. Most frequent was the common assertion that teachers or parents are justified in using their authority (Auth P) to discipline youngsters because kids need and want the adult's superior wisdom and knowledge. Wisdom and knowledge obviously are Auth E, not Auth P. Another common rationalization I often found in the dare-to-discipline books is that power-based authority (Auth P) is justified because the word discipline was derived from the root word *disciple,* meaning a learner. A perceptive reader would see through this deception, recognizing that you use Auth E to teach and instruct disciples, not Auth P.

I also discovered that dare-to-discipline advocates try to make using Auth P sound less authoritarian and coercive than it is by using euphemisms for this type of authority. These are nice-sounding terms interchangeable with authority — such as the 'leadership' of teachers and parents, 'benign' authority, the 'loving leadership' of one's parent, 'guidance,' or 'being authoritative.'

Even when using the Bible to justify adults' punishing children (Auth P), James Dobson, perhaps the most widely known dare-to-discipline advocate, confuses two kinds of authority. He first cites this scriptural admonition, 'Children obey your parents in all things, for this is well-pleasing unto the Lord.' Then he cites another passage (Ephesians 6:4) to further justify parents using authority, but this second scriptural definition of discipline involves giving children suggestions and advice, which is clearly Auth E:

> Don't keep on scolding and nagging your children, making them angry and resentful.
> Rather bring them up with the loving discipline the Lord himself approves, with *suggestions and godly advice.* (my italics)

'Suggestions and godly advice,' as I see it, are ways of instructing or teaching (Auth E) and not demanding obedience (Auth P).

One might assume, as I did, that dare-to-discipline defenders at some deeper level actually disapprove of disciplining children. Why else would they need to use so many euphemisms and Biblical passages to justify using their power? And one might guess that many disciplinarians feel guilty about using their power over persons smaller than they are ('This hurts me worse than it does you').

HOW DISCIPLINE IS SUPPOSED TO WORK

To control children, teachers and parents obviously need some kind of power. What is it and how does it work? Power to control another (not *influence* another) is derived from possessing the means to satisfy some need of the other person or to deprive the other of satisfying some need. To use the terminology of psychologists, power to control others comes from employing rewards and/or punishments. In theory, when behavior that the controller *wants* is rewarded, it strengthens or reinforces that behavior (increases the probability of the behavior recurring); and when behavior that the controller *does not want* is punished, it weakens that behavior (decreases the probability of the behavior recurring).

In practice, however, rewards and punishments don't always produce the results desired by the controller. Parents and teachers seldom can ensure the existence of certain conditions that are necessary for rewards and punishment to work effectively. Let me explain.

For rewards to work (1) the child must be kept completely dependent on the controller to provide the rewards (be prevented from obtaining the rewards himself or herself), (2) the rewards selected by the controller must be needed strongly enough by the child, and (3) the rewards must immediately follow the desired behavior.

For punishment to work (1) the child must be prevented from escaping the punishment, (2) the punishment must be severe enough to be aversive, (3) the punishment must be administered without delay right after the unacceptable behavior occurs, and (4) the child must be kept in a state of fear of the controller's punishment.

With very young children, these conditions may occasionally be met, but with children over eight or ten years of age, it becomes almost impossible to meet some or all of these conditions.

Another severe limitation of rewards and punishment is the fact that both parents and teachers gradually run out of both effective rewards and effective punishments as their children grow older and move into the teen ages. This is one of the principal reasons why the adolescent years bring on so much storm and stress for families and school teachers. Having relied so heavily on *controlling* children with power, adults haven't learned methods of *influencing* them without power, so when their supply of power runs low when the adolescent years are reached, they are literally left impotent.

In fact, I have observed a common scenario both in families and in schools. When children are very young, most adults start using rewards to control them. When they see mounting evidence of the failure of rewards to work, they begin to administer punishment, usually in a mild form. When mild punishment fails to deter unacceptable behavior, as it most often does, then they resort to more severe punishments (harder beatings, more severe deprivations). But at the same time the children are growing older and bigger, and the adults run out of severe punishments. Or the kids learn how to avoid it by lying or escaping from it or by running away. It's then that many parents, recognizing their impotence, give up completely trying to control, a posture incorrectly perceived as 'permissiveness,' when in fact it would more accurately be called 'helplessness.' It's ironic that many so-called permissive parents are actually autocratic parents who have lost all their former power to control their youngsters.

SOME NEGATIVE EFFECTS OF REWARDING

Most people are already aware of many of the negative effects of trying to control children with rewards:
1. Children begin to 'work for the rewards,' as, for example, students working for *grades* instead of for *learning*.
2. Children can become addicted to getting rewards—they habitually seek praise, approval, or compliments, as well as tangible rewards.
3. As children grow older they begin to see the hidden agenda (control) behind adult rewards.
4. Praise often conveys to children a certain element of unacceptance, as in this statement, for example, 'Today you understood the lesson because you weren't daydreaming as you were yesterday.'
5. Children often disbelieve praise when it doesn't match their self-concept.
6. Praise and other rewards heighten rivalries and competitiveness between children.

DEFICIENCIES AND DANGERS OF PUNISHMENT

Punishing children is endemic in the United States. One extensive survey found that 81% of parents said they used physical punishment, with 61% reporting using it at least once a week (Strauss et al., 1980). In schools the frequency of corporal punishment has been decreasing steadily as more and more states have enacted laws prohibiting corporal punishment, yet a recent study reported that the national average is still around 3.5% of students paddled yearly (Maurer, 1984).

We can only guess how many parents and teachers employ other kinds of punishment—for example, deprivations, extra work, confinement, verbal abuse, the silent treatment, and staying after school. No doubt, in my mind, close to 100% of teachers and parents regularly employ some form of punishment to control youngsters despite the proven deficiencies and dangers of punishment. Here are some of the principal ones:

1. For punishment to work, it must be severe, and yet when it *is* severe, youngsters look for all kinds of ways to avoid it, postpone it, weaken it, avert it, escape from it. They lie, put the blame on someone else, tattle, hide, plead for mercy and make promises to 'never do it again.'
2. Boys of 12 years of age whose parents scored high in restrictiveness and punishment showed strong tendencies toward self-punishment, accident proneness, and suicidal intentions (Sears, 1961).
3. Neurotic children had more constraint and excessive control from parents than non-neurotic children (Becker, 1964).
4. Mothers of children with low self-esteem were found to have used less reasoning and discussion and more arbitrary, punitive discipline (Coopersmith, 1967).
5. Children of punitive authoritarian parents tend to lack social competence with peers, to withdraw, to not take social initiative, to lack spontaneity (Baldwin, 1948).
6. Children of controlling (authoritarian) parents who valued obedience and respect for authority showed relatively little independence and social responsibility (Baumrind, 1971).
7. Less than one out of 400 children whose parents did not hit them were found to be violent toward their parents, as opposed to children who *had* been hit by their parents. Half of the latter group had hit their parents in the previous year (Strauss et al., 1980).
8. Studies of the family backgrounds of both male and female juvenile delinquents consistently show a pattern of harsh, punitive, power-assertive parental punishment, in contrast to nondelinquent youngsters (Martin, 1975).
9. Schools using more physical punishment have more vandalism (Hyman, McDowell, & Raines, 1975).
10. In a study of 230 Columbia University graduate students, those who as children had been subjected to the most punishment, as compared with those who had received the least, reported more hatred toward parents, more rejection of teachers, poorer relationships with classmates, more quarrels, more shyness, more unsatisfactory love affairs, more worry, more anxiety, more guilt, more unhappiness and crying, and more dependence on parents (Watson, 1943).

It is quite clear: punitive discipline is hazardous to the mental health of children.

ALTERNATIVES TO DISCIPLINING CHILDREN

Although the philosophy and practice of trying to control children by administering rewards and punishments is nearly universal in both families and schools, promising alternatives to this ineffective method do exist, and pockets of innovation and change can be found, if one looks diligently enough.

Involvement of children in rule-setting

It is a well-established principle that people are more motivated to comply with rules or limits if they have been given the opportunity to participate in determining what they should be.

For a quarter of a century, in my Parent Effectiveness Training and Teacher Effectiveness Training courses (Gordon, 1974) our instructors have been advising parents and teachers to avoid making rules unilaterally. Via tape-recorded examples, demonstrations, and role-playing, we teach methods for involving children in the *process* of determining the policies and rules they will be expected to follow. Among such family policies and rules are those covering bedtime, TV usage, household chores, storage of playthings, use of the telephone, allowances, privacy, homework, and any other activity that has the potential for generating problems or conflicts. Nearly a million parents have been exposed to this new way of determining family rules.

Similarly, in Teacher Effectiveness Training (T.E.T.) we offer the same methodology for involving a class of students in the process of classroom rule-setting. I am grateful to Norma Randolph and William Howe, then working in the Cupertino, California, school district, for convincing me years ago that even first-graders are capable of assuming responsibility for participating with their teachers in setting rules. It was a common practice for children in the lower elementary grades in that district to use posted 'activity cards,' which helped them manage their own classroom behavior and remove the teacher as the major controller (Randolph & Howe, 1966). Here are examples of these 'reminder' cards:
- getting myself into the room
- getting ready to work
- listening
- group discussion
- working with the teacher
- following directions
- working alone
- working with a partner
- working in a group
- getting myself out

Some students, when tempted to ignore a classroom rule they had helped set, rose out of their seats, walked up to the front where the cards were posted, and touched the appropriate card as a reminder of the rules.

Nonblameful 'I-messages'

Another noncontrolling method taught in both P.E.T. and T.E.T. is sending 'I-messages.' Typically, teachers and parents confront children with 'You-messages,' those containing

233

heavy loadings of blame, judgment, criticism, each of which provokes resistance and lowers children's self-esteem:

> *'You're acting like a first-grader.'*
> *'You take your seat right away.'*
> *'You ought to be ashamed of yourself.'*
> *'You're driving me crazy.'*
> *'You're being naughty.'*
> *'You will have to stay after school now.'*

In P.E.T. and T.E.T. we provide a variety of experiences for learning and practicing nonblameful 'I-messages' as the means for telling the child exactly why his or her behavior is unacceptable to the adult:

> *'When there is so much noise, I can't hear what anyone is saying.'*
> *'When the paints aren't put away, I have to take a lot of time to do it myself.'*

I-messages are actually 'appeals for help,' which partially accounts for their superior effectiveness in influencing children to change their behavior. In addition, they place full responsibility on the child for initiating the change, are less likely than You-messages to injure the relationship, and do not damage self-esteem. A teacher reported this incident shortly after taking the T.E.T. course:

> *I was reluctant to try an I-message with the kids I have. They are so hard to manage. Finally, I screwed up my courage and sent a strong I-message to a group of children who were making a mess with water paints in the back of the room by the sink. I said, 'When you mix paints and spill them all over the sink and table, I have to scrub up later or get yelled at by the custodian. I'm sick of cleaning up after you, and I feel helpless to prevent it from happening.' I just stopped then and waited to see what they would do. I really expected them to laugh at me and take that 'I don't care' attitude they've had all year. But they didn't. They stood there looking at me for a minute like they were amazed to find out I was upset. And then one of them said, 'Come on, let's clean it up.' I was floored. You know they haven't turned into models of perfection, but they now clean up the sink and tables every day whether they've spilled paint on them or not.*

Baumrind (1971) found that nursery school children who rated high in self-control and self-discipline had parents who refrained from punitive messages or punishments and instead made extensive use of reasoning and what she termed 'cognitive structuring.' This academic-sounding term turns out to be our I-message — telling children the negative effects of their behavior on others. Baumrind explains that these messages help children internalize the consequences of their behavior and develop conscience or inner control — what I call self-discipline as opposed to externally administered discipline.

To influence infants and toddlers, however, parents and teachers obviously must assume a more active role and employ nonverbal (behavioral) methods. When very young children whine or pester or throw their food on the floor or dawdle or make messes, adults have available a variety of such nonverbal methods:

1. Guessing what the child needs or what deprivation lies behind the unacceptable behavior and then satisfying the need.
2. Substituting for the unacceptable behavior some other behavior that is acceptable to the adult — as, for example, giving the child a damaged pair of nylon hose as a replacement for the new pair the child pulled out of the drawer.

3. Modifying the environment to produce a change in the child's behavior — for example, childproofing the classroom or home, enriching the child's environment so as to capture the full interest of the child, providing designated areas for messing or painting, and assigning storage areas.

Participative management in schools

Today, we are seeing a quiet revolution in the way many companies are being managed. This new leadership style is called 'participative management,' because it relies on extensive employee involvement in making decisions and solving problems related to the workplace environment, the design of products, the methods of production, quality improvement, cost control, and the like.

Over 6,000 U.S. companies have instituted some form of participative management. Some have trained their managers and supervisors with our course, *Leader Effectiveness Training (L.E.T.)*. The benefits of this more democratic style of leadership can be quite remarkable: increases in employee productivity have jumped 100%, grievances have fallen from 3,000 per year to 15, absenteeism has been cut in half, 80% decrease in product rejected because of poor quality (Simmons & Mares, 1983).

Recently, among a handful of teachers, school administrators, and teacher educators we have been witnessing a growing recognition of the importance of increasing student participation in order to improve learning motivation and decrease discipline problems.

Urich and Batchelder (1979) describe how an urban school drastically changed its social climate by increasing student involvement in tackling such important problems as tardiness, absenteeism, apathy, and low achievement. The students worked with teachers and administrators to come up with improvements in each of the problem areas.

In other schools, students have been given the opportunity to monitor their own academic progress and identify areas of needed improvement. In one study, such students were found to make significant gains in study habits and achievement (McLaughlin, 1984).

Some schools have allowed students to participate in academic goal setting and in designing their own tailor-made high school courses (Burrows, 1973). Other schools have involved students in cooperative projects with peer work groups, resulting in enhanced academic and social skills (Johnson & Johnson, 1975).

Students also have been given responsibility for correcting unproductive behavior of their peers (Duke, 1980), for sharing their opinions concerning the quality of their teachers 'instructional skills and teacher-student relationships (Jones & Jones, 1981). Student participation has been extended into some of the schoolwide administrative issues, such as school discipline, school climate, textbook adoptions, new curricula, budget cutting, and energy savings (Aschuler, 1980).

Renowned psychiatrist William Glasser, author of the bestseller *Schools Without Failure* (1961), has recently prescribed a challenging remedy for disciplinary problems in our schools in his new book, *Control Theory in the Classroom* (1986). Students are organized into teams of two to five students made up of low, medium, and high achievers. The high achievers help the lower ones, team members are urged to depend a great deal on themselves and their own creativity, they choose how to offer the teacher evidence of how much they have learned, and each student gets the team score.

The superiority of such cooperative learning efforts over the traditional competitive student-student relationships has been conclusively established in a comprehensive review of 122 studies, published from 1924 to 1980. The results were remarkable: 65 studies found that cooperation produces higher achievement than competition, only eight found the reverse; cooperation promoted higher achievement than independent work in 108 studies, only 6 found the reverse (Johnson, Maruyama, Johnson, Nelson, & Skon, 1981).

In a study of 18 'alternative high schools' in California, where there were personalized teacher-student relations, student participation in school governance, and a nonauthoritarian rule structure, the researchers found that both teachers and students reported fewer and less serious disciplinary behavior problems than in the conventional high schools with minutely defined adult-made rules and rigid ways of dealing with infractions (Duke & Perry, 1978).

Helping children find their own solutions to problems

When children experience some form of deprivation or unmet needs, they often react by behaving in disruptive or noncooperative ways — both in their families and at school. Acting-up children are usually troubled children — youngsters carrying around a lot of frustration, disappointment, resentment, or anger. And troubled children also make poor learners. Consequently, it seems obvious that both discipline problems and low achievement could be reduced in schools if teachers could be taught how to be more effective as helping agents or counselors. This is precisely one of the principal objectives in the T.E.T. course.

I naturally chose the client-centered methodology of counseling as the model to be taught in both T.E.T. and P.E.T., having been trained by Carl Rogers and having many years in private practice as a client-centered therapist. Our training has three principal objectives: (1) to show teachers and parents how their habitual ways of responding when children share their problems can act as communication-blockers and convey nonacceptance. We call these nonfacilitative messages the 'Twelve Roadblocks' — ordering, warning, moralizing (shoulds and oughts), giving solutions, teaching, evaluating negatively, evaluating positively, ridiculing, psychoanalyzing, reassuring (consoling), probing, and kidding (diverting); (2) to help teachers and parents reach a reasonable level of competence in responding to children with Active Listening, which conveys acceptance and shows accurate understanding; (3) to influence parents and teachers to have more trust in children's ability to solve problems themselves.

By and large, I'm convinced that we have succeeded rather well in accomplishing these objectives. Considerable evidence of this can be found in some of the research studies that have evaluated the effects of P.E.T. and T.E.T. We have located over 60 separate studies, many of which unfortunately have flawed designs or inadequate statistical procedures. Recently, however, Robert Cedar at Boston University took 26 of the more carefully designed of these studies and included them in a meta-analysis, a statistical technique for combining and analyzing the findings from many different studies. The results of his meta-analysis were as follows:

1. P.E.T. had an overall 'effect size' of 0.33 standard deviation units, which was significantly greater than the effect size for a group representing alternate treatments — such as behavior modification training, Adlerian-based parent training.
2. The better-designed studies were found to show significantly greater effect sizes of P.E.T. than the less well-designed studies.
3. P.E.T. was shown to have a positive effect on parent attitudes and parent behavior, and this effect endured for some period (up to 26 weeks) after the course was completed.

Cedar (1985) concluded: 'Most of Gordon's claims were (with qualifications) substantiated.'

There is also a wealth of 'hard data' showing conclusively that the same facilitative skills we teach in T.E.T. greatly help teachers better achieve even the traditional and commonly accepted goals of our schools — such as, scholastic achievement, good attendance, creative thinking, and high motivation for learning. In one study (Aspy & Roebuck, 1977), involving 600 teachers and 10,000 students (from kindergarten to grade 12), the students whose teachers were trained in the skills of empathic understanding, acceptance, respect, and positive regard for students as persons were compared with students whose teachers were not trained. The students of the trained teachers were found to:
- miss fewer days of school (four fewer days a year)
- make greater gains on academic achievement measures, including both math and reading scores
- be more spontaneous
- use higher levels of cognitive thinking
- increase their scores on IQ tests
- make more gains in creativity scores
- show increased scores on self-regard measures
- commit fewer acts of vandalism
- present fewer disciplinary problems

Another study showed a significant reduction of disruptive behaviors as a result of teachers being trained in facilitative skills. Roebuck measured the teachers' empathic understanding, respect for students, and the degree of student involvement provided by the teachers. Her findings: more disruptive behavior in classes whose teachers were *low* in empathic understanding, respect, accepting students' ideas, and inviting students' thoughts and opinions (Roebuck, 1980).

Under the leadership and supervision of two German social scientists, Reinhard and Anne-Marie Tausch, a large number of doctoral dissertations and masters' theses produced evaluations of the effects of teachers' facilitative skills on student effectiveness. Here is a clear and beautifully worded summary of the findings:

> In all of the school studies, empathic understanding, genuineness, warm respect, and nondirective activities proved to significantly facilitate the quality of the pupils' intellectual contributions during the lesson, their spontaneity, their independence and initiative, their positive feelings during the lesson, and their positive perception of the teacher. If we want to diminish stress, aversion, and impairment of physical and emotional health in schools and at the same time facilitate the development of personality and the quality of intellectual performance, then we will need a different kind of teacher than we seem to produce at present. Teachers are needed who can create in their classes an atmosphere in which there is empathic understanding, pupils receive warmth and respect, genuineness is encouraged, and the teacher can be facilitative in nondirective ways. (Tausch & Tausch, 1980, pp. 217–18)

The no-lose method of conflict resolution

Although getting youngsters to participate in mutual rule-setting significantly prevents a lot of adult-child conflicts in families and in classrooms, conflicts will always arise for which no rules have been previously established. Parents and teachers have to deal constructively with these unexpected situations or else their relationships will suffer.

Most teachers and parents, with few exceptions, are locked into 'either-or' thinking about resolving conflicts with children: they are either strict or lenient, either tough or easy, either authoritarian or permissive, either *their* solution to the conflict prevails or *the youngster's* solution prevails. In our classes we show how both of these 'either-or' approaches to conflict resolution are win-lose methods — either the adult wins and the child loses or the child wins and the adult loses.

A father shows this either-or thinking when he describes the power struggle in the parents' relationships with their children in this excerpt from a recorded interview:

> *You have to start early letting them know who's boss. Otherwise they'll take advantage of you and dominate you. That's the trouble with my wife — she always ends up letting the kids win all the battles. She gives in all the time and the kids know it.*

Children, too, see their conflicts with adults as win-lose power struggles. Cathy, a bright 15-year-old, expressed this clearly in a recorded interview:

> *What's the use of arguing? They always win. I know that before we ever get into an argument. They're always going to get their way. After all they are parents. They always know they're right. So, now I just don't get into arguments. I walk away and don't talk to them. Course it bugs them when I do that, but I don't care.*

In P.E.T. and T.E.T. we teach parents and teachers how to resolve conflicts with an alternative method called the No-Lose Method (or the Win-Win Method), in which both the adult and the child participate in a process of six separate steps:

Step I: defining the conflict in terms of needs
Step II: generating possible solutions
Step III: evaluating the possible solutions
Step IV: reaching an agreement on the best solution
Step V: determining what is required to implement the solution
Step VI: evaluating the effectiveness of the solution

Readers may recognize that these six steps are similar to John Dewey's six steps for effective *individual* problem solving. We have found they work equally as well as steps for effective resolution of conflicts between individuals.

The No-Lose Method of resolving conflicts requires a firm commitment to an entirely different posture from that assumed in the traditional win-lose methods. The parent or teacher conveys this message to the child:

> *We have a conflict — a problem to be solved. I don't want to use power to win at the expense of your losing. But I don't want to give in and let you win at the expense of my losing. So let's put our heads together and search for a solution we can both accept.*

The No-Lose Method derives its influence from Auth C, the authority derived from people having made a mutual commitment to an agreed-upon solution.

CONCLUSION

Despite the universal use of rewards and punishment in families and schools, I have found abundant evidence of the ineffectiveness of both as a method of control. In addition, punitive discipline itself has been shown to be deleterious to the physical and mental health of children.

I have been deeply involved for a quarter of a century in offering training to parents and teachers in nonpower and noncontrolling methods, which I firmly believe are far more effective than discipline in influencing children to be cooperative, considerate, responsible, and, above all, self-disciplined. I have briefly described these methods, documenting their positive effects on children's mental health.

These nonpower methods add up to a new and far more effective model of parenting and teaching. By giving up using power, parents and teachers will foster self-disciplined children. By relating to children democratically and refusing to be either dictators or doormats, parents and teachers will increase children's compliance with rules through involving them in the process of making the rules. By helping youngsters find their own solutions to problems, parents and teachers will foster more independence, more control over their own destiny, and higher self-esteem. By involving children in their own learning process and in the process of governing their classrooms and school, teachers will make schooling far more interesting, prevent disciplinary problems, and foster higher achievement motivation. And making a commitment to resolve all conflicts with children so nobody loses, parents and teachers will equip children with the skills to become a new species of world citizen—persons who will eschew the use of violence in dealing with conflicts between individuals, between groups, between nations.

No one has expressed more clearly how power-based methods create psychopathology than Abraham Maslow (1970, p. 254):

> Let people realize clearly that every time they threaten someone or humiliate or hurt unnecessarily or dominate or reject another human being they become forces for the creation of psychopathology, even if these be small forces. Let them recognize that every man who is kind, helpful, decent, psychologically democratic, affectionate, and warm is a psychotherapeutic force even though a small one.

All of us working in the field of human relations owe a debt of gratitude to Carl Rogers for his development of an effective method of counseling and psychotherapy, rooted in a basic trust of the client's capacity to find constructive solutions to his or her problems. And all of us have profited from the theory growing out of Carl's experiences as a client-centered therapist— particularly his 'necessary and sufficient conditions' for facilitating therapeutic change or helping another person function more effectively.

Rogers' important contributions became the basic core of my effectiveness training programs—the starting point for the later development of my own model of helping relationships. While Rogers developed his list of characteristics of a helping relationship principally from his experiences as a *professional* helping agent, my model emerged in the context of my attempt to teach lay people how to be more effective as managers, parents, or teachers. In the position of being professional therapists, we seldom get into serious conflict with our clients; we put aside our own needs (and problems) so we can devote nearly full attention to helping our clients meet *their* needs and solve *their* problems; communication is predominantly one-way—from client to therapist; we don't live with our clients, or work with them; and we are not in a dependent (or interdependent) relationship with our clients as we are, for example, in the manager-worker relationship.

Consequently, for me to teach parents how to have better relationships with their children, managers with their workers, or teachers with their students, I found it necessary to offer them additional skills and methodologies, which seldom are required in the counselor-client relationship—for example, modifying the environment (enriching, limiting, childproofing), sending confrontive I-messages, mutual rule-setting, using the No-Lose Method of conflict resolution, and democratic governing facilitating subject-matter classroom discussions.

If I were called upon to find a convenient way to describe my model for effective relationships of the kind we deal with in our training programs, the word 'democracy' first comes to mind. I believe we have been teaching parents, teachers, managers, and spouses how to create and maintain democratic relationships— relationships in which I help you meet your needs and you help me meet mine, relationships that are synergistic (separate persons working cooperatively together with greater total beneficial effects than the sum of their individual effects), and relationships that are equalitarian.

I happen to believe that relationships that are democratic will necessarily be therapeutic, and the more democratic, the more therapeutic. Carl Rogers knew this from his personal experience, and he expressed it in a variety of ways:

> My *influence* has always been increased when I have shared my *power or authority*. (1977, p. 92)

> By refusing to coerce or direct, I think I have stimulated learning, creativity, and self-direction. These are some of the products in which I am most interested. (1977, p. 92)

> Where control is shared, where facilitative conditions are present, it has been demonstrated that vital, sound, enriching relationships occur. (1977, p. 288)

REFERENCES

Aschuler, A. (1980). *School discipline: A socially literate solution.* New York: McGraw-Hill.

Aspy, D. N., & Roebuck, F. N. (1977). *Kids don't learn from people they don't like.* Amherst, MA: Human Resource Development Press.

Baldwin, A. L. (1948). Socialization and the parent-child relationship. *Child development, 19,* 127–36.

Baumrind, D. (1971). Current patterns of parental authority. *Developmental Psychology Monograph,* 4(1, Pt.2).

Becker, W. C. (1964). Consequences of different kinds of parental discipline. In M. L. Hoffman & L. W. Hoffman (Eds.), *Review of child development research* (vol. 1). New York: Russell Sage.

Burrows, C. (1973). The effects of a mastery learning strategy on the geometry achievement of fourth and fifth grade children. Unpublished doctoral dissertation, Indiana University, Bloomington.

Canter, L. (1976) *Assertive discipline.* Los Angeles: Lee Canter Associates.

Cedar, R. B. (1985). A Meta-analysis of the Parent Effectiveness Training outcome research literature. Ph.D. thesis, Boston University, School of Education.

Coopersmith, S. (1967). *The antecedents of self-esteem.* San Francisco: Freeman.

Dobson, J. (1970). *Dare to discipline.* Wheaton, IL: Tyndale House.

Dobson, J. (1978). *The strong-willed child.* Wheaton, IL: Tyndale House.

Duke, D. L. (1980). *Managing student behavior problems.* New York: Teachers College, Columbia University.

Duke, D. L., & Perry, C. (1978). Can alternative schools succeed where Benjamin Spock, Spiro Agnew and B. F. Skinner have failed? *Adolescence, 13,* 375–92.

Glasser, W. (1961). *Schools without failure.* New York: Harper & Row.

Glasser, W. (1986). *Control theory in the classroom.* New York: Harper & Row.

Gordon, T. (1955). *Group-centered leadership.* Boston: Houghton Mifflin.

Gordon, T. (1970). *Parent effectiveness training.* New York: Wyden.

Gordon, T. (1974). *Teacher effectiveness training.* New York: Wyden.

Gordon, T. (1976). *P.E.T. in action.* New York: Wyden.

Gordon, T. (1977). *Leader effectiveness training.* New York: Wyden.

Hyman, I., McDowell, E., & Raines, B. (1975). Corporal punishment and alternative in schools. *Inequality in Education, 23,* 5–20.

Ingraham V. Wright 525 F. 2nd 909 (1976).

Johnson, D., & Johnson, R. (1975). *Learning together and alone: Cooperation, competition and individualization.* Englewood Cliffs, NJ: Prentice-Hall.

Johnson, D., Maruyama, G., Johnson, R., Nelson, D., & Skon, L. (1981). Effects of cooperative, competitive and individualistic goal structures on achievement: A meta-analysis. *Psychological Bulletin, 89,* 47–62.

Jones, V., & Jones, L. (1981). *Responsible classroom discipline.* Newton, MA: Allyn & Bacon.

Martin, B. (1975). Parent-child relations. In M. L. Hoffman & L. W. Hoffman (Eds.), *Review of child development research.* Chicago: University of Chicago Press.

Maslow, A. H. (1970). *Motivation and personality* (2nd ed.). New York: Harper & Row.

Maurer, A. (1984). *1001 alternatives to punishment.* Berkeley, CA: Generation Books.

McLaughlin, T. (1984). A comparison of self-recording and self-recording plus consequences for on-task and assignment completion. *Contemporary Educational Psychology, 9,* 185–92.

Randolph, N., & Howe, W. (1966). *Self-enhancing education.* Palo Alto, CA: Stanford Press.

Roebuck, F. N. (1980, March). Cognitive and affective goals of education: Towards a clarification plan. Presentation to Association for Supervision and Curriculum Development, Atlanta.

Rogers, C. R. (1951). *Client-centered therapy: Its current practice, implications, and theory.* Boston: Houghton/Mifflin.

Rogers, C. R. (1977). *On personal power.* New York: Delacorte.

Sears, R. R. (1961). The relation of early socialization experiences to aggression in middle childhood. *Journal of Abnormal and Social Psychology, 63,* 466–92.

Simmons, J., & Mares, W. (1983). *Working together.* New York: Alfred Knopf.

Strauss, M. A., Gelles, R. J., & Steinmetz, S. K. (1980). *Behind closed doors: Violence in the American family.* New York: Anchor Press/Doubleday.

Tausch, R., & Tausch, A. M. (1980). Verifying the facilitative dimensions in German schools—families—and with German clients. Unpublished manuscript.

Urich, T., & Batchelder, R. (1979). Turning an urban high school around. *Phi Delta Kappan, 61,* 3.

Watson, G. (1943). A comparison of the effects of lax versus strict home training. *Journal of Social Psychology, 5,* 102–5.

Wright, L. (1980). *Parent power.* New York: William Morrow.

Thomas Gordon

Part D

Education

Carl Rogers' Contributions to Education

David N. Aspy *Consortium for Productivity in Education*
Louisville, KY and Amherst MA

Flora N. Roebuck *Texas Woman's University*

Carl Rogers influenced education by the way he thought and lived. In the intellectual area, Carl formulated a theoretical stance that gave structure to the process of enhancing students' growth through interpersonal facilitation. At the most profound level, Rogers taught that teaching and learning and education are all human activities and that truly effective schools should enhance the experience of being human. Scientific investigations validated Rogers' position. Rogers' extended influence in education will depend upon the continued use of his formulations by those who found meaning in them and those who follow Rogers' example of pursuing truth.

Carl Rogers influenced education as he wanted to do. Educators had to consider his ideas and modify their practices in light of them. Rogers was fully aware that his thoughts were so different from those of most mainstream educational thinkers that the chances of total acceptance were slim. Nevertheless, the very nature of his differences with establishment educators meant that his concepts had to be addressed.

Rogers' concepts of education emanated from his core belief in the dignity and power of each human being. Out of this basic value, Rogers formulated an approach to education that not only respected individuals but also enhanced them. His way of thinking was diametrically opposed to most of the current practices in education that in many ways tend to ignore the person.

EDUCATIONAL THEORY

Rogers' advocacy of educational practices that elevate and enhance individuals led him to explicate a theoretical framework that could be tested. Specifically, Rogers held that people's learning varied according to the levels of three conditions communicated to them: empathy, congruence, and unconditional positive regard. He further maintained that these three qualities influenced the amount of learning that occurred in any situation involving people. In fact, he called these factors the 'necessary and sufficient conditions for constructive personality change'; and, in his classic, *On Becoming a Person,* Rogers conjectured that these characteristics were essential to every educational situation (Rogers, 1961).

Rogers' contention that learning situations are enhanced when a teacher (a) understands the students, (b) values the students, and (c) is genuine with the students, seems to make common sense. It appears that no one would support the notion that teachers should (a) not understand students, (b) not like students, and (c) not be genuine with students. Thus Rogers' proposals seemed noncontroversial and there was an early tendency to treat his propositions as a matter of fact. In the beginning, it was common to hear people respond to Rogers' propositions by saying, 'Of course, we all do better when others treat us decently.'

First published in *Person-Centered Review,* Volume 3, Number 1, February 1988.

TEACHING

It was a mistake for educators to treat Carl Rogers' ideas lightly. On several occasions, we heard him say things such as 'I have a core of steel' and 'I can fight very well.' And, so he could. In this spirit, he took his theoretical formulations into the educational context. People soon discovered two things:

1. Rogers was genuine.
2. Teaching according to Rogers' concepts was difficult.

Educators found that providing empathy, congruence, and unconditional positive regard to learners required high levels of facilitative skills. In fact, the acquisition of those abilities involved reorienting most educational practices currently in vogue.

Investigations of classroom interactions had indicated that in a typical class there were *no* responses to students' feelings. This situation contrasts starkly with Rogers' contention that teachers should be aware of their students' deepest emotions. He was asking teachers to turn their attention to their students as persons: rather than attending only to themselves and their goals, they must know how both they and their students felt. It was only in that posture that a teacher simultaneously became both genuine and empathic. In this way, teachers could be aware of things happening both inside the learner and within themselves.

Rogers once wrote that everything he had intentionally taught other people had been irrelevant or hurtful. He believed that people could be taught by manipulating external factors (conditioning), but when we did so, we took them away from their inherent tendency to develop themselves in positive ways (Rogers, 1961).

TEACHER TRAINING

When teachers discovered it was difficult to provide empathy, congruence, and unconditional positive regard to their students, they began to seek ways to acquire these abilities. Again, teachers found the going rough. After a lifetime of living in a climate in which almost no one responds to our feelings, it is difficult to reorient ourselves and behave differently. This is particularly true when the general context in which we live remains unaltered and provides little or no support for our attempts to change.

Carl spoke of this dilemma in a paper he entitled 'Empathic: An Unappreciated Way of Being' (Rogers, 1980). In this statement, Rogers explained his experience that people did not recognize the existence of his empathy when, in fact, he was being most empathic. Some people viewed a Rogerian helper as being a mirror for a client. They extended the metaphor by contending that a good mirror is not seen by people using it. Thus Rogers asked teachers to shift from being the center of attention to a relationship that recognized students as coseekers of learning. To be sure, he recognized that teachers had a different responsibility from that of students; but, for him, the crucial ingredient in any human relationship was a mutual respect for positive growth tendencies.

As Rogers tried to help teachers develop their abilities to provide empathy, congruence, and unconditional positive regard for their students, he found that group procedures could be just as effective as individual contacts. For him, the critical ingredient was an experiential component of learning that forced people to move beyond their frontal lobes (cerebral hemispheres) and include their whole being. This type of learning was given a variety of names such as encounter groups or group facilitation. These group experiences demanded a great investment from teacher participants but since most of them returned to nonsupportive environments, the general impact of these efforts was not as extensive as they might (and should) have been. The power of this type of effort, however, was clear to everyone; those who completed the training successfully felt that they became a more powerful force in all aspects of their lives. Group process was a vital phase of Rogers' work in education.

ROGERS' PHENOMENOLOGICAL EVIDENCE

Educators tried to dissuade Rogers from his educational stance. He was attacked from many angles by adversaries, but he held his ground tenaciously. He stated that, basically, he was a scientist in search of the fundamental laws of human communication. As such, he tested his formulations vigorously, if not always with 'scientific rigor,' in the conventional sense of the term. Rogers was most apt to place prime importance upon phenomenological rather than experimental evidence. He appeared to believe thoroughly that, for human beings, the most important information was what their experience meant to them.

As Rogers applied his experiential 'rule of evidence' to education, he once again collided with conventional practices. The overwhelming majority of educational outcome measures relate to standardized tests. Rogers did not care much about normal distributions and other statistical measures except as they had meaning for learners.

Carl Rogers conducted numerous workshops in education, and often did research on the spot. For instance, in 1968, he conducted a small group demonstration at a conference sponsored by the R. J. Reynolds Foundation for some 500 educators in Winston-Salem, North Carolina. After the small group concluded, Rogers discussed his experience in it. Then, he asked other members to do the same. When questioners from the audience asked Carl about the group's dynamics, he spoke only of his own experiences. Rogers refused to be an 'expert' for the group. Of course, since he had been in many groups, Carl could and would speak of the commonalities and differences in his experiences with various groups (personal observation by the authors).

SCIENTIFIC EVIDENCE

Some of us who relied more on 'scientific' data than did Carl Rogers conducted some research on his position. He did not discourage our approach and, in fact, told us to be bold: 'The facts are friendly.' So, we plunged in.

Our methodology was borrowed from Rogers, Truax, and Carkhuff. Rogers had revolutionized research in psychotherapy by recording his interviews and evaluating them soon after the sessions. Until Rogers used this procedure, a great deal of psychotherapy research relied upon therapists' memory of the events in counseling even though subsequent investigations indicated that recall can be very selective.

We also audio recorded teaching and, using scales designed by Truax and Carkhuff, we evaluated the teachers' levels of empathy, congruence, and unconditional positive regard. (For methodological detail, see Aspy [1972] and Aspy & Roebuck [1977].) The teachers' ratings were compared to their students' level of achievement (test gain), attendance, discipline difficulty, IQ change, and attitudes toward self and school. In multiple-data sets from schools in 42 states and seven foreign countries, we found consistently that students do better when their teachers provide higher levels of empathy, congruence, and positive regard. The phenomenon was independent of sex, race, grade level, subject matter, and geographical setting. These findings were tested cross-culturally by Reinhard Tausch in Hamburg, Germany, where he obtained similar results (Rogers, 1983). The facts were indeed friendly.

Although Rogers cited the scientific data liberally, particularly in *Freedom to Learn in the 80's* (1982) and 'Beyond the Watershed' (1977), for him the most basic and most trusted evidence was his own experience of the events around him. He did not reject the validity of the scientific data; rather he asserted the primacy of human experience in matters that affect human beings. Thus in education, as in all things human, it is human experience that counts.

METAPHOR OF COURAGEOUS LEARNING

Perhaps to those who were fortunate enough to spend time with him, Carl Rogers' greatest lesson was that the most important learnings come from pursuing knowledge honestly. Rogers put himself on the line repeatedly. In fact, he resisted attempts to protect him. He made recordings of his counseling sessions and let others listen — friend and foe alike. He presented his ideas in written and spoken form and answered all questions about them. He demonstrated his counseling techniques (both group and individual) and discussed his experience immediately afterward. He met his behavioristic counterpart, B. F. Skinner, in open debate. He worked in schools across the country, teaching others his formulations. In his later years, Rogers was still visiting foreign countries (including Russia) where he spoke of the rights of individuals to voice their own ideas.

Rogers recalled with amusement a class at the University of Chicago where a young man rose and said, 'I'm furious with you for teaching the way you do.' He replied, 'It's all right with me if you're angry.' The young man huffed and sat down. To Rogers, the salient point was that the young man found it was OK to have and to express angry feelings toward the teacher (Rogers, personal communication, November 1982).

In a contrasting situation, Rogers conducted an individual counseling demonstration session in a class at Texas Woman's University, Denton, Texas, during the summer session, 1982. The client, a lively young woman, came to tears as she talked about her children. So, he took her hand for a moment until she felt better. In the above case he accepted anger; in this incident he recognized caring and responded with tenderness.

Thus in these two classes, Carl Rogers showed that he could and would accept and respond to a broad range of his students' feelings. In short, Rogers did what he said he believed. He got into the fray and demonstrated he could function in it. It seemed that he truly wanted to be the best teacher he could be. Therefore, Carl Rogers was a model for teachers and students who courageously aspire to be their best.

CONCLUSION

Carl Rogers influenced education with his thoughts and actions. He formulated a theoretical stance that gave form and substance to the age old truism that people do better when you treat them well. His formulations gave a structure to the proponents of human decency that enabled them to construct procedures they could use to improve their interpersonal effectiveness. Thus it was possible for teachers purposefully to enhance their interpersonal functioning in a manner that facilitated their students' growth.

Rogers' theoretical formulations included the entire human family by depicting how our individual behavior is related reciprocally. Previously, the prevalent conception of human behavior was that each person was on her or his own. Rogers' conceptualization showed how our destinies are tied together. No longer could a teacher write off a student without understanding that the failure belonged as much to the teacher as to the student. Rogers demonstrated that people's behavior is largely affected by the facilitation they receive from 'significant others.' He argued for a teacher's role that recognized that there was a two-way relationship with students rather than a unidirectional flow of ideas and feelings.

Carl Rogers shook education's foundations by showing teachers two things. *First,* they were ignoring students as people; and, *second,* it was necessary to enter into a relationship with them. He made it clear that teachers did not have to choose between 'being nice' or 'teaching them something.' Rogers' work demonstrated that it is essential to be humanly decent *in order* to teach students something.

Perhaps at the most profound level, Rogers taught that teaching and learning and education are all human activities that first and foremost involve human beings who have experiences. To Carl Rogers, the value of human experience transcended scientific measures that could not assess it. He argued that truly effective schools should enhance human experience and help all students build upon their own. Carl Rogers' popularity among educators ebbed and flowed, but regardless of the level of his acceptability, he remained a rock-solid advocate of the person-centered position. We will miss his supportive presence although his words will ring in our ears to give us strength. Carl Rogers stayed the course. May we do as well.

Carl Rogers' niche in educational history is guaranteed by his explication of the conditions that facilitate personal growth. His extended influence in education's future, however, depends upon the continued use of his formulations by those who found meaning in them. Quite probably, his most lasting influence will be exerted by those who follow his example of pursuing truth.

Our image of Carl Rogers' greatest joy is his joining hands with people of good will throughout human history and reveling in the collective opportunity to contribute to humankind's positive development. We'll just bet that Carl Rogers hoped that all of us would find life as meaningful as he did. We'll also wager that Rogers still wants education to become a process in which people respond to each other as people!

REFERENCES

Aspy, D. N. (1972). *Towards a technology for humanizing education.* Champaign, IL: Research Press.

Aspy, D. N., & Roebuck, F. N. (1977). *Kids don't learn from people they don't like.* Amherst, MA: Human Resource Development Press.

Rogers, C. R. (1961). *On becoming a person.* Boston, MA: Houghton Mifflin.

Rogers, C. R. (1977, May). Beyond the watershed: Where now? *Educational Leadership, 34,* 623–31.

Rogers, C. R. (1980). Empathic: An unappreciated way of being. In C. R. Rogers (Ed.), *Empowering the person* (pp. 137–63). Boston: Houghton Mifflin.

Rogers, C. R. (1983). *Freedom to learn in the 80's.* Columbus, OH: Charles E. Merrill.

The Mental Health of Students:
Nobody minds? Nobody cares?

William W. Purkey   *University of North Carolina at Greensboro*
David N. Aspy   *National Consortium for Productivity in Education*

We first review the background and nature of the present hue and cry for excellence in education. Next we point out that the present overemphasis on cognitive skills and measurable outcomes has been accompanied by an unfair attack on affective education and a growing neglect of the mental health of children. In response to these trends, we maintain that the quality of life in schools and the mental health of young people are important *whether or not* they are associated with academic excellence. We conclude our article by offering five axioms that may help bring the relationship between academic excellence and mental health into better balance.

> Eeyore, the old grey Donkey, stood by the side of the stream, and looked at himself in the water.
> 'Pathetic,' he said. 'That's what it is. Pathetic.'
> He turned and walked slowly down the stream for twenty yards, splashed across it, and walked slowly back on the other side. Then he looked at himself in the water again.
> 'As I thought,' he said. 'No better from *this* side. But nobody minds. Nobody cares. Pathetic, that's what it is.' (Milne, *Winnie the Pooh*, 1926, p. 72)

In light of the present outpouring of new programs, policies, mandates, edicts, and legislations that focus on cognitive outcome performance in education, it seems pathetic that so little attention is being given to the other side: the mental health of students. It is dismaying that the widely publicized reports on education issued during the past several years have almost universally downplayed the affective/social development of students.

The 1983 report released by the National Commission of Excellence in Education was noteworthy for its almost total neglect of such 'nonacademic' areas as student self-esteem, interpersonal relationships and social skills, sensitivity to the feelings and needs of others, personal dignity and integrity, the capacity to give and receive affection, and self-confidence and sense of self-efficacy. It was not alone in this perspective.

The same can be said of *Horace's Compromise* (1984), *A Place Called School* (1984), and nearly every other recently published national report. While some of these are helpful in limited ways, it is easy to conclude from reading them that they do not consider the mental health of students as important as academic excellence in schools.

First published in *Person-Centered Review,* Volume 3, Number 1, February 1988.

THE CRY FOR EXCELLENCE

Regretfully, none of the professional organizations in counseling or related fields has raised a clear voice of concern about the neglect of the emotional well-being of children. In fact, most of the professional organizations have rushed like lemmings to the sea in their cries for excellence: Excel! Exceed! Surpass! Scarcely a state or national conference has met during the last several years without having excellence as its theme. The same can be said of professional journals. Such unabashed endorsement conjures up memories of the old Flash Gordon serial, in which Ming-the-Merciless was always referred to by his minions as 'Your Excellence.' Even the most progressive and socially aware educational groups and journals have been swept up in the tide.

We can conjecture only about the reasons for the current emphasis on excellence as measured by standardized test scores and other narrowly defined cognitive measures, coupled with the relative latest reason for the present *zeitgeist* is that no system of schooling can be separated from the social conditions that surround it, and today America is in a very conservative mood.

ASSAULT ON EDUCATION

Whatever the cause for alarm, America went quickly to its educational system and looked for weaknesses. Many critics, particularly in the popular press, reported that schools were failing because they spent too much time on 'frills' such as counseling services, affective programs, and social development courses. Thus affective education was neatly linked to bad education, and concern for the mental health of children declined.

The linking of affective education and ineffective schools is both unwarranted and inaccurate. What seems to have taken place is that in the continual struggle between 'traditionalists' and 'progressives' in education, the traditionalist saw the reported decline in standardized test scores, the growing use of mind-altering materials by students, the industrial success of the Japanese, and other pressures as a golden opportunity to unleash a major assault on the most progressive aspects of public education. The result is that seldom, if ever, in American history have schools and the people who work there received such condemnation. But regardless of circumstances that brought American education to this point, the evidence is clear: excellence is in! And so the remainder of this article will offer five axioms that we hope will lead to school achievement. Before these axioms are presented, one disclaimer is necessary: *The quality of life in schools and the mental health of young people are important whether or not they are associated with school achievement or academic excellence.* We agree with Rosenshine and McGaw (1972, p. 641): 'Teacher behaviors which demean, humiliate, or deny the rights of students may be judged wrong despite any evidence that these behaviors promote desired outcomes — the end does not justify the means.' With this premise as a beginning point, here are five axioms that may help balance our emphasis on academic achievement with concern for the mental health of children.

FIVE AXIOMS FOR SCHOOL ACHIEVEMENT

1. *Schools that facilitate affective development also facilitate cognitive development.* Studies of classroom contexts have explored the question of the exclusivity of academic and self-concept enhancement. Must educators favor one or the other? In a wide range of

251

elementary and secondary classrooms throughout the United States, a series of investigations by Aspy and Roebuck (1977, 1985) explored the relationship among a facilitative climate and both self-concept and academic achievement. They found that classrooms that facilitated self-concept development also enhanced student achievement. These studies included analysis of 200,000 hours of classroom instruction. Samples were taken from classes at all academic levels as well as from 42 states and seven foreign countries. The clear-cut conclusion from these investigations was that the conditions that enhance self-concept are the very ones that promote academic achievement. Specifically, teachers who respond empathically to their students, who treat them as able, valuable, and responsible, and who present lessons in 'do-able' steps promote both cognitive and emotional growth. Conversely, teachers who do not do these things tend to retard student growth both in self-concept and in school achievement.

2. *'Inviting' practices are related to positive outcomes.* Educational practices based on self-concept theory and that reflect optimism, respect, trust, and intentionality have been named 'inviting' (Purkey, 1978; Purkey & Novak, 1984; Purkey & Schmidt, 1987). In a series of research studies (Amos, 1985; Inglis, 1976; Lambeth, 1980; Ripley, 1985; Smith, 1987; Turner, 1983) involving more than 2,000 secondary and postsecondary, undergraduate and graduate students, these researchers reported a high correlation among inviting teacher practices, identified by Amos as 'consideration,' 'commitment,' 'coordination,' 'proficiency,' and 'expectation' and student affective outcomes, such as attitudes toward course, subject matter, instructor, and self-as-learner. Creating a respectful, caring, and intentionally inviting learning environment is the surest way to encourage student achievement.

3. *Students learn more when they see themselves as able, valuable, and responsible.* Recent brain research provides information that supports the need for emotionally healthy classrooms (Aspy, Aspy, & Roebuck, 1985). When students are placed in environments where they begin to doubt their own value, abilities, or self-directing powers, it appears that the brain physically represses information that is threatening to the perceived self. Apparently, this is the way the brain protects itself from being overwhelmed. In other words, people physiologically block information that intimidates them. Thus the emotional content of material to be learned, as perceived by the teacher as well as the students, is critical. Educators who want students to achieve excellence cannot avoid encountering the emotional aspects of the total learning environment, which includes people, places, policies, programs, and processes.

Of all the things we learn, perhaps none affects our search for personal significance more than our perceptions of self-worth—our view of how valuable and responsible we are and how we fit into the world. The literature on self-concept is so vast that only a few reviews can be cited (Combs & Snygg, 1959; Coopersmith, 1967; Purkey, 1970; Rogers, 1951, 1967; Wylie, 1961, 1974, 1979). Yet the general conclusion from the great majority of these reports is that people tend to behave as they are treated. When students are treated as able, valuable, and responsible, they begin to see themselves as such and tend to act accordingly.

4. *Students learn more when they choose to learn.* Common sense is the usual term for consensual conclusions. Very few people think that humans learn well when they are preoccupied with other concerns. For example, who would think of teaching mathematics to patients in a dentist's waiting room? Who would argue that students learn very little about history when they are 30 minutes away from playing for a state championship? In like manner, who can assert that a person does not learn much about Spanish or trigonometry when his or her concern is that the school is the enemy, where failure is a

constant threat, or even when the student is afraid to go home after school. While some learning is likely to happen in almost any situation, it seems obvious that academic achievement is most likely to occur when both teachers and students see the educative process as a cooperative effort in which students *want* to learn.

It should be noted at this point that in North American schools there are countless teenagers who are so threatened or frustrated with life that suicide is a leading cause of their deaths. And for each student who does commit suicide, there are countless others who attempt it or contemplate it. In addition to suicide, there are the pressures of drug and alcohol abuse, unwanted pregnancies, and unyielding peer expectations. These pressures, when coupled with ever increasing demands for academic performance in an ever toughening competitive environment, suggest that students are not likely to fall in love with learning when their attention is diverted to survival needs. If schools ignore these stress-related pressures or try to force-feed the content of courses, the only thing the schools will accomplish is that students will develop an unquenchable distaste for what is being forced upon them, and/or for the process of learning.

5. *People are the most important components of schools.* When we ask ourselves what is the most significant thing about education, it forces us to reassess the various ingredients we find there. It is difficult to avoid the conclusion that the most important components of schools are the people in the process. A corollary of this judgment is that the mental health of children is of great importance, greater even than improved test scores or 'being number one.'

We have spent billions of dollars on the cognitive components of education, but we have spent next to nothing on creating positive emotional health. Recently, one superintendent related that out of a budget of several millions of dollars he managed to put aside $27,000 for in-service training. He was proud of this amount because he had to struggle with his board to get it. The bad news was that almost none of it was spent to help teachers relate more effectively with their students' feelings, or to help teachers handle their own mental health or that of students. He also reported that his fellow superintendents felt that he had put too much of his budget into this 'frill.' In sum, the mental health of our children and their feelings of self-worth and self-efficacy should be of utmost importance.

CONCLUSION

At some point in the history of education, a myth developed that education has to be either humane or effective, but that it is impossible to be both. The sad part about this myth is that it has been accepted as reality even though there is a wealth of data to refute it. There is no contradiction between firmness and kindness, or between inviting educators and successful ones. The salient point is the attitudinal 'stance' from which we operate. If we concentrate upon students' mental health and self-regard, then our educational practices revolve around them. If we focus on excelling, surpassing, exceeding, then our students' mental health and self-regard revolve around them. The basic issue is the stance we as professional helpers take and maintain.

Since we have a preference for data, we would like for you, the reader, to do a simple experiment with yourself. Just imagine for a moment that right now, we, the authors, tell you how poorly you have read this article or how inadequate your attempts to understand it have been. How would you feel? No child in school will learn much on an empty spirit. It is time that more of us *mind,* more of us *care,* about the mental health of children.

References

Amos, L. W. (1985). Professional and personally inviting teacher practices as related to affective course outcomes reported by dental hygiene students. Unpublished doctoral dissertation, University of North Carolina at Greensboro, NC.

Aspy, D., Aspy, C., & Roebuck, F. (1985). *Third century in American education.* Amherst, MA: HRD.

Aspy, D., & Roebuck, F. (1977). *Kids don't learn from people they don't like.* Amherst, MA: HRD.

Boyer, E. (1983). *High school.* New York: Harper & Row.

Combs, A. W., & Snygg, D. (1959). *Individual behavior: A perceptual approach to behavior* (2nd ed.). New York: Harper & Row.

Coopersmith, S. (1967). *The antecedents of self-esteem.* San Francisco: W. J. Freeman.

Deal, T. E., & Kennedy, A. A. (1982). *Corporate cultures: The rites and rituals of corporate life.* Reading, MA: Addison-Wesley.

Goodlad, J. I. (1984). *A place called school.* New York: McGraw-Hill.

Inglis, S. C. (1976). The development and validation of an instrument to assess teacher invitations and teacher effectiveness as reported by students in a technical and general post-secondary setting. Unpublished doctoral dissertation, University of Florida, Gainesville.

Lambeth, C. R. (1980). Teacher invitations and effectiveness as reported by secondary students in Virginia. Unpublished doctoral dissertation, University of Virginia, Charlottesville, VA.

Milne, A. (1926). *Winnie the Pooh.*

Mitchell, B. (1984). *Nine American lifestyles.* New York: Macmillan.

Purkey, W. W. (1970). *Self-concept and school achievement.* Englewood Cliffs, NJ: Prentice-Hall.

Purkey, W. W. (1978). *Inviting school success: A self-concept approach to teaching and learning.* Belmont, CA: Wadsworth.

Purkey, W. W., & Novak, J. (1984). *Inviting school success* (2nd ed.). Belmont, CA: Wadsworth.

Purkey, W. W., & Schmidt, J. (1987). *The inviting relationship.* Englewood Cliffs, NJ: Prentice-Hall.

Ripley, D. M. (1985). *Invitational teaching behaviors in the associate degree clinical setting.* Greensboro, NC.

Rogers, C. R. (1951). *Client-centered therapy.* Boston: Houghton Mifflin.

Rosenshine, B., & McGaw, B. (1972, June). Issues in assessing teacher accountability in public education. *Phi Delta Kappan,* pp. 640–3.

Sizer, T. R. (1984). *Horace's compromise.* Boston: Houghton Mifflin.

Smith, C. F. (1987). The effect of selected teaching practices on affective outcomes of graduate nursing students: An extension and replication. Unpublished master's thesis, University of North Carolina at Greensboro, NC.

Turner, R. B. (1983). Teacher invitations and effectiveness as reported by physical education students grades 9–12. Unpublished doctoral dissertation, University of North Carolina at Greensboro, NC.

Wylie, R. C. (1961). *The self-concept.* Lincoln: University of Nebraska Press.

Wylie, R. C. (1974). *The self-concept* (Vol. 1, rev. ed.). Lincoln: University of Nebraska Press.

Wylie, R. C. (1979). *The self-concept: Theory and research* (Vol. 2, rev. ed.). Lincoln: University of Nebraska Press.

Is There a Future for

Humanistic or Person-Centered Education?

Arthur W. Combs   *Community Counseling Associates*

The author maintains that humanistic or person-centered education is but a small expression of a much larger worldwide humanist movement. Coping with the human condition has become humanity's number one priority. At the same time, new understandings about people, learning, behavior, and health from the biological and social sciences emphasize the need for person-centered schools. Though currently under attack, the roots of humanism are too deep and the movement is too necessary to warrant a major retreat. If the movement did not exist we would have to invent it.

As a long-time champion of humanistic and person-centered approaches to education, I am often asked, 'But does it have any future?' 'Can it truly endure the "Secular Humanism" label or the vicious attacks of the far right?' 'Can it survive the mechanization of education by computers or the "back to the basics" movement?' Like many of my colleagues, I find these roadblocks misguided and frustrating. I also know that 'this, too, will pass.' Humanistic, person-centered education is an idea whose time has come. Its future is assured. If it did not already exist, we would have to invent it.

The person-centered, humanistic movement is no flash in the pan. It is a vital and necessary response to the world we live in and the future we have embarked upon. The person-centered movement in education is but a small expression of a worldwide shift in human thinking. There are humanist movements, for example, in medicine, anthropology, sociology, psychology, political science, and theology. Humanistic education is only the application in education of ideas growing out of two primary events:

1. A basic shift in human priorities, brought on by breakthroughs in science and industry, and
2. New understanding of the nature and behavior of human beings supplied by the biological and social sciences.

A SHIFT IN HUMAN NEEDS

For untold millennia the primary need of human beings has been how to wrest from the environment the food, clothing, and shelter required for the welfare of one's self and those one cares for. In less than 200 years, but especially in the last 50 or 60, enormous advances in science and industry have changed that picture forever. We have created a world in which we are totally dependent upon other people, millions of whom we have never seen or heard of. We live in the most interdependent, cooperative society the world has ever known since the dawn of history and it is getting more so with every passing day. We are totally dependent upon the cooperation and good will of others for even the

First published in *Person-Centered Review*, Volume 3, Number 1, February 1988.

simplest essentials for daily living. At the same time, the power of individuals to affect the lives of others has increased exponentially. One person at the right time or place, with the right instrument, can disrupt the system. Millions of people can be thrown into jeopardy by assassinating a leader, holding hostages, or setting off a bomb. The lives of thousands can be disrupted by a single person driving while drunk, misguiding an airplane, making unwarranted decisions in government or industry. And, of course, we all live in the shadow of the atomic bomb.

The primary problems of humanity have shifted from things to people. Today, we have the know-how to solve our age-old problem, to feed, clothe, and house the entire world. The most pressing problems we face have become people problems; how to grow and live fully as individuals, on one hand, and how to interact with others in ways that are effective and satisfying, on the other. Make a list of the problems we face: health, education, welfare, war or peace, social security, poverty, population, birth control, environmental pollution, civil rights, Medicare, Women's Lib, equal rights, industrial growth, and efficiency, to name but a few. All these are human problems. Even the bomb. It is not the bomb we need to fear, but the folks who might use it. For a hundred years we have been going through a quiet revolution in which the human condition has become our primary problem. Person-centered education is but a small part of this revolution.

Futurists are generally hesitant to predict the specifics of what the world of tomorrow will be like, and well they should be. On two major points, however, they are practically unanimous: (1) that we are destined to continue current trends toward ever increasing interdependence, and (2) that problems of personal growth and human interaction will continue to increase their critical importance as far ahead as we can see. To prepare tomorrow's citizens for such a future requires an educational system that is aware of the human problems to be confronted and actively engaged in the preparation of youth to meet them. Person-centered education seeks to do just that. It focuses attention on the 'Persons in the Process' and maintains that education must help prepare today's young people to understand and cope with the problems of an interdependent world. Those concerns are not substitutes for the traditional goals of education. Quite the contrary. They represent expanded or additional goals required to prepare young people for the world into which they are moving.

Humanistic, person-centered approaches to education are authentic efforts to meet the challenge of our changing world. The movement is here to stay because it is a necessary response to an increasingly pressing problem. Anything less is a denial of our educational responsibility. Failure to respond to society's changing needs will betray our young people now and, in the long run, can only result in a more rapid drift of public education toward irrelevance and eventual collapse.

New insights about human nature

The basic shift in human needs from things to people has focused attention on personal fulfillment and human interaction. To help us understand these new problems, society has invented a whole series of social sciences: psychology, sociology, anthropology, and political science. To put the findings of these sciences to work, a comparable set of helping professions has sprung into being. Among these are public education, counseling, psychotherapy, social work, applied anthropology, and a wide variety of programs for political and social action.

Out of these sciences and professions has come a flood of new conceptions about the nature and behavior of persons so fundamental as to call for change in many areas in our society but especially in education. The ideas we hold about the nature of human beings and how they behave are basic to educational theory and practice. The attempts of education to put these new conceptions from biological and social science to work in our schools is what person-centered, humanistic education is all about.

For several generations American psychology was dominated by behavioristic thinking. Behavior, we were told, must be understood as response to stimuli or the consequence of action. In other words, people behave according to the forces exerted upon them. Such a view tends to treat students as objects to be shaped and molded through the manipulation of events. Learning, in that frame of reference, is a process for producing appropriate responses through confrontation with information or experience. Teaching, in turn, is accomplished through telling, lecturing, or demonstrating, with heavy emphasis upon recitation, reward, and punishment. Schools are places where students are sent to be taught, whether they want to be there or not. Motivation, in this view, is largely a problem in management: how to get people to do what teachers want them to.

More recently, American psychology has seen the rise of humanistic-perceptual-experiential approaches to understanding human growth and development. These psychologies reject the mechanical views of behaviorism and its view of people as objects. Instead, person-centered psychology sees people as dynamic human beings behaving according to how things seem to them. People behave or misbehave in terms of their perceptions. That is to say it is the feelings, beliefs, attitudes, values, or personal meanings that people hold at the moment of acting that determine how they behave. People are not simply objects responding to the environment. They are persons; active, creative, dynamic beings capable of transcending their environment in the search for personal fulfillment. This shift in fundamental perspective about the nature and behavior of persons has far-reaching implications for all aspects of human interaction. The tenets of person-centered, humanistic psychologies provide the scientific foundations upon which humanistic and person-centered thinking and practice are constructed.

We have become accustomed to 'breakthroughs' in the physical sciences and accept the marvelous contributions they make to our daily lives almost as a matter of course. But breakthroughs occur in the psychological and social sciences too, and have equally profound effects. Some new conceptions lend support to old positions and that is comforting. Some raise serious questions about current goals and practices. That can be distressing. Best of all, more accurate conceptions make it possible to improve old performance and point the way to exciting and promising innovations. Person-centered education attempts to put to work the best of our new understandings from the psychological and social sciences.

THE CURRENT SCENE

Currently, person-centered education is under heavy attack in some quarters. Many people confuse humanistic education with the eighteenth-century philosophy of humanism that suggests that human beings ought not call upon God to solve all their problems. Rather, they need to get about seeking their own solutions utilizing the best that knowledge has to offer in the effort. That philosophy seems, to some fundamentalists, to deny belief in God. Accordingly, they have accused humanistic education of being a religion (secular humanism), a work of the devil. Other critics regard the movement as a sinister communist plot to subvert American youth. Still others fear person-centered education is dangerous subversion of traditional goals brought on by well-meaning, but soft-headed, teachers who have been seduced into liberal thinking. The protestations of these alarmists have even induced Congress to prohibit the use of federal funds for programs smacking of humanism. As a consequence, many humanistically inclined teachers find themselves accused of goals and actions far removed from the realities of their thought and practice.

One casualty of this confusion has been the erosion and redefinition of the word *humanism*. The shrillness and hysteria of the attacks upon humanistic education in many places have converted the word to an epithet and dissuaded many teachers from becoming involved in the movement. Others have carried on their person-centered work without fanfare or have learned to use other language to describe what they do. Despite opposition, misunderstanding, and outright attacks, the movement nevertheless continues, slowly and surely, to grow.

Once before, American education moved in a humanist direction during the progressive movement of the thirties and forties. The progressive movement grew out of the philosophy of John Dewey who held that (1) children have an innate desire to learn, (2) that learning is a social act, and (3) children learn best by doing. Putting these ideas to work, teachers experimented with such humanistic ideas as activity learning, building instruction around the student's own needs or interests, and shifting the role of the teacher from direction and control to 'friendly representative of society.' Like the current humanist movement, progressive education aroused resentment, antagonism, and ridicule from its critics, occasionally exacerbated by the extremes to which some of its advocates carried their innovations. These problems, plus the fact that Dewey's philosophy alone provided too narrow a base for more solid growth, kept the movement barely alive in the forties. It finally succumbed altogether as attention shifted to the country's entrance into World War II.

Today's humanistic, person-centered education is a very different affair. Whereas progressive education in the thirties was a need just being recognized, today's person-centered education has come into being to fulfill a need in full bloom and growing ever stronger. While progressive education was based, almost exclusively, on the work of John Dewey, today's humanistic movement is an expression of far deeper, broader forces that have also spawned humanist movements in medicine, psychology, anthropology, sociology, theology, and political science. It has the strength and resilience to survive and flourish in spite of current resistance.

A GRASS-ROOTS APPROACH TO EDUCATIONAL REFORM

Person-centered, humanistic education is also a quite different approach to educational reform. Most efforts at educational reform over the past 60 years have depended upon ready-made solutions concentrated on 'things' and often accompanied by fanfare, slogans, and hype. Samples of these efforts include:
1. gadgets and gimmicks (movies, TV, computers, psychological testing),
2. rules, regulations, and ways of organizing (team teaching, open classrooms, behavioral objectives, back to the basics),
3. curriculum revision (grade-level textbooks, New Math, New Science),
4. methods (the Palmer method, phonics, discovery learning, contract grading).

Some of these efforts have produced occasional improvements here and there but most have fallen far short of their advocates' fond expectations.

Instead of ready-made solutions or manipulation of things, the person-centered movement seeks for change through people and ideas. This produces change from the bottom up rather than the top down as individual teachers or administrators attempt to implement their humanistic beliefs in their own classrooms or schools. Innovations made in this way may vary widely from person to person or place to place. Their diversity may also make it impossible to identify humanistic education with a particular method or procedure. Indeed, humanistic innovations may be instituted by teachers who would be surprised to hear themselves described so. They see themselves behaving in terms of their beliefs about the nature and needs of their students, what they know of human growth and development, the processes of learning and their own discovery of effective ways for putting all this to work. The accumulation of thousands of local innovations, some notable and explicit, some 'born to flower unseen and unsung,' gives force and substance to the person-centered movement far beyond the comparatively small numbers enrolled in the National Association for Humanistic Education. Person-centered reform comes about as a consequence of the accumulation of solutions to local problems and objectives.

Assessing the impact of humanistic education by counting noses of teachers who ascribe to the name is an exercise in futility. The person-centered movement is not defined by a label. It is the accumulated effect of educators implementing ideas from modern humanistic thought and understanding. When I began teaching in 1935, there were very few humanistically oriented teachers. Today there are thousands modifying their approaches to students and teaching one way and another through the application of person-centered thinking to their daily tasks. Many even manage to do so in schools administered by autocratic and unsympathetic principals and supervisors. A few years ago, antihumanistic critics of education grew apoplectic over teachers who experimented with 'values-clarification' in their classrooms. Today these same critics are bemoaning the lack of values education in their local schools.

The humanist movement in education is here to stay. It is a product of changing human beliefs about the nature of persons, the nature of health, and the human condition. It is the product of and is supported by such massive data from the biological and social sciences that it cannot long be denied. Twenty years from now there may be no humanistic or person-centered education, per se. We may have decided by then to give up those labels. The movement may also be implemented in ways we do not even dream of today. But the fundamental ideas of the humanist movement will still be with us, alive and well and steadily growing in America's schools.

Keeping Person-Centered Education Alive
in Academic Settings

Hobart F. Thomas   *Sonoma State University*

This article deals with the question of how an academic requirement in a university course can be designed to enhance both the emotional and intellectual development of the learner in ways that transcend typical academic expectations. The author describes in detail a method stemming from several years' experience in an alternative educational model that is now employed in the university classroom. A number of examples illustrate how students are encouraged and challenged to transform an academic requirement from 'master' to 'ally' in learning what they themselves determine to be of most importance. Special consideration is given to survival strategies for the person-centered educator operating within institutions that may be disinterested or even antithetical to person-centered values. Of particular importance is the reconciliation of creative expression on the part of the learner with the need for maintaining high academic standards.

The shift in values in the field of education early in the 1980s is captured in the following statement by Notre Dame's president, Theodore M. Hesburgh (1981, p. 77):

> We seem to be passing through a time when education is the more cherished as it is the more vocational, when learning how *to do* something rather than liberal and humanistic learning how *to be* someone, particularly someone human, is in vogue. Thus we must seriously address the future of liberal education—especially in our day when the most popular course on the American college campus is not literature or history, but accounting.

At about the same time the above statement was made, an issue of the *Journal of Humanistic Psychology* (Spring, 1981) was devoted to a discussion of a number of once flourishing alternative education programs, all basically person-centered, which had been phased out of existence.

Rogers (1983) summarizes a voluminous body of research to support the effectiveness of the person-centered approach in a variety of learning situations. At the same time, he is frank to report the eventual cessation of the majority of once successful programs and to speculate on some of the reasons for their demise, such as threat to established systems, limited pool of person-centered leaders, creeping bureaucracy and routinization, no codifiable pattern for the operation of a person-centered institution, and, finally, the unwillingness of leaders to share their power.

For a period of 14 years I devoted my professional life to a small interdis-ciplinary experimental school within the California State University system (the School of Expressive Arts, Sonoma State University), which based its curriculum on the fullest possible development of the individual (Thomas, 1980). This program, once highly successful, was phased out of existence in 1984—another 'sign of the times.'

Those of us who have had the privilege of participating in such unique experiments

First published in *Person-Centered Review*, Volume 3, Number 3, August 1988.

are now challenged to distill the essence of what has been learned and to share it with others. Thus we may search together for new procedures and forms that will enable that which is of the highest value to live and flourish anew. It is with such intent that this article is written.

SOME IMPORTANT QUESTIONS

In telling the story of how I am attempting to keep person-centered education alive within academic settings I would like to direct attention to the following questions:
1. Is it possible to provide a climate conducive to the enhancement of personal values and personal integration within a system that often appears disinterested or even antithetical to such values?
2. How might we redirect an academic requirement to serve the individual's best interests?
3. How can an academic requirement facilitate and enhance such qualities in the student as self-responsibility, eagerness for learning, creativity, affiliation, and cooperation with others?
4. Is it possible to accomplish the above goals while still adhering to acceptable academic standards?

BACK TO THE CLASSROOM

In 1986 I made a decision to engage in what for me was a difficult personal challenge. I agreed to teach several sections of an upper-division required general-education humanities course entitled 'Written and Oral Analysis.' The purpose of the course was to improve student's written and oral communication. What represented a challenge to me was not so much the subject matter of the course itself but the fact that students were in the course involuntarily.

Successful completion of this course is required of all students wishing to graduate from the university. For many years, as a psychotherapist and as an educator, I had been involved in situations in which I had assumed that the voluntary participation of clients or students was an essential factor for successful growth to occur. Here I found myself in a situation that, on the surface at least, appeared to be the very antithesis of what I considered to be person-centered education. Few of these students had asked to be there. Many of them had other priorities: work in their chosen major fields, heavy requirements of other courses, outside employment, family responsibilities, and so on.

Rarely if ever are students consulted as to what they want, are interested in, or might feel are meaningful directions to pursue in the educational process. After all, isn't the teacher expected to know what is to be studied and learned and is it not ridiculous to expect the student to be consulted about these things? When I myself was a student, I was rarely consulted with regard to such matters. Rather, the bulk of my education right through graduate school consisted of following directions, learning what was prescribed for me by a number of different experts, mastering concepts and procedures, meeting others' expectations for me and finding out how to say the right things and give the correct answers on papers in order to pass examinations and get the coveted degree or credential. In fact, in graduate school we students used to say, cynically, 'If you want to succeed, first *study your professor,* then study the subject matter.'

Long after completing the requirements for my degrees I decided that I would never be satisfied with teaching and learning that did not in some way make a significant difference in the life of the learner. So I pursued what often seemed to be an uphill course, namely, the attempt to develop the whole person, insofar as possible, in the educational setting. I found that the success of this attempt depended on a basic shift from a teacher-centered model to a person-centered model of education.

Dealing with the system

I have learned, however, through many years' experience and much trial and error, that if person-centered approaches are to survive and flourish within traditional educational settings one must be well aware of and not ignore certain fundamental realities. One of the most important of these is the fact that most students within our educational institutions are subject to many external demands. The average student in our university system, in addition to the demands of his or her personal life, is probably enrolled at any given time in five or six different courses of study, each of which requires on the average at least two or more hours outside of class time for every hour spent in class. In effect, the student has to serve several masters at the same time. As a consequence, all too often the person gets lost in the process. Far too seldom is the student given the opportunity to integrate the vast amount and variety of information within a personal system of values.

On the other hand, the professor who does not require his or her fair share of the student's time will soon find the student's energies drifting elsewhere. The toughest courses making the most demands on the students get most of their attention, often out of fear of failure. In other words, the squeaking wheels get the grease. So the question becomes one of how to provide the openness and freedom so essential for personal growth within a system that prevents such an opportunity by imposing myriad requirements that far too seldom relate to the personal needs and interests of the individual.

For those of us working on this problem, an important clue existed where we had least expected it—in the requirement itself. 'How,' we asked ourselves, 'can an academic requirement be made to serve the individual, the "master" within each person who at some deep level knows what is right for that person? And, how is it possible to assure that each individual be provided with the time necessary to at least get acquainted with the essential process of self-discovery?'

Another important reality to be dealt with is the necessity of providing some evidence or product of learning that is demonstrable to others and measures up to reasonable academic standards. Academic degrees and credentials are not, nor do I believe they should be, awarded merely for putting in time or 'doing one's own thing' as some people in the heyday of the growth movement believed.

I also would carry the maintenance of standards a step further and challenge myself and my students to look always toward creativity in our productions, toward some unique expression of the self, a new twist, a search for ever-evolving ways of being and expression that offer meaningful contributions to human knowledge and understanding. This, I believe, was the original intent of the Ph.D., to grant the highest academic award only to those who made original contributions to the pool of human knowledge. Is it too much to ask students, at whatever level, to strive for this quality of creativity rather than merely conform to existing patterns. I think not. In fact, the more I encourage the development of creativity in my students, the more I am surprised, delighted, and impressed by what they are capable of accomplishing.

In order to assure that students might have the opportunity for at least a modicum of self-confrontation, I asked myself, 'Why not make the requirement 'demon' the servant rather than the master of the person?' Can we put this "demon" to work in helping us to get as much value as possible out of our educational experience? But who determines what is of most value? Traditionally it is the professor, the expert in charge. But what if the expert who is supposed to know so much shares the responsibility for determining what is of value with every person in the group? What happens when we focus on the values and concerns of each individual?

An experimental model

Following is a description of the tone I attempt to set in the course in Written and Oral Analysis and a general description of the course itself.

I usually begin each course with the following quotation attributed to the late Howard Thurman, a well-known San Francisco clergyman:

Ask not what the world needs, rather ask what makes you come alive and go do that, for what the world needs is people who have come alive.

This is followed by the following instructions:

The basic requirement for this course is to find what makes you come alive. Try to identify just who you are in terms of your basic values and interests. Get interested in *something – anything* you deem to be of value. Try to determine what you need to learn to expand and develop this interest. See where it takes you. Try to discover and develop your own style, your own way of expressing, through oral and written presentation to the group, this quest for your deepest and most important values. The sky's the limit. If you are unclear about what is worthy of your time and effort, then your assignment is to search for it and report on the process. Facing openly your blocks and difficulties, whatever they may be, finding the means of expressing them orally, in written form and in dialogue with others, is often the doorway to new learning. This will be your semester's project underlying most of your work in this course.

You will be expected to begin right away the process of discovering in your own terms what this project will be and to spend a fair measure of time working on it throughout the semester. What is a fair measure of time? Let's adopt the time-honored academic expectation of two hours of study outside of class for every hour spent in class. In this case, since we are spending three hours per week in class, you will be expected to spend an additional six hours per week devoted to work of your own choosing as it relates to your project for this course.

Somewhat paradoxically — and I realize this may appear strange to some of you — you are being *required* to devote this period of time to yourself, to ask what you need to become more fulfilled, to achieve more balance or perspective in your life, or perhaps a bit more modestly, at least to investigate and learn something concerning a topic for which you have some curiosity. Since this is a course in written and oral communication, the other aspect of this requirement is to participate with the rest of the group in the continual process of learning about and practicing effective communication, particularly with regard to those matters that are most alive for each of us.

Each of you will be asked to give a minimum of three oral presentations to the class and complete six written papers for the semester. The last of these will be a more comprehensive written and oral presentation to the group of your final project. Regular attendance and participation are expected of everyone. There will be ample opportunity for you to participate actively both in the large group and in smaller subgroups, to both learn from and teach each other.

After setting the tone, providing general instructions and discussion of questions, the first assignment (beginning with the second class session) is for each person to give a 3–5 minute oral presentation to the class, accompanied by a written paper, introducing themselves to the group. Students are asked to consider such questions as, 'In what ways am I unique; what is there about me that others are most likely to find interesting; what can I share of my interests and values; what makes me come alive; and how can I make this course work for me?' I encourage people to have fun and be as creative as they wish with this initial presentation.

I also ask each student, even at this early date, to share some idea of how they might best use this course for their own purposes. I assure people that I do not expect everyone to be clear or certain about their semester project at this point. What I do ask is a sort of 'position report,' a statement of 'where I am right now' with regard to this question. Students are asked to try to set some goals that can be modified as we proceed.

I cannot emphasize too strongly the value of constantly encouraging people to recognize and accept what is going on for them at any given moment and to find the means of expressing this experience. I have found that the persistent encouragement of authenticity as the first priority is perhaps the best policy I know. Some of my students' most exciting productions have resulted from their willingness first to face honestly the fact that at times they may be feeling ignorant, stupid, inadequate, inept, lost, or even worse, and to engage themselves with the process of turning the struggle into a piece of creative work. It is extremely important that we acknowledge all feelings and, whenever possible, search for ways of expressing them creatively.

During this introductory session I also distribute a course syllabus detailing what the course is about. It includes recommended readings, criteria for different grades, and suggestions for actively participating in the evaluative process. In order to provide a common basis of information I ask all students to read and give written and oral responses to the same two books. Most recently I have used Peter Elbow's (1981) *Writing with Power* and Carl Rogers' (1983) *Freedom to Learn for the Eighties.* The former covers important principles of written communication; the latter provides a conceptual basis for the person-centered approach to learning, something that many students find to be a new and strange experience.

After the initial oral presentation, followed by discussions and sharing of their written work in groups of 3–4 people, I found that it seems to work best to concentrate on the two above mentioned books for the next several weeks and on their continuing consideration of the special interest project. I ask for a written response paper to each of the books (average 3–5 page double-spaced typed paper) emphasizing how they are relating the material to their personal values and their project for the course. These I read and return with comments and personal reactions. In addition to establishing an ongoing dialogue between instructor and student, this process helps me to get some idea of the level at which each student is functioning, her or his strengths and weaknesses, and any areas needing special attention.

A sizable portion of class time throughout the semester is spent in small groups of three or four in which students read each other's work and offer reactions and comments. I purposely encourage the mixing of these groups from time to time so that every student gets to work with every other one at some time. At the end of each class session we devote 15–20 minutes in the total group for the purpose of sharing small group experiences with the entire class.

In addition, much class time consists of various exercises involving a variety of types of writing. Typically this consists of a short presentation by me, followed by a writing period of 10–20 minutes, another period of small group discussion (20–30 minutes) followed by voluntary sharing with the whole class.

Another technique that seems to work quite well is to devote the first 15 minutes of the class session to student oral reports. We usually limit these to 3–4 with a definite time limit of five minutes each. Although these are voluntary, there is the expectation that each student will participate at some time. Students are encouraged to talk about anything of importance to them. The talks vary considerably. They may be informative, persuasive, inspirational, entertaining, or merely a statement of 'what's going on' for the person at the time. Some may be well planned, while others vary from moderately spontaneous to 'off the cuff.' Whatever the case, they provide a good opportunity to speak to a group and practice giving and receiving feedback.

I try to achieve a balance, particularly in the first third to half of the semester, between devoting time to concepts and principles in the two required texts and allowing enough open time and space for pursuit of individual interests. In a way it seems contradictory to assign readings for everyone while at the same time urging people to use the time for themselves. Frankly, I puzzled a lot over this issue and discussed these concerns with the students from time to time. This doesn't seem to pose too great a difficulty once all the concerns are out on the table. For a number of students, the suggestion of readings at the beginning provides a sort of 'security blanket,' a way of easing into the far more difficult, ambiguous, often threatening situation of taking an active and responsible role in their own education. Also, the six hours a week required outside of class, if not exceeded, can protect students from overworking in this course.

I consider it important, however, for me to maintain a gentle but persistent pressure reminding and asking people how the basic project is coming along. Just prior to midterm each person is required to give an oral position report to the class describing in as much detail as possible the progress they are making and/or the difficulties they are having with their project.

It is essential at this point to emphasize that authenticity and honesty in staying true to the process, and describing just what is going on in one's research is infinitely preferable to presenting a slick product designed just to impress others. I've been most impressed with the energy generated by this process and the attention and genuine support students are able to give to each other. The more advanced and creative presentations can inspire while the sometimes awkward but genuine expressions of struggle with work in progress serve to encourage others to be more accepting of themselves and to keep trying. This is a time when individual conferences with students having difficulty can often be of immense benefit in clarifying and removing the blocks to creative expression.

FINDING A SUITABLE PROJECT

The desire to succeed is a double-edged sword. On the one hand, it provides the necessary fuel for each of us to excel in whatever task we undertake. On the other hand, our expectations and standards regarding what constitutes a successful performance or an acceptable product can also become a serious barrier to creative expression.

A bright young woman who had been doing well in the early written assignments and class discussions approached me mid-semester very distressed over the fact that she had not the slightest idea of what to do for her semester project. During her discussion she shared with me a conflict she was having with her parents. She claimed that her parents had threatened to cut off the funds to complete her education if she did not conform to their wishes to spend time at home during her vacation and enroll in what they considered to be a more prestigious institution. She mentioned that this problem appeared to be consuming most of her time and energy. Finally, I remarked to her, 'Do you realize that your "project" just might be staring you in the face?' This had never occurred to her, but she became interested. 'But, is this academic? How could something like this be acceptable?' 'I'm not sure,' I replied. 'That's for you to work on, but whatever the case, you just might have yourself a topic if you want it.' As we talked some more she became clearer about the issues involving the conflict with her parents and the choices she needed to make. She decided to work more intensely on her problem at the counseling center and to go ahead with the task of turning this whole matter into a class project—a written and oral presentation to be given to the class during the last weeks of the semester.

I wish it were possible to convey to you the delightfully creative manner with which she gave her final presentation to the group as well as the enthusiastic response she received from her classmates. By taking charge of her own life and facing many crucial issues with her parents she was in some way speaking for each one of us. With the utmost sensitivity, taste, and humor she described, complete with childhood photos of herself and family, artistic sketches, and even impromptu dramatization, with a number of clever props, her way of dealing with her conflicts and her resulting choices.

To quote a few remarks from her final report:

For the first time in my life, the type of learning I yearned for was taking place. Oh, Humanities class is not the end, merely a delicate taste of a new beginning. One class has not changed me, but it has started the ball rolling within. I am hungry for more similar classes. As it has inspired me, I don't want to stop now. As the class project allowed me to work on things I deemed important, I governed my own learning process. I directed myself to a goal, one which I eventually achieved . . . more importantly, the things that I learned in the class extend well beyond the classroom. They affect me personally, and I shall carry this new information with me for a long time.

I consider, of most importance, her final remarks to the effect that a meaningful process has been set in motion, something that has prospects of continuing in the future.

Another student, a young man 21 years of age, gave a different but equally moving and innovative final presentation to the class in the form of a videotape. He dramatized, in very clever and entertaining form, a variety of incidents in his own life, often humorous but with underlying serious intent, that related to his own growing sense of independence and feeling of personal value. A quote from his final report may give a flavor of what the experience was for him:

In this class I learned what I was excited about because *I* was the curriculum guide. Since my experience here, I hereby proclaim an end to being led as livestock over the educational pasture. I will of course have to follow instructors' guidelines, but preparing my work in a way that motivates me to create, I've found is like a masonry drill spinning through the writer's block.

I find the process of selecting examples from so many exciting pieces of work a difficult one indeed, but here are a few more.

A woman in the class whose sister was dying of cancer used this experience as the basis for her course project. She was able to identify this as her project early in the course.

She shared, from time to time, a number of her experiences in dealing with this very difficult emotional task, both with regard to her own personal feelings and her relationship with her dying sister. In addition, she used her time to learn all she could about the dying process through a fairly systematic study using several resources, relevant literature, tapes, and interviews. Obviously her motivation was very high as the following comments indicate:

> This final project has been a wonderful, enlightening experience for me and one that doesn't stop with this report or the end of the semester. I am a different person due to this course of study and I have been able to share the benefits of my learning with others — family and friends — and keep finding opportunities to share this new experience, strength and hope of mine. I am grateful, too, that I could share this project orally with the class and perhaps diminish the fear of death for others.

Other examples include an art history major, already a competent analytical writer, who for her project developed her creative writing skills; a premed student who began writing poetry for the first time and subsequently elected to enroll in a poetry class; and a business student who did a study of the Isle of Rhodes. This study, in addition to providing him with geographical and historical knowledge, resulted in a deep understanding of his family origins and reestablishment of connection with family members. He then culminated the study with a visit to Rhodes. I include a quote from this student's final report in order to illustrate how the experience of being challenged to assume responsibility for one's own learning may have important ramifications:

> I have seriously taken the questions you had us answer in this class and asked them for each of my other classes and even the Marketing Association. Answering the questions, 'How can I make this course work for me? How much do I already know? And, what do I want to learn?' This has helped me align my classes with my own interests and goals. I have come to realize that learning happens when you have an inherent interest, and a fair amount of time for yourself to study and to devote to the subject.

DOES THIS WORK FOR EVERYONE?

Anonymous end of the semester evaluations from six classes (totaling 128 students) reveal that the vast majority of students claim to have had a highly significant learning experience similar in quality to the examples given. As one might expect, there are bound to be exceptions. A few students self-select out of the course in the beginning weeks of the semester for a variety of unknown reasons. Last year I advised a couple of students who were falling behind to drop the course. To my surprise both reenrolled a year later and are currently taking the course this semester.

A small minority (5%–7%) claim not to have derived anything particularly significant from the course, as illustrated by the following comments:

Need more structure; too ambiguous.
I don't want to dig too deeply; all I want is to graduate.
Needed clearer instructions, more clearly stated objectives.
Class moved at too slow a pace. Could have been more challenging.
Complete waste of time.
Need more grading, more specific assignments. I need to be pushed more to perform.
More written analysis; less psychoanalysis.

Finally, a couple of my favorites:
  Great instructor in an insignificant class.
  More concentration in improving writting (sic) *skills.*

A number of the negative comments remind me of the continuing need to develop meaningful challenges and structures for those students less able to assume personal responsibility for their own learning. Although I consider myself a slow learner in this regard, I am happy to report that the strategies proposed in this article have helped to improve my 'batting average' considerably after many years of trial and error.

CONCLUDING REMARKS

As indicated at the beginning of this report, I had held a number of reservations about whether person-centered approaches to learning that had worked successfully in alternative educational models could be applied to required academic courses. My experience, from which I have drawn a few representative examples, has convinced me beyond a doubt that beneath the facades lies a crying need for personal relevance on the part of vast numbers of students and teachers in our educational institutions. For me, the following observations of a student speak for many of us who participated in the experience:

> I noticed that people worked on subjects that mattered very much to them and they seemed to benefit personally by doing so. I noticed inner conflicts being at least partially solved, career decisions being made, and in general, a true learning process evolving before my eyes. It was good to see real benefits of school happening instead of rote memorization or abstract generalities. It made me feel good to be at a school where this is going on. If only more classes would emphasize learning for yourself, not for the teacher, much more value would be inherent in our system.

A famous educational leader once remarked that all too often school becomes a place where we deal only with things that don't matter. I have learned that if I am willing to share what I know, to admit what I don't know, while staying in touch with what my students have to teach me and each other, then indeed this need never be so.

REFERENCES

Elbow, P. (1981). *Writing with power.* Oxford: Oxford University Press.
Hesburgh, T. M. (1981). Liberal education: What is its future? *Forum for Correspondence and Contact,* 12(2).
Rogers, C. R. (1983). *Freedom to learn for the eighties.* Columbus: Charles E. Merrill.
Thomas, F. F. (1980). Toward a rationale and model for basic education. In E. Bauman, I. B. Brent, L. Piper, & A. Wright (Eds.), *The holistic health lifebook* (pp. 282–93). Berkeley: And/Or Press.

Person-Centered Assumptions
for Counselor Education

Arthur W. Combs   *Greeley, Colorado*

It is suggested that person-centered thinking about counseling requires reexamination of assumptions for counselor training programs. From a background of perceptual psychology, a series of studies on the belief systems of good helpers, and experience gained in several innovative programs, seven assumptions are proposed, discussed, and illustrated with adaptations from sample programs.

Whatever we attempt in the design of programs for the education of counselors will depend upon the fundamental assumptions from which we begin. Over the more than 40 years that I have been deeply involved in the education of helpers such as clinical psychologists, counselors, and teachers, my assumptions have been greatly influenced by person-centered thinking, on the one hand, and a series of studies on the characteristics of effective helpers, on the other.

From person-centered perceptual experiential psychologies I learned to seek understanding of my clients, students, and colleagues in phenomenological terms. I became convinced that behavior is only a symptom whereas the causes of behavior lie inside people, in how things are perceived by them. This frame of reference was so successful in guiding my professional practice that I began to apply it to the task of educating helpers as well.

The second major influence upon my assumptions came from a series of 14 studies on the difference between good and poor helpers in counseling, teaching, nursing, administration, pastoral counseling, and public office. Daniel Soper and I completed the first of these researches in 1962. Most of the rest were carried out as doctoral dissertations at five universities. These studies demonstrated with remarkable agreement that good practitioners in each of the professions explored could be significantly discriminated from poor ones by the nature of their perceptual organizations or belief systems. (See Aspy & Buhler, 1975; Benton, 1964; Brown, 1970; Choy, 1969; Combs & Soper, 1963; Dedrick, 1972; Doyle, 1969; Gooding, 1964; Jennings, 1973; Koffman, 1975; O'Roark, 1974; Usher, 1966; Vonk, 1970.) Because the education of professional helpers must be based upon one's assumptions about what makes a good helper, these studies had a profound effect upon my thinking about professional education.

From these two sources, I have been led to assumptions about the preparation of professional helpers that are extremely different from those I held in my early years as a counselor when I was more behavioristically oriented. I have also had an opportunity to see them put to work for the preparation of practitioners in four helping professions and find they pay real dividends in the development of quality helpers. Here are seven of the most important assumptions currently governing my thinking about the education of helpers:

First published in *Person-Centered Review*, Volume 1, Number 1, February 1986.

1. BECOMING A COUNSELOR

The relationships of counseling require counselors to respond to clients instantaneously. To assure that responses under such conditions are truly helpful and facilitating requires that counselors have in place a broad, accurate, consistent, defensible, and personally relevant belief system from which to select or create appropriate action. The development of such a belief system is not a mechanical process. It is a consequence of deep personal exploration and discovery of meaning, a person-centered process of individual growth and becoming. The medical profession does not speak of its training programs as 'Learning to Doctor,' nor does the legal profession refer to its programs as 'Learning to Law.' Instead, they speak of *becoming* physicians or lawyers. Just so, the education of counselors must be seen not as learning to counsel but as an intensely personal process of becoming a counselor. This represents a basic shift in thinking from a behavioristic philosophy emphasizing teaching, controlling, directing, 'making' counselors to a position focusing upon personal growth and student discovery of personal meaning. The implications of that concept require changes in thinking and practice for many aspects of professional education programs.

2. FOCUSING ON BELIEFS

If it is true that personal beliefs or perceptions determine behavior, as perceptual humanistic psychologies currently suggest, and if it is true that significant differences between good and poor helpers lie in their belief systems, as the studies mentioned above imply, it follows that educational programs must focus on the beliefs or perceptual organizations producing behavior rather than on behavior itself. That is, students and faculty must concentrate more upon the continuous refinement of personal belief systems than upon facts, methods, or behavior. Programs oriented in such terms will be person-centered, focused more upon student experience than curriculum delivery, more on student belief systems than methods and behavior.

Concentrating upon methods and behavior seems logical but, in practice, can actually delay student growth. If behavior is a consequence of personal meaning or belief, then programs focusing on behavior are concentrating upon symptoms rather than causes. My awareness of this has greatly reduced my reliance upon the use of audiovisual equipment. The first time beginning counselors observe themselves on the screen they are shocked or intrigued to see how they look and behave. Left to their own devices, however, they soon give up the use of such equipment, finding it more trouble than it is worth. The scenario often goes something like this: videotaping concentrates attention upon behavior – what the counselor is doing. Such absorption sends the counselor into subsequent interviews preoccupied with his or her own behavior, distracting attention from the primary task of understanding and responding to the client. The counselor is left fumbling about, trying to do 'what I ought to do' instead of smoothly and spontaneously responding to the client.

In my more behaviorally oriented days as a supervisor one might have heard me commenting: 'Why did you – ?' 'You should – or should not have – ,' 'I would not – ' and the like. The series of studies mentioned in the third paragraph of this article agreed that crucial areas of helpers' perceptual organization lay in beliefs about the following: the importance of empathy, what people are like, the helper's self and the purposes he or she sought to fulfill as a person and as a professional helper. In light of these findings, my supervisory remarks these days are more likely to concentrate on those matters. 'How did you feel about Mrs. Jones?' — focusing on counselor feelings and beliefs rather than on what the counselor did. Turning attention to beliefs about people, I may encourage students to explore their beliefs about their clients and people in general. Together we may try to infer the ways clients think and feel about themselves and their relationships with the significant others in their lives. With respect to purposes, I may ask, 'What were you trying to do in this interview?' or 'What do you suppose your client is trying to do?' The comments I make are intended to keep student attention on personal beliefs, understandings, purposes, feelings, attitudes, hopes, and desires — the things that determine behavior. Professional counselors know that concentrating client attention upon personal meanings and basic beliefs is the road to effective growth and change. It is for aspiring student counselors too.

Traditional preparation of practitioners in the helping professions usually involves completion of courses, laboratories, fieldwork, and the like. One 'satisfies requirements' by collecting tickets or grades signifying completion of requirements. When enough have been accumulated, one is graduated and certified as competent. Such a procedure for the preparation of counselors is most inadequate. The acquisition of a complex personal belief system is not a mechanical or cumulative process but a highly personal one. It is achieved by deep personal involvement and the integration of experience through personal exploration and discovery. Such personal growth is not likely to be facilitated in the on again-off again relationships of traditional courses wherein instructors teach subjects, rather than persons, and relationships of student and instructor are mostly superficial. Effective counselor education calls for continuous relationships between faculty and students and among students with each other. Not all of a student's relationships in a program need to have depth and continuity, but such relationships must surely play a prominent role somewhere in a total program.

Close, understanding relationships conducive to deep exploration of meaning take time to develop and maintain. They are too important to be left to chance. They need to be consciously built into the structure and philosophy of the program. What has worked best for me are seminars of about 15 students meeting continuously throughout the program. Membership in such groups includes students at all levels; beginners, old hands, and those about to graduate, continually renewed by replacing graduates with beginners. Other forms of continuous contact can be provided by permanent advisers, student teams, study groups, practicum teams, professional clubs, common projects, and so on.

3. COMMITMENT TO THE LEARNING PROCESS

Because beliefs and perceptions lie inside people, they are not directly open to change. Accordingly, effective professional development requires honest commitment and involvement of students in all aspects of the learning process. Students must be expected to take major responsibility for their own learning. To accomplish such a goal requires more than acceptance of this principle. It requires program structures that aid commitment and a faculty actively facilitating relationships with students based upon mutual respect and cooperation.

In several programs, we sought to implement such goals in the following ways:
  (a) Faculty consensus that student commitment and involvement were basic policy with high priority for action.
  (b) Involvement of students in all faculty committees and meetings with full rights of

    participation and voting. This was usually accomplished by election of student representatives responsible for attending meetings, representing their constituents, and reporting back to the student body.

(c) Active search by faculty and staff for barriers to communication followed by appropriate steps for their elimination or resolution. In my experience, students can and will add much to the functioning and quality of programs, if they honestly feel they have vital roles in the determination of their own destiny.

(d) Encouragement of faculty-student interaction socially as well as professionally.

(e) Continuous involvement of students in planning the next steps for their own growth and for the whole student body.

One could wish that there was a substantial body of definitive follow-up research on the professional preparation of helpers, but such results are extremely difficult to come by, even for long-established programs. Ideally, one would like to have data on the effects new counselors have upon their clientele over a period of time. Such research, however, is extremely costly and difficult to accomplish because students tend to scatter to the four winds upon graduation and follow-up studies are only meaningful some years after students leave the preparation program. I regret, therefore, that the only follow-up data available on the above and other practices mentioned in this article are in the nature of evaluations made by students, faculty members directly involved in implementation of programs, and a few reports from first supervisors and employers following graduation. These tend to be generally, but not exclusively, positive (Combs, Blume, Newman, & Wass, 1974; Wass & Combs, 1974).

4. RESPONSE TO NEED

Perhaps the most certain thing we know about learning is that people learn best when they have a need to know. Despite our certainty about this principle, most educational programs operate as though it did not exist. Faculties assume that students have a need to know — or if they don't, they should! Courses are essentially packages of information, prepared in logical order according to the structure of the subject matter or the convenience of the instructor, then delivered at a 'logically' prescribed spot in the program with little or no reference to the peculiar needs or readiness of students.

    A program truly oriented to the need principle would provide instruction in response to student need. It would (a) seek to discover student needs and provide experiences to fulfill them or (b) expose students to events designed to create new needs. Such a process, however, runs head on into traditional college practices and is almost certain to encounter keen opposition from faculty members, registrars, colleagues, even from students themselves who may be distressed by departures from the way things 'are supposed to be.' Traditional subject matter courses may ignore the need principle and achieve a measure of student retention of information. For programs in the helping professions, dependent upon experiential learning and the development of intensely personal belief systems, the principle demands greater recognition and implementation.

    Here are a few adaptations to the need principle with which I am familiar:

    One program eliminated specific course titles and substituted general ones, around quarters of credit rather than specific content. This left instructors free to organize experiences around student needs, to fulfill current ones or create new ones and facilitate exploration of belief systems without the usual constraints of course time and syllabi.

The above program also arranged to make faculty available to students at any time throughout the program, whether students were registered in a given professor's class or not.

Another substituted student 'demonstrations of competence' for customary courses. Students completed a series of 'learning activities' designed to demonstrate command of an area, ability to utilize resources, deal with significant problems, and critique their own performance (Combs et al., 1974).

Still another program organizes students in teams of eight to ten. Each team selects a representative who meets with the faculty on Thursday of each week. Together, this group plans the following week's program experiences to fulfill current needs and push on to explore new ones.

5. THE FUNCTION OF FIELD EXPERIENCE

Historically, field experience has usually been seen as the place for students to practice what they have learned or for final demonstration of professional competence. Either way, it came near the end of the program. I believe a far more important role for field experience lies in helping students discover what the problems are; that is, field experience is for creating needs to know. For that purpose, field experience should be encountered throughout a program, not reserved for the end. Ideally, students need practical experience running concurrently with all phases of their learning experience, preferably increasing in time on task and level of responsibility assumed.

To be maximally useful, field experience must also deal with real problems. I have serious doubts about the value of 'practice counseling.' At the very heart of good counseling is the need for counselor authenticity. Trying to be authentic when the activity is 'only a game' is frustrating, confusing, and requires concentration on things that don't matter. Worse still, because counselor and client both know the problem is unreal, attention becomes focused on methods so that both parties concentrate upon symptoms rather than the dynamics of the counseling process.

6. DISCOVERING PERSONAL METHODS

Teaching counseling methods, I find, is largely counterproductive. Counseling methods must 'fit.' That is, they must be appropriate for the clients and the circumstances, on the one hand, and must fit the counselor, on the other. They can rarely be taught. They must often be invented on the spot. Nor can the methods of the experts be directly taught to beginners. I once had responsibility for teaching a 'How to Study' course for academic casualties. Not knowing what we ought to teach, the instructors got together and decided to investigate what good students do. We found out that good students don't study much! They go to the movies, study without careful plans, are more involved in campus affairs, and so on. Obviously, the methods of these experts would be suicidal for students in trouble. The methods of experts, like everyone else, arise from their personal belief systems. Employment of their methods without the belief systems behind them can only be accomplished by 'acting them,' a process possible only so long as the counselor can keep his or her mind on the method. That can only be done at the expense of breaking concentration on the client, and runs the risk of being seen by the client as awkward, insincere, or phony.

If authenticity and personal fit are prime requisites, counselor education programs must deemphasize teaching techniques and encourage students to explore and discover their own best ways of working. What is needed is not the teaching of 'right' methods but a cafeteria approach in which students are encouraged to look over the available methods and select what fits their readiness, capacity, and current systems of beliefs. Primary emphasis must be on development of trustworthy belief systems; that is to say, perceptual organizations that are comprehensive, accurate, internally congruent, personally relevant, appropriate to the tasks confronted, and continuously adaptable to modification as required. Such a belief system can be counted upon to guide the counselor's selection and creation of methods required for effective practice. It also makes 'trust in the organism' a defensible principle. A belief system that meets the above criteria deserves to be trusted.

7. PROFESSIONAL EDUCATION AS HELPING MODEL

Finally, an effective program for counselor education must serve as a kind of microcosm in which what students experience is itself a living demonstration of helping principles in action. Teaching, too, is a helping profession. Like counseling, its goal is the facilitation of learning, albeit less personal or intense than therapy. Both professions are based upon the same fundamental principles of learning. There is a widespread belief that teaching and counseling are vastly different functions, probably brought about by unhappy personal experiences and the comparison of good counseling with bad teaching. I find that the best of modern teaching is remarkably like good counseling and the best of counseling is very like good person-centered teaching. It is no accident that the person-centered thinking of Carl Rogers is extremely popular with educators on the cutting edge of the teaching profession. Since I began systematically applying the basic principles of counseling to the planning and practice of teaching, my teaching has immensely improved. Likewise, applying the principles of good teaching has greatly sharpened my counseling skills, especially with groups.

Exposure to excellent teaching can provide students with valuable opportunities to experience basic principles of learning in action. Teacher-student relationships can serve as demonstrations of what good relationships ought to be. Classroom activities can mirror the best we know of good group practice. Administrators and supervisors can model the consulting role. Programs can be consciously designed to reflect good counseling practice. Even the provisions for student interactions in a program can be constructed with an eye to student growth as counselors.

There is an old Indian proverb that states, 'What you do speaks so loudly, I cannot hear what you say.' Many counselor education programs, unhappily, are characterized by mediocre teaching and are often so bound by traditional college regulations and tradition as to provide students with experiences directly contrary to the tenets of effective counseling. Surely, a counselor training program, which hopes to produce effective counselors, ought itself be a model of the philosophy and practices it preaches.

REFERENCES

Aspy, D. N., & Buhler, K. (1975). The effect of teachers' inferred self-concept upon student achievement. *Journal of Educational Research, 47*, 386–9.

Benton, J. A. (1964). Perceptual characteristics of Episcopal pastors. Unpublished doctoral dissertation, University of Florida.

Brown, R. G. (1970). A study of the perceptual organization of elementary and secondary 'Outstanding Young Educators.' Unpublished doctoral dissertation, University of Florida.

Choy, C. (1969). The relationship of college teacher effectiveness to conceptual systems of orientation and perceptual organization. Unpublished doctoral dissertation, University of Northern Colorado.

Combs, A. W., Blume, R. A., Newman, A. J., & Wass, H. L. (Eds.), (1974). *The professional education of teachers. A humanistic approach to teacher preparation.* Boston: Allyn & Bacon.

Combs, A. W., & Soper, D. W. (1963). The perceptual organization of effective counselors. *Journal of Counseling Psychology, 10,* 222–7.

Dedrick, C. V. L. (1972). The relationship between perceptual characteristics and effective teaching at the junior college level. Unpublished doctoral dissertation, University of Florida.

Doyle, E. J. (1969). The relationship between college teacher effectiveness and inferred characteristics of the adequate personality. Unpublished doctoral dissertation, University of Northern Colorado.

Dunning, D. (1982). A study of the perceptual characteristics of Episcopal priests identified and not identified as most effective. Unpublished doctoral dissertation, The Fielding Institute, Santa Barbara, CA.

Gooding, C. T. (1964). An observational analysis of the perceptual organization of effective teachers. Unpublished doctoral dissertation, University of Florida.

Jennings, G. D. (1973). The relationship between perceptual characteristics and effective advising of university housing para-professional residence assistants. Unpublished doctoral dissertation, University of Florida.

Koffman, R. G. (1975). A comparison of the perceptual organizations of outstanding and randomly selected teachers in open and traditional classrooms. Unpublished doctoral dissertation, University of Massachusetts.

O'Roark, A. (1974). A comparison of perceptual characteristics of elected legislators and public school counselors identified as most and least effective. Unpublished doctoral dissertation, University of Florida.

Usher, R. H. (1966). The relationship of perceptions of self, others and the helping task to certain measures of college faculty effectiveness. Unpublished doctoral dissertation, University of Florida.

Vonk, H. G. (1970). The relationship of teacher effectiveness to perceptions of self and teaching purposes. Unpublished doctoral dissertation, University of Florida.

An Experiential, Person-Oriented Learning Process in Counselor Education

Louis Thayer   *Eastern Michigan University*

This article describes an experience that evolved from discussions with counseling practicum students, a survey of their perceptions about their program of studies, and a 60-hour experimental workshop. The feedback from the students on program strengths and weaknesses aided in the design of a person-oriented learning process that is experience based. The learning process is based on student input and is especially designed to help students become aware of counseling concepts and principles, learn basic human relations/counseling skills, review program and professional expectations and opportunities, assess their potential and motivation for different career directions in the helping professions, and examine their career objectives. Graduate students who have participated in the experience have given much positive feedback about the content and process.

The development of an experience-based introduction to counselor education at Eastern Michigan University was initiated with graduate students in counseling who shared their perceptions of a counselor education and training program. The experience to be described was initiated by discussions that were held with requirement — the supervised counseling practicum. Practicum students were very willing to discuss their experiences in training as well as their perceptions of program strengths and weaknesses. They shared ideas about what experiences would have been more beneficial to them in the teaching/learning sequence.

As a result of the discussions, a short questionnaire concerning key areas of the program was prepared with another faculty member, B. Van Riper, to survey prospective counselors during their counseling practicum semester. The discussions with students and the results of the survey stressed a need for changes that would bring more experience-based components into the program of studies prior to the counseling practicum. More than one-half of the 114 practicum students who were surveyed indicated that there were not enough opportunities to practice counseling, to observe effective modeling of counseling skills, or to be involved in practical counseling experiences prior to entering the counseling practicum. Nearly one-half of the students wanted more opportunities to explore their potential for counselor education and indicated that they experienced 'quite a bit' of anxiety about entering the supervised counseling practicum.

This article's purpose is to describe the operational model for the graduate course that I developed as a result of the discussions with counseling practicum students, the questionnaire, and, especially, a 60-hour experimental workshop that I conducted. The learning experience is currently offered in 30 hours in one semester as one of two introductory courses to our master's degree graduate program of studies in counselor education and training. Although other faculty members and visiting lecturers teach the course, the following is a description of the way I offer the experience.

First published in *Person-Centered Review,* Volume 2, Number 1, February 1987.

GOALS FOR THE EXPERIENCE

The process is student oriented, with the following goals making up the main focus of the experience. Before graduate students can decide to make a firm commitment to the helping professions and our program of studies, they need information on program, state, and professional expectations as well as on employment trends and career opportunities. The first goal is to provide the necessary information. A second goal is to help students develop an awareness of key concepts in helping and to aid them in developing competencies in basic counseling skills that reflect these concepts in helping behaviors. A third goal is to offer opportunities for personal growth and for assessment of potential and motivation for different careers in the helping professions. Experiential activities are provided to aid students in assessing their own potential and in selecting appropriate program experiences to meet their career objectives. These activities also include feedback from the counselor educator (facilitator) and other graduate students regarding the students' potential for helping.

As a result of achieving the goals, graduate students learn about expectations and components of the total program, assess their desire and potential for helping, and review expectations of the profession. They are in a better position to decide for themselves about a commitment to our program of studies and a career in helping. *Graduate students have a right to know what is expected of them, what they can expect from their counselor educators, and what they can expect from and for themselves.*

A personal goal that I set for myself as a facilitator is to attempt to establish the crucial conditions for learning (Rogers, 1969) in order to enable students to experience what they are studying. To me, having the opportunity to serve as a facilitator of others is a privilege. I work on decreasing my own feelings of 'self-importance' as the process evolves. In addition, it is my intent to facilitate a process that moves from a facilitator-structured process to a facilitator-learner structured process to a learner-structured process. The goal is to enable students to act in ways that are in accord with their own inner directions. When activities are offered, they are used in an open way to assist students on their journey inward—away from expectations of others, away from pleasing others, away from facades and toward self-direction, openness to experience, trust of self, and acceptance of others (Rogers, 1961c). My hope is to encourage and facilitate students' capacity to develop 'personal knowledge.'

COMPONENTS OF THE EXPERIENCE

Professional and institutional expectations

Students are provided with information on university training program requirements, state and national counselor certification rules and regulations (i.e., substance abuse counselor, national certified counselor, mental health counselor, career counselor, rehabilitation counselor), the State of Michigan psychologist licensure rules and regulations, Michigan public school counselor endorsement, career opportunities in counseling and leadership, and the local, state, and national employment trends and job predictions. Departmental follow-up studies of recent program graduates are also provided to show beginning students what previous graduates are doing with their degrees. I also assist students to explore their expectations of faculty, themselves, and the program.

Personal development

Although the entire experiential process emphasizes a personal development theme for students, a separate component serves to initiate the developmental activities. Strength bombardment (Hall, 1981) is used to begin the experience on a very positive note. Students become acquainted by sharing positive life experiences and then giving and receiving feedback on these initial impressions. Students leave the initial experience with a bookmark that is filled with positive comments from fellow travelers and an uplifted feeling.

In a number of the experiential activities, students are encouraged to use their life experiences and perceptions as the source of the content of the activity. They use their own thoughts and feelings about learning, growing, changing, and counseling. They also begin to look at how personal risk becomes a part of change. Students examine the self-disclosure process (Jourard, 1959, 1971) as it relates to personal development and to counseling with individuals and small groups. By focusing on the students' experiences and perceptions, the 'self of the student as content' idea is encouraged as well as their bringing realness and trust to the group and the learning process.

The personal development component also emphasizes sharing and clarifying personal values (Rogers, 1964) and understanding how these values affect counseling style and process. Students are encouraged to compare their perceptions of themselves and their values with the perceptions of peers and the facilitator (Value Pac, 1970). It is hoped that clarification occurs in an atmosphere of trust and understanding. Often, the discussions focus on personal values and helping another person change by participating in counseling. As students discuss their values, the sources of these values, and the relationship of these values to a career in counseling, they learn that other students experience many of the same feelings, fears, and questions about counselor education and about becoming skilled, competent counselors. Personal values are later related to counseling concepts and styles. I make an additional request to have students take the Value Pac home and complete the exploring activity with a significant other person such as a spouse, partner, boss, child, parent, friend, roommate, or other family member. Students have reported that these processes have stimulated most interesting and serious discussions with others about similarities and differences in values.

I also encounter the following questions in various forms:
- Will the counselor educators in other classes accept and know us as persons while we are in a counselor education and training program?
- Will they make a commitment to us?
- Can they be trusted with personal information about us?

Personally, I encourage students to check me out, test me, and discover whether or not I can be trusted in this learning process, and then, to proceed accordingly.

Learning and its facilitation

As the personal development component progresses, students are assisted in assessing their own learning styles and the conditions under which they learn best (Thayer, 1980). Then students examine these conditions to discover how they learn best. This review leads to careful consideration and discussion of Rogers' principles regarding the facilitation of learning (Rogers, 1957a, 1969). Students discuss the kinds of people that they would seek out for help, the characteristics of these people, and the key components of their counseling approaches (Thayer, 1981c). Students are asked to compare and contrast their own perceptions of counseling and counselors with the writings of experts. Students are encouraged to trust themselves and their personal knowledge of helpers. Counseling is considered as a special relationship (Patterson, 1968, 1985; Rogers, 1961b, 1965b) in which a learning process takes place.

The experiential strategies that are woven into the process offer students opportunities to review their own learning processes and their stance as learners—changing and growing, or stagnant and inhibited. Follow-up discussions focus on the students' views of learning and how these views/attitudes affect the counseling process. My feedback emphasizes the necessity for students to understand their *own* learning processes from a personal standpoint before they attempt to facilitate the learning and development of others in counseling.

Developing knowledge of counseling concepts and competencies in basic human relations skills

As an introduction to this component, students participate in a dyadic encounter in which they share their perceptions and previous experiences of counseling with a partner (Peterson & Thayer, 1980). The dyadic encounter also provides an early review of key concepts and skills to be learned. This structured two-person sharing process often leads to the development of helping friendships that are based on similar career aspirations and reservations.

Basic counseling concepts are studied. The core conditions of *congruence, unconditional positive regard,* and *empathic understanding* (Rogers, 1957a, 1957b, 1965b) are emphasized. The skills developed reflect these three counselor qualities. The skill learning component receives a major time commitment for learning and practicing skills and receiving feedback after practice sessions. Some of the skills I emphasize that convey the three core qualities are being attentive and fully present; being relaxed and comfortable with people and their concerns; sensing and communicating an understanding of thoughts (verbal messages); sensing and communicating an understanding of feelings and meanings (verbal and nonverbal messages); being aware of one's own personal experiencing and sharing relevant thoughts and feelings; experiencing positive regard and appreciation for clients as persons; showing respect for others and oneself; and trusting and expressing intuitive hunches (Thayer, 1981b). Two additional skills are: (1) responding to the part of the client's reality that is most conspicuous by its absence, and (2) paying attention to one's own mental images about the client's story (Thayer, 1984). Learning 'to be silent' also has come to have increased meaning as an important skill worth learning. I have moved away from using the terms *reflection of feelings, paraphrasing,* and *reflection of content* as they do not accurately describe the 'intent' of the counselor in experiencing the core conditions of empathic understanding, congruence, and unconditional positive regard for the client. As the learning process continues, students discover how these counselor qualities and their respective behaviors form a climate for helping, provide the basis for the counseling relationship, and facilitate the evolution of a helping process.

The skill learning process provides students with opportunities to discuss their concerns, fears, and joys about entering counseling, to consider value-laden questions about counseling, to aid peers in discussing similar concerns, to observe both client and counselor roles, and to become personally acquainted with other students. The skill practice gives students a unique chance to share and know each other while establishing a support network with other graduate students. The process is an exciting part of learning. A more complete description of the skill learning component may be found in Thayer (1977).

After thorough discussion of the core conditions and how these qualities are manifested in counseling behavior, a skill learning process occurs in several steps. As a first step in the skill practice, students participate in a preassessment to begin the process of examining their own responses to others. After Step I is completed, students participate in Steps II–IV for each of the several skills noted earlier. Steps V–VIII follow the skill practice sessions to provide additional practice, feedback, learning resources, and discussions on counseling principles and practice. The counseling concepts and skills component of the class uses about 18 of the 30 class hours.

Components of counseling skills practice:

Steps I–VIII
I. *Preassessment.* Students respond to videotaped counseling vignettes (Carr, Merz, Peterson, & Thayer, 1969) and then assess their mode of responding to these simulated clients. In addition to assessing their own responses, they have the opportunity to learn a method (Jones, 1973; Porter, 1950) of discriminating among various types of counselor responses (evaluative, interpretive, supportive, probing, and understanding). Students are encouraged to begin examining their own and others' *response patterns* in daily interactions.
II. *Minilecture.* I give a minilecture (5–7 minutes) on the basic counseling skill to be learned (Thayer, 1981b). Afterward, a short discussion is held concerning the use and value of the skill, and its relationship to a core counseling concept.
III. *Modeling.* I model the appropriate and inappropriate use of the skill. After the modeling, I ask for feedback about my behavior and its effects. The critiquing process provides excellent opportunity to introduce constructive feedback principles (Johnson, 1986). Students need to learn good feedback principles if they are to be of help to each other during the learning process. After the modeling ends, students seem to have more confidence in me since I have demonstrated the skill.
IV. *The triad encounter.* The students practice the basic counseling skill in a learning triad composed of an observer, a counselor, and a client. After having the group split into triads, I coach the clients for the practice situations. *Clients* are encouraged to discuss issues and concerns relevant to entering a counseling education program. At other times, clients are asked to express personal concerns that they feel comfortable in sharing with their peers. My hope is that they experience some feelings of *being real clients* even though the encounter is brief (approximately 8–10 minutes). The opportunity affords students time to discuss their feelings about counselor education and what their own potential appears to be. The presentation of real but minor concerns and incidents facilitates trust and cohesiveness in the total group. Because class time is limited and students are inexperienced, it is not appropriate to work with major concerns. I briefly observe in several triads and make notes for general discussion. After the members of the triads have participated in each of the three roles, a general discussion is held to review questions and comments about the skill. Later in the skill learning process, videotaping of some students in the skill practice sessions becomes a key aid in the feedback and discussion process. Usually, I seek the assistance of a graduate assistant to videotape several practice sessions while the class continues to practice in the triads. Then the videotaped segments are played for the entire class for review and discussion.
V. *A professional tape film.* After several counseling skills have been practiced using

Steps II–IV, I select a professional audiotape or film to show to the group. Students critique the professional counselor and notice the way in which the skills become part of a caring, facilitative counseling process. The film *Three Approaches to Psychotherapy 1* (Rogers, 1965a), in which Carl Rogers works with Gloria, is offered as an excellent example of a 'client-centered' approach. Although time is not usually available, the other two films in the series by Fritz Perls and Albert Ellis and a subsequent series (Rogers, 1978) provide students with contrasting approaches such as rational emotive, Gestalt, actualizing, and multimodal therapy. I sometimes use additional videotaped stimulus materials such as *Critical Moments in Counseling* (Carr, Merz, Peterson, & Thayer, 1969) for further practice and discussion on responding to clients. The videotape contains 32 simulated counseling vignettes, each of which contains 30–90 seconds of a client sharing a problem or some aspect of a problem.

VI. *The counseling lab.* After the skills have been practiced, the learning sessions are moved from the classroom to the counseling lab, where the students practice and observe minicounseling sessions with each other. The sessions are observed through one-way mirrors. After a designated amount of time passes, the observers join the counselors (students) and clients in the counseling cubicles and give feedback to the counselors. Throughout the training process, I may coach the clients (Whitely & Jakubowski, 1969) to present or role play more difficult and complex concerns with increased emotionality.

VII. *A real counseling session.* Near the end of the skill learning process (approximately 24 hours into the course) each student is scheduled for one *real* 30-minute interview in the counseling class. Each interview has two observers who give feedback. After the session has concluded, the interviewees, along with the observers, share their feelings and perceptions about the interview with the counselor. Discussions continue with the learning group members about their performance, their potential for helping, and their motivation to be effective helpers.

VIII. *Postassessment.* Again, students are shown several short simulated counseling vignettes (Carr et al., 1969) and are asked to respond. Students receive feedback on changes in their demonstrated abilities to listen, observe, and respond effectively to others.

The steps involved in this component are extremely important in helping the students understand that practice, study, and hard work will be part of the counselor education program. The steps focus on skill learning, but also serve the purpose of desensitizing students to the process of videotaping, giving and receiving feedback, being supervised, and working in the counseling lab with observers. The skill learning component seems to be a good practical beginning to the counselor education program.

Information on related counselor education topics

A small amount of time (one to two hours) in one of the last three class sessions is spent presenting and discussing topical subject areas to be covered in the counselor education program. The intent is to expose students to upcoming topics of study. Handouts are prepared to complement this component. Several examples of these future areas of study are counseling process, theories of counseling, group process, educational and occupational information, administration and interpretation of tests, crisis intervention, cross-cultural counseling, stress management, life development theory, substance abuse, supervised counseling practicum, supervised fieldwork, and others.

Professional activities

Students are informed in one of the last three class sessions about professional organizations and activities as well as how these groups support counselors' work. They are also informed about groups such as the Center for Studies of the Person in La Jolla, California, whose activities serve to enhance individuals' personal growth. The students are shown newsletters, journals, and materials published by local, state, and national groups. Several position statements of professional organizations are briefly introduced to give students a better idea of professional activities—for example, the American Association for Counseling and Development's statement on ethical standards, privileged communications guidelines, and the role and function of counselors. Handouts and short discussions are used with the topical area.

After the discussion on professional activities, three questions are posed to students. It is believed that the questions will help prospective counselors approach a program of studies with seriousness and commitment. The questions are intended to stimulate thinking about counseling practices and are often discussed in class. The questions (Carkhuff, 1969) are as follows:
- What right do I have to intervene in the life of another?
- What are my responsibilities once I have intervened?
- What is my role in helping another?

KEY ASPECTS OF THE EXPERIENTIAL PROCESS

Facilitator-student relationships

Perhaps the interaction between students and the facilitator/educator is one of the most significant parts of the entire experience. My goal is to establish a facilitative climate for learning that is positive, open, and encouraging. I attempt to treat students in the way they would like to be treated as *persons* and as students beginning a counselor education program. I try to be myself and share openly with the group while extending an invitation for more openness and honesty between students and myself. My personal sharing seems to help open the way for more closeness among students. I hope that my beliefs about people and myself will be reflected in my behavior (Combs, 1969). Like Combs (1969), I believe the *self* of the facilitator is a key *instrument* in helping others. Students are encouraged to test me and other students in whatever way necessary to make sure that we are trustworthy.

If time is available, other counseling program faculty members are invited to class to consult with students on selected topics. Students are encouraged to talk with the professors about the professors' views of counseling, students, and the program of studies. My hope is that students will come to know more professors and form impressions about their competencies and commitment to students.

Self-assessment and self-selection

Student self-assessment and self-selection are parts of the process that are strongly emphasized. Students are encouraged to begin a process of reviewing their own potential for counseling and personal development. The goal is for students to become more independent and responsible for assessing their learning and the accomplishment of their objectives. Another goal of mine is to enable students to move away from their need for me to structure their learning activities toward a process that is more student structured and self-directed. As the experience progresses, I seek to help students place an increasing amount of trust in their own perceptions and experiences as they relate to counseling (Thayer, 1981a). A self-assessment inventory (Thayer, 1976) aids in the process and also helps students discover the qualities and characteristics that are emerging in them as persons (Rogers, 1977). The self-assessment process helps students self-select *in or out* of the counselor education program of studies. Since a number of students are on a conditional admission or have a special student status, the process assists them in determining whether or not to pursue a counseling program.

Complementary readings

I assign a group of selected readings that complements the ongoing experiential process at a pace of one per week for approximately the first 8–10 weeks. The students are asked to write a *personal reaction paper,* not a summary, on each of the foundation articles (approximately ten). Several of these counseling-related articles are listed in the reference section. I respond extensively and personally in writing to each of the students' papers without evaluating the papers. The reaction papers enable me to communicate individually with students during the learning process. Students also have the opportunity to listen to several audiotapes (5–7 minutes each) from the *Counseline* series (Hill & Harmon, 1977), which provides basic information on topics such as assertiveness, interpersonal relationships, and recognizing suicidal potential in others. These tapes were developed for people who have never sought counseling but who will call an information service for help. Students are also welcomed and encouraged to borrow from my library of counseling books and audiotapes.

An experience model

In an effort to personalize the total process, the students are asked to design, plan, complete, and assess a learning experience *outside* the classroom (Thayer, 1978, 1984) during the semester. I trust the students to prepare an *experience* that is personally relevant to their lives, needs, and desires. I ask them to determine their own goals, the nature of the learning process, the level of the risk, any necessary materials and conditions, the location or setting, the time commitment, how the experience will be reported, and how the experience will be assessed in terms of significant affective and cognitive learning outcomes. I serve as a resource person and listener but not a director for the project. The students determine the parameters and the process of the experience. Although some students are bewildered by the expectation that they create their own experience, other students know exactly what they need or wish to do. For me, it is exciting as I watch students wrestle with questions about their own needs, desires, learnings, and risk-taking.

The experience module takes many forms as students tackle relevant learning goals in their lives. Experiences range from repairing or enhancing a personal relationship to learning about new and different aspects of counseling to observing community agencies at work to looking deep within oneself. Although each experience module is different, several examples are provided here:
- Reestablish 'feeling'-level communication with my husband in order to enhance our relationship.

- Talk with my father and mother about their coming to the United States from the old country. They have never discussed their struggles and adventures of coming to the United States.
- Attend several counseling sessions as a client to explore and understand myself and my career directions better. My goal is to make some decisions about graduate study.
- Learn more about my father, who died when I was young, by interviewing relatives, talking with my mother, visiting places where he lived, and putting together a photo album. I want my memories of my father. I have missed him.
- Interview several divorced males to gain an awareness of their thoughts and feelings on their divorce and related events.

The experience module is a step toward increased self-directed learning. According to students, it has resulted in exciting, risky, challenging, real, meaningful, and significant learning experiences.

Beginning group process

Group process sessions are sprinkled throughout the experience. The purpose of the groups is to provide an exposure to group process, to enable students to view me in a group facilitation role, and to offer students the opportunity to talk about themselves and to consider important issues such as personal development, commitment to counselor development, goal setting, potential for counselor education, and career direction. Students have a brief exposure to the beginning development of a group (Ohlsen, 1977).

A personal interview

In addition to the group sessions, I attempt to have at least one personal interview with every student near the end of the experience. Although the interviews are not structured, most students talk about themselves, their plans for the future, their skill progress, and their potential for counselor development. Every effort is made to help students explore and resolve personal concerns and fears related to entering the program.

An offer of assistance

At the end of the semester, I offer to help anyone seeking further assistance with personal concerns and/or career directions. If persons prefer outside assistance because of my participation in the program, aid is offered in locating appropriate counseling services at the university or in the community. During the experience, some students take the option of participation in counseling by attending several individual sessions with advanced counseling practicum students in the counseling lab. These students have an opportunity to explore their own potential, resolve concerns, and experience counseling from the client's position.[1]

Experience assessment

A formal assessment is conducted at the beginning of the concepts and skills learning

---

1. The practice of offering to help students was learned from Dr. Merle Ohlsen.

component and at the end of the experiential course. At the end of the semester, assessment is made in the areas of basic counseling skills, basic counseling concepts and knowledge, discrimination of counselor response types, student perceptions of their own progress, student perceptions of the learning climate and resources, and student perceptions of me as the facilitator. Several assessment methods and tools are used. Paper-and-pencil methods are used to gather students' perceptions of the course and to review their abilities to discriminate among various types of counselor responses.

Methods such as videotaping short counseling sessions, observing short counseling sessions in the counseling lab, and writing responses to audiotaped client stimulus statements have been used to examine student responses to clients.

On the last day, I convene the total group for a critique of the experience. Students have consistently indicated that the experience is highly beneficial as a beginning course.

Here are a few representative samples of the students' written comments.

> *It is the first time I really felt as though my thoughts and feelings were the most important part of the learning experience. It felt good and has made some positive changes in the direction of my personal growth. It is the first time that I really sensed a lack of threat in a college classroom. That may sound strange, but I mean that most of us seemed to feel free to express ourselves without fear of being attacked or put down. Our views were accepted.*

> *The course expectations are designed to promote introspection and force us to develop our own ideas and philosophies about counseling — once again, a rare and enjoyable aspect of your teaching style.*

> *The timing of reading material was excellent for me. It seemed to come forth at precisely the right moment to answer questions that were forming for me.*

> *I believe I experienced 'listening' for the first time. I will carry this asset into my classroom.*

> *LT is the kind of facilitator that practices what he preaches in a dynamic, exciting way. His personal comments on my papers were thought-provoking and personal.*

> *I felt the personal unconditional regard of the instructor at all times. This, most of all, gave me confidence to grow and learn.*

> *This course may be the best thing that ever happened to me. It has provided insight about myself and counseling skills.*

> *He created an environment which maximized the learning process.*

> *He allowed us to do our own learning.*

> *Have some skill development assignments for homework.*

> *Caused me to think a lot about who I really am and how important it is to value self and others for who they are.*

> *The self-directed learning was truly an enjoyable and worthwhile experience. I worked harder for that project than any other in my academic career.*

THOUGHTS ON THE EXPERIENCE

Student feedback on the experience is very positive, and I continue to believe that it is an excellent beginning to a counselor education program. The students in my classes and I remain highly enthusiastic about the goals, structured and unstructured processes, and outcomes. Feedback from students indicates that the major course goals are being met. Many positive *person-to-person* relationships are developed at the start of the graduate program instead of at the end, including relationships between students and between students and me.

Graduate students can be more involved in providing perceptions and information about what is needed and desired in a program of studies. They are capable of pinpointing program strengths and weaknesses as well as recommending revisions, restructuring, and new components. Students can also be trusted to participate responsibly, efficiently, and effectively in contributing to their own learning directions and outcomes.

The experience has had a positive effect on graduate students and the career selection process. Many students, but not all, who select the counseling program have selected it because of a desire to be a helping person. Their commitment to the program and the profession seems strong and begins at the start of a program rather than at the end. Students are getting involved in professional activities earlier by joining professional groups, writing for professional newsletters, attending conferences and workshops, and seeking field-based experience for their own learning. Because I have come to know these students, I have found that they have had special life experiences about which they have valuable insights and knowledge to contribute. Consequently, it has been my privilege to help a number of these talented individuals prepare their experiences to share with the professional community. Their contributions have included poems, quotable quotes, interviews, articles on personal life experiences, and book reviews. Students learn that they have significant and meaningful contributions to make. Some have been encouraged to participate in state and local counseling organizations. They bring excitement and new ideas to the groups. In addition, they have exhibited increased readiness and enthusiasm for subsequent courses in the learning sequence.

There seems to be better balance among knowledge (knowing), practice (doing), and relationships (being) in the experience. An early start in the experiential mode has facilitated the personal growth of students and encouraged movement toward student-directed learning experiences. Students also come to expect balance among knowledge, practice, and caring in their future courses. Students enter other classes with a better knowledge of counseling concepts and how these concepts are manifested in counseling behaviors. There has been a positive effect on student-facilitator planning. And students expect me to *practice what is preached.*

When the experience is successful, the outcomes are reflected in positive student-professor and student-student relationships. Students begin a program with greater awareness of expectations — their own, the program's, and those of the profession.

In keeping with the experience I have described, my goals as a facilitator continue to be to create the most positive learning climate possible with the primary focus on the person rather than the content, to help students experience the basic concepts and skills that are part of the course, to encourage the development of 'personal' knowledge through experiencing, to encourage self-directed learning, to provide opportunities for self-assessment, and to offer many resources as students develop their inner potentials for becoming counselors.

EXPERIENCING THE PRIORITIES

For me, the most important goal remains that of creating a positive and facilitative atmosphere for learning. When the facilitative conditions of congruence, unconditional positive regard, and empathic understanding are perceived by the students, then a process almost invariably occurs in the learning situation. Learning outcomes are often unpredictable. These outcomes are based on the uniqueness of the students, their potential, the climate, the process, and the facilitator. A natural and logical order of events seems to unfold.

It helps me to ask myself several key questions that have often been shared by Carl Rogers. First, is it possible for me to be congruent in this classroom situation? I suspect that I never quite reach this state; however, it is a most worthy goal I hold before myself. When I come closer to this goal and students perceive a realness in me, they tend to become more genuine in their papers, in their responses in class, and in their interactions with others. They move in a direction of more immediacy of experiencing and more openness to experience. The classroom comes alive in the 'here and now.' Students seem to be more in tune with their own thoughts, feelings, and meanings and how these relate to personal growth, counseling knowledge, and helping others. Students seem to learn that it is okay just to be themselves. They find that the approach is holistic.

Second, can I experience an unconditional positive regard for students as persons and as learners? When students perceive that they are respected and accepted, they seem to find themselves more acceptable as students. They tend to have higher degrees of self-acceptance and self-confidence. Their limitless potential begins to blossom. They tend to trust themselves more and create significant self-directed learning plans.

Third, will I be a good listener for them and try to understand their inner worlds with all their hopes, dreams, and feelings? For me, listening has been a strength for many years. When students are heard and understood, they tend to listen to themselves more. They, in turn, also become better listeners. While developing greater sensitivity to their own inner experiencing, they tend to seek learning directions that are more in accord with their own 'paths' in life. They can be trusted because it is themselves with whom they are dealing.

When the conditions are perceived as present to some minimal degree, students' potentials begin to emerge and a process of learning evolves. Students become more self-directed and move to a more internal locus of evaluation—self-assessment.

The person entering the program is the focus. And I, as a facilitator, try to set the climate and begin the process by encouraging the development of good human relationships. In many ways, *the process is the lesson. The experience is the message.*

AUTHOR'S NOTE

An earlier version of this article was presented at the First International Forum on the Person-Centered Approach, Oaxtapec, Mexico, June 1982.

REFERENCES

Andrews, H. B., & Weekley, A. W. (1981). An encounter for couples: Enhancing interpersonal relationships. In L. Thayer (Ed.), *50 strategies for experiential learning: Book two.* San Diego,

CA: University Associates.

Carkhuff, R. R. (1969). *Helping and human relations: A primer for lay and professional helpers* (Vol. 2). New York: Holt, Rinehart & Winston.

Carr, E., Merz, D., Peterson, J. V., & Thayer, L. (1969). *Critical moments in counseling* [Videotape]. Urbana: University of Illinois.

Combs, A. M. (1969). *Florida studies in helping professions* (Social Sciences Monograph No. 37). Gainesville: University of Florida Press.

Hall, L. (1981). The AMP miniseminar: Successes and strengths. In L. Thayer (Ed.), *50 strategies for experiential learning: Book two.* San Diego, CA: University Associates.

Hill, F. E., & Harmon, F. M. (1977). *Counseline* [A series of audiotapes on mental health]. Austin: University of Texas Press.

Johnson, D. W. (1986). *Reaching out: Interpersonal effectiveness and self-actualization* (3rd ed.). Englewood Cliffs, NJ: Prentice-Hall.

Jones, J. E. (1973). Helping relationship inventory. In J. E. Jones & J. W. Pfeiffer (Eds.), *The 1973 annual handbook for group facilitators.* San Diego, CA: University Associates.

Jourard, S. M. (1959). Healthy personality and self-disclosure. *Mental Hygiene, 43,* 499–507.*

Jourard, S. M. (1971). *The transparent self* (rev. ed.). New York: Van Nostrand Reinhold.

Ohlsen, M. M. (1977). *Group counseling* (2nd ed.). New York: Holt, Rinehart & Winston.

Patterson, C. H. (1968). The nature of counseling: Some basic principles. *Michigan College Personnel Association Journal, 5,* 1–11.*

Patterson, C. H. (1985). *The therapeutic relationship. Foundations for an eclectic pychotherapy.* Monterey, CA: Brooks/Cole.

Peterson, J. V., & Thayer, L. (1980). *A dyadic encounter on counseling (helping).* Ypsilanti, MI: LT Resources.

Porter, E. H., Jr. (1950). *An introduction to therapeutic counseling.* Boston: Houghton Mifflin.

Rogers, C. R. (1957a). Personal thoughts on teaching and learning. *Merrill-Palmer Quarterly, 3,* 241–3.*

Rogers, C. R. (1957b). The necessary and sufficient conditions of therapeutic personality change. *Journal of Counseling Psychology. 21*(2), 95–103.*

Rogers, C. R. (1961a). A process conception of psychotherapy. In C. R. Rogers, *On becoming a person.* Boston: Houghton Mifflin.*

Rogers, C. R. (1961b). The characteristics of the helping relationship. In C. R. Rogers, *On becoming a person.* Boston: Houghton Mifflin.

Rogers, C. R. (1961c). To be that self which one truly is: A therapist's view of personal goals. In C. R. Rogers, *On becoming a person.* Boston: Houghton Mifflin.*

Rogers, C. R. (1964). Toward a modern approach to values: The valuing process in the mature person. *Journal of Abnormal and Social Psychology, 68,* 160–7.

Rogers, C. R. (1965a). Client-centered therapy [Film No. 1]. In E. Shostrom (Ed.), *Three approaches to psychotherapy* [Film]. Santa Ana, CA: Psychological Films.

Rogers, C. R. (1965b). The interpersonal relationship: The core of guidance. In R. L. Mosher, R. F. Carle, & C. C. Kehas (Eds.), *Guidance: An examination.* New York: Harcourt, Brace & World.*

Rogers, C. R. (1969). The interpersonal relationship in the facilitation of learning. In C. R. Rogers, *Freedom to learn.* Columbus, OH: Charles E. Merrill.

Rogers, C. R. (1977). The emerging person: Spearhead of the quiet revolution. In C. R. Rogers, *Carl Rogers on personal power: Inner strength and its revolutionary impact.* New York: Delacorte.*

Rogers, C. R. (1978). Client-centered therapy [Film No. 1]. In E. Shostrom (Ed.), *Three approaches to psychotherapy – II* [Film]. Santa Ana, CA: Psychological Films.

Thayer, L. (1976). Self-assessment: A focus on classroom and small group behavior. In L. Thayer (Ed.), *50 strategies for experiential learning: Book one.* San Diego, CA: University Associates.

Thayer, L. (1977). An experiential approach to learning skills. *Humanist Educator, 15*(3), 132–9.

Thayer, L. (1978). Experience modules complement courses. *Walkabout: Exploring New Paths to Adulthood* (Phi Delta Kappa newsletter), 3(2), 5.

Thayer, L. (1980). Self-assessment: The learner and the learning process. Unpublished manuscript, Eastern Michigan University.

Thayer, L. (1981a). A person-centered task: Focusing on interpersonal relationships. In L. Thayer (Ed.), *50 strategies for experiential learning: Book two.* San Diego, CA: University Associates.

Thayer, L. (1981b). Toward experiential learning with the person-centered approach. In L. Thayer (Ed.), *50 strategies for experiential learning: Book two.* San Diego, CA: University Associates.

Thayer, L. (1981c). Trust yourself: Personal knowledge of helpers and the helping process. In L. Thayer (Ed.), *50 strategies for experiential learning: Book two.* San Diego, CA: University Associates.

Thayer, L. (1984). On person-centered experiential learning and effective development. In G. Jennings (Ed.), *Affective learning in industrial arts* (pp. 52–103). Peoria, IL: McKnight.*

Value Pac. (1970). Rosemont, IL: Combined Motivation Education Systems.

Whitely, J. J., & Jakubowski, P. A. (1969). The coached client as a research and training resource in counseling. *Counseling Education and Supervision, 9*(1), 19–29.

* These articles are used as reading for reaction papers in the course.

Louis Thayer

Part E

Person-Centered Research Methods

Research with People:

The paradigm of cooperative experiential inquiry

Peter Reason   *University of Bath*

John Heron   *University of London*

A methodology of cooperative inquiry in which all those involved work together as coresearchers is described. The epistemological and ontological issues underlying this methodology are briefly discussed, and the argument made that the inquiry rests on an attitude of critical subjectivity within an epistemological heterogeneity. Issues of validity within the paradigm are discussed, and practical steps for exploring threats to validity are outlined.

As Rogers (1985) has pointed out, there is currently a burgeoning of new models for research and inquiry in the human sciences. We have been involved in the development of this 'new' or 'post-positivist' paradigm of inquiry for over ten years (Heron, 1971; Reason, 1976), and have developed an approach we call cooperative experiential inquiry. In this article we wish to summarize the considerations that led us to this practice, and to describe briefly the cooperative inquiry process. We will also draw attention to the worldview that underlies our approach, and set out some practical steps that can be taken to enhance the validity of this kind of inquiry.

We do not wish to pursue the critique of orthodox inquiry method in detail here: it has been developed by many writers and is thoroughly summarized in Reason and Rowan (1981a). At the heart of this critique is the idea that these methods are neither adequate nor appropriate for the study *of persons,* for persons are to some significant degree self-determining. Orthodox inquiry methods, as part of their rationale, exclude the experimental human subjects from all the thinking and decision making that generates, designs, manages, and draws conclusions from the research. Such exclusion treats the subjects as less than self-determining persons, alienates them from the inquiry process and from the knowledge that is its outcome, and thus invalidates any claim the methods have to being a science of persons.

In essence, science is creative thinking and then careful thinking, with systematic observation and public examination of ideas and predictions against experience. We do not necessarily need experimental or quasiexperimental designs, or questionnaire surveys, or any other particular methodology to do this. These are only ways that may or may not help us inquire clearly and carefully. Rather than depend on method, we can return to the self-directing person as the primary source of knowing, and thus the primary 'instrument' of inquiry, in what we have described as experiential and cooperative inquiry. This means research *with* people, rather than research *on* people (Reason & Rowan, 1981a). It is this approach to research with people that this article addresses.

First published in *Person-Centered Review,* Volume 1, Number 4, November 1986.

BASES OF COOPERATIVE INQUIRY

A full account of the philosophical bases of a new paradigm of research has been set out elsewhere (Heron, 1981). Here we summarize two ideas that were particularly important in the development of our thinking.

1. *Persons as self-determining.* We regard persons as self-determining, that is, as the authors of their own actions — to some degree actually, and to a greater degree potentially. To say that persons are self-determining is to say that their intentions and purposes, their intelligent choices, are causes of their behavior. One can only do research on persons in the full and proper sense of the term if one addresses them as self-determining, which means that what they do and what they experience as part of the research must be to some significant degree determined by them. I can only properly study who you are if your intentionality contributes to what you do in the inquiry. This means that you need to help plan the inquiry as coresearcher as well as be subject in it. So in cooperative inquiry all those involved in the research are both coresearchers, whose thinking and decision making contributes to generating ideas, designing and managing the project, and drawing conclusions from the experience; and also cosubjects, participating in the activity that is being researched.

2. *The nature of knowledge.* It is useful to distinguish at least three kinds of knowledge: (a) *experiential knowledge* is gained through direct encounter with persons, places, or things: (b) *practical knowledge* concerns how to do something — it is knowledge demonstrated in a skill or competence; (c) *propositional knowledge* is knowledge about something, and is expressed in statements and theories. In research on persons the propositional knowledge stated in the research conclusions needs to be rooted in and derived from the experiential and practical knowledge of the subjects in the inquiry. If the propositions are generated exclusively by a researcher who is not involved in the experience being researched, and are imposed without consultation on the practical and experiential knowledge of the subjects, we have findings that directly reflect the experience of neither the researcher nor the subjects.

METHODOLOGY

In traditional research, the roles of researcher and subject are mutually exclusive. The researcher contributes all the thinking that goes into the project, while the subject contributes the research action to be studied. In the new model of inquiry these mutually exclusive roles give way to a cooperative relationship with bilateral initiative and control, so that all those involved work together as coresearchers and cosubjects. Ideally there is full reciprocity, with each person's agency fundamentally honored both in the exchange of ideas and in the action. There can be no other base for researching the human condition from the standpoint of the person as experiencing agent.

We should note that full reciprocity does not necessarily mean that all those involved in the inquiry enterprise contribute in identical ways. In an inquiry group, as in any human group, people will take different roles, and there will be qualitative differences in contribution. While in a 'pure' or ideal form of cooperative inquiry, full consensus will be reached on all decisions, this may not always be practical. At a minimum everyone involved needs to be initiated into the inquiry process and give their free and informed assent to all decisions about process and outcome.

294

Cooperative inquiry takes place in four phases of action and reflection.

Phase 1

A group of coresearchers agree on an area for inquiry and identify some initial research propositions. They may choose to explore some aspect of their experience, or agree to try out in practice some particular actions or skills. They also agree to some set of procedures by which they will observe and record their own and each other's experience. This phase involves primarily propositional knowing.

For example, we initiated a cooperative inquiry into the theory and practice of holistic medicine and invited general medical practitioners to join us as coresearchers (Heron & Reason, 1985). After early meetings to establish the group and agree on the nature and scope of the inquiry, the whole group discussed the issues involved in holistic medical practice. From this discussion we developed a conceptual model of holistic medicine, a variety of strategies for applying this model in surgery, and ways of observing and recording the experienced results of this endeavor.

Phase 2

The group then applies these ideas and procedures: they initiate the agreed actions and observe and record the outcomes of their own and each other's behavior. At this stage they need to be particularly alert for the subtleties and nuances of experience, and to ways in which the original ideas do and do not accord with experience. This phase involves primarily practical knowing.

Returning to our example, the group of doctors applied diverse holistic health strategies within the British National Health Service. For example, they attempted to engage cooperatively with their patients to define the nature of the latter's complaints; they tried to make their diagnoses in terms of psychological, social, and spiritual influences as well as physical symptoms, and so on. The doctors recorded these activities in various ways, writing a report on each full cycle of application for the next meeting of the group.

Phase 3

The coresearchers will in all probability become fully immersed in this activity and experience. At times they will be excited and carried away by it; at times they will be bored and alienated by it; at times they will forget they are involved in an inquiry project. They may forget or otherwise fail to carry out and record the agreed procedures, or they may stumble on unexpected and unpredicted experiences and develop creative new insights. This stage of full immersion is fundamental to the whole process. It is here that the coresearchers, fully engaged with their experience, may develop an openness to what is going on for them and their environment, which allows them to bracket off their prior beliefs and preconceptions and so see their experience in a new way. This phase involves mainly experiential knowing. For example, some of our holistic doctors found that significant self-development and personal growth is fundamental to effective holistic practice. This was not an hypothesis that all members took into the inquiry.

Phase 4

After an appropriate period engaged in stages two and three, the coresearchers return to consider their original research propositions and hypotheses in the light of experience, modifying, reformulating, and rejecting them, adopting new hypotheses, and so on. They may also amend and develop their research procedures more fully to record their experience. So this phase involves a critical return to propositional knowing. Thus our medical inquiry group met periodically over a year to revise and develop our overall model of holistic medicine as well as particular strategies for implementing it.

This cycle of movement from reflection to action and back to reflection needs to be repeated several times so that ideas and discoveries tentatively reached in early cycles may be clarified, refined, deepened, and corrected. This 'research cycling' clearly has an important bearing on the empirical validity of the whole inquiry process, and is discussed in more detail later in this article.

EPISTEMOLOGICAL HETEROGENEITY

Having outlined the cooperative inquiry method, we wish now to turn to some of the epistemological and ontological issues that underlie it. We do this even though it means touching only briefly on complex questions of fundamental importance, and in doing so we may be seen as oversimplifying and overstating. However, our disciplines are involved in a shift in paradigms; maybe our Western culture is involved in an epochal shift in worldview: the old perspective is passing, and there is as yet no 'official' or generally accepted alternative. The ground of our understanding is shifting under our feet, and these are anxious, confusing, and exciting times when debate must inevitably verge on the polemical. As Feyerabend (1978) points out, it is impossible to translate between paradigms, they are incommensurable. Whatever we write, we will necessarily upset and disturb some people. Therefore it is important to us to state clearly, if briefly, how work with our method has affected our thinking.

Cooperative inquiry is inquiry with people; it is participatory. While it overlaps with qualitative and naturalistic research methods, it is also significantly different from them because it invites people to participate in the cocreation of knowing about themselves. Texts on qualitative method suggest that research must be 'grounded' in data (Glaser & Strauss, 1967), or that findings must be 'negotiated' with participants (Lincoln & Guba, 1985). We argue that this is not enough.

Skolimowski (1985) maps out how our prevailing worldview and associated epistemology is in the process of change. The worldview based on Cartesian rationality and Newtonian physics, with 'an empirical view of the mind based on notions of objectivity' (p. 12), is giving way. It is under pressure from new ideas in physics, from systems thinking and ecological awareness, and from the realization of the dark side of our culture, the 'ecological devastations, human and social fragmentation, the spiritual impoverishment' (p. 22).

Skolimowski argues that as the mechanistic metaphor collapses, an evolutionary-holistic cosmology is emerging, and that this goes hand in hand with a participatory methodology:

> Wholeness means that all parts belong together, and that means that they partake in each other. Thus from the central idea that all is connected, that each is part of the whole, comes the idea that each participate in the whole. *Thus participation is an implicit aspect of wholeness.* (Skolimowski, 1985, p. 25)

As we participate in the Whole we cocreate with it. In some sense we choose our reality and our knowing of it; therefore, valid human inquiry essentially requires full participation in the creation of personal and social knowings.

In our own practice we started to develop and use cooperative inquiry primarily for pragmatic reasons: we could find no other way of doing justice to the experience and action of self-directing persons. But once we started working this way—both initiating our own inquiries and supervising research students—we were in a sense forced, by our experience of what worked and what didn't work, further and further away from an orthodox scientific worldview. We found that we were almost inevitably adopting a radical philosophical position that affirms the centrality of critical subjectivity and epistemological heterogeneity. While this position is related and indebted to the work of many modern writers on science (Bateson, 1972; Berger & Luckmann, 1966; Bohm, 1978; Capra, 1982; Hainer, 1968; Koestler, 1978; Macmurray, 1957; Maslow, 1966; Mitroff, 1974; Mitroff & Kilmann, 1978; Polanyi, 1958; Schwartz & Ogilvy, 1980; Wilber, 1981), it has evolved out of our practical work as researchers in the fields of humanistic psychology and holistic medicine.

Orthodox scientific inquiry within the positivist paradigm is based on at least six presuppositions with which we take issue: (1) that there is one 'reality'; (2) that this one reality can be known objectively; (3) that this knowledge is identical for all knowers; (4) that knowledge is expressed in propositions that are validated empirically, in the ideal form in the carefully controlled experiment; (5) that the whole may be explained in terms of the sum of the parts, and the aim of inquiry is to discover more and more fundamental elements and processes; and (6) that explanation is sought in terms of linear, energetic cause and effect. (For a useful review of the positivist paradigm, see Lincoln & Guba, 1985.)

While we believe that this view of the scientific enterprise is no longer fully secure, it still prevails at heart both among laypeople and many professionals. While sophisticated theoretical discussions may argue that science has moved beyond this position, in fundamental ways many people remain attached to it: it underlies our Western civilization and is the basis of its success and of its troubles, and is extremely difficult and anxiety provoking to get away from. As Bateson (1972, p. 462) argues, 'The most important task today is, perhaps, to learn to think in the new way.' Our own attempts to think in a new way have led us to the following tentative position.

First, we hold that reality is both one and many in the sense that we can only have knowledge of objective reality (accepting, for pragmatic purposes, that there is one or are some) from many different subjective perspectives as we choose or cocreate our reality (Rogers, 1980). Thus knowledge is subjective-objective, always knowing from a perspective (Schwartz & Ogilvy, 1980) in the sense of being a 'personal view from some distance' suggesting 'neither the universality of objectivity nor the personal bias of subjectivity' (p. 51). As Bateson puts it:

> The word 'objective' becomes, of course, quite quietly obsolete: and the word subjective, which normally confines you within your skin, disappears as well . . . The world is no longer 'out there' in quite the way it used to be . . . There is a combining or marriage between an objectivity that is passive to the outside world and a creative subjectivity, neither pure solipsism nor its opposite . . . Somewhere between these two is a region where you are partly blown by the winds of reality and partly an artist creating a composite out of inner and outer events. (in Brockman, 1977, p. 245)

And as we have argued before,

> We have to learn to think dialectically, to view reality as a process, always emerging through a self-contradictory development, always becoming; knowing this reality is neither subjective nor objective, it is both wholly independent of me and wholly dependent on me. (Reason & Rowan, 1981b, p. 241)

Thus there will be as many knowings as there are knowers, we must accept an epistemological heterogeneity. Truth about reality (or realities) may be more fully revealed in the way these different knowings or perspectives overlap and inform each other.

It also follows from the tripartite nature of knowledge that these multiple knowings are not only sets of propositions or theories about the subject matter, but also the validating competences (practical knowledge) and experiences (experiential knowledge) of those participating in it. This point is echoed by Torbert (1981, p. 145) who argues that the important thing is 'not how to develop a reflective science *about* action, but how to develop genuinely well informed action — how to conduct *action science.*'

Within this paradigm we seek to understand and act in whole systems and whole situations as such, not fragmenting wholes into the simple sum of the parts but understanding the parts in terms of their interaction within the whole, realizing also that we are a part of that whole. Finally, arising from this ecological view, explanation is sought in terms of mutual action and interaction within the total system, not solely in terms of linear cause and effect (Bateson, 1972).

In conducting cooperative inquiry we seek not objectivity but what might be termed *critical subjectivity:* we seek a 'rigor of softness.' It is to the establishment of that rigor that we now turn.

VALIDITY IN COOPERATIVE INQUIRY

Cooperative inquiry claims to be a valid approach to research with people because it 'rests on a collaborative encounter with experience' (Reason & Rowan, 1981b). This is the touchstone of the approach in that any practical skills or theoretical propositions that arise from the inquiry can be said to derive from and be congruent with this experience. The validity of this encounter with experience in turn rests on the high quality, critical, self-aware, discriminating, and informed judgments of the coresearchers. Of course, this means that the method is open to all the ways in which human beings fool themselves and each other in their perceptions of the world, through cultural bias, character defense, political partisanship, spiritual impoverishment, and so on. As we have argued earlier (Reason & Rowan, 1981b; Heron, 1982), cooperative inquiry is threatened by unaware projection and consensus collusion.

Unaware projection means that we deceive ourselves. We do this because to inquire carefully and critically into those things that we care about is an anxiety-provoking business that stirs up our psychological defenses. We then project our anxieties onto the world we are supposed to be studying (Devereaux, 1967).

The coresearchers on our holistic medicine inquiry had invested half a lifetime, years of education, practice and commitment in being orthodox doctors. To set this aside to explore new attitudes and ways of practice was a formidably difficult task, involving the personal risk of error and shame, and the possibility of injury and death. It is much more comfortable to hold onto the worldview one already knows. Therefore it is easy for one's defenses to give rise to a whole variety of self-deceptions in the course of the inquiry, so one cannot or will not see the new truth.

Consensus collusion means that the co-researchers may band together as a group in defence of their anxieties, so that areas of their experience which challenge their worldview are ignored or not properly explored.

PROCEDURES FOR ENHANCING VALIDITY

We suggest the following procedures may serve to counteract (but not eliminate) these threats to validity (Reason & Rowan, 1981b; Heron, 1982).

1. *Development of discriminating awareness.* Unless human beings adopt some practices for cultivating the quality of their awareness—what might be called *mindfulness* or *wakefulness* (Masters, 1981)—they cannot practice critical subjectivity, but merely lapse into subjectivism, and 'life is but a dream.' This applies particularly to experiential inquiry. There are many disciplines, both ancient and modern, from which we can borrow for this purpose. In our own work we have adapted from Gestalt therapy, T'ai Chi and Circle Dancing, Alexander's Inhibiting Technique and the Gurdjieff 'Stop!' exercise (Masters, 1981), the work of Jean Houston (1982), and Charlotte Selver (in Brooks, 1974).

2. *Research cycling, divergence, and convergence. Research cycling* means taking an idea several times around the cycle of reflection and action. Primarily, this provides a series of corrective feedback loops; it may also clarify and deepen the ideas being explored (Heron, 1982). Divergence and convergence are complementary forms of cycling. We may choose to explore one aspect of our inquiry in closer and closer detail over several cycles, or we may choose to diverge into different aspects so we can see phenomena in context, or both. Through convergent cycling the coresearchers are checking and rechecking with more and more attention to detail. Through divergent cycling one may affirm equally the values of heterogeneity and the creativity that comes with taking many different viewpoints, and in addition place one's work in a wider context.

This interweaving of convergence and divergence over several cycles has the effect of knitting together various strands of the inquiry into a comprehensive whole. It assures that, while any one piece of data or conclusion may be tentative or open to error, the final outcome is a network of interrelated ideas and evidence that together have a holistic or contextual validity (Diesing, 1972; Reason, 1985).

Thus in our holistic medicine project we completed six cycles of action and reflection in the course of a year's study. We started the project with each person following her or his own interests. Some explored power sharing with their patients by organizing self-help groups for particular ailments; some set out to widen the kinds of issues they explored with patients in the surgery; others decided to look critically at their own lifestyle, and so on. It seemed right to continue this degree of divergence through the first two cycles, since it sustained creativity and commitment, and enabled the group as a whole to range freely over the whole field. At the third meeting, however, we established two subgroups. One explored power-sharing strategies and another the use of spiritual interventions, thus seeking a balance between divergence and convergence in our research cycling.

3. *Authentic collaboration.* It is clearly not possible to do this kind of research alone; the diversity of viewpoint, the loving support of colleagues, the challenge when we seem to be in error, are all essential. Since collaboration is an essential aspect of this form of inquiry, it must be in some sense authentic: it must not be a relationship overdominated by a charismatic leader or a small clique, but rather the kind of experience in which all persons can in time find a place to be themselves, to make their own contribution to decision making and creative thinking, and in which the differences among all concerned may be celebrated. Our experience with a variety of learning groups convinces us that it is possible to facilitate the emergence of intimate collaboration with appropriate

amounts of both support and confrontation. We know that this also takes time, willingness, and skill.

In our holistic medicine inquiry, we met for one three-hour session each cycle in an encounter group format. During this time we attempted to establish norms of open and direct critique of our behavior during the inquiry. We discovered several aspects of our group process with which we were unhappy, and those we attempted to change. For example, discussion was at times dominated by vocal cliques; the men tended to be more outspoken than the women; and our leadership as initiating facilitators was challenged and criticized. Our conclusion at the end of the project was that we had managed to establish authentic participation in the group, but to a modest degree.

4. *Falsification.* We have mentioned above the danger of consensus collusion. It is essential that inquiry groups build in norms that will counter this tendency: we need what Torbert (1976) described as 'friends willing to act as enemies.' We have found the Devil's Advocate procedure helpful in this. The Devil's Advocate is a member of the group who temporarily takes the role of radical critic. The Devil's Advocate is charged with the paradoxical duty of challenging all assumptions the group appears to make, all occasions when actual behavior appears to diverge from espoused behavior and ideology, all occasions when the group appears to be colluding to bury some issue, and so on. The Devil's Advocate may be appointed as part of a regular session; or special sessions may be arranged where the Devil's Advocate's role is evoked and systematically exercised – such as when critically challenging tentative findings. We have found it helpful if the Devil's Advocate has some concrete symbol of authority – something can usually be found that will serve as a mace.

5. *Management of unaware projections.* We have pointed out above how unacknowledged distress and psychological defenses may seriously distort inquiry. Some systematic method is needed that will draw the distress into awareness and either resolve it or allow it creative expression. Devereaux (1967) suggested that the researcher should undergo psychoanalysis; we have used cocounseling (Jackins, 1965; Heron, 1973). That is a method of reciprocal support through which each person, working as client in a pair relationship, can explore the ways in which their own defenses are being caught up with the research thinking and action. Psychodrama can be similarly used (Hawkins, 1986).

6. *Balance of action and reflection.* Collaborative inquiry involves both action and reflection, and somehow these need to be brought into appropriate balance. Too much action without reflection is mere activism; too much reflection without action is mere introspection and armchair discussion. The right sort of balance will depend on the inquiry in question, and on the judgments of those involved.

7. *Chaos.* From our early inquiries we came to the conclusion that a descent into chaos would often facilitate the emergence of new creative order. There is an element of arbitrariness, randomness, chaos, indeterminism, in the scheme of things. If the group is really going to be open, adventurous, exploratory, creative, innovative, and put all at risk to reach out for the truth beyond fear and collusion, then once the inquiry is well under way, divergence of thought and expression is likely to descend into confusion, uncertainty, ambiguity, disorder, and even chaos with most if not all coresearchers feeling lost to a greater or lesser degree.

There can be no guarantee that chaos will occur; certainly one cannot plan it. The key validity issue is to be prepared for it, to be able to tolerate it, to go with the confusions and uncertainty; not to pull out of it anxiously, but to wait until there's a real sense of creative resolution. We make this argument for openness to extreme uncertainty to counterbalance the human being's enormous capacity for creating and sustaining order, even when such order is no longer appropriate.

Application of validity procedures

These validity procedures are useful for systematically reviewing the quality of inquiry work. Use of them does not mean that the experiential, practical, or propositional knowing that comes out of the research is valid in any absolute sense of the term, but rather that it is possible to see more clearly and communicate to others the perspective from which that knowing is derived, and to illuminate the distortions that may have occurred.

It is important to distinguish between the influence of perspective and distortion. For example, the perspective of our holistic medicine inquiry is that of a group of general medical practitioners who are interested in and committed to the development of holistic practice. Other groups — patients, professional medical researchers, hospital doctors, and so on — would have worked from equally valid but different perspectives. Dialogue between these would increase the comprehensiveness of our knowing. The perspective of the inquiry also derives from the aware choices of the inquiry group as they carry out their work, for example, how they chose convergent and divergent cycles of inquiry. On the other hand, distortions in inquiry derive from the group's *unaware* choices arising from simple carelessness and unsystematic inquiry, from anxiety, false consensus, and so on.

Full use of the validity procedures will assist an inquiry group to make decisions that will clarify the perspective of its work, and draw its attention to ways in which the inquiry is likely to be distorted. In our own inquiries we have used the validity procedures to review systematically our work at the end of each cycle of research. In the early cycles of the holistic medical inquiry this review was completed entirely by ourselves as initiating facilitators. As the inquiry progressed the validity procedures were increasingly adopted, internalized, and developed by members of the inquiry group, so that by the fourth meeting the validity review was undertaken by the group as a whole.

ASSESSMENT OF COOPERATIVE INQUIRY

We have been asked by the editors of this journal to provide an assessment of the effectiveness of the cooperative inquiry approach. We have decided to take our own advice and do this in the form of a critical dialogue between ourselves and a more orthodox Devil's Advocate, who expresses some of the objections of our critics.

Devil's Advocate: What do you two think you're up to, anyway? It is not clear whether you are putting forward a whole new approach to research, or just offering additional tools that may be useful in some circumstances.

Authors: No, it's not just another tool. We are attempting to work our way toward a new, genuinely postpositivist paradigm for inquiry with persons. We argue strongly that the only basis for inquiry with persons is cooperation, participation, dialogue, whatever term is preferred. Here we have set out our way of cooperation; we know that other inquirers and other inquiry groups will find their own different approaches.

Devil's Advocate: But how on earth can you expect people to devote so much time and energy to it? The method just won't work unless people really want to work with you.

Authors: That's right. We don't see any point to inquiry unless people genuinely want to change their experience or behavior, personally or professionally, on the basis of new knowings. Much research is quite useless in practice, because no one is committed to the questions posed or the answers obtained, so it becomes an academic exercise, in the worst sense of that term.

Devil's Advocate: But then you can really only work with very small samples, and your results will not be generalizable!

Authors: When you use the term 'sample' you reveal your continuing commitment to positivist assumptions and methods. We want to work with *people*, not with samples. And generalization is problematic anyway, since you cannot, in our epistemology, generalize knowings beyond the particular person or group who holds them. What you *can* do is tell others, 'This is what we found for ourselves, maybe you would like to try it out as well,' which seems to us to be a much more healthy way of spreading ideas and practice.

Devil's Advocate: Well then, all you are really doing is offering us another 'exploratory' research method. There really is no way of testing theories and confirming your findings.

Authors: You really are attached to the old ideas, aren't you! We don't find the distinction between 'exploratory' and 'confirmatory' inquiry particularly helpful. They belong to an epistemology in which it is possible to be absolutely 'right' or 'wrong' that we have rejected. In cooperative inquiry, if we wish to examine tentative findings carefully, we would arrange for our research cycling to converge on the relevant issues so they could be looked at several times in increasing detail; and we would attempt to establish the contextual validity of our discoveries by knitting together a complex view of the whole.

Devil's Advocate: So you'd never be properly rigorous and use an experiment or a questionnaire.

Authors: Oh yes, we might! Although on the whole we prefer holistic inquiry that views each aspect of the subject in its context, it is possible to conceive of a situation in which we wanted to test one variable with considerable rigor, in which case a controlled experiment *might* be the best way. However, we would require all those involved in the inquiry to be party to its design and to the interpretation of results. Questionnaires and surveys can be used on the same basis. But this is very different from having someone else make sense of our answers to questions that we were not involved in asking in the first place.

Devil's Advocate: You haven't told us anything about the outcomes of the holistic medicine inquiry. Did you discover anything useful?

Authors: We reviewed the project in terms of the validity procedures and concluded that it had been a modest success. We were able to use the cooperative inquiry model successfully, developing and beginning to explore critically in practice a model for holistic medicine. Certainly involvement in the inquiry brought about far-reaching changes in the medical practice of most of the participants: a deeper care for their own well-being, shifts toward cooperative diagnoses and treatment, and a deeper understanding of psychological and spiritual aspects of their practice. It has been more difficult to communicate these changes to others who were not part of the original inquiry, although several members of the inquiry are active participants in the newly formed British Holistic Medical Association. Obviously there is a place for further inquiries to explore both the model as a whole and the detailed strategies implied by it.

Devil's Advocate: Well, despite all you say, I think you are offering an interesting approach to problem solving rather than a general research paradigm.

Authors: From our perspective it is really important not to split these two. We want to develop an experiential and practical science, in which sound research findings consist of a mix of experiential, practical, and propositional knowings. There is no such thing as a 'body of knowledge' separate from the practice or application of that knowledge.

Devil's Advocate: I find all this very difficult to fit in with all I was taught about research methods.

Authors: Well, it is. We have outlined an approach to human inquiry based on assumptions about persons and human capacities radically different from those of positivist science. In practice the research process and outcomes are also very different. The kind of inquiry we are advocating is very much alive, very much an existential struggle with understanding and practice in a real world context. Managing this kind of inquiry is a complex and multifaceted process, involving questions about the creativity and pathology of the inquirers as persons, about the behavior of groups, as well as more traditional questions concerning the logic of the inquiry process. We have tried to develop a *rigour of softness,* or a *rigour of participation* that takes into account the person as a whole being capable of critical awareness, and hence capable of human inquiry. The intellectual, emotional, and practical challenge of doing this kind of research well is formidable. It is also enormously rewarding.

AUTHOR'S NOTE

While the ideas in this article were developed collaboratively by both authors, the final version was written by Peter Reason. I am deeply grateful for the loving support and critical comments from Judi Marshall and Adrian McLean in the final stages of preparing the article for publication.

REFERENCES

Bateson, G. (1972). *Steps to an ecology of mind.* San Francisco: Chandler.
Berger, P. L., & Luckmann, T. (1966). *The social construction of reality.* New York: Doubleday.
Bohm, D. (1978). 'The enfolding-unfolding universe: A conversation with David Bohm conducted

by Renee Weber.' *Re-Vision, 1,* (3/4).

Brockman, J. (Ed). (1977). *About Bateson.* New York: F. P. Dutton.

Brooks, C. (1974). *Sensory awareness: The rediscovery of experiencing.* New York: Viking.

Capra, F. (1982). *The turning point.* London: Wildwood.

Devereaux, G. (1967). *From anxiety to method in the behavioural sciences.* The Hague: Mouton.

Diesing, P. (1972). *Patterns of discovery in the social sciences.* London: Routledge & Kegan Paul.

Feyerabend, P. (1978). *Science in a free society.* London: Verso.

Glaser, B. G., & Strauss, A. L. (1967). *The discovery of grounded theory.* Chicago: Aldine.

Hainer, R. (1968). Rationalism, pragmatism, and existentialism: Perceived but undiscovered multi-cultural problems. In E. Glatt & M. S. Shelly (Eds.), *The research society.* New York: Gordon & Breach.

Hawkins, P. (1986). Living the learning: An exploration of learning processes in primary learning communities and the development of a learning perspective to inform team development. Unpublished Ph.D. dissertation, University of Bath.

Heron, J. (1971). *Experience and method.* England, University of Surrey, Human Potential Research Project.

Heron, J. (1973). *Re-evaluation counselling: A theoretical review.* University of Surrey, Human Potential Research Project.

Heron, J. (1981). Philosophical basis for a new paradigm. In P. Reason & J. Rowan (Eds.), *Human inquiry, a sourcebook of new paradigm research.* Chichester: John Wiley.

Heron, J. (1982). *Empirical validity in experiential research.* University of Surrey, Human Potential Research Project.

Heron, J., & Reason, P. (Eds.) (1985). *Whole person medicine.* University of London, British Postgraduate Medical Federation.

Houston, J. (1982). *The possible human.* Los Angeles: J. P. Tarcher.

Jackins, H. (1965). *The human side of human beings: The theory of re-evaluation counselling.* Seattle: Rational Island.

Koestler, A. (1978). *Janus.* London: Hutchinson.

Lincoln, Y.S. & Guba, E. G. (1985). *Naturalistic Inquiry.* Beverly Hills, CA: Sage.

Macmurray, J. (1957). *Persons in relation.* London: Faber & Faber.

Maslow, A. (1966). *The psychology of science.* New York: Harper & Row.

Masters, R. (1981). Introduction to mindfulness in the sacred psychologies. *Dromenon, 3,* (3).

Mitroff, I. (1974). *The subjective side of science.* Amsterdam: Elsevier.

Mitroff, I., & Kilmann, R. (1978). *Methodological approaches to social science.* San Francisco: Jossey-Bass.

Polanyi, M. (1958). *Personal knowledge: Towards a postcritical philosophy.* London: Routledge & Kegan Paul.

Reason, P. (1976). Explorations in the dialectics of two person relationships. Unpublished Ph.D, dissertation, Case Western Reserve University.

Reason, P. (1985). Innovative Research Techniques: Critical subjectivity and holistic inquiry. *Complementary Medical Research, 1,* (1).

Reason, P. & Rowan, J. (Eds.) (1981a). *Human inquiry, a sourcebook of new paradigm research.* Chichester: John Wiley.

Reason, P. & Rowan, J. (1981b). Issues of validity in new paradigm research. In P. Reason & J. Rowan (Eds.), *Human Inquiry, a sourcebook of new paradigm research.* Chichester: John Wiley.

Rogers, C. (1980). Do we need 'a' reality? In *A Way of being.* Boston: Houghton Mifflin.

Rogers, C. (1985). Toward a more human science of the person. *Journal of Humanistic Psychology, 25,* (4)

Schwartz P. & Ogilvy, J. (1980). *The emergent paradigm: Changing patterns of thought and belief*(Analytical Report No. 7). Values and Lifestyles Program, SRI International: Menlo Park, CA.

Skolimowski, H. (1981). *Eco-philosophy: Designing new tactics for living.* London: Marion Boyars.

Skolimowski, H. (1985). The co-creative mind as a partner of the creative evolution. Paper presented at the First International Conference on the Mind-Matter Interaction. Universidada Estuadual De Campinas, Brazil.

Torbert, W. (1976). *Creating a Community of Inquiry: Conflict, collaboration, transformation.* New York: John Wiley.

Torbert, W. (1981). Why educational research has been so uneducational: The case for a new model of social science based on collaborative inquiry. In P. Reason & J. Rowan (Eds.), *Human Inquiry, a sourcebook of new paradigm research.* Chichester: John Wiley.

Wilber, K. (1981). Reflections on the new age paradigm: An interview with Ken Wilber. *Re-Vision, 4,* (1).

Human Science Inquiry into the Person:

Methodological issues and an illustration

Judith E. Crothers and Paul R. Dokecki

George Peabody College, Vanderbilt University

We argue for a postpositivist, human science, interpretive approach to inquiry into the person and emphasize the importance of giving priority to the phenomenon of the person, with choice of method following from the phenomenon and not vice versa. We illustrate our methodological argument through a discussion and critique of a human science investigation we conducted. In that investigation, we chose an important life event, the birth of a first child, as the context in which parents were invited to participate in open-ended interviews, each one conducted as a cooperative dialogue between the parent and researcher. We endeavored to fit interpretations derived from theory to these qualitative phenomenological data and drew theoretical, methodological, and clinical implications for future human science inquiry.

Where would American psychology be today if it had given priority to the phenomenon of the person rather than to methodology? Recall Abraham Kaplan's (1964, p. 11) metaphor of the behavioral scientist as an inebriated person searching for missing keys under the street lamp rather than in the dark where the keys were lost. Why? Because, said our besotted scientist, 'It's lighter here!' Kaplan claimed that the behavioral sciences are all too easily characterized by this 'principle of *the drunkard's search*,' by an emphasis on method, typically natural science method. We are often led to know precisely where and what things *aren't* — we will come to know that the keys aren't under the lamppost — rather than to an understanding of the human phenomena of interest. How can we characterize, then, the body of thought psychological research has produced about the person? Sigmund Koch has characterized much of it as *a meaningful thought,* thought long on method and short on meaning. This type of criticism today is being issued from an intellectual movement many are coming to call *human science* (e.g., Giorgi, 1970; Polkinghorne, 1983).[1]

KNOWING THE PERSON THROUGH HUMAN SCIENCE

Human science is not particularly new. Bloom's (1987) historical analysis traces its development in the modern era to Kant's criticism of the Enlightenment's attempt to render all things knowable by reason, especially by Newtonian natural science. Kant accepted Rousseau's argument that freedom defines the human realm, rendering natural

---

1. Our purposes here are to are to argue for a human science approach to knowing the person and to illustrate this methodological argument by describing a study based on human science principles.

First published in *Person-Centered Review,* Volume 4, Number 4, November 1989.

science notions of causality inadequate to understanding the human person:

> Man understood as a free, moral individual — as creative, as producer of cultures, as maker and product of history — provided a field for humane research taking man seriously as man, not reduced to the moving bodies that now constituted the realm of natural science. (Bloom, 1987, p. 301)[2]

Human science thereby came on the intellectual scene, and there was active debate in Europe throughout the nineteenth century over whether the nomothetic natural sciences (*Naturwissenschaften*) or the idiographic and historical human sciences (*Geisteswissenschaften*) constituted the best approach to understanding the human person. American psychology, for its part, declined the bid offered by the human sciences and sought entry into the fraternity of the natural sciences. And if we follow Koch (1981), the result has been much a meaningful thought. Since the 1950s, however, there has been a rising tide of criticism of positivism in the natural sciences and of its dominance in psychology (e.g., Dokecki, 1986, 1987; Hanson, 1958/1965; Kuhn, 1962/1970; Toulmin, 1953/1960). Contemporary versions of the human sciences typically have a postpositivist (not necessarily anti-positivist) cast, in which 'the traditional narrow and limited positivist methods are complemented with a wide variety of methods, chosen to be adequate to the particular phenomena to be studied at this or that time in varying contexts' (Dokecki, 1986, p. 5). One way of understanding the postpositivist human sciences is that they reverse Kaplan's principle of the drunkard's search by seeking methods that fit phenomena rather than unnecessarily distorting phenomena by fitting them to methodological prescriptions. Moreover, rather than claiming that there is one royal road to knowledge — positivism's claim about natural science method — multiple methodological perspectives are allowed and encouraged. For example, Bernstein (1971, 1978, 1983) makes a case for methodological conversation among the perspectives of empiricism, Marxism, existentialism, phenomenology, pragmatism, critical theory, and hermeneutics. Morgan (1983) suggests that an array of methodological choices is available to students of human social phenomena, including quasi-experimentation, action research, interpretive interactionism, structuralism, life history method, critical theory, collaborative inquiry, and several others. Morgan argues the case for 'a reflective social science . . . [in which] a knowledge of technique needs to be complemented by an appreciation of the nature of research as a distinctively human process' (p. 7).

One of our most important personality theorists, George Kelly (1955), emphasized that theoretical and methodological approaches to the person must account equally well for the theorist as for the one theorized about and must recognize that persons are studying persons. Taking Kelly seriously would require reconceptualization of the research situation. When free intentional persons try to understand other free intentional persons in a research context, there is a significant potential for distortion if experimental manipulation and control are the exclusive order of the day. And there are ethical overtones here as well, since society has come to accept the ethical dictum that persons should be accorded dignity, that is, be treated as persons not things, as ends not means. How often in mainstream research are persons treated as objects to be manipulated, as means to the researchers' ends? Although we do not intend our argument to be extreme — after all, life inevitably involves people interacting in manipulative ways to a greater or lesser extent, and great benefits may accrue to society from such interactions in research — it is

---

2. See Rychlak's (1981) textbook on personality for a systematic analysis of different meanings of causality as applied to the person.

nonetheless important to keep the dignity of the person in mind as an ethical imperative and regulative ideal. Reason and Heron (1986), in this journal, have expressed appreciation for these notions and described an inquiry in which researchers and research participants collaborated to develop knowledge about a topic meaningful to both. Many of the usual experimental canons were not only out of place in Reason and Heron's kind of investigation, they could even be construed as destructive of the purposes of their collaborative and experiential inquiry (see also Heron, 1971; Reason & Rowan, 1981).

In human science inquiry, a different methodological mind set from that of positivism must be employed. Polkinghorne's (1983) *Methodology for the Human Sciences* elaborates such a perspective in order to 'investigate all of the experiences, activities, constructs, and artifacts . . . [including] the study of personal consciousness and experience, as well as social, political, and economic systems . . . [constituting] the realm of the human' (p. 289). Such investigations require the view of knowledge as *assertoric:*

> Assertoric knowledge uses practical reasoning and argumentation. It requires a decision among alternatives, none of which provides certainty. A supporter of a knowledge claim is expected to argue cogently before the appropriate community, providing evidence pertinent to his or her proposal and defending his or her position as the most likely correct position among various alternatives. (Polkinghorne, 1983, p. 287)

This notion of assertoric knowledge suggests an important methodological point, namely, the human science affirmation that the knower contributes to the construction of knowledge (Dewey & Bentley, 1949/1973; Plas & Dokecki, 1982). In line with current thinking in the history and philosophy of science since the 1950s (e.g., Brown, 1977), human scientists affirm that knowledge of reality is always theory laden, value laden, and socially constructed. They deny, therefore, the existence of naively realistic facts independent of the knower. In this regard, Woolfolk, Sass, and Messer (1988), writing about human science inquiry under the rubric of hermeneutics, have cogently argued:

> Perhaps the most radical implication of a hermeneutic [human science] outlook for psychology is the attitude it fosters toward the nature of evidence, data, and empirical investigations. Most contemporary psychology researchers write as if they believe themselves to be accumulating neutral, objective facts in a value free, transhistorical, epistemological arena. From a hermeneutic perspective, such an approach ignores the extent to which such facts are inextricably interwoven with theory, with the researcher's biases, with the choice of language used to describe the terms employed, and with sociocultural and historical influences — all of which preclude the notion of facts existing apart from interpretative process. This is not to say that traditional psychological data-gathering approaches are without value in the study of personality, psychopathology, and psychotherapy. It does say, however, that such methods have no epistemic pedigree that renders them superior to other methods, including clinical case analysis, phenomenological description [and others]. (pp. 24–5)

Human science methods typically entail a person (the researcher) attempting to understand (construct the meaning of) the world of another person (the research participant) within specific, concrete, intersubjective contexts. Understanding emerges in the form of the human scientist's interpretations of the meanings manifest in these contexts. The issue here is not one of methodological convention, for example, quantitatively establishing interobserver reliability of observations or categories, an endeavor that assumes a theory-free and value-free reality 'out there' to be discovered by so-called objective observers (Lincoln & Guba, 1985). Rather, reality and its categorizations are understood as socially constructed (Berger & Luckmann, 1966) and communicated by a human scientist who is intimately and uniquely involved in the particular interpersonal context of the investigation. Crucial is the human scientist's interpretation of this context.

An interpretation, then, arises from a concrete experiential context. Rather than acceding to the positivist demand that an 'independent' interpreter come up with the same interpretation—a questionable demand, since observations and categorizations cannot be independent of the specific contexts from which they arise—the human science demand is that the interpretation be communicable, trustworthy, credible, reasonable, and persuasive, and that its generalizability be explored. Although the human scientist actively participates in constructing knowledge in a concrete human situation, he or she does so within a systematic and rigorous framework and makes knowledge known— and thereby objective (Rychlak, 1981)—through presenting arguments to and inviting arguments from the community of scholars. The human scientist communicates how his or her typically qualitative or phenomenological data were generated (inviting other researchers to do similar work), outlines the nature of these data, and argues for the interpretations that make most sense of the data. Along the way, the *trustworthiness* (Lincoln & Guba, 1985) of the data are established through the human scientist describing the care and rigor of the interactions that generated them. Again, the focus is not on methodological conventions, such as interobserver reliability ratios, but on the reasonableness, persuasiveness, and utility of the interpretations advanced through the arguments presented in the public communications of the human scientist (Polkinghorne, 1983). Positivist scientists assume that methodological conventions guarantee truth; postpositivist human scientists, rather, deny the preeminence of method and stress the need for meaningful interpretation, assertion, and argumentation presented through the medium of dialogue within a community of scholars (Gadamer, 1975; Polkinghorne, 1983).

We intend the following report of a human science inquiry to be illustrative in order to point out issues to consider in this type of research; therefore, we briefly describe the particulars of the study (for a more complete description see Crothers, 1987). The methods for qualitative human science inquiry are evolving, and this investigation was a means for our exploring some of these methods.

As such, it has some weaknesses, and readers are asked to focus first on the methodological issues and only secondarily on the particular results.

A HUMAN SCIENCE INQUIRY INTO THE INDEPENDENT-CONNECTED SELF-DIALECTIC

The inquiry began with our interest in theories about the self that characterize the person's basic psychological task as the differentiation of an independent self while maintaining connection with others. We termed this task the independent-connected self-dialectic. To explain briefly, this task is twofold. Persons wish to experience and view themselves as separate and unique from others. At the same time, they wish to experience a connection to others. Each of these experiences becomes meaningful only by being set dialectically against the other. In other words, they can be described as polar opposites, or perhaps as figure-ground phenomena, with each pole emerging as figure or fading into ground, depending on the individual's developmental phase and life circumstances.

Theorists from a variety of orientations have highlighted this dialectical developmental tension. For example, among early psychologist-philosopher theorists,

Baldwin (1897/1968) and Cooley (1902/1968) wrote of the self as developing along the two lines of differentiation and connection. From the psychoanalytic perspective, Freud (1923/1950, 1930/1961) had at least an implicitly dialectical view of the self, and Fromm (1941) saw that being connected to others is necessary for the development of the self, but only after the self has become differentiated. Furthermore, developmental psychologists have described the self dialectically. For example, Kegan (1982) offered a model for the development of the self that takes the shape of a helix, wherein the tension in self-development between differentiation and connection gets resolved more in favor of one pole or the other of the dialectic at different times over the life span. And Gilligan (1982) asserted that traditional theories of development have described the self as developing only toward the pole of differentiation, typically ignoring the self as developing also toward the pole of connection.

Beyond psychology, other social scientists have written of the dialectical nature of self-development. In *Habits of the Heart,* Bellah, Madsen, Sullivan, Swidler, and Tipton (1985) described the struggle of hundreds of Americans they interviewed to reconcile the desire for independence with the desire for interdependence with others, and concluded that American culture makes this struggle particularly difficult. Social historian Christopher Lasch (1984) observed that American society promotes either total differentiation of self or total connection of self, both of which are illusions and, therefore, unsatisfactory. And in the spirit of Buber's (1937) I-Thou relationship, philosopher John Macmurray (1957, 1961) described the field of the personal in which the self emerges only in its relations with the other, and therefore, needs the other in order to exist. In a related vein, Bakan (1966) has discussed two aspects of the self, calling the desire for separation and mastery, 'agency,' and the desire for connection and cooperation, 'communion.'

Diverse disciplines and theorists, therefore, have suggested that the person's basic psychological activity entails a dialectical self task. How can one investigate this phenomenon? We believed that this dialectic would be clearly manifest in people's experience of important life events, such as the birth of a first child. The importance of the birth event was demonstrated by Berger and Luckmann (1966) in their phenomenological analysis of the crucial changes that take place in parents' perceptions of social reality when a child is born. The effect on a marriage of having a child has been studied extensively (e.g., Belsky, Lang, & Rovine, 1985; Belsky, Spanier, & Rovine, 1983; Russell, 1974), and the life transition nature of the birth event is well-established (Hobbs & Cole, 1976; Rossi, 1968; Russell, 1974). Moreover, Leifer (1977) concluded that most women experience early parenthood as a crisis, but they also experience a sense of growth and expansion of the self.

These lines of theory and research led us to conduct a phenomenological and cooperative human science inquiry. Our guiding theoretical perspective was that since the dialectical task of differentiating an independent self and maintaining connection to others is basic to the person, the experiences parents report of the life event of having a first child are meaningfully interpretable by means of the independent-connected self-dialectic theory.

Participants

Six married couples (one pilot couple and five formal research couples) participated in this study, each couple having only one child (the first child for all parents) who was under two years, so that the birth experience was still vivid. The parents were Caucasian, ranging in age from 26 to 34 years, had at least a bachelor's degree, and could be considered middle- to upper-middle socioeconomic class.

Procedure

The first author (who has a Master's Degree and several years experience in interviewing and counseling and is an advanced doctoral student in clinical psychology) conducted two open-ended interviews separately with each parent. The interviews were tape-recorded and transcribed.

Initially, the first author interviewed a married couple (meeting the foregoing stated criteria) as a pilot case to test the interview method. The authors and members of their research group had drafted a list of open-ended questions to ask the parents concerning their experiences. These questions were originally meant to provide some 'standardization' to the analysis of the interviews. However, following the pilot interviews, we questioned whether we had understood the experience from the parents' perspective or had tended to impose our own framework. For example, one question had been, 'What are some of the positive and negative aspects of your experience of having a child?' The 'pilot' father had remarked that he did not view his experience in terms of positives and negatives. As a result of misgivings about our understanding of the pilot parents' views, and of our growing conviction of the importance of cooperative inquiry (as in Reason & Heron, 1986), we decided to allow the parents in the study to state for themselves the important topics for inquiry. Therefore, the first interview with each parent opened with this question: 'If you were wanting me to understand your experience of having this child, what questions would I need to ask you, or about what topics would I need to inquire?' The interviewer took notes on the parent's responses and then asked the parent the questions that had been provided. If a parent had difficulty responding to the opening question or verbalizing his or her experience, the interviewer responded with nondirective and reflective statements.[3] Direct questions about topics that the interviewee had not introduced were avoided. After the first interview with a parent had been transcribed, the second interview was scheduled to follow up on any topics judged to be unclear and to provide the parent with an opportunity to add or change any information. The second interview opened with the same interviewer saying, 'These are the topics that we talked about last time. Did you have any thoughts after our discussion that you want to talk about now, or anything that you want to add or change?' Again, the interview was tape-recorded, notes were taken, and the interview was transcribed.

Reflecting on this method now, we believe that its advantage was that it let us see what was important to the parents, uninfluenced by overt questions from us. The disadvantage was that the parents might not have listed topics that were important merely because the topic did not occur to them at the time or because they might have thought a particular topic was not appropriate. In future research, one could allow the first interview to be open, as we did, but have the second interview include certain structured questions such as, 'Other parents have said that "X" was important to them, and you have not mentioned it. What do you think about that now?' Structured questions developed by the researcher might also be included. These tactics, while losing the complete spontaneity of the parents' responses, would enhance the coverage of the topics discussed and introduce a further element of standardization.

---

3. See Tandon (1981) for a discussion of how dialogue itself can change an 'underorganized system' into an organized system.

Analysis

Units, construed as molar topics, were coded from the transcripts. Coding began at the point in the transcript where the parent began elaborating on his or her first chosen topic. The two authors used a three-part coding scheme for each molar topic unit of the interview, as follows: (a) a notation was made of the *person* to whom the parent was referring (e.g., child or spouse), (b) a notation was made of one of three *time* references in the parent's statements (past, present, or future), and (c) a notation was made of the parent's *psychological commentary* (e.g., thoughts, feelings, beliefs) expressed in the particular unit. The molar topic units were typed onto index cards, one coded unit per card. The first author sorted individual cards for each parent according to superordinate topics or themes, and thereby identified three or four main themes for each parent. These themes were then used both to compare all the parents in order to identify overall main themes and to identify an individual's themes.

Trustworthiness

In cooperative experiential research of this type, according to Reason and Rowan (1981), validity is threatened by two processes: unaware projection and consensual collusion. *Unaware projection* occurs when the researcher projects her or his own internal problems onto the phenomenon being studied. We addressed unaware projection by (a) frequent dialogue with at least two persons not formally involved in the study for the purpose of checking perceptions and obtaining feedback on the logic and rationale of the themes being derived and the interpretations being made, and (b) effort on the part of the investigators to maintain a 'realized' level of thinking (Reason & Rowan, 1981), in other words, by continually questioning results and interpretations. For example, we had at first considered using a two-part coding scheme entailing the person referred to and the psychological commentary. During a dialogue with our colleagues, however, we became convinced that a third coding element — the time reference — should be included to document changes over time. This use of dialogue with other persons to refine coding categories is one of a number of validation or trustworthiness strategies that might have been employed (see Lincoln & Guba, 1985).

The second threat to validity, *consensual collusion,* occurs when a group of researchers 'sustain a tacit norm to the effect that certain areas of experience, ranges of human potentiality, behavioral possibilities, shall be overlooked, so that the adequacy of the theory is not called experientially into question' (Heron, 1971, p. 15). We addressed consensual collusion by (a) ongoing dialogue with colleagues who were invited to take 'devil's advocate' roles in order that conclusions be questioned and examined, and (b) going around the research cycle many times (i.e., two interviews with each of the several participants) and checking information with each participant in the second interview. This aspect of validity might have been enhanced by including a question in the second interview about topics that other parents had mentioned, but that the particular parent had omitted, as discussed here. We might also have returned to the participants a third time with the coded categories, requested their feedback on the categories, and adjusted the final data and interpretations accordingly. This procedure is costly in time and effort; however, the parents might thereby become even more intimate collaborators in the research.

In research analyzing narrative data, the calculation of interjudge reliability, a common trustworthiness convention in traditional research, is sometimes used for both validity and reliability purposes. We did not do this. Because of the interpersonal and dialogical nature of the interviews, the perspective that the interviewer-researcher brought to the analysis of the typed transcripts of the interviews was not duplicable. Another person with a typed transcript or even a tape-recording to analyze would encounter a version of the interview minus the interviewer's situationally derived experiences and interpretations. This is not to say that the main contents of the interviews were opaque to an 'outsider.' As stated, two other persons did read the transcripts and engage in dialogue with us about the plausibility of our interpretations. But to compare our specific data codings with those they might have given would have been neither useful nor in line with the logic of our interpretive inquiry. On the other hand, we now believe that our results might have been made more convincing by systematically documenting the process and the conclusions of the discussions with the two colleague-readers of the transcripts. Points of concurrence and dissonance in the coding categories and interpretations might have been described and the resulting modifications and rationale for doing so noted, thus enhancing trustworthiness.

Results

Results were analyzed on several levels. First, the overall group themes were compiled and examined in light of dialectical self-theory. Then, each parent's experiences were summarized and similarly subjected to theoretical interpretation. Some might argue that our method could have produced no other results than those we expected, and that unbiased methods should have been employed to check the validity of our results and interpretations. In our inquiry, however, we did not 'test' a hypothesis; rather, we examined a theoretical perspective to see if it was a plausible mode of interpretation and understanding. Alternate interpretations could also be offered, but this is the case in *any* investigation, including those that follow standard methods of hypothesis testing (Rychlak, 1981). Readers are invited, therefore, to ask themselves (a) whether our interpretations of the reported themes and experiences in light of dialectical self-theory tells a coherent and meaningful story, (b) whether our interpretations concur with their own scholarly and professional experiences, and (c) whether our interpretations help facilitate further research and clinical interactions.

Again, since this article is but an illustration of human science inquiry into the person, only the group themes phase is presented.

Enjoyment of the relationship and self-growth. Two of the most commonly stated themes, that of enjoying the relationship with the newborn child, and that of experiencing a growth in self, illustrate the dialectical task of differentiating self by maintaining connections to others. For example, most (nine) of the parents found themselves immersed in a deeply satisfying relationship with the child. More than half of the parents even expressed surprise over the extent of their attachment to the child. As one father said, 'I sort of marvel at the emotions that I feel toward [child's name] that I didn't anticipate, and how strong they are.' None of the parents spoke of the relationship with the child as negative; but perhaps they would have felt reluctant to report negative experiences if they had had them. Eight parents found that the intense and satisfying relationship with the newborn contributed to their perceptions of themselves as separate individuals, which they then used to enhance their relationship with their child as well as relationships with others. One father in particular gave a clear and touching description of the dialectical nature of how the relationship with the child affected his sense of self, which in turn affected his sense of self in his extended family relationships.

Some (four) of the parents did not specifically mention experiencing self-growth. Two mothers in particular mentioned that they did not feel different; however, they thought perceptions of themselves by others had changed.

Sense of responsibility. Another frequently stated theme (eight parents), experiencing a profound sense of responsibility for the child, is an example of the boundaries between self and other being indistinct. In other words, care of the child was found to be alarmingly important, at least as important as care of the self. A number of aspects of this care were mentioned, such as financial and basic child care responsibilities. For some of the parents, however, the child was not explicitly felt to be a separate being, and the realization that the child was getting his or her sense of self from the parent(s) reverberated deeply in their sense of responsibility. One father said, 'It makes you think about, well, if [child's name] is soaking up everything that I'm doing, [and] everything that I am, then I have a responsibility to try to make that a decent thing, to make it the best I can.'

Conflict about time. Seven parents reported experiencing a conflict in dividing time between child and other interests, such as career, illustrating the tension in the dialectic. The conflict could be due to the parents' paradoxical desires to feel both the connected relationship with the child and the separate concept of self, and feeling that not enough time could be spent on each. Several mothers in particular, who had always seen themselves as 'career' persons, seemed to struggle painfully with this conflict.

Change in marital and other relationships. The themes of experiencing a change in the marital relationship (five parents) and experiencing a change in the relationship with parents and siblings (four parents), illustrate how the intense involvement in the relationship with the child affects other relationships, either directly or indirectly. Some direct changes in other relationships resulted from the demands of the relationship with the child leaving less time for other relationships. Some indirect changes came from a parent's self-concept changing, affecting sense of self in other relationships (as noted), or from a parent's own perceptions of others and even of world issues changing. One mother, struggling to articulate the complex interactions of perceptions of herself, her child, and her parents, said:

> I think I've gotten rid of a lot of baggage about my family in realizing that my parents say things and do things which are not intentional. I probably have better relationships with my family because I guess I don't have the expectations that I've always had of them. And [having a child has] also let me give up a lot of the expectations I have had of myself, which has been a real positive thing.

Each of the main themes discussed by the parents can be interpreted as an issue in the parents' struggle to differentiate a separate self, while being connected to others. *Without much deviation from the parents' own words, the dialectic of this struggle was manifest.* The themes of (a) finding growth in the sense of self through the relationship with the child, (b) strongly feeling the self's responsibility for the child's growth, (c) feeling conflicted about allocations of limited and precious time, and (d) seeing the self change in relationships, which in turn changes the self, were all themes that provided evidence consistent with dialectical self-theory.

Parents' reported experiences of the birth of a child, therefore, can reasonably and plausibly be interpreted by means of dialectical self-theory. The parents related their experiences in terms of effects on themselves, their interpersonal relationships, and the dialectic between the two. The interpretations we have offered can also be seen to exemplify how this theory could be useful to clinicians in understanding clients' experiences of self and relationships. In a clinical situation, of course, the clinician would formulate the specifics of the interpretations as working hypotheses, subject to reformulations in the clinical interaction. Clinicians, by recognizing the individual's dialectical need for relatedness in order to find separateness, can avoid emphasizing only growth toward differentiation or growth toward relatedness. While individuals do grow toward differentiation, the growth takes place in the context of relationships with others. Keeping in mind both aspects of the dialectic can help a clinician more fully understand the person's experiences.

DISCUSSION

Our investigation was limited by several factors. Because of the relatively small number of participants, about as many as could be accommodated given the intensive study of each individual, we can generalize findings of the specific content of the overall themes only with caution. In addition, the participants were somewhat an elite group, being highly educated and professionally employed people. The intelligent and articulate characteristics of the participants, however, contributed to the overall high quality of the information gained through the unstructured interviews. This relationship raises an important issue in this type of research. On the one hand, a qualitative researcher needs to study participants who are able to reflect and report their experiences in a somewhat abstract manner. On the other hand, there is the need for participants who are representative of the population in general, or of a population of interest, and representatives of the population may not easily give usable information in a face-to-face unstructured interview. We made a trade-off that suggests caution in generalizing our findings.

Returning to the issue of validity, the evidence we found for dialectical self-theory was largely a matter of our interpretation of parents' reported experiences. Other researchers might find evidence for another theory. Our interpretations, however, were made in the context of a community of researchers. On numerous occasions, we engaged in dialogue with several others in order to probe the plausibility of our applications of the theory. A further test of theory would be its usefulness in describing and explaining persons' phenomenological experiences of self and other in a clinical context. Would clinicians find dialectical self-theory helpful in formulating strategies and techniques for working with clients? What might some of these applications entail? Further research would be useful.

In conclusion, we found evidence consistent with the theoretical assertion that parents' reports of their experiences of the birth of a child entail a dialectic of independence and connection. We offer this inquiry and its findings as an illustration of the power of human science inquiry into the person. Contributors to and readers of the *Person-Centered Review* in particular are invited to reflect on the methodological issues raised in giving priority in inquiry to the phenomenon of the person.

AUTHOR'S NOTE

This study was supported in part by a Vanderbilt Biomedical Science Research Grant. Thanks are due to Julius Seemen for insightful suggestions.

REFERENCES

Bakan, D. (1966). *The duality of human existence: An essay on psychology and religion.* Chicago: Rand McNally.

Baldwin, J. M. (1968). The self-conscious person. In C. Gordon & K. I. Gergen (Eds.), *The self in social interaction* (Vol 1; pp. 161–9). New York: John Wiley. (Original work published 1897.)

Bellah, R., Madsen, R., Sullivan, W., Swidler, A., & Tipton, S. (1985). *Habits of the heart.* New York: Harper & Row.

Belsky, J., Lang, M., & Rovine, M. (1985). Stability and change in marriage across the transition to parenthood: A second study. *Journal of Marriage and the Family, 47,* 855–66.

Belsky, J., Spanier, G., & Rovine, M. (1983). Stability and change in marriage across the transition to parenthood. *Journal of Marriage and the Family, 45,* 567–77.

Berger, P., & Luckmann, R. (1966). *The social construction of reality.* New York: Doubleday.

Bernstein, R. J. (1971). *Praxis and action: Contemporary philosophies of human activity.* Philadelphia: University of Pennsylvania Press.

Bernstein, R. J. (1978). *The restructuring of social political theory.* Philadelphia: University of Pennsylvania Press.

Bernstein, R. J. (1983). *Beyond objectivism and relativism: Science, hermaneutics, and praxis.* Philadelphia: University of Pennsylvania Press.

Bloom, A. (1987). *The closing of the American mind.* New York: Simon & Schuster.

Brown, H. I. (1977). *Perception, theory and commitment: The new philosophy of science.* Chicago: University of Chicago Press.

Buber, M. (1937). *I and Thou.* New York: Scribner.

Cooley, C. H. (1968). The social self: On the meaning of 'I.' In C. Gordon & K. J. Gergen (Eds.), *The self in social interaction* (Vol. 1; pp. 78–91). New York: John Wiley. (Original work published 1902.)

Crothers, J. E. (1987). Parents' experience of a dialectic of differentiating self through connections to others in the context of the birth of their first child. Unpublished master's thesis, Vanderbilt University, Nashville, TN.

Dewey, J., & Bentley, A. (1973). Knowing and the known. In R. Handy & E. C. Harwood (Eds.), *Useful procedures of inquiry.* New York: Irvington. (Original work published in 1949.)

Dokecki, P. R. (1986). Methodological futures of the caring professions. *Urban & Social Change Review, 19(Winter, Summer),* 3–7.

Dokecki, P. R. (1987). Can knowledge contribute to the creation of community? *Journal of Community Psychology, 15,* 90–6.

Freud, S. (1950) *The ego and the id* (J. Rivere, Trans.). London: Hogarth Press. (Original work published 1923.)

Freud, S. (1961). *Civilization and its discontents* (J. Strachey, Trans.). New York: Norton. (Original work published 1930.)

Fromm, E. (1941). *Escape from freedom.* New York: Avon.

Gadamer, H. G. (1975). *Truth and method* [G. Burden and J. Cumming, Trans]. New York: Seabury Press. (Original work published 1960.)

Gilligan, C. (1982). *In a different voice: Psychological theory and women's development.* Cambridge, MA: Harvard University Press.

Giorgi, A. (1970). *Psychology as a human science: A phenomenologically based approach.* New York: Harper & Row.

Hanson, N. R. (1965). *Patterns of discovery.* Cambridge: Cambridge University Press. (Original work published 1958.)

Heron, J. (1971). *Experience and method: An inquiry into the concept of experiential research.* University of Surrey, England, Human Potential Research Project.

Hobbs, D., & Cole, S. (1976). Transition to parenthood: A decade replication. *Journal of Marriage and the Family, 38,* 723–31.

Kaplan, A. (1964). *The conduct of inquiry: Methodology for behavioral science.* San Francisco, CA: Chandler.

Kegan, R. (1982). *The evolving self: Problem and process in human development.* Cambridge MA: Harvard University Press.

Kelly, G. A. (1955). *The psychology of personal constructs.* New York: Norton.

315

Koch, S. (1981). The nature and limits of psychological knowledge: Lessons of a century qua 'science.' *American Psychologist, 36,* 257–69.

Kuhn, T. S. (1970). *The structure of scientific revolutions* (2nd ed.). Chicago: University of Chicago Press. (Original work published 1962.)

Lasch, C. (1984). *The minimal self: Psychic survival in troubled times.* New York: Norton.

Leifer, M. (1977). Psychological changes accompanying pregnancy and motherhood. *Genetic Psychological Monographs, 95,* 55–96.

Lincoln, Y. S., & Guba, E. G. (1985). *Naturalistic inquiry.* Beverly Hills, CA: Sage.

Macmurray, J. (1957). *The self as agent.* London: Faber.

Macmurray, J. (1961). *Persons in relations.* New York: Harper.

Morgan, G. (Ed.) (1983). *Beyond method: Strategies for social research.* Beverly Hills, CA: Sage.

Plas, J. M., & Dokecki, P. R. (1982). Philosophy-based education: A transactional approach. *Professional Psychology, 13,* 279–82.

Polkinghorne, D. (1983). *Methodology for the human sciences: Systems of inquiry.* Albany: State University of New York Press.

Reason, P., & Heron, J. (1986). Research with people: The paradigm of cooperative experiential inquiry. *Person-Centered Review, 1,* 456–76.

Reason, P., & Rowan, J. (1981). Issues of validity in new paradigm research. In P. Reason and J. Rowan (Eds.), *Human inquiry: A sourcebook of new paradigm research* (pp. 239–50). Chichester, England: John Wiley.

Rossi, A. (1968). Transition to parenthood. *Journal of Marriage and the Family, 30,* 26–39.

Russell, C. (1974). Transition to parenthood: Problems and gratifications. *Journal of Marriage and the Family, 36,* 294–302.

Rychlak, J. F. (1981). *Introduction to personality and psychotherapy: A theory-construction approach* (2nd ed.). Boston: Houghton Mifflin.

Tandon, R. (1981). Dialogue as inquiry and intervention. In P. Reason & J. Rowan (Eds.), *Human inquiry: A source book of new paradigm research* (pp. 293–301). Chichester, England: John Wiley.

Toulmin, S. (1960). *The philosophy of science.* New York: Harper & Row. (Original work published 1953.)

Woolfolk, R. L. Sass, L. A., & Messer, S. B. (1988). Introduction to hermeneutics. In S. B. Messer, L. A. Sass, & R. L. Woolfolk (Eds.), *Hermeneutics and psychological theory: Interpretive perspectives on personality, psychotherapy, and psychopathology* (pp. 2–26). New Brunswick, NJ: Rutgers University Press.

A Person-Centered Research Model

Phillip Barrineau   *Pembroke State University*
Jerold D. Bozarth   *University of Georgia*

This article poses the thesis that the core conditions postulated by Rogers (1957) along with the fundamental philosophical position of open inquiry in Person-Centered Therapy are appropriate basic components for qualitative research of a heuristic nature. The article reviews (1) the basic principles of the Person-Centered Approach, (2) heuristic inquiry as a research approach, (3) similarities and differences of the Person-Centered Approach (PCA) and heuristic inquiry, and (4) the qualities and principles of the PCA as a model of heuristic inquiry.

Fueled by a concern that humanistic psychology is having relatively little impact on mainstream psychology, Carl Rogers (1985) sounded a call for a more human science of the person. This article contends that the core conditions postulated by Rogers (1957) as essential to therapeutic personality change, and the fundamental philosophical position of open inquiry in Person-Centered (PC) Therapy can be basic components in qualitative research. As such, the philosophy and principles of the Person-Centered Approach (PCA) are adequate bases for heuristic inquiry. Thus we contend that Rogers not only sounded a call for new approaches to research but, in fact, provided a model for an approach that is consistent with fundamental characteristics of heuristic inquiry. One implication of this model is that qualitative researchers may benefit from developing and fostering the attitudinal qualities Rogers postulated to be necessary and sufficient conditions for therapeutic personality change.

This article will (1) review the basic principles of the Person-Centered Approach, (2) review heuristic inquiry as a research approach, (3) examine the similarities and differences between the PCA and heuristic research, and (4) identify the PCA as a model of heuristic inquiry and note the potential contributions of the person-centered approach to qualitative research.

THE PERSON-CENTERED APPROACH

The PCA in therapy essentially requires a complete dedication of the therapist to the client's world and process. The stance of the approach is open inquiry. Bozarth (1988), after reviewing several studies and the theory of Client-Centered/Person-Centered (CC/PC) Therapy, concludes the following: 'The essence of CC/PC Therapy is the therapist's dedication to going with the client's direction, at the client's pace, and with the client's unique way of being' (p. 1).

A basic definition of Person-Centered Therapy is offered by Bozarth and Schwartz (1988). It is defined as 'a certain psychological climate that is experienced (by the client,

First published in *Person-Centered Review,* Volume 4, Number 4, November 1989.

family, couple) with the locus of control for their own lives belonging to them that the actualizing and formative tendencies are promoted' (p. 1).

In Person-Centered Therapy, the goal of therapy is to create an atmosphere that promotes the client's actualizing tendency. There is no other goal! The therapist's role is that of going with the client's pace, in the client's direction, and in the client's preferred manner. The therapist does this by experiencing and communicating certain attitudinal qualities that create this atmosphere. This process of therapy may be viewed as open inquiry. O'Hara (1986, p. 174) conceptualizes PC therapy as a process of discovery in which 'both therapist and client become engaged in a joint study of the rich and mysterious world of the client. Client-Centered Therapy is, itself, a heuristic investigation into the nature and meaning of human experience.'

HEURISTIC INQUIRY

Webster defines the adjective *heuristic* as 'helping to discover or learn, guiding or furthering investigation.' Douglass and Moustakas (1985) define *heuristics* as 'passionate and personal involvement in problem solving, an effort to know the essence of some aspect of life through the internal pathways of the self.' Thus research that is heuristic is characterized by an exploration for the discovery of the meaning and essence of human experience.

As a qualitative research approach, heuristic inquiry contrasts with quantitative research methods. It is not a substitute for quantitative methods but is a different mode of scientific inquiry. Just as in traditional quantitative research designs, the acquisition of qualitative data requires a disciplined and systematic series of methods and procedures that have been carefully designed to yield information to the researcher. A key difference is that in heuristic inquiry spontaneous creation of new methods or changing methods in midstream is not only allowed, but is encouraged. Douglass and Moustakas (1985, p. 49) point out that 'this license stems from the recognition of the contribution that subjectivity makes to knowledge and from the dynamic nature of subjective reality.'

Further, whereas traditional empirical studies presuppose the actuality of cause/effect relationships, heuristic inquiry seeks to uncover that which is, as it is, so that the object is not to prove or disprove a hypothesis, but to discover the nature of some phenomenon.

> To carry the contrast further, heuristics is concerned with meanings, not measurement; with essence, not appearance; with quality, not quantity; with experience, not behavior. Formal hypotheses play no part, though the researcher may have initial beliefs or convictions regarding the theme or question, based on intuition and on prior knowledge and experience. (Douglass & Moustakas, 1985, p. 42)

Polanyi asserts that scientific knowledge consists of 'discerning Gestalten that are aspects of reality . . . Every interpretation of nature, whether scientific, non-scientific or anti-scientific, is based on some intuitive conception of the general nature of things.'

Rogers (1959) referred to the need for research that would allow for more subjectivity as a vital and central part of a developing philosophy. He applauded new paradigms and methodologies for scientific research. Perhaps the most cogent reason for this type of research was one that 'would keep the scientist as a human being in the picture at all times, and we would recognize that science is but the lengthened shadow of dedicated beings' (Rogers, 1968).

Qualitative research is a tradition of inquiry that comes primarily from the anthropological and sociological tradition. Kirk and Miller (1986, p. 12) summarize qualitative research as involving 'sustained interaction with the people being studied in their own language, and on their own turf.'

A seminal study in heuristic research is Moustakas' (1961) study of loneliness. The study is rooted in a life experience of the author who was making a decision whether or not to elect heart surgery for his daughter. Douglass and Moustakas (1985) assert that the power of heuristic inquiry is in its potential for disclosing truth. Since his focus was to know as fully as possible the truth of the phenomenon of loneliness, his decision was to become steeped 'in a world of loneliness, letting my life take root and unfold in it, letting its dimensions and meanings and forms evolve its own timetable and dynamics' (p. 40).

HEURISTIC INQUIRY AND THE PERSON-CENTERED APPROACH: SIMILARITIES AND DIFFERENCES

The essential similarity of the Person-Centered Approach and heuristic inquiry is that the intention of each is to create an atmosphere of open inquiry. As noted, O'Hara (1986) identifies the person-centered therapeutic approach as being heuristic inquiry. The inquiry is 'open' inasmuch as it includes no presupposition or expectations about the inner world or meaning or experience of the client. The therapist in the process is open to the discovery of the world of the data experienced subjectively and honestly. As Douglass and Moustakas (1985, p. 48) further suggest: 'Immersion of this kind is more impulsive than deliberate, more a wandering than a goal, more a way of being than a method of doing.'

The difference between therapy and heuristic research of the person-centered model is a moot one. The model, for therapy, promotes the actualizing tendency. The model, for research, promotes the same process that includes, for the participant, clarity of discourse. Person-Centered research in this tradition is likely to be therapeutic for subjects. Person-Centered therapy in this tradition opens the way for increased understanding of oneself and life phenomena.

Specific therapist behaviors may differ from specific researcher behaviors in idiosyncratic ways with particular clients or particular 'subjects.' The foundations for both are in the existence and communication of the attitudinal qualities (of either the therapist or researcher) within the particular context. The expectations of a client in therapy usually may be different in that the intention is, in some way, to grow. The research participant does not usually have this intention. However, the therapist and researcher are, in terms of the model, doing the same thing by creating the facilitative atmosphere with the particular individual. The specific involvements of either the therapist or the researcher depend upon the particular client or research participant.

The major difference between the therapeutic and research intentions come after the gathering of 'data.' The therapist generally does nothing with the data and is dedicated to fostering the continuation of the client's actualizing process. The researcher generally undertakes the task of placing the data in some form to begin to derive meaning from it. Various methods of coding and analysis that are prominent in the qualitative research literature are used and employed in heuristic research.

For example, Moustakas' study (1981) began with inner, subjective musings that propelled him ultimately to a systematic and definitive exposition of loneliness. Initially, he interviewed hospitalized children to gain a sense of their experience of loneliness. His focus was on listening objectively, without making any kind of record. Objectivity, writes Moustakas (1981, p. 67), consists in seeing what an experience is for another person, not what causes it, not why it exists, not how it can be defined and classified. It means seeing attitudes, beliefs, and feelings of the person as they exist for him at the moment he is experiencing them, perceiving them whole, as a unity.

Further, Moustakas read and listened to school children's accounts of their experiences of loneliness. He interviewed parents, young adults, and colleagues to gain a sense of their experiences. Finally, he read any published reports on loneliness, and studied the biographies and autobiographies of people known to have experienced loneliness, including Emily Dickinson and Abraham Lincoln. The literature on loneliness was included near the end of the study, so as not to predispose or predetermine the researcher's growing awareness. In short, Moustakas immersed himself in the world of his investigation in much the same way person-centered therapists immerse themselves in the world of their clients.

Bozarth and Mitchell (1984) contend that the person-centered therapist approaches the client with no preconceived suppositions of what the client may do or become in therapy in any specific sense. The therapist does not have specific outcome or process goals for the client in person-centered therapy. The therapist's goal is to create an atmosphere, which then promotes the ongoing, natural growth tendency. The atmosphere that the person-centered therapist attempts to create is a nonthreatening one of open inquiry. In person-centered therapy, the therapist's embodiment of the attitudinal conditions of empathy, genuineness, and unconditional positive regard, along with disciplined attention to the clients' experiential worlds are considered to be the conditions that are necessary and sufficient for client personality growth. Similarly, these attitudinal conditions create the atmosphere for open inquiry critical for heuristic research. Definitions of the attitudinal values as they apply to therapy and to research are as follows:

Genuineness refers to the therapist or investigator being a real person who is not playing a role. In therapy and research, this augments the relationship and enhances open responsiveness. The therapist as investigator is 'a congruent, genuine, and integrated person. It means that within the relationship he is freely and deeply himself, with his actual experience accurately represented by his awareness of himself' (Rogers, 1957, p. 97).

Unconditional positive regard refers to the prizing of the client (or subject) in a way that the person is free to 'be whatever immediate feeling is going on — confusion, resentment, fear, anger, love, or pride. Such caring on the part of the therapist is nonpossessive' (Rogers, 1980, p. 116). The researcher holds this attitude toward the subject and the data. Subjects are totally affirmed in this way, which frees them to present the truest data. This attitude of unconditional positive regard may be held regarding the data per se. That is, the data related to the phenomenon are allowed to be, to unfold, and to evolve in empirical reality and in the growing experience of the researcher.

Empathy refers to the understanding of the person's world as if the therapist (or researcher) were the other person. The biases and views of the empathizer are virtually eliminated with this stance. In therapy, such understanding promotes growth. In research, it promotes the ideal climate for open inquiry.

The therapist's philosophy of following the direction, pace, and being of the client while embodying these core attitudinal values are likewise related to heuristic inquiry as expressed by Douglass and Moustakas (1985). They suggested that the challenge is

to examine all the collected data in creative combinations and recombinations, sifting and sorting, moving rhythmically in and out of appearance, looking, listening carefully for the meanings within meanings, attempting to identify the overarching qualities that inhere in the data. (p. 52)

Conceptually, heuristic inquiry offers an attitude with which to approach research, but does not provide a particular methodology. Moustakas' study may be best viewed as an example of heuristic research, and while the work done to date does suggest a series of inquiry processes 'each heuristic study is a unique, creative challenge aimed at revealing the intimate nature of reality and thus requiring methods that fit the particular investigation' (Douglass and Moustakas, 1985, p. 42).

The similarities of application between the person-centered therapist and the heuristic researcher are obvious. There are few differences in the fundamental stance of the therapist and researcher. The stance of the researcher is an empathic attitude accompanied with the attitudinal values of genuineness and unconditional positive regard that are the core of person-centered therapy; and the focus is on allowing the data to emerge as the natural expression of the phenomena to be studied.

THE PERSON-CENTERED RESEARCH MODEL

It is the development of the person-centered attitudinal qualities that enables an individual's actualizing tendency to be promoted. Methods and techniques are secondary since the development of these attitudes are reflective of the basic philosophy of open inquiry. In therapy, this philosophy is manifested by the therapist's lack of presuppositions regarding what the client might do, be, or become. Likewise, heuristic inquiry requires that the investigator be capable of holding an attitude that does not presuppose the nature of the data or findings. It is the discipline and dedication of the investigator to finding the truth, rather than external rules and methods of control for objectivity espoused by the scientific method. The manner in which person-centered therapists are prepared is an equally valid approach for the preparation of heuristic investigators. When the investigator can embody the attitudinal qualities in a manner similar to the person-centered therapist, the unfolding process is most apt to occur.

The person-centered research model, then, focuses on the attitudinal values of the researcher in the way that person-centered therapy focuses on the attitudinal values of the therapist. These values are the critical bases for acquiring emerging data. As such, person-centered researchers value the discipline of divesting themselves of personal beliefs and biases in order to attend to the always new, emerging world of the their 'subjects.' The researcher provides total attention to the person's world with complete receptivity of perceptions, feelings, cognition, and being of the person. Some guidelines for the person-centered researcher include the following:
- embodying oneself as much as possible in the attitudinal qualities of genuineness, unconditional positive regard, and empathy
- working toward freeing oneself of presuppositions about the individuals or phenomenon being investigated
- striving toward total attention and receptivity to these individuals or phenomena
- focusing on understanding the person's world (including feelings, cognition, and meanings) and testing these understandings

CONCLUSION

The person-centered research model is a functional model for allowing the material to find its own patterning. This method actually underlies all phenomenological research. A major addition of the person-centered research model is that there is a more determined emphasis on the importance of the attitudes and stance of the investigator.

It is thus our contention that Carl Rogers did more than just sound a call for a more human science of the person. He also provided, through his basic hypotheses about constructive therapy, a model that readily lends itself to heuristic inquiry, and offers a dimension seldom considered in qualitative research. Namely, the attitudes of the researchers as those experiencing unconditional positive regard and empathic understanding while being genuine human beings can be an important contribution in such inquiry.

REFERENCES

Bozarth, J. D. (1988, September). The essence of the client-centered approach. Paper presented at the Client-Centered and Experiential Therapy Conference, Leuven, Belgium.

Bozarth, J. D., & Mitchell, S. (1984). Functional dimensions of the person-centered approach. *Renaissance* 1(1), 1–3.

Bozarth, J. D., & Schwartz, A. (1988, May). The family way. Paper presented at the meeting of the Association for the Development of Person-Centered Approach, New York.

Douglass, B. G., & Moustakas, C. (1985). Heuristic inquiry: The search to know. *Journal of Humanistic Psychology* 25(3), 39–54.

Kirk, J., & Miller, M. L. (1986). *Reliability and validity in qualitative research. Qualitative Research Methods, Series 1.* Beverly Hills, CA: Sage.

Moustakas, C. (1961). *Loneliness.* Englewood Cliffs, NJ: Prentice-Hall.

Moustakas, C. (1981). Heuristic research. In P. Reason & J. Rowan (Eds.), *Human inquiry: A source book of new paradigm research.* Chichester, England: John Wiley.

O'Hara, M. (1986). Heuristic inquiry as psychotherapy. *Person-Centered Review, 1*(2), 172–84.

Rogers, C. R. (1957). The necessary and sufficient conditions of therapeutic personality change. *Journal of Consulting Psychology* 21(2), 95–103.

Rogers, C. R. (1959). A theory of therapy, personality and interpersonal relationships as developed in the client-centered framework. In S. Koch (Ed.), *Psychology: A study of a science* (Vol. 3; pp. 184–256). New York: McGraw-Hill.

Rogers, C. R. (1968). Some thoughts regarding the current assumptions of the behavioral sciences. In W. Coulson & C. R. Rogers (Eds.), *Man and the science of man.* Columbus, OH: Charles Merrill.

Rogers, C. R. (1980). *A way of being.* Boston: Houghton Mifflin.

Rogers, C. R. (1985). Toward a more human science of the person. *Journal of Humanistic Psychology* 25(4), 7–22.

Can there be a Human Science?
Constructivism as an alternative

Egon G. Guba   *Indiana University*
Yvonna S. Lincoln   *Vanderbilt University*

Conventional science cannot qualify as a *human* science because it is tied to an inquiry paradigm — positivism — that is not resonant with the character of humans as entities to be studied. This article examines three alternative paradigms — post-positivism, critical theory, and constructivism — that currently are providing strong challenges, and makes the case that constructivism is the most viable of these. The grounds for this assertion are that constructivism restores humans to the center of the inquiry process, is educative to all participants, tilts the inquirer toward ethical behavior, provides a new perspective on the change process, is empowering and emancipatory, rescinds the special privilege of science, and emulates the emergent paradigm in the 'hard' sciences.

The proposition that science, as conventionally practiced, is not resonant with the character of humans as entities-to-be-studied seems beyond debate. It ignores the strong possibility that humans are unlike the many other objects which science studies. It overlooks uniquely human qualities. While stressing reason and logic, it not only downplays the emotional, valuational, ethical, and relational aspects of humans, but it literally declares them to be *inimical* to the aim of science to discover how things 'really are' and how they 'really work.'

In his provocative book, *Paradigms Lost,* John L. Casti (1989) raises the question, 'Are humans really something special?' He examines this question from six major perspectives (pp. 492 ff.):

1. *Origins of life.* Chemical and biological evidence suggests, Casti concludes, that the emergence of life is a unique phenomenon with virtually zero probability of being repeated.
2. *Sociobiology.* Although the evidence is not conclusive, Casti opines that 'human behavioral repertoires could very well be special, differing in essential ways from the basically genetic determination of other living things.'
3. *Language acquisition.* Casti comes down squarely in support of Chomsky's assertion that humans are possessed of a special language acquisition 'device.'
4. *Artificial intelligence.* While recognizing that his reading of the evidence in this arena runs counter to his interpretation in the other arenas, Casti argues that he finds 'no essential contradiction in thinking that perhaps a genuine thinking machine is yet a possibility.'
5. *Extraterrestrial intelligence.* Casti comes to the 'sad conclusion that we probably are alone, at least in the galaxy . . . and very likely . . . in the universe as well. So on the strength of these . . . considerations, humans again start looking like something very special indeed.'
6. *Quantum reality.* While noting that there are no compelling grounds for accepting any

First published in *Person-Centered Review,* Volume 5, Number 2, May 1990.

ontological position on reality, Casti concludes that 'a variety of aesthetic considerations make it at least plausible, if not desirable, to lean toward the romantics [those who believe a human presence is necessary to bring reality into existence], thereby thrusting mankind into the role of creator as well as observer and participant.'

Casti concludes:

> To my eye, the overall conclusion is that *homo sapiens* is a very special creature, at least here on earth, and maybe in the universe as a whole. While it may not yet be a conclusion to bet your pension on, I think the odds favoring our uniqueness are high enough that my bookie would tell me, 'Off the board, doc.' (p. 497)

If Casti is right, and we believe he is, the question we wish to raise is whether conventional science is the appropriate process to use in the study of humans. Obviously, the answer to that question depends on what one means by science. We undertake in this article to define *science* as our effort to know. Conventionally, we shall argue, science has assumed the form of positivism, a posture now hardly tenable to anyone, as we shall show. Positivism is being challenged by a variety of alternative approaches, which we shall characterize as falling into three broad schools: post-positivism, critical theory, and constructivism. It shall be our claim that of these alternatives, constructivism comes closest to producing knowledge (constructions) that is resonant with humans qua humans rather than as objects.

BASIC BELIEF SYSTEMS

Science, in all its forms, is concerned with coming to know. Historically, philosophers concerned with knowing have found it necessary to ask three fundamental and interrelated questions: (a) What is there that can be known? (b) What is the relationship between the knower and the known? and (c) How can one go about finding out? These three questions may be termed, respectively, the *ontological,* the *epistemological,* and the *methodological* questions. The answers that are given to these three questions may be termed, as sets, 'basic belief systems.' These are the starting points, or givens, that determine what inquiry is and how it should be practiced. They cannot be proven or disproven, any more than, say, one religion or one system of jurisprudence can ultimately be shown to be better than another. If it were possible to demonstrate, let us say, that Papal pronouncements and the Bible are equally valid sources of divine revelation, the distinction between Catholics and Protestants would have disappeared long ago. If it could be demonstrated that presuming innocence of an accused until he or she were proven guilty, as in Anglo-Saxon common law, was preferable to presuming guilt until proven innocent, as in the Napoleonic Code, all countries would be practicing before the bar in identical ways. If it could be demonstrated that one ontological/epistemological/methodological belief system were superior to all others in some ultimate (let us say, foundational) sense, there would be no doubt about how to practice science.

But the rules of science are human constructions. Despite the apocryphal tale that Moses actually carried *three* tablets down the mountain but broke one *en route* — unfortunately, the one that prescribed science as *the* way to determine truth — it is nevertheless the case that the means we have devised to guide our forays into knowledge are *human inventions,* subject to all the foibles and errors that inevitably accompany human endeavors.

There are certainly many different ways in which to define basic belief systems, that is, to answer the three fundamental questions. That assertion might be primarily of academic interest, however, were it not for the fact that *every aspect of our humanness is touched by our preferred definition.* Parker J. Palmer (1987) has noted that:

> My thesis is a very simple one. I do not believe that epistemology is a bloodless abstraction; the *way* we know has powerful implications for the *way* we live. I argue that every epistemology tends to become an ethic, and that every way of knowing tends to become a way of living. I argue that the relation established between the knower and the known . . . tends to become the relation of the living person to the world itself. I argue that every mode of knowing contains its own moral trajectory, its own ethical directions and outcomes. (p. 22)

While Palmer's comments are directed specifically at the epistemological question, it is clear that they apply equally well to the ontological and methodological questions. These questions are intimately related: a given epistemology implies a parallel ontology while leading logically and inevitably to a resonant methodology. The *entire belief system* constitutes not only a way to pursue knowledge but also an ethic and a way of living.

THE BASIC SYSTEM (PARADIGM) OF CONVENTIONAL (POSITIVIST) SCIENCE

Historically, there have been many different ways to define basic belief systems (Lincoln & Guba, 1985). But it is only since the time of Descartes (1596–1650) that science can be said to approximate its recent, conventional form. Descartes was obsessed by the fear that he might be gulled into believing things that were not certainly true. His search for a sure foundation is legendary, culminating in the only proposition he could make to himself of which he was utterly convinced: *Cogito, ergo sum* – I think, therefore I am. His overriding concern with certain or foundational knowledge has come to be called *Cartesian anxiety,* a dis-ease that is still reflected today by the continuing search to find out 'how things *really* are' and 'how things *really* work.'

Those latter phrases, it should be noted, are ontological creeds. The basic belief system of modern science, especially of the last 200 years, is rooted in a *realist ontology,* that is, in the belief that there exists a reality *out there,* driven by natural and immutable laws, irrespective of the notice that any human may take. The business of science, then, is to discover the 'true' nature of reality and of how it 'truly' works. The ultimate criterion of science's success is its ability *to predict and control* those natural phenomena (presumably with humankind's best interests in mind). To predict and control implies knowledge of the putative causal mechanisms, often metaphorically understood to be machine-like in nature (e.g., Isaac Newton's 'great clockwork in the sky' – planetary motion). A realist ontology thus implies the existence of underlying causal linkages, whose operations are time- and context-free, described as scientific generalizations.

Once committed to a realist ontology, the conventional scientist is constrained to an *objectivist epistemology.* The relationship between knower and known must be circumspect, lest, on the one hand, Nature's operations are adversely influenced by the inquirer's efforts to pry loose her secrets, or, on the other hand, the inquirer's observations and subsequent interpretations are unduly influenced by either Nature's confounding ways or by rampant subjectivity; that is, the inquirer's own preconceptions and biases (note how those terms can have meaning only within a realist ontology). Objectivity is the 'Archimedean point' (Archimedes, having articulated the law of the lever, is said to have boasted that given a long enough lever and a place whereon to stand, he could move the earth) that permits the scientist to wrest Nature's secrets without altering them in any way; he or she can discover 'how things really are' and 'how things really work.' The inquirer, so to speak, can stand behind a thick wall of one-way glass and observe Nature as 'she does her thing.'

But how is that possible? How can one go about finding out things if committed to a realist ontology and an objectivist epistemology? The answer, the conventionalist responds, lies in the use of an appropriate *methodology: experimentalism* (manipulation). Experimentalism in this sense means more than just laboratory work; it means positing propositions based on what is already known or can be additionally hypothesized (usually derivative from an a priori theory), and subjecting those propositions to empirical tests (falsification) under the most careful control that can be managed (usually less than ideal). Those tests involve manipulations in order to set up the required experimental conditions ('treatments'); such manipulations, even if requiring deception, are necessary in order to lead the inquirer to some 'higher truth' or to serve some 'greater social good.'

We may thus summarize conventional science's (positivism's) basic belief system (paradigm) as follows:

Ontology: Realist. Reality exists 'out there' and is driven by immutable natural laws and mechanisms. Our knowledge of these entities, laws and mechanisms is conventionally summarized in the form of time- and context-free generalizations. Some of these generalizations take the form of cause-effect laws.

Epistemology: Dualist/objectivist. It is both possible and essential for the observer to adopt a distant, noninteractive posture that facilitates 'putting questions directly to nature and getting nature's answers directly back.' Values, whether those of the inquirer or anyone else, are automatically excluded from exerting influence on outcomes.

Methodology: Experimental/manipulative. Questions and/or hypotheses are stated in advance in propositional form and subjected to empirical test (falsification) under carefully controlled conditions, to prevent bias or confounding.

There are many ways in which this belief system can be undermined; we shall review three major schools of thought on that subject momentarily. But it may be appropriate, before turning to that task, to ask why conventional science is so often seen as an inappropriate approach by those who are interested in developing a *human* science.

Given the belief system described above, we may point to the following disabling characteristics.

Its absolutist character

Within the conventional paradigm, any proposition *must be true* if correspondence exists between the proposition and that aspect of reality which it is intended to describe (or predict or control). That is, there must be correspondence between the theoretical language in which the proposition is couched and the observational language in which data are collected. When science has established such a truth, it is incumbent upon everyone to believe it. Hannah Arendt (1963) has commented on the *coercive* nature of putative truth. What is so is so, and what is not is not. Human judgment and experience play no role; the data 'speak for themselves.'

Its objectivist character

Within the conventional paradigm, all entities that may be studied are defined as objects, *including humans.* All such objects obey certain natural laws and are determined by them. Human behavior is reduced to the same level as animal behavior, or indeed, even inanimate 'behavior,' such as the behavior of a flying projectile. This deterministic, reductionist posture must be repugnant to anyone who considers humans to be in any way 'special'; it certainly flies in the face of the human experience of free will.

Its disempowering character

Within the conventional paradigm, it is solely the inquirer's province to decide about the propositions to be studied and the methodology by which to study them. The propositions emerge from the interests of the inquirer (who is pursuing the next aggregatable 'chunk' of truth, identified as accessible on theoretical or substantive grounds), while the methodology is chosen in ways that ensure the 'technical adequacy' of the study (read: makes it impervious to critique from the inquirer's peer group). Such an approach exploits the 'subjects' and subverts their interests to those of the inquirer. It ignores any inputs from the humans involved, either on the grounds of their substantive irrelevance (the questions and/or hypotheses have, after all, already been articulated) or because of threats they may pose to technical adequacy. Such inquiry tends to maintain the status quo, since the questions and/or hypotheses are generated by the inquirer, and his or her funders, sponsors, dissertation committees, and other authority figures, who pursue only those things relevant to their already existing, etic constructions. Persons with alternative views (including, we note with some irony, those who challenge the conventional paradigm of inquiry) are routinely shunted aside.

Its unethical character

The belief in some ultimate or final truth (or some foundational way to judge the quality of inquiries) is a powerful warrant to engage in unethical practices. For example, it may be judged appropriate to engage in deceptive research on the grounds that deception is warranted for the sake of discovering some 'higher truth' or achieving some 'higher social good.' Moreover, the findings of scientific inquiries take on the character of norms; by a curious twist, the outputs of a putatively value-free inquiry mode become, themselves, values that have all the sanction and authority that science parades in Western culture. The manipulative character of conventional methodology denies the right of individuals to choose their own fates — the myth of 'fully informed consent' notwithstanding. And, of course, the firm belief in cause-effect chains makes it possible to assign culpability or blame (usually under the guise of 'accountability') to politically weaker persons in the context, while protecting both the inquirer and his or her sponsors/funders, who stand aside in their objective postures.

These four characterizations of the conventional, positivist paradigm are more than sufficient to uphold our claim that it is totally deficient as a model for the conduct of human inquiry. It denies personhood in a multitude of ways and is dissonant with human qualities. But, it should be noted, its dissonance with personhood is not the only reason for arguing that positivism is an obsolete paradigm. We turn now to an examination of some alternative paradigms currently being proposed. We shall keep paramount, however, the question of which of these emergent alternatives is most resonant with personhood.

Some alternatives to the conventional (positivist) paradigm: post-positivism, critical theory and constructivism

We believe that the variety of emergent paradigms currently challenging conventional positivism can conveniently be subsumed under three broad headings: post-positivism, critical theory, and constructivism. While adherents of these alternatives are united in what they oppose, they are divided in what they espouse. Each camp sees certain problems with positivism, and proposes countermeasures that sometimes eliminate, but at least ameliorate, the problems they identify. We consider each in turn:

Post-positivism

The critics who may be subsumed under this label (a heterogeneous category indeed) believe that the conventional paradigm suffers from certain imbalances that must be redressed to make positivism serviceable again — albeit in new clothes. Essentially, these imbalances, not all of which are identified by every post-positivist, are these:

That between rigor and relevance. The concern with laboratory-like control in order to ensure what is commonly called 'internal validity' has virtually destroyed external validity or generalizability. Laboratory results can, strictly speaking, be generalized only to another laboratory. To redress this imbalance, it is proposed to eliminate such 'context-stripping' by carrying out inquiry in 'natural settings.' Ecological psychology is a type case (Barker & Associates, 1978).

That between objectivity and subjectivity. In an effort to restore some humanness to inquiry, to acknowledge the impossibility of a detached stance for the inquirer, and to grant license for use of the 'human instrument,' it is proposed that more qualitative rather than quantitative (intersubjective reliability) measures of objectivity be used (Scriven, 1971), or that an 'objectivity/subjectivity' continuum be defined that affords the inquirer the opportunity to 'move back and forth' between 'poles' (Reason & Rowan, 1981).

That between precision and richness. Precision is critical to a science that defines its major goal as the ability to predict and control. Moreover, that the resulting press for precision should lead quickly to an emphasis on quantitative methods — that epitome of precision — is not surprising. Post-positivists propose to redress this imbalance by including more qualitative methods (or, if one chooses, more ethnographic, phenomenological, or case-study methods). Proposals by Patton (1982) and Miles and Huberman (1984) are examples. *It should be noted that much of the current agitation for the qualitative paradigm does not touch the paradigm level of discourse at all. it is simply a reflection of the effort to redress this imbalance.*

That between elegance and applicability. The need to formulate a priori propositions or questions require that the inquiry begin with an overall theory, or at least some form of logical structure, that provides the rationale. Simultaneously, the interest in providing very broadly based (reductionist?) generalizations has furnished an impetus for 'grand' theory. But such broad theories (and at times their junior-grade versions, 'middle-range theories'), while abetting generalizability, have often not been found to 'fit' or 'work' in local contexts. Locality and specificity are incommensurable with generalizability. The proposed solution: 'ground' theory in local circumstances (i.e., conduct the inquiry so that theory is the *product* rather than the *precursor* of the inquiry). The pre-eminent example is the work of Glaser and Strauss (Glaser & Strauss, 1967; Glaser, 1978).

That between discovery and verification. Discovery, that is, the process by which a priori theories and their implied hypotheses and questions emerge, is not a formal part of the conventional paradigm. Discovery is a precursor, it is claimed, rather than an integral part of the scientific process, whose major (only?) component is verification (falsification?). Virtually all of Einstein's work, based as it is on 'mental experiments' ('gedankenexperimente') would not qualify under this distinction as science. Such a posture is increasingly seen as absurd. The solution: define a continuum of inquiry ranging from discovery at one end to verification at the other (Kennedy, 1985), with any given inquiry occupying some point along that continuum

.

These are laudable accommodations indeed, and there is hardly a scientist to be found (excluding proponents of other alternatives) who would not place himself or herself in this post-positivist camp, rather than in the positivist camp. But it must be clear that these adjustments, or redressings of imbalances, constitute little more than *damage control,* to appropriate a naval term. *The basic belief system is touched hardly at all.* While post-positivists no longer espouse what has now come to be called 'naive realism,' they continue to use labels such as 'critical realism.' The concession does *not* abandon the notion of an objective, foundational reality, but rather argues that reality can never be 'fully known.' While post-positivists no longer argue that it is possible to achieve ideal objectivity, they continue to assert that one can work at it through devices such as self-revelation ('coming clean'), the critical tradition (the literature), the critical community (are journal editors and referees appropriately critical?), or meta-analysis. Post-positivists continue to assert that manipulative experimentalism remains the ideal inquiry form, conceding only that adjustments must be made (e.g., quasi-experiments) because of real-world constraints (social, political, ethical, legal, and the like). Fundamentally, post-positivism is no more satisfactory as a human science than is conventional positivism. It remains absolutist, objectivist, disempowering, and unethical to virtually the same degree as its logical predecessor.

Critical theory

The label *critical theory* is undoubtedly inadequate to encompass all of the alternatives that we have swept into this category. Perhaps a more appropriate label would be 'ideologically oriented inquiry,' for we mean to include perspectives such as neo-Marxism, materialism, feminism, Freireism, participatory inquiry, and other similar movements, as well as critical theory itself. We believe it appropriate to place these seemingly disparate approaches into a single category, however, because they converge in rejecting the putative claim of value-freedom made by positivists (and largely continuing to be made by post-positivists).

Values, proponents of this position argue, permeate every paradigm that has ever been or will ever be proposed. As human constructions, paradigms cannot be impervious to the influence of human values. Values enter into the inquiry at such points as the choice of problem selected for study, the choice of paradigm within which to carry out the study, the choice of instrumental and analytic modes, the choice of interpretations to be made, and the choice of the conclusions to be drawn or recommendations to be made. Nature, they say, cannot be seen as it 'really is' or 'really works' but only as constructed through some 'value window.'

Now, if values *do* enter into inquiry (and the evidence on that point seems incontrovertible), then the question of what values and whose values enter becomes paramount. If the findings of studies can vary as a function of the value system brought to bear, then the arbitrary choice of a particular value system tends to empower certain persons and to disempower or disenfranchise others. It is for this reason that the conventional paradigm is often labeled as an 'instrument of the status quo,' or worse, as an instrument of oppression. If these critiques are taken seriously, as we believe they must be, then the conventional mode of inquiry is as much a *political* act as any act can be. To accept this position is to reject the claim of value-freedom, and to redefine the doing of inquiry to account for the possibility that values can and do influence findings and interpretations.

Given this radical posture, one would expect critical theorists (and the other ideologues in this group) to reject the idea of a dualist, objectivist epistemology, and indeed, they do. But one would equally expect that, as a result of this dramatic epistemological reorientation, proponents of this position would also reject a realist ontology. For if there is a *real* state-of-affairs, then it seems unreasonable to argue that the value positions which inquirers — or anyone else — might take could influence that reality. A *real* reality requires an objective epistemological stance to ferret it out. Here the critical theorists fail us.

That there is adherence to the idea of an objective reality is easily inferred from the phrase commonly heard among critical theorists: 'false consciousness.' The task of inquiry is, by definition, to raise people to a level of 'true' consciousness so that they can appreciate how oppressed they are, and by what means, so that they can then *transform* the world to their greater satisfaction. The close relationship between the goal of *transforming* the world, on the one hand, and *predicting and controlling* it, on the other, should not be lost on us.

Thus we are confronted with a logical disjunction: a *realist* (albeit critical realist?) ontology joined to a *monist, subjectivist* epistemology. There is surely little argument from us that the move to a subjectivist epistemology represents a forward-looking and useful step, but so long as that epistemology is enlisted in the service of a realist ontology, it seems to lose much of its force, perhaps even its *raison d'être.*

At the methodological end of the belief system, critical theorists seem more consistent. If the aim of inquiry is to transform the (real) world by raising the consciousness of the participants so that they are energized and facilitated toward transformation, then something other than an experimental, manipulative methodology is required. Critical theorists take a dialogic approach that seeks to eliminate false consciousness and rally participants around a common (true?) point of view. In this process, features of the real world are apprehended and judgments are made about which of them can be altered. The result of effective action is transformation.

We may summarize the basic belief system of this critical theory (or more broadly, ideological) belief system as follows:

Ontology: Realist (albeit critical realist)
Epistemology: Monist, subjectivist
Methodology: Dialogic, transformative

There is no doubt in our minds that this formulation is superior to that of either positivism or post-positivism. It suffers, we believe, from the logical disjunction we have pointed to: Realist ontologies and subjectivist epistemologies seem illogically connected. But more seriously, it fails (as does post-positivism) to take account of certain problems of positivism that are so pervasive as to require, we believe, abandoning that paradigm altogether. We turn now to an alternative that takes this stance. As the reader will have surmised, it is the alternative we favor.

Constructivism

It is our belief that proponents of both the post-positivist and critical theory (ideological) positions feel that, given the reforms they propose, there can be an accommodation between their positions and conventional positivism. Constructivists, on the other hand, feel that the positivist paradigm is fatally flawed and must be entirely replaced. Among the more telling arguments they bring to bear are these; they are short-handed here, but available in much extended form in Lincoln and Guba (1985) and Guba and Lincoln (1989):

The theory-ladenness of facts

It is now well established that it is *not* possible 'to put questions directly to Nature and get Nature's answers directly back.' Theoretical and observational languages are *not* independent. If empirical tests are to have any ultimate meaning as arbiters of propositions (questions and hypotheses) put to Nature by human inquirers, it must be possible to phrase those propositions in ways that cannot influence the empirical observation. The 'facts' that are collected must be independent of the propositional statements (and of the theory that espouses them) if the test is to be valid. However, philosophers of science now uniformly believe that facts are facts *only within* some theoretical framework (Hesse, 1980). The positivist paradigm thus loses its rationale for claiming to be able to produce findings that represent nature as it 'really is and really works.'

There seems to be two possible responses to this dilemma. One can argue that reality does exist but that human inquirers will never be able to comprehend it 'fully.' Or, one can argue that no ultimate reality exists in the first place. The former position is widely espoused by post-positivists and critical theorists; the latter is the ontological bastion of constructivism.

The under-determination of theory

Even if it could be argued that facts and theories are independent (but the weight of the evidence is preponderantly against that assertion, as we have just seen), no theory can ever be fully tested because of what is often called 'the problem of induction.' As is now well understood, the fact that we have examined a million swans and found them all to be white is nothing more than a probabalistic argument for the proposition, 'All swans are white.' The fact that research has validated a million propositions derived from a given theory is no ultimate proof for the theory's validity. Given a body of 'facts' (tested propositions) to be explained, there is always a large number of theories that will explain those facts equally well. No matter how far it may go, inquiry will never be able to establish unequivocally a given explanation (theory) as ultimately true. There are again two possible responses: continue pushing anyway, so that we can approach the 'barrier of ignorance' as closely as possible, believing that then we will not have missed the truth by much; or accept the fact of multiple interpretations and see the major task of inquiry to be a working toward some consensus among the holders of different constructions. The former position is widely held by post-positivists; the latter is the challenge of constructivism.

The value-ladenness of facts

We need not repeat again the argument already made, in the case of critical theory, for the value-dependence of inquiry carried out by human agents. The position taken by constructivists is exactly parallel to that taken with respect to theory-ladenness. If reality can be apprehended only through a theory window, it is equally apprehendable only through a value window. Again one must choose between the two horns of a dilemma: settling for 'in-principle' less-than-full knowledge, or denying the existence of an objective reality.

The interactive nature of the inquirer/inquired-into dyad

Virtually everyone would now agree that the ideal objective relationship between the inquirer and the object of inquiry (if the 'object' is a human being, we prefer the term *respondent)* is not attainable: there is no Archimedean point. This fact has been apprehended in the so-called hard sciences for almost all of this century, but seems to be making considerably less headway in the social sciences. Before 1930, the Heisenberg Uncertainty Principle and Bohr's Complementarity Principle had made it plain to physicists that objectivism was dead. The well-known particle physicist John Wheeler has noted,

> May the universe in some strange sense be 'brought into being' by the participation of those who participate? . . . The vital act is the act of participation. 'Participator' is the incontrovertible new concept given by quantum mechanics. It strikes down the term 'observer' of classical theory, the man who stands behind the thick glass wall and watches what goes on without taking part. It can't be done, quantum mechanics notes. (Cited in Zukav, 1979, p. 29)

The scientific community is now almost entirely supportive of what is, by now, and 'old, new' view. And if there is such an intimate interconnectedness between inquirer and inquired-into in the physical sciences (not called 'hard' for nothing), how much more likely is it that inter-connectedness also works to shape social inquiry, in which the inquired-into is always either one or more humans or one or more of their human characteristics? The well-known phenomenon of so-called reactivity in human research is but the nose of the camel!

This problem of interaction is, we think, especially devastating to positivism. First, it renders the historical distinction between ontology and epistemology obsolete; what can be known and the individual who comes to know it are fused into a single, coherent whole. Second, it makes the outcomes or findings of an inquiry not a report of what is 'out there,' but the residue of a process that *literally creates them* as it proceeds, depending on the particular time, place, circumstances, and persons involved (the creators). Third, it depicts knowledge as the outcome, residue, or consequence of *human* activity; knowledge is a *human construction,* never certifiable as absolutely or ultimately true, but problematic and ever-changing.

Given this critique, we hope it is apparent why constructivists feel that what is needed is to create an entirely new belief system or paradigm, one radically different from conventional science or positivism. Ontologically, if the constructivist argues that there are always many formulations and interpretations — constructions — that exist in any inquiry situation — and further argues that there is no foundational process by which the truth or falsity of these several constructions can *finally* be determined (note that we do not rule out *provisional* determination; that topic is beyond the scope of this paper, however) — then there seems to be no viable alternative to taking a position of *relativism.* The constructivist does not *deplore* relativism, for we are not dealing here with either an immobilizing radical skepticism or an anarchic 'anything goes' posture. Instead, the constructivist *celebrates* relativism, because it is the key to openness and the continuing search for ever more informed and sophisticated constructions: the multiple mental realities formed in individual minds.

Epistemologically, if the constructivist argues that the outcomes of any inquiry are a literal creation stemming from the interaction between inquirer and inquired-into, then there is no viable alternative to taking a *subjectivist* position. Note that the constructivist does not *deplore* subjectivity (in the manner of post-positivists) but instead *celebrates* it, because it is the key to unlocking the constructions held by persons in the context of interest. If realities exist only in respondents' minds, subjective interaction with them seems to be the only way to tease them out.

If the constructivist operates from the above ontological and epistemological presuppositions, then, methodologically, constructivist inquiry must take the form of determining the variety of constructions that exist and bringing them into as much consensus as possible. There are two aspects in this process: hermeneutics and dialectics. The hermeneutic aspect consists in depicting each individual construction as accurately as possible (the degree of accuracy to be judged by the respondent, not the inquirer); that is to say, individual *emic* or insider constructions are delineated to the insiders' satisfaction. These individual constructions are examined in the inquiry process not only by the inquirer (who must obviously work in the context of his or her *etic* or outsider construction), but by the individual respondents as well, so that each respondent understands the content of other constructions and is required to take those other constructions into account in shaping his or her own. Since constructions are heavily shaped by the local context (including, of course, the manifold aspects of local cultural socialization), generalization cannot be an aim. However, information from other contexts, from the literature, from the experience of others, and so on (including the construction that the inquirer brings) *can* be introduced into this process in order to increase the amount of information and the level of sophistication that locals have to work with.

The dialectic aspects consist in processes of comparing and contrasting existing constructions (their number inevitably decreases over time, but probably never reaches unity) so that each respondent must confront the constructions of others and come to terms with them. If there are elements in other constructions that do not fit his or her own, it is their responsibility to face those conflicts head-on and decide what to do about them. Whatever they do must be supported by a reason. Of course, it is the case that persons committed to the process can continue to disagree (if for no other reason than constructions suffer from the same disease as theories: underdetermination). But all have the responsibility to engage in dialectic interchange in the hope that consensus may emerge.

The hermeneutic/dialectic methodology of constructivism aims to produce as informed and sophisticated a construction (or more likely, constructions) as is possible, given the amount of information and the degree of sophistication available in the local context. At the same time, the methodology works to keep channels of communication open so that information and sophistication can be continuously improved. New constructions that may thereby emerge cannot be considered 'more true' than those they replace, but simply 'more informed and sophisticated.' Constructivism thus aims neither to predict and control the 'real' world nor to transform *it*, but rather to reconstruct the 'world' at the only point at which it exists: in the minds of constructors, human beings. It is the mind that is to be transformed, not the 'real world.'

It is impossible within the scope of an article such as this to provide more than a fleeting glimpse into the possibilities of this approach, or to demonstrate the fact that it is practical and useful. The interested reader is referred to our two works, *Naturalistic Inquiry* (Lincoln & Guba, 1985), and *Fourth Generation Evaluation* (Guba & Lincoln, 1989), for a more detailed exposition.

We may summarize the constructivist belief system as follows (retaining the three-fold organization for contrast's sake, despite having argued that in constructivism, the ontology/epistemology distinction is obliterated):

Ontology: *Relativist.* Realities (not reality) exist in the form of multiple mental constructions, socially and experientially based, local and specific, and dependent for their form and content on the persons who hold them.

Epistemology: *Monist, subjectivist.* Inquirer and inquired-into are fused into a single (monistic) entity. Findings are literally the creation of the process of interaction between the two.

Methodology: *Hermeneutic, dialectic.* Individual human constructions are elicited and refined hermeneutically, and compared and contrasted dialectically, with the aim of generating one (or a few) constructions on which there is substantial consensus.

If this summary describes the position of constructivism, wherein is the warrant for labeling it *the* preferred form for a human science?

THE WARRANT FOR CONSTRUCTIVISM AS *THE* HUMAN SCIENCE

We agree at the outset that constructivism has at best an imperfect warrant. Winston Churchill once opined that while democracy was not the best form of government, it was the best form that humankind had been able to invent thus far. Our feeling about constructivism is similar. We do not believe that it represents the ultimate prescription for conducting human science, but we believe that a strong case can be made for its superiority over other contemporary forms. It is our position that if the constructivist has a moral imperative, it is not simply to be open to the arguments of other constructors but to seek them out and to be challenged by them. In that spirit, we hope that constructivism will soon be replaced by a superior form. But for now, there are strong reasons for considering constructivism to be the preferred paradigm among contenders to guide *human* inquiry.

Constructivism restores humans to the center of the inquiry process

Knowledge is defined in terms of human constructions, and hence, humans are acknowledged as the *creators,* not simply the discoverers or the receivers, of knowledge. Every individual is the developer and arbiter of his or her own construction, which does not consist simply of 'scientific' knowledge, that is, empirically verifiable knowledge, but is open to *all* human experience: history, socialization, values, context, and of course, human relationships and interchanges. Cartesian anxiety is set aside as humans struggle to do the best they can with their own insights and information, having accepted the fact that there is, finally, *no* secure or foundational knowledge. Human knowledge and scientific knowledge become one; the artificial distinction disappears. And with Jefferson, we may assert that if we believe that humans are incompetent to carry out such a formidable task, the remedy is not to bar them from pursuing it but to 'inform their discretion.' Indeed, it is not possible to bar them from it; our professional task is to furnish them with as much information and sophistication as we can, in the hope and with the conviction that, in the last analysis, people will be able to think and act not only more rationally, but also with greater care and feeling.

Constructivism is educative to all participants in the inquiry process

In any inquiry, all participants, including the inquirer(s), begin with certain constructions — biases, positivists would say. But, of course, the term *bias* suggests some distortion of 'reality,' a concern to positivists but hardly to constructivists, who argue realities are mental constructions. The hermeneutic/dialectic methodology engages all participants in the task of delineating their constructions (whose contents when explicated may come as something of a surprise even to the constructors), and then contrasting and comparing them in an effort to formulate a *joint* construction on which all can come to consensus. It is inevitable that such a process will be educative, whether or not consensus finally occurs. The need to become aware of other constructions and the commitment to take them into account produces movement in everyone's construction, *including that of the inquirer,* toward more informed and sophisticated *forms. All* teach and *all* learn. To the positivist who would declaim, 'Yes, but you've *changed* what people think and do; you haven't found out how things really are,' the constructivist replies, 'Of course they've changed — I have too! Isn't that what inquiry is for? And what makes you think that information about constructions collected in ways that would *not* change people (were that possible) would be any more real?'

Constructivism tilts toward ethical inquirer behavior rather than away from it

A realist ontology provides an unusual warrant for unethical behavior. In the interest of discovering 'the real truth' or 'serving some higher social good,' it may be necessary to deceive the 'subjects' about the true purpose of the inquiry. But, of course, if reality is seen as a mental construction, that warrant disappears. Indeed, to deceive the respondents about the nature and aims of the inquiry is *completely dysfunctional* to the constructivist, who is interested in finding out what respondents' constructions are and in engaging them in a dialectic. Respondents who are deceived cannot disclose what is needed. Further, in conventional inquiry, humans are treated as objects in the same way that any other entity being studied is treated. As such, they may be manipulated and, at times, even deprived of some possibly useful treatment in the interest of maintaining the 'controls' needed. Fully informed consent often turns out to be a myth, since laypersons cannot understand in what ways they are placed at risk, or may be forced by circumstances to comply even when they do understand (what dying person refuses an untried drug protocol?). None of these circumstances can obtain in constructivist inquiry; the discussion is always at the level at which the respondent can communicate (that is the nature of the process), and there is no need to hide anything from respondents. Of course, constructivism has its own coterie of ethical problems (Lincoln & Guba, 1989), but it does not, as a belief system, provide a *warrant* for unethical behavior; indeed, it does just the reverse.

Constructivism sees social change as resulting from changed constructions, not from engineering

It is a hallmark of our society that when some unsatisfactory state-of-affairs is identified (please note the value-laden nature of the scientific identification process, as in a needs assessment!), efforts are usually made to identify its *cause,* on the assumption that, when the 'real' cause is known, appropriate countermeasures can be engineered to eliminate or ameliorate it. Virtually all social programs in education, health care, criminal justice, social work, and the like are developed on this basis. Constructivism sees change as occurring only by mediating changes in people's constructions; if their constructions change, so will the unsatisfactory state-of-affairs. Since constructions are always local in some sense (the vast majority of respondents' experience is local), there can be no universally useful engineered solutions anyway. Again, it is the humans who are placed center stage; it is in their heads, and not in the putative 'real world,' that change can occur.

Constructivism is empowering

In constructivist terms the pursuit of inquiry, by definition, requires collaborative, participatory action. One way to think of this is to say that if an outside observer were to follow the action in a constructivist inquiry, it would be hard to tell who is the inquirer and who are the respondents, since they would *all be doing much the same thing*. Constructivism aims to devise a joint construction to which all can assent (at least that is the ideal); by virtue of their participation, all are enfranchised to assist in determining what to do and how to do it, and all are expected to take responsibility for carrying out those plans. Theory and praxis are united so closely as to make Catholic marriage look like rampant free love.

Constructivism is emancipatory

So long as human science is viewed in reductionistic, deterministic ways, human beings will be seen as regulated by a system of natural laws, pushed and pulled by them, while making their own (relatively insignificant) contribution to action. They are literally cogs in a machine (the pervasiveness of that metaphor is astonishing!). Knowledge of the laws of human behavior makes it possible to manipulate, indeed, to exploit humans. It is hard to believe otherwise when we see how research in such areas as marketing, personnel supervision, leadership, teaching and learning, and similar areas is conducted. Constructivism takes the position, however, that there are no natural laws 'out there' in terms of which humans are constrained to behave. If we behave in predictable ways, it is because we share constructions to which we have been socialized and by which we feel ourselves bound. The posture of constructivism suddenly breaks humans out of this constraining mold. Perhaps most importantly, the posture of constructivism places a wholly new interpretation on the concept of *accountability*. It is no longer possible to determine who is accountable for what in any definitive way. Instead, *all* must *jointly* take responsibility for devising a working construction and for implementing it. Failures cannot be charged to the account of the weakest link in the political chain. All share the glory, or the disgrace.

Constructivism rescinds the special privilege of science; scientists are human too

If there is a way things 'really are' and 'really work,' then the community of persons who know how to find out about those things is indeed special. Its members are the ones who know what questions to put to nature (and how to put them), as well as how to understand nature's answers. They are a priesthood, standing between other humans and nature as the Cabots stand between the Lowells and God. Their special status seems to give many of them license for arrogance, as in the case of the eminent social scientist who proclaimed at a recent national professional meeting that one could not expect much from 'subjects' who 'don't know a fact from a bag of popcorn.' Because they stand outside on their Archimedean points, scientists cannot be held responsible for the data they discover; one ought not to kill the messenger because one does not like the message. But constructivism requires scientists to take the same measure of responsibility for their actions that other humans take. The scientists' values are as much a part of the process as anyone else's; their constructions must be equally open to critique in the hermeneutic/dialectic process. If constructions are human creations, *not* nature's, there can be no special warrant for a priesthood that claims to know how things 'really are' and 'really work.'

Constructivism emulates the emergent hard sciences

In 1842, John Stuart Mill urged his social science colleagues to adopt the posture of the hard sciences, which at that time were reveling in the full glory of Newton's *Principia*. One must acknowledge that his advice has been taken to a far greater extent than Mill would have believed possible. There is, of course, debate about whether Mill was right to give such advice, but let us assume for the moment that he was. Let us further assume that the same advice might be given today: what social scientists should do, to 'clean up their act,' is to emulate the physical sciences. For, if we were to decide on that basis, it is likely that constructivism would be the modern choice. While no doubt the majority of *practicing* scientists believe in an objective reality, leading philosophers of science, such as the later Ludwig Wittgenstein, Imre Lakatos, Paul Feyerabend, and Thomas Kuhn have declared in favor of the relativist belief that reality is what the community says it is (Casti, 1989, p. 46). It seems to us that once that ontological shift is made, the remainder of constructivism's belief system must follow as the night the day. Mill's advice leads us away from all alternatives except constructivism.

We began by arguing that humans were special, different from other entities-to-be-studied. We have proposed a shift in ontology and epistemology that places humans in the center of the inquiry process, and that defines them not simply as discoverers or receivers of knowledge but as its *creators*. The answer we give to John Wheeler's question, quoted earlier, 'May the universe in some strange way be "brought into being" by the participation of those who participate?' is a resounding 'Yes.'

If these two propositions accord with *your* construction, can there be any doubt that a human science *is* possible, and that constructivism is the best among the alternative paradigm candidates for pursuing it?

REFERENCES

Arendt, H. (1963). *On revolution.* New York: Viking.
Barker, R. G., & Associates (1978). *Habits, environments, and human behavior.* San Francisco, CA: Jossey-Bass.
Casti, J. L. (1989). *Paradigms lost: Images of man in the mirror of science.* New York: Morrow.
Glaser, B. G. (1978). *Theoretical sensitivity: Advances in the methodology of grounded theory.* Mill Valley, CA: Sociology Press.
Glaser, B. G., & Strauss, A. L. (1967). *The discovery of grounded theory.* Chicago: Aldine.
Guba, E. G., & Lincoln, Y. S. (1989). *Fourth generation evaluation.* Newbury Park, CA: Sage.
Hesse, M. (1980). *Revolutions and reconstructions in the philosophy of science.* Bloomington: Indiana University Press.
Kennedy, J. (1985). Remarks made as part of the debate, 'Is the distinction between quantitative and qualitative research meaningful?' Annual meeting of the Midwestern Educational Research Association, Chicago, Illinois. Reprinted in *Midwest Educational Researcher, 7,* Spring, 1986.
Lincoln, Y. S., & Guba, E. G. (1985). *Naturalistic inquiry.* Beverly Hills, CA: Sage.
Lincoln, Y. S., & Guba, E. G. (1989). Ethics: The failure of positivist science. *Review of Higher*

Education, 12(3), 221–4.

Miles, M. B., & Huberman, A. M. (1984). *Qualitative data analysis: A sourcebook of new methods.* Beverly Hills, CA: Sage.

Palmer P. J. (1987). Community, conflict, and ways of knowing. *Change, 19*(5), 20–5.

Patton, M. Q. (1982). *Practical evaluation.* Beverly Hills, CA: Sage.

Reason, P., & Rowan, J. (Eds.) (1981). *Human inquiry: A sourcebook of new paradigm research.* New York: Wiley.

Scriven M. (1971). Objectivity and subjectivity in educational research. In L. G. Thomas (Ed.), *Philosophical redirection of educational research.* 71st yearbook of the National Society for the Study of Education, Part 1. Chicago: University of Chicago Press.

Zukav, G. (1979). *The dancing Wu-Li masters.* New York: Bantam.

Heuristic Research:
Design and methodology

Clark Moustakas
Centre for Humanistic Studies, Detroit and The Union Institute, Cincinnati

'Heuristic Research: Design and methodology' offers an invitation to consider a theory and methodology of investigating human experience. The article emphasizes the essentials of self-processes in discovering the nature, meaning, and essence of things. Self-search, self-dialogue, indwelling, and intuition are openings toward the illumination and explication of problems, questions, and human concerns. From the initial immersion into a topic, followed by periods of activity and rest, the heuristic design enables a significant illumination and clarification of a question, deepened and extended in awareness and meaning through dialogues with others. The article describes the qualities that distinguish the heuristic research question; presents a design that guides the heuristic researcher in conducting the study; suggests a methodology for preparation, collection, and analysis of data; and provides an outline for creating the research manuscript. In developing the article, the author employed heuristic processes to shape his conception of heuristic design and methodology, while also keeping alive poetic and autobiographic sensings and markings.

Heuristic research, as an organized and systematic form for investigating human experience, was launched with my study of *Loneliness* (1961) and continued in my explorations of *Loneliness and Love* (1972) and *The Touch of Loneliness* (1975). Other works which influenced the development of heuristic methodology include Maslow's research on self-actualizing persons (1956, 1966) and Jourard's investigations of self-disclosure (1968). Also of significance in the evolution of heuristic concepts are Polanyi's elucidations of the tacit dimension (1983), indwelling and personal knowledge (1962); Buber's explorations of dialogue and mutuality (1958, 1965); Bridgman's delineations of subjective-objective truth (1950); and Gendlin's analysis of meaning and experiencing (1962). Rogers' work on human science (1969, 1985; Coulson & Rogers, 1968) added theoretical and conceptual depth to the heuristic paradigm presented in *Individuality and Encounter* (Moustakas, 1968) and *Rhythms, Rituals and Relationships* (Moustakas, 1981) and to its phenomenological underpinnings developed in *Phenomenology, Science, and Psychotherapy* (Moustakas, 1988).

As part of my own heuristic process in creating this work, I gathered before me the relatively recent investigations for which I served as research guide. These included the inner world of teaching (Craig, 1978), shyness (MacIntyre, 1981), self-reclamation (Schultz, 1982), being sensitive (McNally, 1982), being inspired (Rourke, 1983), return to Mexican-American ethnic identity (Rodriguez, 1984), feeling unconditionally loved (Hawka, 1985), the psychologically androgynous male (Clark, 1987), feeling connected to nature (J. Snyder, 1988), growing up in a fatherless home (Cheyne, 1988), rejecting love (R. Snyder, 1988), interaction rhythms in intimate relations (Shaw, 1989) and the experience of poetry (Vaughn, 1989).

First published in *Person-Centered Review*, Volume 5, Number 2, May 1990.

Along with the above works, I brought together my personal notes and spontaneous self-reflective writings for study and analysis. I also reviewed heuristic literature and reexamined my seminar outlines and presentations on heuristic design and methodology. I returned to lyric poetry, autobiography, and biography. I engaged in an immersion process, open and receptive to the nature of discovery, welcoming alternating rhythms of concentrated focus and inventive distraction. I searched within my knowledge and experience for deepened and extended awareness that would further illuminate structures and essences of heuristic discovery. I found particular meaning in heuristic studies that exemplified the heuristic paradigm and that provided practical methods and procedures for its operational effectiveness in investigating human experience.

From the beginning and throughout an investigation, heuristic research involves self-search, self-dialogue, and self-discovery. The research question and the methodology flow out of inner awareness, meaning, and inspiration. When I consider an issue, problem, or question, I enter into it fully. I focus on it with unwavering attention and interest. I search introspectively, meditatively, and reflectively into its nature and meaning. My primary task is to recognize whatever exists in my consciousness as a fundamental awareness, to receive it, accept it, support it, and dwell inside it. I awaken to it as my question, receptive, open, and with full and unqualified interest in extending my understanding. I begin the heuristic investigation with my own self awareness and explicate that awareness with reference to a question or problem until an essential insight is achieved, one that will throw a beginning light on a critical human experience.

In the process of heuristic search, I may challenge, confront, or doubt my understanding of a human concern or issue, but when I persist I ultimately deepen my knowledge of the phenomenon. In the heuristic process, I am personally involved, searching for the qualities, conditions, and relationships that underlay a fundamental question or concern.

I may be entranced by visions, images, and dreams that connect me to my quest. I may come into touch with new regions of myself, and discover revealing connections with others. Through the guides of a heuristic design, I am able to see and understand in a different way.

If I am investigating the meaning of the delight then delight hovers nearby and follows me around. It takes me fully into its confidence and I take it into mine. Delight becomes a lingering presence. For awhile, there is only delight. It opens me to the world in a joyous way and takes me into a richness, playfulness, and childlikeness that moves freely and effortlessly. I am ready to see, feel, touch, and hear whatever opens me to delight.

In heuristics, an unshakable connection exists between what is out there, in its appearance and reality, and what is within me in reflective thought, feeling, and awareness. It is 'I' the person living in a world with others, alone yet inseparable from the community of others; I who sees and understands something, freshly, as if for the first time; I who comes to know essential meanings inherent in my experience.

Moffitt (1971) captures this kind of seeing and knowing in his poem 'To Look At Any Thing.'

> *To look at any thing*
> *If you would know that thing,*
> *You must look at it long:*
> *To look at this green and say*
> *'I have seen spring in these*
> *Woods,' will not do — you must*
> *Be the thing you see:*
> *You must be the dark snakes of*

Stems and ferny plumes of leaves,
You must enter in
To the small silences between
The leaves,
You must take your time
And touch the very place
They issue from. (p. 149)

In Moffitt's sense, I am the person who brings existence into its essence and returns essence to ongoing life. Whatever else may enter my awareness, I provide the light that guides the explication of something and knowledge of it. When I illuminate a question, it comes to life. When I understand its constituents, it emerges as something solid and real.

Emphasis on the internal frame of reference, self-searching, intuition, and indwelling is the beginning place of heuristic inquiry and the foundation stone for the evidence of what something is and means. An example of the opening of a heuristic search may be found in Roads' *Talking with Nature* (1987).

Before anything else could become part of his knowledge, Roads entered into a dialogue with trees, plants, animals, birds, and the earth. He heard nature speak to him, 'Help yourself, if you wish to tell the story of our connection, then write from the point of contact which you are' (p. 1). Roads responded: 'How can we write of unseen realities, hint of unheard concepts, or even demonstrate the practicality of inner truths, without disturbing the slumbering Self within?' (p. 22). The answer:

> Let go and fall into the river. Let the river of life sweep you beyond all aid from old and worn concepts. I will support you. Trust me. As you swim from an old consciousness, blind to higher realities beyond your physical world, trust that I will guide you with care and love into a new stream of consciousness. I will open a new world before you. Can you trust me enough to let go of the known and swim in an unknown current? (p. 26)

It is just that swimming into an 'unknown current' that is so striking in heuristic beginnings. The dawning or awakening may be refreshing and peaceful, or it may be disturbing and shocking.

In 'Heuristic Inquiry' (Douglass & Moustakas, 1985), we contrasted heuristic research from the traditional paradigm, noting that traditional empirical investigations presuppose cause-effect relationships, while the heuristic scientist seeks to discover the nature and meaning of the phenomenon itself and to illuminate it from direct first-person accounts of individuals who have directly encountered the phenomenon in experience. We also contrasted heuristic inquiry from phenomenological research pointing out that:

> (1) Whereas phenomenology encourages a kind of detachment from the phenomenon being investigated, heuristics emphasizes connectedness and relationship. (2) Whereas phenomenology permits the researcher to conclude with definitive descriptions of the structures of experience, heuristics leads to depictions of essential meanings and portrayal of the intrigue and personal significance that imbue the search to know. (3) Whereas phenomenological research generally concludes with a presentation of the distilled structures of experience, heuristics may involve reintegration of derived knowledge that itself is an act of creative discovery, a synthesis that includes intuition and tacit understanding. (4) Whereas phenomenology loses the persons in the process of descriptive analysis, in heuristics the research participants remain visible in the examination of the data and continue to be portrayed as whole persons. Phenomenology ends with the essence of experience; heuristics retains the essence of the person in experience. (p. 43)

The focus in a heuristic quest is on re-creation of the lived experience, full and complete depictions of the experience from the frame of reference of the experiencing person. The challenge is fulfilled through examples, narrative descriptions, dialogues, stories, poems, art work, journals and diaries, autobiographical logs, and other personal documents. The heuristic process is congruent with Schopenhauer's (1966) reference to lyric poetry: the depicted is 'also at the same time the depicter' (p. 248), requiring vivid perception, description, and illustration of the experience.

A typical way of gathering material is through an interview, which often takes the form of dialogues with oneself and co-researchers. Ordinarily, such an 'interview' is not ruled by the clock, but by inner experiential time. In dialogue, one is encouraged to permit ideas, thoughts, feelings, and images to unfold and be expressed naturally. One completes the quest when one has had an opportunity to tell one's story to a point of natural closing.

In his essay 'Toward a Science of the Person,' Rogers (1969) describes his heuristic process. He states,

> Within myself—from my own internal frame of reference—I may 'know' that I love or hate, sense, perceive, comprehend. I may believe or disbelieve, enjoy or dislike, be interested in or bored by . . . It is only by reference to the flow of feelings in me that I can begin to conceptualize an answer . . . I taste a foreign dish. Do I like it? It is only by referring to the flow of my experiencing that I can sense the implicit meanings . . . (p. 23)

FORMULATING THE QUESTION

The crucial processes in heuristics, once one understands the values, beliefs, and knowledge inherent in the heuristic paradigm, are: *concentrated gazing* on something that attracts or compels one into a search for meaning, *focusing on a topic* or formulation of the question, and using *methods* of preparing, collecting, organizing, analyzing, and synthesizing data.

All heuristic inquiry begins with the internal search to discover, with an encompassing puzzlement, a passionate desire to know, a devotion and commitment to pursue a question that is strongly connected to one's own identity and selfhood. The awakening of such a question comes through an inward clearing and an intentional readiness and determination to discover a fundamental truth regarding the meaning and essence of one's own experience and that of others.

Polanyi (1969) has stated that,

> It is customary today to represent the process of scientific inquiry as the setting up of a hypothesis followed by its subsequent testing. I cannot accept these terms. All true scientific research starts with hitting on a deep and promising problem, and this is half the discovery (p. 118).

Polanyi points to the imperative nature of the problem as such.

> To see a problem is to see something that may yet be accessible . . . It is an engrossing possession of incipient knowledge which passionately strives to validate itself. Such is the heuristic power of a problem (1969, pp. 131–2).

Discovering a significant problem or question that will hold the wondering gaze and the passionate commitment of the researcher is the essential opening of the heuristic process. It means finding a path. The question, as such, will determine whether or not an authentic and compelling path has opened, one that will sustain the researcher's curiosity, involvement, and participation, with full energy and resourcefulness over a lengthy period of time.

The way in which the investigator poses the question, the words and ordering of the words, will determine what activities and materials will bear on the problem and what one will discover.

In order to design a heuristic research study that will reveal the meanings and essences of a particular human experience in an accurate, comprehensive, and vivid way, it is essential that the question be stated in simple, clear, and concrete terms. It is necessary that the key words and phrases be placed in the proper order. The basic elements of the search are found in the primary words stated in the ordering of the question. The question, as such, should reveal itself immediately and evidently, in a way that one knows what one is seeking. The question itself provides the crucial beginning and meaning, the nature of the searcher's quest. The way in which the investigator poses the question will determine what fundamental events, relationships, and activities will bear on the problem.

The question grows out of an intense interest in a particular problem or theme. The researcher's excitement and curiosity inspire the search. Associations multiply as personal experiences bring the core of the problem into focus. As the fullness of the theme emerges, strands, and tangents of it may complicate an articulation of a manageable and specific question. Yet this process of allowing all aspects to come into awareness is essential to the eventual formulation of a clear question.

The heuristic research question has definite characteristics:
1. It seeks to reveal more fully the essence or meaning of a phenomenon of human experience.
2. It seeks to discover the qualitative aspects, rather than quantitative dimensions.
3. It engages one's total self and evokes a personal and passionate involvement and active participation in the process.
4. It does not seek to predict or to determine causal relationships.
5. It is illuminated through careful descriptions, illustrations, metaphors, poetry, dialogue, and other creative renderings, rather than by measurements, ratings, or scores.

Suggested steps in formulating the question:
1. List all aspects of particular interests or topics which represent curiosities or intrigues for you. Do this freely, jotting down questions and thoughts, even if they are not complete.
2. Cluster the related interests or topics into sub-themes.
3. Set aside any sub-themes which imply causal relationships. Set aside any sub-themes which contain inherent assumptions.
4. Look at all the remaining sub-themes and stay with them until one basic theme or question emerges as central, one that passionately awakens your interest, concern, and commitment.
5. Formulate it in a way that specifies clearly and precisely what it is that you want to know.

Then, as Pearce (1971) exclaims,

> If you hold and serve the question, until all ambiguity is erased and you really believe in your question, it will be answered; the break-point will arrive when you will suddenly be 'ready.' Then you must put your hand to the plow and not look back; walk out onto the water unmindful of the waves. (p. 108)

In heuristic research, the openness of the researcher in elucidating the question, clarifying its terms, and pointing to its directions provides the essential beginnings of the discovery process. From there, as Kierkegaard (1965) has so aptly stated, the researcher must strive to be humble and not hold a single presupposition, to be in a position to learn the more.

HEURISTIC METHODOLOGY

Having formulated the question and defined and delineated its primary terms and meanings, the next step is a careful and disciplined organization of methods of preparing to conduct the study. This step is followed by construction of methods and procedures to guide a collection of data that will illuminate an answer to the question. After the data are collected, they must be organized and presented in a way that depicts and illustrates the themes, meanings, and essences of the experience that has been investigated.

Methods of heuristic research are open-ended. They point to a process of accomplishing something in a thoughtful and orderly way, a manner of proceeding that guides the researcher. There is no exclusive list that would be appropriate for every heuristic investigation, but rather each research process unfolds in its own way. Initially, methods may be envisioned and constructed that will guide the process through preparation for, collection of, and analysis of data. They facilitate the flow of the investigation and aim toward yielding rich, accurate, and complete depictions of the qualities or constituents of the experience. Keen (1975) has remarked that, 'The goal of every technique is to help the phenomenon *reveal itself more completely* than it does in ordinary experience' (p. 41). Every method or procedure must relate to the question and facilitate collection of data that will disclose the nature, meaning, and essence of the experience.

Bridgman (1950) has emphasized that 'science is what scientists do . . . there are as many scientific methods as there are individual scientists' (p. 83). The purpose of a method of scientific inquiry is to obtain an answer to the problem in hand. The working scientist, Bridgman observes, 'is not consciously following any prescribed course of action, but feels complete freedom to utilize any method or device whatever which in the particular situation . . . seems likely to yield the correct answer' (p. 83).

The heuristic researcher constructs methods that will explicate meanings and patterns of experience relevant to the question, procedures that will encourage open expression and dialogue.

METHODS OF PREPARATION

When I began to study loneliness, it became the center of my world. Everything appeared to be connected with loneliness. I found loneliness everywhere in my waking life, a crucial component of hospitalized children separated from their families; an inherent quality of making decisions that importantly impacted on other's lives. It became a significant focus of the people I met with in therapy — whatever their presenting problems — and of my reflections on my own life. I recognized loneliness as a crucial component of solitude and creativity. My dreams were filled with lonely awakenings and encounters. I walked the streets at night and noticed especially isolated stars, clouds, trees, and flowers. I was once confronted by municipal police and told that I was violating a local ordinance and that lonely middle-of-the-night sojourns were forbidden. If I did not cease these nocturnal walks, I would definitely be arrested. On one occasion, I was escorted home with rotating, flaring lights illuminating my every step.

Loneliness, for awhile, was the mainstream of my life and colored everything else, influenced the meaning of everything else. This kind of autobiographical immersion provides the initial essential preparation for discovering the nature and essence of a particular experience.

Methods of preparation in heuristic research include:

1. *Developing a set of instructions* that will inform potential co-researchers of the nature of the research design, its purpose and process, and what is expected of them.

2. *Locating and acquiring the research participants.* Developing a set of criteria for selection of participants, for example, age, sex, socio-economic, and education factors; ability to articulate the experience; cooperation, interest, willingness to make the commitment; enthusiasm; and degree of involvement.

3. *Developing a contract* which includes time commitments, place, confidentiality, informed consent, opportunities for feedback, permission to tape-record, permission to use material in a thesis, dissertation and/or other publications, and verification of the findings.

4. *Considering ways of creating an atmosphere* or climate that will encourage trust, openness, and self-disclosure.

5. *Using relaxation-meditation activities* to facilitate a sense of comfort, relaxation, and at-homeness.

6. *Constructing a way of apprising co-researchers* of the nature of the heuristic design and its process, the importance of immersion and intervals of concentration and respite.

George Kelly's (1969) guidance is helpful here:

> Each person who participates should at some point be apprised of what the 'experimenter' thinks he is doing, and what he considers evidence of what. It is of equal importance to ask what the 'subject' thinks is being done, and what he considers evidence of what. Since this can change during the course of the experiment, it is appropriate to ask 'subjects' what their perception of the experimental design was at each important juncture in the experience. (p. 56)

METHODS OF COLLECTING THE DATA

Heuristic research investigations ordinarily employ an informal conversational approach in which both researchers and co-researchers enter into the process fully. Dialogue aims toward encouraging expression, elucidation, and disclosure of the experience being investigated. Jourard (1968) has shown that self-disclosure elicits disclosure. There may be moments in the interview process when the primary investigator shares an experience that will inspire and evoke richer, fuller, and more comprehensive depictions from the co-researcher.

The heart of the heuristic 'interview' is dialogue. In *Disclosing Man to Himself,* Jourard (1968) has borrowed from Buber's writings to emphasize that, 'Dialogue is like mutual unveiling, where each seeks to be experienced and confirmed by the other . . . Such dialogue is likely to occur when the two people believe each is trustworthy and of good will' (p.21). Buber (1965) expands on the values of dialogue:

> Where the dialogue is fulfilled in its being, between partners who have turned to one another in truth, who express themselves without reserve and are free of the desire for semblance, there is brought into being a memorable common fruitfulness which is to be found nowhere else. At such times, at each such time, the world arises in a substantial way between men who have been seized in their depths and opened out by the dynamic of an elemental togetherness. The interhuman opens out what otherwise remains unopened. (p. 86)

345

In heuristic interviewing, the data generated is dependent upon accurate, empathic listening, being open to oneself and to the co-researcher, being flexible and free to vary procedures to respond to what is required in the flow of dialogue, being skilful in creating a climate that encourages the co-researcher to respond comfortably, accurately, comprehensively, and honestly in elucidating the phenomenon.

Questions that might guide a heuristic 'interview' include:
• What does this person know about the experience?
• What qualities or dimensions of the experience stand out for the person? What examples are vivid and alive?
• What events, situations, and people are connected with the experience?
• What feelings and thoughts are generated by the experience? What bodily states or shifts in bodily presence occur in the experience?
• What time and space factors affect the person's awareness and meaning of the experience?

In the process of exploring these questions with co-researchers,

> We cannot and should not be unaffected by what is said . . . On the contrary it is only in relating to the other as one human being to another that interviewing is really possible . . . when the interviewer and the participant are both caught up in the phenomenon being discussed. (Weber, 1986, p. 68)

The researcher must keep in mind throughout the process that the material collected must depict the experience in accurate, comprepensive, rich, and vivid terms. In heuristic research, depictions are often presented in stories, examples, conversations, metaphors, and analogies.

The interview should be tape-recorded and later transcribed. The basic data for illuminating the question and providing a basis for analysis of constituents, themes, and essences of the experience come from transcriptions and notes taken immediately following the interview.

To supplement the interview data, the heuristic researcher may also collect personal documents. Diaries, journals, logs, poetry, and art work offer additional meaning and depth and supplement depictions of the experience obtained from observations and interviews.

METHODS OF ORGANIZING AND SYNTHESIZING DATA HEURISTICALLY

Immersion and incubation

The transcriptions, notes, and personal documents are gathered together and organized by the investigator into a sequence that tells the story of each research participant. This may be done in a variety of ways from the most recent to the most remote event connected with the experience, or vice versa, the order of actual collection of data, or in whatever way will facilitate full immersion into the material. Essential to the process of heuristic analysis is intimate knowledge of all the material for each participant and for the group of participants collectively. The task involves timeless immersion inside the data, with intervals of resting and returning to the data. The condition of again and again, of repetition, is essential until intimate knowledge is obtained.

Organizing and analyzing heuristic data during the immersion and incubation process may take many forms. Clark (1987), in his study of the psychologically androgynous male, describes the process over a period of five months. Gradually, the core themes and patterns began to emerge and take shape. To convey a direct contact with the process, I offer this excerpt from Clark's dissertation:

> I listened to the interview tapes for several weeks before beginning to take notes on them. Very detailed notes were done on each take, including extensive quoting and notes on the affect of the co-researcher as he provided the data.
>
> After immersing in the tape and notes of each co-researcher for some time, I developed a reflective portrait of each and contacted him for feedback on the portrait. I received very positive responses. Three co-researchers added information or emphases on certain aspects of the experience, which were then included in their portraits.
>
> The clustering process utilized to place the data before me in one viewable panorama required many days of painstaking work transferring the essential components of the reflective portraits to a six foot by six foot diagram. This was the androgyny . . . This resulted in a diagram of over 200 components of the experience of the psychologically androgynous male. As the map grew, the color coding system used to cluster related ideas revealed a system of quadrants. Some individual aspects of the experience appeared in more than one quadrant, but each quadrant represented a unique thematic matrix of closely connected components of psychological androgyny. The process of watching these quadrants take shape was fascinating. When the androgyny map was complete, I spent several weeks alternately immersing myself in studying it and incubating by attending to other interests. During this time many shifts occurred in my perception of the map, and I began to note themes and relationships between ideas which had not been apparent previously . . . ' (pp. 94–6).[1]

Illumination and explication

Once full knowledge of an experience is ingested and understood, the researcher enters into a process of illumination in which essential qualities and themes are discovered. This is followed by an elucidation and explication of the themes until an *individual depiction* of the meanings and essences of the experience investigated can be constructed. The *individual depiction* may include descriptive narrative, examples, and verbatim exemplary material drawn from the data. It also may include verbatim conversations, poetry, and art work. From the individual depictions, a *composite depiction* of the experience is constructed. Then, the heuristic researcher returns to the individual co-researchers. Through immersion and analysis of the 'individual' data, two or three *exemplary portraits* are developed, profiles that are unique, yet which embrace and characterize the group as a whole.

The creative synthesis

Finally, the heuristic researcher develops a *creative synthesis,* an original integration of the material that reflects the researcher's intuition, imagination, and personal knowledge of the meanings and essences of the experience. The *creative synthesis* may take the form of a lyric poem, a song, a narrative description, a story, a metaphoric tale, or an art work.

To sum up, the data are used to develop *individual depictions,* a *composite depiction, exemplary portraits* of individual persons, and a *creative synthesis* of the experience. In this way, the experience is illuminated. A creative vision of the experience is offered, and, unlike most research studies, the individual persons remain intact and fully alive in the experience.

Outline Guide of Procedures for Analysis of Data

1. In the first step in organization, handling, and synthesizing, the researcher gathers all of the data from one participant (recording, transcript, notes, journal, personal documents, poems, art work).

2. The researcher enters into the material in timeless immersion until it is fully understood. Knowledge of the individual participant's experience, as a whole and in its detail, is comprehensively apprehended by the researcher.

3. The data are set aside for awhile, encouraging an interval of rest and return to the data, procedures which facilitate the awakening of fresh energy and perspective. Then, after reviewing again all of the material derived from one individual, the researcher takes notes, identifying the qualities and themes manifested in the data. Further study and review of the data, and the notes, enable the heuristic researcher to construct an *individual depiction* of the experience. The *individual depiction* retains the language and includes examples drawn from the individual co-researcher's experience of the phenomenon. It includes qualities and themes that encompass the research participant's experience.

4. The next step requires a return to the original data of the individual co-researcher. Does the *individual depiction* of the experience fit the data from which it was developed? Does it contain the qualities and themes essential to the experience? If it does, the researcher is ready to move on to the next co-researchers. If not, the *individual depiction* must be revised to include what has been omitted or deleted, what is or is not an essential dimension of the experience. The *individual depiction* may also be shared with the research participant for affirmation of its comprehensiveness and accuracy, and for suggestions for deletion and addition.

5. When the above steps have been completed, the heuristic researcher undertakes the same course of organization and analysis of the data for each research participant until an *individual depiction* of each co-researcher's experience of the phenomenon has been constructed.

6. *The individual depictions,* representing each co-researcher's experience, are gathered together. The researcher again enters into an immersion process, with intervals of rest, until the 'universal' qualities and themes of the experience are thoroughly internalized and understood. At a timely point in the development of the researcher's knowledge and readiness, the researcher constructs a *composite depiction* that represents the 'universal' or common qualities and themes that embrace the experience of the co-researchers. The *composite depiction* (group depiction reflecting the experience of individual participants) should include exemplary narratives, descriptive accounts, conversations, illustrations, and verbatim excerpts that accentuate the flow, spirit, and life inherent in the experience. The *composite depiction* should be vivid, accurate, alive, and clear and should encompass the core qualities and themes inherent in the experience. It should include all of the core meanings of the phenomenon as experienced by the individual participants and by the group as a whole.

7. The heuristic researcher returns again to the raw material derived from each co-researcher's experience and the *individual depictions* derived from the raw material. From these data, the researcher selects two or three participants who clearly exemplify the group as a whole. The researcher then develops *individual portraits* of these persons, using the raw data, the *individual depiction,* and autobiographical material that was gathered during preliminary contacts and meetings or that is contained in

personal documents or that was shared during the interview. The *individual portraits* should be presented in such a way that both the phenomenon investigated and the individual persons emerge as real.

8. The final step in heuristic presentation and handling of data is the development of a *creative synthesis* of the experience. The *creative synthesis* encourages a wide range of freedom in characterizing the phenomenon. It invites a recognition of tacit, intuitive awareness of the researcher, knowledge that has been incubating over months through processes of immersion, illumination, and explication of the phenomenon investigated. The researcher as scientist-artist develops an aesthetic rendition of the themes and essential meanings of the phenomenon. The researcher taps into imaginative and contemplative sources of knowledge and light in synthesizing the experience, in presenting the discovery of essences — peaks and valleys, highlights and horizons. In the *creative synthesis,* there is a free reign of thought and feeling that supports the researcher's knowledge, passion, and presence; this infuses the work with a personal, professional, and literary value that can be expressed through a narrative, story, poem, art work, metaphor, analogy, or tale.

This presentation of heuristic research design and methodology has embraced beliefs, values, theory, concepts, processes, and methods that are essential to an understanding and conduct of heuristic research and discovery. Additional parameters of heuristics may be found in my chapter, 'Heuristic Research,' in *Individuality and Encounter* (Moustakas, 1968); in 'Heuristic Methods of Obtaining Knowledge,' in my book, *Rhythms, Rituals and Relationships* (1981); and in the article 'Heuristic Inquiry' (Douglass & Moustakas, 1985).

CREATING THE RESEARCH MANUSCRIPT

Once heuristic 'interviews' have been completed, transcribed, organized, depicted, and synthesized, the research is nearing completion. It is time to present the research process and findings in a form that can be understood and used. I have developed an outline for the manuscript, a guide for presentation of the work of an heuristic investigation. I offer it as one way of bringing together an experience which has profoundly affected the investigator and which holds possibilities for scientific knowledge and social impact and meaning.

Introduction and Statement of Topic and Question. Out of what ground of concerns, knowledge, and experience did the topic emerge? What stands out, one or two critical incidents in your life that created the puzzlement, curiosity, passion to know? Does the topic have social relevance? How would new knowledge contribute to your profession? To you as a person and as a learner? State your question and elucidate the terms.

Review the Literature. Discuss the computer search, data-bases, descriptors, key words and years covered. Organize the review to include an *introduction* which presents the topic reviewed and its significance and provides an overview of the methodological problems; *methods* that describe what induced you to include the published study in your review and how the studies were conducted; *themes* that cluster into patterns, and which organize the presentation of findings; and a *summary* of core findings relevant to your research that differentiate your investigation from those in the literature review with regard to the question, model, methodology, and knowledge sought.

Methodology. List and discuss methods and procedures developed in *preparing* to conduct the study, in *collecting* the data, and in *organizing, analyzing,* and *synthesizing* the data.

Presentation of Data. Include verbatim examples that illustrate the collection of data and its analysis and synthesis. Discuss thematic structures and illustrate. Include depictions of the experience as a whole and exemplary portraits that are vivid, comprehensive, alive, and accurate. In the presentation of data, include individual depictions, a comprehensive depiction, two or three exemplary individual portraits and a creative synthesis.

Summary, Implications, and Outcomes. Summarize *your study* in brief, vivid terms from its inception to its final synthesis of data. Now that your investigation has been completed, how, in fact, *do your findings differ* from findings presented in your literature review? *What future studies* might you or others conduct, as an outcome of your research? Suggest a design for one or two future studies. *What implications* of your findings are relevant to society? To your profession? To you as a learner and as a person? *Write a brief creative conclusion* that speaks to the essence of your study and its significance to you and others.

CLOSING REFLECTIONS

This has been a lengthy journey. The heuristic process is rooted in experiential time, not clock time. Once one enters into the quest for knowledge and understanding, once one begins the passionate search for the illumination of a puzzlement, the intensity, wonder, intrigue, and engagement carry one along through ever-growing levels of meaning and excitement. It is as if a new internal time rhythm has awakened, one rooted in a particular absorption and in a sustaining gaze, a rhythm that must take its own course and that will not be satisfied or fulfilled until a natural closing occurs and the rhythm has carried out its intent and purpose.

Heuristic research processes include moments of meaning, understanding, and discovery that the researcher will forever hold onto and savor. Feelings, thoughts, ideas, and images have awakened that will return again and again. A connection has been made that will forever remain unbroken and that will serve as a reminder of a life-long process of knowing and being. Polanyi (1962) touches on this relationship in the following passage:

> Having made a discovery, I shall never see the world again as before. My eyes have become different; I have made myself into a person seeing and thinking differently. I have crossed a gap, the heuristic gap, which lies between problem and discovery. (p. 142)

REFERENCES

Bridgman, P. (1950). *Reflections of a physicist.* New York: Philosophical Library.

Buber, M. (1958). *I and thou.* New York: Scribner.

Buber, M. (1965). *The knowledge of man.* New York: Harper & Row.

Cheyne, V. (1988). *Growing up in a fatherless home: The female experience.* Ann Arbor, MI: University Microfilms International. Dissertation.

Clark, J. (1987). *The experience of the psychologically androgynous male.* Ann Arbor, MI: University Microfilms International. Dissertation.

Coulson, W., & Rogers, C. R. (Eds.) (1968). *Man and the science of man.* Columbus, OH: Charles E. Merrill.

Craig, E. (1978). *The heart of the teacher: A heuristic study of the inner world of teaching.* Ann Arbor, MI: University Microfilms International. Dissertation.

Douglass, B., & Moustakas, C. (1985). Heuristic inquiry: The internal search to know. *Journal of Humanistic Psychology, 25(3),* 39–55.

Gendlin, E. (1962). *Experiencing and the creation of meaning.* Glencoe, IL: Free Press.

Gendlin, E. (1978). *Focusing.* New York: Everest House.

Hawka, S. (1985). *The experience of feeling unconditionally loved.* Ann Arbor, MI: University Microfilms International. Dissertation.

Jourard, S. (1968). *Disclosing man to himself.* New York: Van Nostrand Reinhold.

Keen, E. (1975). *A primer on phenomenological psychology.* New York: Holt, Rinehart & Winston.

Kelly, G. A. (1969). Humanistic methodology in psychological research. *Journal of Humanistic Psychology, 11*(1), 53–65.

Kierkegaard, S. (1965). *The point of view for my work as an author.* B. Nelson (Ed.). New York: Harper & Row.

MacIntyre, M. (1981). *The experience of shyness.* Ann Arbor, MI: University Microfilms International. Dissertation.

Maslow, A. H. (1956). Self-actualizing people: A study of psychological health. In C. Moustakas (Ed.), *The self.* New York: Harper.

Maslow, A. H. (1966). *The psychology of science.* New York: Harper & Row.

McNally, C. (1982). *The experience of being sensitive.* Ann Arbor, MI: University Microfilms International. Dissertation.

Moffitt, J. (1971). *Since feeling is first.* J. Mecklenberger & G. Simmons (Eds.). Glenview, IL: Scott, Foresman.

Moustakas, C. (1961). *Loneliness.* Englewood Cliffs, NJ: Prentice-Hall.

Moustakas, C. (1968). *Individuality and encounter.* Cambridge, MA: Howard A. Doyle.

Moustakas, C. (1972). *Loneliness and love.* Englewood Cliffs, NJ: Prentice-Hall.

Moustakas, C. (1975). *The touch of loneliness.* Englewood Cliffs, NJ: Prentice-Hall.

Moustakas, C. (1981). *Rhythms, rituals and relationships.* Detroit, MI: Center for Humanistic Studies.

Moustakas, C. (1988). *Phenomenology, science and psychotherapy.* Sydney, Nova Scotia, Canada: Family Life Institute, University College of Cape Breton.

Pearce, J. C. (1971). *The crack in the cosmic egg.* New York: Julian.

Polanyi, M. (1962). *Personal knowledge.* Chicago: University of Chicago.

Polanyi, M. (1969). *Knowing and being.* Marjorie Grene (Ed.). Chicago: University of Chicago.

Polanyi, M. (1983). *The tacit dimension.* Gloucester, MA: Peter Smith.

Roads, M. (1987). *Talking with nature.* Tiburon, CA: H. J. Kramer.

Rodriguez, A. (1984). *A heuristic/phenomenological investigation of Mexican American ethnic identity.* Ann Arbor, MI: University Microfilms International. Dissertation.

Rogers, C. (1969). Toward a science of the person. In A. J. Sutich & M. A. Vich (Eds.), *Readings in Humanistic Psychology.* New York: Macmillan Company.

Rogers, C. (1985). Toward a more human science of the person. *Journal of Humanistic Psychology, 25*(4), 7–24.

Rourke, P. (1983). *The experience of being inspired.* Ann Arbor, MI: University Microfilms International. Dissertation.

Schopenhauer, A. (1966). *The world as will and representation.* (E.F.J. Payne, Trans.). New York: Doves.

Schultz, D. (1982). *The experience of self-reclamation of former catholic religious women.* Ann Arbor, MI: University Microfilms International. Dissertation.

Shaw, R. (1989). Interaction rhythms in intimate relations. Unpublished dissertation.

Snyder, J. (1988). *The experience of really feeling connected with nature.* Ann Arbor, MI: University Microfilms International. Dissertation.

Snyder, R. (1988). Rejecting love. Unpublished dissertation.

Vaughn, L. (1989). The experience of poetry. Unpublished dissertation.

Weber, S. J. (1986). The nature of interviewing. *Phenomenology and Pedagogy, 4*(2), 65–72.

Ethnomethodology and Person-Centered Practices

Melvin Pollner   *University of California, Los Angeles*

David Goode   *College of Staten Island*

Ethnomethodological studies focus on the practices through which members of society enact what they regard as a meaningful reality. Ethnomethodology provides a distinctive resource for person-centered perspectives by describing how versions of the person are created, sustained or dissolved in everyday, organizational and research contexts. The ethnomethodological approach is illustrated through a discussion of studies, conducted by the authors, of families with children diagnosed as severely limited in their capacity for communication. The studies show that versions of the children's competence are constituted by the practices of the families, the clinics, and those of the ethnomethodological investigators themselves.

Person-centered theory and research are predicated upon the capacity of individuals to reflect on their own lives, make meaningful choices, and creatively participate in the social world; person-centered institutions construct identities which respect and enhance these fundamental capacities. As a practice, or even as an ideal, however, person-centering is less than universal. Everyday life abounds in transactions in which individuals' voice and perspective are dismissed or ignored. Various therapeutic modalities reduce the individual to psychobiological processes. Numerous paradigms in the social and behavioral sciences define the individual through metaphors which either obviate his or her point of view or explain it away as the specious by-product of processes regarded as more 'real.' To *their* practitioners, the alternatives often have the aura of necessity and good sense that readers of this journal — ourselves included — might attribute to person-centered perspectives. Thus, person-centering is but one among alternative and often conflicting ways of defining and responding to individuals.

This context of contention invites two kinds of response. On the one hand, it sounds a clarion call for intensifying efforts to deepen and promote person-centered paradigms. On the other hand, it invites examination of the processes through which person-centered paradigms come to be dominant — or, for that matter, subordinate or inconceivable — ways of defining and responding to fellow humans. In this article, we gesture with both hands: first, we provide a synopsis of the *ethnomethodological* perspective which, we suggest, augments the person-centering repertoire through its appreciation of the richly textured practices or 'methods' intricated in human conduct. We illustrate the application of the ethnomethodological perspective by a discussion of two studies conducted by the authors. Each of the studies analyzes how different families construct the personhood of a child who has been diagnosed as severely retarded. Secondly, through our commentary, we explore some of the processes enhancing or inhibiting a person-centered approach in our own studies and, by implication, in other studies as well.

First published in *Person-Centered Review,* Volume 5, Number 2, May 1990.

ETHNOMETHODOLOGICAL INITIATIVES

Ethnomethodology originated as a reaction to the prevailing Parsonian orthodoxy of mid-century American sociology (Heritage, 1984). Despite its aspiration to be *the* theory of social action, Talcott Parsons' (e.g., 1951) massive effort neglected or distorted significant aspects of the organization of social action. The emphasis on shared, internalized norms as an explanation of patterned social behavior, for example, disregarded the interpretive judgments necessarily involved in the application of a norm or rule (Garfinkel, 1967; Cicourel, 1972); the emphasis on abstract 'top-down' theorizing precluded close examination of the features of actual 'bottom-up' interaction; the invocation of the ideals of scientific inquiry as a model of everyday rationality pre-empted consideration of the indigenous processes used by members to organize and assess the 'rationality' of their own activities in everyday life (Schutz, 1967).

Originating as a critique of the prevailing Parsonian paradigm, ethnomethodology evolved into a cluster of initiatives that provided a distinctive view of socially organized activity. In its pristine form (Garfinkel, 1967; Heritage, 1984), ethnomethodology is not a 'theory,' but rather research initiatives, heuristics, and exemplars which focus analytic attention on the 'folk methods' (i.e., ethnomethods) used in the construction of social activities. Key initiatives emphasize the enacted nature of social reality, respect for the indigenous order, the reflexivity of socially organized activities, and immersion and estrangement as research methodologies.

The enacted nature of social settings

Ethnomethodology is predicated on the recognition that the meaningfulness and intelligibility of social worlds is constituted through shared practices of reasoning, interaction, and interpretation. Rather than treat 'meaning' as an intrinsic feature of social settings or as being lodged in the minds of social actors, ethnomethodology views meaning as a construction which is continuously and collaboratively sustained through a range of practices or 'ethnomethods.' Thus, in contrast to versions of social action which dismiss or disregard the 'common sense' practices implicated in ordinary conduct, ethnomethodology brings these background skills, assumptions, and informal bodies of knowledge to the foreground. Whatever 'imprecision' and 'vagueness' they may display when assessed by extrinsic criteria, these practices constitute the social reality of everyday activities — in the home, the clinic, and even the scientific laboratory (Garfinkel, Lynch, & Livingston, 1981).

The ethnomethodological perspective entails a transformation of the ordinary or 'natural' attitude (Husserl, 1913/1962) toward the everyday world; features in everyday life ordinarily treated as given, natural, or real are ethnomethodologically examined as the product of interpretive and interactional 'work.' To highlight the transformation, ethnomethodologists speak of a setting's 'accountable' features; an accountable feature refers to the setting as it is sanctionably or accountably oriented to and sustained in discourse, interaction, and cognition (Garfinkel, 1967). In some societies, to give a crude example, 'witches' are accountable identities; reasoning and actions are predicated upon and reproduce the 'knowledge' that 'witches' exist. Competent membership in such contexts consists of speaking, reasoning, and even experiencing the reality of witchcraft (Evans-Pritchard, 1937). In industrialized, urbanized societies, on the other hand, witches are accountably non-existent; members sanctionably require one another to honor and orient to the non-existence of witches in their actions, reason, and discourse. Similarly, the authority and validity of a clinical diagnosis as an accountable feature refers to the various ways in which patients, colleagues, and staff acknowledge the diagnosis as authoratitive and valid and use it as the grounds for further inference and action. The issue of the ultimate ontological reality of accountable features such as witches or diagnoses (or whatever) is suspended in order to focus on the feature as it is socially oriented to, addressed, assessed, and used in the actions, discourse, and reasoning of members.

Respect for the indigenous

Just as an anthropologist suspends the biases and assumptions of his or her home culture to more fully enter the social world of the group, the ethnomethodologist suspends received versions and 'isms' in order to encounter social reality as it is known, experienced, and enacted from 'within.' The ethnomethodological stance precludes characterizations of members as deficient, pathological, or irrational (or superior, normal, or rational); such characterizations are of interest only in the ways in which they are constructed from *within* the setting under consideration. Thus, to anticipate the materials we shall be discussing, in the study of families with ostensibly unusual versions of reality, the ethnomethodological approach requires the researcher to refrain from invoking an external criterion of rationality or correctness in order to examine the practices as they are orchestrated and assessed by family members.

The reflexivity of social action

Ethnomethodology appreciates reflexivity in several senses. First, as we noted, actions are not 'reactions' to a priori features or objects, but are 'enactions' of those features. Although the chair in everyday life invites us to sit upon it, the accountable chair is *constituted* by activities such as sitting upon it, acknowledging that it can and ought to be sat upon, and admonishing children when they stand upon it. Thus, in a cyclical and reflexive way, human conduct not only occurs within an accountable order, but folds back to create and preserve that very order.

A second sense of reflexivity derives from the ethnomethodological appreciation that *every* feature of *every* setting is an accountable feature. The 'ethno' in ethnomethodology includes every category of member and activity from astrologers to astronomers, from diviners to physicists, from soothsayers to psychologists and, of course, ethnomethodologists themselves. Their work, no less than that of the lay member, may be approached as an achievement constituted through assumptions and practices for constructing 'diagnoses,' 'findings,' or 'truth' (Garfinkel, 1967; Garfinkel et al., 1981). These determinations themselves are accountable products emerging from the interactional, technological, and textual (Cicourel, 1981) exchanges that compose the practical settings within which they are produced.

Immersion and distance

While the ethnomethodological stance emphasizes the enactive, indigenous, and reflexive aspects of socially organized settings, ethnomethodological research strategies oscillate between estrangement and immersion. Depending upon the issue or the setting, one or another of the movements predominates. Because everyday practices are taken for granted, for example, Garfinkel (1967) undertook exploratory studies which destabilized 'routine' interaction in order to discover the assumptions and practices through which the mundane character of everyday life is enacted. In ethnomethodological studies of specialized (e.g., technical) settings, by contrast, the problem is not developing 'amnesia for common sense' (Garfinkel, 1967), but acquiring familiarity with what may appear to be opaque assumptions, background knowledge, and practices. Thus, studies of scientific work (Garfinkel et al., 1981) and the life world of groups in problematic situations emphasize acquiring the background knowledge used to make intelligible features which, from the 'outside,' are either unintelligible or unrecognizable. In his study of communicational practices in families of children who are deaf, blind, and mentally retarded, for example, Goode (in press) stayed with and observed the children and their families in the course of their daily life in a variety of different contexts. Moreover, in order to gain insight into the communicational environment of children with Rubella Syndrome, Goode (1979) simulated aspects of their condition by, for example, blind-folding himself for extended periods of time.

The ethnomethodological initiatives establish three levels of approach to the study of person-centering and, indeed, to the very notion of 'person' itself: conceptual, empirical and reflexive. On the *conceptual* level, the ethnomethodological perspective cultivates an appreciation of the skills, practices, and assumptions through which persons create and sustain their social worlds. Through interpretive practices, judgmental work, and skilled coordination of practical action, persons make sense of, manage, and constitute the complex, fluid, and ambiguous environments in which they participate. At the conceptual level, then, there is considerable respect for the creative, enactive capacities of social actors. Indeed, because these competencies and sensitivities are taken for granted, ethnomethodology succeeds in highlighting capacities and achievements to which social actors are often oblivious.

In turning to the organization of social settings and social worlds as *empirical* topics, ethnomethodology treats 'persons' as it might any other feature of a social setting, that is, as indigenously produced and accountable features of a setting. In institutional and everyday settings, individuals are described, analyzed, and diagnosed. These activities are themselves steeped in taken-for-granted assumptions and organizational practices which provide for the sensible and intelligible nature of interaction and discourse pertaining to personhood. In moving from the conceptual to the empirical level, the focus shifts from elaborating theoretical conceptions of what persons 'really' are, do, or need to detailed study of how conceptions of personhood are developed and sustained in action and discourse by participants to a particular setting. Thus, for example, in studying medical settings, an ethnomethodologically oriented study examines the assumptions and discourse used by medical personnel to conceptualize and describe patients, and the practices through which these schemes of interpretation are applied and used (cf. Anspach, 1988).

As a consequence of ethnomethodology's commitment to *reflexivity*, ethno-methodological studies are not exempt from the scrutiny to which they subject other professional and institutional settings. The reflexive turn entails that ethnomethodological concepts and empirical studies pertaining to persons (or any other topic) are themselves examined as the product of taken-for-granted practices and presuppositions. All of the ethnomethodological initiatives are framed at a high level of abstraction; their application and realization in any particular study is suffused by interpretations and practices that shape the final textual product. In taking the reflexive turn, the ethnomethodological portrayal of practices and assumptions peculiar to a particular setting is itself attended to as the product of practices and assumptions through which 'data' are collected, interpreted, and textually rendered into a determinate version of social reality. An exegesis

355

of two actual studies will provide concrete illustrations of the conceptual, empirical, and reflexive thrust of ethnomethodology.

ETHNOMETHODOLOGICAL STUDIES OF PERSON-CENTERING

In the following pages, we summarize and comment upon studies we have separately undertaken of families with children diagnosed as having disabilities that severely impaired their capacity to communicate. Each study examined the practices through which family members interacted with, interpreted, and generally made sense of what impressed non-family members, most especially clinical personnel, as unintelligible or, indeed, as simply non-existent communications from the child. Given that the families are prodigious in their efforts to maximize the competence of their children, the reports, in effect, are case studies of person-centering in the family. Our explication of these studies highlights their ethnomethodologically informed conceptual underpinnings and empirical findings, and provides illustrations of what we have referred to as 'practices,' 'assumptions' and 'skills.' In addition, we begin to explore reflexively how these studies are themselves the product of practices shaped by the organizational contexts in which they were conducted.

'The Social Construction of Unreality: A Case Study of a Family's Attribution of Competence to a Severely Retarded Child' (Pollner & McDonald-Wikler, 1985) is a case study of a family which came to a major psychiatric clinic requesting diagnosis and help with their 5½-year-old daughter. Family members were in agreement that Mary was a bright and gregarious child within the family, but refused to behave normally or to speak in public situations. The child was observed in the clinic over an eight-week period by the staff, including numerous specialists in developmental disabilities. Mary was diagnosed as severely retarded and virtually incapable of speech. The family's resistance to the diagnosis was itself diagnosed as symptomatic of a *folie famille* – a shared family delusion – initiated by the mother.

The analysis is devoted to describing the 'skills, practices, and strategies' employed by the family 'to create and then "discover" Mary's competence.' Intensive analysis of the video-taped interaction revealed a variety of practices. Through the practice of *framing,* family members invoked a definition of the situation and assigned significance to Mary's behaviors – even if they were seemingly non-responsive – in terms of the definitional frame. Thus, for example, the sister proposes a game of 'catch' and places a ball in Mary's hands. As the ball tumbles from Mary's hand, the sister characterizes the event in terms of the imposed frame in saying, 'Almost dropped it.' In *postscripting,* family members embedded Mary's behaviors in a context of meaning which made them appear to be autonomous or responsive actions. Thus, for example, family members 'requested' Mary to 'open the door' *after* Mary had begun to move toward the door in a manner which made it seem likely that she would open it. Through *puppeteering,* family members physically maneuver Mary through actions while narrating the scene to imply that Mary was performing as an autonomous and responsive agent.

Although Mary was never observed to speak in the hospital or in video-taped sequences, family members' responses to Mary implied that they were reacting to something she had said. The practice which was referred to as *putting words in Mary's mouth* appears most dramatically on an audio-tape which the family was invited to make to secure samples of Mary's language abilities with family members at home. The family reported difficulty in making the tape and was dissatisfied with the quality of Mary's performance. The taped transactions, however, included several sequences in which Mary does not utter an intelligible utterance, and typically does not utter anything at all, but is nevertheless responded to as though she had made an intelligible, meaningful statement. Thus, in an episode in which Mary is given a newly bought robe, the following transaction occurred:

FATHER:	*Want to see it in the mirror?*
MARY:	*(Gurgling sound)*
FATHER:	*She doesn't like it.*
MOTHER	*You don't like the robe? It fits you.*
MARY:	*(Gurgling sound)*
MOTHER:	*What did you say about Daddy?*
MARY:	*Mmmmmmm(Gurgling sound)*
FATHER:	*She thinks it's too cheap!*

In numerous sequences, family members found Mary to be doing other or less than what they felt she should or could do. Indeed, the parents' dissatisfaction with Mary's performance led them to the clinic. Family members, however, accounted for Mary's failures by reference to her obstinacy, playfulness, or manipulativeness. In *accounting in the 'bright' direction,* family members explained Mary's failure to behave appropriately as expressions of a character trait or intentional choice not to behave appropriately. Thus, for example, in one sequence in which Mary makes no response to her father's repeated requests to 'get the ball,' the father refers to Mary as a 'bad girl.'

Within the terms of the clinical diagnosis of Mary's capacity for communication, the analysis shows how the family created and sustained their world. The ethnomethodological sensitivity to the enacted character of social reality furnished a means of examining the nature of Mary's personhood as it is attributed and sustained by family members. The analysis provides insight into the insistence and persistence of their claims regarding Mary's competence; the family furnished itself with a continuous stream of evidence testifying to their child's normal, if not precocious, level of intelligence and responsiveness.

The analysis, however, is not entirely respectful of the indigenous family world. To be sure, the study recognizes and enters into the world of what is referred to in the article (using Elsa First's [1975] phrase) as a 'little tribe in distress.' Yet the inchoate appreciation of the family's indigenous world is suffused by irony. Every aspect of the analysis is predicated upon the authority of the clinical diagnosis of Mary as incapable of expressive speech. From the title of the study onward, the family's version is defined as a 'delusion' and the family's practices are portrayed as ingeniously sustaining a massive error. The entire analysis presupposes the clinical diagnosis, and virtually every characterization of every action is made from within the terms of the clinical diagnosis. The unusual marriage of the ethnomethodological emphasis on the enactment of social reality and the clinical determination of deficiency and delusion portrays the family as ingeniously creative on one level — and thus endows them with a person-centered identity — yet victimized by a pathological process on another — which renders specious their discourse, practice and, indeed, their reality.

For many of the characterizations of the family practices proffered in the article, an alternative, arguably plausible interpretation that is consonant with the *family's* claims is possible. Thus, for example, Mary's sister's efforts at 'framing' (with its negative implications), might have been formulated as 'cajoling' a recalcitrant child into an activity — or even as a form of humor. The sister's characterization of Mary's unresponsiveness to the ball as 'dropping' is plausibly an ironic commentary on Mary's complete indifference. Our point, however, is not to argue for one or another substantive interpretation, but rather to highlight the arguably different interpretations of family members' actions. How the 'practices' will be characterized is not necessarily determined by the transactions alone, but reflects commitments and choices embedded in the researchers' stance which in the current case, we suggest, is firmly planted within the clinical order.

From a clinical point of view, of course, such an approach is appropriate. The clinical mandate, after all, is to diagnose and treat problems. The diagnosis in this case, moreover, was the product of assiduous and extensive observation and analysis by clinic staff. Thus, use of clinical diagnosis to formulate and address the family's 'problem' is precisely how the clinic and staff member accomplishes accountable competence. As an ethnomethodological analysis of the family, however, the use of clinic determinations and discourse makes the analysis, at best, only ambiguously respectful of the indigenous. The possibility that the clinic's version of Mary and her family might be viewed as a construction is raised, but, in a fashion characteristic of practical endeavors, the reflexive possibility is deferred. The empirical findings of the article thus emerge from a lamination of perspectives in which ethnomethodological initiatives are subordinated to the accountable order of the clinic.

The ethnomethodological initiatives are realized in a very different manner in Goode's (in press) ethnography of a family with a deaf, blind, and profoundly retarded daughter. Goode spent nine months collecting data through extensive observation of Brenda at home and at school. In addition to audio tapes of family interaction with Brenda, Goode took extensive field notes. These procedures resulted in a wealth of data regarding interaction with Brenda in a variety of different contexts and a detailed and intimate view of the family over an extended period of time.

There was an interesting parallel between Brenda and Mary. Brenda had Rubella Syndrome, resulting in severe damage to the central nervous system and particularly to perceptual and motor systems. She had multiple handicaps, including bilateral cataracts, profound mental retardation, cerebral palsy, and other sequelae from prenatal rubella. She had no language or symbols of any sort and few self-help skills. She was regarded as a low functional child by the school and clinical observers, without much prospect of improvement. Like Mary's family, Brenda's family (especially her mother) was regarded by the school as making excessive claims for Brenda's competence. Her mother had indicated to clinical personnel, for example, that Brenda could tell her 'everything' and that she understood her completely. Clinic staff noted in the file that Brenda's mother was not reasonable about the degree of her daughter's handicap, and at one point Brenda's mother is referred to as 'delusional'.

An important difference between these two studies, however, is the organizational context and discourse framing the study. In the study of Mary, the point of departure was the clinical frame within which the family was initially encountered by Wilder (a clinical social worker). Thus, family practices were formulated from the vantage (or dis-advantage) point of the clinical determination that the family was 'delusional.' Goode, on the other hand, did not have a clinical responsibility to the family. Without a clinical concern to define the family's 'problems,' he was not committed to clinical diagnoses or assumptions regarding what was 'really' going on in the family. In point of fact, he was being advised by Pollner and Garfinkel as graduate teachers to operate phenomenologically, suspend extrinsic judgments, and find 'family life as lived.'

In order to attenuate the effect of the numerous evaluations of Brenda and her family which emphasized pathology and deficiency, Goode explicitly elected as a research policy to 'go with' or believe the parents unless explicit observations required otherwise. Thus in Goode's analysis there is a prejudice of sorts, albeit one which is deliberately adapted as a bulwark against other prejudices. One of the most significant consequences of the policy is that Brenda and her family are not relegated to a specious world of 'unreality,' 'deficiency,' and 'pathology' from the outset of the analysis. The respect for the indigenous reflected in the maxim also invites a broader methodology; Goode observed the family in their daily round of activity outside the contexts of clinic offices and waiting rooms.

While it is not possible to present the extensive observations gathered by Goode, the family practices for communicating with Brenda at home are examined without asking the question of their fit to other versions of family reality (for example, such as the clinic's). Consequently, the practices are presented in a different light than in the analysis of Mary's family. Rather than being seen as the product of a deficiency or a delusion, the practices are portrayed as features of a communicational network in which both Brenda and her family are involved in subtle, *collaborative* activity. Although Brenda could make only a few basic gestural responses such as indicating pleasure or displeasure, for example, these responses were interpreted in terms of a complex web of routines that allowed them to take on a variety of meanings and nuances. Grunting displeasure after eating often meant 'get me away from the table, to the next part of my routine.' A similar-sounding grunt during a meal could mean 'get me my milk,' which the mother would literally hear as a demand to 'get me my milk.' Similarly, the layout of the home, known and understood to all in the home, was another way of establishing effective non-language-related communication. Thus Brenda could head to places that she knew were forbidden to her by her parents. In this way she could 'get them,' as the family put it. Or, she could get a hold of forbidden objects to similarly anger her mother.

Other practices of communication made less common sense. Brenda's mother sometimes claimed, for example, that she 'just knew' what Brenda was thinking. These were esoteric (i.e., extraordinary) forms of communication that persons having relationships with persons like Brenda or Mary sometimes report to others. Again, the fact that the family claimed communication lacking in common-sense plausibility did not lead Goode to interpret them as pathological or deficient. Indeed, that Goode had also known a child with Rubella Syndrome intimately allowed him to empathize with the mother and father's position. In Goode's analysis, parents are characterized as striving to tell professionals about communication practices that do not fit conventional notions of communication. They are presented by Goode as participating in communicational patterns that they do not know how to describe, rather than as parents who cannot accept their daughter's handicaps and profound retardation, and who invent mentalistic communication as a fantasy to compensate. Similarly, Brenda is presented not as just a person with profound retardation and multiple handicaps, but as someone who participated in the reality construction of her family situation. Admittedly, the participation is asymmetrical, with the parents forming much of the contexting and interpretation work, but it is participation nonetheless.

As we reflected on these studies, we came to appreciate a number of ironic aspects: they reach different interpretations of similar phenomena; they were done at the same place (UCLA) and each work was known to the other authors; and Pollner served as a primary author on one study and primary advisor on the other. Although each study began with comparable appreciations of the ethnomethodological initiatives and a similar research issue, the interpretation and implementation of the initiatives led to very different portrayals of family practice. Although there may well have been significant differences between the families, we suggest that the differences partly reflect critical choices and commitments made at the outset regarding how the families' work was to be construed.

A critical decision in shaping the two studies was the authority accorded clinical judgments and diagnoses. In the study of Mary's family, the priority given to clinic assumptions suffuses the choice of data and the discourse used to describe Mary and her family. In the study of Brenda, by contrast, the suspension of the authority of clinical judgments about family reality contributes to an alternative style of data collection and a different discourse for describing the family and their 'ethnomethods.' Thus, the researcher's stance with regard to the clinical diagnosis ramifies every aspect of the study ultimately shaping how these families are conceived and described.

Because of the practical need of organizations and professions to produce versions of reality, it is not likely that ethnomethodological initiatives will be given priority over pragmatic organizational concerns. Practitioners and professionals require a specific diagnosis or determination of what is really happening, rather than an infinitely regressing consideration of how such versions are produced. Thus, there is a pragmatic incentive to terminate questioning at some point and to treat some determinations as 'adequate for all practical purposes' (Schutz, 1967). Insofar as the ethnomethodological initiatives are 'useful' to clinicians, it is likely they will be subordinated to clinical concerns and discourse – as in the study of Mary. Such studies can add to clinical knowledge about the construction of particular social worlds, although the increment will, of necessity, be in terms pre-figured by clinical-professional discourse.

Despite the practical aversion to suspending one's own frame of reference or, worse, conceiving of it as a construction, we suggest that ethnomethodological studies which suspend the authority of established clinical discourse and which reflexively consider their own construction have the greatest potential for developing new insight into the ways of persons and personhood – and ultimately into the ways of clinicians and researchers. Goode's radical respect for the indigenous world of Brenda and her family which entailed 'going with' the family and suspending clinical portrayals, for example, revealed layers of communicative activity which seemed to have been disattended, discounted, or gone unnoticed by clinical personnel (cf. Bogdan & Taylor, 1989). Further, although reflexive inquiry can be fruitless or paralyzing, a properly proportioned appreciation of the extent to which inquiry and diagnosis is organizationally embedded and suffused by taken-for-granted practices and presuppositions may secure 'therapeutic' benefits. At the very least, the potential of reflexive awareness brings into view the deeply personal character, not only of 'subjects,' but of researchers as well. In contrast to positivist versions of inquiry, which encourage or require the researcher to cast him- or herself as a passive agent in the production of knowledge, the reflexive dimension of ethnomethodology reminds the researcher that, like his subjects, he or she is endlessly and irremediably implicated in the construction of social reality. Thus, in embracing the ethnomethodological initiatives in full measure, a researcher may find that not only has he or she realized a person-centered stance with regard to his or her subjects, but he or she has also established a person-centered stance with regard to his- or herself.

CONCLUDING REMARKS

The image of persons rooted within ethnomethodology is of creative, interpretative, and skilled actors participating in the construction of what they regard as intelligible and meaningful worlds. The ethnomethodological imperative is to examine in rich, fine detail the actual instant-by-instant 'work' – the shared practices of talking, reasoning, and cognizing—through which members accomplish these worlds. Because these practices are typically taken for granted, ethnomethodological studies afford the opportunity for participants to become aware of and then change or self-consciously continue the work through which they make their world.

'Persons' are themselves features of the constructed world (cf. Gergen & Davis, 1985). Common-sense thinking often conceives of personhood as lodged in psychobiological processes. The ethnomethodological perspective, however, emphasizes the socially sanctioned reasoning, cognizing, and talking through which versions of personhood are developed, used, and sustained in particular social settings. Thus, ethnomethodology provides a resource for describing the actual practices through which versions of persons and personhood—be they compatible with person-centered approaches or not—are constructed and reproduced.

Ethnomethodological inquiry is itself a creative, interpretative activity through which a community—the community of researchers—constitutes what it regards as an intelligible, sensible, and meaningful world. This recognition is a continual invitation to turn to ethnomethodological studies, as they are themselves embedded within taken-for-granted practices, assumptions, and skills. With regard to personhood per se, reflexivity entails examining how the ethnomethodological rendering of the construction of person in any particular setting is itself suffused by implicit and explicit assumptions and practices for constructing person (or whatever the particular aspect under study happens to be). As might be anticipated, the invitation to reflexivity is often declined because of its unsettling ramifications. Nevertheless, the potential of a reflexive turn is a reminder that, like the members of the communities and settings he or she investigates, the ethnomethodologist is engaged in the tacit labor of the construction of social reality.

The case studies we described illustrate the movement of ethnomethodologically informed inquiry through conceptual, empirical, and reflexive phases. Moreover, they suggest that the implementation of perspectives which respect and promote the competence and creativity of persons is a contingent accomplishment in everyday life *and* in the research activities which explicate everyday life. Each study displays a family's unceasing efforts to discern and maximize the communicative competencies of their children through finely detailed practices of cognition, reasoning, and interaction. Our reflexive commentary suggests, however, that the portrayal of family practices in person-centered terms is itself a contingent accomplishment which may be transformed, despite the investigators' intentions. The ethnomethodological sensitivity to the subtle, multi-leveled nature of the construction of social reality provides a significant resource for uncovering the actual practices through which families, clinics, and researchers form, transform, and enact versions of one another.

References

Anspach, R. R. (1988). Notes on the sociology of medical discourse: The language of case presentation. *Journal of Health and Social Behavior, 29*, 357–75.

Bogdan, R., & Taylor, S. J. (1989). Relationships with severely disabled people: The social construction of humanness. *Social Problems, 36*, 135–48.

Cicourel, A. V. (1972). Basic and normative rules in the negotiation of status and role. In D. Sudnow (Ed.), *Studies in Social Interaction* (pp. 229–58). New York: Free Press.

Cicourel, A. V. (1981). Notes on the integration of micro and macro levels of analysis. In A. V. Cicourel and K. Knorr-Cetina (Eds.), *Advances in social theory and methodology: Toward an integration of macro and micro-sociologies* (pp. 51–80). London: Routledge & Kegan Paul.

Evans-Pritchard, F. F. (1937). *Witchcraft, oracles and magic among the Azande.* London: Oxford University Press.

First, E. (1975). The new wave in psychiatry. *New York Review of Books, 22,* 8–15.

Garfinkel, H. (1967). *Studies in ethnomethodology.* Englewood Cliffs, NJ: Prentice-Hall.

Garfinkel, H., Lynch, M., & Livingston, F. (1981). The work of a discovering science construed with materials from the optically discovered pulsar. *Philosophy of the Social Sciences, 11,* 131–58.

Gergen, K. J., & Davis, K. E. (1985) (Eds). *The social construction of the person.* New York: Springer-Verlag.

Goode. D. A. (1979). The world of the congenitally deaf-blind. In J. Jacobs & H. Schwartz (Eds.), *Qualitative sociology* (pp. 381–96). New York: Free Press.

Goode, D. A. (in press). On understanding without words: communication between a deaf-blind child and her parents.

Heritage, J. C. (1984). *Garfinkel and ethnomethodology.* Cambridge, England: Polity.

Husserl, E. (1962). *Ideas: General introduction to pure phenomenology* (W. R. Boyce Gison. Trans.). New York: Collier. (Original work published in 1913.)

Parsons, T. (1951). *The social system.* New York: Free Press.

Pollner, M., & McDonald-Wikler, L. (1985). The social construction of unreality: A case study of a family's attribution of competence to a severely retarded child. *Family Process, 24,* 241–54.

Schutz, A. (1967). *Collected papers I: The problem of social reality.* The Hague: Martinus Nijhoff.

Part F

Issues, Controversies, Discussions

The Paradox of Nondirectiveness
in the Person-Centered Approach

David J. Cain   *Carlsbad, California*

Directiveness. The very thought of directiveness makes many client-centered therapists cringe. In many ways it seems to represent the antithesis of a person-centered way of being. Yet the issue of directiveness raises some fundamental questions about the meaning and practice of person-centered approaches.

In this article I will examine the concepts of directiveness and nondirectiveness and propose that nondirectiveness may not always be a compatible component of client-centered therapy, student-centered teaching, or various applications of the person-centered approach.

HISTORICAL PERSPECTIVE

In its early stages of development, Rogers' approach to therapy was, in part, a *reaction* to the directive therapies of the period. In his first text defining the parameters of his new approach to therapy, Rogers (1942) devoted a chapter, 'The Directive Versus the Non-Directive Approach,' to this issue (pp. 115–30). In this text Rogers often attacked, sometimes quite fervently, a number of counseling techniques and methods that were common between 1900 and 1940. These included ordering and forbidding, exhortation, suggestion, reassurance, encouragement, catharsis, advice, interpretation, and persuasion, among others. Rogers' stated objection to these methods was that they 'have deeply ingrained in them the idea "The counselor knows best"' (p. 27). As Rogers articulated his newly developing position, he placed great emphasis on what counseling was *not*. What it wasn't was those methods listed here. In contrast, he indicated that the 'basic aspects of a therapeutic relationship' *were:* 'counselor warmth and responsiveness,' 'permissiveness in regard to expression of feelings,' 'therapeutic limits' and 'freedom from any type of pressure or coercion' (pp. 87–9).

Rogers' intent in developing this position was *to free* the client to grow in his or her own way. He stated that the counseling relationship 'is not a mere negative restraint, a wooden refusal to influence the client. It is the positive ground for personality growth and development, for conscious choice, for *self-directed* integration' (p. 90, italics added). Obviously Rogers' main objection to *therapist* directiveness was that it impaired the possibility for client-directed behavior. He wished to free the client from the therapist's authority, believing that 'therapy and authority cannot exist within the same relationship' (1942, p. 109). Understandably, Rogers had associated therapist directiveness with authority or control over the client.

In contrasting directive with nondirective approaches, Rogers cites a study by Porter (in Rogers, 1942) in which directive counselors are compared with nondirective counselors. Rogers interpreted the differences between nondirective and directive counselors as follows:

First published in *Person-Centered Review*, Volume 4, Number 2, May 1989.

> The more directive counselors are more active in the counseling situation—they do much more of the talking . . . In nondirective counseling the client comes to 'talk out his problems.' In directive contact the counselor talks to the client . . . We find . . . that differences in method center around such techniques as persuading the client, pointing out problems needing correction, interpreting test results, and asking specific questions, all of which are more characteristic of the directive approach than the nondirective . . .
>
> We note the fundamental contrast in emphasis, the directive group stressing those techniques which control the interview and move the client toward a counselor-chosen goal, the nondirective group stressing those means which cause the client to be more conscious of his own attitudes and feelings . . .
>
> It might be said that counseling of the directive sort is characterized by many highly specific questions to which specific answers are expected, and by information and explanation given by the counselor . . . The counselor further gives the client opportunity to express his attitudes on specified topics, and points out to the client problems and conditions which he, the counselor, has observed to be in need of correction . . . He endeavors to bring about change by proposing the action the client should take, and by bringing to bear both evidence and personal influence to insure that such action will be taken.
>
> On the other hand, counseling of the nondirective sort is characterized by a preponderance of client activity, the client doing most of the talking about his problems. The counselor's primary techniques are those that help the client more clearly to recognize and understand his feelings, attitudes, and reaction patterns, and which encourage the client to talk about them. (Rogers, 1942, pp. 122–4)

Rogers' main objection to the directive approach was that the 'unstated implication is that the counselor is superior to the client, since the latter is assumed to be incapable of accepting full responsibility for choosing his goals' (p. 126). Another objection was that 'The directive viewpoint places a high value on social conformity and the right of the more able to direct the less able' (p. 127).

Interestingly, the word *nondirective* does not appear in the *title* of any of Rogers' published articles after 1947, and he barely addresses the issue in any of his books after *Counseling and Psychotherapy* (1942). Why? One possible explanation is that Rogers tired of facing attacks on the nondirective nature of his counseling. John Shlien (personal communication, 1989) recalls (circa 1947) that Rogers moved away from the 'nondirective' descriptor because his approach was viewed by some critics as wishy-washy and directionless. Rogers wanted to make it clear that therapy did have direction, but it was client-determined direction. Another possibility is that Rogers' thinking was evolving over the years and the issue of directiveness became increasingly less central to what he believed was the essence of his approach. Instead of therapist nondirectiveness, he spoke more of *self-directed* behavior on the part of the client or student.

SOME INTENDED EFFECTS OF NONDIRECTIVE BEHAVIOR

As a nondirective therapist and teacher, Rogers' apparent intents were to avoid determining or controlling: (1) *what* the client talked about or *how* or *when* the client talked about it, (2) the client's goals, or (3) the actions or means by which the client attained those goals. Instead, he wished to provide his clients with a sense of *freedom* to use their sessions in any way they saw fit. He trusted that the client would eventually make constructive choices in a permissive, supportive, and understanding atmosphere. Rogers also wanted to allow the client to be *active* and encouraged client-initiated activity by restraining the nature and amount of his activity. Obviously, Rogers wanted clients to assume responsibility for their lives and felt that this was more likely in an atmosphere free from any pressure to adhere to the authority of the counselor.

As Rogers applied his ideas to education, he defined the aim of education as the *facilitation of learning.* He aptly titled his two major texts on learning *Freedom to Learn* (1969, 1983). The pervasive theme of these texts, and Rogers' thinking on education, is to free students from the typical constraints of the educational systems in which they find themselves. He clearly wished to empower students to take control over the course of their learning—to choose what was to be learned and how it would be learned. The role of the 'teacher' was defined in terms of a facilitative co-learner who would provide the student with both personal and informational *resources* for learning.

THE PROBLEM OF INDIVIDUAL DIFFERENCES

On the surface it seems hard to argue with the goal of providing optimal levels of freedom for our students and clients to facilitate their learning and growth. Yet, curiously enough, an approach that places enormous emphasis and value on the individual tends to take a 'one approach fits all' stance toward the facilitation of growth. That is, the same basic attitudinal qualities in the therapist or teacher are viewed as necessary and sufficient for all clients (students) regardless of individual differences in the person, even enormous ones. Not surprisingly, there is generally fairly little variation in the ways person-centered practitioners interact with their clients. Therefore, the person-centered approach seems to deny or minimize the evidence that individuals have different learning styles or preferences that are more conducive than others to their learning.

At this point, I will review briefly some research that addresses the issue of individual learning styles. Dunn and Dunn (1978), in their text titled *Teaching Students Through Their Individual Learning Styles,* summarize learning style research as follows:

> Recent research concerned with identifying the relationship between academic achievement and learning style has provided consistent support for the following: (1) students do learn differently from each other; (2) student performances in different subject areas are related to how individuals do, in fact, learn; (3) when students are taught through the methods each prefers, they do learn more effectively. (p. 389)

Their Learning Style Inventory identifies a wide range of factors related to learning preferences. Some of these include preferences for: quiet, light, and temperature regulation, learning alone, auditory, visual, and tactile and kinesthetic learning. Obviously the factors affecting a given individual's learning are varied and complex.

Witkin and his colleagues (in Slavin, 1988) have identified two learning-perceptual styles: field dependent and field independent. The field-dependent individuals 'tend to see patterns as a whole, and have difficulty separating out specific aspects of a situation or pattern' (Slavin, 1988, p. 312). In contrast, field independent people 'are more able to see the parts that make up a large pattern [and] . . . are more likely to do well with numbers, science, and problem-solving tasks' (Slavin, 1988, pp. 312–13).

Entwistle (in Slavin, 1988) identified differences in cognitive style along the dimensions of impulsivity versus reflectivity. Impulsive students 'tend to work and make decisions quickly, while reflective types are more likely to take a long time considering all alternatives' (Slavin, 1988, p. 313).

Witkin's research (1968) in the field of psychotherapy provides some evidence that more highly differentiated individuals (field independent) are likely to respond differently in therapy from clients whose degree of differentiation is low (field dependent). For example, results of one study provided evidence that less differentiated clients show more shame, less guilt, more diffuse anxiety reactions, and more inner-directed hostility, and are less verbal than more differentiated clients.

The apparent equivalency of a wide variety of therapeutic approaches on client outcome would seem to suggest that clients learn and grow in many different ways. While there is as yet little evidence on the issue, it would seem that any therapeutic approach might be made more effective to the degree that it 'fits' the client's individual styles of learning and growth.

IMPLICATIONS FOR PRACTICE

Person-centered practitioners share a belief that their clients have the capacity to know or recognize that which promotes their learning and growth. Consistent with this notion, clients' perceptions of themselves and their worlds are viewed as the ultimate criterion for determining whether therapists' or teachers' attitudes, manner of relating, or specific behaviors are facilitative or not. Therefore, the truly person-centered practitioners would be continuously receptive to learning how their clients learn effectively. By doing so, they would then be more likely to interact in a manner that best fits their client's needs and preferences. In their attempt to create an optimal atmosphere for learning and growth, person-centered practitioners would be less concerned about whether they are being directive or not and more concerned about whether whatever they do facilitates or impairs learning. Receptivity, flexibility, and differentiated responses in practitioners are likely to maximize learning in their clients.

In contrast, rigid adherence to nondirectiveness may be experienced as an *imposition* by our clients or students if this is the only way we are willing to interact with them. By remaining nondirective, despite direct and indirect feedback from our clients that this is not helpful, we are essentially requiring our clients to do our thing. Despite our good intentions to provide freedom for our clients, they may well feel constrained by our limited manner of interacting. While we may wish to empower through nondirectiveness, our clients may experience themselves as having less power and freedom because they are likely to view us as authorities regarding how they can best change. They may infer from our nondirective behavior that 'the best way to learn is to find your own way.' And while this may well be consistent with person-centered values and beliefs about how growth optimally takes place, it may not, in fact, be true for a given client or student with specific needs or goals.

Perhaps an illustration will help. An individual approaches a 'student-centered' tennis instructor with the goal of learning to develop an effective forehand. If the tennis instructor remains nondirective in his or her teaching style, and only encourages the student to experiment with different ways to hit a forehand, the student may eventually develop an adequate forehand. However, if the instructor was fully student-centered, I believe he or she would be more likely to inquire or notice how the student learns best and pursue that approach with the student. In this example, the student may be able to inform the instructor that he or she learns best by first spending time watching and developing a visual image of an effective stroking pattern *before* beginning to practice hitting the ball.

I wish to make it clear that I am not attempting to make a case for or against nondirectiveness. Rather, I wish to make the point that nondirectiveness is neither a defining nor essential component of person-centeredness. In fact, to the degree to which person-centered practitioners feel compelled to be nondirective, the more likely they are to impose limits on their clients because they constrain their own behavior. By doing so, they limit the variety of ways they interact with their clients and, in turn, the variety of ways their clients are likely to interact with them. Jules Seeman (1965) articulated this dilemma as he reflected on the implications of the early phases of the development of nondirective and client-centered therapy. He stated:

> If the beginning was a time of innovation and daring, it can now be seen also as a time of caution and constraint. The client was to be made free, but the cost turned out to be high structure and low freedom of movement for the counselor. The counselor could lock himself into a ritual of verbal response which was anything but spontaneous. And in the end, a situation so much structured for the counselor could not be free for the client. (p. 216)

Rogers, too, was aware of what might be called the 'freedom dilemma.' In responding to an interview by David Ryback regarding the desirability of competition and an honor roll in schools, Rogers commented: 'We often forget that you can give people alternatives. I don't like to "impose" freedom or "impose" a new set of values.'

In order for our clients to experience genuine freedom it seems necessary that we too must feel free to interact in a variety of ways that may or may not include nondirectiveness. In fact, it is almost impossible to be completely 'nondirective' in terms of the perceptual viewpoint of the client. No matter how one acts (or responds) the behavior will be *perceived* as having some degree of directiveness, however subtle or minimal. Even if one says or does nothing (assuming this is possible) while in the presence of another person, some inference is likely to be made about the possible intents and meanings of such behavior.

In my view, the issues of power and control are much more basic to person-centered practice than the issue of directiveness. Person-centered practitioners seem to share a fundamental value and desire to empower their clients. Very few show any inclination to guide, manipulate, or control those with whom they work. Yet this conscious intention not to direct or control another person sometimes has a constraining instead of a freeing effect. By adhering to strongly ingrained values of nondirectiveness, person-centered practitioners sometimes lose sight of the fact that they too need to feel free and act freely if they are to offer or create optimal conditions for growth in their clients. Our clients are not likely to experience any manipulative or controlling intent on our part if whatever we offer (e.g., exercises, strategies, tools and techniques, information, structures) derives from our understanding of their individual needs and is done in a manner that clearly communicates that 'this is an *option* you may wish to consider.' If we truly trust our clients' capacity to recognize and choose what they need to move forward in their lives, then we are more likely to feel free to offer our personal and professional resources to them. As we consider the actual (as opposed to intended) impact we have on our clients, it would seem helpful to consider whether we inadvertently impose our ideologies and values on our clients, or trust them to guide us in providing that which will best meet their individual needs in a manner compatible with their preferred learning styles.

REFERENCES

Dunn, R., & Dunn, K. (1978). *Teaching students through their individual learning styles.* Reston, VA: Reston.

Rogers, C. R. (1942). *Counseling and psychotherapy.* Boston: Houghton Mifflin.

Rogers, C. R. (1969). *Freedom to learn.* Columbus, OH: Charles E. Merrill.

Rogers, C. R. (1983). *Freedom to learn for the 80s.* Columbus, OH: Charles E. Merrill.

Ryback, D. (1989). An interview with Carl Rogers. *Person-Centered Review, 4*(1), 103.

Seeman, J. (1965). Perspectives in client-centered therapy. In B. Wolman (Ed.), *Handbook of clinical psychology* (pp. 1215–29). New York: McGraw-Hill.

Slavin, R. E. (1988). *Educational psychology.* Englewood Cliffs, NJ: Prentice-Hall.

Witkin, H., Lewis, H., & Weil, E. (1968). Affective reactions and patient-therapist interactions among more differentiated and less differentiated patients early in therapy. *Journal of Nervous and Mental Disease, 146*(3), 193–208.

Principled and Instrumental Nondirectiveness in Person-Centered and Client-Centered Therapy

Barry Grant *Chicago, Illinois*

Nondirectiveness is a focal point in the debate about the nature of person-centered and client-centered therapy. In my view, the debate is essentially about the morally best way of doing therapy. Conceptions of nondirectiveness differ primarily in whether they emphasize pragmatic concerns for promoting growth and 'meeting needs' or respect for persons. Two conceptions of nondirectiveness—instrumental and principled—are described and compared. Principled nondirectiveness is elaborated, and a justification for it is sketched.

The defining characteristics of person-centered therapy and client-centered therapy have been debated in *Renaissance*, the *Person-Centered Review*, and at ADPCA meetings for at least the past three years (e.g., Bozarth & Brodley, 1986; Cain, 1986; Rogers, 1987). One of the focal points of the debate, perhaps *the* focal point, is nondirectiveness: what nondirectiveness is, and the extent to which consistent adherence to it is a feature of person-centered therapy and client-centered therapy. Conceptions of nondirectiveness seem to differ primarily in the extent to which they emphasize either pragmatic concerns for promoting growth and 'meeting needs,' or respect for persons. What I will call 'instrumental nondirectiveness' and 'principled nondirectiveness' embody the different emphases. Instrumental nondirectiveness is seen as essentially a means of facilitating growth: principled nondirectiveness is essentially an expression of respect. In this paper, I describe and compare the two notions, and elaborate on and sketch a justification for principled nondirectiveness.[1]

In the instrumental version of nondirectiveness, which I take to be exemplified in a recent essay by Cain (1989), the purpose of the therapist's actions is to bring about growth or empower clients. If being nondirective facilitates growth for a client in a particular instance, then it is valuable; if it does not, then the therapist decides whether continuing to be nondirective or adopting a different approach would be more effective. Respect for the client is not absent, but is allied to or tempered with a pragmatic concern with promoting growth. In the principled version, the therapist's actions are derived from the fundamental idea of respect for persons (Brodley, 1986; Grant, 1986). The therapist does not attempt or intend to make anything happen—growth, insight, self-acceptance— in the client, but rather provides the therapeutic conditions in the belief that they are expressions of respect and with the hope that the client will make use of them. Following Brodley's (1988) distinction between the person-centered therapies and client-centered therapy, principled nondirectiveness is essential to client-centered therapy, while

---

1. This essay is a revision of a paper presented at the Third Annual Meeting of the Association for the Development of the Person-Centered Approach in Atlanta, May 1989.

First published in *Person-Centered Review*, Volume 5, Number 1, February 1990.

instrumental nondirectiveness is part of the other person-centered therapies.

The two conceptions of nondirectiveness are part of different moral visions. To describe them in this way may seem odd and out of place, but I believe it precisely describes the most important difference between the two views. The debate about the nature of person-centered therapy, and about nondirectiveness, is essentially an argument about right and wrong in psychotherapy. Before discussing nondirectiveness, I want to give this claim some substance.

ON THE QUESTION OF THE NATURE OF PERSON-CENTERED THERAPY

One way of looking at the question of the nature or definition of person-centered therapy is to see it as asking what is the correct interpretation of Rogers' theory of psychotherapy. Rogers originated person-centered therapy. When we ask what it is, we ask about what he thought. This is important both to historians of psychology and to those of us who call ourselves person-centered or client-centered. We have chosen these labels because we believe our views on therapy are identical, or significantly similar, to Rogers' views.

Any body of complex thought that has developed over a period of time will be open to more than one compelling reading. There is no one correct answer to the question of what Rogers' therapy is, any more than there is one correct understanding of Freud's, Jung's, or any other person's therapy. Debate about the correct interpretation of Rogers' work can continue for as long as his readers can come up with new and persuasive ways of making sense of his writings. The debate will end when we all agree or lose interest. Neither is likely to happen soon.

The danger of debating the definition of person-centered therapy or client-centered therapy solely in terms of what Rogers wrote is that it can distract us from explicitly addressing a more important question. Certainly none of the disputants are just arguing about how to read Rogers. We are exercised about 'misreadings' of Rogers because we have judgments about the practices they imply. We think it is wrong or right, better or worse, to help people to focus, to give advice, to be nondirective, and so on. We don't just think Rogers did or did not advocate these things. The debate is not essentially (or should not be) about the correct understanding of Rogers. It is a way of addressing a basic question every form of psychotherapy must answer: How *ought* one to practice therapy?

The debate about what person-centered therapy or client-centered therapy is or is not is better understood as a dispute about what is the morally best way of doing therapy. Taking a position on the matter begins with Rogers' work, but it should not end there. It begins there because the participants in the debate have been heavily influenced by Rogers. We take our vocabulary and guiding ideas from him. Because we are different and he isn't unitary, we don't take the same things in the same way, and we argue about what he said. But, defining terms, offering interpretations, and declaring ourselves are not adequate justifications for our practices. We must also give moral reasons for our views. We must be able to argue why it is good to engage in the practices we advocate. We should be able to do this because psychotherapy is a moral enterprise. It is an activity which can and does affect the well-being of others, and which is based on ideas about right and wrong in human relationships (see, of many authors who make this point, Grant, 1985; London, 1986; Szasz, 1978; Watson, 1958). Thus, principled and instrumental nondirectiveness are not only competing interpretations of Rogers, they are competing ideas about how one ought to conduct oneself as a therapist, what is most important in therapy, what it serves, what its goal is.

INSTRUMENTAL NONDIRECTIVENESS

In instrumental nondirectiveness, the therapist's primary commitment is to the client's growth. Cain (1989) argued that strict adherence to nondirectiveness does clients a disservice when it does not serve the client's growth. He sees nondirectiveness as a way of bringing about certain effects in clients; it is valuable insofar as it can do this, and an obstacle insofar as it cannot. He reads Rogers as advocating nondirectiveness because it promotes freedom and growth: 'Rogers' intent . . . was to *free* the client to grow in his or her own way' (p. 124). The 'paradox' of nondirectiveness in the title of his paper refers to the therapist, whose purpose in being nondirective is to empower, free, and bring about growth in clients, and who may, at times, actually disempower clients, and hamper and frustrate their growth. Cain (1989) wrote:

> To the degree to which person-centered practitioners feel compelled to be nondirective, the more likely they are to impose limits on their clients because they constrain their own behavior . . . In order for our clients to feel genuine freedom it seems necessary that we too must feel free to interact in a variety of ways that may or may not include nondirectiveness. (pp. 129–30)

The major point of his essay is that this is especially true for clients whose 'learning style' is not compatible with nondirectiveness. He argued, in effect, that it is wrong to be nondirective when being so is counterproductive. Cain did not explicitly describe what actions are consistent with his conception of nondirectiveness, but he seems to have a common view of it which holds that it is usually expressed through empathic responses. Indications from the client for a different response are likely to be met with emphatic responses, by simply listening or by encouraging the client to experiment or figure things out alone.

In this view, efficacy is the most important criterion that nondirectiveness or any attitude or technique has to meet. 'Does it facilitate growth?' is the first question a therapist of this ilk asks. Growth is necessarily defined to some extent independently of the client's frame of reference. The therapist must have an idea of what constitutes growth in order to decide when to be nondirective.

PRINCIPLED NONDIRECTIVENESS

'Does it respect the client?' is the first question a therapist who has a principled conception of nondirectiveness asks about an intervention. For this sort of therapist, the question about efficacy is not absent. Because therapists claim to offer service, they may ask clients if therapy is helpful. But the client-centered therapist's rationale for being nondirective is not that nondirectiveness works. Being nondirective in a principled manner is not a way of making something happen, not a way of causing growth or freedom or empowerment or self-acceptance. Client-centered therapists are not nondirective because they believe that by declining to exercise power they are more likely to 'free' clients than if they did something else. They are nondirective because they respect their clients' voices. Principled nondirectiveness is an attitude that provides a 'space' for growth, not one that intends to cause it. Nondirectiveness, like love, is not acted upon for what it achieves, but for what it honors. Excepting instances in which other moral considerations prevail, it is, within this framework, always right to be nondirective and always wrong not to be.

Principled nondirectiveness is an attitude, not a set of behaviors. Having the attitude does not mean having a stock or a 'hands off' approach to relating to clients, although the most common expression of it is empathic understanding responses (Brodley, 1988). Living the attitude means being open and responsive to clients' requests and indications for other types of response. So, for example, a tennis instructor who holds to principled nondirectiveness would not respond to a request for instruction by encouraging the student to experiment, as Cain's, or a directive instructor would, *unless* he or she thought that this was the best way to develop a stroke. If the instructor thought that there were better ways, those would be offered instead. A request for help would get the instructor's best answer. If the instructor did not know, or was not sure, that would be indicated.

Principled nondirectiveness is an expression of an absence of the *intention* to make anything in particular happen, and of an openness to following the client's direction.

How can the principled nondirective attitude be justified? I think there are a couple of reasons for it which I will sketch briefly. One derives from the 'Attitudes and Orientation of the Counselor' chapter of *Client-Centered Therapy* (Rogers, 1951). There, Rogers wrote about the dignity and worth of the individual, the individual's capacity for self-direction and right to self-direction, all values of liberalism. Client-centered therapy can be understood as liberal values enacted in a therapeutic setting (see Van Belle, 1980). 'The liberal idea of freedom . . . claims for man, by reason of his humanity, the right, within limits . . . to order his life as seems good to him' (Plemenatz, 1973). Client-centered therapy fully respects clients' right to determine their path in life. It makes no assumptions about what people need or how they should be free. It respects clients as authors of their own lives and provides them with a space to rewrite their story, if they want to. Ibsen describes liberty as giving each individual the right to liberate himself, each according to his personal needs. Client-centered therapy offers this liberty. It does it in such a way that its ends are consistent with its means (Tomlinson & Whitney, 1970). This is very important. The liberation that can come from client-centered therapy is accomplished by respecting clients as autonomous beings, not by making them autonomous beings.

Principled nondirectiveness can also be seen as an expression of a nearly religious attitude toward the world. The attitude is religious in that it has to do with what Edwards (1982) calls 'a fundamental and pervasive stance to all that is' (p. 236). Edwards very beautifully expresses an attitude that can serve as a basis for nondirectiveness in his description of an aspect of Wittgenstein's thought:

> Wittgenstein's [notion of sound human understanding] is the expression of a religious commitment; it is the expression that is, of a fundamental and pervasive stance to all that is, a stance which treats the world as a *miracle*, as an object of love, not of will. The sound human understanding is the mark of such love, for it is a feature of love that it never literalizes any perception; love is always ready to go deeper, to see through whatever has already been seen. From the perspective of loving attention, no story is ever over; no depths are ever fully plumbed. The world and its beings are a miracle, never to be comprehended, with depths never to be exhausted. Thus the sound human understanding is essentially a religious response . . . It is a response that makes sheer acknowledgement, not control, central. (p. 236)

This attitude is one of being humbled before the mystery of others and wishing only to acknowledge and respect them. Client-centered therapy is a way of making this acknowledgment — an almost aesthetic appreciation for the uniqueness and otherness of the client.

The paradox of principled nondirectiveness is that a therapist who wholeheartedly lives the attitude may at times appear to be extremely directive. A client may request direction, advice, interpretations, or instructions, and the therapist may offer these. The decision to do so does not depend on a determination of the client's needs, best interests, diagnosis, or learning style. It rests, rather, on whether the therapist wants to honor the request, judges himself or herself competent to honor it, and believes it moral to do so. The therapist has no stake in having things come out one way rather than another.

Answering questions is not only inconsistent with nondirectiveness, it may at times be required by it. The leading edge of growth is the client's voice — the client's requests, stated intentions, wishes, self-descriptions, and desires. Growth is what the client says and does. It is not a hypothetical process happening somewhere 'inside' the client; nor can it be defined from outside of the client's frame of reference. Answering questions meets clients at the edge of their growth — at the actions they initiate. Giving a personal response to a question is an encounter of one sovereign being with another. It is not a distortion or subversion of a process; it is a response to the only thing a person can know about the particular form of growth of a particular client.[2]

Principled nondirective therapists take their lead from the client and do not adapt to any determination of the client's 'learning style.' They do not try to figure out clients' learning styles any more than they try to figure out their diagnoses or anything else about them — unless they are asked and have an opinion. Principled nondirectiveness is incompatible with any programmatic use of the hundreds of notions such as 'learning style,' 'diagnosis,' 'level of experiencing,' which a therapist can use to conceptualize the client and link to an understanding of the nature of growth.

Client-centered therapists are, to use Cain's word, 'constrained' by the attitude of principled nondirectiveness. The freedom he advocates for the therapist as a means of facilitating freedom in clients is not consistent with principled nondirectiveness. Client-centered therapists do not intend to free or constrain their clients. They do limit themselves and the variety of ways in which they interact with clients. But this does not, as Cain argues, impose freedom or anything else on clients. To say so is to misuse language. It is not an imposition to not wish to direct or influence someone anymore than it is an imposition to speak English rather than Spanish, to love rather than hate.

The claim that client-centered therapists limit or constrain themselves needs to be clarified. Beginning and developing therapists should constrain themselves. It is wrong to act on every impulse or idea that occurs while doing therapy. Client-centered therapy is a discipline. Those who are gifted or who have done it for a long time may come to do it 'naturally' and spontaneously. As one develops as a therapist, there is less need for self-restraint because there is less inclination to exercise power and control and more regard and love for others. The desire to change other people, to make things happen, dissipates.

Nondirectiveness, and the attitudes that express it — unconditional positive regard, empathy, and congruence — are moral virtues. They are praiseworthy characteristics of persons. Being able to act spontaneously and idiosyncratically on them does not happen by instructing oneself to loosen up and be free. This emerges out of discipline in the attitudes — e.g., by working on seeing in loving and accepting ways, by detecting and getting rid of the desire to exercise power, or by accepting oneself. No religious or moral tradition that I am aware of trusts that people left to their own devices will acquire the virtues valued by the tradition. They all recognize that character development takes work.

---

2. Rogers often defers answering questions. Sometimes, apparently, he does this because he believes the client ought to figure things out without his ideas and gives indirect instruction to do this. This is not principled nondirectiveness. Other times, apparently, he doesn't answer questions because he doesn't have an answer and doesn't believe he could have one. This is consistent with principled nondirectiveness. Sometimes he does answer questions (Brodley, 1989).

Because there is no telling exactly how a client-centered therapist will develop the attitudes, or what 'new and more subtle ways of implementing [the] client-centered hypothesis' (Rogers, 1951, p. 25) a person will devise, empathic responses and personal responses to direct and indirect questions are not the only forms of response consistent with the nondirective attitude. Offering unsolicited opinions, suggestions, and the like *can* also be consistent with having the attitude. Nondirective client-centered therapy is a way of being, and not a method, because it allows the therapist to make novel, personal, unplanned responses. There is a place in client-centered therapy for

> the therapist . . . in a spontaneous and non-systematic way [to] offer reactions, suggestions, ask questions, try to help the client experience feelings, share aspects of his or her own life, etc., while maintaining a basic and continuing respect for the client as the architect of the process. (Raskin, 1988)

Cain sanctions these sorts of responses if they are well-intentioned attempts to empower the client, offered as options, and based on an understanding of the client's needs and preferences. This rationale implies that the therapist is sizing up the client and judging what might be of most help. They are consistent with principled nondirectiveness if they are just things the therapist feels like saying. They are not justified by what they intend to accomplish, but by being personal expressions of the attitudes. These spontaneous and nonsystematic actions must be understood as coming from someone in whom the attitudes are deeply ingrained. Buddhists say that whatever an enlightened person does is faultless. Maybe so, but those of us who are less than perfect should usually stay to the well-worn path of common virtue. I am often suspicious of these actions in myself when I do them, and in others when I hear about them. I doubt the purity of the motivation. I doubt that they are gifts of love and regard given with no desire to influence.

Perhaps those who are gifted with the attitudes or who have acquired them through discipline agree with the following lines from Rogers and Segel's (1955) film and from Weil (1951), and have no desire to do anything but understand. According to Rogers:

> The most that can be given to another person, not the least, but the most that can be given to another person, is to be willing to go with them in their own separate feelings as a separate person. (Rogers & Segel, 1955 [Film])

In a similar vein, Weil writes:

> Those who are unhappy have no need for anything in this world but people capable of giving them their attention . . . The love of our neighbor in its fullness simply means being able to say to him, 'What are you going through?' (pp. 114–15)

CONCLUSIONS

I have discussed two conceptions of nondirectiveness. Instrumental nondirectiveness is expressed by empathic responses and by encouraging clients to find solutions to problems within themselves. It is an often helpful and sometimes unhelpful way of promoting growth. On the principled conception, nondirectiveness is an ideally unwavering expression of respect that is manifested in many and unpredictable ways, but usually in the form of empathic responses. Many of the same behaviors are consistent with both versions of nondirectiveness, but they are done for different reasons, in different spirits.

Different conceptions of nondirectiveness, and of person-centered therapy and client-centered therapy, are not just private personal ideas about how to do therapy that are justified because Rogers supports them or because they are an expression of one's process of growth. They are ideas about how one should conduct oneself as a therapist, and so they require moral justification. I have sketched two justifications for nondirectiveness in client-centered therapy. One appeals to a principle of respect for persons, the other to an attitude of 'sheer acknowledgement' of others. The adequacy, implications, and appropriateness of these notions can, of course, be argued about. Indeed, we may disagree about what constitutes adequate justification. These are the sorts of discussions that come up when the moral dimension of psychotherapy is seen as central.

REFERENCES

Bozarth, I., & Brodley, B. (1986). Client-centered psychotherapy: A statement. *Person-Centered Review, 1*(3), 262–71.

Brodley, B. (1986). Client-centered therapy: What is it? What is it not? Unpublished manuscript.

Brodley, B. (1988). Untitled article. *Renaissance, 5*(3–4), 1–2.

Brodley, B. (1989). Carl Rogers' responses to questions in client-centered interviews. Unpublished manuscript.

Cain, D. (1986). What does it mean to be 'person-centered'? *Person-Centered Review, 1*(3), 251–6.

Cain, D. (1989). The paradox of nondirectiveness in the person-centered approach. *Person-Centered Review, 4*(2), 123–31.

Edwards, J. (1982). *Ethics without philosophy: Wittgenstein and the moral life.* Tampa, FL: University of South Florida Press.

Grant, B. (1985). The moral nature of psychotherapy. *Counseling and Values, 29*(2), 141–50.

Grant, B. (1986). Etica y psicoterapia: Prolegomeno a una terapia centrada en el cliente sin una teoria centrada en el cliente [Ethics and psychotherapy: A prolegomenon to client-centered therapy without client-centered theory]. *Revista de Psiquiatria y Psicologia Humanista, 17*(4), 82–6.

London, P. (1986). *The modes and morals of psychotherapy.* New York: Hemisphere.

Plemenatz, J. (1973). Liberalism. In P. Weiner (Ed.), *Dictionary of the history of ideas* (Vol. III, pp. 36–61). New York: Scribner.

Raskin, N. (1988). Untitled article. *Renaissance, 5*(3–4), 2.

Rogers, C. (1951). *Client-centered therapy.* New York: Houghton Mifflin.

Rogers, C., & Segel, R. (Producers). (1955) *Psychotherapy in process: The case of Mrs. Mun* [Film]. Transcribed in J. Bozarth (1984), Beyond reflection: Emergent modes of empathy. In R. Levant & J. Shlien (Eds.), *Client-centered therapy and the person-centered approach: New directions in theory, research, and practice* (p. 62). New York: Praeger.

Rogers, C. (1987). Client-centered? Person-centered? *Person-Centered Review, 2*(1), 11–14.

Szasz, T. (1978). *The myth of psychotherapy.* Garden City, NY: Anchor Press.

Tomlinson, T., & Whitney, R. (1970). Values and strategies in client-centered therapy: A means to an end. In Hart & Tomlinson (Eds.), *New directions in client-centered therapy.* Boston: Houghton Mifflin.

Van Belle, H. (1980). *Basic intent and therapeutic approach of Carl R. Rogers.* Toronto: Wedge.

Watson, G. (1958). Moral issues in psychotherapy. *American Psychologist, 13*(9), 574–6.

Weil, S. (1951). *Waiting for God.* New York: Harper & Row.

Further Thoughts about Nondirectiveness and Client-Centered Therapy

David J. Cain   *Carlsbad, California*

In this article I address some comments by Dr. Barry Grant (this issue) on the issue of nondirectiveness, and offer some further thoughts on client-centered therapy. Grant has responded to a previous article of mine (1989) regarding the issue of nondirectiveness, while providing his own perspective. I appreciate his concern about this important issue and value the dialogue he has initiated.

As I read Grant's paper, I found that we shared some common ground. We agree that respect for the person is a basic and essential value of the client-centered therapist. We also agree that, while what Rogers wrote and said (and demonstrated) is basic to understanding the meaning of client-centeredness, his ideas do not represent an endpoint in our thinking, nor should they.

WHY BE NONDIRECTIVE?

In addressing the issue of nondirectiveness in client-centered therapy, the most basic question one might ask is: 'Why be nondirective?' or 'What is the purpose of nondirectiveness?' The answer to this question would seem to derive from Rogers' view of people and the nature of the therapist-client relationship. To place the issue in historical context, Rogers' advocacy of therapist nondirectiveness was originally reactive in nature. He was reacting to therapeutic approaches that he viewed as *therapist-centered* and directive. His primary objection to directive therapies was that: 'the unstated implication is that the counselor is superior to the client, since the latter is assumed to be incapable of accepting full responsibility for choosing his goals' and that 'The directive viewpoint places a high value on social conformity and the right of the more able to direct the less able' (1942, pp. 126–7). As I understand Rogers' message, it is that people are *capable* and, therefore, do not need to be directed or guided by someone who is 'more capable.' Based on this assumption of client capability, Rogers initially advocated strongly that therapists remain nondirective in their responses in order to free or release clients' 'capacity to achieve reasonably adequate solutions for their problems' (1942, p. 128).

Another reason for nondirectiveness is to *avoid* controlling the client. Obviously, if one believes that clients are capable of directing their own lives and solving their own problems, then one would not find it necessary or desirable to influence clients' perceptions or behavior. A related rationale for nondirectiveness is that such behavior is less likely to make clients dependent on their therapists. The assumption here is that the more clients depend on their therapists, the less likely they will be to develop and rely on their own resources. Implicitly, therapists' disinclination to influence or control clients communicates trust in their resourcefulness and a respect for their autonomy and integrity.

First published in *Person-Centered Review*, Volume 5, Number 1, February 1990.

A practical reason for nondirectiveness is to provide clients with adequate time and freedom to talk about whatever they want, when they want, and how they want. Simply put, if the therapist talks less, the client may talk more. The client-centered therapist assumes that, given this freedom, clients will be most able to identify those issues that are personally relevant. It is also assumed that clients have the right to choose their own goals and will assume responsibility for changing themselves.

It should be made clear that these justifications for nondirectiveness represent the *external* perspective of the client-centered therapist. They are assumed to be in the best interests of the client. In the abstract, it is difficult to argue with such altruistic motives on the therapist's part or with Grant's view of 'principled nondirectiveness' as 'essentially an expression of respect' (this issue). However, the client-centered approach is phenomenological in nature. An individual's experience, then, constitutes his or her reality. Thus, the problem with Grant's view is that it remains external to that of the client. Consequently, his implicit assumption that therapist nondirectiveness is respectful to the client is just that, an assumption.

Without knowing the client's experience, one can only speculate about the effect of the therapist's nondirectiveness. Clinical experience suggests that, for many clients, therapist nondirectiveness is experienced in a positive manner. For other clients, the therapist's nondirectiveness is experienced variously as frustrating, constraining, counterproductive, annoying, and possibly indicative of passivity, lack of involvement, caring, or willingness to help. Sometimes our clients tell us how our nondirective behavior affects them. Sometimes they don't. I suspect that more than a few of our clients have quietly withdrawn from therapy because their therapists' nondirectiveness didn't fit them. The point is that we should not and cannot assume that therapist nondirectiveness has the constructive effects in a particular client that are in accord with our positive intentions and beliefs.

Person-centered therapists believe that clients are the best judges of their experiences. Therefore, it seems appropriate that therapists be mindful and inquire about the impact of nondirective and all other therapeutic behaviors. By doing so, the therapist is much more likely to be affected by the client's direct and indirect feedback regarding whether his or her responses are having a constructive impact. In contrast, Grant believes that the therapist should not be concerned with his or her impact on the client, but only with whether the client is respected. He states: 'the therapist does not attempt or intend to make anything happen—growth, insight, self-acceptance—in the client, but rather provides the therapeutic conditions *in the belief* that they are expressions of respect and *with the hope* [italics added] that the client will make use of them' (this issue). Once again, it should be made clear that the therapist's beliefs and assumptions remain outside the client's perspective, and, therefore, are subject to question. As Rogers made clear, 'Unless some communication of these attitudes has been achieved, then such attitudes do not exist in the relationship as far as the client is concerned, and the therapeutic process could not, by our hypothesis, be initiated' (1957, p. 289). Rather than assume that my nondirective behavior communicates respect, I would prefer to determine, from the client's perspective, the impact of this or any other behavior. In my view, client-centered therapy is a collaborative endeavor, one in which I depend heavily on my client to inform me how I can be maximally helpful. This conscious concern with being helpful raises another issue regarding the therapeutic endeavor: intent.

ON BEING HELPFUL AND MORAL

I cannot imagine that client-centered therapists, or any other type for that matter, are not concerned about being helpful to their clients. An enduring value of client-centered therapy is its *pragmatism.* As Rogers wrote about his formative years in Rochester, ' . . . my only concern was in trying to be more effective with our clients . . . There was only one criterion in regard to any method of dealing with these children and their parents, and that was Does it work? Is it effective?' (Rogers, in Burton, 1972, p. 47). In my mind, this concern with our effectiveness is and should remain an ongoing concern of the client-centered therapist. Grant, however, seemed to downplay the importance of the therapist's concern with being helpful by emphasizing the primary importance of therapist respect, which is communicated, he believes, by a nondirective 'attitude.' While I fully agree that it is essential for the therapist to be respectful, I am unwilling to assume that nondirectiveness is experienced by all clients at all times as respectful. When Grant states that, 'Excepting instances in which other moral considerations prevail, it is, within this framework, *always* right to be nondirective and *always* [italics added] wrong not to be,' I am left with the impression that the tail is wagging the dog. That is, Grant's moral beliefs seem to have interfered with his ability or inclination to determine if nondirectiveness is right for his clients.

Grant also stated that the 'the therapeutic conditions' are provided 'with the hope that the client will make use of them.' As essential as therapist hopefulness is in therapy (if perceived by the client), I believe we must be more than hopeful that our therapeutic attitudes and moral beliefs will result in constructive change in our clients. In addition, we must remain aware of our clients' direct and indirect feedback regarding whether we are meeting *their* goals for growth. To me, it seems morally right to be concerned about whether we are being helpful. Therapy is a relationship with a purpose — to assist the client. And while therapists must be concerned with the quality of the relationship they provide their clients, this is not a sufficient goal. They also need to remain cognizant of the fact that the purpose of the relationship is to facilitate constructive change as defined by the client.

ON HONORING DIVERSITY

The client-centered approach does not, in any systematic way, address the issue of the existence of meaningful individual differences between clients. Although a few practitioners (e.g., Prouty, 1977; Gendlin, 1967) have suggested modifying practice for clients who experience specific disorders, the client-centered approach tends to view and treat clients as unitary phenomena. That is, the same therapeutic attitudes and response styles are believed to be appropriate and effective for all clients. As Rogers had been known to say, 'that which is most universal is most personal.' This is not to say that Rogers and other client-centered therapists were not aware of the great variety of differences in clients. They were. My point is that this awareness has not led to significant modifications in practice, at least as reported in the person-centered literature.

A paradox of the client-centered approach is that it acknowledges and values the uniqueness of persons, yet does not specify how the differences in clients might affect therapeutic practice. Rogers and most other client-centered scholars and practitioners offer little in terms of how therapists might modify their response styles to meet specific client needs or preferences. This can be understood, in part, as Rogers' way of moving away from the heavily technique-oriented and nondirective phase of the 1940s. It also represents Rogers' eschewing of the caricatured view of client-centered therapy as the mindless parroting of the client's words. More importantly, however, Rogers increasingly disavowed therapeutic technique as his conviction deepened that the most human elements in the therapeutic relationship were most healing. The emphasis on the *person* of the therapist on the therapeutic relationship as opposed to techniques and methods is what sets the client-centered approach apart from most others, and appropriately so. Another distinguishing characteristic of the client-centered approach is its strong emphasis on discovery learning. While this approach to learning may fit many persons, it is clearly not suitable to all. Therefore, I do not believe the client-centered approach has realized, or will realize, its full potential unless it more fully acknowledges the compelling reality that important differences in clients (persons) require modifications in therapists' responses, if they are to be optimally effective in helping their clients.

A basic issue facing the client-centered therapist is to identify ways of understanding persons that are accurate, and that acknowledge the complexity and diversity of their being. Diagnostic categorization is clearly not the answer. Categorization of people focuses one's attention on dimensions of the person that are too limited and limiting. A more comprehensive and differentiated view of the person as an active and evolving being is needed. Obviously this is a tall order, but there are some possibilities worthy of consideration.

One useful way to understand people is in terms of how they comport themselves. Comportment refers to the ways in which people outwardly manifest their personalities. Fischer (1985, p. 37) describes comportment as 'the way one carries one's self' and the 'actional, decisional, stylistic, and habitual aspects' of the person. Comportment describes a person in motion as opposed to a static view of the person. It refers to an individual's ways of being and, therefore, to aspects of the individual's self.

Another way to honor the diversity in persons is to acknowledge differences in the way they learn and the specific conditions that optimize learning and change. Two basic premises are relevant in considering the importance of learning style and therapeutic change. First, all persons are viewed as having the capacity to change. Second, the potential for therapeutic change is optimized when the therapist works with the client in a manner compatible with the client's preferred learning style. A corollary of this premise is that therapeutic learning will be enhanced when factors that affect learning style (e.g., environmental conditions) are also optimized. Some of these factors include considerations regarding whether individuals learn best alone or in groups, in bright or low light, in warm or cool temperatures, require quiet or sound, or learn best at specific times of the day.

In its simplest meaning, learning style refers to how a person prefers to learn. For our purposes, learning style is defined as the relatively persistent cognitive, affective, and physiological qualities that affect how persons perceive, process, and interact with experience and information. While all individuals learn in many ways, all learners would appear to have particular preferences and strengths that enhance their ability to learn. There are many ways to conceptualize the varieties of learning styles. Some examples include: auditory, visual, tactile, kinesthetic, reflective, field-dependent and field-independent, divergent and convergent, and abstract and concrete. The implications for therapy are enormous. Stated simply, if clients comport themselves and learn in a variety of ways, then it seems essential that therapists modify their therapeutic approach to fit the client. In this approach, the therapist's primary concern is to adapt and accomodate to the specific needs of each client.

Some therapeutic illustrations

Within the last year or so, I have become increasingly and consciously attuned to individual differences in my clients, and especially to how they learn best. As a psychologist in private practice, I often invite prospective clients to ask anything they might like to know about me or my therapeutic approach. Frequently, I hear more knowledgable clients ask if I will do more than just listen. As I inquire about this concern, they often tell me that they want to see someone who will give them some 'feedback' — either about themselves or the problem with which they are concerned. Frequently, these are clients who have expressed dissatisfaction with a previous therapist who they found to be too passive or nondirective. I accept their concern at face value and try to determine, with them, if what I might offer them will meet their needs. When the client asks for something I can't provide (e.g., Christian counseling) I tell them so and try to refer them to someone who can.

Several months ago I was contacted by a single woman in her late twenties who expressed concerns about her eating problems and about her relationship with her family. She indicated that she needed someone who would give her feedback about herself and her relationship with her mother and father. I took her request at face value and, during our first session, shared with her my personal reactions to her and the problems she discussed. She reported that the session had been extremely helpful. I also felt that it had been a productive session and that I had been fully myself in it, though I tend to talk less in most of my sessions.

About a year and a half ago I began seeing Sherry, a writer in her mid-twenties who was suffering from a medical condition called environmental illness, a condition in which the person is extremely allergic and/or reactive to a large number of substances or toxins in the environment. Such persons require an extremely sterile environment in which to live. Sherry is reactive to woods that have been treated, to shampoo, to soaps, perfumes, carbon monoxide, most foods, formaldehyde, tar, and pesticides — to name only a few of the substances to which she is highly reactive. Our sessions are conducted outside because Sherry was having an adverse reaction to many objects and subtle odors in my office. For Sherry, most days are a struggle. More often than not she feels tired, experiences a variety of pains, gets rashes and headaches, cries without reason, and is functionally immobilized. She writes only on those days when she feels well enough. Remarkably, Sherry is a surprisingly well-adjusted person who keeps herself going, despite the enormous strain of everyday life. I deeply admire her courage and strength to live as best she can under the circumstances.

Most of my therapeutic work with Sherry is supportive. I try my best to understand what it must be like to face the daily and unrelenting challenges she does. Since there are no known effective medical or psychological treatments for environmental illness (Sherry has consulted numerous physicians), I sometimes wonder if I am being of much use to her. On occasion, when my personal concern and understanding seem inadequate, I have asked her what would help her *now*. Usually, she would request some practical ideas to help her with a pressing problem. Thus, some of my 'help' has consisted of suggesting that she buy a laptop computer so she could work outside, reading and critiquing some of her queries to magazine editors regarding articles she would like to write, offering her my back yard to camp out in until she could find an apartment she could tolerate, and giving her ideas about how she could make more money until she found steady writing assignments. Although Sherry has expressed her appreciation for my support and understanding, it is my practical assistance that she often seems to find most helpful. As must be clear by now, my therapeutic work with Sherry is far from traditional, but it is surely person-centered.

Linda, an attractive single woman in her late twenties, came to see me about her tendency to lose interest in men she thought of as possible marital partners. Linda's manner of comportment and learning style soon became factors in our work. In the initial phase of therapy, Linda talked a lot about what might have caused her feelings to change in a previous relationship, but seemed to reach a plateau after about five sessions. Our sessions tended to start out slowly because Linda was not currently involved in a serious relationship and found it difficult to talk about an experience unless it was immediate.

After beginning one session by saying that nothing had happened recently for her to talk about, she asked me to 'get her going.' I decided to accept her request and asked 'What do you want?' She replied that she wanted to (1) assess more accurately how her relationship with a man is going, (2) learn to express her feelings, and (3) understand her decision-making process in her relationships with men. During our sessions Linda realized that she was not very good at recognizing her feelings or reflecting on their meaning. She also became aware that she wasn't inclined to sit down and take time to reflect on her life. Linda described herself as a 'hyper' person who always had to be doing something. Sitting still, even to watch TV or read a book, was not something she could do very easily. It was becoming clear to both of us that she learned better from her immediate experience, and that she needed a specific activity to help her benefit more from therapy. With a little assistance from me, she devised a plan whereby she would notice her feelings when they were occurring and express them at that time. During our next session, she indicated that she had followed through on her plan and was pleased that she had done so. She also indicated that this was a better approach because of her inability to sit still, do nothing, or just focus on herself.

As I began to reflect on my therapeutic work with Linda, I began to realize that, in some ways, she was not an ideal client for client-centered therapy as typically practiced. For one thing, Linda was not a very reflective person, or one who was inclined to spend time with her feelings. Her manner of comportment was active, fast-paced, practical, cognitive, and structured. She learned best by doing things, rather than reflecting on things. A shift from a more reflective to a more active and structured approach seemed to fit her needs and enabled her to get more out of therapy.

Natalie Rogers' person-centered expressive therapy is an approach which, in my view, acknowledges and honors the diversity of individuals. By combining movement, art, writing, guided imagery, music, therapeutic touch, dream exploration, and other expressive forms, she provides an opportunity for her clients to select and combine therapeutic modalities that are compatible with their personalities and learning styles. Approaches like Natalie Rogers' have the advantage of offering a person-centered alternative to clients who may express themselves more effectively in forms other than verbal.

THE CLIENT KNOWS

I have been a client-centered therapist for over 15 years. As I review my own evolution, I believe I have become more client-centered, though I am probably more divergent in style than I was earlier. Let me explain. My faith in each person's capacity to change in a constructive manner remains strong. I have yet to meet a person who I didn't think could change for the better. I also believe that change is most likely to occur within the context of a loving, understanding, and accepting relationship with a therapist who is fully present and knowable. As a therapist, I prefer to be nondirective with my clients because I trust their ability to identify what they would like to change and to find a way of doing so that suits them. My desire is to be a sensitive and perceptive listener who enables my clients to see themselves and life more clearly. I strive to be fully present with my clients.

I have a deep appreciation for the wide range of individual differences that exist in people. Sometimes these differences astonish, puzzle and, occasionally, flabbergast me. And while the most human of experiences may well be those that are most universal, I have come to believe that the variety of ways in which people comport themselves and learn are crucial factors in the process of therapeutic change. Therefore, a guiding question I ask of myself and of my clients is, 'Does it fit?' It has become increasingly clear to me that people can be relied upon to recognize that which suits them and that which does not. Sometimes what fits a given client is readily evident to the client and therapist. Sometimes it is not. In the latter case the client can be asked directly. At times when the answer is not clear, further exploration may be necessary to determine what does fit. Regardless of how the therapist and client determine what is right for the client, doing so is an essential part of serving and assisting the client to meet his or her needs.

More than any other therapeutic system, the client-centered approach allows and encourages persons to become their unique selves. In my view, clients are most likely to realize their unique potential if therapists remain mindful that each person is different from every other, and that each therapy needs to be individualized if we are to be optimally helpful to our clients. To do so means that the therapist attempts to see with the client's eyes, hear through the client's ears, and learn from the client what fits.

REFERENCES

Cain, D. J. (1989). The paradox of nondirectiveness in the person-centered approach. *Person-Centered Review, 4*(2), 123–31.

Fischer, C. T. (1985). *Individualizing psychological assessment.* Monterey: Brooks/Cole.

Gendlin, E. T. (1967). Therapeutic procedures in dealing with schizophrenics. In C. Rogers (Ed.), *The therapeutic relationship and its impact* (pp. 369–400). Madison: University of Wisconsin Press.

Grant, B. (this issue).

Prouty, G. F. (1977). Pre-therapy, a method of treating pre-expressive psychotic and retarded patients. *Psychotherapy: Theory, Research and Practice, 13,* 290–4.

Rogers, C. R. (1942). *Counseling and psychotherapy.* Boston: Houghton Mifflin.

Rogers, C. R. (1957). The necessary and sufficient conditions of therapeutic personality change. *Journal of Consulting Psychology, 21,* 95–103.

Rogers, C. R. (1972). My personal growth. In A. Burton (Ed.), *Twelve therapists* (pp. 28–77). San Francisco: Jossey-Bass.

Symposium on Psychodiagnosis

(i) Psychodiagnosis: A person-centered perspective

Angelo V. Boy   *University of New Hampshire*

Psychodiagnosis has become more of a routine and accepted first step in psychotherapy not because of its inherent logic and objectivity but because of a variety of influences. This article raises fundamental questions about psychodiagnosis. These questions are not new. They are part of a past and continuing controversy surrounding psychodiagnosis.

EDITOR'S NOTE: Four authors served as respondents to Dr. Boy's article on psychodiagnosis. They were invited to react to his article in any way they wished or to present their own ideas on psychodiagnosis. Readers are encouraged to add their perspectives to those presented.

Bohart and Todd (1988) state that 'the medical model holds that the first step in dealing with a disorder is to diagnose what it is, so that its cause can be discovered and a treatment can be scientifically developed' (p. 27). The medical model of diagnosing, determining cause, and developing a treatment plan has recently become a more significant part of psychotherapeutic practice than ever before.

The purpose of this article is to review some historic questions about the usefulness of psychodiagnosis. Many of the issues raised in this article are not new (Rogers, 1942). They still need to be raised today, however, before psychodiagnosis becomes so routinized that its adherents cease to accept 'questions from the floor' regarding its purpose and accuracy.

In the past, psychodiagnosis was a controversial part of counseling and psychotherapy (Patterson & Eisenberg, 1983). In recent years, however, psychodiagnosis has become more routine for an increasing number of clients and patients (Seligman, 1983). A review of the literature, however, reveals no new information, procedures, or breakthroughs to account for the current increase in the use of psychodiagnosis. Other reasons, however, are identified. Patterson (1985) indicates that the tradition of behaviorism continues to stimulate interest in psychodiagnosis. Seligman (1983) links the interest to the accountability movement. Corey (1986) and Kottler and Brown (1985) state that the recent interest may be due to the insurance requirement that financial reimbursement cannot occur unless the client's problem is first classified through a psychodiagnosis. Robins and Helzer (1986) indicate that diagnostic systems are used by administrators of hospitals, by departments of health for annual reports and budget requests, by those making insurance claims, and by the research community interested in developing new knowledge about disorders and their treatment (p. 422).

First published in *Person-Centered Review*, Volume 4, Number 2, May 1989.

THE PURPOSE OF PSYCHODIAGNOSIS

The rationale for psychodiagnosis ('to know') emerges from the logic of an organic medical diagnosis (Patterson & Eisenberg, 1983). Since the human body is physically the same for all persons, excluding gender of course, the logic of medical diagnostic procedures is obvious. When a patient's organic symptoms can be accurately categorized, a judgment can be made regarding what's wrong with the patient and what needs to be done; and when large numbers of patients have the same patterns of symptoms, and those patterns can be summarized by a diagnostic label, we can link more accurately the treatment process to the diagnosis.

Some would assume that a psychodiagnosis can produce a psychological picture of a client with the same degree of accuracy achieved in a medical diagnosis. Many humanistically oriented therapists, however, have taken the position that a person's psychological characteristics are unique and complex, and that they cannot be objectively identified, understood, judged, or labeled (Rogers, 1951; Frankl, 1969; Arbuckle, 1975; May, 1981; Bugental, 1981). There is a great deal of difference in the accuracy of the process used to identify a person's organic disorder and that applied to determine a person's psychological disorder. The body possesses physical qualities that can be seen, touched, and objectively evaluated. These physical qualities can be altered and changed and the field of medicine is able to categorize and label the agents causing these changes. Even in medicine, however, patients are encouraged to seek second opinions. Psycho-diagnosticians feel that they can evaluate the health of the human psyche with the same degree of accuracy that medicine assesses the health of one's body. As Patterson and Eisenberg (1983) have stated, however, 'Because models of medical diagnosis do not seem to apply well to mental health work, the meaning of diagnosis in mental health work has become ambiguous and confusing' (p. 136).

Those who support psychodiagnosis assert that since all clients are different from each other, treatment processes must be tailored to meet individualized psychological needs than can be known only through a psychodiagnosis (Bohart & Todd, 1988). Patterson (1985) presents the counterview that people are psychologically alike in their desire to experience loving, supportive, real, and empathic relationships with each other. Such relationships produce psychological stability. When such relationships are not available people become vulnerable and at higher risk for becoming psychologically disordered. Patterson (1985) indicates that successful treatment is related to the therapist's ability to create a helpful therapeutic relationship rather than being dependent upon the (assumed) accuracy of a psychodiagnosis.

As was noted, Seligman (1983) observed that an increase in the use of psychodiagnosis became an important part of the accountability movement. On the surface, the psychodiagnostic process appears to be scientific and objective. Belkin (1987) indicates that psychodiagnosis has the capacity to heighten the mystique of professionalism:

> The employment of diagnostic categories has found less favor than the approaches of the anti illness movement in recent years, especially among partisans of the community health and humanistic positions. Such critics have argued that the main reason diagnosis is still so widely used is that it heightens the professional mystique. When a therapist is able to articulate what is 'wrong' with a patient in a language that only other professional colleagues are able to understand, it invests the therapist with an authority that is lacking if he or she uses language that is comprehensible to lay people as well. Critics argue that this use of diagnosis insulates the practitioner from uninvited comments from the lay public. (p. 4)

Psychiatrist Torrey (1972) says that the mystique of professionalism can also be heightened by the use of a diagnostic name or label — the magic of the 'right' word:

> Every therapist who has ever had the experience of observing a patient's relief after solemnly telling him that he was suffering from ideopathic dermatitis or pediculosis knows how important the name is. It says to the patient that someone understands, that he is not alone with his sickness, and implicitly that there is a way to get well. (p. 14)

Glasser (1984) indicates that a psychodiagnostic label enables the client to evade responsibility for a disorder since the client didn't cause the disorder just as a medical patient didn't cause a kidney to malfunction. The client is able to react to a psychological disorder with the same lack of responsibility and detachment as a medical patient. Glasser further states that it is precisely this lack of personal responsibility that is the root cause for psychological disorders.

Another reason for today's increased interest in psychodiagnosis may be 'to satisfy the record keeping requirements of insurance companies' (Kottler & Brown, 1985, p. 161) so that health insurance requests for reimbursement will be accepted.

THE TOOLS OF PSYCHODIAGNOSIS

The two tools that are most frequently used in psychodiagnosis are personality and projective tests (George & Cristiani, 1986). Anastasi (1982) warns that these kinds of instruments are the least valid and reliable (along with aptitude and interest tests) when compared with individual measurements of intelligence and academic achievement tests. In other words, psychodiagnosticians make judgments about clients that are based upon instruments that have low levels of validity and reliability. Intelligence and achievement tests are far more accurate in their ability to measure intelligence and academic achievement than are personality and projective tests to give an accurate picture of a person's psychological disorder. Intelligence and achievement can be defined and measured more objectively than a psychological disorder. Psychometricians can more easily agree on what constitutes intelligence and achievement but have difficulty in determining what constitutes a psychological disorder (Anastasi, 1982).

Some sources of information used in a psychodiagnosis are highly subjective. The information is often colored by the perceptions of the evaluator. These may include statements and evaluations appearing in anecdotal and cumulative records, and behavioral observations and evaluations (Belkin, 1987). Patterson and Eisenberg (1983) state that face-to-face interactions with a client are included in a diagnosis without acknowledging the possible influence of the clinician's subjective biases, perceptions, and interpretations.

In its attempt to emulate the scientific nature of medical procedures, the psychodiagnostic process falls short. Since a medical diagnosis primarily relies on the data derived from medical tests, psychodiagnosis attempts to bring scientific objectivity to the evaluative process by using tests also. A review of the instrumentation used in medical diagnoses reveals a vast difference in the technological and objective sophistication of these instruments when compared to personality and projective tests. Yet even when using technically accurate instruments, no physician will guarantee the accuracy of a diagnosis.

THE METHODOLOGY OF PSYCHODIAGNOSIS

The methodology of psychodiagnosis is lacking in its ability to identify a problem, its etiology, and cure with accuracy. If one looks at the nature of human nature, psychodiagnosis barely scratches the surface of a person's essence, that person's inner world of feelings, beliefs, perceptions, values, and attitudes, let alone the presubconscious and unconscious material that continually influences how, when, and why we respond to particular stimuli. As Hansen, Stevic, and Warner (1986, p. 391) have said, a psychodiagnosis 'oversimplifies the client.' Existential psychotherapists tell us that inner feelings are too complex to be revealed by psychodiagnostic procedures and that psychotherapy has the best chance to identify and penetrate these feelings (Albee, 1970; Arbuckle, 1975; May, 1981). This is due, in part, to the length of a relationship between a counselor/psychotherapist and a client. That relationship may last weeks, months, or years, while a psychodiagnostician's face-to-face contact with clients is generally limited to several hours at the most. The talk-centered and self-revealing methodology of psychotherapy lends itself more readily to entering the client's inner and presubconscious feelings than the structured, brief, and evaluative nature of psychodiagnosis.

The methodology of psychodiagnosis often fails to take into account cultural (Levine & Padilla, 1980), ethnic (Sue, 1981), economic (Kottler & Brown, 1985), and social (Corey, 1986) influences on a client's disorder. A psychodiagnosis must be viewed in the context of these influences in order to understand a client's behavior, its causes, and the degree to which it can be judged to be disordered. As Corey (1986) has noted, 'Certain behaviors and personality styles might be labeled neurotic or deviant simply because they are not characteristics of the dominant culture' (p. 303). Anastasi (1982) confirms Corey's view when she says: 'Errors may arise when clinicians make diagnostic or prognostic inferences about a client whose cultural background, education, or socioeconomic levels differ markedly from their own' (pp. 488–9).

Psychodiagnosis looks at the client, primarily, from an external frame of reference. For nearly half a century Rogers (1942, 1987) presented evidence that indicated that the only accurate and reliable viewpoint for understanding a client is from the client's internal frame of reference. A psychodiagnosis doesn't often include the client's internal frame of reference. When it does, it is not given a high level of credence. The data derived from an external frame of reference is trusted more because of its assumed objectivity, an objectivity that cannot always be guaranteed. Clinicians are human. They are not mistake-free. A diagnosis may be influenced by the clinician's cultural background, education, and socioeconomic level (Anastasi, 1982).

Kottler and Brown (1985) indicate that the methodology of psychodiagnosis errs in its emphasis on pathology instead of health. Psychodiagnostic methodology prompts the clinician to identify what's 'wrong' with the client with little or no consideration of what's 'right.' Kottler and Brown further indicate that psychodiagnostic methodology contains no concept or indices of normal behavior against which the client's behavior can be compared. Psychodiagnostic procedures enable the clinician to define a client as 'disordered' without a model of 'ordered' behavior. If clients are classified as disordered there must be a norm or prototype from which they are deviating. As Albee (1970) has noted, 'We do not use, in psychology, a nomenclature or diagnostic system for normal behavior, and if we agree that disturbed behavior is continuous with normal behavior it seems inappropriate to try to formulate a nomenclature for disturbance' (p. 386).

The methodology of psychodiagnosis contains no systematic or recommended procedure for correcting an inaccurate, wrong, or erroneous diagnosis (Kottler & Brown,

1985). Once the psychodiagnosis has been made, the label sticks. Rosenhan (1973) reports on eight experimenters who were admitted to psychiatric hospitals as patients after complaining, as instructed, that they were 'hearing voices.' Immediately after admission, the eight experimenters were instructed to behave normally as they would in their everyday lives. Regardless of the normalcy of their behavior after admission, the eight experimenters were never considered normal or sane regardless of how much contact they had with the hospital's staff of professionals.

The methodology of psychodiagnosis also has the capacity to make the client a victim of reductionism. It reduces the complex and mysterious nature of the human personality to a diagnostic label. But the label is convenient, and as Torrey (1972) has indicated, it contains the 'magic' of the 'right' word. Monahan (1977) indicates that a psychodiagnostic label can also prompt some clients to evade responsibility by imitating the behavior associated with a diagnosis rather than working to get well. The label enables a 'self-fulfilling prophecy' to manifest itself because the label comes from an 'expert' in human behavior.

The methodology of psychodiagnosis can also induce the client to become dependent during the process itself or during treatment. Psychodiagnostic procedures place the clinician in a dominant and authoritative role. The message to the client is that if he or she cooperates with the diagnostic process and furnishes accurate information, then a precise diagnosis can be made. The more the psychodiagnostician is perceived as expert, the greater the tendency for the client to become dependent (Rogers, 1942, 1951; Albee, 1970; Boy & Pine, 1986).

THE PSYCHODIAGNOSTICIAN

If psychodiagnosis were to acquire a more sophisticated rationale, the tools used were to achieve an acceptable level of validity and reliability, and the problems surrounding the methodology of psychodiagnosis were solved, we would still need to face the problems associated with the personality of the psychodiagnostician. The psychodiagnostician's personality is assumed to be psychologically stable. Impairments in the psychodiagnostician's personality, however, will affect the trend, scope, and accuracy of a diagnosis.

Corey (1986) identifies the following factors that can influence a clinician's skills and cast doubt on psychodiagnostic conclusions: the theory of personality used to evaluate a client; the clinician who tends to be biased and expresses that bias by looking for behavior that fits a certain favorite diagnostic category; and the influence of the clinician's cultural, ethnic, and socioeconomic background upon psychodiagnostic conclusions.

Brammer and Shostrom (1982) raise some questions about the person performing a psychodiagnosis when they indicate that he or she can become preoccupied with a client's history while neglecting current attitudes and behaviors; rely on tests too heavily in the psychodiagnostic process, thus heightening the client's expectation that these instruments will produce 'answers' to a disorder; become preoccupied with signs of pathology while ignoring those healthy and creative dimensions of personality; assume the mantle of 'expert'; and contribute to the process of reducing a psychologically complex human being to a simple and convenient diagnostic category.

Kottler and Brown (1985) observe that a psychodiagnostician's socioeconomic background, basic values, observational skills, and theoretical orientation will influence the scope and focus of a psychodiagnosis. Kottler and Brown (1985) conclude that different judgments can be made when evaluating the data derived from a diagnosis:

> Suppose a client presents symptoms of irritability, listlessness, low energy, failed performances at work, lack of sex drive, and loss of appetite; these symptoms may be diagnosed in a number of ways, ranging from anorexia nervosa to depression to an acute stress reaction. Errors are possible not only in the conclusions drawn about a case but also in the ways chosen for working with a client. (p. 274)

In pointing out the lack of agreement that can occur among psychodiagnosticians, George and Cristiani (1986) state that

> the most common examples are the multitude of professional opinions expressed in evaluating individuals who are on trial for various crimes, and the studies of individuals who are readmitted to hospitals for various mental conditions and are seen by different psychiatrists or psychologists. The diagnostic reliability among professionals in these cases seems to be lacking. (p. 223)

The reliability of psychodiagnosis has also been questioned by Eysenck (1986) and Garfield (1986). Garfield (1986) adds a personal observation when he says that 'anyone who has worked in a large clinical setting has probably noticed that there is no unanimity among the staff in diagnostic conferences. I have participated in staff conferences in which the final decision was conclusively settled by an eight to seven vote of the staff members present' (p. 101).

Anastasi (1982) indicates that clinical assessments rely on judgment in some aspects of the process and the observer often relies upon an assumed similarity to oneself in those judgments (p. 488). She goes on to indicate that biased data gathering techniques may diminish the accuracy of a clinician's judgment.

> If clinicians are unduly influenced by their early hypotheses, they may look only for data that support those hypotheses. By the type of questions they ask and the way they formulate them or by subtle expressions of agreement or disagreement, they may influence what the client reports. Such biased data-gathering techniques probably account for the remarkably uniform etiologies found among the clients of some psychoanalysts. (p. 489)

and

> Undoubtedly the objectivity and skill with which data are gathered and interpreted — and the resulting accuracy of predictions — vary widely with the abilities, personality, professional training, and experience of individual clinicians. (p. 492)

and

> We regularly perceive the world in three dimensions without being able to specify the cues we employ in the process. Similarly, after exposure to a test protocol, a set of test scores, a case history, or a face-to-face interaction with a client, the clinician may assert that the patient is creative, or a likely suicide, or a poor psychotherapy risk, even though the clinician cannot verbalize the facts he or she used in reaching such a conclusion. Being unaware of the cues that mediated the inference, the clinician may also be unaware of the probabilistic nature of the inference and may feel more confidence in it than is justified. (p. 490)

Arkes (1981) points out that many clinicians are not aware of the subjective factors, the interplay among them, and how they can influence a psychodiagnostic conclusion. Beyond the influence of shared experiences between clinician and client, Arkes (1981) also indicates that a clinician's theory of personality needs to be carefully monitored and controlled since it has such an overpowering influence on the clinician's judgment. It may prove to be more powerful than the data gathered and could prompt the clinician to add or not add new data that would change both the psychodiagnosis and treatment plan.

Hansen, Stevic, and Warner (1986) are concerned about the issue of clinical overconfidence and its possible inverse relationship to accuracy. They point to research that indicates that as clinicians are given more information, they may become more confident in their judgments without becoming more accurate. They also conclude that the most confident judges tend to be the least accurate (p. 398).

Weitz (1961) points out the difficulties faced by a clinician when attempting to define and classify human behavior.

> Psychological behavior is a continuous, unbroken stream of events. It is impossible in objective reality to segment and examine this flow. If we take a bucketful of water from a swift-running brook, we have only a bucketful of water to analyze and evaluate. We have lost the magic bubbling of the brook; the sparkle and the sound are gone. What is left is no longer the gaily running brook we sought to understand. So it is with human behavior. Observation of the continuous stream of human life is impossible in objective reality, for the events that make up human behavior merge one into the other in such ways as to be one moment cause and the next moment effect. (p. 550)

Albee (1970) reinforces the preceding when he says:

> Psychologists have also known for a long time that traits are not absolute invariant qualities of the individual but appear and disappear, and change dramatically, depending upon a number of interacting variables, including the social situation. Yet we keep talking about our need to develop our own rigid diagnostic system for classifying human behavior. (p. 390)

THE DSM-III

The third edition of the Diagnostic and Statistical Manual (DSM-III) (American Psychiatric Association, 1980) is the major reference used today in the psychodiagnostic process. The clinician observes the client's behavior, takes samples of that behavior through assessment instruments and procedures, and comes to some conclusions. Those conclusions are matched with one or more of the descriptive behaviors contained in DSM-III and a diagnostic decision is reached and a label identified. Because a diagnosis has been reached it is assumed that the clinician is now able to plan an appropriate treatment process.

Those on the front edge of scientific inquiry in psychodiagnosis are alarmed that the DSM-III has been enthusiastically accepted and used. Their criticisms focus on DSM-III's violation of the principles of taxonomy (Eysenck, 1986), its reliability (Eysenck, 1986; Garfield, 1986; Robins & Helzer, 1986), its new and questionable diagnostic categories (Garfield, 1986), its structure and content; namely, the axes, major categories on the axes, the coverage, the text, hierarchies, and the rigidity of criteria (Robins & Helzer, 1986). Robins and Helzer (1986) also direct their DSM-III criticism to other basic issues: categories versus dimensions of human behavior, the organization of the nomenclature, and the development of criteria for evaluating a diagnostic system.

How did the DSM-III gain such wide acceptance among clinicians when members of the scientific community raised so many questions about it? Zubin (1977–8) states that 'Scientific values were bent to suit the needs of psychiatry, third party payments, certification and economic exigencies of one sort or another including territoriality rights' (p. 5).

Garfield (1986) especially questions the integrity of the new diagnostic categories included in DSM-III.

> Among the new developmental disorders are 'specific reading disorder' and 'specific arithmetic disorder.' These are most frequently viewed as specific learning problems and would appear to be diagnosed and handled most appropriately by persons in the field of education or educational psychology. Not only are psychiatrists not the professionals best able to deal with such problems, but there is also some potential stigma associated with having a psychiatric disorder and having to see a psychiatrist. There were undoubtedly a number of possible reasons why these and related categories were included in DSM-III, but they would appear to be self-serving interests. As a result of the inclusion of such disorders in DSM-III, psychiatrists and other mental health providers are more likely to be reimbursed by third party payers for the diagnosis and treatment of specific reading disorder or specific arithmetic disorder. Thus, it seems likely that considerations other than those of a primarily clinical and research nature entered into this determination. The net result is to weaken the classification system and to cast doubt on the overall enterprise. (pp. 109–10)

Eysenck, Wakefield and Friedman (1983) concluded that

> research conducted during the development of DSM-III was mostly concerned with the reliability of diagnosis and the acceptability of the proposed categories to clinicians. (p. 177)

and

> Our survey of the available evidence on the DSM-III leaves us with the impression that while an improvement on previous schedules, the new scheme is based on foundations so insecure, so lacking in scientific support, and so contrary to well established fact that its use can only be justified in terms of social need. Psychologists may have to use the system because of social pressures of various kinds, but this should not blind them to the fundamental weaknesses of any such scheme based upon democratic voting procedures rather than on scientific evidence. (p. 183)

Eysenck (1986) clarified the meaning of 'democratic voting procedures' when he said:

> DSM-III, like its predecessors, is the outcome of large-scale committee work, designed not so much to ascertain facts and to arrive at the truth, but rather to reconcile different power groups and pacify semipolitical Tammany Hall-type organizations whose influences are incommensurate with their scientific status. (p. 74)

Robins and Helzer (1986) also provide insight into how conclusions were reached regarding the names used for some diagnostic categories in DSM-III.

> Many of the names have been altered, in part because the old names were sometimes being used with different meanings by different groups, but more often because they had become associated with one or another adversarial group, a new term was intended to be politically neutral. (p. 413)

Robins and Helzer (1986) indicate how the psychoanalytic and psychodynamic branches of American psychiatry influenced the content of DSM-III.

> They fought for the term 'neurotic' because it had come to symbolize the etiologic theory of the psychodynamic school that certain disorders are the product of intrapsychic conflict. The outcry from psychodynamic psychiatrists and their threats to scuttle the whole enterprise finally resulted in a compromise. A new diagnosis 'Dysthymia' was created to

fulfill the role previously filled by depressive neurosis and for Dysthymia, Panic Disorder, and Obsessive Compulsive Disorder, a parenthetical phrase allowing the use of the term neurosis was included. (pp. 421–2)

CONCLUSION

It is interesting to note that, according to Robins and Helzer (1986), 'At best, diagnoses are imperfect descriptions of reality' (p. 430). The psychodiagnostic process has been inherited from the field of medicine (Belkin, 1987). Medical diagnosis is logical. When something ails us we want to find out what it is so that the healing process can be assisted. But medicine's logic cannot be applied to psychotherapy since medical and psychological disorders are different. Medical disorders tend to be concrete and can be more readily differentiated into discrete groups or classes, each with a common etiology, symptomatology, course, and outcome. Psychological disorders tend to be abstract and are not easily differentiated into discrete groups or classes, each with a common etiology, symptomatology, course, and outcome. Organic functioning can be measured with a reasonable degree of accuracy. The psychological characteristics of a person are far more subject to biased interpretations. Their identification is so deeply influenced by the psychodiagnostician's values, socioeconomic background, culture, ethnic identity, and psychological needs, that we cannot give a psychodiagnosis the same credibility that we give a medical diagnosis. The foundation of a medical diagnosis is generally objective, while the foundation of a psychodiagnosis is considerably more subjective in its purpose, tools, methodology, and the judgment required of its practitioners. However, it must also be noted that although medicine is more scientific and objective in its scientific tools and procedures the human element enters into a medical diagnosis and may affect its accuracy.

Psychotherapy's attempt to improve its methodologies must continue, but we must admit that our attempts to emulate medicine in diagnostic procedures have not produced equivalent results. We must be willing to admit that the human psyche cannot be known, studied, measured, and evaluated with the same degree of accuracy as can the human body.

Patterson (1969) was one of the first to point out that the analogy between medicine and psychopathology is weak.

> The two differ in many respects. The nature of the etiology is quite different. In the case of physical disease, though there are common factors of stress, there is always a specific ultimately verifiable, physical or external agent, whether chemical, bacteriological, or viral in nature. Such a statement cannot yet be made regarding mental disorders. In the case of physical disease, the process is primarily one of chemical and physiological malfunctioning. In mental disturbance, on the other hand, the process is primarily a psychosocial disturbance. In physical disease, patients having the same disorder follow rather closely the same course and in most cases with the same predictable outcome. In mental disturbances, on the other hand, there are wide differences in the course and outcome among those classified as having the same diagnosis. For the physical diseases there exist either known, or as yet unknown, specific remedies. Again, though the search and hope for such specific remedies continue, none has been found for the presumed different personality disturbances. (pp. 8–9)

There are better ways of starting the psychotherapeutic process with clients and patients than those contained in psychodiagnostic procedures. These better ways may require psychotherapists to acquire a very different attitudinal and intellectual disposition from that of the medical model. Torrey (1974) sees the medical model as an unnecessary burden that has been carried too long by the counseling and psychotherapeutic professions. Belkin (1987) offers a phenomenological alternative to the medical model. It requires a very different way of perceiving a client or patient. It is one of many alternatives available.

> The phenomenological approach attempts to reconstruct the world from the point of view of the patient. Free of value judgments, undistorted by perceptual biases, the world of the patient opens up to the therapist in all of its pristine clarity and internal logic. The phenomenological approach precludes the designation of mental illness by eliminating such broad categories as diagnosis and curative terminology. More importantly, it works independently of and in contradiction to the medical model of treatment. By embracing the phenomenological approach, partisans argue, the therapist frees himself or herself of the difficulties implicit in the medical model and inherent in the theory of mental illness.
>
> The phenomenological approach is not part of any specific form of therapy; it is a philosophical framework that infuses all the therapist's attitudes and understanding of the patient. Specifically, it suggests that we must strip away all our biases and preconceptions and attempt to grasp the world from the point of view of the patient. In this way, phenomenologists suggest, the patient's 'is-ness'—essential sense of being and self-coherence—emerges through the therapeutic process. Thus the phenomenological approach runs counter to the medical model, which subordinates the patient's essential being to the diagnostic categories. (Belkin, 1987, p. 9)

If psychodiagnosis truly improves the accuracy of psychotherapy so that we can more effectively help clients achieve positive and enduring results, then it must be retained as the necessary first step in the psychotherapeutic process. This, however, has yet to be established. We still need to establish if psychodiagnosis is a necessary part of psychotherapy.

Person-centered therapists have nothing inherently against the development of a broad classification system for categorizing human behavior as a scientific endeavor. This is a well-intended effort that may someday contribute to our understanding of the variety of ways in which humans behave. But when a questionable classification system like DSM-III becomes the standard requirement for starting psychotherapy, then the tail is clearly wagging the dog.

The requirements of scientific inquiry would be better served if several different concepts of psychodiagnosis were used and evaluated in clinical settings. The range of concepts would have to meet scientific standards and procedures. Some psychodiagnostic procedures would emphasize the clinician's external locus of evaluation while others would emphasize the client's internal locus of evaluation. By evaluating both procedures we could learn which yields the most reliable diagnostic results. Having more reliable diagnoses will lead to more accurate treatment procedures. Such an evaluation, over a period of time, would serve the needs of clients, clinicians, the scientific community, and third party payers. We would then have a more accurate psychodiagnostic system instead of perpetuating one that many question.

One model of psychodiagnosis that could be included in such an evaluation is that proposed by Carl Rogers (1951). He developed 'The Client-Centered Rationale for Diagnosis' and based it upon the following propositions:

> Behavior is caused, and the psychological cause of behavior is a certain perception or a way of perceiving. The client is the only one who has the potentiality of knowing fully the dynamics of his perceptions and his behaviors.
>
> In order for behavior to change, a change in perception must be experienced. Intellectual

knowledge cannot substitute for this.

The constructive forces which bring about altered perception, reorganization of self, and relearning, reside primarily in the client, and probably cannot come from outside.

Therapy is basically the experiencing of inadequacies in old ways of perceiving, the experiencing of new and adequate perceptions, and the recognition of significant relationships between perceptions.

In a very meaningful and accurate sense therapy is diagnosis, and this diagnosis is a process which goes on in the experience of the client, rather than in the intellect of the clinician. (pp. 221–3)

I believe client-centered therapists would welcome having Rogers' propositions given equal status to those supporting the use of DSM-III. They would welcome comparative studies that evaluate different psychodiagnostic concepts, procedures, and outcomes. If no studies are done, justice would be better served by allowing competing concepts of psychodiagnosis to be used in clinical settings.

Many person-centered therapists would support Eysenck's (1986) reaction to DSM-III: 'It is clearly necessary to throw out the whole approach, hook, line, and sinker before anything better can take its place. DSM-IV, if ever such a misshapen fetus should experience a live birth, can only make confusion worse confounded and make the psychiatric approach to classification even less scientific than it is at the moment. What is needed is a complete rethinking of the whole approach, a consideration of the underlying problems, and an attempt to formulate experimental and psychometric approaches to these problems which may generate a universally agreed answer in due course' (p. 96).

Client-centered therapists desire nothing more than the opportunity to contribute to development of a 'universally agreed answer.' Our profession must reconsider its support of existing psychodiagnostic process that may have compromised its integrity, and therefore, its reliability, by being hurried to the marketplace before all viewpoints were heard and evaluated.

REFERENCES

Albee, G. W. (1970). Notes toward a position paper opposing psychodiagnosis. In A. H. Mahrer (Ed.), *New approaches to personality classification.* New York: Columbia University Press.

American Psychiatric Association (1980). *Diagnostic and statistical manual of mental disorders* (3rd ed.). Washington, DC: Author.

Anastasi, A. (1982). *Psychological testing* (5th ed.). New York: Macmillan.

Arbuckle, D. S. (1975). *Counseling and psychotherapy: An existential humanistic view.* Boston: Allyn & Bacon.

Arkes, H. (1981). Impediments to accurate clinical judgments and possible ways to minimize their impact. *Journal of Consulting and Clinical Psychology, 49,* 323–33.

Belkin, G. S. (1987). *Contemporary psychotherapies* (2nd ed.). Monterey, CA: Brooks/Cole.

Bohart, A. C., & Todd, J. (1988). *Foundations of clinical and counseling psychology.* New York: Harper & Row.

Boy, A. V., & Pine, G. J. (1986). Mental health procedures: A continuing client-centered reaction. *Person-Centered Review, 1,* 62–71.

Brammer, L., & Shostrom, E. (1982). *Therapeutic psychology: Fundamentals of counseling and psychotherapy* (4th ed.). Englewood Cliffs, NJ: Prentice-Hall.

Bugental, J.F.T. (1981). *The search for authenticity: Existential analytic approach to psychotherapy* (rev. ed.). New York: Holt, Rinehart & Winston.

Corey, G. (1986). *Theory and practice of counseling and psychotherapy* (3rd ed.). Monterey, CA: Brooks/Cole.

Eysenck, H. J. (1986). A critique of contemporary classification and diagnosis. In T. Millon and G. L. Klerman (Eds.), *Contemporary directions in psychopathology.* New York: Guilford.

Eysenck, H. J., Wakefield, J. A., & Friedman, A. F. (1983). Diagnosis and clinical assessment: The DSM-III. *Annual Review of Psychology, 34,* 167–93.

Frankl, V. (1969). *The will to meaning: Foundations and application of logotherapy.* New York: New American Library.

Garfield, S. L. (1986). Problems in diagnostic classification. In T. Millon and G. L. Klerman (Eds.), *Contemporary directions in psychopathology.* New York: Guilford.

George, R. L., & Cristiani, T. S. (1986). *Counseling theory and practice* (2nd ed.). Englewood Cliffs, NJ: Prentice-Hall.

Glasser, W. (1984). *Reality therapy.* In R. Corsini (Ed.), *Current psychotherapies* (3rd ed.). Itasca, IL: Peacock.

Hansen, J. C., Stevic, R. R., & Warner, R. W., Jr. (1986). *Counseling theory and process* (4th ed.). Boston: Allyn & Bacon.

Kottler, J. A., & Brown, R. L. (1985). *Introduction to therapeutic counseling.* Monterey, CA: Brooks/Cole.

Levine, E. S., & Padilla, A. M. (1980). *Crossing Hispanic.* Monterey, CA: Brooks/Cole.

May, R. (1981). *Freedom and destiny.* New York: Norton.

Monahan, L. (1977). Diagnosis and expectation for change: An inverse relationship? *Journal of Nervous and Mental Disease, 164,* 214–17.

Patterson, C. H. (1969). A current view of client-centered or relationship therapy. *Counseling Psychologist, 1,* 2–25.

Patterson, C. H. (1985). *The therapeutic relationship: Foundation for an eclectic psychotherapy.* Monterey, CA: Brooks/Cole.

Patterson, L. E., & Eisenberg, S. (1983). *The counseling process.* Boston: Houghton Mifflin.

Robins, L. N., & Helzer, J. E. (1986). Diagnosis and clinical assessment: The current state of psychiatric diagnosis. *Annual Review of Psychology 1986.* New York: American Psychological Association.

Rogers, C. R. (1942). *Counseling and psychotherapy.* Boston: Houghton Mifflin.

Rogers, C. R. (1951). *Client-centered therapy.* Boston: Houghton Mifflin.

Rogers, C. R. (1987). The underlying theory: Drawn from experience with individuals and groups. *Counseling and Values, 32,* 38–46.

Rosenhan, D. L. (1973). On being sane in insane places. *Science, 179,* 250–8.

Seligman, L. (1983). An introduction to the new DSM-III. *Personnel and Guidance Journal, 61,* 601–5.

Sue, D. W. (1981). *Counseling the culturally different: Theory and practice.* New York: John Wiley.

Torrey, E. F. (1972). *The mind game.* New York: Emerson Hall.

Torrey, E. F. (1974). *The death of psychiatry.* Radnor, PA: Chilton.

Weitz, H. (1961). Guidance as behavior change. *Personnel and Guidance Journal, 39,* 550–5.

Zubin, J. (1977–78). But is it good for science? *Clinical Psychologist, 31,* 3–7.

Symposium on Psychodiagnosis

(ii) A Reaction to 'Psychodiagnosis: A person-centered perspective'

Julius Seeman   *Vanderbilt University*

David Cain has asked me to reflect upon the article by Angelo Boy and to set forth some of my own perspectives on psychodiagnosis. For me the issues are complex, and my comments will reflect that complexity. Specifically, there are four aspects to consider: the value aspects of psychodiagnosis, the technical validity of tests used in psychodiagnosis, the human judgments involved, and the useful functions served by psychodiagnosis.

The value aspects of psychodiagnosis. It is on this point that I have the clearest concurrence with the view that Angelo Boy expressed. The process of thinking *about* a person rather than thinking *with* a person is likely to have the effect of creating a subject-object split, of distancing the client from the examiner, and of creating a one-up one-down hierarchy. None of these elements is consistent with relationships congruent with client-centered theory.

In a related vein, the attitudes and procedures of client-centered therapy make psychodiagnosis irrelevant to the internal aspects of client-centered therapy. Nathaniel Raskin said it well many years ago in this way:

> He (the counselor) tries to get *within* and to live the attitudes expressed rather than observing them ... And in struggling to do this, there is simply no room for any other type of counselor activity or attitude; if he is attempting to live the attitudes of the other, he cannot be diagnosing them, he cannot be thinking of making the process go faster. (quoted in Rogers, 1951, p. 29)

Raskin here has indicated another kind of risk that the psychodiagnostic process involves for the student of client-centered therapy. The thought processes involved in thinking about a client diagnostically engender an external frame of reference in the examiner; she or he is formulating constructs relevant to a diagnostic framework. Contrarily, the therapeutic process in client-centered therapy involves the development of an internal frame of reference, which is a very different kind of listening. Students who learn diagnosis first are sometimes simply unable to develop the kind of listening required to do client-centered therapy.

The technical validity of diagnostic tests. The article by Boy developed the thesis that psychodiagnosis, unlike medical diagnosis, lacked validity. There are two issues that I have with this view. The major one is that the validity or invalidity of diagnostic testing is not the point with respect to client-centered therapy. The nub of the matter lies in the issue of theoretical consistency enunciated here, that is, psychodiagnosis has no role in client-centered therapy.

The second point is that in my judgment, recent advances in psychological testing permit better-than-chance description and classification of persons where that activity is

First published in *Person-Centered Review*, Volume 4, Number 2, May 1989.

relevant. Tests that provide valid research information can also provide valid diagnostic information. For example, a student in our department has just completed a doctoral dissertation in which she was interested in advancing her understanding of women with eating disorders—specifically, women who binged and purged with food. She recruited women in this category and a contrast group of nonbulemic women. Tests used provided information on (a) the level of self-esteem reported by women in each group and (b) their description of their interpersonal relationships. These two measures provided 100% accuracy in differentiating women in the two groups. Every woman in the bulimic group had scores lower than those in the nonbulimic group. There are many other examples in the literature of testing procedures that produce valid information, but that fact does not make the information relevant to client-centered therapy.

The human judgments surrounding psychodiagnosis. While tests can provide valid information about persons, there is also plenty of evidence to support Boy's view that the more complex human judgments involved in the total psychodiagnostic process are error-ridden. I want to cite just one collection of such errors. The study to which I am referring, by Daniel and Rabin (1985), followed four patients whose maladies were labeled functional. The article's summary is as follows:

> In four patients, each of whom displayed overt signs and symptoms of a delirious state, the delirium was overlooked [by the psychiatrists]. We describe in detail the features of delirium because this syndrome is protean in its etiology and clinical presentations. It can be life-threatening, and it may not be recognized because the behavioral correlates are often attributed to a functional disorder. (p. 666)

Daniel and Rabin go on to cite other studies that found that 'the frequency of undiagnosed major medical illness in psychiatric patients varies from 24% to 49%' (p. 666).

There is one parenthetical point that I want to make here, having to do with the relationship between psychodiagnosis and psychotherapy. While client-centered theory has no role for psychodiagnosis, that does not make psychodiagnosis inherently 'bad,' but simply irrelevant. There are some theories of psychotherapy that involve constructs obtainable through prior testing, and it is possible to do testing with competence and with due attention to ethical standards.

In the foregoing context, I want to call attention to one statement in Boy's article where I read history differently. Boy subscribes to the view that 'the tradition of behaviorism continues to stimulate interest in psychodiagnosis.' That is not my reading of behaviorist theory. As I indicated here, psychodiagnosis fits some theories but not others. Behaviorist theory has little use for traditional diagnostic procedures that tend to be either trait-oriented or psychodynamically oriented. Behaviorists seek specifically for an understanding of those conditions that maintain a maladaptive behavior, and then apply reinforcement contingencies designed to extinguish the maladaptive behavior and/ or to enhance adaptive behavior. As to their view of psychodiagnosis in general, Ullman and Krasner (1969), behaviorist-oriented writers, say, 'The present authors think the problems of the current diagnostic system arose from the application of an inappropriate medical model to social behavior' (p. 35)—a view in some degree like that of Boy.

The positive function served by psychodiagnosis. I believe that there is a limited but necessary role for diagnostic functions. I can visualize this role best in the context of a comprehensive human-system model of organismic health and its aberrations. Brody (1973) and Schwartz (1980) have each put forth similar human-system models of health. The human system is a unified system consisting of interrelated subsystems (biochemical, physiological, perceptual, cognitive, interpersonal). All of these component behavioral subsystems are linked. In a state of health 'Each of these component systems on each hierarchical level are intact and functioning. All feedback loops must be intact' (Brody, p. 76). When these conditions exist, the system is functioning harmoniously and can be said to be in a healthy state. Schwartz similarly says that an intact system is self-regulating through intricate networks of information exchange. The system, however, can go awry. Brody talks about perturbation or disruption in the system. Schwartz refers to this phenomenon as disregulation. The crucial point here is that the system can be stressed and disregulated at any hierarchical level from biochemical to interpersonal. We also know that, given the connectedness of these subsystems, disregulation may affect multiple aspects of the system. However, we as therapists have access to some aspects of the system but not to others. A common problem for therapists is that we are sensitized to the psychological-emotional aspects of disregulation more than to others. The illustrations that I cited in the Daniels and Rabin paper indicate this kind of selectivity.

It is the case that many instances of biological disruption call for biomedical intervention, but it is also a fact that psychodiagnostic procedures can track some forms of disregulation. In particular, recent advances in neuropsychological testing make it possible to detect organic brain dysfunction in ways that are not open to direct observation in therapy. We can refer a client for psychodiagnostic procedures that provide valuable information; we can do so in ways that maintain respect for the client and, also important, leave the client in control of the information. Thus the client-therapist relationship need not be compromised through this information-generating process. Indeed, there are times when such a procedure is necessary in order for us to fulfill our professional/ethical responsibilities.

In summary, I argue here that psychodiagnosis is irrelevant to the internal process of client-centered therapy, and that there are occasions when referral for psychodiagnosis is part of our ethical/professional responsibility.

REFERENCES

Brody, H. (1973, Autumn). The systems view of man. *Perspectives in Biology and Medicine*, pp. 71–92.

Daniel, D. G., and Rabin, P. L. (1985). Disguises of delirium. *Southern Medical Journal, 78*, 666–72.

Rogers, C. R. (1951). *Client-centered therapy*. New York: Houghton Mifflin.

Schwartz, G. E. (1980). Behavioral medicine and system theory: A new synthesis. *National Forum*, 25–30.

Ullman, L. P., & Krasner, L. (1969). *A psychological approach to abnormal behavior*. Englewood Cliffs, NJ: Prentice-Hall.

Symposium on Psychodiagnosis

(iii) Boy's Person-Centered Perspective on Psychodiagnosis: A response

John M. Shlien   *Harvard University*

Overall, the case against diagnosis as presented by Boy is pretty complete. The force of his argument seems dulled by repetition and an overly conciliatory style. Perhaps the meek will inherit the earth, but only after it has already been ravaged by the brazen.

There are a few other fundamental questions that might have been raised. It might be pointed out that studies as early as those by Hollingshead and Redlich (1958) showed the influence of social class (of both client and clinician populations) on the diagnostic categories applies.

It would also help to have some numbers in the text. If psychodiagnostic instruments have low levels of validity and reliability, how low are they? After all, intelligence and achievement tests, at their best, have average correlations of no more than .70 with validation criteria. That accounts for only half of the variance for a population, and makes predictions for any individual quite precarious. The average validity for clinical measures is not even that high. No wonder. The criteria of clinical judgments are so unstable, and the diagnostic measures plus their interpretations are so unreliable, that the result is like the multiplication of fractions. Of course the numbers will be terrible. The instruments and clinical judgments in diagnosis are all but useless except in the extremes (just where they are least needed). Why not make this clear, aside from philosophy or theory?

'Diagnostics' is an area that was assigned to psychology by psychiatry. The early history of treatment is medical. No wonder that diagnosis played a large part. In fact, since treatment was so confused and ineffective, diagnosis was the main area of 'success.' Psychologists were simply the hired hands in the psychiatric field, and generally all too willing ones. As psychologists acquired the 'right to practice' (psychotherapy), they held onto their previously assigned specialty of psychodiagnosis. That is not surprising. The diagnostics were their security blanket as well as their entering wedge. Further, psychological therapists were either 'eclectic,' (i.e., 'confused' or 'uncommitted' or 'open-minded' or 'pragmatic' or some combination thereof) or were invested in a form of therapy with theoretical attachments to diagnosis — psychoanalysis, for instance.

From my point of view, Boy gives away too much. For instance, speaking of the 'assumed objectivity' of an external evaluation, he says only that such objectivity 'cannot always be guaranteed.' Not always? It can *never* be guaranteed. It does not exist. The so-called external frame of reference is really only some other person's internal frame; a subjectivity that passes for 'objectivity' only in a foolish logic that assumes judges to be nonsubjective simply because they judge from outside the judged one. Why should you dignify my judgment of you with the honorific 'external frame of reference,' translated as 'objectivity?' To be sure, it is external to you, but that is all. Further, the agreement of two or more judgments from 'external frames of reference' is only intersubjectivity. There

First published in *Person-Centered Review*, Volume 4, Number 2, May 1989.

is no objectivity to it. Not always, and not ever.

All of the work cited by Boy, that is, from Anastasi, Eysenck, Garfield, Zubin, and others, approach this point in their well-founded and well-stated criticisms of the instruments, the psychodiagnosticians, the Diagnostic Manuals, and so on. But critical approaches in the literature aren't enough. How is it that there have been dozens of lawsuits about the misuse and abuse of those tests of 'intelligence' and achievement, and none (to my knowledge) about the misuse of psychodiagnosis? How is it that *our* controversy doesn't lead to client assertions in defense of their fair treatment and equal opportunity? And we claim to be so 'caring' and vocal about 'empowerment.' A few malpractice suits regarding diagnostic misclassification could have a salutary effect on clinics and hospitals, as it has had on schools, admissions procedures, and test suppliers.

For that matter, how did we leave it for those others (Eysenck, for instance) not so closely identified with 'humanistic' psychology to make the more forceful testimony that Boy has collected? Are we turning the other cheek? Or is it the client's cheek? When Boy writes that 'client-centered therapists desire nothing more than the opportunity to contribute' (to the reconstruction of diagnostic measures and systems) he does not speak for this client-centered therapist. I stand much more with the critics such as Eysenck, Garfield, Zubin and others. I am in favor, in fact, of *de*construction.

It is not that psychodiagnostics 'may' become routinized. It already is. Universities must teach it because internships demand it. Internships demand it because the internships make money from it. That is what it is all about, not treatment, and not research either, except insofar as those are ways psychologists make a living. We are not as much in a 'helping profession' as in a major industry. It is run by accountants who work for the physicians or corporate administrators who own the health insurance systems. Psychologists are, by and large, trying to be more a part of this system, to have hospital privileges and the like. They are willing tools of the system. Much of the appeal of the 'medical model' comes from the fact that many psychologists wish they were 'real doctors.'

Take the money out of psychodiagnostics, and as a routine it will disappear within five years. It will also diminish in research practice. But that would be very hard to do. There is a lot of money and a lot of professional benefit involved. The psychologists who spent considerable time and money in a successful legal action to gain entrance to the Psychoanalytic Association Training Programs weren't just looking for access to learning. Something like $60,000–$200,000 per patient is available as income for the therapist. And, as for the influence of insurance and 'third party payments,' one does not need merely to suggest a possible connection. It is a blatant fact. There are studies that document it. Treatment (which begins with diagnosis required for insurance) frequently ends when the limit of payment is reached. Have you not noticed the great interest in short-term and time-limited therapy? That coincides, but not coincidentally, with the onset of limited third-party payments.

Economics and status and security considerations aside, what about the client-centered point of view? One can have a science based on classification, prediction and control, or one can have a quite different science based on understanding. The latter is the only science that fits psychotherapy. But for me it is no longer necessary to relate therapy to science at all. We can have appropriate science for our research, but therapy (as practice) can just as well be considered art and philosophy. (In fact, I was delighted to read of a Dutchman with a Ph.D. in philosophy who, for a comparable-to-psychotherapy fee, meets with clients, advertises for clients, listens to and discusses their philosophy of life. Diagnosis does not rear its head.)

There is more to it. Rogers did not really develop a 'rationale for diagnosis.' He made one of his many mistakes of a particular academic sort: he paid momentary lip service to the positivistic logic he felt stuck with at that period. The mistake was to call his own statement (quoted by Boy) as a 'rationale for diagnosis' (Rogers, 1951, p. 223). On the same page Rogers says it is really a rationale for psychotherapy *without* (not built upon) external diagnosis. It does not pay to make even temporary concessions to logic you believe to be false, or professional conventions you believe unworthy. They haunt one forever.

It is not only for philosophical and 'treatment-related' reasons so well developed by Boy that diagnosis does not fit client-centered therapy. For the 'psychodynamic' therapist whose theory is based on pathology, or for the eclectic who thinks he has many different methods in his armory of equipment, diagnosis makes some sense.

But client-centered therapy has only *one* treatment for *all* cases. That fact makes diagnosis entirely useless. If you have no specific treatment to relate to it, what possible purpose could there be to specific diagnosis? Nothing remains but the detrimental effects.

Then, diagnosis is not good, not even neutral, but bad. Let's be straightforward and flat out about it. The facts might be friendly, but what are the facts? Diagnosis comes not just from a medical model, but from a theory of psychotherapy that is different from ours, antagonistic to ours. It is not only that its diagnostic predictions are flawed, faulty, and detrimental to the relationship and the client's self-determination, they are simply a form of evil. That is, they label and subjugate people in ways that are difficult to contradict or escape. There is no value in being 'reasonable' about that, in wanting to participate in reformulation of the psychodiagnostic endeavor that will generate a universally agreed-upon answer. Why petition to be a partner to reformulation when it is wrong from the beginning?

These last two paragraphs are my main points. Tactically, it strikes me as too passive or compliant when Boy suggests that client-centered therapists 'would welcome' having Rogers' propositions given equal status, or welcome comparative studies or the allowing of competing concepts in psychodiagnostics to be used in clinical settings. That is a gift not likely to be given. Asking for an invitation to participate only acknowledges that the diagnosticians are in control. Why should they take this initiative? A more positive action would be to mount a national conference ourselves, with well-prepared positions, evidence, and challenges. There is no advantage in cooperating with the dominant clique. The lion and the lamb may lie down together, but if it is in the lion's den, the lion is probably quite relaxed, looking forward to breakfast in bed. Want a good basis for some interesting research on what kind of person makes what kinds of judgments about others? Try this: propose that everyone who uses diagnostic measures must also be measured by them, with the measures on file in the office of the secretary of state. Your state legislators would enjoy the idea. After all, if it is good enough for the clients, it should be good enough for the clinicians as well.

REFERENCES

Hollingshead, A., & Redlich F. C. (1958). *Social class and mental illness: A community study.* New York: John Wiley.
Rogers, C. R. (1951). *Client-centered therapy.* Boston: Houghton Mifflin.

Symposium on Psychodiagnosis

(iv) A Life-Centered Approach to Psychodiagnostics: Attending to lifeworld, ambiguity and possibility

Constance T. Fischer   *Duquesne University*

This article assumes the validity of longstanding criticisms of psychodiagnostics. Nevertheless, all therapy should be planned in accordance with assessment of the client's circumstance. Such assessment need not await improved taxonomies and instruments. No matter what our tools, we can address our clients' worlds and ways of moving through them. This task entails: (a) collaboration directly with the client throughout the assessment process, (b) respect for the ambiguity and intersubjectivity of truth, and (c) exploration of possibility. This article describes such life-centered assessment practices.

Person-centered counselors and therapists have consistently criticized psychodiagnostics and testing (see the overview by Boy, in this issue). This astute criticism has highlighted the irrelevance of labels and scores for working with individuals, as well as the demeaning character of the evaluation process, and the detrimental emphasis on limitation and pathology. I strongly agree with these criticisms of test- and nomenclature-oriented evaluation, which is indeed the prevailing approach to psychodiagnostics. However, I value the earlier, deeper meaning of psychodiagnostics: to know thoroughly a psychological life.

Psychological life includes the ways one takes up — perceives, gives over to, and makes sure of — his or her environment, neurophysiology, culture, community, and other persons. To best serve a client, the counselor or therapist should understand that person's life and assist accordingly. It is not enough to provide a positive therapeutic climate in which the client feels understood, empathized with, respected, cared for, and protected, and in which he or she is invited to grow via reflection, action, and communication. It is essential that a therapeutic strategy take into account the person's life circumstance, including developmental level. I will present some examples from my clinical practice to remind us of the importance of assessment. Then I will briefly address philosophical aspects of life-centered assessment, and I will go on to describe concrete assessment practices that engage the client as coassessor, respect intersubjectivity and ambiguity, and explore not just what has been but what might be possible. Throughout, the client's world is the focus, with test data, diagnostic categories, and theory serving as tools to better understand the lifeworld and its relation to contexts (history, body, family, socioeconomics, and so on).

First published in *Person-Centered Review,* Volume 4, Number 2, May 1989.

Necessity of assessment

Most often, a new client and I agree on our goals and approach by the end of our first therapy session. We may revise our goals in light of any new information that shows up on my take-home packet of background information. No formal testing is needed. As our understanding grows, and as the client grows (or does not), I may modify my approach. At any time, I can explain a requested diagnosis in terms of what I have learned directly of the person's life.

There are many occasions, however, when I assess the client's circumstance before agreeing to enter a therapeutic relationship. The assessment might include a family interview, referral to a medical specialist, review of records, objective tests, projective techniques, or a structured inquiry into a particular area such as alcohol use. Sometimes I realize within therapy that we ought to investigate an issue through a separate assessment. I also receive assessment referrals from colleagues.

Three years ago, a woman in her sixties came to me saying that she needed to get her act together, to stop irritating her family, and to not feel so sorry for herself. She derided herself for failing to remember to put items on her shopping list and to record social invitations. After testing provided instances of memory loss and of related anxiety, I arranged for a neuropsychiatrist to coordinate new medications with those prescribed by her cardiologist. The woman participated in family conferences where everyone came to understand that this family member's forgetfulness and confusion were not motivated. Earlier, the family had been impatient that the woman had not responded to psychotherapy and to tricyclics aimed at her 'depression.' The family now provides more structure and support. The woman and I continue to meet weekly for half-hour visits during which I support this woman's struggles with her Alzheimer's-affected life.

Parents brought their college freshman daughter home after hearing that she had told friends she was suicidal. The young woman agreed to talk to a psychologist, but the latter could not determine in just two sessions whether the student could safely return to school. The psychologist referred the student to me because an efficient assessment was necessary so the student either could return without missing further classes or could withdraw without penalty. Using a range of objective and projective materials, the student and I discovered that she was not academically well prepared for college, and that she resented her siblings' achievements, which made it all the more difficult to study effectively. Apparent contradictions between the MMPI and Rorschach led to the discovery of a history of undiagnosed depressive episodes, not now present. Her statement about suicide was ready at hand from prior depressive periods, but mostly she was just 'down' about being away from her boyfriend and about the difficulty of her courses. Eventually all of this would have been clarified in therapy, but it arose in an especially timely fashion through formal assessment. In the latter, our joint observations about the student's comportment with the testing materials allowed her to recall similar lifeworld instances, and to make sense of them herself. She decided to continue that process with the psychologist on weekends. The psychologist found that our work fit her earlier suspicion of familial bipolar depression. If the student again becomes depressed, she and the psychologist will look into medical intervention.

A man in his thirties came to me saying that he wanted to begin therapy to determine whether he would live as a homosexual. Shortly into our first meeting, I advised him that I would need to spend several sessions gathering information from him so we could plan if and how to work together. In that course we came to agree that intimacy with anyone, sexual or not, was the more critical issue. We also agreed that we wouldn't be surprised if we lived out some of his old patterns: getting close, becoming demanding, then being afraid of being hurt, becoming angry, and finally threatening harm or termination. We developed rules for each of us to follow (e.g., he would not call my home; I would acknowledge irritation toward him), and agreed that extended therapy was in order.

In these cases, my familiarity with life patterns of disordered living allowed for planning that saved clients unnecessary anguish and effort. Assessment procedures respected clients as individuals, and therapeutic approaches were tailored to each client. None of these persons would have been well served by immediate pursuit of my preferred therapeutic style of encouraging growth and integration through self-exploration. As the text here will indicate, clients also can participate in assessments to make their own decisions independent of any therapy.

Philosophical aspects of life-oriented assessment

Life-oriented assessment addresses the person going about his or her life. Test scores, diagnostic categories, theoretical constructs, and other nomothetic devices are derived notions to be used as tools to understand the person's circumstances. The tools should not be confused with results. Until the practitioner can say what the derived findings mean in terms of the person's daily life, that practitioner doesn't know 'what in the world' he or she is talking about.

In life, as we all know, people behave at least in part according to their perceptions and goals. In addition, we simultaneously live in accordance with our biology, culture, and so on, all structurally related. Explanations in terms of simple dimensions are indeed simplistic. Even complex explanations cannot attend to all dimensions at once; they are always deficient. But this is our condition; our knowledge is always in part constructed by us, and hence is always limited, perspectival. Psychodiagnostic assessment ought not to pretend to greater precision and clarity than being human allows. Ironically, truly disciplined accounts respect ambiguity. Reporting life events with their contexts, along with specifying the observer's perspective, avoids the pretense of precision, and leaves the way open for development of multiple understandings.

Life-oriented assessment considers the environments and contexts that the person moves through. These might include family, community prejudices, work setting, and physical health.

When one individual assesses another, that person inevitably uses his or her own life as access to the other person. Tests and diagnostic schemes are, of course, devised within historically situated values and assumptions. All assessment is intersubjective. Rather than pretend to objectivity, we ought to seek discipline in our use of subjectivity.

Finally, life-oriented assessment continues to respect the reflective and planning capacities of persons who became clients. When we address our tools to the lifeworld, clients can help us to explore the possible meanings of even projective devices and MMPI profiles. Moreover, client and assessor together can look into alternative goals, pathways, and styles. Personal viability of possibilities can be investigated with clients, more often than not for the client to pursue on his or her own.

INDIVIDUALIZING PSYCHOLOGICAL ASSESSMENT

The following practices are presented more elaborately with many illustrations in my textbook, *Individualizing Psychological Assessment* (Fischer, 1985). This approach is intended not only to assist professionals in making service decisions, but to involve clients as coassessors and as users of the individualized findings. Even when a major purpose is to determine placement (gifted program, closed ward, e.g.), the client can participate collaboratively. Life events are the point of departure into tests, theory, and categories. Those life events are also the point of return, now understood freshly and with appreciation of options. Some of these understandings should find their way into any assessment report.

A first step is to identify with the referring party the events that led to the request for assessment, and what decisions are to follow. Constructs are unfolded until actual events are recovered. For example, a differential diagnosis request in regard to a possible borderline personality disorder turns out to be about the practitioner's feeling uncomfortable with odd breaks in discussion, the client's references to past suicide attempts, and sudden barbs. The client recognizes the concrete examples I share, and describes what was going on from his perspective. Together we identify similar instances that occur during the assessment, and that are similar to past occurrences. From leads provided by the MMPI and Rorschach, we agree that the client is feeling agitated, despondent, and isolated in much the way he did when he had given into impulsive, violent suicide attempts. We agree that these understandings match the pattern named in DSM III-R as borderline personality disorder. Client, practitioner, and I agree that (a) the problematic cluster is just what the client sought help with, (b) this practitioner is uncomfortable working with such life patterns, (c) careful selection of an alternative therapist is in order. The client notes that this has been a surprisingly meaningful process. He now understands that there is not some 'thing' wrong with him, that both he and the other person usually have given each other reason (if not justification) for being irritated, and that the troublesome events we had identified were the ones to work on in and out of therapy.

Individualized assessment addresses how the person has been co-authoring his or her life and world. For example, a young woman complains that she's tired of parents and employers characterizing her as cocky. Then we note that I am surprised at how well her Bender-Gestalt comes out, given that she had made casual remarks throughout, punctuated with dismissive hand gestures and gum snapping. It turned out that she had privately counted all the dots, had calculated spacing for all the designs, and had taken more time than most people do to complete the task. She, in turn, was surprised that her overt stance created an impression opposite of her desire to do well and to mask her fears that her work would be inferior. We then discover other instances that share the same pattern.

We also move on to explore ways she could help people to understand her seriousness. On Block Design, she interrupted her own flippant remarks about Rubic's cube, nodded at me self-consciously, and said, 'Actually, I'm nervous because I want to do well, but I can't decide whether I'm supposed to go for speed or whether the idea is to avoid mistakes.' We are struck that we both experience her as sincere in this moment. Later we role-play similar situations. My written report included this shift in style as one of the suggestions we developed. In these ways, lifeworld assessment evaluates what else is possible for the person, and often explores possibilities by trying them out and tailoring them until an approach is personally viable for the client.

No constructs or reductions are necessary. We do not ask whether a person is 'really' a schizophrenic or whether hostility explains a behavior. The goal is to understand the structure of an event—how it unfolds in relation to its context. Such an understanding accounts for the event adequately to anticipate it, and to influence it from within and from outside.

The language of the assessment and of reports is that of everyday life, with any jargon explained in terms of what it says about such life. Description is representational; that is, representative events from the assessment are represented in the report with their meanings for the person's life spelled out. Reports are written in first person ('Mr. Smith and I talked about his being ill at ease . . . '). Concrete events rather than constructs are reported, and past tense is used to indicate that events will not necessarily continue to evolve as they have ('Mr. Smith scowled when I read the Picture Arrangement instructions' versus 'Mr. Smith resents authority'). The assessor's involvement and participation are presented as part of the assessment context and as part of the data ('I found myself wanting to reassure her').

In short, life-centered psychodiagnostics serves the client's interests. It empowers the client by recognizing personal agency and by exploring positive possibility. It respects the ambiguity and intersubjectivity that are inherent to human understanding. Emphasis on life context alerts client and others involved in the assessment to the larger contexts of comportment, and to our responsibilities for grappling with systems as well as with individuals.

REFERENCE

Fischer, C. T. (1985). *Individualizing psychological assessment.* Monterey, CA: Brooks-Cole.

Symposium on Psychodiagnosis

(v) The Client's Role in Diagnosis: Three approaches

David J. Cain   *Carlsbad, California*

The basic premise of this article is that what clients learn about themselves is much more important than what diagnosticians learn in the assessment process. Three approaches to diagnostic assessment and remediation are compared in terms of their advantages and disadvantages for the client-consumer. It is also argued that the process of diagnosis, defined as 'knowing the self,' is compatible with client-centered theory and practice.

The term *diagnose* is derived from a Greek word which means 'to know' or 'to discover.' Scribner's dictionary defines diagnosis as follows: 'to identify or determine the cause of a disease, malfunction, or problem.' Both the notion of 'knowing' and 'determining the cause' of a problem are appealing on logical and practical grounds. Daily life presents us with an almost endless array of problems, personal and otherwise, that require understanding and skill to remedy them. Whether one is dealing with a car that won't start or a feeling of depression, diagnosis of the problem would seem to be the logical first step toward remediation of the problem.

In this article I will explore the usefulness and limitations of the diagnostic endeavor as it is applied by various 'helpers' who address problems ranging from the mechanical to the personal. I will argue that the diagnostic approach to remedying problems may have desirable or undesirable effects depending on the role played by the diagnostician and the person seeking assistance. The issue of the *purpose* of diagnosis and *who* it is intended to benefit will also be addressed.

Basically, the diagnostic procedure is aimed at finding out what is *wrong* with something so it can be *fixed.* Therefore, the person one consults for help will usually focus his or her attention on discovering whatever has broken down or gone awry—something that is undesirable and that one wants to eliminate or modify (e.g., toothache, TV without sound). The basic premise operative here is that one must first know what is wrong *before* one can fix it. Another basic assumption is that whatever is wrong (e.g., flat tire) has a *cause,* an etiology (e.g., nail puncture). Thus, as the diagnostician searches for the cause of what is wrong, he or she will tend *not* to focus on the whole of the object (or person) of the diagnosis or on what might be *right* with it. Diagnosis, then, is a procedure in which the diagnostician typically delimits his or her focus to that part of a whole that is believed to be the cause of the malfunctioning of the person or thing.

There are some problems for which a diagnostic focus on malfunction seems appropriate and others for which this focus would appear to be inadequate, limiting, or potentially harmful. Three approaches to diagnosis and remediation that are prevalent in American culture are presented here. Each will be discussed in terms of its benefits and disadvantages for the person seeking assistance. The three approaches are as follows:

First published in *Person-Centered Review,* Volume 4, Number 2, May 1989.

(1) the Mechanical, (2) the Prescriptive, and (3) the Collaborative. A comparison of these three approaches is presented in Figure 1.

THE MECHANICAL MODEL

In the mechanical model, an expert, defined as someone with a high level of technical skill and knowledge, is sought out by a person in need of assistance to determine the cause of the problem and to fix it. The car mechanic is a prototype for the mechanical model of diagnosis and remediation. When one notices a malfunction or symptom in one's car, one

Figure 1: Models of diagnosis and remediation

H = high   M = moderate   L = low

Relevant Expert-Client Issues	Mechanical Model	Prescriptive Model	Collaborative Model
1. Degree of responsibility for diagnosing problem			
Expert	H	H	L-M
Client	L	L-M	H
2. Knowledge and skill required to remediate problem			
Expert	H	H	M-H
Client	L	L-M	H
3. Degree of active participation in solving problem			
Expert	H	M-H	L-M
Client	L	L-M	H
4. Importance of the development of new learning of skill in client	L	L-M	H
5. Feeling of accomplishment in remediating problem			
Expert	H	M-H	L-M
Client	L	L-M	H
6. Importance of critical assessment of diagnosis, remediational procedures and effectiveness of solution			
Expert	H	M-H	L-M
Client	L	L-M	H
7. Client's level of dependence on helper	H	M-H	L
8. Likelihood client will need expert's services in future	H	M-H	L-M

generally calls a car mechanic to diagnose and repair the malfunction. The mechanical model is, of course, practiced by other helping or service professionals. They would include dentists, engineers, business consultants, lawyers, radio and television repairmen, some types of therapists, and a host of others. What all of these professionals have in common is that they offer their specific expertise and skill for a fee to persons who do not have adequate knowledge, skill, or motivation to remedy the problem themselves.

Consumers of these experts' services, however, often do not wish to develop their own skills or knowledge in the problem area. In fact, most consumers who prefer the mechanical model do so *because* it is convenient, efficient, and requires little of them. Many a clinical practitioner has received requests from prospective clients who ask: 'Can you hypnotize me' (to get rid of a problem) or clients who bring in their problem children hoping the therapist can 'fix them up.' The point here is that the mechanical model of diagnosis and remediation has established itself firmly because it meets the needs of many consumers. As our everyday lives and the world of technology become increasingly complex, the mechanical model may well become more appealing.

There are, of course, some disadvantages to the mechanical approach to problems. The consumer's ability to evaluate the effectiveness of the expert's work is limited, since all that can be seen is that the problem or symptom has apparently been remediated. Therefore, the consumer must trust that the expert made the correct diagnosis, did not overlook anything essential, and remedied the problem correctly. Since no new learning or skill development has taken place in the consumer (client), he or she remains dependent on the expert should a similar or new problem arise in the future. As a consequence of the consumer's turning the problem over to an expert, the consumer does not derive any satisfaction, or sense of pride or accomplishment, that would normally occur by participating in the solution of the problem.

THE PRESCRIPTIVE MODEL

In the prescriptive approach, one consults an expert who makes a diagnostic assessment of one's problem and *prescribes* a treatment or course of remediation. The physician is a prototype of the prescriptive approach. This approach to helping is also characteristic of many helpers, including teachers, consultants, nutritionists, physical trainers, coaches, and therapists from a wide range of helping professions. Similar to the mechanical approach, practitioners of the prescriptive approach are sought out because they have special knowledge and skill generally not possessed by their clients. After diagnosing their clients' (students', patients') problem the practitioner either prescribes a plan of action (treatment, remediation) to be followed or treats the problem directly. For example, a physician or dietitian may prescribe a specific diet for a male over 50 who wishes to lose 30 pounds. In contrast to the mechanical approach, however, the client must participate in the remediation of the problem. However, the client's participation tends to be *passive* since the practitioner does not engage the client very much in the diagnostic assessment or remediation planning. While most practitioners of the prescriptive model have a genuine concern for their clients' well-being, relatively few actively collaborate with their clients in developing a course of action. Instead, the client is urged and expected to comply with the expert's recommendations. Clients may be taught a skill (e.g., speed reading) or instructed in a procedure (e.g., self-administration of insulin) and may receive some information about the nature of their problem. Generally, however, the prescriptive approach practitioner does not encourage new learning in the client.

The main appeal of the prescriptive approach, like the mechanical, is that it is convenient and requires relatively little of the client in terms of knowledge or skill. The client may be required to spend some time and energy on remediational or aftercare activities, but basically the client relies on the expert for direction and supervision.

The main limitation of the prescriptive approach is that the client tends to remain passive and dependent on the helper. The client must trust that the helper's training, experience, competence, and integrity are adequate since the client has placed him- or herself in the hands of the expert. Unfortunately such trust or even blind faith can be misguided and risky. If the 'doctor' *always* knew best or never made a mistake such faith might be justified. However, there is ample evidence that well-intentioned helpers are sometimes unknowledgeable, incompetent, and fallible. To illustrate this dilemma, within the last year I have: (1) been misdiagnosed as having high blood pressure, (2) received contradictory treatments and advice for elbow, back, and hamstring problems, and (3) witnessed a physician whose lack of knowledge about a drug could have been life-threatening to an 11-year-old girl in respiratory crisis. In each of these cases, I believe the caregivers' (physicians, rehabilitation therapists, and chiropractor) sincere desire was to provide good treatment. However, to the degree one turns one's well-being over to an 'expert,' one is increasingly vulnerable to the limitations of the caregiver. Sometimes the appeal of convenience and the desire to be taken care of by a trusted expert without having to engage in treatment actively and critically undermines clients' awareness that they are ultimately responsible for their own well-being.

THE COLLABORATIVE MODEL

In the collaborative approach, the client is an active and involved *partner* in the diagnosis and remediation of his or her problems. Clients engaged in this approach are also involved in the critical assessment of all aspects of their diagnosis and treatment and in the evaluation of its effectiveness. The client-centered therapist (teacher, consultant) is a prototype of the collaborative approach. The collaborative approach is also compatible with existential therapists (e.g., Fischer, 1985) and with practitioners from any field whose intention it is to empower their clients.

Before proceeding further, I wish to make it clear that I view psychodiagnosis, defined as 'knowing the self,' as entirely compatible with client-centered theory and practice. Consistent with this view, the use of a variety of assessment procedures, including psychological testing, is both desirable and appropriate *if* such procedures are requested or desired by clients for client-defined purposes. Tests or testing are not antithetical to client-centered values or practice. Indeed, clients often request testing to help them gather information about themselves, usually with the goal of making a decision or modifying their behavior. From our clients' frames of reference, tests are often viewed as means of serving them.

Who is diagnosis for?

The objection many client-centered practitioners have to diagnosis is that it is something *done to* the client from an *external frame of reference* (the diagnostician's), and without the client having adequate influence regarding the purpose and use of the information gathered. While this is a legitimate objection, it is relevant to the mechanical and prescriptive approaches to diagnosis but not to the collaborative approach described here. The basic issue, as I see it, revolves around the question 'Who is diagnosis for?' That is, who is diagnosis intended to serve? In traditional approaches to diagnosis (mechanical and prescriptive), the diagnostic assessment is usually done so that someone other than the client can use the information gathered, usually in an attempt to assist the client. In a typical scenario, a client is referred for diagnosis by a therapist who hopes to use the diagnostic data to understand the client better and to plan a course of treatment. Sometimes the diagnostic findings are shared with the client; sometimes they are not. Since the traditional approaches emphasize the treating agent's use of the data, relatively little importance is placed on the client's development of relevant self-knowledge. Consequently, the process is, at worst, dehumanizing and frequently of little direct value to the client.

The collaborative practitioner's answer to the question 'Who is diagnosis for?' is clearly 'the client.' That is, the purpose of diagnosis from a collaborative viewpoint is to assist clients in learning relevant information about themselves that they can use to remediate problems and move forward in their development. The diagnostician who engages collaboratively with the client basically states: 'I am here to assist you to learn anything that will help you define and meet your needs.' Practitioners engaged in a collaborative approach with their clients recognize that what they learn about the client is of far less importance than what the client knows. While this may seem like a minor shift in emphasis, it is in fact quite radical. In the collaborative model, the client is assisted in a process of self-diagnosis. In this model the diagnostic and therapeutic processes are essentially the same. Rogers (1951) expressed a similar position over 35 years ago.

> In a very meaningful and accurate sense, therapy *is* diagnosis, and this diagnosis is a process which goes on in the experience of the client, rather than in the intellect of the clinician . . . In client-centered therapy one could say that the purpose of the therapist is to provide the conditions in which the client is able to make, to experience, and to accept the diagnosis of the psychogenic aspects of his maladjustment. (p. 223)

Timothy Leary (1970) has articulated a compatible view about the diagnostic endeavor.

> The patient or subject should be seen and treated not as a passive thing to be done to but as the equal of the psychologist in the collaborative research. The patient, after all, is the world's leading authority on the issue at hand — his own life and the transactions in which he is involved. Here I am urging *phenomenological-equality.* Always get the viewpoint of the patient on every issue, question, and decision, and treat this viewpoint as equal to your own. (p. 213)

Leary goes on to say, 'The aim of psychodiagnosis should be to make the patient feel wiser and feel good' (p. 219) and 'Accurate diagnosis, collaboratively worked out with the patient, is effective therapy for both patient and doctor' (p. 234).

Constance Fischer (1985) has played a central role in the development of a collaborative approach to diagnosis and treatment. She identifies her approach as individualized assessment and indicates that it goes 'beyond normative data and classification [and] addresses a particular person's situation as he or she experiences it and simultaneously contributes to it. Hence the client can contribute throughout the psychological assessment' (p. 5). Fischer (1985) also views the assessment process as a growth-enhancing experience for the client. She states: 'An effective assessment is necessarily growthful because clients begin to experience themselves as able to assess and change their lives' (p. 49).

CHARACTERISTICS OF THE COLLABORATIVE APPROACH

The collaborative approach has several important characteristics. Collaborative practitioners view their clients holistically, realizing that psychological, biological, and sociocultural aspects of the person are interrelated. Consequently, the practitioner will be more person-focused than problem-focused as he or she engages in the diagnostic process with the client. Such practitioners will attend as much to what is right with their clients as to what is wrong. Therefore, their clients are more likely to gain a more complete picture of themselves and the factors that affect their 'problems' than clients of mechanical or prescriptive model practitioners.

Collaborative practitioners take a phenomenological approach to their clients. They place observation of immediate experience above explanation. Fischer (1985) articulates some of the essential characteristics of a phenomenological approach to diagnosis as follows:

> All knowledge is human knowledge . . . We do not simply discover data; we inevitably prefigure it through our interests and perspectives . . . [It] takes into account the necessarily perspectival character of all perception and knowledge . . . It addresses the individual as a particular individual in order to explore and describe that person's lived world [instead] of describing the person in terms of preestablished kinds of measurements and categories . . . It attends to how [clients'] approaches to situations preform what they can see and do. (p. 351)

Collaborative practitioners are more interested in enabling their clients to engage in an ongoing process of *self-diagnosis* rather than limiting themselves to understanding a problem in isolation. As a result, their clients are more likely to continue to assess the meaning of their experiences and to transform it into *personal knowledge* that can be applied to present and future problems. Clients who have participated in collaborative approaches will tend to want to develop individualized remediational programs for themselves rather than accept remedies in which 'one approach fits all.' They are likely to feel satisfied about the active and significant role they have played in the remediation of their problems and are less likely to feel (or become) dependent on their professional caretakers.

A major strength of the collaborative approach is that it helps create in clients a new consciousness about the significant and crucial role they can play in determining the nature and quality of care afforded to them. It enables them to realize that they are the best judge of their needs—physical, psychological, and otherwise—and that they can learn to take more charge of and influence the course of their lives, even in areas in which they have relatively little 'expertise.' Clients are more likely to insist that any remediations proposed to them by 'experts' are compatible with what they know (or have learned) about themselves and with their values.

In the personal example mentioned earlier, I have been treated for (mechanical approach) and have had treatments prescribed for (prescriptive approach) lower back, elbow, and hamstring problems with modest results. Recently, I have become more involved in assessing the messages of my body, learned more about anatomy and physiology and alternative treatment approaches while collaborating more assertively with my caretaker (a chiropractor) regarding which treatments he and I will use. We also consult with each other about the effects of the treatments and about exercises to do or avoid. The result is that I have experienced more significant and encouraging results than with any previous treatments. I might add that my chiropractor was both pleased and supportive of my increased involvement and feedback regarding what was and was not working. As a consequence of this experience, I have become more optimistic about

413

my ability to identify and utilize resources, professional and personal, that enable me to take care of myself, even in areas in which I know relatively little.

The main disadvantage of the collaborative approach is that it requires much more of the client in terms of time commitment, effort, and active involvement. It may also be more difficult to find a collaborative practitioner for one's area of concern.

CONCLUDING THOUGHTS

For better or worse, diagnosis is here to stay. It is firmly embedded in American culture and many others as well. As long as people have problems they will seek the help of experts to remedy them. For many, the logic of diagnosis is appealing and pragmatic. That is, when something doesn't work or function as it's supposed to, find out what's wrong and fix it. It is hard to deny that life is made easier because experts ranging from the mechanic to the psychotherapist are apparently able to diagnose and remedy our problems. The degree to which one's active involvement is necessary or desirable can vary from none to a considerable amount. Therefore, one's level of participation in assessing and remedying one's problems is often a matter of choice. Yet this very choice is crucial in shaping one's view of life and oneself as well as the quality of care one is likely to receive.

Each approach to diagnosis and remediation has legitimate and desirable benefits for the consumer-client. Few, if any, people have the time or inclination to become even minimally expert in the areas in which they may need help. We can hardly blame others for trying to find the simplest and most painless solutions to their problems. Such tendencies may well be universal. Yet, when the well-being of a person is involved, the stakes are obviously high. Turning over one's care, partially or entirely, to another person, however expert or trustworthy, involves an unknown degree of risk.

In the fields of psychology and psychiatry our ability to establish a reliable and meaningful diagnosis for our clients remains in a rudimentary stage of development. Even if we could accurately diagnose and categorize disorders within people, we have not yet established specific treatments for specific disorders. Since an extremely diverse range of therapeutic approaches are roughly equivalent in treating a variety of problems, it seems more likely that the crucial element is the person of the therapist rather than the therapist's ideology. Yet even the most talented of therapists (or other caretakers) are faced with the challenge of attempting to assist a person who, in some essential ways, is unlike any client that therapist has ever seen or will see again. In addition, each client brings to the therapeutic endeavor his or her own capacity and limitations to engage profitably in the diagnostic and treatment process. As Rogers (1951) suggested, 'The constructive forces which bring about altered perceptions, reorganization of self, and relearning, reside primarily in the client, and probably cannot come from outside' (p. 222). If we accept this assumption, then it seems to me that we must make every attempt to engage our clients as fully as possible as collaborators in the diagnostic-therapeutic process.

REFERENCES

Fischer, C. T. (1985). *Individualizing psychological assessment.* Monterey, CA: Brooks/Cole.

Leary. T. (1970). The diagnosis of behavior and the diagnosis of experience. In A. Mahrer (Ed.), *New approaches to personality classification* (pp. 211–36). New York: Columbia University Press.

Rogers, C. R. (1951). *Client-centered therapy.* Boston: Houghton Mifflin.

Special discussion: A Countertheory of Transference

(i) A Countertheory of Transference

John M. Shlien   *Harvard University*

Transference or the 'transference neurosis' is reexamined. This analysis suggests that transference is a defense mechanism used to deny or disguise the reality and natural consequences of the therapist's behavior. Two of these behaviors, understanding and misunderstanding, are featured as archetypical causes of love and hate, unnecessarily called 'positive' and 'negative' transference. The analysis starts with the uneasy origin of the concept illustrated in the case of Anna 0. It continues through variations in definition and use of transference, and observations on the self-concept of the therapist. The repetition-logic of psychoanalysis is disputed, and a countertheory is proposed, based on clinical experience and phenomenal evidence of the normal human response to understanding. The act of understanding is described not only as the first cause of 'transference' but also as the essential healing factor, the main contribution and the proper objective of all psychotherapies.

Editor's Note: John M. Shlien has taken a provocative and controversial position on the issue of transference. While Shlien's ideas are likely to be acceptable to some, they will likely be unsettling to others. Whatever one's position on the phenomenon of transference, one's thinking about the client's seemingly unfounded reactions to the therapist will inevitably be stimulated. Since the issue is one of significance to therapists of all persuasions, notable therapists within and outside the client/person-centered approach have been invited to respond to Shlien's article. Their responses will be included in the next issue of the *Person-Centered Review*. Readers are encouraged to submit to the Editor their own reactions to Shlien's article or to the articles of the respondents.

> *'Transference' is a fiction, invented and maintained by therapists to protect themselves from the consequences of their own behavior.*

To many, this assertion will seem an exaggeration, an outrage, an indictment. It is presented here as a serious hypothesis, charging a highly invested profession with the task of reexamining a fundamental concept in practice.

It is not entirely new to consider transference as a defense. Even its proponents cast it among the defense mechanisms when they term it a 'projection.' But they mean that the defense is on the part of the patient. My assertion suggests a different type of defense: denial or distortion, and on the part of the therapist.

Mine is not an official position in client-centered therapy. There is none. Carl Rogers has dealt with the subject succinctly, in about 20 pages (1951, pp. 198–217), a relatively brief treatment of a matter that has taken up volumes of the literature in the field.[1] 'In

---

1. Transference does not appear in the index of his earlier volume, *Counseling and Psychotherapy* (Rogers, 1942).

First published in *Person-Centered Review,* Volume 2, Number 1, February 1987.

client-centered therapy, this involved and persistent dependency relationship does not tend to develop' (p. 201), though such transference attitudes are evident in a considerable proportion of cases handled by client-centered therapists. Transference is not fostered or cultivated by this present-time oriented framework where intensive exploration of early childhood is not required, and where the therapist is visible and available for reality testing. While Rogers knows of the position taken here and has, I believe, been influenced by it since its first presentation in 1959, he has never treated the transference topic as an issue of dispute. This is partly so because of his lack of inclination for combat on controversial issues, where he prefers to do his own constructive work and let evidence accumulate with new experience.

Why then should client-centered therapy take a position on an issue of so little moment in its own development? For one reason, the concept of transference is ubiquitous. It has a powerful grip on the minds of professionals and the public. And, while client-centered practice has the popular image of a relatively self-effacing therapist, it holds to a standard of self-discipline and responsibility for the conditions and processes it fosters, and it could not fail to encounter those emotional and relational strains so often classed as transference.

There are many separate questions raised by the assertion at the start of this article. *What* behavior of the therapist? Leading to *which* consequences? *Why* invent[2] such a concept? *How* does it protect? In reexamining the concept of transference how do we, to use Freud's words, 'inquire into its source'?

Throughout we will consider only the male therapist/female patient data. Such was the critical situation when the term was invented. The first five case histories in the 1895 landmark *Studies on Hysteria* (Breuer & Freud, 1957) are Anna O., Emmy von N., Lucy R., Katharina, and Elisabeth. It set up the image of the most sensitive relationship (older man, younger woman) most suspect in the minds of the public (whether skeptic or enthusiast) and the combination most common for many decades.[3] Indeed it is possible that without the sexually charged atmosphere thus engendered, the concept of transference might not have developed as it has, if at all! For it is not insignificant that Breuer, and Freud, were particularly vulnerable. As Jewish physicians, admitted to the fringes of anti-Semitic Viennese society by virtue of their professional status, they could ill afford any jeopardy.

For psychoanalysis, transference seems to be the essential concept: 'sine qua non,' 'an inevitable necessity,' 'the object of treatment,' 'the most important thing we [Freud and Breuer] have to make known to the world,' without which 'the physician and his arguments would never be listened to.' In addition, it contains and subsumes all the elaborate support structures: the primary significance of sexual instincts, psychic determinism, the unconscious, psychogenetic theory, and the power of past experience. It is crucial in theory! In practice, it comforts, protects, and explains.

Transference is also supposed to distinguish psychoanalysis from other forms of therapy. Perhaps it is meant to do so, but this becomes moot through contradictions in

---

2. Inventions are human-made. Thus *invent* is used to offset Freud's use of the word *discovered,* which inaccurately implies a fact found or truth revealed.

3. Social and economic conditions that create anxiety neuroses in women and enable men to become physicians have changed enough to bring about some evening of opportunity. Fortunately, women can now more easily find female therapists. There are also more cross-sex, same-sex, bisex, and other permutations. We know relatively little of these many parallels of the transference model, but may be sure that the concept is now so well established that it will appear as a 'demand characteristic' in its own right. It has become part of the pseudosophisticated belief system of informed clients.

the literature, which variously asserts that transference is peculiar to psychoanalysis while also common in everyday life. Whether unique or universal, it is in widespread use throughout most psychodynamic systems. One distinction it surely serves: that between professional and paraprofessional, or sophisticate and literalist, and in general between those in and out of power. If transference is no longer the singular hallmark of psychoanalysis, it at least marks those 'in the know,' whether novices or not.

It was in Freud's mind 'a new fact which we are thus unwilling compelled to recognize' (Jones, 1953, p. 385). 'Unwilling' does not truly describe Freud's attitude. That word is an artful form of argument to make a welcome conjecture seem an unavoidable fact. Currently, 'unwilling' more aptly describes the attitude of psychotherapists toward reexamination of the idea. But reexamination is necessary if we are to reevaluate the usefulness of the concept.

HISTORICAL CONTEXT

It seems most appropriate to begin this reevaluation with the early history of the concept. The case of Anna O. provides the cornerstone on which the theory of transference is generally thought to be based. More than a dramatic and moving affair, it is of momentous importance to the field, and its effects still influence the majority of theory and practice. Though psychoanalysis and/or other forms of psychotherapy would somehow have developed, all present forms owe much to these few pioneers and their struggles. To honor them properly, it is necessary to study these human points or origin.

The accounts begin in the *Studies on Hysteria* (Breuer & Freud, 1957), first published in 1895, 13 years after treatment ended. Details of treatment were reported cautiously, out of respect for the still-living patient, and for other reasons having to do with questions about the outcome, and growing tensions between Freud and Breuer. Anna O. was, by all accounts, remarkable, and, for that time, so was her treatment. In her twenty-first year, she was described by Breuer and others as a person of great beauty, charm, and powerful intellect, with a quick grasp and surplus energy. Living in a comfortable but monotonous environment at home, she was hungry for intellectual stimulation. She was poetic and imaginative, fluent in German, English, Italian, and French. Much of her waking time was spent in daydreaming, her 'private theatre.' She was also sharp and critical, and therefore, Breuer notes, 'completely unsuggestable' (though he routinely used hypnosis), needing to be convinced by argument on every point. She was tenacious and obstinate, but also known for immensely sympathetic kindness, a quality that marked most of her life's work. She had never been in love. In short, she was young, attractive, intelligent, and lonely; it was she who named psychotherapy 'the talking-cure,' and she was a near-perfect companion for the also remarkable physician-pioneer in this form of treatment. (He was 38 at the time, admired, loved, respected, and of high professional and social status.) Both deserved all the tributes given, and Breuer perhaps even more. While Freud was the conceptual and literary genius without doubt, and Anna O. the central figure of the famous case, Breuer was probably the therapeutic genius of the time. And that in a new, dangerous exploration where there were few precedents, guidelines, or previous personal experiences.

Through the experience of Anna O. with Breuer, the material used as the basis for the theory of *transference-love* (as it was then called) was gathered, but it was Freud alone who later invented that theory to interpret that material to Breuer and the world. In the meantime, Freud's invention had been fostered by experience of his own with at least one other female patient.

The case of Anna O. is described in 1895 by Breuer (Breuer & Freud, 1957, pp. 21–47), who wrote that he had 'suppressed a large number of quite interesting details' (true), and that she had left Vienna to travel for a while, free of her previous disturbances (not quite so true, for she was taken to a sanatorium where she 'inflamed the heart of the psychiatrist in charge' [Jones, 1953, p. 225], and was temporarily addicted to morphine). By the time Breuer reported the *Studies* a decade later, he could write that 'it was a considerable time before she regained her mental balance entirely' (p. 41). Even so, he had confided sorrowfully to Freud in an earlier discussion that he thought sometimes she were better off dead, to end her suffering. The 'suppressed details' may in part be related to his sudden termination of the treatment and the patient's shocking emergency regarding her 'pregnancy' and his 'responsibility.' James Strachey, editor of the 1957 translation of *Studies on Hysteria,* says Freud told him of the end of Anna O.'s treatment: 'The patient suddenly made manifest to Breuer the presence of a strong unanalysed positive transference of an unmistakably sexual nature' (Breuer & Freud, 1957, p. 41, fn.). This is a retroactive interpretation, of course, since at the time of its occurrence neither Breuer nor perhaps even Freud yet had any idea of 'transference.' That idea builds, and more complete information is released, as Freud describes the case in both oblique and direct references in lectures and other writings from 1905 to his autobiography in 1925. Still more explicit communications are released in Ernest Jones's (1953) biography of Freud. In 1972, Freeman, a well-known popular writer, published a 'novelized' biography and report of Anna O. and her treatment. (None of these is exact, verbatim, or anything like 'verification data.')

Even so, the somewhat guarded report by Breuer gives us a privileged view of his work. The editor of *Studies on Hysteria* tells us that Breuer had little need of hypnosis because Anna O. so readily 'produced streams of material from her unconscious, and *all Breuer had to do was to sit by and listen to them without interrupting her*' (Breuer & Freud, 1957, p. xvii; emphasis added). That is *all*? As you will see later, I argue that this is no small thing. It may not seem much to that editor, himself a lay analyst in training, but to the lonely, grieving, and desperate young woman, it must have seemed a treasure. At that period, young ladies were given placebos, referred from one doctor to another, and generally treated with patronizing attention or benign neglect. Breuer and Freud were precious rarities in that they listened, took her seriously. Would that Breuer had done more of that, and had done it steadfastly *through the end.* Listening is behavior of great consequence. The pity is that he felt forced to cut it short at the critical last moments.

Meanwhile, there were many other behaviors and we can only estimate their consequences. He fed her. She was emaciated, and he alone was able to feed her. He could give her water when she otherwise would not drink. No doubt there were other nourishing figures in her life, but he was clearly one himself. He paid her daily visits. She held his hands in order to identify him at times when she could not see. When she was exhausted, he put her to sleep, with narcotics or suggestion. He restored mobility to paralyzed limbs. He hypnotized her, sometimes twice a day, taught her self-hypnosis, and then 'would relieve her of the whole stock of imaginative products she had accumulated since [his] last visit' (1957, p. 36). He took her for rides in his carriage with his daughter (named Berthe, which was also Anna O.'s real name). He read her diary — a notably tricky business either with or without her permission. He forced her to remember unpleasant experiences.

From this alone, would you think that Anna O. had reason (real, not imaginary) for feelings such as gratitude, hope, affection, trust, annoyance, intimacy, resentment, and fear of separation?

Finally, there was the ending. Breuer had been preoccupied with his patient, and his wife had become jealous and morose. There had been improvement, indeed. But also, according to Jones's account, Breuer confided to Freud that he decided to terminate treatment because he divined the meaning of his wife's state of mind. 'It provoked a violent reaction in him, perhaps compounded of love and guilt, and he decided to bring the treatment to an end' (Jones, 1953, p. 225).

Exactly how he announced this decision to Anna O. we do not know. That evening he was called back by the mother and found his patient 'in a greatly excited state, apparently as ill as ever.' She was 'in the throes of an hysterical childbirth' (Jones, 1953, p. 224).

Certainly that is an interpretation of her 'cramps' and utterances that might commonly occur. We have no firsthand information as to what the patient thought or meant. Every report is second- or thirdhand, *through* Freud *about* Breuer, and that usually through Jones, who wrote, 'Freud has related to me a fuller account than he described in his writings,' and some of that account is quoted as follows:

> The patient, who according to him [Breuer] had appeared as an asexual being and had never made any allusion to such a forbidden topic throughout the treatment, was now in the throes of an hysterical childbirth (pseudocyesis), the logical termination of a phantom pregnancy that had been invisibly developing in response to Breuer s ministrations. Though profoundly shocked, he managed to calm her down by hypnotizing her, and then fled the house in a cold sweat. The next day he and his wife left for Venice to spend a second honeymoon . . .
>
> Some ten years later, at a time when Breuer and Freud were studying cases together, Breuer called him into consultation over an hysterical patient. Before seeing her, he described her symptoms, whereupon Freud pointed out that they were typical products of a phantom pregnancy. The recurrence of the old situation was too much for Breuer. Without saying a word, he took up his hat and stick and hurriedly left the house. (1953, pp. 224–6)

A somewhat more explicit (but still far from direct or verbatim) report is cited in Freeman (1972, p. 200). Freud writes to Stefan Zweig (a relative of Anna O. by marriage): *'What really happened* with Breuer I was able to *guess* later on, long after the break in our relations, when I *suddenly remembered* something Breuer had told me in another context before we had begun to collaborate and which he never repeated. On the evening of the day when all her symptoms had been disposed of, he was summoned to the patient again, found her confused and writhing in abdominal cramps. Asked what was wrong with her, she replied: "Now Dr. B's child is coming!"' (emphasis added).[4]

---

4. One point must be stressed. There is only, but *only* Freud's reconstruction in this momentous history. No other source whatever. How much Freud wanted these data, how much and how often he pressed Breuer for them, we have a few hints. In his autobiography (1948, first published in 1925): 'When I was back in Vienna I turned once more to Breuer's observation and made him tell me more about it'(p. 34). In 1925 he still speaks of 'a veil of obscurity which Breuer never raised for me' (p. 36). This prodding, however, eventually cost them their friendship. How much Breuer's support meant to Freud we do know. How highly motivated to get this information, which he sometimes says Breuer would never repeat for him, we also know. Yet it is all Freud's reconstruction; and in 1932, when he wrote the cited letter to Stefan Zweig, he still seems wanting of confirmation: 'I was so convinced of this reconstruction of mine that I published it somewhere. Breuer's youngest daughter read my account and asked her father about it shortly before his death. He confirmed my version, and she informed me about it later' (Freeman, 1972, p. 200). To what 'reconstruction' does this refer, that he published 'somewhere' (and *where?)* because he was so convinced yet unconfirmed? Hot pursuit, without a doubt, but the facts are still reported with slight discrepancies, and never by anyone but Freud.

Freud, speaking of Breuer, added, 'At this moment he held in his hand the key,' but 'seized by conventional horror he took flight and abandoned his patient to a colleague' (Freeman, 1972, p. 200).[5]

Here is one final quotation from Breuer himself in his own report: 'The element of sexuality was astonishingly undeveloped in her. The patient, whose life became known to me *to an extent to which one person's life is seldom known to another,* had never been in love' (Breuer & Freud, 1957, pp. 21–2; emphasis added).

What then 'really happened'? We will never know. Two exceptional (in my opinion, magnificent) people of great intelligence and noble spirit came close to understanding. He knew her well. Probably she knew him better than he thought. The knowing appears to have been precious to both. Understanding failed at a critical point. They dropped the key. It is tragic; so much was lost. Thankfully, we know that both carried on vital and constructive lives for many years.

If you are a woman, reading this will probably bring different reactions than those of the typical man. Perhaps you feel more sympathetic to the patient. If you put yourself in the therapist's place, supposing this could be your case, you know at least that you could think to yourself, and possibly say to Anna O., 'Unlikely that it is my child in the physical sense, since I am woman like yourself, but perhaps you mean that I am somehow parent to your pain, your growth, your condition, whatever.' (If you think that logically a woman therapist would never face such a situation, because of the reality, consider the implications of *that* for transference theory!)

More difficult if you are a man, putting yourself in this imaginary situation. You might say, 'I submitted to voluntary sterilization in order to make my life less anxious, as it were, so it is unlikely, etc.' as above. Not only a condition with which few readers would identify, but in this case useless, since Anna knows Breuer has recently fathered a child. (There is another possible source of security, transference theory, but it had not yet been invented.)

Meanwhile, return to the fact that it is Dr. Breuer who is directly and immediately involved, and involved with Anna O. What might they be thinking, *meaning,* saying to each other in this perilous moment, at best and at worst? God knows what words she uttered in which four languages (for she was known to speak a 'gibberish' of mixed tongues when ill), nor what she heard, what he said, or what he told Freud was said. Nor what Freud told Jones; nor how accurate Jones's translation (not always, we know). But let us take it that Freud's letter to Zweig is the most authentic; in it, Anna, on one page, says, 'Now Dr. B's child is coming' (Freeman, 1972, p. 200) or, in a slightly different quotation from the same scene, same book, 'Now Dr. Breuer's baby is coming. It is coming!' (p. 56).

Anna might have thought, felt, or said, for example:

Dr. B – a baby. I feel like a baby!

Would you abort my child? Then don't abort my treatment.

You know me so well, but you thought I was sexually underdeveloped, had never been in love, had no romantic feelings – although you knew, for instance, that I loved to dance. Well, I've grown. Thanks to you in good part. Now Dr. Breuer's child has become a woman. I'm ready at last for that sexual release. It is coming!

When you were late for our appointment one morning, you apologized and told me [as he had] that it had to be so because your wife was having a new baby and you had to stay up

---

5. The key to what? Not necessarily the arcane lock Freud had in mind. Perhaps the door to a more literal and still more courageous exploration, and Breuer might have founded an enlightened form of psychotherapy to advance the field by decades. But he was frightened off by the event, his circumstances, and perhaps his colleague as well.

all night. If that is what is more important to you, look, I'm having one too.

Why did you tell me so suddenly that you could not continue to see me? Your reasons sounded false. I know so well your voice, your eyes. What is the real reason? If you must lie to me to leave me, I must lie to you to keep you.

Only hear me out. I mean you no harm as you leave. We have touched. You massaged me, fed me, gave me life, comfort, discipline; made me tell things I would not tell anyone else. I felt loved, and I must tell you in the ultimate way, I love you too. You are handsome, kind, distinguished. If all of this does not justify my excitement and love, what does? Life together is impossible, I know that. Sex is really not that important to me either. But love is. A child would be. I want someone to love. I am in great pain over it.

None of these possibilities begins to describe conversations to which they might have led. But meanwhile, Dr. Breuer, on his part, might have thought, felt, or said something like the following:

What did I do to deserve this?

My God, you are really out of your mind (again).

You cannot think that I . . . (or can you?)

We've never even discussed such a thing (which they hadn't).

It never entered my mind (if indeed it hadn't).

Is this more of your 'private theatre'? Not amusing.

You are punishing me.

Damned embarrassing. I already have problems at home.

This is a trap! How to get out of it.

Here is the ruination of my reputation/family/livelihood/method/hope/everything.[6]

Or, in a more benign mood:

You don't want me to leave you.

Perhaps I have been both too caring and careless, left you unfairly.

What are you growing, laboring to deliver?

What part did I play?

I am touched and honored that you choose me.

Have I led you to expect more than I can give?

Or, best of all:

You are in pain. Let's try to understand. I will postpone my trip and work with you.

Freud, as we already know, discussed this case with Breuer more than once. There is some evidence that Breuer felt not only uncertainty about it, but guilt and shame as well. In the late 1880s, years after *Studies in Hysteria* was written, Freud tried to persuade Breuer to write more about it. Breuer had declared the treatment of hysterics an ordeal he could not face again. Freud then described to Breuer one experience so well known now through his autobiography (1948, p. 48) in which he too had faced 'untoward events.' As Jones (1953, p. 250) described it:

---

6. I have personally known psychologists and psychiatrists who far exceeded Breuer's relatively innocent transgressions, that is, their 'sins' by the informal definition, 'included exchange of bodily fluids.' Results included divorce, marriage to the patient, suicide, murderous thoughts and a probable attempt, career changes, and the development of new theories. The late O. H. Mowrer's therapy based on real guilt and compensation (1967) is an example of the latter, as he often announced to professional colleagues.

So Freud told him of his own experience with a female patient suddenly flinging her arms around his neck in a transport of affection, and he explained his reasons for regarding such 'untoward occurrences' as part of the transference phenomena characteristic of certain types of hysteria.[7] This seems to have had a calming effect on Breuer, who evidently had taken his own experience of the kind more personally and perhaps even reproached himself for indiscretion in the handling of his patient.

Momentarily this comforted, explained to, and protected Breuer, but only momentarily. At first, Breuer agreed to join in the publication and promotion of the idea of transference. As Freud writes many times, 'I believe,' he told me, 'that this is the most important thing we two have to give the world' (Breuer & Freud, 1957, p. xxviii). But then, Breuer withdrew his support for the theory and the complete primacy of sexual etiology of neuroses — support Freud needed and urgently sought. 'He [Breuer] might have crushed me . . . by pointing to his own patient [Anna O.] in whose case sexual factors had ostensibly played no part whatever' (Freud, 1948, p. 6).[8] That Breuer was ambivalent, that he neither crushed nor supported, Freud put down to Breuer's suppressed secret of the case. Breuer may have had serious and sincere doubts on other scores. They agreed to disagree, citing 'the natural and justifiable differences between the opinions of two observers who are agreed upon the facts and their basic reading of them, but who are not invariably at one in their interpretations and conjectures.' It was signed 'J. Breuer/S. Freud, April 1895'; (Breuer & Freud, 1957, p. xxx). Breuer, quite possibly intimidated by the nature of his suppressed material and his loyalty to both colleague Freud and patient Anna O., did not press his arguments, whatever they might have been. Freud did, and swept the field. Now we have transference.

DEFINITIONS AND DEFINERS

A few definitions are in order. There are dozens. They change over time and between authors. The main theme is constant enough that the proponent of any form of 'depth psychology' can sagely nod assent, though Orr (1954, p. 625) writes, 'From about 1930 onward, there are too many variations of the concept of transference for systematic summary.'

Circa 1905

What are transferences? They are new editions or facsimiles of the tendencies and phantasies which are aroused and made conscious during the progress of the analysis; but they have this peculiarity, which is characteristic for their species, that they replace some earlier person by the person of the physician. To put it another way: a whole series of psychological experiences are revived, not as belonging to the past, but as applying to the person of the physician at the present moment. Some of these transferences have a content which differs from that of their model in no respect whatever except for the substitution. These, then — to keep the same metaphor — are merely new impressions or reprints. Others are more ingeniously constructed; their content has been subjected to a moderating influence — to

---

7. This is either the instance that Freud sometimes described in his autobiography and elsewhere, as the patient being just aroused from a hypnotic trance, and with a maidservant unexpectedly knocking or entering, or it is a separate but prototypic scene.
8. Breuer knew better. Had he walked into this trap, it is he who would have been crushed.

sublimation, as I call it — and they may even become conscious, by cleverly taking advantage of some real peculiarity in the physician's person or circumstances and attaching them to that.[9] These, then, will no longer be new impressions, but revised editions. (Freud, 1959, p. 139)

The new fact which we are thus unwillingly compelled to recognize we call 'transference.' By this we mean a transference of feelings on to the person of the physician, because we do not believe that the situation in the treatment can account for the origin of such feelings. (Freud, 1935, p. 384)

By transference is meant a striking peculiarity of neurotics. They develop toward their physician emotional reactions both of an affectionate and hostile character, which are not based upon the actual situation but are derived from their relations to their parents. (Freud, 1935, p. 391)

There can be no doubt that the hostile feelings against the analyst deserve the name of 'transference' for the situation in the treatment gives no adequate occasion for them. (Freud, 1935, p. 385)

Why should anyone feel hostility toward Freud? 'Actually I have never done a mean thing,' wrote Freud to Putnam (Jones, 1957, p. 247). Not many can make this disclaimer, and not all believe it borne out by Freud's record (compare Roustang, 1982).

Still, if he only *thinks* this of himself it is more likely that hostile feelings toward him would be seen as unjustified by his behavior. What matters here is the analyst's proclamation of innocence — a stance that permeates transference theory throughout. While an ad hominem argument is of limited use, there is a principle to which readers in this field must surely subscribe. It is that *every honest theory of personality and psychotherapy must reflect the personality and experience of its author.* How could it be otherwise?

Freud (1935, p. 385) continues this definition:

The necessity for regarding the negative transference in this light is a confirmation of our previous similar views of the positive or affectionate variety.

This 'necessity' is part of that strange logic in which the second assertion confirms the first!

Is transference useful? Yes, it overcomes resistance, enables interpretation; it is your chief tactical ally. 'The father-transference is only the battlefield where we conquer and take the libido prisoner '(Freud, 1935, p. 396).

In sum, the patient's feelings '*do not originate in the present situation,* and *they are not deserved by the personality of the physician,* but they repeat what has happened to him once before in his life' (Freud, 1927, p. 129; emphasis added). The 'once before' is experience 'in childhood, and usually in connection with one of his parents.' As put most simply in *The Problem of Lay Analysis* (Freud, 1927, p. 129): 'The attitude is, to put it bluntly, a kind of falling in love.' We must not forget, 'This affection is not accounted for by the physician's behavior nor the relationship nor situation' (1935, p. 383).

So, the analyst is not responsible, the situation is not responsible, even though there may be some 'real peculiarities' visible in the physician or circumstances. Transference is a neurotic peculiarity. Whether it is a normal (common) trait also is unclear, but the transference neurosis is a feature of analysis — that is certain.

There are some updatings. They will not make a basic difference, but it is worth noting that Fenichel (1941, p. 95) tried to alter the absolute exemption of the therapist's

---

9. Women are especially good at this, he writes. They 'have a genius for it' (Freud, 1935, p. 384).

responsibility when he wrote:

> Not everything is transference that is experienced by a patient in the form of affects and impulses during the course of the analytic treatment. If the analysis appears to make no progress, the patient has, in my opinion, the right to be angry, and his anger need not be a transference from childhood – or rather, we will not succeed in demonstrating the transference component in it.

Later positions (Macalpine, 1950; Menninger, 1958) suggest that the analytic situation itself is regressive, and thus somewhat influential if not responsible. Waelder (1956, p. 367) says, 'Hence transference is a regressive process. Transference develops *in consequence* of the conditions of the analytic situation and the analytic technique' (emphasis added). Waelder's statement directly contradicts some of Freud's basic definitions, but to what effect?

The qualifications make concessions and corrections, but no one anywhere questions the basic concept, per se. Oddly, they serve only to strengthen, never to cast doubt. The situation *is* regressive because it turns all the patient's attention inward and backward toward earliest experience, and the therapist is made to seem bland, neutral, indistinct, even invisible. It is like a form of sensory deprivation. Other forms are elevated into unusual prominence. So it is with the presence and with the pronouncements of the therapist in this regressive situation.

Or, if transference is considered as a matter of 'projection,' the question arises, *what is the screen?* The answer was implied, though it seemed not to be recognized, in the first deep crack in transference theory – 'countertransference.' The instant that concept was developed, it should have become clear that the analyst's presence was more than a blank. Presumably countertransference was to be kept at a minimum. Until recently, definitions of and attention to it have been relatively minimal (except for one sector where it seems most nearly innocent, appropriate, and 'natural': that is, work with children).

As Freud began to give attention to countertransference, he viewed it as responsive or reflexive rather than as an originating characteristic of the analyst. 'We have become aware of the "countertransference" which arises in [the physician] as a result of *the patient's influence*[10] on his unconscious feeling' (Freud, 1910, p. 122; emphasis added). This is a far cry from the notion of one of my students, who thinks that transference lies in wait with the therapist and his wishes or expectations, while the countertransference is on the part of the patient! Not so farfetched as it first seems, for it may be only a reversal of Freud's statement just preceding. Which comes first?

The psychoanalytic positions on countertransference range from treating it as a hindrance to be overcome[11] to welcoming it as a sensory asset ('third ear') (Epstein and Feiner, 1974, p. 1). In any event, one can hardly claim 'no responsibility' on a 'nobody home' basis if it is admitted that somebody, with *some* palpable characteristics, is there.

---

10. This too is the patient's doing? Does this material not reside in the being of the physician? Or, if an interactive quality, does the transference, in reverse, arise in the patient as a result of the *physician's* influence?

11. In a letter dated 1909 about a case now become infamous, Freud wrote to Jung, 'After receiving your wire I wrote Fraulein Sp. a letter in which I affected ignorance' (McGuire, 1974, p. 230) and says of Jung's mishap, 'I myself have never been taken in quite so badly, but I have come very close to it a number of times and had a *"narrow escape"* [in English]. I believe that only grim necessities weighing on my work and the fact that I was ten years older when I came to psychoanalysis saved me from similar experiences. But no lasting harm is done. They helped us to develop the thick skin we need and to dominate "countertransference" which is after all a permanent problem for us' (McGuire, 1974, p. 231).

The question now becomes, What is the nature of these characteristics?

The therapist is in truth a person of some distinctiveness, some identity, no matter how discreetly hidden. He has some self-concept—an image of what he is and wants to be. Perhaps the more truly modest and humble, the more he will be surprised by intense idealizations of himself by others. If plain (he thinks), how much more inappropriate for the patient to think him handsome.

But perhaps he is not really modest or humble. That may be only a professional attitude. When Freud wrote to his wife Martha, telling her of Anna O.'s strenuous affection for Dr. Breuer and of the consternation on the part of Breuer's wife, Martha replied that she hoped that would not happen to her (a common concern of the therapist's spouse). Freud 'reproved her for her vanity in supposing that other women would fall in love with *her* husband: "for that to happen one has to be a Breuer"' (Jones, 1953, p. 225). Yet it was not really *her* vanity at issue, it would seem, but her concern over *his* exposure. Having first miscast the problem, he then did not quite give the assurance that she wanted,[12] and additionally, it *did* happen to her husband, as the theory predicted that it would. Perhaps it already had. At some point, reported in his autobiography, Freud had discontinued hypnosis after an 'untoward event' of his own. The patient, being aroused from a trance, threw her arms around him 'in a transport of affection.' At any rate, Freud dropped the method of hypnosis (was 'freed of it') shortly after, and took a position behind the couch. Some aspect of self-image certainly was a factor: hypnosis he compared to the work of a 'hod carrier or cosmetician,' while analysis was 'science,' 'surgery.' Perhaps it was more dignity at stake than modesty.

Though modesty was a thread often pulled. He wrote to Martha, 'To talk with Breuer was like sitting in the sun; he radiates light and warmth. He is such a sunny person, and I don't know what he sees in me to be so kind.'

To Martha herself, 'Can there be anything crazier, I said to myself. You have won the dearest girl in the world quite without any merit of your own'[13] (Jones, 1953, p. 110). Granted that this is the romantic hyperbole of courtship, and that there are fluctuations in mood and tone as situations change, so that we hear this humility from the same powerful genius who called his real nature that of the *conquistador*. Still, the literary license we give to 'without merit' is like that we give to the supposedly indistinguishable therapist who receives what *he* says *he* does not deserve in the service of carrying out the conditions for transference.

'Can there be anything crazier, I said to myself.' Yes, a few things. One is institutionalizing false modesty such as that, by denying the characteristics in the situation and the personality of the analyst—denying so completely that a neurosis is cultivated by and for both parties while it is the very object of treatment. And all in the name of sanity, clarity, and honest scrutiny.

INTERIM THOUGHTS

On the way to proposing a countertherapy, permit me to describe some experiences that, over the years, led me to depart from the common beliefs in psychoanalytic theory that I once held.

---

12. 'Later he assured her that the anatomy of the brain was the only rival she had or was likely to have' (Jones, 1953, p. 211).
13. 'But a week later he asks why he should not for once get more than he deserved. Never has he imagined such happiness' (Jones, 1953, p. 110).

1. For 15 years, at the University of Chicago Counseling Center, I worked through the ranks from student-intern to senior faculty and chairman of the Interdepartmental Clinical Program, and occupied the office of my former mentor Carl Rogers after he left for Wisconsin. In such a position, one develops the reputation of a 'therapist's therapist.' It is a privileged learning opportunity. My clientele consisted largely of junior professionals. Three were interns on a psychiatric rotation from the university hospital. They were taught by their medical faculty a good deal about transference. They discussed their experiences as psychiatrists in training. One, a shy, diffident young man, was especially articulate about the onset of transference as he perceived it in a slightly older woman patient. He felt a rising excitement—'This is it.' He also felt that he was being handed a power about which he was both pleased and embarrassed, and of course embarrassed by his pleasure and embarrassment. Not only was transference theory an 'armor in his ordeal,' but a source of *downright satisfaction.* He felt 'as if I were wearing a mask. I smiled behind it. I could have taken it off. I thought of that, but I was too confused about what I'd have to uncover. Behind it, I could be detached, amused, be more thoughtful and responsive.' It was a revealing bit of information on the inner experience of transference in a young adherent of the theory. I wondered how many therapists acknowledge their pleasure so honestly. Weeks later, I took a neighbor and his four-year-old son to the emergency room. My client was on duty. I helped hold and soothe the little boy while Dr. G. sewed stitches in his head wound. We worked in a kind of harmonic unison over this child of French-Iranian extraction, who knew little English and was pained and frightened. We did it well. In our next session, Dr. G. told me that he had felt as if the boy were 'our child.' Did he mean his feminine qualities and my masculine ones (or the reverse)? No. If it must be put in familial terms, we were brothers, he thought. So did I (though neither of us actually had brothers). One might easily see in this an expression of transference and/or countertransference. I found neither. We had an experience that made us feel like brothers.

2. I attended a discussion of religion between Bruno Bettleheim and Paul Tillich. Bettleheim took the general position outlined in Freud's *Future of an Illusion* (1949) to the effect that the urge toward religious belief was a projection of the longing for a father. That seemed most plausible to me. Tillich answered, 'But what is the screen?' Not a weighty reply, to my way of thinking at the time, but increasingly I realized that 'it' cannot be nothing.

3. One evening I overheard a client in the next office. She wept and shouted, 'No one has ever treated me this way before. I love it, I can't believe it, but I'm afraid every time I come.' I thought she was banging on the desk to emphasize her points. At the end of the evening I went to that counselor's office. 'For God's sake, Russ, what were you doing?' He explained, and I heard fragments of a primitive audiodisc recording. The banging was the steam pipes. The client was saying, 'No one has ever understood me this way before. No one. I can't believe it. I love the feeling of "at last, someone knows, someone cares." But when I come back next week, with the rest of my garbage, will you still understand? I couldn't bear it if you didn't.' I do not know the content of what was understood, but was most struck by what understanding meant to her, and thought about it for a long time.

4. I once taught a course with the prominent Adlerian Dr. Rudolph Dreikurs—a hearty, gruff bear of a man. In one class he seemed especially heavy-handed. Students were angry and critical. During the intermission, he said, 'Do you notice the hostility? There is a lot of negative transference here.' I told him my observations, and he was perplexed, crestfallen. He had taught hundreds, even thousands, and no one had complained. They usually loved him.

5. In 1971, during the period of the 'revolution in mental health' (community

organization, demystification, 'radical therapy' and politics to fit, and so on), a consulting psychiatrist and practicing analyst told me, 'It is amazing. Some of these paraprofessionals I'm supervising can do anything we can do — except the handling of the transference.' I wondered — what would he say if there *is* no 'transference'?

6. Over many years, I have been perceived in many different ways. Humble and proud, kind and cruel, loyal and unreliable, ugly and handsome, cowardly and brave, to name a few wide-ranging contradictions. Someone must be mistaken? No, they are all true. This sense of my self, sometimes selfish, sometimes generous, makes me hesitate before characterizing someone's perception as a distortion. One client dreamed of me as a little boy, one she held on her lap — and I a white-haired father of three grown children, as she knew. But she too was correct (and she had her own reasons for that caretaking dream). There is that childlike side of me. I could cast it off, but keep it for my enjoyment. I have been seen as a lion and a rabbit. True, I can be hard and soft. Is that unusual? Though happy to have been married for 40 years, I could, when young, have fallen in love frequently — with ease, passion, and tenderness. Seriously? Sometimes seriously enough to last another lifetime, probably, but not so seriously that I think I am the only man for this only woman for me.[14] While I do not respect the philanderer because of the damage he is likely to do, reading Jones's (1953, p. 139) judgment that 'Freud was not only monogamous in a very unusual degree but for a time seemed to be well on the way to becoming uxorious' struck me as curious and doubtful. It is, however, a condition that would more readily incline one toward transference theory — at least as a supporting illusion. But if that is not my condition or my personality, should his theory be my theory?

Then, about my granddaughter. I dearly love this child. From what previous experience do I transfer this affection? Yes, I dearly loved my two daughters and my son when they were three-year-olds, too — but whence came *that?* Sooner or later, experience has to be *de novo,* original. We know from work in comparative psychology that most women and many men show autonomic signs (such as pupillary change) of great attraction to the typical 'configuration of infant' large head and small body. In short, it is an instinct, and it *produces its natural consequences each time for the same instinctive reasons, as if each time were the first.* This child knows, trusts, and loves me, too. Is *her* experience transference? Transfer of what? From where? Is mine transference and hers countertransference? Neither one; the trust is earned, the love is natural. That is the answer.

The real question is, what conditions bring about the original experience, the first of its kind without precedents? Then, what if those conditions again prevail? Put another way, if every perception depends on the past, what if there is no past?

The next step

History of its origins aside, transference is a shorthand term for qualities and characteristics of human interaction. Any shorthand will fail to represent the particulars of a unique relationship. Rather, the shorthand will obscure (in a sometimes comforting way) the realities of the relationship. The concept of 'father figure,' for instance, needs to be unraveled; what characteristics is it supposed to represent? What do such concepts as 'parent' or 'infantalizing' mean? In the remaining pages, an alternative view is presented to clarify the realities that the shorthand forms fail to represent.

---

14. My wife, with good taste and judgment, advises ('after all, this is not your biography') omitting this entire section. I would like to, but a main point of the article is that theory is in part biographical, stemming from thought, observation, and self-concept.

A COUNTERTHEORY

If transference is a fiction to protect therapists from the consequences of their own behavior, it is time to examine some behaviors — and their normal consequences. This does not start with any implication of villainy. It is simply that since 'transference-love' is the consequence most fraught with concern, and since that was the original instance in development of transference theory (from which all its extensions come), we should examine the behaviors responsible for the development of affectionate and erotic feelings. What is the truth? What are the facts?

First, there is the situation, its true conditions. Dependency is a built-in feature for the petitioner at the beginning, and the treatment itself often promotes further dependency. The patient (or client) is typically anxious, distressed, in need of help, and often lonely. The therapist, presumably, is not. Instead, he holds a professional role (especially if a physician) that ranks at or near the top in sociological surveys of romantic attractiveness to women seeking husbands (ahead of astronauts and other celebrities).[15] The situation is set for intimacy, privacy, trust, frequent contact, and revelation of precious secrets.

Second, it is also the case that there is an ongoing search, on the part of most adolescents and adults, for sexual companionship. It requires only the opportunity for intimacy. One does not need to look into therapy for arcane and mysterious sources of erotic feelings. They are commonplace, everywhere, carried about from place to place. Psychotherapy will encounter sexual attraction as surely as it encounters nature. The simple combination of urge and situation is a formula for instant, if casual, romantic fantasy.

Third, there is a supremely important special factor in a behavior to which most therapists subscribe and try to provide. It is *understanding*. Freud put it bluntly, (of transference) 'It is a kind of falling in love.' Let me put this bluntly too: *Understanding is a form of lovemaking*. It may not be so intended, but that is one of its effects. The professional Don Juan knows and uses it to deliberate advantage. That alone may make it an embarrassment to the therapist who does not wish to take advantage and is hard pressed to deal in an accepting but nonpossessive way with natural feelings that conventionally call for either some response in kind or rejection. Such difficulty does not relieve him of the responsibility. Intentionally he has been understanding, and this alone will, over time, activate in the patient some object-seeking components of trust, gratitude, and quite possibly affection or sexual desire.

In this same context, *misunderstanding is a form of hatemaking*. It works equally well since being misunderstood in a generally understanding relation is a shock, betrayal, and frustration.[16]

Understanding and misunderstanding and their ambivalent interplay are the primary factors in this thesis about 'positive and negative transference,' but there are numerous supplementary behaviors. To supplement misunderstanding, for example: waiting, asking

---

15. A current viewpoint in social psychology suggests that love, especially sexual love, is the result of status and power factors — 'a love relationship is one in which at least one actor gives (or is prepared to give) extremely high status to the other' (Kemper, 1978, p. 285).

16. This should not be overlooked: the therapist wants, and sometimes demands, to be understood by the patient, or client. Whether dealing in reflections, interpretations, or hypnotic suggestion, the therapist wants these understood — he or she feels good about it if they are, and inadequate and 'resisted' if they are not. Indeed, *the therapist may have the same response to understanding as does the patient* — tempered, of course, by wisdom, maturity, self-awareness, and other (not always present) virtues.

for the bathroom key, paying (possibly for missed appointments), cigar smoke, and various other subordinating and infantalizing conditions.

The most convincing evidence for this simple but profoundly effective thesis probably lies in one's own experience. It was, however, called to my attention by a combination of events, such as that overheard client in the next office, and another fortuitous circumstance. A Catholic priest took a year of sabbatical study at the University of Chicago, and I was able to see some of the basic data on which he based his study of how it feels to be 'really understood' (van Kaam, 1959). A seemingly simple question, but of great significance. By chance, the first questionnaire respondent was an adolescent girl, a 17-year-old student in a parochial school. This midwestern bobby-sox type is hardly a match for the sophisticated European Anna O., but they are equally real and, I suspect, would have understood each other. As to how she feels, in substance and spirit, when she experiences understanding, she wrote:

> I felt as if he, my boyfriend, had reached into my heart and had really seen my fears and understood how much my religion meant to me. My whole being wanted to cry out how much I loved him for that understanding. My body felt so alive and I wanted to tell everyone how happy and exuberant I was. I wanted everyone to be happy with me. I wanted to hang on to that understanding and pray it would never be lost to me.
>
> Whenever I am understood by anyone, I feel a fresh onset of love for anyone or anything. I can't sleep right away because I don't want that understanding to fade, and somehow it seems to me that it will probably be lost in the morning.
>
> My body seems to have a terrific pounding sensation and I want to cry out something which I don't know how to express in words. I feel more sure of myself. I want to give. I want to give everything I have to make this person who understands happier. I want to live the full minute of every day. Life seems so much richer when you know someone understands, because to me, one who understands is the one who cares and loves me and I feel love and security and peace. (A. van Kaam, personal communication, 1961)

I submit that this is not an atypical reaction, but simply one heightened by the enthusiastic vigor of an adolescent girl. She tells us how being understood affects a human being psychologically or physiologically. Why should such effects be labeled 'transference'? They do in fact originate in the situation and through the performance of psychotherapy (when that is indeed benevolent). The reaction might better be called 'originalence.' It is not transferred, not inappropriate. It is the normal and appropriate reaction. It might come about in someone who had never been so understood before. Thus it might come from no past experience, but from a wish that the past had been different, or from the hopes and dreams of the future!

For example, there is the filmed interview between Carl Rogers and Gloria (Rogers, 1965), of which a portion is reproduced below. Near the final section, she feels deeply understood in a way that brings tears and a feeling she calls 'precious.' She wishes her father had been so understanding—but that had not been the case. The typical professional audience witnessing this becomes tense and alert. There is uneasy laughter. They have been taught what to think of this, and the moods range from scornful to sympathetic, for there is a general feeling that transference has reared its head (and the anticipation that Rogers might be caught in a dangerous 'Freudian' situation). It can be read that way. It can equally be read as her response to understanding such as she never had from her father, her wish that she could have a father like that, not like her own. Is that transference?

Rogers, on display and well aware of this issue, makes certain that he does not deny or reject, and while his response may not be the perfect model, it acknowledges her admiring wistfulness, his appreciation in kind of her, and continues in an understanding mode.

> ROGERS: *I sense that, in those utopian moments, you really feel kind of whole. You really feel all in one place.*
>
> GLORIA: *Yes. [Rogers: M-hm.] Yeah. It gives me a choked up feeling when you say that, because I don't get that feeling as often as I like. [Rogers: M-hm.] I like that whole feeling. It's really precious to me.*
>
> ROGERS: *I suspect none of us gets it as often as we'd like, but I really do understand. [pause] M-hm, that [referring to her tears] really does touch you, doesn't it?*
>
> GLORIA: *Yeah, and you know what else, though, I was just thinking . . . I feel it's a dumb thing that, uhm, all of a sudden when I'm talking, gee, how nice I can talk to you, and I want you to approve of me, and I respect you, but I miss that my father couldn't talk to me like you are. I mean I'd like to say, gee, I'd like you for my father. [Rogers: M-hm.] [pause] [Rogers: You . . .] I don't even know why that came to me.[17]*
>
> ROGERS: *You look to me like a pretty nice daughter. [a long, long pause] But you really do miss the fact that you couldn't be open with your own dad.*
>
> GLORIA: *Yeah, I couldn't be open, but . . . I want to blame it on him. I think I'm more open than he'd allow me. I mean he would never listen to me talk like you are. And, ah, not disapprove, and not lower me down.*

'ORIGINALENCE' VERSUS A FORM OF 'REPETITION-COMPULSON' IN PSYCHOLOGICAL THOUGHT

'Originalence' is a not very good word for another way of thinking about the problem. It refers, if you can believe in such a possibility, to new experience. That could mean 'fresh perceptions,' or 'first loves' and could also refer to an experience previously known or an act previously performed but new in spite of its appearance of being old. It is an orientation toward present or even future influences on behavior. 'Originalence' is merely a word counterpart to 'transference' and is not designed to 'catch on' as a theory. The purpose here is to balance and then dispense with these particular theories so that the facts can once more be observed with what the phenomenologists call 'sophisticated naivete.'

One of the errors in transference theory is the illogical assumption that any response duplicating a prior similar response is necessarily replicating it. Similar responses are not always repetitions. They appear to us to be repetitions because, in our effort to comprehend quickly, we look for patterns, try to generalize. There is breathing as a general respiratory pattern, but my most recent breath is not taken because of the previous one: rather, for the same reason the previous breath was taken, and the first breath was taken.

---

17. The typical audience thinks it knows why—'looking for a father.' Popular wisdom says that young women seek 'father figures.' A less popular and somewhat hidden knowledge is that men also may seek 'daughter figures.' Freud might have known this from his dream about 'overaffectionate feelings' for his ten-year-old daughter Mathilde (letter to W. Fliess, May 31, 1897), but such reciprocity, or seeking from both directions, does not so readily fit to transference theory. Whatever motives for either party—whether benign caring, dependency, exploitation, fulfillment or various hopes and desires—the seeking moves in *both* directions. So neither party may be justly accused of entirely uninvited or unrewarded responsibility. This is not necessarily to explain the particular case of Gloria, but to add a statement of general interest in the reanalysis of transference theory.

It is not habit. It is normal function, repeated but not repetition.

In the first instance, the original love of the child for the parent is not transferred from the past. There was no earlier instance. What then? This original love developed for the same sorts of reasons or conditions that will again produce it in later life. Provide those conditions again and they will produce (not reproduce) it again and again, each time on its own merits. The produced experience is mingled with memories and associations, but those are not the conditions. Memories may seem to reproduce. If so, they reproduce the *conditions* (for fear or passion, for example), and it is again the *conditions*, not the memory, that account for the response.

How did any particular affect come into being in the first place? If love developed through the parents' understanding (of what the child needs in the way of care, in the development of its whole mental life from language to thought), further understanding should elicit love too; but consider, *every second instance might as well have been the first.* Warmth feels good to the body, not only because it felt good when one was an infant, but because it *always* feels good. The need is 'wired in' as an innate physiological requirement. When one tastes a lemon at age 30, does it taste sour because it tasted that way at age three? It *always* tastes sour, the first time at any age, whether or not it ever tasted so before, and all following times for the same but original reason each time.

A QUESTION OF LOGIC

This logic is functional; the logic of transference is historical. The difference is very great. Historical logic in psychoanalysis goes even beyond looking into the past of an individual's life. Anna Freud writes: 'Long ago the analytical study of the neuroses suggested that there is in human nature a disposition to repudiate certain instincts, in particular the sexual instincts, indiscriminately and independently of individual experience. This disposition appears to be a *phylogenetic inheritance, a kind of deposit accumulated from acts of regression practised by many generations and merely continued, not initiated, by individuals'* (1946, p. 171; emphasis added). In contrast, the logic of a present (or future) orientation does not deny the past, but looks at immediate experience, or even imagination.

From experiential evidence, this newer logic explicitly asserts that any therapist has an active and response-arousing set of roles and behaviors. Therapists are loved for what makes them lovable, hated for what makes them hateful, and all shades in between. *This should be the first hypothesis.* Whatever it does not account for may then be described as proof of another phenomenon, such as transference, but understanding and misunderstanding will, I believe, account for the major affects of love and hate.

This does not begin to analyze the complex interactions beyond understanding and misunderstanding. Whatever they are in any given case, there too therapists play their part. The first principle remains; for the therapist to eschew the pretense of innocent invisibility and to reflect upon what, in the situation and his or her behaviors, does in fact account for those 'untoward events' that brought transference theory into being. Adoption of this principle may engender a sense of vulnerability and remove not only the shield but some of the most ornamental of therapeutic trappings as well. This is not the most inviting prospect for the contemporary psychotherapist. It is easier to have an exotic treatment for an intriguing disease. For the patient there may be some allure and pleasure in disguise as well.

Is there no transference, whatever, at any time? Of course there is, if you wish it. The material is there at the outset. It can be cultivated, and it can be forced. Emotional attitudes *will* be expressed, through indirect channels if open expression is discouraged. Like seeds, emotions and perceptions will grow straight and true in nourishing soil or crookedly through cracks in the sidewalk. One can encourage distortions, and then analyze them. It is a matter of choice. As with any fiction, 'transference' can be turned into a scenario to be acted out, creating a desired reality.

At the beginning, there is always incipient prejudice. Upon first meeting, stereotyped judgments and appraisals based on prior experience will be applied to the perception of the new unknown. Some call it 'stimulus generalization.' In a state of ignorance, what else can one do to make meaning? – unless it is the rare instance of those who are able and willing to approach new experience with suspended judgment, and a fresh, open view.

Except in such cases, prejudgment applies. Then if the reality of the new experience is concealed, attention turns inward to make meaning. If, however, the new reality is available to be known as needed, prejudice fades; judgments and appraisals appropriate to that reality will develop. For example, if red suspenders (and it could be blue eyes, swastikas, peace symbols, skin color) are worn by a person you meet, and if you have been mistreated by someone wearing red suspenders, you will be wary of this new person. If you are permitted to know more, and wish to do so, the effect of red suspenders will be canceled or supported or become trivial, depending upon your whole knowledge of the new reality. But if the new reality is concealed, attention searches for focus and meaning and, from a relationship standpoint, projections reign. Transference, or what passes for transference, can then be cultivated. Yet it is neither inevitable nor necessary. It is an obstruction.[18] That some derive benefit from its analysis may come from the concentrated self-examination and the presence of attentive intelligence on the part of the therapist – both of which are possible in at least equally pure form *without* the transference neurosis.

Will there be any change in basic transference theory? Is it possible to bring balance through corrective criticism? Not likely. Such 'balance' is only a temporary concession. The theory itself does not allow for balance. It is too heavily weighted (nearly all or none) because its logic cannot bear disturbance. As for the basic position, it is as entrenched as ever. For the public, it is high fashion and popular culture – diverting and entertaining. For the professional it is a tradition, a convenience, a shield, stock-in-trade, a revealed truth and a habit of thought.

How strong a habit of thought is illustrated by an instance described in the study by a sophisticated and sympathetic journalist, Janet Malcolm, under the title 'Trouble in the Archives' (1983). It reports as 'striking example of Eissler's[19] remarkable freedom from self-justification' (p. 132) a case history. 'He treated a wealthy older woman during the years before her death, and was so helpful that, in gratitude, she changed her will and left him a huge amount of money.' He could not accept it for himself and ordered it returned to beneficiaries or donated to charities. However, 'the husband of a relative of the deceased whose legacy had been diminished because of the change in the will, formally objected to the probation of the will. He happend to be an analyst, and his argument was

---

18. Without doubt, the transference neurosis is an illness, deliberately contrived to benefit the treatment. Perhaps this is part of what is meant by the statement, 'Psychoanalysis is the disease it is trying to cure.'

19. Kurt Eissler is a towering figure in the psychoanalytic movement, of whom one of his colleagues says, 'Eissler is not lovable, and he knows it' (Malcolm, 1983, p. 152). Yet his patient may have found him so, and rightly, for the very reason of his understanding behavior – when, if, and inasmuch.

that Eissler had exercised "undue influence" on the patient through "the unconscious utilization of the transference"' (p. 132). Malcolm writes, 'The case history ends with a wonderful twist.' Since the matter had caused painful embarrassment, what had first been seen as a 'loving gesture' was reinterpreted by Eissler as 'an expression of her hatred of him—an expression of the negative transference that had never been allowed to emerge during treatment' (p. 137).

It can be interpreted in other ways as well. The ex-patient may indeed have wished him well, may even have expected that if he could not use the money for himself he could choose to support charitable interests of importance to him. On the other hand, she may have enjoyed the amusement afforded by anticipation of cleverly hurting both her analyst and her relatives with one stroke. Two other observations remain. First, she was treated, even after her death, like a psychiatric patient and therefore a minor or incompetent. She could not exercise her choice about what was, after all, her money, because (a) her judgment was forever suspect, (b) it dispensed something of considerable value to others, and (c) it did not suit those who survived her and who either could call upon or were called upon by transference theory. Second, everything suffers (not entirely without compensation) *except* the concept of transference. One might think that since it was born of embarrassment, it might now die of embarrassment. But no, that is its charm. It merely changes color, never seriously questioned, only reconfirmed.

Conclusion

I have offered a brief for a countertheory, not in the sense of a complement or counterpart, as in 'transference and countertransference,' but in the sense that *counter* means opposite, alternative. If transference is a theory, this is the counter. Personality and situation aside for the moment, *the therapist is responsible for two fundamental behaviors — understanding and misunderstanding — which account for love, or for hate,* and their associated affects. These, as well as other behaviors and the situation and personality of the therapist, may account — should first be held accountable — for the whole of what passes for transference.

The power of understanding has been featured to account for the phenomenon called 'transference.' That use should not hide the point that it is this very power of understanding (not the transference, transference-love, or love itself) that heals. Understanding makes for healing and growth; misunderstanding makes for injury and destruction.

The proposition that 'understanding heals' does not make understanding the exclusive property of client-centered therapy. Far from it. Client-centered therapy has a constant theme in its focus on understanding: early, in its method of seeking confirmation from the client; later, in its stress on empathy (as a form of understanding and even a 'way of being') and how such understanding is best achieved. That is its emphasis, not its proprietary claim.

The emphasis on understanding is stressed at this final point to indicate that, while love is a blessing, love is not enough. Ultimately, we are trying to account not only for transference-love, or for love in general, but for *healing*. Even romantic love ('falling in,' or choosing to be in) gives promise of, and is given in the hopes of receiving, understanding (which may or may not be delivered). Being 'in love' often assumes understanding to exist even where it does not. When love *is* present, it is an environment for or the consequence of *understanding*. Though the two are strongly associated, love does not heal. Understanding heals. It also makes one feel loved, or sustains love already felt, but the healing power is in the understanding.

Knowing that does not make the conduct of therapy easier in the slightest. It may, however, help us to separate therapy from the rest of life. It seems that we can quite well love, and take love from, those to whom we do not devote the considerable or sometimes near-consuming effort to understand fully. *That* is the difference between real life in ordinary relations and equally real life in therapy. If and to such extent as they could be brought together, so much the better; if not, so much the good in either case.

To conclude that it is not love that heals may be a disappointment to many. The role of the healer is appealing. So is that of the benefactor who dispenses love. Therapists and others find these roles all too gratifying. But no, the 'healer' takes credit for a process inherent in the organism, if released, and love is therapeutic or enduringly beneficial only if expressed through understanding. The act of understanding may be the most difficult of any task we set ourselves — a seemingly mundane 'service role' yet requiring kinds of intelligence and sensitivity so demanding that some people are truly seen as gifted. Even that is not the final cause. It still remains for the client to feel understood. Of course, in doing so, clients understand themselves — that is the source of their confirming the understanding.

To realize that it is the *understanding* that promotes the healing will direct us to the remaining problem for psychotherapy and psychology: we do not know the mechanisms by which understanding promotes healing or even the mechanisms of understanding itself. That knowledge cannot come from a theory such as transference, which has been a roadblock and a pointer in the wrong direction for almost a century. That knowledge may not come from *any* present version of psychotherapy, but rather from more neutral realms of cognitive, social, and developmental psychology, or neuroscience, to the ultimate benefit of a new theory and practice.

AUTHOR'S NOTE

This article is a revised version of a chapter in the book *Client-Centered Therapy and the Person-Centered Approach* (Levant & Shlien, Eds., 1984) and I would like to thank the publisher, CBS-Praeger, for permission to reprint it here. It has previously been translated into Italian, French and Hungarian. Working with translators taught me, too late for this chapter, that my writing should have been translated into better English at the beginning. I apologize for difficulties to the reader.

REFERENCES

Breuer, J., & Freud, S. (1957). *Studies on hysteria.* New York: Basic Books.
Epstein, L., & Feiner, A. (1974). *Countertransference.* New York: Aronson.
Fenichel, O. (1941). *Problems of psychoanalytic technique.* Albany, NY: Psychoanalytic Quarterly.
Freeman, L. (1972). *The story of Anna O.* New York: Walker.
Freud, A. (1946). *The Ego and the mechanisms of defense.* New York: International University Press.
Freud, S. (1910). The future prospects of psychoanalytic theory. In J. Strachey (Ed. and Trans.), *The standard edition of the complete psychological works of Sigmund Freud* (Vol. 7, pp. 3–122). London: Hogarth.
Freud, S. (1923). *The ego and the id.* London: Hogarth.
Freud, S. (1927). *The problem of lay analysis.* New York: Brentano.
Freud, S. (1935). *A general introduction to psychoanalysis* (Vol. 1). New York: Liveright.
Freud, S. (1948). *An autobiographical study.* London: Hogarth.
Freud, S. (1949). *The future of an illusion.* New York: Liveright.

Freud, S. (1959). *Collected papers* (Vol. 3). New York: Basic Books.

Jones, E. (1953). *The life and work of Sigmund Freud* (Vol. 1). New York: Basic Books.

Jones, E. (1957). *The life and work of Sigmund Freud* (Vol. 3). New York: Basic Books.

Kemper, T. (1978). *A social interactional theory of emotions.* New York: John Wiley.

Macalpine, I. (1950). The development of the transference. *Psychoanalytic Quarterly, 19,* 501–39.

Malcolm, J. (1983, December 5). Annals of scholarship: Trouble in the Archives I. *New Yorker,* pp. 59–152.

Masson, J. (Ed.) (1985). *The complete letters of S. Freud to W. Fliess 1887–1904.* Cambridge: Belknap-Harvard.

McGuire, W. (Ed.) (1974). *The Freud-Jung letters.* Princeton, NJ: Princeton University Press.

Menninger, K. (1958). *The theory of psychoanalytic technique.* New York: Basic Books.

Mowrer, O. H. (Ed.) (1967). *Morality and mental health.* Chicago: Rand McNally.

Orr, D. (1954). Transference and countertransference: An historical survey. *Journal of the American Psychoanalytic Association,* 621–70.

Rogers, C. R. (1942). *Counseling and psychotherapy.* Boston: Houghton Mifflin.

Rogers, C. R. (1951). *Client-centered therapy.* Boston: Houghton Mifflin.

Rogers, C. R. (1954). The case of Mrs. Oak. In C. R. Rogers & R. F. Dymond (Eds.), *Psychotherapy and personality change.* Chicago: University of Chicago Press.

Rogers, C. R. (1965). *Three approaches to psychotherapy I* [Film]. Santa Ana, CA: Psychological Films.

Roustang, F. (1982). *Dire mastery.* Baltimore: Johns Hopkins University Press.

Shlien, J. M. (1963). Erotic feelings in psychotherapy relationships: Origins, influences, and resolutions. Paper presented at the annual meeting of the American Psychological Association, Philadelphia.

van Kaam, A. (1959). Phenomenal analysis: Exemplified by a study of the experience of 'really feeling understood.' *Journal of Individual Psychology, 15,* 66–72.

Waelder, R. (1956). Introduction to the discussion on problems of transference. *International Journal of Psychoanalysis, 37,* 367–84.

Special discussion: A Countertheory of Transference

(ii) Comments on 'A Countertheory of Transference'

Ernst G. Beier   *University of Utah*

Transference is a condition in which patients 'transfer' the significant feelings they had originally experienced with their parents to their psychotherapists. Shlien bases his article on the assumption that this theoretical position removes the therapist's sense of responsibility for his or her own feelings. Shlien believes that the significant feelings between the patient and the psychotherapist are an interaction and claims that analysts see transference as a one-way street. He overlooks the fact that the psychoanalyst sees the whole concept of transference/countertransference as an interaction. To argue who starts this interaction is like arguing whether the chicken or the egg came first or how many angels can dance on the head of a pin.

If you wish to prove scientifically that a thousand angels do certain deeds you can do so with reasonable ease. You propose the following 'null' hypothesis: 'Angels always support keys floating in the air.' You hold a bunch of keys in the air, remove your supporting hand, and watch carefully whether they drop. When they drop you have disproved that angels always support keys in the air. Shlien's article has approximately the same consequences as the scientific effort above. Does it really matter who sends the first subtle, mostly nonverbal cues of love or hate? Even if the patient sends the first subtle cues, the therapist's responsibility is obviously to understand them and not to respond to them in kind. That is the theory both in psychoanalysis and in other therapies. The first 12 pages of this article represent the author's effort to use his learnedness in the service of a bias. Shlien tries to convince us that the discovery of transference was not based on sound interpretation of the original experiences. This is like arguing that penicillin must be useless because it was discovered accidentally or that the discovery of the benzene ring is unimportant because it may have been first seen in a dream. If Shlien had first looked at the function of the concept in theory, the use of the concept in psychotherapy, and the ways in which this concept leads to inadequate service to the patient, then these pages may have made some sense. By devoting more than one-half of the article to the errors committed in the process of discovery, Shlien's countertheory got off to a slow start.

On page 15, Shlien gives us at least a hint why he believes he has to discuss transference in this article. He states that 'transference is a fiction to protect therapists from the consequences of their own behavior.' Unfortunately, he fails to elaborate on this challenging statement. Just how does transference serve this complicated purpose? Just how do therapists shift the responsibility for their own feelings to their patients? What does the therapist say or fail to say or fail to understand? The implications are that when we make a genetic or historical statement about the patient we shift responsibility away from ourselves. Does that mean that when I say that a patient has parents who are alcoholics, I in fact shift responsibility away from myself to the patient, or does this

First published in *Person-Centered Review*, Volume 2, Number 2, May 1987.

knowledge make me work perhaps a little harder in my understanding of the patient's problems and needs? The therapist, by knowing some of the conditions under which the patient grew up and the feelings of love and hate he has previously experienced, is probably in a better position to understand the patient, and even to understand what he or she is saying at a given moment. In fact I have argued elsewhere (Beier and Young, 1984) that this knowledge will enable the therapist to stay emotionally disengaged from the patient's emotional demands and help him or her to make new choices.

There are indeed many ways in which therapists can fail to accept responsibility for their behavior in the session. They can do so by 'sitting' on their own biases and remain unaware of certain information that the patient sends them or they may fall into social engagement patterns that I have described elsewhere(Beier and Valens, 1975). These social engagement patterns simply mean that individual psychotherapists are still children of this culture who will react to verbal as well as nonverbal cues with the types of response designed for them by the culture. Therapists should use their skill to understand what the patient is telling them rather than react emotionally to the emotional demands of the patient. We can deny responsibility by failing to understand the continuity of life, that there are repeated patterns in life that frequently are acted out in the therapeutic hour. Shlien argues that transference, or something like transference, may very well occur, but it might be better called 'originalence' because it should be seen as a new experience rather than a historical one. There is no explanation regarding what consequences the different views would have on the psychotherapist who held one view or the other in his or her relationship to the patient.

On page 38, Shlien remarks that 'Gloria,' in response to her therapist (Rogers), expresses the wish for a father like Rogers. Shlien questions whether that is transference. Obviously, Shlien does not know the difference and mistakes the use of the word *father* with transference. Later, on page 40, he argues that every event is always new and stresses that 'every second instance might as well have been the first.' I believe he means to say that only when one views every instance in life as new and unique will one be able to accept full responsibility for one's own feelings. His is a strange argument that calls the understanding of history and the continuity of life an irresponsible act.

Whatever the name, there are 'silent rules' or transference demands, traits, fixed action patterns, or just guidelines that appear to focus a person's manner of behavior throughout life and give him or her a sense of consistency. I prefer to call them silent rules or guidelines that are learned early in life. The exploration of these is essentially the objective of psychotherapy.

Shlien's article represents an extreme attempt to celebrate 'experiencing.' Perhaps experiencing in the psychotherapeutic process should be modified by at least some participation of the therapist's left brain.

REFERENCES

Beier, E. G. & Valens, E. G. (1975). *People reading*. New York: Stein & Day.
Beier, E. G. & Young, D. M. (1984). *The silent language of psychotherapy* (2nd ed.). New York: Aldine.

Special discussion: A Countertheory of Transference

(iii) Beyond Transference

Constance T. Fischer   *Duquesne University*

In this response to John Shlien's (1987) revised 'Countertheory of Transference,' I affirm his major points, and I mention minor divergences in opinion. My main departure from Shlien's argument is indeed more of a departure than a disagreement. To my way of thinking, the issue is not whether transference is an invention, but rather 'What have we meant by this construction?' and 'How else might we understand the phenomena the term points to?' These are hermeneutic issues, which for me assume that sociocultural-historical contexts and personal motives inevitably are part of the questions and answers we formulate. Hence, for me, Shlien's case for how 'transference' was manufactured does not detract from a certain validity and usefulness.

Shlien has addressed the above two issues thoroughly enough that I see no requirement for further investigation of what 'transference' is. Moreover, it seems to me that although the construct once served a positive purpose it is no longer uniquely helpful, and it unnecessarily impedes the growth of client and therapist and of theory and research. To free ourselves from the limiting and sometimes destructive aspects of believing in transference, we would do well to go *beyond* explanatory constructs altogether. Before making some remarks on going beyond transference, I will review and comment on Shlien's major contributions. His main points remain valid, even in the face of developments in contemporary psychodynamic and alternative therapies.

SHLIEN'S CONTRIBUTIONS

The social construction, obsolesence, and restrictiveness of transference. Shlien documents, most effectively, how Freud came up with his notion of love transference to account for the emotional/sexual feelings that women patients (notably Anna O.) expressed toward Breuer and himself. The excerpts from Freud's writings show clearly how critical it was, for both his theory of infantile sexuality and for his posture as an objective and disinterested scientist, that expressions of emotion toward the analyst be seen only as manifestations of childhood desires. Theory, method, and personal (moral) reputation would be endangered by admission of genuine, interpersonal feelings between patient and analyst. Through Shlien's presentation we can see that transference is not only a construction but one that has already served its purpose. The theory, method, and professionalism of psychoanalysis have survived, and in turn have given rise to the expanding field of psychotherapy.

Part of the staying power of the transference construction, however, is that it was not purely an invention. Freud was of course correct in his observation that desires that arose in earlier forms and times carry impressions from those times into current

First published in *Person-Centered Review*, Volume 2, Number 2, May 1987.

expressions. But the therapist can help the client become aware of habitual comportment that is inappropriate to the therapy situation without having to evoke a transference complex. From my perspective, Shlien's presentation makes a convincing case that the construct is now obsolete, problematic, and deserving of retirement.

Belief in transference allows both patient and therapist to avoid examination of their actual, present interpersonal relationship. Belief in 'transference resolution' as the goal and sign of therapeutic achievement deadens the present as attention is focused on a past that is said to account for current events. Agency and responsibility are attenuated when therapist and client view the present as largely predetermined. Albeit unintentionally, this stance particularly demeans and disempowers the client, who remains subordinate to the therapist's intimations of what is relatively fresh versus what is transferred from the past. Opportunities for the client to test interpersonal perceptions and to voice intimate feelings directly to the therapist are lost.

To the extent that the therapist bases psychotherapy on the vicissitudes of transference, the therapist, too, is restricted. No matter how liberated from the old notion of the analyst as blank screen, and no matter how humane in attitude, the therapist who observes principally in terms of transference risks curtailing examination of his or her personal involvement in the therapy case and thereby also risks foregoing opportunities for self-knowledge and growth. Moreover, to the extent that transference phenomena are viewed as essential to effective therapy, the therapist is unlikely to expand his or her skills to include brief forms and alternative methods of therapy. Perhaps it is not incidental that alternative methods generally encourage clients toward *self-help* by providing cognitive or behavioral tools and/or by helping clients to articulate and act on their self-understandings.

Finally, to the extent that therapists place emphasis on the past as determinative of the present, and to the extent that they disallow exploration of the therapeutic relationship as an interpersonal event in its own right (a cigar is also a cigar), they forgo opportunities to revise both the theory and practice of depth psychology.

It is time to deconstruct transference, to look beyond it and to re-ask basic questions about how people function, get unstuck, and grow. But I certainly would want to retain the professionalism that belief in transference has protected. Clients should be able to count on therapists to be objective, and to not use the therapy relationship in pursuit of personal interests. Therapists should remain humbly aware that who they are for clients is shaped by the clients' historical and continuing experiences, goals, and conflicts. Events between therapist and client should continue to be used to alert the client to habitual but presently inappropriate ways of relating.

Therapy as interpersonal

An implicit but pervasive theme running through Shlien's article is that psychotherapy is interpersonal; it is a relationship in its own right. True, one can be guided by this acknowledgment and thus pursue transference aspects of therapy in an advised way. Still, the notion of transference is likely to lead the therapist to discount his or her own contribution to the relationship, and thereby lose opportunities for clients to explore their perceptions of shared events. In his discussion, Shlien addresses standard 'talk' therapy. I would add that too many practitioners whose therapeutic contact with clients is brief in form are unmindful that they, too, inevitably are in an interpersonal relationship as they, for example, prescribe neuroleptics, provide biofeedback, present a paradoxical instruction, or assign cognitive/behavioral homework.

Originalence versus repetition compulsion

Shlien introduces the term 'originalence' not so much as a claim that everything that occurs in therapy is brand new, but as a dramatic challenge to the prevailing assumption in some circles that whatever happens in therapy is a repetition or contemporary replication of unresolved childhood desires and conflicts. The term serves Shlien's purposes well. However, for my own interest in providing a corrective to the deterministic version of transference, I prefer the term 'continuance.' My term is meant to remind us that current behavior is not merely a replaying or transferring of infantile or childhood tensions from parental figures of yore to the therapist. Rather, we bring with us the influences of where we have been as we *continue* our course into our present on our way to anticipated futures. Growth occurs when we use our past as a springboard or as stepping-stones or markers for changing course, rather than as walls, millstones, or permanent flagstone paths. Always our past is alive in the present, reunderstood in terms of where we have been more recently. A therapy that focuses too much on the past as-it-was encourages clients to tread on old flagstones rather than look for fresh horizons available from the next step up or next turn in the course. However, it is also true that a therapy that focuses too much on clients' present curtails their making sense of, integrating, and revising their lives as they *continue* their journeys.

Understanding and misunderstanding as the occasions for love and hate

Here is Shlien's major contribution. Through Anna O. and contemporary clinical and nonclinical vignettes, he evokes the power of a major constituent of therapy: the client's desire to understand and to be understood. Shlien implicitly invites the reader to recall the satisfaction of mutual understanding, the frustration over nonagreement or misunderstanding, a client's joy and gratitude for being understood, another client's relief that some aspects of his or her life is understandable in itself, and another client's rage that one will not understand him or her as he or she wishes.

Psychological integration and growth require new sense making, which is all the more powerful when it occurs in and is tested and affirmed in an interpersonal context. The strong affect and emotion that attend understanding and misunderstanding go a long way toward accounting for what is often thought of as transference and countertransference. Other affects, as Shlien points out, are quite often also reactions to the actual situation, for example, sexual attraction and resentment. In short, an abiding problem with the notion of transference is that its positive value (namely, its pointing to the past that still is alive in present form) too often is overridden by failure to respect the power of the present-future dynamic.

My concerns with Shlien's brief presentation on understanding are twofold. First, I hope that readers do not assume that understanding is an adequate condition for growth. Some form of self-understanding and of feeling understood are helpful for growth, but they are not sufficient, and may not be essential for all kinds of growth. Second, I do not agree that we should look for 'the mechanisms' of understanding, or that we should look to developments in neuropsychology, cognitive psychology, and so on to comprehend understanding and transference phenomena.

BEYOND TRANSFERENCE

Constructs and mechanisms lead us to think causally. When we do, we underattend to our sense making and future building, whether as individuals, clients, therapists, theorists, or researchers. When we look at persons' lives holistically, and as much as possible without hypotheses, we see that we are all traveling through life, making meaning of it and evolving our 'personalities' through the ways we live in our environments. I would say that who we are (personality) is the way we comport ourselves as we journey toward our chosen and circumstantial destinations while, at the same time, maneuvering to avoid what we experience as threatening to our carriage or plans. Psychological history, depth, and dynamics are directly visible in our habitual comportment and in our efforts to be and not be certain kinds of people as we go about our journeys. Tension and disruption are apparent in our doomed efforts to get to places that are not on the same route, as well as in our struggles to bypass the significance of finding ourselves at particular waystations.

We develop our sense of who we are and who we might become as we encounter obstacles and invitations, and as we find ourselves stymied or fulfilled. We know who we are as social beings through our encounters with other people—who affirm and disconfirm our assumptions from previous experience. Other travelers can show us alternate routes, styles of travel, ways of being, and even new horizons and different ways of seeing. Although looking back at how we got to where we are helps us take stock, regroup, and make considered decisions, actual changing of course or of attitude or style of travel occurs only in the present, in the face of viable options (Fischer, 1985).

Within this context, when a client behaves toward a therapist as though the therapist were the client's parent, we can understand this 'transference' either as resistance to the therapist's expectations, or simply as an habitual response to a similar figure. Medard Boss (1963) understood transference in terms of the client having only limited ways to respond to a situation. Similarly, I see psychopathology as the person's unnecessarily restricted way of going through life (Fischer & Fischer, 1983), and resistance as clients' response to feeling that they cannot continue to be who they are and still go where the therapist is pointing. The most efficient and straightforward therapeutic strategy is to look for ways to expand clients' sense of what is already personally viable, and to help them discover that old ways are understandable but no longer necessary. Sometimes this can be accomplished through short-term behavioral instruction, paradoxical prescription, and so on, as well as through 'talk therapy.'

Interpersonal encounter, with the sharing of impressions and of present interpersonal perceptions, is a powerful avenue toward correcting one's course, discovering additional pathways, and of confirming one's general destination. Direct sharing often reveals not only clients' 'baggage' from earlier trips, but therapists' present contribution to the so-called transference. Therapists' open exploration and acknowledgment of clients' perceptions of the therapeutic relationship facilitates openness to growth, and does so more powerfully than traditional analysis of transference.

Psychological researchers also can look beyond constructs to see what else might be visible when their inclination to categorize is held in abeyance as much as possible. The results are narrative descriptions that try to be faithful to the structural whole of reported experiences (e.g., Giorgi, 1985). Valdeane Brown's (1986) dissertation, among about two-dozen Duquesne University empirical phenomenological studies of psychotherapeutic process, most directly addresses the concepts of transference and countertransference. He asked six therapists to describe 'reacting strongly within a session.' He found that regardless of the therapist's approach, training, and experience, strong reactions were emblematic of constrictions and foreclosures shared by both therapist and client. In acknowledging to clients their reaction, therapists discovered meanings for both themselves and their clients that were not fully available before. Both participants later recalled this moment as 'having inaugurated a radically transformed world, one with new possibilities, struggles, hopes' (abstract). Therapists who did not acknowledge their reaction remained reflectively captivated by it, and did not report related transformative experiences.

In short, although the notion of transference has served its purpose, and continues to be a viable construct for some therapies, by now it is an unnecessarily restrictive way of thinking. Shlien's article effectively documents the latter case. An alternative view suggests going beyond efforts to explain transference. Instead, we can look at how people continue their lives, taking on new encounters in terms of the sense they make of their pasts and their anticipation of the future. The insights and techniques of most approaches to therapy may be used within this framework.

References

Boss, M. (1963). *Psychoanalysis and daseinsanalysis.* New York: Basic Books.

Brown, V. W. (1986). Psychotherapists' strong reactions: An empirical phenomenological investigation (Doctoral dissertation. Duquesne University, Pittsburgh, 1986). *Dissertation Abstracts International, 42,* 1713B.

Fischer, C. T. (1985). *Individualizing psychological assessment.* Monterey CA: Brooks-Cole.

Fischer, C. T., & Fischer, W. F. (1983). Phenomenological-existential psychotherapy. In M. Hersen, A. E. Kazdin, & A. S. Bellack (Eds.), *The clinical psychology handbook* (pp. 489–505). New York: Pergamon.

Giorgi, A. (Ed.) (1985). *Phenomenology and psychological research.* Pittsburgh: Duquesne Univ. Press.

Shlien, J. M. (1987). A countertheory of transference. *Person-Centered Review, 2*(1), 15–49.

Special discussion: A Countertheory of Transference

(iv) Yes, John, There is a Transference

Harold Greenwald   *Direct Decision Institute, San Diego*

John M. Shlien has done a fascinating job researching a variety of sources and quotations about transference. However, he has offered so many points of view on the subject that it is somewhat difficult to discuss what is actually his position.

In his opening sentence he writes: 'Transference is a fiction, invented and maintained by therapists to protect themselves from the consequences of their own behavior.' Toward the end of this lengthy essay, he states: 'Therapists are loved for what makes them lovable, hated for what makes them hateful, and all shades in between. *This should be the first hypothesis.* Whatever it does not account for may then be described as proof of another phenomenon, such as transference.'

Of course transference does not account for every emotional reaction to another and therefore it seems to me that Shlien has set up a straw man that he then proceeds to destroy with articulate logic. Unfortunately, his basic definition of what transference is supposed to be suffers from incompleteness.

It may well be, as I heard Dr. Thomas Szasz comment in a lecture several years ago, that transference was a brilliant invention by Freud to prevent psychoanalysis from being regarded as an obscene undertaking. Nineteenth-century Vienna was a very different place from California in the 1980s. The arousal of amorous feelings in a patient of the opposite sex may happen for a variety of reasons and is not regarded in the same manner it would have been in Victorian Vienna.

There is a charming naiveté in Shlien's assumption that understanding and misunderstanding lead to love and hate, respectively. Apparently he has never encountered patients who are furious at being understood. As one man said to me, 'It's not that my wife doesn't understand me; she understands me too well and I could just kill her for that.' He experienced her total acceptance of his negative feelings as indifference on her part. To him it meant that she was totally unmoved and unresponsive to anything he said or did.

Unfortunately, many of us are engaged in creating new and glittering theories and countertheories. Psychoanalysis, like every other scientific endeavor, has had a long history of controversy, much of which has been productive in clarifying our theory and our practice. But we are now mature enough to start building bridges between the various approaches. It would be helpful if we could offer fellow practitioners the same understanding that Shlien so eloquently espouses for our patients.

When transference occurs, it may be extremely helpful to promote precisely the understanding that Shlien sees as a sine qua non of therapy. The existence of transference makes it possible for the therapist to understand the patient's earlier conflicts in the 'here and now' of the interview. The problem of understanding a complex human being can be looked at in a variety of models or even as explanatory fiction. As Freud (in Fodor, 1963,

First published in *Person-Centered Review,* Volume 2, Number 2, May 1987.

p. 158) noted in discussing transference in the 'Problem of Lay Analysis': 'So what he is showing us is the very core of his most private life.' Obviously, Freud and Shlien are not in disagreement about the essential process of therapy.

The familiarity of the therapist with several modalities and the ability to employ them flexibly may be compared to the advantage of stereophonic sound over monaural. In a luncheon conversation with Nat Raskin and Carl Rogers about two years ago, I suggested the importance of graduate students being taught a number of approaches. Raskin disagreed but Rogers agreed about the importance of such a well-rounded education.

In my own practice, I have had a number of examples of behavior that can most economically be understood as transference phenomenon. For example, one patient viewed me very much like her mother and kept sending me Mother's Day cards for several years. In group, some would see me as a benign influence and others as a malignant force who had to be defeated so that they could grow.

Even when I was a comparatively 'pure' psychoanalyst, I made the distinction in my teachings between transference in which a patient projects upon the therapist characteristics of significant figures in the past, and induced feelings created by the behavior of the therapist. They are not the same.

It should also be noted that recent research, such as that undertaken by the National Institute of Mental Health, indicates the value of the cognitive approach for the treatment of depression. Shlien's emphasis on understanding may be appropriate, but understanding is not a monopoly of any single school. Perhaps cognitive therapists also show understanding from their point of view; even behavioral therapists may behave in such a manner as to impress the patient with their understanding of the human dilemma. There are many paths to therapeutic salvation and it is still too early in our history to shut off any of them. Rather, let us join in searching for the commonalities that seem to indicate that many therapists, regardless of orientation, are effective in about the same proportion.

REFERENCE

Fodor, N. (1963). *Freud dictionary of psychoanalysis.* New York: Fawcett.

Special discussion: A Countertheory of Transference

(v) A Brief Commentary on Shlien's Countertheory

Arnold A. Lazarus   *Rutgers University*

Trenchant criticisms of psychoanalytic theory and practice (e.g., Jurjevich, 1974; Rachman, 1963; Salter, 1952; Wells, 1963; Wohlgemuth, 1923) have gone virtually unheeded. Those who are wedded to psychoanalysis do not assimilate any facts aimed at their dogma. It has often been observed that theories are not killed by criticism; they are superseded — replaced by others that hold greater promise. Nevertheless, the will to believe prevails, and those who need explanatory fictions (e.g., 'transference') will rise fervently to the defense of their doctrine. In my case, Shlien's article was merely preaching to a longtime convert. For me, the flimsy, subjective, speculative foundation of psychoanalytic thought was reaffirmed. Shlien has deftly documented the manner in which two prudish, sexist, chauvinistic gentlemen, Breuer and Freud, generalized way beyond their anecdotal observations. Moreover, he described the origins of the (now) widespread penchant to read far-reaching, occult meaning and significance into seemingly innocent events. Shlien reaffirms that Freud became a victim of his suggestible patients; that he conditioned them to supply the supposed confirmations of his theoretical ideas.

While I agree that 'transference' as embroidered by the Freudians and neo-Freudians is a fiction, one might inquire whether there is any substance to the central notion. The essence of the concept of transference is that human beings are capable of behaving toward people in the present as they once behaved toward significant others in their past. This important insight, if left at that, could be considered a pivotal psychological truth. We are all aware of the fact that people tend to repeat past relationships that are sometimes inappropriate to the present. Unfortunately, there is more. Transference is not simply the attribution to new relationships of characteristics belonging to old (or former) ones. Rather it is a matter of reliving or reestablishing, with whomsoever will permit it, an infantile situation that is deeply desired, because it had previously been either greatly enjoyed or greatly missed. Thus statements such as 'You are like my father,' or 'You remind me of my Uncle Fred,' are not transference. The point about transference is that it is unconscious.

Psychodynamic theorists draw a distinction between 'transference reactions' and 'transference neurosis.' The former are presumed to be the basis of all human relationships. Upon meeting someone for the first time, positive and negative impressions are presumably based on transference reactions (implying simply that one will relate unconsciously to that person in terms of memories and associations that he or she triggers vis-à-vis past people and events). Since *reality* is the opposite of transference, when the stranger self-discloses and becomes known for himself or herself, possible projections and distortions recede. In analytic jargon, genuine friendships are predicated on transference objects becoming real objects. Thus to promote the transference neurosis, the analyst avoids self-disclosure and encourages regression in the analysand. In so doing, it is assumed that repressed fantasies originating in significant conflictual childhood

First published in *Person-Centered Review,* Volume 2, Number 2, May 1987.

relationships can be projected onto the therapist. As Shlien points out, this state has to be fostered or cultivated, and it presupposes that the therapist is unavailable for reality testing. The clinical virtues of this modus operandi have yet to be experimentally demonstrated.

Shlien's emphasis on 'originalence' brings to mind the quotation of an unknown author (quoted in Salter, 1963, p. 6):

All of psychoanalytic theory can be derived from three postulates:

1. Whatever it looks like — that isn't it.

2. If you can measure it — it's something else.

3. Whatever it is — it isn't nice.

I strongly recommend three brilliant chapters (2, 3, and 4) by Crews (1986) documenting Freud's egregious errors and distortions and their impact on the entire edifice of psychoanalytic theory and practice.

REFERENCES

Crews, F. (1986). *Skeptical engagements.* New York: Oxford University Press.

Jurjevich, R. M. (1974). *The hoax of Freudism.* Philadelphia: Dorrance.

Rachman, S. (Ed.) (1963). *Critical essays on psychoanalysis.* New York: Pergamon.

Salter, A. (1952). *The case against psychoanalysis.* New York: Holt. (2nd edition, 1963, New York: Citadel Press.)

Wells, H. K. (1963). *The failure of psychoanalysis.* New York: International Publishers.

Wohlgemuth, A. (1923). *A critical examination of psychoanalysis.* London: Allen & Unwin.

Special discussion: A Countertheory of Transference

(vi) On the Importance of the Present: Reactions to John Shlien's article

Salvatore R. Maddi   *University of California, Irvine*

John Shlien's (1987) sensitive and discerning critique of the transference concept is a service to all who practice psychotherapy. I regard him as right in spirit, and he paves the way for further thoughts.

To appreciate what there is to appreciate in the transference concept, it is well to remember that psychoanalysis is a contrived relationship designed by theory and practice to have a therapeutic effect. Thus determined by particular rules, the therapeutic interaction is not free to go in whatever direction the wishes and individualities of therapist and patient might otherwise encourage. Although patients become vulnerable by revealing their psyches and trusting their therapists, they are protected from destructive hurt by the therapist's commitment to, and skill in implementing, their recovery. Presumably, this rule-determined nature of the therapeutic relationship is what Freud meant in absolving Breuer of any responsibility for Anna O.'s love reaction. Breuer had 'done nothing' to justify this reaction in the sense that the therapeutic relationship is not the same as an open-ended (to say nothing of a romantic) encounter. Probably, Breuer neither presented himself as 'available' nor took emotional or sexual liberties with his patient. Instead, he had attempted to be therapeutic.

But no amount of commitment to psychoanalytic theory and skill in using its techniques will produce complete therapist uniformity, and that is one way in which the transference concept gets undermined. Not only is it impossible for psychoanalysts to shed their long-developed individuality, they badly need it in order to achieve a therapeutic effect. That complex, imaginative, subtle, interpretive, persuasive interaction psychoanalysts engage in with their patients is still best characterized as an art. Perhaps at a very general, abstract level of interpretation, all psychoanalysts take their therapies in the same direction. But at the more concrete interactional level at which persons influence each other, the therapy is infused with the psychoanalyst's personal style and content preoccupations. That was true when the psychoanalyst sat behind the patient's couch, and is even more true now that the interaction is usually face-to-face.

The presence of therapist style and content in the therapeutic interaction makes application of the transference concept very difficult. How can therapists separate the patient's reaction to their persons from something that is purely an emotional legacy from the past? It probably does not help much for therapists to become aware of their style and content. To remove themselves from the therapeutic interaction, therapists would have to avoid using their style and content, not merely be aware of it. But then what would they use, if not themselves? Psychoanalytic theory and practice must be employed by a palpable human being if they are to have any effect. Could Breuer have disguised his handsome figure? Should he have been less attentive? Should he even have avoided

First published in *Person-Centered Review,* Volume 2, Number 2, May 1987.

holding Anne O.'s hands, if doing so had a facilitative effect? It is unlikely that even if therapists could shed their personhood that would make them better therapists. What this means is that when patients love or hate in the psychotherapeutic relationship, they are at least in part reacting to the style and content, or personhood, of their therapists.

And then there is the human significance of the therapeutic interaction itself. Shlien is at his best in explicating how the therapist gives the gift of understanding to the patient, or fails in attempting this. Whatever the particular style and content of the psychotherapist, to offer understanding is to be lovable, to withhold understanding is to be hateful. These conditions in the therapeutic interaction that engender love and hate are inextricable from what it means to be in psychotherapy. This too makes it difficult to apply the transference concept. How can therapists separate their patients' legitimate reactions to the successes and failures of the therapeutic interaction from something more clearly expressive of past unresolved conflicts?

It strikes me here that Shlien's case could be made even stronger by recognition of other legitimate functions of psychotherapy in addition to that of providing the patient with understanding. Perhaps if Shlien's predilection were less person-centered he would have also emphasized the change function of therapy. After all, the patient is likely to be fed up with what seems like a failed life. When therapists help patients to change, however painful that may be in the short run, are they not legitimately lovable? And when the suffering patient derives little benefit in terms of changing, is the therapist not legitimately hateful? Once again, this would appear to have more to do with the functions of the therapeutic interaction itself than with either the therapist's style and content or the patient's unresolved conflicts from the past.

None of this is to deny that the pasts of persons have a role to play in what and how they love and hate. Our past experience may well influence the range of styles and contents in others that we can easily love or hate. Further, our susceptibility to loving those who understand us and help us to change, and hating those who do not, may also express our pasts. But this means that there are at least three factors influencing the patients' emotional reactions in the therapeutic interaction: the past, the therapist's style and content, and the functions of the therapeutic interaction. The last two factors are in the present and cannot be curtailed lest there be no therapeutic interaction left. In this sense, if the concept of transference requires explication of the patient's love or hate reactions as merely expressive of the past, it is an untenable idea.

In discussing the psychoanalytic concept of countertransference, Shlien seems primarily concerned with showing its asymmetry with the transference concept. It is not particularly believable that the therapist is regarded as making no contribution to the 'transference' reaction, whereas the patient is a contributant to the 'countertransference' reaction. The therapist appears here to be taken more seriously than is the patient. I think there is a reason for this asymmetry beyond that of absolving the therapist of any taint of taking advantage. This reason is the therapist's attempt to produce change, and I shall return to it soon. First, however, I want to explore further the whole business of the therapist's reactions of love and hate for the patient.

There is every reason to believe that the same three factors influencing the patient's emotional reactions in the therapeutic interaction operate on the therapist as well. The style and content of the patient's personhood can provoke love or hate from the therapist. Mere awareness of what is happening is not really an antidote here. No doubt the therapist's past will influence the range of style and content in patients in ways that can provoke emotional reactions.

The third factor, the functional events of the therapeutic encounter itself is, as hinted by Shlien, extremely important. Of course, the therapeutic relationship is intentionally one-sided. It is the patient who is to be understood and helped to change. In understanding the patient and encouraging needed change, therapists use all their talent, humanity, imagination, and skill in a massive, continuing act of giving. Especially where this giving has the intended effect — the patient is grateful and encouraged — it is not at all surprising that the therapist would feel something reasonably called love. Remember that some theorists, such as Fromm (1956), long ago defined love as more the result of giving than of receiving. Furthermore, Freud himself once called doing psychotherapy an act of love. Nor is it surprising that when the patient is imperfectly understood and not provoked to change, the therapist might legitimately feel something like hate rather than love. Whatever the role of the past here, it cannot be a complete explanation of the therapist's emotional reactions, which are to a significant degree a function of the success or failure of the therapeutic interaction. The concept of countertransference would not seem very useful, therefore, in understanding these emotional reactions.The style and content of the patient's and therapist's personhood, and the successes and failures of the therapeutic interaction are factors having their emotional effects in the present, not the past. This is not at all changed by recognition that the past may well have influenced who these two persons are and how they interact. Whether and when they love or hate each other expresses what is going in the here and now. To try to interpret this in the strict sense of transference and countertransference, as mere reflections of unresolved interpersonal conflicts from the past, is to misunderstand. To liberalize the transference and counter-transference concepts so as to include forces from the present interaction along with forces from the past is to so water down the intent of psychoanalysis that it loses its distinctiveness in theory and practice.

On the horns of this dilemma, psychoanalysts have generally chosen to stay within the strict limits of the transference and countertransference concepts. They have tried to insist that they are blank screens to their patients, and that awareness of their own personhood permits minimizing its effects in the treatment. Not only is this stance implausible for reasons already given by Shlien and elaborated here, it also falls into a dangerous misunderstanding of the nature of psychotherapy.

The special, generic characteristic of psychotherapy, it seems to me, is a relationship of intimacy brought about by and serving contractual aims. Intimacy is ensured by clients (this seems to me a more generic term than patients) who struggle to reveal the innermost recesses of their minds, and therapists who struggle to support, understand, and appreciate these efforts. To be sure, the intimacy is typically rather one-sided, revealing its contractual purposes. The therapist is selfless because the client is paying for psychological help. Though selfless, however, the therapist enters into the intimacy by the kind of giving discussed before.

Looked at this way, the psychotherapeutic relationship has much by way of present, unfolding experience for both parties to provide explanations of their mutually changing loves and hates. The pasts, remote and immediate, that they bring to the relationship certainly influence the nature and intensity of their emotional reactions. But to insist that the past is all important is to explain away the present. The danger in this misunderstanding of emotional reactions is that it becomes paradoxically harder to learn from them what will help in fashioning and valuing intimacy.

There are many varieties and qualities of love and hate. We need not assume, for example, that all love is sexually tinged. A client might love the therapist the way a child loves a parent. Or a therapist might love the client the way a parent loves a child. This would be quite understandable in here and now terms, given the imbalance in experience, authority, and sometimes even age between client and therapist, and the fact that the client is seeking help. This is not to say, however, that neither client nor therapist can legitimately feel sexual love in the therapeutic relationship. After all, one might feel physical attraction for the other as a function of that person's stylistic features. More important, the mental intimacy of psychotherapy might be quite sufficient to initiate a more organismically comprehensive emotional response including a sexual component. It is even possible that the client or therapist love the other sexually in part because they are the kind of persons who need to be on the short or long end of power imbalances in order to feel aroused. But this in no way means that the love should not have occurred or is somehow not real. If the concepts of transference and countertransference can fully appreciate the reality of loves and hates in the present or therapeutic relationships, so much the better. I imagine, however, that to do this, the concepts will have been so liberalized as to remove its uniqueness from psychoanalysis.

Having recognized their loves and hates for each other and accepted them as expressions of forces in the present, client and therapist must still decide how to act on these emotions. In this, the contractual basis of therapy is important. Vulnerable and paying for help, the client is not to be exploited. Take, for example, the case of a female client who falls in what feels like sexual love with her male therapist. Suppose it has been her pattern to love men who abuse her, and to find the others boring. Suppose the therapist is the first kind, giving man she can remember finding interesting enough to love. Perhaps the therapist is a bit more interesting than the general run of nonabusive men she has been meeting. But it may be even more important that he is the first nonabusive man she has remained in a relationship with long enough—because she is paying for psychotherapeutic help—to appreciate how good it feels to be understood and supported. Because she feels safe and valued rather than bored, perhaps the love she experiences is more totalistic, and therefore vigorously sexual, than any she has previously felt. She would be badly served, it seems to me, by a therapist who persuades her, through a long process of interpretations, that her feelings expressed unresolved conflicts involving parents. Rather, she should be applauded for her emotional breakthrough.

What about the therapist's feelings? Suppose he came to respond with a sexualized love of his own, based on her beauty, openness, appealing vulnerability, and ability to change constructively? Should he try to maintain the semblance of being a blank screen, of having 'done nothing' to justify her sexual love? Should he rush to get supervision in hopes of conquering his feelings? Perhaps he should reciprocate by admitting his love to her. In addition to being true, this would constitute a wonderful reward for the risk she took in loving a different kind of man. Handled well, all this increases the likelihood that she will relate to nonabusive men in the future.

The approach suggested in the extended example requires great care at the level of actions taken as a consequence of shared emotions. The client may well want to start an affair with the therapist. Clearly, the therapist should decline, on the grounds of the contract that therapy represents. Suppose the therapist is a happily married family man. He could still have entered legitimately into the therapeutic contract because it is a contrived or limited relationship of intimacy. He did not advertise himself as available for an open-ended intimacy. The contract explicitly or implicitly excluded sexual intercourse in its emphasis on mental interaction. Even if all this were not true, it is not clear that he could help his client best by having a sexual affair with her. The most he can do, and it is a great deal, is to admit his sexual love for the client (if that is true), so that she may experience herself as desirable by a nonabusive man she desires. The reasons for their not having an affair are not, properly speaking, a rejection of her.

I deliberately fashioned an extended example that would take the position Shlien has taken, and with which I agree. Negative emotions generated in the therapeutic interaction can also be handled in this present-oriented approach. The therapist who is bored enough to have difficulty remaining awake by a client who insists on repeating some theme without making any progress toward change might be well advised to admit this. Done supportively, admission of negative emotional reactions on the therapist's part can help clients recognize their responsibility not only to contribute to relationships but to grow themselves. The road to using negative emotions supportively involves admitting but not acting on them in such ways as withdrawing support from the client. Once again, the therapeutic contract is a good guide.

Why did Freud and the other psychoanalysts get so committed to such an implausible concept as transference? There may be something in Shlien's contention that Freud wanted to insulate Breuer (and future analysts) from social criticism. This would have been understandable, given the radical and unfamiliar nature of psychoanalysis at the time. But I suspect there was also another reason, namely, the need to evolve in theory and technique some mechanism for inducing change in the patient. All therapies have such a mechanism. Witness the confrontation of clients with their supposed irrationality in rational-emotive therapy, and the unflagging unconditional positive regard given clients in person-centered therapy. In psychoanalysis, the patient is rendered dependent on the therapist's judgment largely through identification and interpretation of what are regarded as transference manifestations. Patients learn that they cannot trust their own emotions to be accurate reactions to events, and that these emotions reflect instead the unresolved parental conflicts constituting their psychic problem. Because the therapist emerges as the best guide to the true meaning of these emotions, patients become simultaneously less sure of themselves and more dependent on their therapists. In this fashion, the psychoanalyst is able to influence the direction of change in the patient.

Although I accept the functional need of psychotherapists to develop some mechanism for effecting client change, the transference concept seems an unwise choice. It is unwise not only because, as Shlien and I have concurred, transference is logically implausible. Beyond that, transference interpretations may have dangerous side effects. Here it is important to recognize that the underlying formulation of transference—that emotions in the here and now are best understood as expressions of unresolved parental conflicts from the past—is not restricted to the therapeutic interaction only. You will recall Freud's (1930, 1938) contention that all love and hate experiences are determined by past experiences in the nuclear family. When we are normal (not abnormal), we love the person we love because he or she resembles, at an unconscious level of awareness, our opposite-sexed parent. When we are normal (not abnormal), we work and make contributions to civilization out of displaced emotions and impulses that still arise unconsciously from unresolved loves and hates toward our parents.

What all this means is that, if we are to be honest and sophisticated, we must not trust our emotional reactions to reflect accurately our experiences in the present. We do not love or hate the persons and activities in our here and now out of their own characteristics except insofar as those characteristics are unconscious reminders of past parental interactions. This version of psychoanalytic reality has had a great influence on contemporary culture, directly through analyses, and indirectly through intellectual influences in literature, films, and even political analysis and literary criticism.

It is a very dangerous influence. If you cannot trust your reactions to things in the present, then you have no decision-making grounds to stand on. You also have no basis for taking the present seriously. This major thrust of psychoanalytic theory is toward

451

skepticism, self-preoccupation, inertia, nihilism, and finally, meaninglessness. Elsewhere, I (Maddi, 1970) have suggested that it is not surprising, given the impact of the transference notion on our general culture, that depressive disorders are so rampant these days. If the ground for taking the present seriously is cut out from under people, it is understandable that they would react with depressive affect. In attempting to understand depression, we should look less to physiological imbalances (which could, after all, result from certain chronic thought patterns anyway) and more to the perhaps unexpected side effects of psychoanalytic theory and other similarly nihilistic worldviews.

Perhaps psychoanalysis should not be held accountable for its indirect effects on general culture. I suppose it could be argued that when a person undergoes a competently done course in psychoanalytic therapy, the end result is not self-preoccupation, nihilism, and meaninglessness, despite the centrality in this process of the transference concept. But if the psychoanalytic version of truth is that our emotions in the present inevitably reflect the legacy of the past, then there is no changing this, and that would seem to be a source of meaninglessness. The heavy emphasis in this approach on the unconscious as a ubiquitous fact of life, and the childhood events of the nuclear family as formative, leave little room for hope that psychoanalysis can free persons to have experiences in the present that are independent of the past. This is one reason why Malcolm (1980) entitled her book about psychoanalysis *The Impossible Profession,* and quoted a psychoanalyst who was undergoing his third personal psychoanalysis as hoping that this time he would make some developmental progress. It is easy to conclude that the seeds of self-preoccupation, nihilism, and meaninglessness are built into the very practice of psychoanalysis through the transference concept. Therefore can depression be far away?

Certainly psychoanalysis has changed since its inception by Freud. It might be argued that ego psychology has provided a basis for taking present experiences seriously. After all, the content and energy of present functioning may, in ego formulations (e.g., Kernberg, 1976), be rather autonomous of unresolved childhood conflicts involving one's parents. Although ego psychology helps in avoiding the dangerous side effects of meaninglessness, its theoretical plausibility is a little shaky. What, for example, is this 'neutralized' energy that somehow is and is not libidinous at the same time? Perhaps the best hope that psychoanalysis will transcend the limitations epitomized in the transference concept lies beyond ego psychology in so-called psychoanalytic self-psychology (Kohut, 1977). In such notions that the kind of self the child takes into the Oedipal conflict may well influence the outcome of that drama there is an implicit basis for deemphasizing the transference concept and taking the present seriously. But as this self-psychology develops further, it may raise an insistent question of just how psychoanalytic it is.

References

Freud, S. (1930). *Civilization and its discontents.* New York: Norton.
Freud, S. (1938). Three contributions to the theory of sex. In *The basic writings of Sigmund Freud.* New York: Modern Library.
Fromm, E. (1956). *The art of loving.* New York: Harper.
Kernberg, O. F. (1976). *Object relations theory and clinical psychoanalysis.* New York: Jason Aronson.
Kohut, H. (1977). *The restoration of the self.* New York: International Universities Press.
Maddi, S. R. (1970). The search for meaning. In M. Page (Ed.), *Nebraska symposium on motivation.* Lincoln, NE: Univ. of Nebraska Press.
Malcolm, J. (1980). *The impossible profession.* New York: Harper.
Shlien, J. M. (1987). A countertheory of transference. *Person-Centered Review, 2*(1), 15–49.

Special discussion: A Countertheory of Transference

(vii) Comment on Shlien's Article

'A Countertheory of Transference'

Carl R. Rogers   *Center for the Studies of the Person*

I shall leave to others the detailed and critical assessment of Dr. Shlien's article. My own overall reaction is that it is competently done, deals straightforwardly with important issues, and is very timely. I find myself in agreement with its major thrust. I believe it is important that this challenging statement is written by a man who was an enthusiastic student of Freudian analysis long before he became aware of any other mode of therapy. I am pleased that it is written out of many years of involvement as a therapist, and as a teacher and supervisor of therapists. The views Shlien expresses grow out of long experience, as well as out of careful scholarly research.

My own comments will be limited to an explication of the way in which a therapist may deal with attitudes and feelings directed toward herself or himself, including those termed 'transference.'

Feelings and emotions directed toward the therapist fall primarily into two groups. First are those feelings that are an understandable response to some of the attitudes and behaviors of the therapist. There may be resentment originating in an attitude of superiority of expertness in the therapist. The client feels looked down upon, and responds negatively. Such resentment may also be caused by incorrect or premature interpretations by the therapist, resulting in the client's feeling pushed or misunderstood. There may be anger at therapist prescriptions for client behavior. One client cooperated very well with Fritz Perls during an interview. Later, seeing a film of the interview, she was indignant at him and at herself. *'Why* did I *do* all those things he told me to do?!' In such instances as these, therapists may or may not be aware of the fact that negative client attitudes are simply a natural response to their statements or actions.

Positive feelings may also result from therapist behavior. Warm and loving feelings may arise in the client from an unexpected and very welcome depth of understanding on the part of the therapist; from small actions showing concern for the client's comfort; from such behavior as laying a hand on the client's arm during a moment of painful struggle; from such behavior as Heinz Kohut offering 'two fingers' to a desperate analysand; from such things as helping a client put on a heavy coat, or casually offering transportation during a heavy rain storm. It is entirely reasonable that the client should, in these circumstances, come to like or love the therapist, and want a loving response in return. Again, the therapist may or may not be aware of the fact that it is his or her statements or actions that are at the base of the client's feelings.

The second category of client reactions are the emotions that have little or no relationship to the therapist's behavior. These are truly 'transferred' from their real origin to the therapist. They are projections. They may be triggered by something in the therapist — 'You look like my father,' or 'You resemble a man I despise' — but the intensity

First published in *Person-Centered Review,* Volume 2, Number 2, May 1987.

of the feeling comes from within the client, and is not due to the behavior of the therapist.

These projected feelings may be positive feelings of love, sexual desire, adoration, and the like. They may be negative — hatred, contempt, fear, mistrust. Their true object may be a parent or other significant person in the client's life. Or, and this is less often recognized, they may be negative attitudes toward the self, which the client cannot bear to face.

From a client-centered point of view, it is not necessary, in responding to and dealing with these feelings, to determine whether they are therapist caused or are projections. The distinction is of theoretical interest, but is not a practical problem. In the therapeutic interaction all of these attitudes — positive or negative, 'transference' feelings, or therapist-caused reactions — are best dealt with in the same way. If the therapist is sensitively understanding and genuinely acceptant and nonjudgmental, therapy will move forward *through* these feelings. There is absolutely no need to make a special case of attitudes that are transferred to the therapist, and no need for the therapist to permit the dependence that is so often a part of other forms of therapy, particulary psychoanalysis. It is entirely possible to accept dependent feelings, without permitting the client to change the therapist's role.

All of this is well illustrated in a case example previously published, but still worthy of careful examination.

The client was an unmarried woman in her thirties, a decidedly disturbed individual. In her early interviews she struggled with painful feelings of guilt arising out of possible incestuous relations with her father. She could not be certain whether the events she described really occurred, or whether they were products of her imagination. She was slow in her speech, enabling the therapist to keep unusually complete notes, so what follows is nearly verbatim. Several excerpts from three interviews will indicate the depth of her 'transference' feelings, and the way in which the therapist responded to them. They illuminate the way in which 'transference' disappears when the feelings are expressed in a client-centered climate.

From the ninth interview

S: *This morning I hung my coat out there instead of here in your office. I've told you I like you, and I was afraid if you helped me on with the coat, I might turn around and kiss you.*

C: *You thought those feelings of affection might* make *you kiss me unless you protected yourself from them.*

S: *Well, another reason I left the coat out there is that I want to be dependent — but I want to show you I don't have to be dependent.*

C: *You both want to be, and to prove you don't have to be. [Toward end of interview.]*

S: *I've never told anyone they were the most wonderful person I've ever known, but I've told you that. It's not just sex. It's more than that.*

C: *You really feel very deeply attached to me.*

From the tenth interview

S: *I think emotionally I'm dying for sexual intercourse but I don't do anything about it . . . The thing I want is to have sexual intercourse with you. I don't dare ask you, 'cause I'm afraid you'd be nondirective.*

C: *You have this awful tension, and want so much to have relations with me.*

S: *[Goes on in this vein. Finally.] Can't we do something about it? This tension is*

> *awful! Will you relieve the tension . . . Can you give me a direct answer? I think it might help both of us.*

C: *[Gently.] The answer would be no. I can understand how desperately you feel, but I would not be willing to do that.*

S: *[Pause. Sigh of relief.] I think that helps me. It's only when I'm upset that I'm like this. You have strength, and it gives me strength.*

Twelfth interview

S: *[Silent for two minutes. Then begins to talk in hard flat voice, quite unlike her usual tone. Does not look at therapist. There was much repetition, but the following excerpts give the major thoughts.] You feel I want to come, but I don't! I'm not coming anymore. It doesn't do any good. I don't like you. [Her voice becomes venomous.] I hate you! I wish you never were born.*

C: *[His tone matching the depth of her feeling.] You just hate me — very bitterly!*

S: *I think I'll throw you in the lake. I'll cut you up! You think people like you, but they don't . . . You think you can attract women, but you can't . . . I wish you were dead.*

C: *You detest me and you'd really like to get rid of me!*

S: *You think my father did bad things with me, but he didn't! You think he wasn't a good man but he was. You think I want intercourse, but I don't!*

C: *You feel I absolutely misrepresent all your thoughts.*

S: *You think you can get people to come in and tell you everything, and they'll think they're being helped but they're not! You just like to make 'em suffer. You think you can hypnotize them, but you can't! You think you're good, but you ain't. I hate you, I hate you, I hate you!*

C: *You feel I really like to make 'em suffer, but that I don't help them.*

S: *You think I haven't been straight, but I have. I hate you. All I've had is pain, pain, pain. You think I can't direct my own life, but I can. You think I can't get well, but I can. You think I had hallucinations, but I didn't. I hate you. [Long pause. Leans on desk in strained, exhausted pose.] You think I'm crazy, but I'm not.*

C: *You're sure I think you're crazy.*

S: *[Pause.] I'm tied, and I just can't get loose! [Despairing tone of voice, and tears. Pause.] I had a hallucination and I've got to get it out! . . . [Goes on about her own deep conflicts, and tells of the hallucination she has experienced, with terrific tension in her voice, but with an attitude very different from that at beginning of interview.]*

Later in interview

S: *I knew at the office I had to get rid of this somewhere. I felt I could come down and tell you. I knew you'd understand. I couldn't say I hated myself. That's true but I couldn't say it. So I just thought of all the ugly things I could say to you instead.*

C: *The things you felt about yourself you couldn't say but you could say them about me.*

S: *I know we're getting to rock bottom . . .* (Rogers, 1951, pp. 211–13)

Here are several comments about these excerpts. They show — again — that when the therapeutic conditions are present, the process of therapy moves forward. They show that this hypothesis holds for the exploration of so-called transference feelings, just as it does for the exploration of all other feelings.

This case shows that when the therapist's understanding is accurate and his acceptance is genuine, when there are no interpretations given and no evaluations made, 'transference' attitudes tend to dissolve, and the feelings are directed toward their true object. In a climate of such safety, there is less need to deny feelings of awareness, and as a consequence the client becomes more accurately aware of the meaning of her experience, and develops new insight.

It is noteworthy that when the therapist responds to her question and states his unwillingness (on ethical grounds) to engage in sex, he speaks solely for himself, and of himself. There is no interpretation of her behavior, no judgment of her request.

In my opinion, interpretations tend to delay — not hasten — the process. If the therapist had said, 'I think perhaps you are asking to recreate the incestuous relationship with your father' — an interpretation that might well be true — it would almost certainly have met strong resistance.

Psychoanalysts speak often of resistance and the difficulties in dealing with it. It is well to recognize that there are two types of resistance. There is the pain of revealing — to oneself and another — the feelings that have hitherto been denied to awareness. There is also the resistance to the therapist, created *by* the therapist. Offering interpretations, making diagnoses and other judgments — these are the usual way by which resistance is brought about — the resistance with which the therapist then must deal.

Here is the special virtue of the client-centered approach. By creating a relationship that is *safe,* the client has no need to resist the therapist, and hence is more free, as in this case, to deal with the resistance she finds in herself. She finds the situation safe enough to realize that all the thoughts and feelings she has projected onto the therapist are in fact thoughts and feelings she has about herself.

To me it seems clear that the most effective way of dealing with *all* feelings directed toward the therapist is through the creation of a therapeutic relationship that fulfills the conditions set forth in client-centered theory. To deal with transference feelings as a very special part of therapy, making their handling the very core of therapy, is to my mind a grave mistake. Such an approach fosters dependency and lengthens therapy. It creates a whole new problem, the only purpose of which appears to be the intellectual satisfaction of the therapist — showing the elaborateness of his or her expertise. I deplore it.

There is one additional point I would make. If dealing with the 'transference neurosis' is so important to therapy, and brings about a greater depth of change in personality and behavior, why are there no data to back this up? Where are the recorded interviews that would demonstrate that the psychoanalytic view is more effective, more far-reaching in its results? Why the reluctance to make known what actually happens in the therapist's dealings with this core of the analytic process?

Having, years ago, read a transcript of a complete psychoanalysis, and having had the opportunity to listen to brief segments of psychoanalytic therapy, I believe I can understand the reluctance to make such data public. So the questions about transference will be debated and argued, but always one step removed from the data. The questions cannot be finally answered until psychoanalysts are willing to open their work to professional scrutiny.

References

Rogers, C. R. (1951). *Client-centered therapy.* Boston: Houghton Mifflin.

Special discussion: A Countertheory of Transference
(viii) Transference and Psychotherapy

Julius Seeman   *Vanderbilt University*

I have been invited to read John Shlien's article and to write some comments of my own concerning the topic of transference. What will work best for me is to approach the topic not as a response to John Shlien's article but rather in terms of my own understanding and views about the topic.

In approaching the question of transference, I believe that its meaning for me will be illuminated if I consider separately its application to experiences of the client and experiences of the therapist. In this article I will discuss each in turn and then talk about the meaning of transference in therapies other than the person-centered approach.

'TRANSFERENCE' AS OBSERVED IN THE CLIENT

I have placed quotation marks around the term 'transference' as a signal that the term is not part of my own language as a therapist. Once that is clear, I can deal with the term readily as a widely used construct that has meaning for many therapists. For me the most useful definition of the term comes from its root form 'transfer.' I can understand this process best in a learning theory context through the application of the two closely related concepts of generalization and transfer. Persons who have generalized constructs (e.g., who have generalized the concept 'older person' to the concept 'authority') are in a position to transfer this learning to any new situation in which an older person is involved.

There are no surprises in this construct from the standpoint of personality theory. Most theories of personality, including person-centered theory, postulate an evolving structure of personality that has form, substance, and continuity. It is also the case that this ongoing structure shapes the meaning that new experiences have for us.

Thus far, then, the concept of transfer(ence) is simple, logical, and straightforward. Complications arise, however, when two additional boundaries are placed upon the meaning of the concept. One such boundary concerns the view that transference behavior is necessarily a distortion of current reality. I believe that this misconception arises simply through sampling error. The concept arose through observation of a truncated range of persons — that is, through the observation of troubled persons. If a broader sample had been used, it would have become obvious that some generalization and transfer served very useful learning needs and represented reality quite well.

The second complication arises when transference is construed as a literal replication and reenactment of earlier behavior. This argument may be a 'straw man' argument to begin with, since psychoanalysis is more interested in the psychodynamics underlying the behavior than in the details of the behavior itself. Nevertheless, some accounts that appear in the literature suggest that the writer finds the behavior fully explainable by construing it as the reappearance of unfulfilled infantile needs. It is as though the current

First published in *Person-Centered Review,* Volume 2, Number 2, May 1987.

situation has no reality of its own, but only a symbolic meaning. I find this idea too illogical to take seriously.

Having said all that, I believe that client behavior defined in the usual sense as transference behavior can and does occur in psychotherapy. What I mean is that clients may misconstrue the meaning of a current experience in psychotherapy on the basis of the personal meanings and structure that they bring with them into therapy. But then this phenomenon is readily explained not only by psychoanalytic theory but also by self-theory. For example, if we refer to the theory as put forth by Rogers (1951) we find two propositions that are quite applicable, as follows:

> (IX) As a result of interaction with the environment, and particularly as a result of evaluational interaction with others, the structure of self is formed — an organized, fluid, but consistent conceptual pattern of perceptions of characteristics and relationships of the 'I' or the 'me,' together with values attached to these concepts. (p. 498)

> (XI) As experiences occur in the life of the individual, they are either (a) symbolized, perceived, and organized into some relationship to the self, (b) ignored because there is no perceived relationship to the self-structure, (c) denied symbolization or given a distorted symbolization because the experience is inconsistent with the structure of the self. (p. 503)

The two foregoing propositions jointly assert that (a) persons evolve enduring self-structures and (b) threats to the self-structure may lead to distorted constructions of subsequent experience. These two assertions readily encompass behavior that can be construed as transference behavior.

Transference and the Person-Centered Therapist

There are a number of elements in person-centered theory and therapy that make the concept of transference irrelevant to the person-centered therapist. The three considerations that I see as most germane to this issue are as follows:

1. *Phenomena and constructs.* Person-centered theory as a phenomenological theory has two corollaries: (a) the therapist is interested in the client's phenomenology — that is, the data of the client's immediately given and lived experience are the data to which the therapist attends. (b) Since all of the therapist's attention and energy are centered on these data (the phenomena), the therapist has no need for intervening constructs to guide his or her understanding of these phenomena. Indeed, the therapist would find nothing more distracting and counterproductive than the intrusion of nondata. Who needs it?

2. *Therapy now.* The person-centered therapist stays with the client fully in the current moment of immediate experience. The process is thus completely ahistorical. The past of course is not thereby ignored (I have never worked with a client who failed to refer to her or his past). But that past is engaged only when it is being lived in the current moment by the client, and it is thus very much present.

3. *Therapy as a present relationship.* Finally, person-centered therapy is a relationship between two people, a here-and-now relationship experienced fully in the present and not in the past. Thus what matters is the present relationship as a reality and not as a symbol or a reenactment of something else.

If we now integrate all of the foregoing considerations, we can conclude that all of the client's experiential data are received by the therapist in the same manner, with no filtering through a system of constructs. Thus no construct such as transference intrudes upon the therapeutic process.

Transference, Rankian therapy and psychoanalysis

One way to understand the concept of transference more fully is to view it through the eyes of other theories. To this end I have chosen to set forth my understanding of the ways in which Rankian theory and modern psychoanalytic theory view the transference concept.

The most eloquent interpreter of Rankian theory and therapy is Jessie Taft (1933/1962). Her view of transference is strikingly similar to that of the person-centered approach, and highlights the influence that Rankian theory has had upon the development of person-centered theory. In discussing the task of the therapist, Taft (1933/1962, p. 9) made the following observation regarding the psychoanalytic concept of transference.

> According to this transference concept, the worker is being used in the present but only as a lay figure on which to project experiences and feelings from the client's past. An utter confusion results, a practical denial of the reality of the present which is functioning for the sake of the past. Once more the worker is effectively hidden behind the screen of father, mother, brother, sister, while all the time her value for the client is that she is none of these and he knows it.

It is evident from the foregoing passage that Taft gives high priority to the immediacy and reality of the real relationship between client and therapist and rejects the concept of role projection implicit in classical transference theory.

The perspective of psychoanalytic theory is quite another matter and far more complex. This complexity is largely a function of the long-term evolution of psychoanalytic theory and the attendant variability in viewpoint that has emerged over time. I will limit my comments here to an exploration of concepts put forth in recent years by Kohut (1977) and others writing from the same framework (e.g., Goldberg, 1980).

In many ways Kohut's viewpoint is markedly different from that of classical psychoanalytic theory, and those differences have a bearing on formulations of transference. Classical psychoanalysis held that neurosis was rooted in conflict between infantile impulses and the demands of the real world. Transference was seen as the projection of this conflict upon the person of the therapist. The transference neurosis, fostered by the analyst, was seen as the vehicle by which the conflict was brought into the present and worked through.

My understanding of Kohut's concept is that it is quite different, leaning as it does on developmental theory rather than conflict theory. On this basis, the goal of analysis 'must now also be evaluated in terms of achieving self-cohesion, particularly in terms of the restitution of the self with the aid of a re-established empathic closeness to responsive self objects' (Kohut, 1977, p. 281).

The foregoing statement makes no mention of transference neurosis, and indeed the theory as stated here does not require such a process, though transference is still part of the theory. The dynamics of the transference appear to be rather different, and make room for a view of transference based more on a relational context.

The case illustrations in Goldberg (1980) strengthen the impression that the relationship assumes a greater role in this new formulation. For example, Schwaber (in

Newman, 1980) discusses the case of a woman in psychoanalysis and says, 'After revealing a particularly shameful aspect of her life, a young woman patient appeared to feel touched by an emotional response I made in attempting to understand her feelings' (p. 271). Such a response is a far cry from the 'surgical' objectivity advocated by Freud.

Since I have no direct experience with psychoanalysis I cannot evaluate with any depth the significance of these trends. There are nevertheless several implications that seem logical to me. First, the theory itself is plainly a self-theory, oriented more along developmental lines than on concepts of intrapsychic conflict. Second, the terms of the theory evidently lead to a more direct relational involvement of the therapist with the client. And finally, these changes are bound to result in modifications of transference theory. This is so because classical transference required that the therapist be a screen rather than a present person, so the patient could more readily project his or her conflicts in a pure form, free of complications that might emanate from the therapist. Since the newer theory permits the therapist to be more nearly a real person, it is reasonable to expect that continuing modifications in theory and practice may lead to progressively more emphasis on relational components of the therapy. There is an open-ended quality here that permits departure from role and ritual, and so I remain an interested bystander, eager to see what may happen next.

REFERENCES

Goldberg, A. (Ed.) (1980). *Advances in self psychology.* New York: International Universities Press.

Kohut, H. (1977). *The restoration of the self.* New York: International Universities Press.

Newman, K. (1980). Discussion: Defense analysis and self psychology. In A. Goldberg (Ed.), *Advance in self psychology.* New York: International Universities Press.

Rogers, C. R. (1951). *Client-centered therapy.* New York: Houghton Mifflin.

Taft, J. (1933/1962). *The dynamics of therapy in a controlled relationship.* New York: Dover.

Special discussion: A Countertheory of Transference

(ix) Response to 'A Countertheory of Transference' by John M. Shlien

Hans H. Strupp *Vanderbilt University*

Dr. John Shlien anticipates that the major thesis of his article will seem 'an exaggeration, an outrage, an indictment.' To some, it may be any or all of these things. I personally regret most, Shlien's misunderstandings and misconceptions. There is little recognition that psychoanalytic theory — and therapy — have advanced significantly since the time of Freud and that Freud's formulations of transference have been modified in a number of ways. I also question whether many psychodynamic therapists today view transference in the manner depicted here. In this brief commentary I can do no more than state my own views, which are heavily influenced by contemporary thinking in psychoanalysis and interpersonal theory. For more detailed discussions, I refer interested readers to my recent book, *Psychotherapy in a New Key* (1984). I also recommend Anchin and Kiesler's *Handbook of Interpersonal Psychotherapy* (1982).

First, it seems essential to place transference in the context of the psychodynamic theory of psychotherapy. What does the latter attempt to do? How does it seek to resolve the patient's problems in living? What kinds of problems does it seek to ameliorate?

Above all, the dynamic psychotherapist attempts to mediate a constructive experience in living. I adopt as a basic working assumption that patients suffer from the ill-effects of previous interpersonal experiences, notably those with significant figures of their childhood. As part of these earlier experiences they have acquired attitudes, cognitions, and beliefs that are associated with troublesome feelings (notably anxiety) that serve them poorly in their current lives. These maladaptations encompass the 'symptoms' of which the patient currently complains. As therapists we assume that if one human relationship has made the patient 'ill,' another human relationship can, within limits, make him or her 'well.'

To achieve desired goals, the therapist proceeds on two major fronts by (1) providing the patient with a new — and different — interpersonal experience, and (2) seeking to effect changes in the faulty learning that the patient has carried forward from the past. Parenthetically, the patient's past is of no interest per se; it does, however, become crucially important in terms of unresolved issues that continue to bedevil the patient's adult life.

Together with many therapists (including Shlien), I place great importance on the quality of the therapeutic relationship and the patient's experience in that relationship. I believe that the latter is the alpha and omega of all forms of psychotherapy. The benefits the patient derives away from his or her interaction with the therapist is the product of that experience. Prominent factors are the therapist's empathic understanding, commitment, reliability, respect, and trustworthiness that are communicated by word, attitude, and action. In this regard, I am in full agreement with client-centered therapy (Rogers, 1957). Indeed, Rogers deserves great credit for having emphasized these qualities

First published in *Person-Centered Review,* Volume 2, Number 2, May 1987.

at a time when such views were far from being generally accepted. I also agree with Shlien that 'love is not enough,' but I do so for different reasons. Furthermore, I have reservations about accepting Rogers' facilitative conditions as necessary *and* sufficient. I believe they are necessary but often not sufficient. Let me elaborate.

The problem for dynamic psychotherapy, as I see it, is precisely the patient's impaired ability to take advantage of what a good human relationship can offer; if it were otherwise, there would be no great need for a professionally trained psychotherapist. If we assume that the adult patient who comes to psychotherapy lives in a human environment in which satisfying relationships are potentially available, we must wonder why he or she failed to solve the problem of relatedness. This failure is precisely the problem for psychotherapy. Instead of being able to use existing opportunities, the patient operates on the basis of faulty beliefs and assumptions. Furthermore, he or she continually courts defeat by engaging in behavior patterns that predictably produce untoward results. In these respects, the patient resembles a laboratory animal that has learned a single set of techniques for solving a problem but is unable to modify them in light of new information or changing conditions. These forms of stereotypy and rigidity are defining characteristics of neurotic behavior. How can psychotherapy promote new learning and/or modify old patterns of behavior? At this point, transference enters the picture and becomes the *raison d'être* of psychodynamic psychotherapy.

Before expanding on this topic, I wish to emphasize that psychotherapeutic change comes about in many different ways and no 'school' of psychotherapy has a monopoly on 'techniques.' Laypersons, paraprofessionals, wives, friends, and so on can all play therapeutic roles and the available research evidence supports this conclusion. Thus when I speak of dynamic psychotherapy, which has as its central feature the analysis of transference, I am not asserting that it offers a *unique* approach to the solution of problems in living. What I do assert is that the approach is theoretically sound, teachable, and potentially based on solid empirical data. It is also rational and makes good sense. Many colleagues clearly share this view, which accounts for the thriving interest in psychoanalytic psychotherapy.

To return to the main topic, why is transference important and what function does its 'analysis' play in psychodynamic psychotherapy? The answer lies in the well-established observation that people tend to enact with significant others (including the therapist) strategies and patterns of behavior they have learned in the past. This is particularly true of unresolved difficulties in the areas of autonomy and intimacy. Thus they treat significant others in the present as if they were significant persons in the past, and they unwittingly create and perpetuate maladaptive patterns of interpersonal behavior. They seek to derive from dyadic relationships gratifications that are no longer appropriate (e.g., dependence on a powerful parent) or were never available; they persist in anachronistic struggles with parents who were once inadequate or hurtful; and they refuse to act on the basis of realistic adult needs (e.g., love that is based on a mutually rewarding relationship). Although they consciously seek relatedness on an adult level, they cannot accept what a 'good relationship' has to offer.

Since a good deal of human activity is embedded in social, interpersonal contexts (Kiesler, in Anchin and Kiesler, 1982, Chap. 1) and since all individuals, from early life on, are 'object-seeking,' the therapist presently comes to assume the role of a 'significant other.' This is particularly true because patients are unhappy in their current interpersonal relationships and intent upon turning to someone who might alleviate their suffering. For these reasons, the patient soon begins to use the therapist and the therapeutic relationship as a vehicle for enacting unresolved wishes, fears, and impulses. Specifically, he or she attempts to evoke from the therapist the very responses that are an integral part of 'the problem.' However, not all of the patient's problems are 'transference.' It is generally recognized today that there is always a 'real' relationship between patient and therapist, that is, the patient relates to the therapist *both* as an adult peer *and* as a personification from the past.

To illustrate: if the therapist is recurrently late for appointments, the patient has a right to be angry; however, if there is no ostensible 'cause' for the patient's feelings of anger, we must look elsewhere for an explanation. Since patients keep from themselves, as well as from the therapist, their 'true' motives, it may take considerable effort to ferret out the patient's underlying scenario.

There is ample evidence that all individuals continually *transfer* feelings, attitudes, and action patterns to others. It is a matter of clinical judgment whether and to what degree such transference reactions interfere with productive and satisfying living and whether therapeutic efforts are called for. By virtue of the working alliance, the therapist is gradually enabled to say to the patient: 'Perhaps you can see that you are treating me as if I were someone from your past. What transpires here also goes on with a significant other in your current life, and perhaps you can also see that there is a relationship between this pattern and your relationship with your father (mother, etc.).' In Kiesler's words: (in Anchin and Kiesler, 1982, p. 13)

> Problems in living reside in the recurrent transactions of a person with others, especially significant others, in his life. Problems in living are defined as disordered, inappropriate, or inadequate interpersonal communications. They result originally and cumulatively from a person's not attending to and not correcting the self-defeating, interpersonally unsuccessful aspects of his communications. Largely by nonverbal messages, the disturbed person consistently communicates a rigid and extreme self-presentation, and simultaneously pulls for a rigid and constricted relationship from others. (italics in original)

It was one of Freud's greatest and, in my opinion, most lasting contributions to have discovered — not invented, as Shlien would have it — this basic dynamic in human relationships. The patient's 'illness,' therefore, is found in his or her tendency to transfer and to elicit complementary reactions from others. If these transferences can be identified in *statu nascendi*, and if the therapist declines to play a complementary role (i.e., gives an 'asocial' response), a therapeutic intervention becomes possible. Much here depends on timing and the quality of the working alliance. Needless to say, this process takes time and the therapist's job is often difficult. However, progress occurs as the patient can experience his or her transference reactions against the backdrop of a realistic 'good' relationship with the therapist in the here and now. The lessons can eventually be put to use in other interpersonal relationships.

To repeat, dynamic psychotherapy proceeds on a dual track: It provides the patient with a good relationship that is therapeutic in its own right; and, secondly, it seeks to clarify via transference analysis, maladaptive cyclic patterns that impede good relationships with significant persons outside of therapy.

In Freud's linear conceptions (based on nineteenth-century thinking), the relationship between patient and therapist was seen as a one-way street, that is, the patient transferred and the therapist was considered a mirror that simply reflected the patient's feelings, wishes, and so on. Correspondingly, untoward responses on the therapist's part were described as 'countertransference.' Today we realize that therapist and patient form a dynamic unit. Just as the patient continually reacts to the therapist, so does the therapist react to the patient. Since the patient's behavior tends to evoke certain (often maladaptive) responses from the therapist, the latter can experience these subtle 'pulls' and, one hopes, place them in the service of obtaining a better understanding of the patient. If, without realizing it, the therapist reacts to the patient's evoking messages with problematic patterns of his or her own, the therapy may reach an impasse, the patient may leave therapy, or a power struggle may ensue. To some degree, the therapist, in order to be effective, must become a coactor in the patient's scenario (via empathy); but then he or she must be able to extricate himself or herself and *metacommunicate* with the patient about their interaction. In other forms of therapy, this step is typically omitted, that is, troublesome aspects of the patient-therapist relationship are not being 'analyzed.' In my opinion, only a well-trained therapist can execute these tasks that, to a significant extent, define the skills of a professional psychotherapist.

Finally, I wish to comment on a few additional points. Although transference reactions develop in any therapeutic relationship in which the therapist provides a modicum of empathy, warmth, commitment, and caring, it is true that the classical 'transference neurosis' is now generally considered an undesirable artifact, a development that should not be fostered. It is counteracted by therapies in which the therapist remains less 'anonymous' and emerges as a real person; when sessions, as is now typically the case, occur on a once- or twice-a-week basis; when the therapist desists from cultivating a highly charged atmosphere; and when systematic attention is paid to the troublesome problems in the patient's current life, including prominently the therapeutic relationship. Regression that occurs inevitably in a therapeutic relationship should be analyzed rather than encouraged. Idealization of the therapist, a common occurrence, is likewise dealt with as a therapeutic problem. Throughout, it is critically important for the therapist to differentiate 'real' feelings from 'transference feelings' and to treat the latter as a problem for therapy. One would expect that in a well-conducted therapy the patient would develop positive and affectionate feelings toward the therapist that are altogether legitimate. By the same token, it is to be expected that a patient who after a period of time takes leave from therapy will experience feelings of loss that need to be tolerated and worked through. Franz Alexander was quite correct in regarding overtreatment a greater problem than undertreatment. In our era in which a patient's personal finances and insurance benefits have set rather strict limits on the length and intensity of therapy, overtreatment is becoming less of a problem, although there are certainly cases in which intensive and prolonged therapy is a necessity, not a luxury.

Transference, as I have been at pains to point out, is neither a fiction in the mind of the therapist nor is it an artifact. Rather it is the essence of the problem in need of resolution. A therapist who understands these dynamics will neither suppress nor cultivate the patient's transference reactions. He or she will neither succumb to the snares of the patient's adulation nor punish the latter for the expression of negative, hostile feelings. The therapist's professional skills are demonstrated by his or her ability to guide the relationship toward therapeutic ends while concurrently fostering a genuine experience of understanding, nurturance, and trust.

REFERENCES

Anchin, I. C., & Kiesler, D. J. (Eds.) (1982). *Handbook of interpersonal psychotherapy.* New York: Pergamon.

Rogers, C. R. (1957). The necessary and sufficient conditions of therapeutic personality change. *Journal of Consulting Psychology. 21*, 95–103.

Strupp, H. H., & Binder, I. L. (1984). *Psychotherapy in a new key: A guide to time-limited psychotherapy.* New York: Basic Books.

Special discussion: A Countertheory of Transference

(x) Further Thoughts on Transference:

Responses to Drs. Ernst Beier, Constance Fischer, Harold Greenwald,

Arnold Lazarus, Salvatore Maddi, Carl Rogers,

Julius Seeman and Hans Strupp

John M. Shlien   *Harvard University*

An article, *A Countertheory of Transference,* was published in this journal, volume 2, number 1, 1987. Eight eminent psychologists wrote critiques from various points of view. These were published in volume 2, number 2. It is necessary to have read these previous exchanges in order to make sense of the present reply. Client-centered therapy and other viewpoints have had an engagement with the psychoanalytic concept of 'transference.' In this article I continue a dialogue with the respondents and offer additional perspectives on the transference controversy.

First, thanks to all of you for your thoughtful attention. Many of the comments were polished papers in themselves. What a privilege to have such readers, and from Editor Cain, the opportunity to reply, as well.

Perhaps our exchanges will have illuminated the problem for others. It is doubtful that any of us have changed our minds, and I really did not expect anyone to alter, much less reverse, her or his point of view. For many reasons of deep investment, this topic of 'transference' is highly resistant to change, very durable in one form or another. Since I consider it a defense, I would never expect it to yield to attack. My purpose is to declare a position, one that can take its place in a range of opinions, so that people can exercise critical judgments and think in a more informed way about their choices.

The journal containing your comments reached me in Rome, and I carried it to read at various stops — Budapest, Vienna, Prague, Geneva and Paris, making notes for each of you, but lacking access to your references and your own books or articles. Having just returned, I wrote without benefit of those materials. Meanwhile, let me recommend an American book now popular in Europe — *In Dora's Case: Freud, Hysteria and Feminism* (Berheimer and Kahane, 1982).

Why return to Dora? Many reasons. It, not Anna O., is the case in which Freud gave us the first view of his transference theory at work, and his technical prescriptions and interpretive methods. It is the model to which the world still refers, which makes others pale, and which illustrates not only the origin but the core of the idea.

It is this period to which some of you refer when you speak of 'classical transference' or 'classical psychoanalytic theory.' But it was *never* classical. It was baroque from the beginning. Consider the case: Dora was brought to Freud by her father, who was angry and embarrassed about her complaints regarding the hypocrisy of the adults in her family circle. Her father had been treated by Freud for syphilis and introduced to Freud by Herr

---

First published in *Person-Centered Review*, Volume 2, Number 4, November 1987.

K., who was Dora's would-be seducer and also husband to Frau K., the mistress of Dora's father. Frau K. was Dora's confidante, mother of the children Dora sometimes took care of, and the woman Dora really desired, according to Freud. Meanwhile, Freud was struggling with his own analysis of his homosexual tendencies and hysteria, not to mention his 'countertransference' (a concept not yet published if even known at that time) and his apparent identification with Herr K.

Out of this nest of complication, how could we expect the cleanliness and elegance of 'classical' theory? I wish only that psychoanalysis had the beauty and definition of pure form, somewhere, sometime.

Poor Dora. Although Freud did not fail her at first, he did not at once oblige her father and join in the sham and denial of her family. For a while, he listened, understood her on her terms, besieged as she was, better than anyone else had. Later she wanted to kiss him, and he traces her desire to the smoky connection between himself and Herr K., who should have been, in Freud's view, sexually and romantically attractive to a healthy teenage girl.

Some of you make the case for 'transfer.' Was this just a matter of transfer (both did smoke cigars) or stimulus generalization? Freud thought it was *'the* transference,' which he had handled badly, that caused Dora to terminate the interviews.

Suppose that Freud had recognized the emotional consequences of the precious service he *(unlike* Herr K.) had given Dora, that is, understanding in the beginning that her perceptions were valid, her feelings legitimate. For such value received, gratitude and affection come naturally, and if Freud had the humility to accept such an expression for its meaning, we might not have had 'the transference.' He *could* have simply realized the emotional value of understanding, that is. Freud had such inclinations. He sometimes wanted to transform neurotic complexities into ordinary human unhappiness. He once thought that the theme of psychoanalysis should be, 'Oh my poor child, what have they done to you.' But he had other and more clever tendencies on his way to the company of Darwin and Copernicus. 'We have disturbed the sleep of the world' sounds terribly important, but seems to me a terrible state. What the world needs is *fully awakened consciousness.* Does 'transference' promote or obscure it? That is one of the main issues throughout this dialogue.

In one particular dimension, some (Fischer and Maddi, at least) believe that 'transference' reveals more the past at the expense of concealing the present. This raises questions of differences in viewpoint: Why are some of us more oriented to the past, others more to the present? It is simply a theory of determinism? A personal inclination? On this same dimension, Seeman (1987, p. 193) quotes Jessie Taft:

> According to this transference concept, the worker is being used in the present but only as a lay figure on which to project experiences and feelings from the client's past. An utter confusion results, a practical denial of the reality of the present which is functioning for the sake of the past. Once more the worker is effectively hidden behind the screen of father, mother, brother, sister, while all the time her value for the client is that she is none of these and he knows it.

It is interesting to note that she stated her version of our current debate in 1933, more than 50 years ago. Not many heard her voice. Note also the gender difference. The 'she' is the therapist (social worker) and 'he' the client.

You may recall that I asked in my article whether the idea of transference would have occurred if Anna O.'s therapist had been a woman. I think not. My view is that transference is defense. Who needs it? Whoever is vulnerable. I expect that 'transference' will remain the major convention for some time. It may be 'retired' (see Fischer) as more women enter the field. They seem more alert to what some call 'countertransference,' and more open witnesses to their own contributions as nourishing figures, for instance. Our profession has been dominated by males. 'Transference' has been a valuable protection for males with female patients.

Freud and most of his colleagues were Jewish males. They had a narrower range of sanctioned behavior. New opportunities were promising and important, but in fact, and in memory, life was precarious. Freud's father was a 'tolerated Jew' in Moravia. Families moved gingerly, not all at once. The culture was skilled in protestations of innocence and denial of wrong-doing when persecuted, as was often the case. To be the object of a woman's affections, especially one of higher class and/or the dominant culture, was simply dangerous as well as embarrassing. When one makes house calls, hypnotizes patients, and a servant enters just as a woman recovering from a trance throws her arms about the doctor's neck (an 'untoward incident') it is likely that the technique of hypnosis will soon be dropped. The therapist's responsibility is all too evident and the risks too great. Not that there were no temptations; Freud warned, 'there is an incomparable fascination in a woman of high principles who confesses her passion' (in Malcolm, 1987, p. 102). Is it any wonder, with these declared crosscurrents of desire, that there was private suspicion in the minds of professionals and public? This suspicion, not mentioned in our academic discussions either, is that transference is a name for a kind of extended sexual excitement, half forbidden and half encouraged, and deliberately frustrated in the service of the treatment. The combination of envy, shame, and disgust thus engendered surely contributed to the therapist's sense of vulnerability.

Does any of this hypothesized vulnerability and defense have validity for the present day? My interview data, collected over 20 years from therapists and patients of various persuasions, says it does. It is for this reason that I return again to early cases and origins. They are not simply of historical interest. They represent the same factors present in current cases. (There is also the problem of finding new published cases equally authentic and with more complete data, that is, transcripts.)

Throughout our dialogues, there are complaints about definitions, and attempts to supply these with useful distinctions. They range from 'transfer,' accepted as a reality by all, to the quintessential, 'the transference neurosis,' generally abandoned as an artifact or a vanished extreme. In between we find transference, and 'transference' wherein they sometimes mean skepticism or 'so-called,' and transfer(ence), and so on. I struggled to find a template for common meaning, but could not. Each contributor has his or her own definition and usage(s) and they vary just as did the ones I quoted originally. It is only part of the source of our confusion and disagreement, however. Another, but still fractional part, is the apparent belief that one can start with the innocuous 'transfer' and move along the scale of meanings, stopping wherever one wants, but certainly short of the neurosis. I believe it is a pregnant concept, not limited as one might wish, but moving with its own imperative to its end point.

There is one related major point left untouched. Lazarus (1987, p. 169) put his finger on it quite directly: 'The point about transference is that it is unconscious.' That is a still bigger issue, one I deliberately avoided. For the moment let me quote from the aforementioned book about Dora (Berheimer & Kahane, 1982, p. 106) a comment regarding Freud's growing realization that 'there is no "indication of reality" in the unconscious so that it is impossible to distinguish between truth and emotionally charged fiction.' Exactly. And, although that kind of fiction is just what I call transference, I cannot draw any support from the above statement, because I do not subscribe to the notion of the unconscious. Client-centered theory relates to a framework of levels of awareness, and that is quite a different matter.

Here is the definition given by Lazarus. He starts by making the case for what is called 'transfer,' the human capacity to generalize, and considers that 'a pivotal psychological truth.' He continues,

> We are all aware of the fact that people tend to repeat past relationships that are sometimes inappropriate to the present. Unfortunately, there is more. Transference is not simply the attribution to new relationships of characteristics belonging to old ones. Rather it is a matter of reliving or reestablishing, with whomsoever will permit it . . . an infantile situation that is deeply desired, because it had previously been either greatly enjoyed or greatly missed. Thus statements such as 'You are like my father,' or 'You remind me of my Uncle Fred,' are not transference. The point about transference is that it is unconscious. (1987, p. 169)

This is an opportune moment to comment on the rest of Lazarus' response. It is both brief and complete. I would hope that anyone who could not tolerate my article would simply read his. If only he had not closed with those aphorisms from Salter. Psychoanalysis is not so easily written off.

We have relatively little clinical material in the commentaries, but that which is given is richly illustrative. Maddi (1987, p. 175) draws an unusual picture of therapy as an 'unfolding experience for both parties to provide explanations of their mutual changing loves and hates.' I have never before heard such courage and candor. There is more requirement for energy, alert intelligence, and self-disclosure in Maddi's exposition than most therapists would care (or dare) to risk. Rogers, as usual, provides direct descriptions and word-by-word accounts. Strupp provides an illustrative prototype of a stylized statement directly related to transference. Greenwald expressed his own particular style and personality at several points in his 'Yes, John' address. That form moves me to respond in kind.

Dear Dr. Greenwald,

Ho ho ho. Your paraphrase of the famous 'Yes, Virginia' editorial represents, I suppose, your geniality. Perhaps it also means that no matter how much rational and secular examination of the ritual, there is always transference as there is always Santa Claus – a wish – (and therefore a fact?). Yes, transference and Santa Claus have much in common. Drama, a mythology of partial truth, an economic benefit to its merchants, a celebration that draws all participants at least momentarily into a preoccupation with childhood, and so on.

Perhaps you also invoke that spirit in which you suggest that we all 'join in searching for the commonalities' (1987, p. 167). It's not for me. I'm interested in clarification and depth of differences. Eclecticism seems shallow, hopelessly confounded for research purposes, and usually undisciplined in thought.

Now to be more personal. Your address of 'Yes, John,' like your attribution of 'charming naivete' to my views, is not entirely genial. These have the character of smiling insults. Aren't they ways in which you might speak to children? Then again, you mention my eloquence or articulate logic. Are you friendly or unfriendly? That is, *do you present two aspects?*

I say that you do, in your behavior with me. It is important because you give us examples 'most economically understood as transference phenomena' (1987, p. 166). Fine. Let us see. One example is your experience in a group, where some see you as 'a benign influence,' others see you as a 'malignant force.' The question is, do *you* see yourself as just one person, a single uniform aspect, so that at least one part of this group must be misperceiving you?

Please answer. The theory in my article and my knowledge of self and others suggest that *you* can be *both ways*. To introduce a transference explanation, wouldn't you have to present only one steady image, or else none at all? It seems to me that any practitioner using transference theory tries to hide his or her ambivalence behind a mask of ambiguity. It doesn't work. It confuses. Transference *may* be, as you say, the most economical explanation, but it is not the most accurate.

Your other example, the patient who saw you as 'very much like her mother, and kept sending me Mother's Day cards for years' (1987, p. 167) I find charming, and myself willing to ask some naive questions. *Were* you like her mother? Do you *know* her mother? Is your patient quite mistaken? *How can you judge that?*

As for the cards she continued to send, either you 'failed to resolve the transference,' as they say, or your patient developed the most marvelous sense of humor and you are both to be congratulated.

You write of patients who are furious at being understood. Your example is not about a reaction to yourself, but your patient's reaction to his *wife's* 'understanding.' It doesn't work. I have not the necessary evidence that she understood in the manner we call empathic. Of course people hate to be 'seen through,' made to feel transparent against their will, and so on. None of that pass for understanding as I meant it, so I continue to believe that 'understanding and misunderstanding lead to love and hate respectively,' as you put it.

Strupp also provides some examples, prototypic, of the therapist's behavior. We find it in the context of his reasoned, persuasive, diplomatic presentation. We have a few areas of agreement, but for the most part, our differences are fundamental and not, as he puts it, misunderstandings or misconceptions. The one point on which we wholeheartedly agree is his statement that 'transference' should be neither fanned nor suppressed.

He believes that psychoanalytic theory has been modified in significant ways. I do not. I think that there are concessions from time to time, but that the system is fixed. It can be stretched, but returns to its form. To my mind, transference is a trap, it is permanent, and it snares both patient and therapist.

It may be that the 'transference *neurosis'* is no longer cultivated as the object of treatment. In Europe, however, especially where Lacan has been influential in 'bringing back Freud,' transference in the more traditional model is considered 'the motor that drives the therapy.' And, when Strupp answers his own question as to how therapy can promote change, transference 'becomes the *raison d'être.'*

If that is the case, what does it matter that 'not all of the patients' problems are "transference"' or that there is always a 'real' relationship in which the 'patient relates to the therapist *both* as an adult peer *and* as a personification of the past' (1987, p. 199). Given this *personification* (my emphasis) and the *'raison d'être'* quoted above, all the weight seems to be on the examination of *transference,* and not of that 'real' relationship.

Strupp tries to show that this imbalance is not the case. 'To illustrate,' he continues, 'if the therapist is recurrently late for appointments the patient has a right to be angry; however, if there is no ostensible "cause" for the patient's feelings of anger, we must look elsewhere' (1987, p. 199). True, and how long and hard may we look for 'ostensible cause'? Why is the therapist late? What will he tell about it, and do about it? What other causes might be judged 'ostensible' by the therapist? Being late is rather blatant. What about misunderstandings? These may not be so obvious, to the therapist. Really, the question is, how closely will therapists examine *their* behaviors in this system?

Strupp seems to reserve his most alert attention for the concealments on the part of the patient, 'since patients tend to keep from themselves, as well as the therapist, their "true" motives, [and] it may take considerable effort to ferret out the patient's underlying scenario' (1987 p. 199). What has changed? Freud used the terms 'pick-locks' (or skeleton key); Strupp chooses the ferret. In either case, the assumption remains: you cannot trust the patient to reveal, you must be watchful and shrewd. Meanwhile, what about the *therapist's* 'underlying scenario'? Does it create an adversarial relationship, or a competition in which the rule says that the patient must lose if he or she is ever to win? Or, does anyone believe that the therapist does not *have* an underlying scenario? What else *is* transference theory?

In the next paragraph, Strupp draws us deeper into the complexities, which require careful analysis. Here Strupp (1987, p. 199) tells us of, 'ample evidence that all individuals continually *transfer* [his emphasis] feelings, attitudes, and action patterns.' Often they do, but not continually. I made the same assertion in my original article. Well then, what's to quarrel about? That comes in Strupp's (p. 199) next sentence, which begins, 'It is a matter of clinical judgment whether and to what degree such *transference reactions* [now my emphasis] interfere.' My objection is to the way these two different ideas (transfer, and transference reactions) have been condensed as if they were the same. Is that intentional or by accident? In so many of our exchanges the disputed concept 'transference' hides behind the undisputed one, 'transfer.' And since psychodynamic determination does not allow for accident, the problem should be intentionally resolved. Otherwise it is like Jell-O; sometimes liquid, sometimes semisolid, always slippery, changed at will by heating and stirring.

Then, to the heart of the matter, Strupp's next sentence reads, 'By virtue of the working alliance' (and I interrupt to say how much more friendly this sounds than does 'the transference neurosis,' which Freud called, 'the battlefield where we conquer and take the libido prisoner'), 'the therapist is gradually enabled to say to the patient:

> Perhaps you can see that you are treating me as someone from your past. What transpires here also goes on with a significant other in your current life, and perhaps you can also see that there is a relationship between this pattern and your relationship with your father (mother, etc.). (1987, p. 200)

I see this as an improvement in style over the battlefield metaphor, and thank Hans Strupp for his kindness, to both the hypothetical patient and to us for whom he provides the example. But didn't the trap just spring? We see the therapist 'gradually enabled' to do what he or she has intended from the beginning. The trap is preset, in his underlying scenario. Is this gently instructive statement by Strupp a difference in kind or in degree? I say degree. The adjustments do not modify the system. They only muffle and temper it.

That was the heart of it. There are other points at which we do agree, and while not meaningless, they are superficial in that all people of good will share similar views. Regarding the quality of the relationship, Strupp (1987, p. 197) is 'in full agreement with client-centered therapy' when it comes to such factors as 'the therapist's empathic understanding, commitment, reliability, respect, and trustworthiness.' It is appreciated that he gives Rogers credit for promoting these virtues when they were not fashionable. It is also a sad commentary on the character of a profession that needed such prompting. Actually, Strupp mentions only one of the 'conditions' Rogers has specified as necessary and sufficient, empathic understanding. That is enough to demonstrate the limits of agreement. The condition called 'congruence' (or genuineness) would present special problems for one committed to 'transference' in practice.

Strupp has represented well his approach, which he justifies as (1) theoretically sound, (2) teachable, and (3) 'potentially based on solid empirical data.' Of course it is 'potentially based' and that reservation makes his assertion true until proven otherwise. I believe that this assertion expresses his hopes, for few have worked as earnestly to develop that solid base. We are all waiting for those data, including the clinical/case material within it.

As for 'theoretically sound,' it seems to me that we are debating the point, and probably will for some time to come. Meanwhile, is it 'teachable'? Eminently so, at all levels down to and including the popular. It is universally appealing and useful.

Take, for example, the case of the pornographer who claims, when criticized by a group of feminists, that 'these women attack me because they hated their fathers.' What a perversion, what abuse of clinical method. But how useful as a defense, as a way of explaining the behavior of others and thereby avoiding critical examination of one's self. And, therefore, how eager the whole world is to learn about 'transference' if only superficially. So it is no surprise that there is a thriving professional interest in psychoanalytic psychotherapy. It is a fascinating and intricate body of knowledge whose practice provides access to professional status, power and income (after all, we are talking about the way in which people make a living, and not just the correctness of a theory). Why should students look elsewhere? Nor is there any question but that it is teachable. The question, it seems to me, is whether a concept such as transference can be taught and used in such a way as to distinguish it clearly from the vulgar application in the example of the pornographer. Of course that does not discourage (but rather demands) a clear and equal evaluation of the therapist's responsibility in the interaction— *unless* there is something inherent in the concept to prevent that.

Still speaking to old acquaintances, let me reply to Jules Seeman. Independent as he is, he did not reply to my article but wrote his own. Truly liberal as he is, he apportions his support in noncommitted impartiality. He can afford to be calm and judicious, since, when it comes to transference, he doesn't use the stuff himself.

As with many others, his analysis begins with 'transfer' as a given. Seeman's description is perfectly balanced. Next he moves to a midposition with the word 'transfer(ence).' If only we could all be persuaded to use the same delicate distinctions in our vocabulary! His next step in the language and thought of the subject is 'transference' and the *danger* that it might be considered a *sure* sign of the distortion of current reality, since transference behavior is not *necessarily* a distortion. If not, tell us *when is it not* and how to decide. This is the problem with which everyone must wrestle.

Once past that danger, we reach a second danger, 'when transference is construed as a literal reenactment of earlier behavior.' This Seeman (1987, p. 190) considers 'too illogical to take seriously.' Oddly, I take it seriously, because some other theorists do.

Finally, having cleaned up the definitional problem, Seeman concludes that transference 'in the usual sense' does occur. Not only that, but we need not go outside Rogerian self-theory for an explanation, and Seeman gives us the appropriate propositions from Rogers' theory to show that transference can be domesticated and kept in our house as well as in the psychoanalytic edifice. True, client-centered theory does contain statements pertaining to distortion, denial to awareness, and other relevant observables. Seeman, like others in this conversation, is looking for conciliation, bridges, commonalities. He too believes that modification has removed many of the dangerous features of transference. One might ask, didn't Rank and Taft change views of transference within psychoanalysis? The answer is, no, they did not. Other analysts (and they themselves) considered their ideas to be departures, not modern psychoanalysis. Seeman also looks with hope at Kohut's thinking as an encouraging development in another self-theory, bringing reapproachment and evidence that 'classical transference' is fading. I say, not so fast. Take, for example, this recent title—a 1985 publication by Luborsky et al., 'A Verification of Freud's Grandest Hypothesis: The Transference.' In it the authors quote what they call 'a usual definition: transference is a revival in a current object relationship, especially to the analyst, of thought, feeling, and behavior derived from repressed childhood fantasies originating in significant conflictual childhood relationships' (Luborsky et al., 1985, p. 241). It does not appear to me that there are such open-ended qualities in the trends as Seeman and others perceive. Meanwhile, he will 'remain an interested bystander, eager to see what will happen next' (1987, p. 194). But who will make it happen?

The reactions of Salvatore Maddi constitute a significant contribution. There is a base of long experience and thought, and much originality. He is writing about a level of interaction far beyond simply taking the curse off the 'one-way street' image of psychotherapy. I wonder if any of us can remember an interview, published or not, that approaches his vision of the psychotherapeutic relationship. It sounds like the work of a lifetime.

In truth, I have nothing to add to Maddi's ideas. There is a question that no one answers but most ask. As he puts it, 'how can therapists separate the patient's reaction to their persons from something that is purely an emotional legacy from the past' (1987, p. 172)? He adds that 'it probably does not help much for the therapists to become aware of their own style and content' (p. 172). I should think it would help a great deal, especially since he also says that 'patients are reacting at least in part to that style and content' (p. 172).

Some of Maddi's most cogent comments are in his observations about the social effects of transference theory. The general cultural influence is so strong and prevailing that people must now be very sophisticated indeed in order to trust themselves and the validity of their decisions. Otherwise, the situation becomes one in which 'We do not love or hate the person or activities (in our present) out of their own characteristics except insofar as these characteristics are unconscious reminders of past parental influence' (1987, p. 179). Has it really come to this? Is a whole society befuddled, or can we keep this a provincial clinical debate? *I* think that Maddi is correct, and that psychoanalysis has much to answer for on the broader scale.

Rogers throws in two novel twists. In the 1951 transcript material, he first acknowledges two factors, projection and transfer. First, he illustrates the projection of feeling, *not* from those held toward parents or early significant others, but from *the self*. Hatred of self is first expressed as hatred of therapist. By no present definition would that qualify as transference. Next, in the second (and recent) case, presented here, he illustrates again the process of *transfer*, this time in what we might call *reverse*. That is, a benign experience with the therapist is assumed to generalize 'outward.' This does not support the concept of 'transference' either.

Rogers really doesn't care about that. He simply says,

When a client is angry at us, or affectionate, or seductive, etc., why can't we respond to that in the same way as when he is angry at someone in his family, or some other person? We don't have trouble dealing with *that*. Why treat it differently when it is directed toward us? (Recorded comments during a seminar in Szeged, Hungary, 1986)

Rogers is unconcerned *theoretically* whether a client's attitudes are projections or are therapist caused since he believes the therapist's response should be the same in either case. His is essentially a *practical* theory about how one gets from here to there. It is not really developmental since the principles apply to any age, stage, or time of life, and are therefore not related to causes. The question is not how did one get sick, but how does one get well.

The second case (a recent one) was described in a cross-cultural conference, organized by Dr. Charles Devonshire, held in the summer of 1986 in Hungary. Rogers and I were jointly interviewed before a small audience for the Hungarian Public Television. Our interviewer, Dr. Sandor Klein, asks a question about transference and countertransference. My beginning answer is briefly summarized as follows:

> *Transference is a fiction to defend the therapist against the consequences of his own behavior. This behavior is, in the positive case, by no means villainous. It is the valuable act of understanding — something therapists of every persuasion try to provide. To put it simply, understanding is a form of love making — not as courtship, but in its response effects nevertheless. If you do not comprehend this, or if you want to distance yourself from the personal discomfort resulting, you are likely to look for another explanation.*

What follows is verbatim

SHLIEN: *As for how we deal with it, I'd like for Carl to speak first to that.*

ROGERS: *I think it is quite natural that at different times — and John points out the reasons for it — clients will feel loving feelings, or negative and hostile and hateful feelings towards the therapist. The question is, what do you do about that. In client-centered therapy, we endeavor to treat that as we do* any other feelings — namely, *really to understand it, understand how it seems to the client, and to accept it.*

I could illustrate it with minor examples but I think I'll choose one that I remember very well because I felt it was very important and I felt somewhat pleased with the way I was able to handle it.

It was an attractive young woman with whom I'd been working for quite a long time. It was clear that she liked me, and in one interview she said, 'I would like very much to sleep with you because I feel that would help me so much in my relations with men. My relations with men have been so unsatisfactory, and I think you are different. I think if I could sleep with you that would help a great deal.'

And I said, 'I feel flattered to know that you would like to go to bed with me. I feel that if we had sexual intercourse it would be very enjoyable for me, but I have deep ethical convictions which make me take the point of view that no, not now, nor in the future, will I go to bed with you — but I can understand very well your desire for that and I certainly understand your feeling that if you had a better relationship with me, it would help you in your relationship with other men.'

Months later she told me how relieved she was that I'd said no to her request, and also how released she felt because I didn't reject her request — didn't condemn it, didn't judge it — I simply accepted it and understood it, and I feel that, to my mind, is the way in which transference feelings — no, wait a minute — the way positive or negative feelings toward the therapist, should be dealt with. And it's not easy.

Because it is much easier to understand feelings of hatred toward his or her father or his or her mother than it is hatred toward me, I think that therapists get uneasy when feelings are directed toward them.

But if the therapist can really be aware of feelings that are directed toward himself or herself, understand those, and accept those, it is a big step forward in

473

therapy.

It means that from a client-centered point of view, there is really no – [pause] [starts over] – from a client-centered point of view, feelings that are transferred are of no great importance. Perhaps this man feels, 'I love you because you look like my grandfather.' Okay, that's fine. I can recognize that and I can accept that. Or perhaps you dislike me because I look like your father. Either of these things I can accept.

But it is not easy for a therapist to accept feelings that are directed toward them. So whether the feelings are transferred from someone else to the therapist, or whether they are developed by the therapist in the way that John describes, they can be dealt with in exactly *the same fashion with all other feelings.*

And often therapists say, 'Yes, you understand, you accept, but then what?' There is no 'then what.' If you understand and accept, and it becomes part of the real situation, then the client will cope with it, will deal with it. So that – I feel that one of the most profound mistakes in psychoanalysis was to elevate these feelings directed toward the therapist into this enormous superstructure about transference, which I feel is profoundly mistaken.

It is especially difficult to reply to Ernst Beier. It should be easy. Beier's (1987, p. 153) definition of transference as 'a condition in which patients "transfer" the significant feelings they had originally experienced with their parents to their psychotherapists' is both narrow and traditional. It might set the stage for more useful dispute. The problem is that in almost every sentence thereafter, I must correct a misattribution or a distorted meaning of my words, to which he then has taken exception.

For example, I did not say that transference theory 'removes the therapist's sense of responsibility for his own feelings' (1987, p. 153). Not feelings, but the consequences of his or her own *behavior.* There is quite a difference.

Beier believes that I 'overlook the fact that the psychoanalyst sees the whole concept of transference/countertransference as an interaction' and also thinks that 'to argue who starts this interaction is like arguing whether chicken or egg came first' (1987, p. 153). To begin, I do not believe that the interaction is much acknowledged by the analyst. Almost nothing of the analyst's contribution is revealed to us. In short, I think that the current reliance on the *idea* of interaction is another line of defense, something to pacify the critics. If I am wrong, prove it. Where is the evidence?

Second, of the transference/countertransference, Beier (1987, p. 153) asks, 'Does it really matter who sends the first subtle cues . . . of love or hate?' Of course it does. This is again a question of responsibility. If the first cues are sent by the therapist's demands or activities, denying this would be unfair and untruthful. It would be that self-fulfilling, self-confirming situation in which the instigator blames the victim.

Beier (1987, p. 155) writes: 'Shlien remarks that "Gloria," in response to her therapist (Rogers), expresses the wish for a father like Rogers. Shlien questions whether that is transference. Obviously, Shlien does not know the difference, and mistakes the use of the word *father* for transference.' Actually, I think that there is a difference, and I asked that question as a rhetorical device. Audiences viewing the film often laugh nervously at that point, unsure whether indeed this is or is not transference. They might well wonder, not because of the trigger word *father* but because they might have in mind the kind of definition expressed at least twice (by Lazarus and by Strupp). That kind of definition includes the transfer of what is *missed,* or *was not available,* and thus would indeed fit Gloria's statement!

There is one point that I would like to leave clearly corrected. My article does not 'represent an extreme attempt to celebrate experiencing' (Beier, 1987, p. 155). Above all, I am trying to get people to *think* about what they experience.

Finally, from Constance Fischer, the only woman commentator, I learned a great deal. She comprehends my article so well that I would be content if readers studied hers alone, instead of my own. She takes us into the modern world of 'deconstructionist' philosophy, and beyond transference to alternatives we can consider only insofar as we are unbound. Fischer, like Maddi, firmly promotes the safeguards of 'professional' responsibility. Probably for the same reason; both are taking us into new territory.

Fischer's (1987, p. 157) questions about transference bear repeating: (1) 'What have we meant by this construction' and (2) 'How else might we understand the phenomena the term points to'? The first question has a number of different meanings. I do not know how to resolve that. The second question is the crucial one, but not all of us wish to address it. To ask 'How else might we understand it?' is to challenge the ideology itself.

Inquiry into the origins of the concept, how it was 'manufactured,' rests again on my belief that the reasons for its invention are still the reasons for its being maintained now. Fischer believes that these reasons do not detract from a certain validity and usefulness. The validity must be on the order of what Lazarus called 'a pivotal truth,' in an earlier reference. And the usefulness was the 'positive purpose it once served,' the protection of the theory, method, and professionalism of psychoanalysis, so that ultimately we might have our present expanded field of psychotherapy? If that is what is meant, I think that these present-day developments might have come, with more widespread acceptance and application if psychotherapy had not carried the baggage of psychoanalysis. There is no doubt, however, that Freud was the Great Packager and that the magnetic attractiveness of his ideas in the fields of literature, drama, history, myth, anthropology, and so on, helped to promote his clinical theory whether or not it worked well.

Fischer prefers to go beyond explanatory constructs altogether! I suppose that intention comes from her clear phenomenological orientation. It is certainly the right posture for one who wants to 're-ask basic questions about how people function, get unstuck, and grow' (1987, p. 159). In what way is the question 'how?' different from my interest in finding the 'mechanisms'? For me, this is not finding cause-effect relationships, but discovering *how* understanding *works*. We who talk about the value of understanding do not know how it works. If we did, we might make it more effective. If not, just knowing would be a great achievement in itself.

Fischer understands quite well the meaning of my term 'originalence.' Her term, to provide 'a corrective to the deterministic view of transference' (1987, p. 160), is *continuance*. I consider that a better term for a more advanced concept. 'Originalence' merely cautions against assuming that every event duplicating a prior event is also *repeating* that prior event, and the further assumption that a repeated act is a habitual response rather than a functional response. *Continuance* does not stop with that. It moves the process to the next steps in meaning and living. One could almost say that her version of therapy begins where psychoanalysis ends.

We do have one significant difference of opinion. Fischer (1987, p. 161) hopes that 'readers will not assume that understanding is an adequate condition for growth.' But I think it is. In my view, understanding is more than warm soup. It is not love or comfort. Those may be motives or consequences. Empathic understanding is active, rational, cognitive. It is consciousness expanding. It restores the sanity lost through isolation or misunderstanding. It supplies the energy, attention, and reflection to facilitate new levels of thought and intelligence. It involves more brain, more knowing, more vision. Those valued positive emotions or attitudes, such as trust, self-esteem, and the like, are happy by-products. Our interaction is a case in point. Because she understands me so well, I trust Fischer to explore the benefits of other activities in therapy, even though my own experience tells me that 'Understanding is enough.'

Fischer (1987, p. 158) says, 'Belief in transference allows both patient and therapist to avoid examination of their actual present interpersonal relationship.' 'Allows avoidance' is one way to put it. 'Disallows examination' (1987, p. 159) is stronger and more to the point. Either way, that prohibition is unhealthy, to put it mildly. I am reminded of the prophecy, 'Those who do not remember the past are doomed to repeat it.' It may or may not be true, but it sounds so ominous that few want to question it. What Fischer points to is something even worse. That is, those who cannot remember the *present* are losing part of their mind. Cannot remember the present? That's right; cannot remember because they are not allowed to examine what they witness. A new neurosis is being manufactured while an old one is being analyzed!

The beauty of Fischer's (1987, p. 160) term 'continuance' is that it points in a different direction to the question, 'who might we become on our way to our anticipated futures?' In fact, I believe that the future determines the present more than does the past. How could this be, when the future hasn't happened yet? It is as Fischer says—'in our anticipation.' So I applaud not only Fischer's critique, but her own ideas, which move us theoretically beyond historical constructions and constrictions. It is a proper orientation, facing forward, for the end of these exchanges.

REFERENCES

Beier, E. G. (1987). Comments on 'A countertheory of transference.' *Person-Centered Review, 2*(2), 153–6.

Berheimer, C., & Kahane, C. (Eds.) (1982). *In Dora's case: Freud, hysteria and feminism.* New York: Columbia University Press.

Fischer, C. T. (1987). Beyond transference. *Person-Centered Review, 2*(2), 157–64.

Greenwald, H. (1987). Yes, John, there is a transference. *Person-Centered Review,2*(2), 165–7.

Lazarus, A. A. (1987). A brief commentary on Shlien's countertheory. *Person-Centered Review, 2*(2), 168–70.

Luborsky, L. et al. (1985). A verification of Freud's grandest hypothesis: The transference. *Clinical Psychology Review, 5*(3), 231–46.

Maddi, S. R. (1987). On the importance of the present: Reactions to John Shlien's article. *Person-Centered Review, 2*(2), 171–81.

Malcolm, J. (1987, April 20). J'Appelle un Chat un Chat. *The New Yorker*, pp. 84–102.

Rogers, C. R. (1987). Comment on Shlien's article 'A countertheory of transference.' *Person-Centered Review, 2*(2), 182–8.

Seeman, J. (1987). Transference and psychotherapy. *Person-Centered Review, 2*(2), 189–95.

Shlien, J. M. (1987). A countertheory of transference. *Person-Centered Review, 2*(1), 15–49

Strupp, H. H. (1987). Response to 'A countertheory of transference' by John M. Shlien. *Person-Centered Review, 2*(2), 196–202.

Special discussion: A Countertheory of Transference

(xi) On the Therapeutic Value of Both the 'Real' and the 'Transference' Relationship: A reply to John Shlien

Edwin Kahn

Queensborough Community College, The City University of New York

In response to John Shlien's fascinating article, 'A Countertheory of Transference,' I suggest that the therapist utilize both the 'real' and the 'transference' relationship. Just as free will and determinism are able to exist side-by-side, so can the real relationship (with its emphasis on the present and the future) and the transference relationship (with its emphasis on the past and the present) exist together. During the real, empathic interaction of the moment it is distracting to reflect upon transferred material from the past. This empathic interaction may be the most important facilitator of growth (Rogers), when growth is defined as the maturation of the person's self (Kohut). However, the transference relationship is ever present and should not be ignored since it helps both patient and therapist understand how the self was formed.

As someone intrigued by the similarities as well as the differences between the approaches of Heinz Kohut and Carl Rogers (Kahn, 1985; Kahn, n.d.), I was fascinated by Shlien's excellent article 'A Countertheory of Transference.' Shlien (1987, p. 15) feels that the concept of transference is a fiction, that it is a defense mechanism used by therapists 'to protect themselves from the consequences of their own behavior.' In contrast, Kohut (1984, p. 208) said, 'self psychology does not advocate a change in the essence of analytic technique. The transferences are allowed to unfold and their analysis . . . occupies, now as before, the center of the analyst's attention.' More recently, Stolorow (1986, p. 401), in an excellent critique of Kohut's work, said 'the analysis of transference . . . produces the greatest yields in both maximizing our therapeutic effectiveness and advancing our psychoanalytic theories.' However, I wonder, in partial agreement with Shlien, whether the transference is the primary therapeutic vehicle.

Before going further, several terms should be defined. Gill (1982, pp. 9–13) noted that there has been some confusion with the concept of transference in the analytic literature. Some analytic investigators restrict the use of transference (and countertransference) to 'the distortion of a realistic patient-analyst relationship by additions from past unconscious and repressed object relations' (Anna Freud, quoted in Gill, 1982, p. 12). This definition would involve only the transferring of material that is inappropriate to the present, such as negative and erotic feelings. According to Gill (1982, pp. 10, 13), Freud, however, included in the transference not only the repetition of the repressed material that is inappropriate to the present, but also conscious and appropriate elements, such as the friendly feelings that make up the unobjectionable positive transference, and that do not require analysis. Gill sided with Freud, defining transference as including both what is conscious and facilitates relating, as well as what is repressed and obstructs relating. This broader definition of transference is the one that I will use in this report.

First published in *Person-Centered Review*, Volume 2, Number 4, November 1987.

Gill emphasized that the patient's experience of the analytic relationship is always determined by both the past and the present. Gill (1982, pp. 85–6) said,

> all behavior is built on the past as it is intrapsychically represented and the individual nuances of even apparently similar adaptive behaviors will reflect this past. On the other hand, since total estrangement from reality is well-nigh impossible, all behavior bears some relationship to a 'stimulus' in the present, however idiosyncratically interpreted. Even a deteriorated schizophrenic will show some response to the current situation. No matter how inappropriate behavior is, it has some relation to the present, and no matter how appropriate it is, it has some relation to the past.

In this article, I define, as Gill has, the 'real' aspect of the relationship as the person's appropriate reaction to the stimulus in the present. Just as being kind will naturally elicit a positive response, being hostile will naturally provoke a negative reaction. On the other hand, the 'transference' aspect of the relationship is what the person brings to the current interaction from the past. In classical psychoanalysis, therapeutic gain has been thought to occur mainly via the analysis of the transference. With few exceptions, until recently, the real relationship has not been considered a vehicle for permanent change. But recognition of the importance of the real relationship is occurring (Gill, 1982, pp. 118–20, 178–9). For example, Gill (1982, p. 119) states:

> This estimation of not only the inevitability but even the desirability of the new experience with the analyst seems counter to the analyst's reluctance to intervene in an effort to minimize the role of the analytic relationship as a factor in the result. Yet it is becoming increasingly recognized in our literature that the effects of an analysis are due not merely to insight but to the experience of a new relationship.

However, the nature of this new relationship is not discussed in Gill's book, which is devoted to the therapeutic technique of transference analysis.

In an ideal therapeutic moment, a therapist will understand his or her patient optimally, as part of a real, genuine human interaction (Rogers, 1951). Kohut referred to this empathic understanding as the self-object function of the analyst, which describes in a more abstract way the kind of attunement that the client-centered therapist seeks to provide for the client.

As noted by two of the respondents to the Shlien article (Maddi, 1987, p. 181; Seeman, 1987, pp. 193–4), the psychoanalytic self-psychologist, more so than the classical psychoanalyst, is willing to engage the patient as a real person in the therapeutic relationship. For example, the self-psychologist may be willing to supply information about himself or herself so that the patient may be willing to do likewise. Wolf (1983, pp. 500–1) said, 'the analyst may reveal that he or she is ignorant or clumsy in attempting to understand the analysis and, or perhaps, the analyst's own self-object needs may seek some surcease in the psychoanalytic situation, even at times using the patient as a self-object.' In such a context the analysand may gain 'courage from these self-revelations of the analyst to know that the analyst does not need to feed on the patient to achieve cohesion and harmony' (Wolf, 1983, p. 501). Surely each of the two participants in the process is transferring experiences and feelings from the past into the present, and these experiences and feelings, on one level of discourse, constitute 'transferences.' These transferences are readily apparent in the therapeutic situation, as when one patient may 'idealize,' while another 'devalues' the same therapist (see Greenwald's [1987, p. 167] comment on Shlien's article). However, when the empathic interaction is ongoing and real, there is no need to explain or account for the transferred material from the past. As a matter of fact, considering a genuine, caring interaction as merely the medium for the transference is both distancing and distracting (Rogers, 1986, pp. 132–3). Focusing on the transference diverts attention away from the constructive human interaction of the moment, which may be the most important facilitator of growth (Rogers, 1951, 1959, 1986), when *growth* is defined as the maturation of the patient's self (Kohut, 1971, 1977, 1984).

Just as determinism (with its focus on the past) and free will (with its focus on the future) are able to exist side by side even though they appear to be contradictory (Rogers, in Kirschenbaum, 1979, p. 269; Kohut, 1980, pp. 540–6), so can transference (with its emphasis on the past) and genuine human interaction (with its emphasis on the here-and-now) exist side by side. When dealing with the past and how the past affects the present, the concept of transference is useful. But when dealing with the present and the hopes and plans for the future, the transference relationship becomes irrelevant; it is the real, genuine human interaction that enhances the self. Both ways of viewing the relationship, I think, are essential in order to maximize therapeutic benefits.

I would disagree with Shlien about eliminating the concept of transference entirely. The transference relationship is essential when trying to understand the past, that is, when trying to explain the present behavior of the person using the deterministic principles of natural science. The concept of transference is especially helpful during a block or difficulty in the therapeutic relationship, where a therapist can help a patient see the origin of an exaggerated response. A tentatively offered transference interpretation may help to restore empathic attunement. And perhaps it is during these moments of attunement, the importance of which has been documented in infant research (e.g., Beebe, 1985; Stern, 1985), that maximum therapeutic progress, that is, maturation of the self, occurs.

Kohut (1977, pp. 244–5) stated that

> determinism holds limitless sway so long as the observer conceives of man's psychological activities as being performed in analogy with the processes in the external world that are explainable with the aid of the laws of classical physics. This is mental-apparatus psychology, governed by the laws of psychic determinism — and it explains a great deal. But while it is thus true that many psychological activities and interactions lend themselves to being satisfactorily explained within this framework, it is equally true that there are some phenomena that require for their explanation the positing of a psychic configuration — the self — that, *whatever the history of its formation,* has become a center of initiative: a unit that tries to follow its own course.

And elsewhere Kohut (1980, p. 540) said,

> man's self, once it has been established, is, in its essence, an energized pattern for the future that, lying in the area of free will and initiative, has a significance all of its own, independent of the genetic factors that — in the area of cause-and-effect determinism — had originally laid down its contents and had given it its shape. It is this aspect of man . . . which has been neglected by analysis heretofore.

Taking Kohut's statements seriously, it follows logically that psychoanalysis has overemphasized the transference relationship and the determinism inherent in that concept. The simple truth may be that the maturation of the self is optimally facilitated in the real, empathic interaction of the here-and-now. In this empathic interaction the self becomes more able to choose freely its destiny. This genuine interaction is obscured in classical psychoanalysis, which has been overly preoccupied with the analysis of the transference. The focus on the transference has had the effect of restraining the 'analyst' from being more real and human in the relationship (Gill, 1982, p. 107), which is tragic and unfortunate. However, the deterministic concept of transference, I believe, should not be completely ignored since it is essential in helping both patient and therapist understand how the self was formed.

REFERENCES

Beebe, B. (1985, October). Mutual influence in mother-infant interaction. In M. Tolpin (Chair), Frontiers in developmental studies. Symposium conducted at the eighth annual conference on the psychology of the self. New York.

Gill, M. M. (1982). *Analysis of transference: Vol. 1. Theory and technique.* New York: International Universities Press.

Greenwald, H. (1987). Yes John, there is a transference. *Person-Centered Review, 2,* 165–7.

Kahn, E. (1985). Heinz Kohut and Carl Rogers: A timely comparison. *American Psychologist, 40,* 893–904.

Kahn, E. (n.d.). Heinz Kohut and Carl Rogers: A constructive collaboration. Manuscript submitted for publication.

Kirschenbaum, H. (1979). *On becoming Carl Rogers.* New York: Delta.

Kohut, H. (1971). *The analysis of the self.* New York: International Universities Press.

Kohut, H. (1977). *The restoration of the self.* New York: International Universities Press.

Kohut H. (1980). Reflections on advances in self psychology. In A. Goldberg (Ed.), *Advances in self psychology* (pp. 473–554). New York: International Universities Press.

Kohut, H. (1984). *How does analysis cure?* Chicago: University of Chicago Press.

Maddi, S. R. (1987). On the importance of the present: Reactions to John Shlien's article. *Person-Centered Review, 2,* 171–81.

Rogers, C. R. (1951). *Client-centered therapy.* Boston: Houghton Mifflin.

Rogers, C. R. (1959). A theory of therapy, personality, and interpersonal relationships, as developed in the client-centered framework. In S. Koch (Ed.), *Psychology: A study of a science: Vol. 3. Formulations of the person and the social context* (pp. 184–256). New York: McGraw-Hill.

Rogers, C. R. (1986). Rogers, Kohut, and Erickson: A personal perspective on some similarities and differences. *Person-Centered Review, 1,* 125–40.

Seeman, J. (1987). Transference and psychotherapy. *Person-Centered Review. 2,* 189–95.

Shlien, J. M. (1987). A countertheory of transference. *Person-Centered Review, 2,* 15–49.

Stern, D. N. (1985). *The interpersonal world of the infant.* New York: Basic Books.

Stolorow, R. D. (1986). Critical reflections on the theory of self psychology: An inside view. *Psychoanalytic Inquiry, 6,* 387–402.

Wolf, E. S. (1983). Concluding statement. In A. Goldberg (Ed.), *The future of psychoanalysis: Essays in honor of Heinz Kohut* (pp. 495–505). New York: International Universities Press.

Index